PIMLICO

569

THOMAS & JANE CARLYLE

Rosemary Ashton studied at the universities of Aberdeen and Cambridge, and is now Professor of English at University College London. Her previous books include studies of German thought and German exiles in Victorian England, and three highly acclaimed biographies of G.H. Lewes, Samuel Taylor Coleridge and George Eliot (shortlisted for the Whitbread Biography Prize, 1996).

Praise for *Thomas & Jane Carlyle*

'Ashton is one of the country's leading authorities on the intellectual and literary culture of the Victorians . . . Her deep knowledge and immaculate scholarship allow her to put every passing person, book, debate and piece of legislation in its proper context.' Kathryn Hughes, *Guardian*

'In her erudite and clear-eyed attention to telling detail, her thorough scholarship and sympathetic humour, she is dependable and convincing on everything – and there's a lot – relating to the Carlyle marriage.' *The Times*

'Rosemary Ashton's book is a scholarly distillation of the thousands of letters and diaries which make the Carlyle ménage the best documented of all nineteenth-century marriages.' Jackie Wullschlager, *Financial Times*

'This portrait of the Carlyle's marriage is full of fascinating things and is finely written.' Craig Brown, *Mail on Sunday*

'Immaculately researched and presented . . . The author draws on many sources for her remarkably complete and fresh portrait of two of mid-Victorian England's most astonishing literary figures . . . it is her picture of Jane, an intelligent woman who never found an appropriate outlet for her talents, that makes this book so original . . . she has produced a scholarly and readable book that adds considerably to our understanding of this odd, but vital couple in our literary history.' Simon Heffer, *Country Life*

'Entertaining . . . diligently researched and scrupulously fair.' D.J. Taylor, *New Statesman*

'Rosemary Ashton ably captures the impetuousness of Thomas Carlyle . . . a fine reference book.' Imogen Gassert, *Observer*

'Professor Ashton is not partisan; she is fair to both sides in her balanced and thorough study of the relationship.' Alethea Hayter, *Times Literary Supplement*

'Rich, measured and thoughtful . . . uses with tact and skill the treasury of letters, the mass of general information about a time of tumultuous growth and change, and the profusion of opinions expressed by contemporaries about both Carlyle and Jane.' J.B. Pick, *Scotsman*

'Rosemary Ashton . . . chronicles the turbulence, frequent separation and passionate wretchedness of their alliance with scholarly exactness and a preference for fact over psychological enquiry or the lively gossip which was Jane Carlyle's particular talent.' Jane Shilling, *Evening Standard*

'Wonderfully written . . . brilliant.' *Herald*

'Ashton's grasp of her material is impressive . . . one can only praise the persistence and fluency with which she has knitted together disparate sources.' Pamela Norris, *Literary Review*

'In this fascinating and exhaustive biography, Rosemary Ashton gives us a complete and intriguing insight into the married life of one of the most legendary couples of the nineteenth century.' *Sunday Independent*

THOMAS & JANE CARLYLE

Portrait of a Marriage

ROSEMARY ASHTON

PIMLICO

Published by Pimlico 2003

2 4 6 8 10 9 7 5 3 1

First published in Great Britain by Chatto & Windus 2002
Pimlico edition 2003

Pimlico
Random House, 20 Vauxhall Bridge Road,
London SW1V 2SA

Random House Australia (Pty) Limited
20 Alfred Street, Milsons Point, Sydney,
New South Wales 2061, Australia

Random House New Zealand Limited
18 Poland Road, Glenfield,
Auckland 10, New Zealand

Random House (Pty) Limited
Endulini, 5A Jubilee Road, Parktown 2193, South Africa

The Random House Group Limited Reg. No. 954009
www.randomhouse.co.uk

A CIP catalogue record for this book
is available from the British Library

ISBN 0-7126-6634-6

Papers used by Random House are natural,
recyclable products made from wood grown in sustainable forests;
the manufacturing processes conform to the environmental
regulations of the country of origin

Printed and bound in Great Britain by
Mackays of Chatham plc, Chatham, Kent

Contents

Illustrations

I

27 Geraldine Jewsbury, photograph, 1855.

28 Ellen Twisleton.

29 'A "Latter-Day Nightmare", brought on by reading Thomas Carlyle his Pamphets', *Punch*, April 1850.

30 Jane Carlyle with Nero, photograph, July 1854.

31 Carlyle, photograph, July 1854.

32 Carlyle in back garden at Cheyne Row, photograph, 1857.

33 Carlyle, portrait by Robert Tait, 1856.

34 Carlyle Township, New South Wales, sketch by Charles Gavan Duffy, 1858.

35 Carlyle on Fritz in Hyde Park, photograph, August 1861.

36 *Work*, by Ford Madox Brown, 1852–63.

37 Carlyle's handwriting (to John Carlyle, 25 September 1855).

38 Jane Carlyle's handwriting (to Mary Russell, 30 December 1858).

39 Carlyle and Lord Ashburton, photograph, Vernon Heath, October 1862.

40 Carlyle, photograph, Elliott and Fry, 1865.

Illustration Acknowledgements

The author and publishers gratefully acknowledge permission to use the illustrations in this book, as follows:
Carlyle's House, Chelsea (The National Trust), 1, 2, 13, 14, 15, 16, 18, 21, 25, 32, 33, 35, 39; Thomas Carlyle Albums, Rare Book and Manuscript Library, Columbia University, 4, 20, 22, 23, 24, 27, 30, 31; National Portrait Gallery, London, 6, 12; Scottish National Portrait Gallery, 7; Victoria and Albert Picture Library, 10, 11; Houghton Library, Harvard University, 17; National Library of Scotland, 19, 34, 37, 38; English Heritage © Crown copyright, National Monuments Record, 26; © Manchester City Art Galleries, 36; Beinecke Rare Book and Manuscript Library, Yale University, 40.

A Note on Spelling

Victorian spelling and punctuation are sometimes irregular, Jane Carlyle's particularly so, and Carlyle's occasionally. I have not modernised spellings, and have not, in most cases, corrected punctuation. In a few cases, where there might be obscurity or ambiguity, I use [*sic*] or add missing letters or punctuation in square brackets, but on the whole I follow the originals without comment.

Preface

There is no shortage of material, published and unpublished, about Thomas and Jane Carlyle, whose marriage is the subject of this book. Both were prolific letter writers; over 9,000 of their letters survive. These are currently being published in full in the excellent ongoing edition of *The Collected Letters of Thomas and Jane Welsh Carlyle* (abbreviated in footnotes to *CL*), a joint project of the University of Edinburgh and Duke University, North Carolina, currently under the senior editorship of Professor K. J. Fielding. Twenty-eight volumes have been published so far, taking the letters up to the end of 1853. Like all Carlyle scholars, and like Victorianists with interests in the period generally, I am indebted to the scholarly scrupulousness of the editors, their clear introductions and informative notes. To Professor Fielding I owe an extra debt; he has been generous enough to open to me the files of the letters from 1854 to 1858, already transcribed by the editorial team but not yet published. I am most grateful to Professor Fielding and his Edinburgh colleagues Ian Campbell, Aileen Christianson, and Sheila McIntosh for their help.

For letters from 1858 until Jane Carlyle's death in 1866 and beyond, I have used the many selections of Carlyle letters published since the 1880s, supplemented by research in several archives of as yet unpublished correspondence. Students of the Carlyles are fortunate in having so many published sources to draw on; on the other hand, they have to wrestle with the textual inaccuracies and omissions of the early editors, and the controversies surrounding the papers. Carlyle chose as his biographer his younger friend James Anthony Froude, handing over a mass of papers in the years before his death. Only a few weeks after Carlyle's death in February 1881, Froude published, with what seemed to some like indecent haste, Carlyle's own *Reminiscences*, including his long, self-reproachful reminiscence of Jane. Froude brought out the first two volumes of his four-volume *Life* of Carlyle in 1882; the following year he published three volumes of Jane's letters, collected and annotated by Carlyle himself, under the title *Letters and Memorials of Jane Welsh Carlyle*; the last two volumes of the *Life* appeared in 1884.

Froude's work is of immense importance, but his procedures were controversial. He became involved in a long argument with Carlyle's niece Mary Aitken Carlyle, and her husband (and cousin) Alexander Carlyle, over the ownership of the papers, and, more damagingly, over his interpretation of Carlyle's wishes, particularly in the matter of *Reminiscences*, of which Carlyle had written that he was not sure they were suitable to be published as they stood. The Carlyle family believed that Froude had betrayed his friend by publishing letters and notebooks of the Carlyles which showed the strains of the marriage; they particularly disliked the publication of Carlyle's expressions of grief and guilt after Jane's death, and of those letters of Jane's in which she criticised her husband and expressed unhappiness.

Alexander Carlyle went into print with his own selection of letters, supplementing those Froude had used; he aimed to correct the impression Froude had left of a marriage made unhappy by Carlyle's selfishness. Alexander Carlyle published *New Letters and Memorials of Jane Welsh Carlyle* in 1903, with a preface by an eminent psychiatrist, Sir James Crichton-Browne, in which Jane was diagnosed as neurotic, addicted to drugs, and – in her middle years, when she kept a miserable diary – suffering from menopausal depression. These suggestions contain some truth, but the attack on Froude was excessive, as was the whitewashing of Carlyle; while Crichton-Browne and Alexander Carlyle attacked Froude for suppressing and distorting material to create a monster out of Carlyle, they silently did the same thing in order to save him from criticism and make Jane out to be at fault. Alexander Carlyle published *New Letters of Thomas Carlyle* in 1904, after a bitter exchange with Froude's children, who brought out their late father's self-justificatory account, *My Relations with Carlyle* (1903), to which Crichton-Browne and Alexander Carlyle replied with *The Nemesis of Froude: A Rejoinder to J. A. Froude's 'My Relations with Carlyle'* (1903).

Another disciple was David Alec Wilson, who published a massive six-volume biography of Carlyle between 1923 and 1934. Though he constantly obtrudes his harsh opinion of Jane, Wilson's biography is exhaustive and wide-ranging; he is also, on the whole, more scrupulous with his materials than either Froude or Alexander Carlyle, though he omits certain passages which would show Carlyle in a poor light, particularly when quoting from his infatuated letters to Lady Ashburton in the 1850s. I have used Froude, Alexander Carlyle, and Wilson for letters and journals not yet published in the *Collected Letters*, but wherever possible I have quoted from the original manuscript rather than their sometimes inaccurate or incomplete texts.

Many other scholars have produced selections from the huge mass of letters. These include several volumes of Carlyle's letters edited by his American friend Charles Eliot Norton between 1883 and 1888 (all of which have been superseded by *Collected Letters* except for *Correspondence between Goethe and Carlyle* (1887), which includes Goethe's letters); a selection of Jane's letters and another of Carlyle's letters to her, both edited by Trudy Bliss (1949, 1953); Carlyle's correspondence with Ralph Waldo Emerson, edited by Joseph Slater (1964); his correspondence with his brother Alexander (Alick), edited by Edwin J. Marrs, Jr. (1968); a selection of Jane's letters by Alan and Mary McQueen Simpson (1977); and the Carlyle–Ruskin correspondence, edited by George Allan Cate (1982); see Bibliography. There have been several modern biographical studies of Carlyle, notably by Fred Kaplan (1983) and Simon Heffer (1995); and of Jane by Lawrence and Elisabeth Hanson (1950) and Virginia Surtees (1986). Phyllis Rose, in her *Parallel Lives: Five Victorian Marriages* (1984), gives an astute brief account of the Carlyles' relationship. I have found these, and the many other books and articles on the Carlyles to be found in the Bibliography, helpful in the course of my research.

When quoting from Carlyle's works in this book, I do not refer to any particular edition, as no completely reliable scholarly edition of the *Works* exists. The Norman and Charlotte Strouse Edition of Carlyle's writings, now under way, promises to fill the gap; I have used *Sartor Resartus*, expertly edited by Rodger L. Tarr and Mark Engel, which came out in 2000 as part of the Strouse Edition.

For unpublished material, there are two main sources. The largest collection of letters, journals, and related material is in the National Library of Scotland (NLS). I am indebted to the Principal Curator of Manuscripts, Dr Iain Brown, and his colleagues for access to the documents and permission to quote from them.

The second largest collection is in the Houghton Library, Harvard University, which holds letters from, to, and about the Carlyles, as well as Carlyle's richly annotated library of books used in his research for his history of Frederick the Great, a collection he bequeathed to the library. I am grateful to the Curator of Manuscripts, Leslie A. Morris, for permission to quote from the unpublished Twisleton and Parkman Family Papers, which contain fascinating accounts of the Carlyles in the letters of Ellen Twisleton and her sister Elizabeth Dwight. I am indebted to Lord Saye and Sele for permission to quote from Ellen Twisleton's 1855 memoir of Jane's early married life, and to Professor K. J. Fielding, who found the memoir in the Houghton and published it in the *Times Literary Supplement* in 1999. Other collections in the Houghton which I have used are the Charles Eliot Norton Collection and the Charles Sumner Collection of Autographs.

My thanks go also to the librarians and curators of manuscripts at the following institutions for permission to quote from unpublished Carlyle-related material: Edinburgh University Library and the Library of New College, Edinburgh; Dr Williams's Library, the National Art Library at the Victoria and Albert Museum, the Royal Institution of Great Britain, and the National Trust (Carlyle's House), all in London; the Bodleian Library in Oxford; the Jagiellonian University Library, Cracow, Poland; the Henry E. Huntington Library, San Marino, California; Duke University Library, Durham, North Carolina.

Individuals who have helped me with material, information, encouragement, suggestions, and in some cases hospitality, are: Margaret Ainslie, Anthea Brook, Sandie Brown, Ian Campbell, Aileen Christianson, Lesley and Mike Cullen, Julia Cumming, Mrs. Mary Davidson, Rufus Exton, Ken Fielding, Monica Fryckstedt, Peter Funnell, Sam Gilpin, Robin Hamlyn, Mary Harland, Philip Horne, Elisabeth Jay, Danny Karlin, Alastair Laing, Sheila McIntosh, Gerard O'Daly, Bob and Kitty Preyer, Charles Pugh, Michael Slater, Gerry Slowey, David Sorensen, Ron and Sue Speirs, Guilland Sutherland, John Sutherland, Emmanuella Tandello, Uta Thompson, Ann Totterdell, Hazel Vickery, Henry Woudhuysen. To all these I owe a debt of gratitude.

I am grateful to the Arts and Humanities Board of the British Academy for an award of Research Leave to finish the book. Warm thanks go to my editor at Chatto, Jenny Uglow, to my copy editor, Beth Humphries, and indexer Vicki Robinson, to Alex Butler, to my erstwhile agent Alexandra Pringle, and to my present agent Victoria Hobbs. My children, Ben, Kate, and Tom, have preserved a welcome balance in my life; my deepest debt is to my late husband, Gerry Ashton.

Introduction

In May 1858 the Scottish painter Robert Tait contributed his most recent work to the annual exhibition of the Royal Academy of Arts. Entitled *A Chelsea Interior*, it depicts Thomas Carlyle and his wife Jane at home in their sitting room at 5, Cheyne Row. In the foreground, standing by the fire, is Thomas, widely known as 'the Sage of Chelsea', the one man of the age whose writings and lectures had sounded a trumpet note to a whole generation of thinkers, writers, politicians, social reformers, and ordinary enthusiastic, if often perplexed, readers and hearers. His friends W. M. Thackeray and Edward FitzGerald nicknamed him 'Gurlyle' on account of the apocalyptic tone of his written works, with their gloomy prophecies and pronouncements on the 'condition of England', and, more especially, on account of the vehemence of his extraordinary conversation.[1]

Carlyle was never one to temper his talk out of deference to the opinions, tastes, or sensibilities of his listeners; nor did he pay any attention to the current fashion. In Tait's painting he stands by the fire, tall, lean, somehow both elegant and homely in a full-length checked dressing gown, filling a long 'churchwarden' pipe. He looks handsome and relatively young for a man of sixty-two, with hair still thick and brown, and a modest (three-year-old) beard. In the picture he is for once not talking, but is occupied in calm contemplation.

At the other side of the fire, seated, in pensive pose with chin in hand, looking away from her husband, is Jane. She is fifty-six, small, thin, pale, neatly dressed, with rather sharp features and an expression suggestive of unhappiness, even bitterness, but also determination and a certain pleased consciousness of herself as sitter. She, her husband, their dog Nero, and the whole ground floor of their little Chelsea house are, she knows, to be exhibited to the picture-viewing public in this work of 'Vandyke fidelity'. It is the most private of subjects – a married couple in their own home – yet the painting is intended to satisfy the curiosity of that large abstract entity known as 'the public'.

Towards the end of 1857 Jane commented expansively on Tait's work in progress. She complained to her Scottish friend Mary Russell of that weary Artist who took the bright idea last spring that he would make a picture of our sitting room – to be 'amazingly interesting to Posterity a hundred years hence' – I little knew what I was committing myself to when I let him begin . . .; for the last six weeks he has been overshadowing me like a night-mare *every day*!! Except when, please God, the fog is so black that he can't *see*! . . . a whole day painting at my portfolio! another whole day over my workbox and so on! not the minutest object in these three rooms, opening into one another, but what is getting itself represented with Vandyke fidelity! . . . I suspect he aims at more than posthumous fame from this picture – hopes perhaps some admirer of Mr C's, with more money than wit to guide it, may give him a thousand pounds for Mr C's 'Interior' – the portraits of Mr C himself, and Mr C's wife, and Mr C's dog inclusive! – The dog is the only member of the family who has reason to be pleased with his likeness as yet![2]

By summer 1858, when the painting was on show at the Royal Academy, Jane had changed her mind about Nero's reason for rejoicing. She told the young sculptor Thomas Woolner that she wished Tait had not painted Nero 'as big as a sheep! *That* is what provokes me; more than being transmitted to "Posterity" in "wrong perspective" and with a "frightful table cover!" '[3] Here Jane is echoing some critical remarks John Ruskin had made on seeing the work. He objected playfully (but respectfully, as befitted a younger admirer of Carlyle) to the colours of the books behind Jane's head: 'Books should always be grave in colour, especially books behind the head of a historian's wife.' And he told her frankly that Tait had violated 'the first rule of perspective by making his point of station imaginary, or rather impossible – the perspective is only true for a point within about six inches of the picture's surface which is at *least* a foot too little'.[4]

Perhaps Jane passed on Ruskin's criticisms to Tait, for she told Mary Russell as late as March 1858 that he was still putting 'the finishing touches to my portrait, in that immortal picture of his'.[5] Tait defended the painting's perspective on the back of the canvas:

Painted by me Robert Tait/ 5 Queen Anne Street, London/ Commenced 26th May 1857, and finished on this 5th April 1858.
The proper point of sight is about 18 inches in front of the picture exactly opposite this point [1¾ inches to left (from front) of the dead centre of the picture]. A near point of sight was thus adopted in order to get in as much as possible of the front room. The picture having been painted from the recess of one of the two windows in the front room, a spectator looking properly at the picture, sees everything in the interior as if he were seated in the said recess.[6]

A Chelsea Interior caused little immediate stir at the Exhibition, where it competed with works by Sir Edwin Landseer, Frederic Leighton, and W. P. Frith, whose *Derby Day* was that year's sensation, so much so that a protective rail had to be erected to prevent it from being damaged by the crush.[7] As Tait's picture measured only 22 by 34 inches, it was hung in one of the smaller rooms towards the end of the Exhibition. The *Art-Journal* review included it in a list of pictures 'which ought to have had better places', but the reviewer was unable to give column space to any of the smaller pictures.[8]

A Chelsea Interior did achieve fame, however. Tait, better known as a pioneer in the new art of photography than as a painter, took photographs of the painting; so also did another famous London photographer, Leonida Caldesi.[9] Friends and admirers either bought or were presented with copies. In 1861 the Italian exile and patriot Giuseppe Mazzini, long an admirer of both Carlyles and a close friend of Jane in particular, wrote to thank an English friend for sending him 'the little interior'. He thought the likeness of Jane particularly good.[10] Carlyle himself had a low opinion of the picture, but another friend admired it exceedingly. Jane may have been joking when she suspected Tait of wishing to sell the painting to some admirer of Carlyle's for £1,000, but he did, in fact, sell it to Lord Ashburton, who was happy to pay the huge sum of £500 for it – 'just £495 pounds too much!' was Carlyle's reported response.[11]

William Bingham Baring, second Baron Ashburton, heir to the Baring banking concern, was one of the richest and most generous of men and a great admirer of Carlyle, as was his clever society wife, Lady Harriet, eldest daughter of the sixth Earl of Sandwich. The couple were intimate with royalty and with leading politicians. They hosted glittering dinners and balls at their London home, Bath House on Piccadilly; the Christmas and New Year house parties at their Hampshire country house, the Grange, were legendary.

On 27 June 1858 Jane gave Carlyle an elaborate account of how she suspected Tait of inducing an Edinburgh friend, George Combe, to praise the picture in Lord Ashburton's presence, thereby seeming to suggest that Jane herself was eager for him to offer for it. Jane's story is full of minute descriptive detail – Vandyke fidelity in words – interspersed with expressions of her opinions and quotations of phrases from acquaintances which had amused her and Carlyle:

Yesterday Tait called, and said: 'you know of course Lord A has bought the Picture', and 'on that hint I spake!' frankly taxed him with having *put* Combe *up* to *reminding* Lord A; and of implicating *me*, as it were, *in picking* the pocket of a friend (making me a forenoon visit) to the extent of 500£! Explaining to him that, so little did Lord A *wish* for the picture, he had pressed it on *my* acceptance, &c. &c. 'If the transaction were not solemnly finished off, he Tait ought to break it off'! A more frank exposition of my feelings could not have been made! . . .

Tait took Combe and his Wife to the Exhibition – of course pointed out to them his own picture – which Combe, very much his friend and 'maybes nae great jooge'! went into rapture over. From the Academy the female Combe and

Tait drove to the Royal Institution, dropping the male Combe at Sir James Clark's, where he was engaged to lunch, and where he found himself sitting next Lord Ashburton. Of course he began talking of the Academy pictures he had just come from, and, with pure zeal of friendship, mentioned with special approbation *The Chelsea Interior* – 'Ah! said Lord A, listening with a pleased look: I *rather think* that picture belongs to *me*! I said I should be glad to buy it of the artist' . . . Now, really that sounds very like Lord A! – carried away by the impulse of the moment – pleased to say *he* was possessor of a picture the person *next him* was praising! – and so far poor Tait was blameless . . .

What Tait regrets is, that Lord A never having heard the price of the picture, may have bought it dearer than he likes – For Tait himself considers the price a sort of fancy one – put on it '*to prevent it falling into vulgar hands*' (as he wrote to Lord A). He would really have taken off a hundred or two, I think, if it had not been 'for the honour of the thing' – tho' the price being set down 500 in the catalogue, Lord A *might* have known it from the beginning, had he liked – I believe it was from Tait himself Lord A got the idea that the price was high. Wonderful Lord A! at all events it was Tait's conscience about the *price* that made him take my rating so meekly![12]

In due course the picture was loaned to Carlyle's House by Louisa, the second Lady Ashburton; it has hung since 1895 in the very ground-floor sitting room it depicts with such faithful Dutch realism. Fittingly, number 5, Cheyne Row (since renumbering in 1877, number 24), has been restored to the décor of 1858, mainly through recourse to Tait's picture and to his many photographs.[13] The house was first opened as a museum in 1895, when the Carlyle's House Purchase Fund was established, with a distinguished committee chaired by Leslie Stephen and including Tennyson, Lord Houghton, Lord Rothschild, Sir Frederic Leighton, the Earl of Rosebery, Thomas Henry Huxley, and the United States Ambassador. The committee raised money through subscriptions, gathering amounts ranging from £100, given by the German Emperor, to one shilling from 'a Poor Parson'.[14]

★

Even before the purchase of the house, the area immediately around it had become full of monuments and memorials to Chelsea's most famous nineteenth-century resident. As one of Carlyle's biographers, John Nichol, pointed out, as early as 1892 the visitor to Chelsea would step off an excursion steamer at Carlyle Pier and pass the imposing bronze statue of Carlyle on the Embankment, where Cheyne Row comes down at right angles to the Thames. Behind the statue stood (and stands) Carlyle Mansions, and a little further away from the river was (and is) Carlyle Square.[15] The statue, done at the Earl of Rosebery's request soon after

Carlyle's death in February 1881, was a life-size version of several smaller statuettes in terracotta and bronze which the sculptor Joseph Edgar Boehm had modelled from the life during the 1870s, with commissions from Louisa, Lady Ashburton, and the German Emperor, Wilhelm I, among other distinguished admirers.[16]

Though Chelsea is now one of the most fashionable districts of London, it was little more than a shabby, muddy backwater for most of the nineteenth century. Cheyne Walk, the wide street running parallel to the river, boasted handsome houses and several celebrated residents in the Victorian period, among them George Eliot and Dante Gabriel Rossetti. Several famous people had lived in the immediate area before the nineteenth century, from Sir Thomas More – also commemorated by a statue on the Embankment – through Donne and Herbert to Sir Isaac Newton, Swift, Addison, Steele, Smollett, and Sir Hans Sloane.[17] It did not, however, begin to be fashionable until the Chelsea Embankment was completed in 1874. Before then, as David Masson wrote, recalling his first acquaintance with the Carlyles in the 1840s,

Cheyne Walk was a quaint riverside street of shops and antique houses, looking down upon an unembanked shore, – pleasant enough to the sight when the stream was full, but not so pleasant when the low tide left its margin of mud and ooze. One way of getting to Cheyne Row from the City or the Strand region was by one of the river steam-boats. Having sailed up the river, you got out at a pier at the Chelsea riverside below Battersea Bridge; and a few paces along Cheyne Walk, with its shops and antique houses, brought you to the quieter Cheyne Row, at right angles to it; and there, about the middle of the Row, on your right hand, you found No. 5.

Alternatively, you could go by Chelsea omnibus 'along Piccadilly, down Sloane Street, and so into Chelsea by the long King's Road'.[18]

The Carlyles' street changed little during the almost thirty-two years they lived there together, from June 1834 until Jane's death in April 1866, and not much from then until Carlyle's death. Frederic Harrison noted in 1872:

I was struck with humiliation when I went to see the Old Prophet at Chelsea. He seems to live in a very dismal corner of this foul city. When I thought of the poor, soured, wild old genius, coiling himself up in his own virtue in that alley where one might expect to find one's washerwoman, I could not help contrasting it with the luxurious homes and lovely scenery wherein sundry articles against luxury are produced and the royal palace of the 'Bard' at Blackdown [Tennyson's home near Haslemere in Surrey] – who is after all but an organ-grinder to the true Bard at Chelsea.[19]

That Harrison, liberal lawyer and man of letters, was no wide-eyed follower of Carlyle, differing markedly from him in politics and philosophy, only makes this testimony to Carlyle's stature the more striking.

When Carlyle was house-hunting in London in May 1834, he was fully aware of the disadvantages of Chelsea. However, funds were limited and he was looking for somewhere cheap. He wrote to Jane saying he had been diligently tramping the London streets in search of somewhere suitable for a couple with small savings, no regular income, but a strong determination to risk settling in the capital in hopes of something turning up for Carlyle in the way of editors' and publishers' (overdue) recognition of his genius. He had already seen some houses in Bayswater and Kensington before trying Chelsea on the advice of Leigh Hunt, the London poet and journalist, friend and collaborator of Keats, Shelley, and Byron. Hunt lived in picturesque poverty with his large family in nearby Upper Cheyne Row. Carlyle was invited to tea, an occasion which he described to Jane:

The Frau Hunt lay drowsing on cushions 'sick, sick' with thousand temporary ailments, the young imps all agog to see me jumped hither and thither, one strange goblin-looking fellow about 16, ran ministering about tea-kettles for us: it was all a mingled lazaretto and tinkers camp, yet with a certain joy and nobleness at heart of it; faintly resembling some of the maddest scenes in *Wilhelm Meister* [Goethe's novel, which Carlyle had translated in 1824], only madder . . . I soon got out with Hunt in wide quest of houses. Chelsea lies low close by the side of the river; has an ancient, here and there dilapidated look; the houses apparently a tenth cheaper; some market articles, especially coals said likewise to be cheaper. I liked it little; and, to say truth, cared not to be so near the poetic Tinkerdom.[20]

A few days later Carlyle addressed his 'dearest Wifekin' again, telling her of his wandering about 'like the shoemaker of Jerusalem', of his viewing a small house near Regent's Park, available to rent for 45 guineas, with a garden 'which in my spleen I likened to something between a bed-quilt and a pancake; unjustly, for it was bigger than either', and of finally deciding in favour of 'unfashionable' Chelsea, where number 5, Cheyne Row was to be had for a very reasonable £35 a year. The Hunts, though 'tinkerish-nomadic' and 'within a gunshot' of Cheyne Row, he now thought would not be 'intrusive', and he warmed to the solid old house, built by Lord Cheyne in about 1708, as well as to the area with its 'traces of great men'.[21]

And so Cheyne Row it was to be. Jane travelled by stages to London, after sending the furniture and heavy items by 'Pickford's huge waggons'. She arrived on 4 June with her canary, Chico, who had 'sung violently all the way by sea or land, nay struck up his *lilt* in the very London streets wherever he could see green leaves and feel the free air', as Carlyle reported romantically to his brother John.[22] They moved in on 10 June, determined to make their mark in literary London.

★

The story of the Carlyles' marriage is one of psychological and emotional tension; it is also a story of astonishing literary, intellectual, and social success. When Tait painted them at home, he crystallised what was remarkable about them. Carlyle had frequently been asked to sit for portraits and photographs since he achieved fame with his history of the French Revolution in 1837. Tait had already exhibited a portrait at the Royal Academy (in 1856), as had Samuel Laurence, the most famous of nineteenth-century portraitists, who made his first drawing of Carlyle in 1838.[23] As the wife of a famous man, celebrated on her own account for her sparkling conversation, Jane too was painted by Laurence and photographed many times by Tait and others.

Images of both Carlyles travelled to America at the request of a number of Carlyleans grouped round Ralph Waldo Emerson, and Carlyle's head on a medallion fashioned in March 1851 by Thomas Woolner was 'constantly' being asked for in Australia when Woolner visited there in 1854.[24] Four years later Carlyle was further celebrated in Australia by the naming of a whole new township after him, its main streets being the intersecting Thomas Street and Jane Street, while neighbouring roads were called after friends of the Carlyles such as John Forster, John Sterling, John Stuart Mill, and Thackeray. A young admirer – a rather surprising one, the 'Young Ireland' nationalist Charles Gavan Duffy – was responsible for the laying out of this Carlyle Township on the Murray River in New South Wales in 1858. Having been imprisoned on charges of treason in 1848 and released a year later, Duffy had finally settled in Australia in 1855, soon becoming Minister of Land and Works. When Carlyle, who had sympathised with Duffy and supported his release from prison, saw the map Duffy sent him, 'especially Jane Street', he almost wept, as he confessed, at such 'strange handwritings on the wall'.[25]

The Carlyle Township gives evidence of the extent of the Carlyles' fame, as does Tait's picture. No other married couple featured so prominently in the art and photography of the nineteenth century. Samuel Laurence and others exhibited famous pictures of literary celebrities – Dickens, Thackeray, and Tennyson in particular – but their wives did not appear.[26] None of them had any pretensions to fame, whereas Jane Carlyle did, though she never published a line of poetry or prose in her lifetime.

Jane herself was alert to her 'value', though she put it down (sometimes bitterly) to Carlyle's fame rather than her own. In July 1865 she wrote to him – he was visiting his family in Scotland – playing on her feelings of mingled outrage and pride about some photographs (done by the firm of John and Charles Watkins):

The greatest testimony to your fame seems to me to be the fact of *my* photograph – the whole three, two of them very ugly (Watkins's) – stuck up in Macmichael's shop-window!! Did you ever hear anything so preposterous in your life! And what impertinence on the part of Watkins! He must have sent *my three* along with your *nine* to the wholesale man in Soho Square, without leave asked! But it proves the interest or curiosity *you* excite – for being neither a 'distinguished authoress', nor 'a celebrated murderess', nor an actress, nor a '*Skittles*' [the famous courtesan] (the four classes of women promoted to the shop-windows) it can only be as *Mrs* Carlyle that they offer me for sale![27]

In fact, *Mrs* Carlyle was celebrated not merely as an appendage, but as one of a formidable pair. Tait saw no need to name the Carlyles in the title of his painting. The word 'Chelsea' and the visual representation of Thomas and Jane were deemed enough to identify the subjects to the public.

Ten years earlier, in August 1848, Thackeray wrote to his mother about the possibility of her renting for £60 a year a house which would be large enough for those occasions when he and his two daughters came to visit. 'You might for 60 have the upper part of a house and the use of a cook for the wittles', he explained; 'as for the dignity I dont believe it matters a pinch of snuff'. In order to carry his point he reached for an example: 'Tom Carlyle lives in perfect dignity in a little 40 [actually £35] house at Chelsea with a snuffy Scotch maid to open the door, and the best company in England ringing at it.'[28]

Thackeray probably had in mind chiefly Lord and Lady Ashburton and Lady Ashburton's mother, Lady Sandwich. But he might equally have meant by 'the best company' a wide range of people, British, European, and American, who were prominent in politics, philosophy, literature, or art. Such visitors came in the first instance because they had been inspired by Carlyle's writings. Many continued to come for the sake of his friendship, though his demeanour was often gruff and his rhetoric exaggerated. Several found themselves drawn more to Jane for her kindness, her gift for giving and receiving friendship, her vulnerability, and for the unsurpassed remarks and anecdotes in her conversation and correspondence.

Both Carlyles wrote huge numbers of letters to friends and family. Both possessed energy, imaginative inventiveness, omnivorous curiosity about themselves and others, verbal playfulness and mimicry, a sharp critical eye on the lookout for humbug or stupidity, and a delight in the wonders of everyday life and living. In their letters to one another they show that inwardness of a close couple which is evident from shared jokes and allusions, from self-quotation and even self-parody.

Carlyle's correspondence and journals complement his works – his essays, *Sartor Resartus*, *The French Revolution*, the lectures on heroes and hero worship, *Past and Present*, the account of Oliver Cromwell, *Latter-Day Pamphlets*, the *Life* of his friend John Sterling, and the monumental six-volume history of Frederick the Great. His letters also comment graphically on passing events. Reading them is like reading an intelligent and opinionated distillation of the daily newspapers, with their day-to-day attention to matters large and small, public and private, significant and ephemeral.

Parliamentary news, political and sexual scandals, fashions and fads, criminal cases, the pros and cons of homoeopathy, the parlous state of English education (in 1835 Carlyle quotes estimates that one in twelve adults cannot read or write)[29] – all is filtered through the medium of Carlyle's curious mind. So also are dashed-off pen portraits of his acquaintances, from drunken maids to famous men and women. On meeting Wordsworth in March 1835, for example, he instantly caught hold of the great poet's egotism:

The languid way in which he gives you a handful of numb unresponsive fingers, is very significant. It seems also rather to grieve him that you have any admiration for any body (but him).

I fancy he has fallen into the garrulity of age, and is not what he was: also that his environment (and rural Prophethood) has hurt him much. He seems impatient that even Shakespeare should be admired.[30]

If Carlyle's letters complement his writings, Jane's form a body of literature in themselves. As with Carlyle, no subject escapes her attention. In a letter of 1843 to her Liverpool cousin Jeannie Welsh about a party at the house of the great actor-manager Macready, her tumbling prose expresses the joyful chaos of the occasion:

Dickens and Forster above all exerted themselves till the perspiration was pouring down and they seemed *drunk* with their efforts! Only think of that excellent Dickens playing the *conjuror* for one whole hour – the *best* conjuror I ever saw – (and I have paid money to see several) – and Forster acting as his servant! – This part of the entertainment concluded with a plum pudding made out of raw flour raw eggs – all the raw usual ingredients – boiled in a gentleman's hat – and tumbled out reeking – all in one minute before the eyes of the astonished children, and astonished grown people! that trick – and his other of changing ladies pocket handkerchiefs into comfits – and a box full of bran into a box full of – a live guinea-pig! would enable him to make a handsome subsistence let the bookseller trade go as it please! Then the dancing – old Major Burns with his one eye – old Jerdan of the Literary Gazette, (escaped out of the Rules of the Queen's Bench for the great occasion!) the gigantic Thackeray &c &c all capering like *Mænades*!! . . . Forster *seizing me round the waist*, whirled me into the thick of it – and MADE me dance!! like a person in the tread mill who must move forward or be crushed to death! Once I cried out 'oh for the love of Heaven let me go! you are going to dash my brains out against the folding doors'! to which he answered – (you can fancy the tone) – 'your *brains*! who cares about their brains *here? let them go!*'[31]

The subject of marriage was a frequent topic in the Carlyles' letters. They took an interest in a 'criminal conversation' case brought in 1844 by William Fraser, a literary editor who had published some early Carlyle essays, against his wife. Fraser had used the money his wife brought to the marriage in some speculation, had gone bankrupt, and left her in the care of his friend William Bagley, whom he now accused of adultery with her. Carlyle sums up the situation with a sharp eye for its ironies:

'Attorneys', scoundrels of one or the other hungry sort, again got him in lending; he fell into embarrassments, – at last, he walked off to some obscure quarter of London, and left his poor fidgetting anxious wife to shift with her 4 children as she liked. She supposed him to be living with other women &c; spent much of her time in crying. Last year he wrote to her in the depths of abasement to advance him £200, and he would go out to India, and then retrieve himself with it. He got the £200; staid *where he was*; and now, it all being eaten, he has started a public suit against his Wife for improper conduct with one of his friends who had assisted her sometimes in her distresses![32]

Jane took a similarly dim view of Fraser's doings, but she instinctively related the case to herself, seeing in it the dangerous interpretations that can be put on innocent behaviour between the sexes:

Think of its being made *criminal* to say to a man who for years had been dining four or five times a-week in the house by her husbands invitation 'my dear will you ring the bell'! Merciful Heaven – what criminalities have *I* walked over the top of without knowing it! . . . Sterling sent me daily the Times – and there I sat fuming – wishing to be in the court to show up misstatements which nobody seemed to notice to draw palpable inferences which nobody seemed to draw, or at all rates to be with the poor woman comforting her.[33]

The relative rights of husbands and wives was a subject with which Jane became obsessed a few years later, when she found herself, as she thought, neglected by her own husband. The Carlyles, struggling in their marriage, looked critically at other couples they knew – the Ruskins, the Dickenses, and George Eliot and G. H. Lewes, who could not marry because Lewes was barred from divorcing his estranged wife. They also responded to the current public debates on marriage, an urgent topic of discussion among Victorian legislators and journalists, as were the connected subjects of inheritance, legitimacy, prostitution, married women's property rights, and the unfortunate surplus of unmarried women in the mid-century.[34]

All who visited at Cheyne Row were fascinated by this childless couple, as a couple. The well-known remark made much later by Samuel Butler,

one of the few famous Victorians who did not know them personally –
that it was 'very good of God to let Carlyle and Mrs Carlyle marry one
another, and so make only two people miserable instead of four' – could
have been made by any number of the Carlyles' friends and
acquaintances.[35]

When in 1854 Effie Ruskin sued for the annulment of her marriage on
grounds of non-consummation, there were those who put about the
rumour in the clubs and drawing rooms of London that the Carlyles'
marriage, too, was sexually blank.[36] After Carlyle's death his many
biographers, including his trusted friend J. A. Froude, entered the fray on
both sides of this speculative question, as did a host of other commentators. In 1911 the notorious Frank Harris made the frankly incredible
claim that he had been told of Carlyle's impotence by the elderly sage
himself during a walk in Hyde Park in 1878 or 1879.[37] One later writer,
James L. Halliday, in the transparently named *Mr Carlyle My Patient: A
Psychosomatic Biography* (1949), concludes from Carlyle's writings that the
'patient' was anally fixated, had repressed homosexual feelings, married a
woman who was herself sexually ambiguous, and was a sado-masochist.

The only certain thing is that the relationship between Carlyle and Jane
was not entirely happy. Yet like the unhappy marriages invoked in the
opening words of Tolstoy's *Anna Karenina*, the Carlyle marriage was
unhappy in its own unique, interesting, and often touching way. The
Carlyles themselves found their close yet difficult relationship continually
absorbing; it forms the subject matter of several of the many hundreds of
surviving letters between them. No other nineteenth-century marriage is
so minutely documented from the inside as well as the outside. This is
equally true of their long courtship, which began after an inauspicious
meeting in Scotland in June 1821.

PART ONE

COURTSHIP

CHAPTER I

Strange Meeting 1821

Two striking young men, Edward Irving and Thomas Carlyle, paid a visit at the beginning of June 1821 to Mrs Grace Welsh and her nineteen-year-old daughter Jane at their home in Haddington. Lying eighteen miles east of Edinburgh, Haddington is the pretty county town of East Lothian. It is an ancient Royal Borough, famous as the birthplace of John Knox, who was thought by the Welsh family to be an ancestor, through the marriage of a Welsh to one of Knox's daughters.[1] Jane was the only child of Dr John Welsh and his wife Grace, also born a Welsh, though she was not related to her husband. Born on 14 July 1801, Jane was given the middle name Baillie after her maternal grandmother, who also claimed a famous ancestor, the thirteenth-century patriot William Wallace. Jane was proud of both family legends, though she and Carlyle later doubted the Wallace connection, while believing the Knox story – wrongly – to be true.[2]

Jane Welsh was a bright, precocious, pretty child with huge black eyes and winning manners. In a piece of partly autobiographical fiction, 'The simple Story of my own first Love', she recalled how at the age of nearly ten she set out to attract a boy at a dancing school ball. Her childhood self is described with mingled pride and irony; there are repeated references to her 'elegant attire', 'magnificent eye-lashes', 'lovely dancing', and also to 'her Latin and her wit'.[3] In truth Jane was considered special not only by herself and her doting parents, but also by others who knew the clever and charming, if rather spoilt, only daughter of Haddington's chief doctor. One lifelong friend, Thomas Erskine, recalled in a letter of 1855 'those early days' when he and other friends had 'blessed the sweet bright child, and looked forward to a bright future for her'.[4]

At the local school Jane vied with the boys both intellectually and physically. The story is told of her crawling along the narrow ledge of Nungate Bridge, near her school, to show the boys she could rival them in daring deeds. She also recalled 'taking hissing *Ganders* by the neck' to prove that she could overcome her fear of having to pass the aggressive creatures every day.[5] She later told her friend, the novelist Margaret Oliphant, that Dr Welsh had been ambitious for his daughter, wishing her to have the education that would have been automatic for a boy. Rather against the wishes of his elegant wife, who was more interested in bringing up her daughter to be genteel and ladylike, he allowed her to have a tutor in Latin.[6]

Geraldine Jewsbury, another friend, recorded that Jane was reading Virgil by the age of ten. Geraldine added a story told her by Jane:

She always loved her Doll but when she got into Virgil she thought it shame to care for a Doll. On her tenth Birthday she built a funeral pile of lead pencils and sticks of Cinnamon, and poured some sort of perfume over all − to represent a funeral pile. She then recited the speech of Dido, stabbed her doll and let out all the sawdust after which she consumed her to ashes − and then burst into a passion of tears.[7]

Though Geraldine Jewsbury has been accused of embellishing anecdotes from her friend's life − and she certainly liked a drama, as her letters show − Jane's own account of the episode in a footnote to her 'simple Story' is even more strikingly dramatic. She remembers having become 'pagan' in her morality on reading Virgil, and being so wrapped up in the Roman world of her reading that when her father − 'one whose wishes were law' − told her that 'a young lady *in Virgil* should for consistency's sake drop her doll', she set about ending the doll 'as the doll of "a young Lady in Virgil" should end':

With her dresses which were many and sumptuous, her four-posted bed, a fagot or two of cedar *allumettes*, a few sticks of cinnamon, a few cloves, and a − nutmeg(!) I '*non ignara futuri*' [not ignorant of what was to be] constructed her funeral pire − '*sub auras*' [under the heavens] of course; and the new Dido, having placed herself in the bed − with help − spoke thro my lips − the last sad words of Dido the first, which I had then all by heart as pat as a b c . . . Then however; at the moment of seeing my poor Doll blaze up; for, being stuffed with bran, she took fire, and blazed up, and was *all over* in no time, in that supreme moment my affection for her blazed up also, and I shrieked and would have saved her, and couldn't, and went on shrieking; till every body within hearing flew to me and bore me off in a plunge of tears! − An epitome of most of one's 'heroic sacrifices', it strikes me, magnanimously resolved on, ostentatiously gone about, repented of at the last moment and bewailed with an outcry! . . . Thus was my inner world at that period three fourths *Old Roman*, and one fourth *Old Fairy*.[8]

The Latin tutor engaged by Dr Welsh was Edward Irving, an Edinburgh University theological student from Dumfriesshire who taught at the Mathematical School in Haddington.[9] He was a large, handsome, eloquent youth of eighteen when he arrived there in 1810. Dr Welsh paid him £1 11s. 6d. a month for a one-hour daily lesson of 'private teaching to Jeany', as he called his nine-year-old daughter.[10]

Irving spent two years in Haddington, leaving in August 1812 to divide his time between another teaching post in Kirkcaldy and his theological studies in Edinburgh. Here he became friendly in 1815 with Thomas

Carlyle, a Dumfriesshire youth three years his junior. Irving had preceded Carlyle as a pupil at Annan Academy; both had come to Edinburgh to study for the Church of Scotland ministry. Their families belonged to a small breakaway group, the Burgher Seceders, which protested against patronage and interference in the choice of ministers in the Church of Scotland.[11] This dissenting group worshipped at the little meeting-house in Ecclefechan, a small market town about seven miles north of Annan and sixteen miles north of Carlisle on the coach road between Glasgow and London.

Of the two young Annandale men, Irving was the more striking and attractive; he had a confident, optimistic temperament and was firmly committed to his vocation, in marked contrast to his morose, uncertain young compatriot. In his reminiscence of Irving, written soon after Jane's death in 1866, Carlyle recalled his feelings towards his resented forerunner, his polar opposite, and yet also the man who became his closest friend:

I had heard much of Irving all along, how distinguished in studies, how splendidly successful as Teacher, how two Professors had sent him out to Haddington, and how his new Academy and new methods were illuminating and astonishing everything there (alas, there was one little Pupil he had there, with her prettiest little 'penna, *pennae*' from under the table, and 'let me be a boy, too, Papa!' – who was to be of endless moment, and alone was of any moment to me in all that)! – I don't remember any malicious envy whatever towards this great Irving of the distance: for his greatness in study and learning I certainly might have had a tendency, hadn't I struggled against it, and tried to make it emulation, 'Do the like, do thou the like under difficulties!' As to his Schoolmaster success I cared little about that, and easily flung that out [when] it came across me. But naturally all this betrumpeting of Irving to me (in which I could sometimes trace some touch of malice to myself) had not awakened in me any love towards that victorious man: '*ich gönnte ihm* [I did not begrudge him],' as the Germans phrase it; but in all strictness nothing *more*.[12]

As Carlyle knew when writing this piquant account in 1866 but had not known in 1821, Irving was his predecessor also in winning the heart of the young Latinist, Jane Welsh. She confessed quite late in her courtship with Carlyle that she had, '*once*, passionately loved' Irving when, as a young woman of eighteen, she renewed her acquaintance with her erstwhile tutor on a visit to Edinburgh in 1819.[13] Irving also fell in love with her, but was compromised by having become engaged to another former pupil, Isabella Martin of Kirkcaldy. After a shamefaced request to Miss Martin's father to be released from the understanding, Irving, his request denied, made the best of it, and married Isabella in 1823. This strange young man, already showing signs of the Pecksniffian quack-cum-inspired-preacher he would soon become, wrote to Jane in March 1822:

My well-beloved friend and pupil, when I think of you my mind is overspread with the most affectionate and tender regard which I neither know how to name nor how to describe. One thing I know, it would long ago have taken the form of the most devoted attachment, but for one intervening circumstance . . . When I am in your company my whole soul would rush out to serve you, and my tongue trembles to speak my heart's fulness – but I am enabled to forbear, and have to find other avenues than the natural ones for the overflowing of an affection which would hardly have been able to confine itself within the avenues of nature if they had all been opened. But I feel within me the power to prevail and at once to satisfy duty to another and affection to you.[14]

When Carlyle came to describe the Irving–Isabella–Jane affair in 1866, he used the comic-satirical mode which came as naturally to him as the grandiose-sentimental did to his friend. There is also more than a dash of the revenge of the second choice in his account of Irving's romantic relationships. Shortly before the momentous visit of the two friends to Haddington there had been on Irving's part, says Carlyle,

some movements of negotiation over to Kirkcaldy, for *release* there, and of hinted hope towards Haddington, which was so infinitely preferable! And something (as I used to gather long afterwards) might have come of it, had not Kirkcaldy been so peremptory, and stood by its bond (as *spoken* or as written), 'Bond or utter Ruin, Sir!' – upon which Irving had honourably submitted and resigned himself.[15]

Though Irving's personality invites mockery, he was taken seriously by all concerned. Carlyle reckoned him not only his best friend but for a time his only friend and confidant; Jane treated him much more kindly as a suitor than she did various hapless young men about Haddington. She gave him a lock of her hair: he celebrated it in a sonnet which begins sonorously:

> Thou raven lock! On which mine eyes do rest
> Unwearied. Thou dear emblem of my Jane
> Whose hand did crop thee from her head, fit test
> Of her affection ever to remain.[16]

Jane's mother, too, was smitten by the young man's charm, devotion to his chosen profession, and obvious, if puzzlingly self-aggrandising, sincerity.

When Irving and Carlyle came to call, mother and daughter were still coming to terms with the loss of Dr Welsh, who had died in September 1819, aged forty-four, of typhus fever caught from a patient. His young widow and eighteen-year-old daughter were bereft. Jane wore black until the day of her wedding in 1826, and she told Carlyle frankly during their courtship that she had been happier as a girl than she would ever be again, and that her recollection of Dr Welsh's death 'will darken my being, to the grave'.[17] Her later memory of grasping the hissing ganders by the neck arose in the context of her relationship with her beloved father, as she explained to her cousin Helen Welsh in 1850: 'I suppose my bravery active and passive must have been like most of my other good qualities "for the occasion got up" – *assumed* to gain my Father's approbation, to be *praised* by him, and kissed, and "loved very much indeed".'[18]

On his first entrance into Mrs Welsh's elegant drawing room, Carlyle not only appeared to disadvantage beside the more urbane Irving, but also fell far short of the ideal of manhood which Jane and her mother cherished in their memories of Dr Welsh. Grace Welsh, young, beautiful, concerned with domestic and social elegance, naturally expected to marry her daughter – who had only a small inheritance, her father's birthplace, the house and farm of Craigenputtoch – to a man of settled career or good prospects. She was therefore much more welcoming to Irving, whom she knew and admired (and by whom she was consistently flattered), than to his awkward, undecided, and sullen companion.[19]

Carlyle was aware that he had not impressed his new acquaintances; he also knew immediately that he had been conquered by 'that bright pair of eyes, inquiringly fixed on me'.[20] A few days after the visit he confessed to William Graham, a Glasgow friend, that Irving had had to force him to go on the excursion to Haddington. Irving himself, Carlyle wrote, 'will have told you how sick I was, what work he had to overcome my taciturnity, and then how captious and sophistical I grew, and withal how happy'.[21] He wrote in similarly candid vein to his brother Alick, identifying as the chief source of his sullenness the chronic dyspepsia from which he had suffered since 1818 and which would dog (and disgust) him for the rest of his long and otherwise remarkably healthy life:

Irving was with me lately, during the General Assembly time. The man could not have been kinder to me, had he been a brother. He would needs take me to East Lothian with him for a day or two, to 'see the world'. We went accordingly; and tho' that wretched stomach was full of gall – so that I could neither sleep nor eat to perfection – I was happy as a lark in may.[22]

★

When Carlyle met Jane Welsh, he was twenty-five years old, and had not yet found a firm footing in any career. He was born in Ecclefechan on 4 December 1795, just two months after John Keats, whose tragic death from tuberculosis had taken place in Rome in February 1821, only a few months before the Haddington meeting. If the one young writer came to epitomise Romanticism in his short, breathless career and lyrical, sensuous poetry, the other was slow to start, achieving fame through his rhapsodic and satirical prose only in middle age.

Carlyle's beginnings were humble. His father, James, was born in 1758 in Annandale into a family of uneducated carpenters, stonemasons, and small farmers. James and his brothers were apprenticed to a stonemason; they worked hard and fought hard, by all accounts (including Carlyle's own), though James, at least, did not drink hard, and was all his life known for his strict religious piety.[23] Carlyle told friends that his father had 'walked as a man in the full presence of heaven and hell and the judgment', believing 'with absolute certitude that the greater number of human beings will suffer in literal fire without any end at all!'[24]

In the reminiscence of his father which he wrote in London after hearing of his death in 1832, Carlyle linked James Carlyle's Old Testament faith to his vehement metaphorical speech – 'though he knew not what a metaphor was' – and also to his alarming temper and disinclination to suffer fools. 'He was irascible, choleric, and we all dreaded his wrath.' 'An atmosphere of fear' kept Thomas and his brothers and sisters at a distance; 'I was ever more or less awed and chilled before him', wrote Carlyle. Yet 'I have a sacred pride in my Peasant Father, and would not exchange him even now for any King known to me.'[25] Elsewhere Carlyle recorded that James Carlyle had veracity and '*courage* mostly quiet, but capable of blazing into fire-whirlwinds when needful'. He often showed 'a flash of just *insight*, and of brief natural eloquence and emphasis such as I have never met with in any other man (myself included)', Carlyle wrote in his marginal annotations to a German biographical article sent him in 1866 by its author, Friedrich Althaus. The father laughed seldom, but when he did, it was loud and long. He had a grim, 'Scandinavian' sense of humour, his son remembered.[26]

James married twice, his first wife Janet dying in 1792 after the birth of their son John, known later as 'John of Cockermouth', since he grew up in the Cumbrian town and not with his half-brothers and sisters in Dumfriesshire.[27] James's second wife, Margaret Aitken, was a local girl some thirteen years his junior, whose brother was a stonemason in Dumfries. They were married in March 1795, and together they had nine children, the eldest of whom was Thomas, born when his father was thirty-seven and his mother twenty-four.[28] Though a new sibling was born roughly every two years thereafter until the last, Janet, in 1813, Thomas remained the favourite of both parents, particularly his mother.

Carlyle's authorised biographer Froude almost anticipated Freud in his critical analysis of the extremely close relationship between the mother and the beloved oldest son. 'The strongest passion which he experienced through all his life was his affection for his mother', Froude wrote, and, more dramatically: 'To his mother Carlyle was so loving "That he might not beteem the winds of heaven/ Visit her face too roughly".' 'This was love indeed,' commented Froude, 'love that is lost in its object, and thinks first and only how to guard and foster it.'[29]

The quotation, from Hamlet's first soliloquy describing his father's love for his mother, is suggestive indeed, particularly as Froude goes on to say that Carlyle could never give such unselfish love to his wife. In *The Interpretation of Dreams* (1900) Freud famously linked Hamlet to Oedipus as literary types of the man with repressed sexual feelings towards his mother.[30] For years Froude was attacked for his startlingly frank representation of Carlyle, but there can be no doubting that he recognised a truth about Carlyle's emotional dependence on his mother, from which, though it may well have had little or no sexual element, he never broke free.[31]

'My excellent Mother,' Carlyle wrote in the margin of Althaus's text, 'with perhaps deeper *piety* in most senses [than her husband], had also the most *sport*, – of what is called wit, humour &c.'[32] It was she who taught Carlyle to read, though barely literate herself. In his very last letter to her, written on 4 December 1853, his own fifty-eighth birthday, when he knew she was near death, he thanked her for being such a noble mother. 'For if there has been any good in the things I have uttered in the world's hearing', he wrote, 'it was *your* voice essentially that was speaking through me.' He added, in fairness to the father from whom he had felt more distant yet whom he so frankly admired (and resembled): 'Essentially what you and my brave Father meant and taught me to mean, this was the burthen of all I spoke and wrote.'[33]

Of both parents Carlyle always talked with love and pride, though they remained all their lives in decent obscurity in Dumfriesshire. His father never travelled more than forty miles from home, and the furthest his mother went was Manchester to visit her youngest daughter Janet.[34] A striking and attractive feature of Carlyle's character, seen first in his courtship of Jane and later in his wider social relations, was his lack of shame about his family's poverty and limited social and intellectual horizons. Though his mother taught him to read, she herself could not write until he tutored her in 1834, shortly before he and Jane migrated from Scotland to London.[35] She complied reluctantly with his requests to write, managing such occasional short notes as the following:

My dear Son
I recived your kind letter and am glad to hear you are getting on so well. I hope you will get hounerably through . . . May God by his Spirit acomplish what no other can. You inquier kindly about my health I am full as well as when you saw me. O that I could be as thankfull as I ought . . . You see I come ill at writing yet am still your old Mother.[36]

James Carlyle had written occasionally to his son with similarly approximate spelling and pious wishes. Most of Carlyle's brothers and sisters, too, wrote with difficulty and diffidence, aware of the gap in education between them and their clever older brother. Only John, the third-oldest brother, known in the family as Jack, went to university like Thomas; indeed, Thomas paid for his medical studies at Edinburgh.

Like many another bright child of humble origins, Carlyle was noticed by a friendly schoolmaster and an interested clergyman. He noted on Althaus's memoir:

'Sandy Beattie' (subsequently a Burgher Minister in Glasgow; I well remember his 'examining' us that day) reported me 'complete in English', age then about 7; that I must 'go into Latin', or waste my time; Latin accordingly; with what enthusiasm! But the poor Schoolmaster did not himself know Latin; I gradually got altogether swamped and bewildered under him; reverend Mr Johnstone of Ecclefechan (or *first*, his son, home from College, and already teaching a young Nephew or Cousin, in a careless but intelligent manner) had to take me in hand; and, once pulled afloat again, I made rapid & sure way: a most exact & faithful man Mr Johnstone Senior; my Father & Mother's Minister (Burgher), both of whom he esteemed.[37]

In May 1806, aged ten, he was taken by his father to start secondary school in Annan. Father and son walked the six or seven miles from Ecclefechan on a bright Whitsunday morning, 'I trotting at his side in the way alluded to in Teufelsdrock'.[38] Carlyle refers here to his fictional German alter ego, Diogenes Teufelsdröckh, hero of his first book, *Sartor Resartus* (1833–4). A repository of Carlyle's political, social, literary, and religious opinions and experiences, heightened by a tone alternating between enthusiasm and satire, *Sartor Resartus* is autobiographical, though approximately and often fancifully so. Many of Carlyle's early biographers, including Althaus, understandably used *Sartor* as a key to Carlyle's own early life. It can be so used, but only with caution, as Carlyle himself noted on Althaus's text – 'Fiction *founded* perhaps on fact – a long way off.'[39]

In his 1832 reminiscence of his father Carlyle gives a succinct account of the shock which awaited him at school after the sunshine of his early home life: 'It was a bright morning, and to me full of moment; of flattering boundless Hopes, saddened by parting with Mother with Home; and which afterwards were cruelly disappointed.'[40] The corresponding passage in *Sartor*, written only months before the reminiscence of his father, is more elaborate:

'With my first view of the Hinterschlag Gymnasium', writes Teufelsdröckh, 'my evil days began. Well do I still remember the red sunny Whitsuntide morning, when, trotting full of hope by the side of Father Andreas, I entered the main street of the place, and saw its steeple-clock (then striking Eight) and *Schuldthurm* (jail), and the aproned or disaproned Burghers moving-in to breakfast: a little dog, in mad terror, was rushing past; for some human imps had tied a tin-kettle to its tail; thus did the agonised creature, loud-jingling, career through the whole length of the borough, and become notable enough. Fit emblem of many a Conquering Hero, to whom Fate (wedding Fantasy to Sense, as it often elsewhere does), has malignantly appended a tin-kettle of Ambition, to chase him on; which the faster he runs, urges him the faster, the more loudly and more foolishly! Fit emblem also of much that awaited myself, in that mischievous Den; as in the World, whereof it was a portion and epitome!'[41]

The name Hinterschlag Gymnasium suggests corporal punishment (on the backside); and young Tom Carlyle, like young Diogenes Teufelsdröckh, suffered from the coarseness of some teachers as well as from the brutality of his fellow pupils. Carlyle's memory was bitter in the latter respect:

Unspeakable is the damage & defilement I got out of those coarse unguided tyrannous cubs, – especially till I revolted against them, and gave stroke for stroke; as my pious Mother, in her great love of peace and of my best interests, spiritual chiefly, had imprudently forbidden me to do. One way and another I had never been so wretched as here in that School, and the first 2 years of my time in it still count among the miserable of my life. 'Academies', 'High Schools', 'Instructors of Youth' – Oh ye unspeakable![42]

The sensitive boy, as unhappy in his Scottish rural academy as any middle-class boy (Thackeray, say) at an English public school, left Annan with his temper soured but with the conviction already forming that he was 'like no other'.[43] His parents were proud of his learning and encouraged him to go on to Edinburgh University, where it was their wish, though not particularly his, that he should study for the ministry.

In November 1809, just a month short of fourteen, Carlyle walked the nearly eighty miles from Ecclefechan to Edinburgh, accompanied by an older boy, Tom Smail, who was already a student there. Starting university at such an early age was not uncommon in Scotland then; Edward Irving had done the same, leaving Annan Academy in 1806, just as Carlyle arrived for his three years of torment. Many Edinburgh students were the sons of farmers and poor tradesmen; terms were short and the summer vacation long, to allow boys to help at home with the harvest. The two Toms took three days to arrive in the capital. Having found themselves cheap lodgings, they sallied forth so that the older could show the younger the sights of the town. Carlyle later recalled being (perhaps deliberately and perversely) unimpressed by the splendours, natural and architectural, of the Athens of the North.

By 1809 many of the gracious squares and crescents of the New Town north of Princes Street had been built. Those who could afford it had moved there from the overcrowded, unsanitary 'closes' and 'wynds' of the Old Town near the Castle. Yet the Old Town was spectacular, the Castle perched high up on its rock next to the medieval High Street with its tenement buildings reaching to thirteen storeys at the back, where they tumbled steeply down the hill. Coleridge had made his only visit to the city in September 1803, and had been enchanted by it – 'what alternation of Height & Depth! – a city looked at in the polish'd back of a Brobdingnag Spoon, held lengthways – so enormously *stretched-up* are the Houses!'[44]

Carlyle was not entirely impervious to Edinburgh's beauty and grandeur. His later recollection of his arrival – 'the novice mind was not excessively astonished all at once'[45] – is coloured by the subsequent bitter knowledge that, though he spent a large part of every year in Edinburgh from 1809 to 1827, he made no true friends, acquired no permanent position, and achieved in that great city no reputation commensurate with his abilities.

His comments during his unsettled sojourns in Edinburgh say as much about his own mental and physical health as they do about the city, though they tell truths about the state of Edinburgh too. Thus in February 1821, when he is suffering tortures from dyspepsia, Edinburgh is 'this accursed, stinking, reeky mass of stones and lime and dung'. Auld Reekie, indeed, in a kind of irritating sympathy with his internal complaint. A month later he is feeling better and getting on with some journalistic work. He writes enthusiastically to the same correspondent, his brother Jack, of the pure air at the top of Arthur's Seat, the rocky hill near the Palace of Holyrood:

The blue majestic, everlasting ocean, with the Fife hills swelling gradually into the Grampians behind it on the north; rough crags and rude precipices at our feet ('where not a hillock rears its head unsung') with Edinburgh as their base, clustering proudly over her rugged foundations, and covering with a vapoury mantle the jagged, black, venerable masses of stonework, that stretch far and wide and shew like a city of fairy-land – There's for you man! I saw it all last evening – when the sun was going down – and the moon's fine crescent (like a pretty silver creature as it is) was riding quietly above me.[46]

This is recognisably the Athens of the North, in fine sympathy with the young man's vigour and literary aspirations.

On the whole, however, life in Edinburgh did not agree with him. In May 1824 he would write to his 'dearest' Jane Welsh, announcing that he had finished his translation of Goethe's *Wilhelm Meister's Apprenticeship* and must leave 'poor old Annandale', where he was living on his parents' farm at Mainhill, two or three miles from Ecclefechan,[47] to take the manuscript to the printer: 'I am to be a very very short time in Edinr; Meister is all printed but five sheets; and my business in Athens may very soon be transacted. Within its learned walls, I have not one single friend, not even an acquaintance that I value; which after fifteen years residence says but little for my moral qualities. In truth I care not tho' the intellectual smoke of Athens never more salute my nostrils.'[48]

The 'learned walls' and 'intellectual smoke' describe Edinburgh in general, but the university in particular. Carlyle enrolled there in 1809, as divinity students then did, first in general subjects such as moral philosophy and classics. Ten years later he left the university, finally, without taking a degree. This was not unusual. The university's organisation left much to be desired, with students under no obligation to attend any particular lectures, but paying fees direct to individual professors, who naturally competed with one another, since the class ticket system was their chief source of income. Feuds and scandals were rife, and students often behaved rowdily, shouting and stamping in lectures and writing irreverent articles in student magazines. The main university buildings, though designed by Robert Adam in 1793, were still being built (wartime restrictions having applied from 1793 to the end of the Napoleonic Wars in 1815) when Carlyle was in attendance, as they were a decade later when Charles Darwin and his older brother Erasmus arrived at the university to study medicine in 1825.[49]

For ten years Carlyle was rather loosely attached, studying first the arts curriculum, then mathematics, at which he excelled. As part of his divinity studies, he had to preach some sermons, but as he confessed in 1815, he was feeling 'daily and hourly more lukewarm about this preaching business', and had 'almost come to a determination about my fitness for the study of Divinity'. His unfitness, he meant, using, as he so often did, an olfactory metaphor to express his disaffection: 'Why all this mighty stir – why this ado – about "delivering" a thesis – that in the minds eye seems vile – and in the nostril smells horrible?'[50]

It took him two more years to come to the conclusion finally that he had not the vocation to become a minister. The fact that his parents 'silently much wished for it' weighed heavily on him, as did his gratitude for the financial sacrifices they had made to let him attend the university.[51] A strong feeling of responsibility, a desire not to disappoint them, combined with an odd reluctance to make decisions which always ran through his character alongside extreme forcefulness, kept him from announcing his disinclination. Then in March 1817 he had an experience which allowed him, in what would also be a lifelong characteristic manner, to observe fate taking a hand in his affairs. He went along to see William Ritchie, the Professor of Divinity, to enrol at Divinity Hall and pay his annual fee. Looking back in 1866, Carlyle saw destiny at work, and claimed also to have recognised it at the time:

On one of those visits my last feeble tatter of connexion with Divinity Hall affairs or Clerical outlooks was allowed to snap itself, and fall definitely to the ground. (Old 'Dr Ritchie not at home', when I called to enter myself; – 'Good', answered I; 'let the omen be fulfilled!')[52]

His parents accepted this outcome, his father with silent magnanimity, his mother lovingly but fretfully.[53] That summer Margaret Carlyle suffered some kind of collapse, which 'seemed to threaten the extinction of her reason: we were all of us nigh desperate, and ourselves mad', Carlyle remembered, perhaps connecting at some level his mother's illness with his being the recent cause of deep distress and disappointment to her.[54]

It would not have been surprising if Carlyle had completely lost his religious faith in the environment of the 'Rational University' of Edinburgh, where the memory of David Hume's sceptical philosophy was still strong.[55] His interest in mathematics, logic, and natural science did not, however, wholly undermine his traditional faith in God or reverence for the Bible, which he never completely lost, but his wide reading and natural curiosity made him critical of those apologists for church doctrine who seemed to rest their case on the argument that 'as it is in the scriptures, we have no business to think about it'. This is how he put it in a letter of July 1817 in which he negotiated a path between the position of 'unhappy sceptic' and that of dogmatic apologist.[56] Even more potent in pushing him to the realisation that the ministry was not for him was his observation of his fellow divinity students:

These persons desire, not to understand Newton's philosophy, but to obtain a well 'plenished manse. Their ideas, which are uttered with much vain jangling and generally couched in a recurring series of quips and most slender puns, are nearly confined to the church- or rather kirk-session politics of the place, the secret habits, freaks and adventures of the clergy or professors, the vacant parishes and their presentees, with patrons, tutors and all other appurtenances of the tythe-pig-tail.[57]

His disaffection with the Church arose chiefly, therefore, out of his disgust at the worldliness of its practitioners and would-be practitioners. Though he was also experiencing the beginnings of a long, if intermittent, struggle of faith, one to which he gave famous expression in the 'Everlasting No' chapter of *Sartor Resartus*, he contented himself with merely declaring that he would not be a clergyman. His letters to friends went so far as to say that Christianity 'is only supported by probabilities';[58] to his parents he was careful not to suggest that his doubts reached beyond his own unsuitedness to the ministry.

★

From May 1814 Carlyle, like Irving, had begun to divide his time between Edinburgh and a teaching post undertaken to contribute to family finances. He taught maths at his hated old school, Annan Academy, an experience which he recalled with great clarity and frankness in his reminiscence of Irving:

One attraction, one only, there was in my Annan business: I was supporting myself (even saving some few pounds of my poor £60 or 70 annually, against a rainy day), and not a burden to my ever-generous Father any more; but in all other points of view, I was abundantly lonesome, uncomfortable and out of place there. Didn't go and visit the people there . . .; had the character of morose, dissocial, etc. etc.; – in short, thoroughly detested my function and position, though understood to be honestly doing the duties of it . . . . – As to my Schoolmaster function, it was never said I *misdid* it much ('a clear and correct' expositor and enforcer): but from the first, especially with such adjuncts, I disliked it, and by swift degrees grew to hate it more and more. Some four years, in all, I had of it, two in Annan, two in Kirkcaldy (under much improved *social* accompaniments); – and at the end, my solitary desperate conclusion was fixed, That I, for my own part, would prefer to perish in the ditch, if necessary, rather than continue living by such a trade: – and peremptorily gave *it* up accordingly.[59]

The two years at Kirkcaldy, from November 1816 until he resigned from his post in October 1818, were more bearable because he now had Irving, who was also teaching there, as his friend. Carlyle was taken out of himself by Irving, whose 'honest-heartedness and good humour made him the most delightful of companions'. Together they walked along the beach, in the woods, on expeditions along the coast. 'Such colloquies, and rich rovings about, in bright scenes, in talk or in silence, I have never had since', wrote Carlyle in his reminiscence of Irving, which he recognised was as much about himself as about his friend.[60] Irving's optimistic temperament attracted him, rather than his firm faith, which Carlyle no longer shared and about which they had many a disputatious discussion.

Another element of Kirkcaldy life helped to make schoolmastering there almost tolerable. In an intriguing case of prefigurement, Carlyle became romantically involved with a young woman of higher social rank, an ex-pupil of Irving's, with a female mentor (an aunt in this case) who disapproved of him as a suitor. Carlyle even suggested in his heavily ironised account in *Reminiscences* that, as later with Jane Welsh, his friend had fancied the young woman, Margaret Gordon. 'Irving too, it was sometimes thought', says Carlyle slyly, 'found her very interesting, could the Miss-Martin bonds have allowed; which they never would.' Carlyle himself knew her for only a few months, after which 'she continued, for perhaps some three years a figure hanging more or less in my fancy'.[61]

By 1820 Margaret and her aunt had left for London, where in 1824 she married Alexander Bannerman, described in *Reminiscences* as 'some rich insignificant Aberdeen Mr Something'. Bannerman became an MP and later Governor of Newfoundland, or, as Carlyle put it, making significant use of punctuation and a general vagueness designed to diminish, 'Mr Something afterwards got into Parliament, thence out to "Nova Scotia" (or *so*) "as Governor"; and I heard of her no more.'[62]

He had heard *from* Margaret, however. She sent him two letters in June 1820, gently breaking off relations on the eve of her departure for London, and giving him some 'sisterly' advice, including the (unheeded) suggestion: '*Cultivate the milder dispositions of your heart, subdue the more extravagant visions of the brain . . . Genius* will render you *great*. May *virtue* render you *beloved*!'[63]

Having decided in November 1818 that Kirkcaldy and schoolteaching were not for him, Carlyle left for Edinburgh once more, not hopeful, but thinking he might manage there for two years, living on his savings, which he could supplement by taking private pupils. With preaching and teaching rejected as possible careers, he decided to try the study first of mineralogy, then of law.[64]

Thus began four more years of misery and indecision. Winters were spent in Edinburgh, half-heartedly attending lectures in different subjects, teaching private pupils maths and astronomy, frequently moving lodgings in vain attempts to escape the noises and smells of the city, and in general leading 'a miscellaneous, undescribeable life'.[65] Summers saw him moping on his parents' farm, trying to hide his religious doubts from his mother. As he recalled in 1866, the conversation at home often turned to theology, much to his discomfiture. However, 'I did learn at length, by judicious endeavour, to speak piously and *agreeably* to one so pious, *without* unveracity on my part, nay it was a kind of interesting exercise to wind softly out of those anxious affectionate cavils of her dear heart, on such occasions, and *get* real sympathy, real assent, under borrowed forms.'[66]

At all seasons Carlyle suffered agonies from dyspepsia and from the drastic remedies he applied, in the form of frequent large doses of mercury and sulphate of magnesia.[67] In an unfinished autobiographical novel, 'Wotton Reinfred', begun and abandoned in 1827 and later cut up for passages to use in *Sartor Resartus*, Carlyle describes the equivalent period in the life of his alter ego Wotton as a time of 'eating his own heart . . . like Homer's Bellerophon'.[68]

Some gleams of light relieved the gloom. In February 1819 Carlyle met Dr David Brewster, inventor of the kaleidoscope in 1817 and editor of the *Edinburgh Encyclopædia*, for which he commissioned some twenty articles from Carlyle over the next few years on miscellaneous subjects mainly beginning with M and N (including Montaigne, Newfoundland, Norfolk, and Northumberland).[69] He also began taking German lessons from a Dumfriesshire acquaintance, Robert Jardine, in return for lessons in French, and was soon reading Lessing and Klopstock. On 25 September 1819 he makes the first mention of Goethe.[70] In the same letter he talks of Irving's having found a position as clergyman's assistant to no less a person than the famous Dr Thomas Chalmers of Glasgow. Carlyle rejoices for his friend, while harbouring fears that 'his fervid genius' might 'prompt him into extravagances'.[71]

From now on Carlyle saw Irving only intermittently, but they remained firm friends. Carlyle reported to his friend Robert Mitchell in December 1819 that Irving was hugely popular in Glasgow, where he was conspicuous for his support for starving weavers and other victims of the economic crisis which was sweeping the manufacturing cities of Britain. 1819 was the year of the Peterloo Massacre just outside Manchester; in November Carlyle's 'foolish' namesake, the radical publisher Richard Carlile, was imprisoned for blasphemous libel after reprinting Tom Paine's *Age of Reason*.[72] In Edinburgh, Carlyle wrote in December, 'we are all going mad. Radical Reformers – seditious orators – & warlike burghers are the humour of the day.'[73]

While Carlyle was learning German, he was also engaged in tutoring the brother next to him in age, Alick, who had stayed at Mainhill helping on the family farm, in a course of reading and writing. Alick was told to persevere with Hume's history in January 1820, but to be on his guard against Hume's 'propensities to toryism'. Carlyle also corrected Alick's poor spelling.[74]

At the same time Jane Welsh was writing to her Edinburgh friend Eliza Stodart. Almost overwhelmed with grief at the recent loss of her father, she was trying to fulfil his wishes for her by continuing her own education – learning French and Italian – while also making use of her accomplishments to teach a group of younger girls. '*He* used always to tell me that in giving me a good education he was leaving me the greatest good'; and 'the habits of study in which I have been brought up have done much to support me', she reported early in 1820.[75] Her life was settling into a routine of quiet days at home with her mother, varied by short visits to Edinburgh to stay with Eliza Stodart at Eliza's uncle John Bradfute's house in George Square, and occasional journeys further afield, notably to Liverpool to visit her maternal uncle, John Welsh, and his family. Having lost the person she had loved and admired most in the world, she was vulnerable to the rediscovered attractions of Irving, who was making a name for himself in Glasgow and preparing to be ordained by his native presbytery at Annan in August 1820.[76]

As for Carlyle, nothing seemed to go right. Finding he had a talent for writing, he decided in January 1820 to send a trial review article to Francis Jeffrey, famous editor of the *Edinburgh Review*, the great quarterly journal of literature and Whig politics. Choosing a French work on the theory of gravitation, he wrote his review, 'penned some brief polite Note to the great Editor', and 'walked off with the small Parcel, one night, to his address in George Street'. The result was 'absolute *zero*, no answer, no return of MS, absolutely no notice taken; which was a form of catastrophe more complete than even I had anticipated!'[77] The experience soured for good his view of Jeffrey, in spite of the latter's subsequent kindness towards him; more positively, his crystal-clear memory of his feelings played its part in later years when Carlyle himself was constantly being petitioned by aspiring authors and made it a point of honour to reply.

Dr Brewster was more encouraging than Jeffrey, but a magazine he hoped to found, with Carlyle as chief contributor, never materialised.[78] Another plan, that of using his newly acquired knowledge of German to translate Schiller's history of the Thirty Years War (*Geschichte des Dreissigjährigen Krieges*, 1791–3), was turned down by the publisher Longman.[79] In a further desperate attempt to gain some secure position, Carlyle went to Yorkshire in October 1820 to investigate the prospect of becoming a 'travelling tutor' to a mentally retarded boy. He returned from this venture describing the boy savagely as 'a dotard, a semi-vegetable', and his elder brother, the head of the family, as (in an echo of Swift's *Tale of a Tub*), 'a two-legged animal without feathers'.[80]

To set against these negatives, however, was the growing conviction that he would be a writer. 'Confound the knaves!' he wrote to Jack in January 1821, 'I will write a *book* and shame them all.'[81] The growth of such defiant self-confidence was linked to the discovery, which would be momentous for him, and also, through him, for Victorian culture generally, of Goethe's works. Carlyle confided the first of many expressions of excited admiration to Irving in June 1820. The subject was *Faust*:

I wish Goethe were my countryman, I wish – O, how I wish – he were my friend. It is not for his masterly conception of human nature – from the heroes of classical story down to the blackguards of a Leipsic alehouse – that I admire him above all others; his profound sentiment of beauty, his most brilliant delineations of all its varieties – his gayety of head and melancholy of heart, open all the floodgates of my sympathy. Faust is a wonderful tragedy. I doubt if even Shakespeare with all his powers had sadness enough in his nature to understand the arid and withered feelings of a passionate spirit, worn out by excessive studies and the want of all enjoyment; to delineate the chaos of his thoughts when the secrets of nature are bared before him; to depict his terrible volition and the bitter mockery of the demon [which] gives scope to that volition.[82]

Carlyle was not the first, nor yet the last, discontented youth to respond so heartily to Goethe's drama. For Carlyle, however, Goethe would come to seem nothing less than an aesthetic and spiritual saviour, and he would in due course deliver that message to British readers. In the more immediate future, Goethe and German literature – with its revelation of a 'new Heaven and new Earth'[83] – became a vital ally in the struggle to win, and keep, the affection of Jane Welsh.

CHAPTER 2

Negotiating Romance 1821–1824

They met at the beginning of June 1821. Carlyle was thoroughly smitten and not so shy that he could not gratify his longings by writing to Jane immediately on his return to Edinburgh. Addressing her boldly as 'my dear Friend', he plunged into an impressive list of prescribed reading for her. It might seem 'presumptuous' of him to 'act as your tutor', but he was prepared to take the risk. He advised her to read Robertson, Hume, and Voltaire for history; also Noehden's German grammar when he could procure it for her, and Madame de Staël's famous book on Germany, *De l'Allemagne* (1813).

A novice in the genre of the love letter, he entered self-consciously into the realms of flirtation, asking her to 'tell me in three words what you think of the Lady de Staël' and say whether 'her cousin, the Lady Jane is well and happy; and whether the latter has ever deigned to cast one glance of recollection on those few Elysian hours we spent together lately?' He wound the letter up with an expression of self-irony – 'this wonderful compound of pedagogy and sentimentality and absurdity must conclude' – and a contradictory indication of the relationship he envisaged between them: 'It seems as if we had known each other from infancy upwards, and I were simply your elder Brother', followed by '*Addio, Donna mia cara* [Farewell, my dear Lady]!'[1] The only reply he received to this letter and the accompanying set of books was the following line: 'To Mr Carslile [*sic*], with Miss Welsh's compliments and very best thanks.'[2]

This was an inauspicious beginning. If Carlyle had not been singularly determined, Jane's unfriendly note, accompanying the return of the books he had lent her, might have strangled at birth one of the most extensive exchanges of letters surviving between two people.[3] But he was determined indeed. In 'Wotton Reinfred' he introduces the character Jane Montagu (mainly Jane Welsh, with a dash of Margaret Gordon), who stirs in Wotton an unfamiliar feeling of 'commotion', 'astonishment', and 'agitation'. Wotton responds exactly as his creator did: 'Strange enough! There are moments of trial, of peril, of extreme anxiety, when a man whom we reckoned timid becomes the calmest and firmest. Reinfred's whole being was in a hurricane; but it seemed as if himself were above it, ruling over it, in unwonted strength and clearness.'[4]

Carlyle replied in this spirit to Jane's discouraging note. He did not hide his disappointment or hurt pride, not least at her misspelling of his name, but he quickly moved on to the ground he instinctively knew to be the firmest on which to pursue the relationship – books. He was careful to address her now as 'My dear Madam', rather than presuming on a friendship she had not bestowed:

My dear Madam,
It would have been a pleasant spectacle for Mephistopheles or any of his sooty brethren, – in whose eyes, I understand, this restless life of ours appears like a regular Farce, only somewhat dull at times, – to have surveyed my feelings before opening your parcel, the other night, and after opening it: to have seen with what hysterical speed I undid the grey cover; how I turned over the poor tomes; how I shook them, and searched them through and through; and found – Miss Welsh's 'compliments' to Mr Car*slile*, a gentleman, in whom, it required no small sagacity to detect my own representation! Upon the whole, I suppose, you did well to treat me so. I had dreamed and hoped, indeed; but what right had *I* to hope, or even to wish?
    Those latter volumes of the *Allemagne* will perplex you, I fear. The third in particular is very mysterious; now and then quite absurd. Do not mind it much. – Noehden is not come, the London Smacks being all becalmed. I hope it will arrive in time; to let us begin Lessing and Schiller and the rest, against October, without impediment.[5]

He sensed that this young woman, already well educated at the behest of the father whose memory she held sacred, would respond positively to the pedagogy, while she scorned the sentimentality, in his letters. Encouragingly, her second reply, on 6 July, was a little longer and a little less frosty:

Dear Sir
I return your books; and heartily thank you for the pleasure they have afforded me – I fear you think I have kept them long; nevertheless I have not been idle – I have dismissed my German Master (for the enormous offence of asserting all words beginning with capitals to be the names of towns) and I think I get on faster without him.
    Yours Truly
        Jane Baillie Welsh.[6]

Carlyle was not slow to step into the space so conveniently opened up by the departure of the unnamed fool of a teacher. 'My project', he replied emphatically, 'is no less than *to set out in person to inspect and accelerate your progress in the German tongue!*' For this he planned to visit her in August. 'Will you let me come?' Masterful and pleading by turns, he both lectures and flatters Jane, begging her to 'sit down *instantly*, and say *La Reine le veut*', assuring her that he thinks her more than merely 'a very accomplished young Lady', and asking her 'most humbly' not to address him as 'Car-*slile*' again.[7] Jane graciously accepted the offer of his advice on German matters, but indicated that Mrs Welsh was uncertain about a visit from him. However, she was to be in Edinburgh at Mr Bradfute's house towards the end of July, and Carlyle would be welcome to call on her there.[8]

So began the relationship. There is no record of what Jane thought of Carlyle on first view, though it is clear that she did not fall in love with him. He, on the contrary, laid his cards on the table straight away, yet his feelings were changing and complex. He pursued her single-mindedly, but was capable of procrastination and temporary withdrawal, so that the story of their long courtship is no simple one of the dogged, devoted suitor gradually wearing down the resistance of the fair object of his attentions. A pattern emerged of mutual struggle, of progress and reversal, of shifting mastery and submission, of genuine fondness and sharp criticism, in the letters which travelled between Haddington, Edinburgh, and Dumfries-shire. From the summer of 1821 until they finally married in October 1826, Thomas and Jane met in person only two or three times a year, sometimes less, and then either in snatched half-hours at Mr Bradfute's house in Edinburgh or under the generally baleful eye of Mrs Welsh in Haddington.

The infrequency of their personal contact was due largely to Mrs Welsh's dislike of Carlyle, but the relationship itself often seemed to lack inner urgency, so much so that at various times it looked unlikely that it would ever result in marriage. Though they eventually found they could not live without one another, both showed at times a marked reluctance to find the means to live together. Jane was not, it seems, sexually attracted to Carlyle, while he may well have been frightened of sex altogether. She was later brutally frank (perhaps exaggeratedly so) in a letter of 1843 to her Liverpool cousin Jeannie Welsh about her reasons for marrying Carlyle:

In virtue of his being *the least unlikable* man in the place, I let him dance attendance on my young person, till I came to *need* him – all the same as my slippers, to go to a ball in, or my bonnet to go out to walk. When I finally agreed to marry him, I *cried* excessively and felt excessively shocked – but if I had said *no* he would have left me – and how could I dispense with what was equivalent to my slippers or bonnet?[9]

For his part, Carlyle, who was never critical of Jane in his letters to family and friends in the way she was of him, confessed in the privacy of his journal in September 1825, by which time Jane had finally accepted his proposal, 'My conscience like my sense of pain and pleasure, has grown dull, and *I secretly desire to compensate for laxity of feeling by intenseness of describing*'.[10] His journal, both before and after his marriage, is the repository of much self-pity, mainly about his health, but what is most striking is how frequently its entries express his feeling of complete isolation, even alienation, from his fellow human beings, including Jane.

It is important to understand the strength and permanence of this feeling that he was set apart from the rest of mankind. His case was unusual, for though many another sensitive child suffers bullying and friendlessness at school, and many a shy youth is miserable at university, and many a fledgling author feels hurt to the core by early rejection, it is not often that such a person, once grown up, married, surrounded by friends and family, famous, successful, and admired in his chosen career, continues to suffer from such an intense feeling of loneliness as Carlyle did. It was the dark side of his unique gift as a writer; he himself recognised it as a genetic inheritance which he shared with his brothers Alick and John, though they did not have the genius that was his. 'We Carlyles', he wrote to Alick in December 1820, 'are a clannish people; because we have all something original in our formation, and find, therefore, less than common sympathy with others.'[11]

Jane, from such a different family background, was to find the Carlyle clan difficult to like, and her husband in particular difficult to understand, though it was precisely his unusualness, his unique genius, to which she found herself attracted. She could not know, when she cautiously accepted his attentions in 1821, that, though all Carlyle's hopes of personal happiness rested on her, she would in fact make very little difference to that happiness because he was a man driven by physical and spiritual demons which were impervious to her influence. Perhaps a guilty realisation of this truth lies behind that journal entry of Carlyle's in September 1825, in which he acknowledges a dulling of conscience as well as of feeling.

During the early summer of 1821 Carlyle, back in Edinburgh, corresponded with Jane about German literature and worked hard at writing on the Netherlands and Newfoundland for Brewster's *Encyclopædia*. He wrote to his mother and brothers, indicating that he was 'moderately comfortable or even happy at present', but making no direct mention of Jane.[12] By mid-August he was at home in Mainhill, from where he wrote to Irving, revealing that during his last few weeks in Edinburgh 'sleeplessness and so forth had rendered me a fitter inmate for Bedlam than a study'. His old enemy dyspepsia had taken an unprecedented grip on him; its worst effect was the indignity, the disgust which overwhelmed all other feelings, even love:

The bodily pain is nothing or next to nothing; but alas for the dignity of man! The evil does not stop here. No strength of soul can avail you; this malady will turn that very strength against yourself; it banishes all thought from your head, all love from your heart – and doubles your wretchedness by making you discern it.

O! the long, solitary, sleepless nights that I have passed – with no employment but to count the pulses of my own sick heart – till the gloom of external things seemed to extend itself to the very centre of the mind, till I could remember nothing, observe nothing! All this magnificent nature appeared as if blotted out, a grey, dirty, dismal vapour filled the immensity of space; I stood alone in the universe – alone, and as it were a circle of burning iron enveloped the soul – excluding from it every feeling but a stony-hearted, dead obduracy, more befitting a demon in its place of woe than a man in the land of the living! I tell you, my friend, nothing makes me shudder to the inmost core – *nothing* but this.[13]

Horrid imaginings and terrible sufferings indeed for a man who had just fallen in love.

★

Dyspepsia for Carlyle, as for another sufferer, Charles Darwin, meant more than chronic indigestion. It involved physical weakness and mental depression, and, most alarmingly for both these meticulous men, self-disgust proceeding from the embarrassment of wind and the irregularity and sometimes torture of passing bowel movements. Coleridge, who suffered from constipation as one of the side effects of his opium addiction, described the agony of the condition, which all but stopped him from reaching the lecture hall during a series he was delivering on criticism and literature in 1811. 'Truly for 8 days together', he told Henry Crabb Robinson, 'the Trunk of my poor Body was or seemed to be a Trunk which Nature had first locked, then thrown away the Key.' He added to this graphic description a comic account of the sudden resolution of his problem, achieved, he thought, thanks to his 'morbid delicacy' at the thought of the imminent approach of an old woman with a 'clyster' (enema): 'Flash! like lightning, and roar & rumble! like thunder, it (i.e. the proximate cause) plunged down thro' me – & to the Music loud and visceral and cataractic I sang out, "I do not want the old Lady! – give her half a crown and send her away!"'[14]

Carlyle was unable to be so direct, even in his journals; but his frequent use of unpleasant smells as metaphors or names – Teufelsdröckh means 'devil's dung', the popular name for asafoetida, a strong-smelling resinous gum used as an emetic – represents his striking way of giving vent in vehement social and political criticism to a disgust which, as he well knew, had its roots in his unfortunate physical condition.

Much might be said about the possible causes of digestive ailments in cases such as Coleridge's, Carlyle's, or Darwin's (especially as the latter's illness became chronic when he was writing up a secret diary acknowledging the consequences for orthodox religious belief of his evolutionary

36

conclusions). 'Psychosomatic' is a word which springs to mind, as indeed it did to Coleridge, who coined it.[15] These three men were all original thinkers and men of genius; all of them experienced strong feelings of guilt and exhibited symptoms of fear of sex and marriage. But however their conditions arose, the salient fact is that each of them suffered, and their sufferings seemed often to dictate the course of their lives.

Carlyle looked back at his early life in a fragment of writing done in his last years. On two crammed pages covered in a shaky hand, he speculates on the possibility that he might have been a cheerful person, 'had not Dyspepsia, with its base and unspeakable miseries, kept such fatal hold of me'.[16] That journal entry of September 1825, already quoted in part, perhaps comes nearest to expressing Carlyle's physical and mental anguish; it does so in terms which seem to link his ill health to his sexual fearfulness. This is one of the few instances in which he addresses Jane in the journals; he moves into German to do so:

Unhappy man in whom the body has gained mastery over the soul! Inverse Sensualist, not drawn into the rank of beasts by pleasure, but driven into it by pain! . . .
  Ach Du meine Einzige, die Du mich liebst und Dich an mir anschmiegst, warum bin Ich dir wie ein gebrochenes Rohr! – sollst Du *niemals* glücklich werden! Wo bist Du heute Nacht? Mögen Friede und Liebe und Hoffnung deine Gefährten seyn! Leb' wohl! [Ah my only one, you who love me and cling to me, why am I but as a broken reed for you! Are you *never* to be happy? Where are you tonight? May peace and love and hope be your companions! Farewell!]

The very next entry, for 3 December 1826, opens as follows: 'Married! Married! – *Aber still davon*! [but say nothing of that!]'[17]

We can try to imagine Carlyle's state of mind in June 1821, newly in love but aware that he is not – yet – loved in return, hopeful yet doubtful of his success as a suitor; at the same time he suffers the tortures of dyspepsia and its embarrassments – how can he contemplate intimacy with anyone in such a condition? And then there is his anxiety about religion. Recognising in himself a religious cast of mind, he knows too that his critical faculties are constantly undermining passive acceptance of the old faith. Finally, he is still, at quite an advanced age of young manhood, far from fixed in a career, though he strongly suspects that he has found his *métier* – writing. But what should he write? Who will publish him? How will he survive financially in the meantime?

Carlyle did not know it then, in the midst of his difficulties, but his eventual expression of the chaos of thought and emotions of that summer of 1821 became archetypal, speaking to many who were suffering their own doubts and difficulties. The 'Everlasting No' chapter of *Sartor* annotates the inner experience of Diogenes Teufelsdröckh:

Alas, shut-out from Hope, in a deeper sense than we yet dream of! For, as he wanders wearisomely through this world, he has now lost all tidings of another and higher. Full of religion, or at least of religiosity, as our Friend has since exhibited himself, he hides not that, in those days, he was wholly irreligious: 'Doubt had darkened into Unbelief', says he; 'shade after shade goes grimly over your soul, till you have the fixed, starless, Tartarean black.'

Teufelsdröckh and his author envy those with uninquiring minds and strong stomachs. 'With Stupidity and sound Digestion man may front much', says Teufelsdröckh. 'But what, in these dull unimaginative days, are the terrors of Conscience to the diseases of the Liver!' Carlyle projects his younger self's sense of alienation on to his creation:

I walked solitary; and (except as it was my own heart, not another's, that I kept devouring) savage also, as the tiger in his jungle. Some comfort it would have been, could I, like a Faust, have fancied myself tempted and tormented of the Devil; for a Hell, as I imagine, without Life, though only diabolic Life, were more frightful: but in our age of Down-pulling and Disbelief, the very Devil has been pulled down, you cannot so much as believe in a Devil. To me the Universe was all void of Life, of Purpose, of Volition, even of Hostility: it was one huge, dead, immeasurable Steam-engine, rolling on, in its dead indifference, to grind me limb from limb.

Finally, Carlyle gives utterance to the most famous passage in *Sartor*, in which he mingles autobiographical fact with myth, as Teufelsdröckh recounts a moment of revelation:

Full of such humour, and perhaps the miserablest man in the whole French Capital or Suburbs, was I, one sultry Dog-day, after much perambulation, toiling along the dirty little *Rue Saint-Thomas de l'Enfer*, among civic rubbish enough, in a close atmosphere, and over pavements hot as Nebuchadnezzar's Furnace; whereby doubtless my spirits were little cheered; when, all at once, there rose a Thought in me, and I asked myself: 'What *art* thou afraid of? Wherefore, like a coward, dost thou forever pip and whimper, and go cowering and trembling? Despicable biped! what is the sum-total of the worst that lies before thee? Death? Well, Death; and say the pangs of Tophet too, and all that the Devil and Man may, will or can do against thee! . . . Let it come, then; I will meet it and defy it!' And as I so thought, there rushed like a stream of fire over my whole soul; and I shook base Fear away from me forever. I was strong, of unknown strength; a spirit, almost a god . . .

Thus had the EVERLASTING NO (*das ewige Nein*) pealed authoritatively through all the recesses of my Being, of my ME; and then was it that my whole ME stood up, in native God-created majesty, and with emphasis recorded its Protest.[18]

This is the expression of a turning point. Carlyle noted later that this incident, set in Paris and incorporating a joke on his name – St Thomas of Hell – was based on an actual experience 'which occurred quite literally to myself in Leith Walk, during those 3 weeks of total sleeplessness, in which almost my one solace was that of a daily bather on the sands between Leith and Portobello' (on the Firth of Forth, north of Edinburgh).[19] Inasmuch as Carlyle did reach some kind of peace and resolution (though a peculiarly defiant one, as the *Sartor* passage demonstrates), first in June 1821,[20] and again over the next few years of ups and downs, he owed it to Goethe.

The reading of Madame de Staël on Germany and of Goethe's *Faust* in 1819–20 began a process which continued with his translating *Wilhelm Meister's Apprenticeship* (1824) and *Wilhelm Meister's Travels* (1827), writing several articles on Goethe, quoting him widely as 'the Wisest of our time', and exchanging letters with him from 1824 until Goethe's death in 1832. Over the years Carlyle acquired an intimate knowledge, as his later friend John Tyndall stated, of 'every nook and cranny' of Goethe's huge literary output.[21] To Goethe himself Carlyle wrote in August 1827, in answer to an inquiry about 'my bygone life':

With what readiness could I speak to you of it, how often have I longed to pour out the whole history before you! As it is, your works have been a mirror to me; unasked and unhoped for, your wisdom has counselled me; and so peace and health of soul have visited me from afar. For I was once an Unbeliever, not in Religion only, but in all the Mercy and Beauty of which it is the symbol; storm-tossed in my own imaginations; a man divided from men; exasperated, wretched, driven almost to despair; so that Faust's wild *curse* seemed the only fit greeting for human life, and his passionate *Fluch vor allen der Geduld*! [Cursed above all be patience!] was spoken from my very inmost heart. But now, thank Heaven, all this is altered: without change of external circumstances, solely by the new light which rose upon me, I attained to new thoughts, and a composure which I should once have considered as impossible.[22]

Goethe seemed to have risen above the Faustian torment of soul to land on a high plateau of peace and resignation, and Carlyle felt he had been enabled to follow him there.

To others Carlyle confided at different times that he owed everything to Goethe – even life itself, as Henry Crabb Robinson noted after talking to him in 1832.[23] In a letter to Thomas Spedding in 1851 he answered the question so often asked about his religious beliefs. His 'creed', he writes, 'is all in the most compact quiescent condition', 'and gives me no trouble at all for the last thirty years or so, – fierce as the struggle was, almost to the edge of death or insanity, that I had with it before. But ever since, as Goethe says, "With God, or with the Gods, my affairs have stood on a very tolerable footing!" '[24]

This is evasive; deliberately so, for Carlyle's 'religion' was a strange and shifting entity, as he himself knew. Though he suffered from religious doubt in the 1820s, that doubt was intertwined with other worries, with self-doubt, depression, illness, and anxiety. In his journal for 31 December 1823 he even toyed briefly with the notion of suicide.[25] Goethe, with his Olympian aloofness yet general tolerance of erring humanity, exercised a saving influence across the whole range of Carlyle's troubles, not just in religious questions.

Given this inner turmoil as he began his relationship with Jane, it might strike us as surprising that at no time in their courtship correspondence did the topic of religion arise. One reason was Carlyle's sense of isolation: his spiritual struggles were worked out in the privacy of his journals, and released gradually and in transformed ways in his writings during the 1820s and 1830s. Another reason may have been that Jane, though not yet out of her teens when she met Carlyle, had already given up her religious faith, perhaps chiefly as a result of her father's death. She had written to her paternal grandmother soon after the catastrophe, striving to express her belief in the wisdom of 'the Almighty' in cutting off 'one who was the Glory of his family, & a most useful member of society, one who was respected & beloved by all who knew him'. Though Jane is writing to a religious grandmother and trying to submit to God's will, bitterness is the keynote. One almost suspects satire at God's expense as Jane struggles with the idea that 'the ways of the Almighty are mysterious'

> & though he has afflicted those whom we thought deserved to be happy – *yet* his intention appears to me clear and intelligible – Could the annihilation of a Thousand useless and contemptible beings have sent such terror & submission to the hearts of the survivors as the sudden death of one whom their love would if possible have gifted with immortality – Oh no – Hard it is – but we must acknowledge the wisdom of his sentence even while we are suffering under it – We must kiss the rod even while we are writhing under the tortures which it inflicts.[26]

Carlyle, who read this letter after Jane's death, commented that 'the *religious* expressions I find here' were 'the first and the last instance I have met with' in her.[27] In later years Jane was known for her scepticism; she shocked some acquaintances with her 'sweeping declamation against Christianity and the Church', and led her interlocutors, so Charlotte Williams Wynn declared in 1856, to expect to be 'scalped' if they ventured to disagree.[28] Her decisiveness contrasts markedly with Carlyle's seesawing movement.

★

Religion, then, was not a topic for Jane and Carlyle in 1821, though it formed such an important part of the latter's inner struggles. German literature was the thing, with Carlyle eagerly playing Abelard to Jane's Héloïse. Intriguingly, Irving performed an important function in the early months of this new relationship between his two friends. A three-way correspondence evolved, with Irving voicing his suspicions of the 'entanglements' of German literature generally and of Goethe in particular. He urged Carlyle not to encourage 'our fair acquaintance' in what was already a visible tendency to religious scepticism.[29] Carlyle later recalled that his friend 'did not much know Goethe; had generally a dislike to him, as to a kind of Heathen *ungodly* person and idle Singer, who had considerably seduced *me* from the right path'.[30]

Jane attempted a translation of Goethe's poem 'Der Fischer' ('The Fisherman'); Carlyle, styling himself 'Hypercriticus Minimus', corrected it.[31] German proved useful as a language to convey personal comments which Mrs Welsh, who read his letters to Jane, would not understand – as in September 1821, when Carlyle asked plaintively in German why his 'dearest friend' had not written for three weeks.[32] Jane was hampered by her mother's caprices; one moment she was permitted to invite Carlyle to call, the next forbidden even to correspond with him.[33] Fortunately Carlyle did not know that Irving was writing in February 1822 to 'my dear and lovely Pupil', telling her of his great success during a trial period of preaching in London and thanking 'your affectionate mother, whose indulgence gives me this pleasant communication with her daughter'.[34]

For his part, Carlyle was pleased to hear of Irving's fame, which he reported to their mutual friend John Fergusson in February 1822, describing Irving's offers of employment from the Hatton Garden congregation in London and from New York (where the salary would be an astonishing £1,000). 'I believe him to be about the best man in the Scottish Church, both for head and heart', wrote Carlyle.[35]

He himself, meanwhile, had better prospects, for which he had Irving to thank. While preaching at the Caledonian Chapel in Hatton Garden in December 1821, Irving had met two sisters, Julia Strachey and Isabella Buller, both wives of retired Anglo-Indian judges. Mrs Buller was particularly impressed by the young preacher and sought his advice about the education of her two older sons, Charles, aged fifteen, and Arthur, aged thirteen. Both were at Harrow, and the plan was to send them to a Scottish university. Mrs Buller was looking for a tutor who would live with the family when it moved to Scotland, whereupon Irving generously recommended Carlyle. Mrs Buller, Carlyle later recalled with a deft stroke of the pen, was 'a Calcutta fine lady, a bright princess of the kind worshipped there, a once very beautiful, still very witty graceful airy and ingenuously intelligent woman, of the *gossamer* kind'.[36]

The offer, at £200 a year, came just in time, as Carlyle had had no regular income since giving up teaching three years before. Telling his father of his new prospects, he rejoiced that 'Fate is about to lift its heavy hand off me'.[37]

So it proved, at least for a time. The Buller family came to Edinburgh, and Carlyle began the tutoring experiment, staying for the moment in his old lodgings in Moray Street, which he now shared with his student brother Jack. He found he got on with the Bullers, Charles Buller senior being a good-natured, 'very deaf' type of the English squire, and Mrs Buller gracious, if inclined to show 'a lively appetite' for 'the Ex-Indian accidental English-gentleman, and native or touring *Lion* genus'.[38] Charles junior, reputed to be 'a clever, but too mercurial unmanageable' lad, turned out to be a 'most manageable, intelligent, cheery and altogether welcome and agreeable phenomenon; quite a bit of sunshine in my dreary Edinburgh element'. Carlyle became extremely fond of Charles. He records in his reminiscence, almost with the surprise he must have felt in 1822, that 'the two Youths both took to me with unhesitating liking, and I to them'.[39] The only dampener to this hopeful new beginning was the old enemy, dyspepsia: 'Irving and other friends always treated the "ill-health" item as a light matter, which would soon vanish from the account; but I had a presentiment that it would stay there, and be the Old Man of the Sea to me through life.'[40]

Carlyle was no doubt glad to be able to tell Jane, who would tell her socially conscious mother, about the new appointment with the glamorous Bullers. Despite a brutally clear message from Jane in January 1822 that a visit to Haddington would be unwelcome to both her mother and herself (on account of the 'impertinent conjectures' it might arouse in 'this tattling, illnatured place', as well as his 'too ardent' expressions of devotion), Carlyle persisted in threatening to come and see her. 'Present my kindest respects to your Mother – if you think it worth while', he wrote doggedly on 30 January.[41]

He did go, which was a mistake. Mrs Welsh was cold, and Jane made him feel like a country bumpkin. She told Eliza Stodart about his two-day visit in February, during which they had successfully read German together but he had annoyed her with his clumsiness: 'He scratched the fenders dreadfully – I must have a pair of carpet-shoes and hand-cuffs prepared for him the next time – His tongue only should be left at liberty his other members are most fantastically awkward.'[42]

Carlyle might have felt less discouraged if he could have read the part about 'the next time', but he only knew that the visit had been 'unfortunate' and that Jane and her mother felt socially superior to him. By a lucky chance Irving now enclosed a letter for Jane in one to Carlyle, asking him to send it on to Haddington. This Carlyle did, taking the opportunity to assure her he fully understood 'what is your rank and what your prospects', but asking her to 'forget the roughness of my exterior, if you think me sound within'.[43]

Once more this awkward young man had struck the right note, appealing to the one advantage he had over the other young men in Jane's eyes – his intellect. He would have felt flattered had he seen another recent letter from Jane to her Edinburgh confidante, in which a reading of Rousseau's *Nouvelle Héloïse* was applied light-heartedly to her own case. 'No lover will Jane Welsh ever find like St Preux – no Husband like Wolmar (I dont mean to insinuate that *I should like both*)', she wrote, ticking off a list of recent would-be lovers: 'George Rennie! James Aitken! Robert MacTurk! James Baird!!! Robby Angus!' She went on to muse that Carlyle was *something* like St Preux:

He has *his* talents – *his* vast and cultivated mind – *his* vivid imagination – *his* independence of soul and *his* high souled principles of honour – But then Ah these *buts*! St Preux never kicked the fire irons – nor made puddings in his teacup – Want of Elegance – Want of Elegance Rousseau says is a defect which no woman can overlook.[44]

Carlyle had the common sense not to propose any more visits. He simply resumed the role of epistolary Abelard/St Preux to Jane's Héloïse/Julie, while getting on with tutoring the Bullers, encouraging his brother Jack's plans to study medicine, and translating A. M. Legendre's *Elements of Geometry* for David Brewster. Jane teased him when he wrote about his feelings, telling him rather tartly in April that she was glad to hear that 'the wretched Mr Carlyle has been restored sound in mind and body to his lamenting friends'.[45] She let him know she had other suitors, all of whom had the advantage over him of being able to see her in person, one in particular being very close at hand. This was Dr Alexander Fyffe, who rented the ground-floor surgery of Mrs Welsh's house for his practice, and pressed his unwanted attentions on Jane.[46]

Poor Dr Fyffe became the chief butt of Jane's considerable gift for satire. Carlyle was told about an incident involving this unfortunate suitor in a letter of 1 July in which Jane did not scruple to dangle herself as a desirable object before him:

I was almost forgetting to tell you that I was nearly killed last night. In trying to prevent Dr Fyffe's seeing my ancles (which you may perhaps know are no great things) I lost my balance, and fell from the top of a very high wall – My head proved thicker than I fancied for though I struck it on some stones it sustained no damage – But I lost my gown in the cause and two of my front teeth. – I am bearing this double misfortune with great philosophy so you need not vex yourself about it, the less as one half of it is not true – My teeth being all in my head.[47]

Carlyle kept cool, replying after a decent interval of nearly two weeks, when he let her know how busy he had been, how much he, too, was in demand, with the printer asking for copy (presumably of the Legendre), the Bullers making arrangements about the boys, and Irving arriving on a visit. He was not above doing some dangling in his turn, though not of his (un)desirable person; rather he held up to her the flattering prospect that she might yet become a 'true-minded woman of genius' if she could put her undoubted literary talents to use, under his guidance, on worthwhile subjects.[48]

★

If Carlyle had been a little daunted by the elegance of Mrs Welsh's drawing room, he was now becoming acquainted with quarters much more fashionable, since the Bullers were living in high style in – appropriately – India Street. He told his mother in September that he now took his evening tea 'in the drawing-room of the Bullers with urns and china and splendid apparatus all around me'. Yet, he assured her, he often turned from all that grandeur 'with a soft and pensive recollection to the little *down-the-house* at Mainhill, where kind affections made amends for all deficiences, and would have made rich amends for a thousand more'.[49]

Carlyle appears still to have kept his relationship with Jane secret from his mother, having only once, in December 1821, mentioned in passing that he had 'a standing invitation, from a very excellent Mrs Welsh, to go to Haddington'.[50] On 4 December 1822 he merely mentions in his usual birthday letter to Mrs Carlyle that he is now twenty-seven and 'an unprofitable lout' who has not yet rewarded 'those that had the trouble of my upbringing'. As he often did in his letters to his anxious, pious mother, he adopted the language of the Old Testament:

Great part of an ordinary life-time is gone by: and here am I, poor trifler, still sojourning in Meshach still dwelling among the tents of Kedar! May the great Father of all give me strength to do better in time remaining, to be of service in the good cause in my day and generation, and 'having finished the work which was given me to do' to lie down and sleep in peace and purity in the hope of a happy rising! Amen![51]

This is a good example of his accommodation to his mother's religion. To others he wrote much less biblically, but he was scrupulous not to say anything contrary to his own beliefs in these letters to his mother. In fact, the language he used to her came to be one hallmark of his published writings, especially *Sartor Resartus*. Here, perhaps, lies a clue to its enormous influence; it spoke of spiritual torture and philosophical doubt in terms often borrowed from the most grim biblical landscapes, while a comforting ground-note of faith continued to sound through all the uproar.

As for Carlyle not mentioning Jane to his family, it is likely that his pride played a part in this. After all, his relationship with her was by no means secure. They had not met since his disastrous visit to Haddington in February 1822, and were not to see one another again for a whole year. Meanwhile, Jane blew hot and cold when he returned in his letters to expressions of love and hope. She told him in November 1822 that their first meeting had been memorable for her, but the reason was a troubling one. She had still been full of 'grief at the loss of the only being I ever loved with my whole soul'; the 'pole-star' of her life was lost; she had 'no counsellor that could direct' her. Carlyle had appeared, and 'you spoke like him – your eloquence awoke in my soul the slumbering admirations and ambitions that *His* first kindled there'.[52]

Jane went on sounding this note in their correspondence. Carlyle, cast in the quasi-paternal role, responded sympathetically to her grief for 'that best and truest Friend and Father', while adroitly avoiding acceptance of the impossible role of substitute and quietly reminding her of his hopes as a lover: 'No one will ever counsel you in difficulties with so faithful and disinterested a mind as that good man who is gone; no one! – not even I can speak to you once in ten times without some pitiful sneaking undercurrent less or more of selfish or half-selfish motives – for which I often heartily despise myself.'[53]

They saw one another briefly at Haddington in February 1823, Mrs Welsh, in one of her frequent changes of mood, having wondered why Carlyle did not propose another visit. Jane reported on 23 January that she was now 'formally desired to invite you here, *"in case it may be that you are standing on ceremony"*'. She was pleased at having managed her mother by not seeming herself to be too anxious for such a meeting. 'I am a young lady *"full of devices"*', she boasted on 10 February, when his visit was imminent.[54] This time things went better. Mrs Welsh was pleasant, and Carlyle reported himself, 'in spite of bad health and all its wretched *etceteras*', 'greatly pleased'.[55]

Jane's letters became warmer and more encouraging until, not for the first or last time, he was induced to assume a success he had not fully achieved. 'Jane loves me! she loves me!' he crowed at the end of August, after receiving a letter in which she had declared, 'I owe you much', and, 'in return, I can only love you, and *that* I do, from the bottom of my heart'.[56] Carlyle ought to have heard the tone of gratitude in this declaration, but his heart got the better of him, and he assumed a new understanding between them.

He took the opportunity to assess both their temperaments, first stressing the contradictions in her nature:

The only thing I know is that you are the most delightful, enthusiastic, contemptuous, affectionate, sarcastic, capricious, warm-hearted, lofty-minded, half-devil, half-angel of a woman that ever ruled over the heart of a man; that I will love you, must love you, whatever may betide, till the last moment of my existence; and that if we both act rightly our lot *may* be the happiest of a thousand mortal lots.

In the interests of even-handedness, he then turned the spotlight on himself. He, like her, was 'full of contradictions'. 'Outwardly, on the surface as it were, I am timid as a leveret; while within there are feelings that might suit a tiger – fierce, desperate, deep tormenting feelings.' Before he knew where he was, this strange lover was talking of his 'accursed "physical disease"; Tophet has not in its recesses such a tremendous scourge as thou!'[57] Tophet, which figures prominently in Carlyle's journals and published writings, is the grim and desert place in the Book of Jeremiah, 'the valley of slaughter', where children are sacrificed by the disobedient Jews.

The recipient of this alarming letter drew back, writing on 16 September that she could not understand what she had done to mislead him into thinking she loved him as a wife would a husband. 'Your Friend I will be, your truest most devoted friend, while I breathe the breath of life; but your wife! never, never!'[58] Carlyle's reply reveals the very qualities of head and heart which Jane most admired. He submits, not without bitterness, but it is directed at himself, not at her. He calls himself 'a fool of some standing' and accuses himself of 'accustomed heedlessness'. Then, brilliantly, he casts himself as a kind of cousin of those lovers at cross purposes in Shakespeare's comedies (perhaps not without the hope, conscious or unconscious, that in his case, as in theirs, all will be well that ends well): 'I know very well you will never be my wife. Never! Never! – I never believed it above five minutes at a time all my days. ''Tis all one as I should love a bright particular star, and think to wed it.'''

The quotation comes from Act I, scene i of *All's Well That Ends Well*. Helena speaks the lines about her hopeless love for her social superior, Bertram, who is 'so above me'. The following two lines may also have been in Carlyle's mind:

> In his bright radiance and collateral light
> Must I be comforted, not in his sphere.

Carlyle tells Jane he will never cease to love her, but will seek no engagement; 'I will reverence you as the fairest living emblem of all that is most exalted and engaging in my conceptions of human nature.'[59]

Meanwhile he would carry on with his translation of *Wilhelm Meister's Apprenticeship*, undertaken in March 1823 for the Edinburgh publishing house Oliver and Boyd.[60] Goethe's novel, full of its own romantic entanglements and mistakes, is his steady point of reference while visions of Jane as his wife rise and fade away. He was also writing a life of Schiller, which the *London Magazine* was to publish in monthly parts, thanks to Irving's influence with the editor.[61]

In May 1823 Carlyle went with the Bullers to the Highlands; they had rented Kinnaird House, near Dunkeld, for several months. Here he worked on Goethe and Schiller in a small house near the great one, suffering the tortures of dyspepsia all the while.[62] In September he was a spectator while the Bullers hunted deer. 'A sorrier piece of entertainment, I may observe, is not to be met with in this kingdom', he told Jack; 'they went hallooing, and beating the bushes and talking gaelic', and 'thought it royal sport'.[63] Inevitably, being at such close quarters led him to criticise. Mrs Buller, he complained, 'has the secret of spending seven or eight thousand a year with a *minimum* of comfort', uniting 'extravagance' with 'poorest parsimony'. 'If I were in Buller's place, I would swallow ratsbane', concluded the dyspeptic guest. He was already thinking of extricating himself, though the Bullers very much wanted to keep him.[64] Being as practically indecisive as he was theoretically vehement, he stayed.

*

Irving, from afar, played a significant part in the Carlyle–Jane relationship. Jane, who had not yet told Carlyle of her previous feelings for Irving or his for her, resented the fact that Irving had stopped writing now that he was moving in interesting London circles. She began to write mockingly of him to Carlyle: in July 1823 he was 'the Hero of Hatton Garden'. In her letter of 19 August, the one which led Carlyle to suppose that she returned his love, she noted that Irving's book of sermons had been published and that 'our illustrious Friend', who had promised to send these *Orations* to her and her mother, seemed now too preoccupied with his new friends to remember his old ones.[65] We may suspect, in addition to envy of Irving's success and annoyance at his abandoning his old Haddington friends, some irritation on Jane's part that her erstwhile suitor was publishing a book and achieving fame before her present one. Since Carlyle had also told her in his last letter that Irving was about to marry his Kirkcaldy fiancée, Isabella Martin,[66] Jane's expression of grateful love to Carlyle just at this point may have been connected with her realisation that Irving was finally lost to her.

Carlyle, unaware of the previous status quo between Irving and Jane, was worried less about the Miss Martin business than about Irving's rising fame as a charismatic preacher. 'He is standing *a-tiptoe* on the summit of Fortune's wheel', he commented in September, 'so if it turn, smash he comes with his nose first upon the causeway!'[67] For the moment Irving was enjoying his fame. No less a personage than the Foreign Secretary, George Canning, attended a service with his friend Sir James Mackintosh; Canning then announced during a House of Commons debate on church revenues that he had heard a Scottish minister, trained in one of the most poorly endowed churches, preach the most eloquent sermon he had ever heard. London curiosity was aroused, and soon 1,500 people were said to be applying for seats in the Caledonian Chapel, built to take about 600.[68]

The Times reported the phenomenon, and various pamphlets appeared, several of them already critical of the combination of sanctimoniousness and argumentativeness in Irving's sermons and writings which would eventually lead to his expulsion from the Church of Scotland. A satirical work, *The Trial of the Rev. Edward Irving, M.A., a Cento of Criticism*, appeared in 1823, accusing Irving of being 'a Merry-Andrew', 'a common quack', of 'following divisive courses, subversive of the discipline of the order to which he belongs'. Much fun was made of his squint, the only physical defect in this giant of a man with his handsome face and long black curly hair.[69]

Carlyle knew his friend's foibles better than anyone. He told his mother in September 1823 that he would 'not give his vanity one inch of swing in my company', regardless of 'the fashionable ladies' and 'the multitude of young men' who surrounded him.[70] But he also appreciated Irving's strengths, and was properly grateful for all the good turns his friend had done him, from introducing him to Jane to getting him his appointment with the Bullers and helping him into print with his *Life* of Schiller.

This work, which Carlyle himself thought 'a miserable farrago',[71] appeared in the *London Magazine* from October 1823 to September 1824, and was published as a book the following February. It made little stir, though *The Times* carried an extract, which it praised as 'eloquent'. Carlyle was to remember this in 1866 as 'the *first* public nod of approval I had ever had'.[72] The account he gives of Schiller's life is most interesting for what it reveals about its author. He was obliged to follow the existing German biographies, full of errors and omissions, but he managed to go beyond these and, by an effort of sympathetic imagination, to give a lively picture of the vicissitudes of Schiller's life. With fellow feeling he declares:

Beneath a cold and simple exterior, dignified with no artificial attractions, and marred in its native amiableness by the incessant obstruction, the isolation and painful destitutions under which he lived, there was concealed a burning energy of soul, which no obstruction could extinguish.[73]

One might as easily take this to be about Carlyle as about Schiller. And if he highlighted the gloomy aspects of Schiller's life, he also gave notice of a gift for empathy which would characterise much of his future biographical and historical writing.

In October 1823 Carlyle joined Irving and his new wife at Dunkeld when their wedding journey brought them to Perthshire. The three spent a few days together, time enough for Carlyle to ascertain that Isabella was '*dead ugly*, otherwise a very decent serviceable body', as he told Jack. As for Irving:

> He himself is the same man as ever, only his mind seems churned into a foam by the late agitations and is yielding a plentiful scum of vanities and harmless affectations . . . he puckers up his face into various seamy peaks, rolls his eyes, and puffs like a blast-furnace; talking abundantly a flood of things, the body of which is nonsense, but intermingled with sparkles of curious thinking, and tinctured with his usual flow of warm-hearted generosity and honest affection.[74]

That generosity was in evidence in a letter Irving wrote to Carlyle from Kirkcaldy just before the wedding, as was a characteristic tone of flattery, which Carlyle distrusted, and of patronage, which irritated him. Irving told him he had been showing his parents-in-law 'the place where Thomas Carlyle lived, and where would be found the ghosts of more departed good sense than in any other place in this Kingdom', namely Carlyle's erstwhile lodgings in Kirkcaldy. Here, Irving recalls, he and Carlyle 'were wont to discourse of all things written & unwritten, thought of and unthought of'. Proposing to meet Carlyle at Dunkeld, he held out the prospect of 'revok[ing] from oblivion' 'these our happy communings'; still going on stilts, as he could not help doing, he invited Carlyle to visit him and Isabella in London the following summer: 'I doubt nothing of your speedily finding your way to the level in the Society to which your genius drives you in spite of yourself, and which I hope to see it long adorn'.[75] Carlyle, reporting this invitation to Jack, remarked dryly that he had refused, the offer 'savouring too much of patronage to suit my taste'.[76]

Jane's resentment of Irving, meanwhile, had been swept away by an invitation to *her* to go to London at the same time as Carlyle. 'I am almost out of my wits with joy', she wrote on 14 October; 'you and I are going to London!'[77] To this Carlyle replied discouragingly. He would, of course, like nothing better than to spend three months in London in Jane's company, but he was doubtful whether it could be managed and not at all sure that such a visit would be a success. Though he did not say so in so many words, he clearly had little appetite to spend such a precious three months as was promised – after all, he had not yet spent a total of three weeks in Jane's company – under the roof and the patronage of 'the great Divine'.[78]

He told Jane that she would find Irving's vanity and affectation much increased by his London successes. Caricaturing slightly, though with remarkable prescience in relation to Irving, he mentioned Irving's high, yet somehow insulting, expectations of what London would do for Carlyle's own career:

He seemed to think that if set down on London streets some strange development of genius would take place in me, that by conversing with Coleridge and the Opium eater [Thomas De Quincey], I should find out new channels for speculation, and soon learn to speak with tongues.[79]

Carlyle had no desire to enter London literary life under the auspices of anyone, let alone this friend, in whom he saw unmistakable signs of quackery.

For a time it looked as though Jane would visit London in summer 1824 and Carlyle not. Apart from Carlyle's aversion to accepting Irving's invitation, he may have recoiled from Jane's assumption that he would go simply 'because your own Jane desires it', as she wrote on 14 October.[80] If the trope of the princess and the slave came to anyone's mind, he preferred it to come to his, which could then incorporate a proud and ironic resistance into the concept. In short, he took this rare opportunity to play a little hard to get in his turn.

They resumed their correspondence as before, Carlyle still from Dunkeld, where he remained, despite his grumblings, until February 1824, when he and the Bullers were to separate for three months, after which they would probably join forces again, either in Cornwall or in London. His dyspepsia became so critical that in late November 1823 he travelled to Edinburgh to consult a doctor, George Bell, about whether his condition was curable or not. He was told to give up tobacco, which he did for a time, but to no avail. His recollection in 1866 was bitter: 'I might as well have ridden sixty miles in the opposite direction, and "poured my sorrows into the long hairy ear of the first jack-ass I came upon" as into this select medical man's.'[81]

Two journal entries in December 1823 expressed the fear that he might be dying 'by inches'. 'I do not design to be a *suicide*', he wrote, after dramatising that drastic option.[82] After a snatched visit to Haddington, Carlyle returned to Dunkeld for a few more weeks. He and Jane had agreed well enough on this visit, and Mrs Welsh was kind, but Carlyle seemed now to think the future would be blighted less by Jane's disinclination to marry him than by his own miserable health.[83]

Early in February 1824 he was back in Edinburgh, visiting Jane at Mr Bradfute's house in George Square and seeing the first of two volumes of his translation of *Wilhelm Meister's Apprenticeship* through the press while he continued translating the third. He negotiated £180 for a run of 1,000 copies, thereby impressing Jane, who was anxious that her 'beloved Genius', as she now called him, should finally publish a book.[84] 'I would rather be able to make £180 by my wits than fall heir to a million', she wrote flatteringly in April, though she was far from sure of the merits of *Wilhelm Meister*, which she was then reading. 'The unaccountable propensity to kissing which runs through all your dramatis personae perplexes me sadly', she teased.[85]

Jane was not really much shocked by *Wilhelm Meister*, but she guessed correctly that others might be, and she feared for Carlyle's reputation as its translator. In fact, Carlyle toned down some of the rather direct sexual references in the book; in his preface to the translation he showed some anxiety about these, explaining that he had 'dropped as evidently unfit for the English taste' some 'few phrases and sentences', while assuring his readers that such passages amounted to less than a page in all. The preface is cautiously apologetic about the two criticisms to which he felt Goethe's novel was vulnerable, that of indecency and that of tediousness. He confessed that the novel had its *longueurs*, but claimed, rather diffidently, that if persevered with, it might be found to be

a light airy sketch of the development of man in all his endowments and faculties, gradually proceeding from the first rude exhibitions of puppets and mountebanks, through the perfection of poetic and dramatic art, up to the unfolding of the principle of religion, and the greatest of all the arts, the art of life.[86]

Later Victorian champions of Goethe, notably George Eliot and Henry James, were to argue in similar, though less defensive, terms. That they were able to dispense with apologies for Goethe was due in large part to Carlyle's earlier efforts to persuade the English reading public of Goethe's great merits.[87] In his *Reminiscences* Carlyle looked back at his feelings on finishing the translation in the spring of 1824:

My sally out, after finishing, along the vacant streets of Edinburgh (a windless Scotch-misty Sunday night) is still vivid to me: 'Grand, surely, harmoniously built together, far-seeing, wise and true: when, for many years, or almost, in my life before, have I read such a Book?' Which I was now, really in part as a kind of duty, conscientiously translating for my countrymen, if they would read it, – as a select few of them have ever since kept doing.[88]

During April and May he lived quietly at home in Mainhill, finishing the translation and preparing to go to London, where it was now agreed that he would meet the Bullers. He was to stay with Irving and his wife in Islington for a few weeks first, but Jane was not to go with him after all. Irving had written to put her off, intimating in his usual style that he was not yet emotionally ready to receive a visit from the woman he would have preferred to marry (not to mention that Isabella Irving probably felt no small reluctance to receive her sarcastic rival so soon after her marriage):

My dear Isabella has succeeded in healing the wounds of my heart by her unexampled affection and tenderness; but I am hardly yet in a condition to expose them. My former calmness and piety are returning. I feel growing in grace and holiness; and before another year I shall be worthy in the eye of my own conscience to receive you into my house and under my care, which till then I should hardly be.[89]

Jane railed against 'that stupendous ass the Orator' and expressed her impatience to see Carlyle before he went to London.[90] He stayed at Haddington for a few days at the end of May, when it appears that he and Jane became – albeit secretly and unofficially – engaged. More ups and downs in their relationship lay ahead, but Jane may have felt that, on the eve of Carlyle's departure for the attractions of London, she should secure his affections by promising fidelity. At last Carlyle told his parents about her. On 5 June 1824, an hour before setting sail from Leith, Carlyle wrote to take his leave of his mother, mentioning for the first time in a letter 'my good Jane'.[91]

And so he set off for his first visit to the metropolis, pursued by a giddy letter from Jane, telling him not to write openly of their love, since Mrs Welsh could still spoil things. 'Everything depends upon your appearing as my friend and not my Lover', she wrote, chastising him for his last careless love letter; 'Thou a Man of Genius! thou art an ass.'[92] It remained to be seen what London would make of Carlyle, and Carlyle of London.

CHAPTER 3

A Kind of Engagement 1824–1826

The moment Carlyle arrived at the Irvings' house in Pentonville on the afternoon of 11 June 1824 he sat down to write to his mother, in order to lose 'not a moment in relieving you from all your anxieties about me'. His ship had dropped anchor in the Thames the night before,

and we had a delightful view of the River & its ships in tens of thousands, its coal-heavers, bargemen, mackarel men and variegated population from Purfleet (14 miles down) up to the London Dock. It is an astounding sight: on approaching the city, its dense masses of grim smoky buildings, its forests of masts, and the sound as of a million hammers as if proceeding in louder and fainter notes from many-handed labour, give a strange impression of the bulk and bustle of this mighty place.[1]

It was the usual response of the newcomer to the sheer size and noise of London. In letters to Jane and to his brothers during his first two weeks Carlyle gave brief physical descriptions of 'this heart of all the Earth', 'the great Nineveh of modern Europe', with its 'roomy squares with trees and grass plots intermingled' and, less picturesquely, its brick kilns set up on the 'unbuilt spaces' and giving off a 'sulphurous smell'.[2] But his forte lay where his chief interest did – not in places, but in people.

In all his letters, giving a picture of London meant describing the people he met. There were the Bullers, of course, with whom he agreed that he and Charles junior should spend a short time together in Kew, preparing Charles for entry to Cambridge University. But the Bullers' plans kept changing; Cornwall was now ruled out, and fresh plans followed one another, but none was executed, 'greatly to my annoyance and regret', as Carlyle recalled.[3] By 6 July he was reporting to his mother that he had finally decided he could not continue the 'shifting and trotting about' required by Mrs Buller, 'the "fair Titania" (as the Calcutta Newspapers called her)', who was the chief cause of the whole family's restlessness. Mr Buller was sorry to part with him, as was Charles. A transaction ensued in which Carlyle played an entirely characteristic part. Mr Buller offered him £25 'for my trouble', which Carlyle promptly pronounced 'to be too much, and accepted of *ten*'.[4]

Though Carlyle's feelings towards the Bullers had cooled, the parting was amicable. Meanwhile, he had been introduced to Mrs Buller's sister

53

Julia Strachey, to whom he warmed immediately. 'She is serious and earnest and religious and affectionate', he told his mother, 'while the other is light giddy vain and heartless'.[5] Mrs Strachey was an admirer of Irving, and it was among others of Irving's circle that Carlyle now began, rather uncomfortably, to move.

The Orator himself, Carlyle reported to Jane, was surrounded by some 'notable characters'.[6] Carlyle attended his services and was impressed by their power, but he felt, as he remembered in *Reminiscences*, 'a something of strained and aggravated, of elaborately intentional, which kept jarring on the mind'. The initial excitement about Irving's preaching, which had brought aristocratic carriages rolling to the door, had subsided a little:

The doors were crowded long before opening, and you got in by ticket: but the first sublime rush of what once seemed more than popularity, and *had been* nothing more, – Lady Jersey 'sitting on the Pulpit steps', Canning, Brougham, Mackintosh, etc. rushing, day after day, – was now quite over, and there remained only a popularity of 'the people' (not of the *plebs* at all, but never higher than of the well-dressed *populus* henceforth); which was a sad change to the sanguine man . . . At sight of Canning, Brougham, Lady Jersey and Co. crowding round him, and listening week after week, as if to the message of Salvation, the noblest and joyfullest thought (I know this on perfect authority) had taken possession of his noble, too sanguine, and too trustful mind: 'That Christian Religion was to be a truth again, not a paltry form, and to rule the world, – he, unworthy, even he the chosen instrument!'[7]

Carlyle's stylistic mastery of the double view – sceptical yet sympathetic – is fully in evidence in this account of his friend's well-intentioned folly.

Carlyle found Irving a cordial host. Isabella, though plain and now 'in the family way', was, as he told Jack, 'certainly a very model wife'. His bachelor brother, rather than his volatile semi-fiancée, was the one to hear what constituted perfection in a wife. 'Submissive, helpful, ever good-humoured', he enthused, 'her sole object seems to be her husband's comfort, and that of his friends.'[8] Chief among Irving's admirers was Mrs Anna Montagu, third wife of Basil Montagu, the eccentric lawyer and friend of Wordsworth and Coleridge. Carlyle told Jane that Mrs Montagu had 'a taste for *exciting sentiments*', which was a most astute first impression, as he and Jane were soon to find, when Mrs Montagu decided to help their slow courtship along.[9]

In 1866, when reminiscing about himself and Irving, Carlyle performed a *tour de force* of memory and description which is the more striking because no audience was envisaged for his account. It simply poured from him as he sought to accept the sudden loss of Jane by returning to the past they had shared. Froude, who published the *Reminiscences* immediately after Carlyle's death, interpreting Carlyle's failure to state categorically that they must *not* be published as permission by default, probably did so in part because he recognised the quite astonishing accuracy and detail of the seventy-year-old Carlyle's memory. In his Carlyle biography Froude points out that whereas most retrospective accounts of a life are subject to 'involuntary freaks of memory' which alter past scenes so as to make them 'legendary even to ourselves', Carlyle's 'remain as if photographed precisely as they are to be found in his contemporary letters'.[10]

Carlyle did incorporate the hindsight of subsequent events in the *Reminiscences*; moreover, he wrote these memoirs of Jane, Irving, Francis Jeffrey and others in a spirit of grief and remorse towards the wife whom he half recognised he had neglected. His memorialising is obsessive and in places he obscures as much as he reveals. Nonetheless, he moves between first impressions and later adjustments without losing that sense of freshness and novelty which usually belongs exclusively to contemporary descriptions of first meetings.

The account of Mrs Montagu in *Reminiscences* is a perfect example. Her house contained 'a most difficult miscellany', consisting of Basil's son by his first wife, his three sons by his second wife – young dandies 'who went all and sundry to the bad' – and his two sons by Anna herself – also destined at a later date 'to go astray and be unlucky' – plus two girls, Basil's only daughter and Mrs Montagu's daughter by her previous marriage:

Ruling such a miscellany of a household, with Basil Montagu at the head of it, and an almost still stranger miscellaneous society that fluctuated through it, Mrs Montagu had a problem like few others. But she, if anyone, was equal to it. A more constant and consummate Artist in that kind you could nowhere meet with; truly a remarkable, and partly a high and tragical woman. Now about fifty, with the remains of a certain queenly beauty, which she still took strict care of. A tall, rather thin figure; face pale intelligent and penetrating, nose fine, rather large, and decisively Roman; pair of bright, not soft, but sharp and small black eyes, with a cold smile as of inquiry in them; fine brow, fine chin both rather prominent; thin lips always gently shut, as if till the inquiry were completed, and the time came for something of royal speech upon it.[11]

The description of Mrs Montagu sent to Jane immediately after he had made her acquaintance in June 1824 is less full, but seems nevertheless to penetrate beyond a mere surface impression:

Mrs Montagu (do not tremble) is a stately matron with a quick intellect and a taste for *exciting sentiments*; which two qualities by dint of much management in a longish life she has elaborated into the materials of a showy, tasteful, clear-sighted, rigid, and I fancy cold manner of existence, intended rather for itself and for being looked at, than for being used to any useful purpose in the service of others.[12]

Carlyle, so curious about London life, absorbed its manifestations with gusto. He seemed to have an inner mechanism for sorting people into types. If one of these could be described as sentimental (or 'sentimental') women such as Mrs Buller, Mrs Strachey, and Mrs Montagu, another consisted of the professional 'exiled' Scotsman. One such was Sir Peter Laurie, a follower of Irving whom Carlyle criticised in *Reminiscences* as 'something of an *Ex-Scotchman*'.[13] The worst of these, in Carlyle's eyes, was the poet Thomas Campbell, whom he described to Jane:

He is heartless as a little Edinburgh Advocate; there is a smirk on his face which would befit a shopman or an auctioneer; his very eye has the cold vivacity of a conceited worldling. His talk is small, contemptuous and shallow: the blue frock and trowsers, the eye glass, the wig, the very fashion of his brow proclaim the literary dandy. His wife has black eyes, a fair skin, a symmetrical but vulgar face; and she speaks with that accursed Celtic accent, a twang which I never yet heard associated with any manly or profitable thought or sentiment; which to me is but the symbol of Highland vanity and filth and famine. 'Good heavens', cried I, on coming out, 'does literature then lead to this? Shall I too by my utmost efforts realize nothing but a stupid Gaelic wife, with the pitiful gift of making verses; and affections cold as those of a tinker's cuddie?'[14]

His imagination ran away with him here, as Jane must have felt when she read this fantasy of his being forced to marry a stupid Gaelic wife.

Campbell combined the characteristics of two types for which Carlyle had particularly sharp antennae – the Scot in London and the London literary man. Of the latter sort he met Coleridge, Lamb, and the poet 'Barry Cornwall' – otherwise Bryan W. Procter, who was about to marry Mrs Montagu's daughter Anne. Hazlitt and De Quincey he did not meet, but along with Coleridge and Lamb they people his letters as awful warnings of what can happen to an author who drinks or takes laudanum or slaves for magazines, or undertakes any combination of these activities.

In short, Carlyle was quick to see how humiliating the lives of many London authors were. He sums them up for an Edinburgh friend, Thomas Murray in a letter of 24 August. Lamb is 'a ricketty creature in body and mind', talking as if he were 'quarter drunk with ale and half with laudanum'; Hazlitt 'takes his punch and oysters and rackets and whore at regular intervals; escaping from bailiffs as he best can'.[15] To his brother John he affirms in September that he has no intention of trying the London literary life himself. Significantly, he invokes the Carlyle family pride in the person of his honest, unlettered father: 'A miserable scrub of an author sharking and writing "articles" about Town, like Hazzlitt, Dequincey and that class of living creatures, is a thing which as our Father says, I *canna* be.'[16]

As for the most famous of these authors, Coleridge, with whom Carlyle shared an interest in German literature, particularly Schiller, whose drama *Wallenstein* Coleridge had translated in 1800,[17] he was in the worst situation of them all. Not only was Coleridge notoriously in thrall to opium, but he had lost his independence; he lived as the permanent non-paying guest of his doctor, James Gillman, in whose house in Highgate he held forth conversationally, astonishing all comers with his eloquence. Irving took Carlyle to listen to the oracle, but he was temperamentally incapable of responding positively to Coleridge. Instead, he practised his sketching skills, producing in due course a portrait of the ageing poet which became a much-quoted set piece.

As with Mrs Montagu, the early impression sank deep. On 24 June, after only one visit to Coleridge, Carlyle's pen sketch went off to John Carlyle:

Figure a fat flabby incurvated personage, at once short, rotund and relaxed, with a watery mouth, a snuffy nose, a pair of strange brown timid yet earnest looking eyes, a high tapering brow, and a great bush of grey hair – you will have some faint idea of Coleridge. He is a kind, good soul, full of religion and affection, and poetry and animal magnetism. His cardinal sin is that he wants will; he has no resolution, he shrinks from pain or labour in any of its shapes. His very attitude bespeaks this: he never straightens his knee joints, he stoops with his fat ill shapen shoulders, and in walking he does not tread but shovel and slide – my father would call it *skluiffing* . . . The conversation of the man is much as I anticipated. A forest of thoughts; some true, many false, most part dubious, all of them ingenious in some degree, often in a high degree. But there is no method in his talk; he wanders like a man sailing among many currents, whithersoever his lazy mind directs him – ; and what is more unpleasant he preaches, or rather soliloquizes: he cannot speak; he can only 'tal-k' (so he names it). Hence I found him unprofitable, even tedious: but we parted very good friends I promising to go back and see him some other evening – a promise I fully intend to keep. I sent him a copy of Meister about which we had some friendly talk. I reckon him a man of great and useless genius – a strange not at all a great man.[18]

It is worth noting that Carlyle shows no interest in, or appreciation of, Coleridge's poetry, here or elsewhere in his writings. He lets slip that he expected little of Coleridge's conversation before he went; and his father is invoked once more, as a judge by reference to whom Coleridge is found wanting. Carlyle exhibits great verbal facility in catching Coleridge's image, but he seeks – and therefore finds – only the negative in a Coleridge who was well known by this time to have deteriorated in all respects from what he once was.[19]

Several more such sketches of Coleridge are drawn for his correspondents. His tale is of a man of broken strength and wastefully miscellaneous intellect. In August Thomas Murray is told that Coleridge is 'a steam-engine of a hundred horses power – with the boiler burst'. He 'speaks incessantly', says Carlyle, 'as a rich and lazy housewife might mingle her soup and fish and beef and custard into one unspeakable mass and present it trueheartedly to her astonished guests'. John Carlyle hears in January 1825 that Coleridge is 'a mass of richest spices, putrified into a dunghill'. Most revealing of all, in terms of Carlyle's own fears of what might befall him if he were not so proud and determined, is Carlyle's shrewd remark to Jane that Coleridge is, in effect, a kept man:

A man that is not standing on his own feet in regard to economical affairs, soon ceases to be a man at all. Poor Coleridge is like the hulk of a huge ship: his mast and sails and rudder have rotted quite away.[20]

★

It was easier for Carlyle to perceive clearly what he did *not* want to become than to see his way forward in his still unformed career. He was now nearly thirty and was still waiting, as he recalled much later with that touch of fatalism already noticed, 'till the gloomy whirl of intricacies shd settle itself a little and some beginnings of a clear "road" disclose'.[21] While in London, he made some effort to enter into a new arrangement with a publisher. He offered both Taylor and Hessey, who were bringing out his *Life of Schiller*, and Oliver and Boyd a translation of the sequel, the mysterious *Wilhelm Meister's Travels*.[22]

He was able to point to some encouraging reviews of his *Meister* translation. John Gibson Lockhart, Walter Scott's son-in-law and a Germanist himself, praised it in *Blackwood's Magazine*, and the *Examiner* carried an extract which it described as 'admirable'.[23] However, nothing came of the idea to follow up with *Wilhelm Meister's Travels*, mainly because Carlyle, who had just read it, realised that in its fragmentary state the work was 'unfit for the English market', as he wrote with refreshing frankness to the London publisher James Hessey in August.[24]

Poor Jane, at home in Haddington, received Carlyle's denunciations of London's literary giants and sentimental women, but no settled plan for his – their – future emerged from his letters. Before the end of July he had surprisingly gone off to Birmingham – 'the Wandering Jew or Shoemaker of Jerusalem was but a type of me', he announced, not very reassuringly.[25]

He went in search of health. A friend of Irving's, John Badams, 'a graduate in medicine tho' his business is in chemical manufactories at Birmingham', had invited him to try a month at his home to see if he could cure 'my unfortunate inner man'.[26] Carlyle enjoyed Badams's company so much that he stayed for two months in Birmingham, visiting factories, meeting industrialists, watching the 'hundred and fifty thousand mortals that grind out their destiny there', including coal miners whom he observed, 'literally naked, many of them, all but trowsers; black as ravens;

plashing about among dripping caverns, or scrambling amid heaps of broken mineral; and thirsting unquenchably for beer', as he reported to Alick.[27] His descriptions of Birmingham were appreciated by his father, whom Alick quoted in his reply as 'exclaiming even while we were reading in his own emphatic way – "he is a terrible fallow that too" '.[28]

Carlyle and Badams rode furiously – both were fearless horsemen – around rural Warwickshire, an activity from which Carlyle felt he derived some benefit, though as a medical experiment the Midlands excursion was a failure. 'My Birmingham visit', he wrote in *Reminiscences*, 'except as it continually kept me riding about in the open air, did nothing for me in the *Anti*-dyspeptic way.' 'In the social and spiritually consolatory way', however, 'it was really of benefit.'[29] Carlyle was finding in Birmingham, as he had done in his few weeks in London, that he could make friends and attract others by his personality – a gift he had not noticeably exhibited in his years of trying to settle in indifferent Edinburgh.

Carlyle told Jane that he envied Badams, who seemed to have 'his destiny as it were subdued and lying at his feet, and all things fit around him, like the wheels in an eight-day clock'.[30] The contrast with his own situation was only too clear to him. It was to Jane, too, who hoped he would find his feet in London. She felt the need to entertain the man she had half agreed to marry with some interesting accounts of her own life during his absence. Fortunately, she and her mother had an adventure when they attended a race meeting at Musselburgh, near Edinburgh. Once again Jane conjures up an attractive vision of herself for her distant lover, cleverly undercutting her own vanity with irony:

The Devil put it in my head to go to Musselbro' races – I had been ill of bile or vapours for a day or two before, and I imagined that amusement and exercise would do me good. It was the Devil too that tempted me to go on horse-back, by which means I drew a multitude of eyes on me – Oh the folly of men! . . . one young gentleman (a Sutherlandman) fell in love with me in good earnest . . . , he quite won my Mother's heart, so that she invited him and his Sister (whom, soit dit en passant, neither she nor myself had ever set eyes upon) to visit us on our return to Haddington . . . Well! on the day appointed my Gentleman arrived, accompanied by a little smiling girl from an English boarding-school, and what I had foreseen and dreaded came to pass: the first time that I was left alone with him, out came a matrimonial proposition in due form. In my life, I never felt such difficulty in giving a refusal – not that I had the smallest disposition in the world to consent – oh dear no! my new lover has neither the fire of Lord Byron, nor the wit of Mr Terrot, and in point of elegance he cannot be compared with my steamboat Colonel: but then he has fair silky locks, the sweetest eyes in nature, a voice like music, and a heart so warm and true and so wholely, wholely mine! all which had such a softening effect upon me, that I could not bring myself to say I did not love him; I preferred telling a lie of any magnitude to wounding him with such cruel words; besides my Mother had told me that the *handsomest way of refusing a man was to say that I was engaged*, so I did not scruple to say so in the present instance. Fortunately the distress which this declaration threw him into, saved me from further questioning; I should have found it rather troublesome at the moment to have furnished my beau ideal with a name. Poor youth! he threw himself down on the sopha beside me, and wept and sobbed like a child. I called him 'dear Dugald', to pacify him, and kissed his forehead at least half a dozen times (was not that good of me?) but he would not be comforted: he lay in bed, and cried all the rest of the day; my Mother sat and cried beside him; and his Sister and I cried in another apartment.[31]

This surely made piquant, not to say uncomfortable, reading for Carlyle, who had not been overwhelmed with Mrs Welsh's hospitality and who must have thought Jane could very easily have given a name to the man to whom she was prepared to declare herself engaged.

More was to follow. The afflicted young man, Dugald Gilchrist, 'cried himself into a fever'. Jane's mother, so taken with this young man's charms (where she had been impervious to Carlyle's), made matters worse by becoming hysterical. But in the end his 'whim' subsided, and Jane and her mother returned to normality. She ends her provocative letter by directing some aggression towards Carlyle:

Have you got rid of that infamous accent of yours? remember I can never enjoy your society to the full until you do – my poor ears are in a fever every time they hear it – Why do you speak Annandale? why are you not as elegant as Colonel Alix? my beau-ideal would then be found.[32]

What would Carlyle reply to this? He was already angry with her for not writing earlier. A frantic letter from him, written on 12 August, crossed with this tormenting one of hers. 'What in Heaven's name is the matter?' he asked, before going on to suggest that she might begin a translation of some of Schiller's poems which he could include with a complete version of Schiller's works he was now contemplating. As if to bind her more closely to him, he declared that 'something of thine must and shall be in this book; as I predicted last year that we should go forth together, *umschlungen zärtlich, Seit' an Seite* [tenderly entwined, side by side]'.[33] When he did receive her letter, he left it unanswered for three weeks, then pointedly ignored the jibe about his accent. He matched her slyness about engagements and her 'beau ideal' with some irony of his own:

So you are *engaged*, are you? Would that I had a cast of the Sybilline Books, or the Linen Books, or the future session Books, or any book that would tell me to whom! Is he a genius and 'elegant'? Is he a poet or a philosopher or both in one? Let him look to it that he be a worthy man, and love you with a faithful heart! If he do not, I myself will pull the varlet's nose, and tell him that he merits not to dwell upon our planet![34]

It is a good answer, notable for its picking up of a word or phrase – here 'elegant' – which has resonance for them both. Their letters are henceforth peppered with such quotations, phrases taken from one another and from their acquaintances and recycled, often ironically, for their mutual amusement; they called this Coteriesprache (coterie speech).[35]

Carlyle's next plan in a singularly planless sojourn was to accompany the Irvings and the Stracheys to Dover for a seaside holiday at the beginning of October. He wrote to his father, describing the Kent countryside and, knowing where his correspondent's interest lay, comparing the farming habits with those of Dumfriesshire: 'They plough with *five* horses and two men (one *ca-ing*); and the plough has wheels! Many a time have I thought of Alick with his Lothian tackle, and two horses, setting these inefficient loiterers to the right about.'

The country people in Kent are less poor than their Scottish counterparts, he says. Introducing an idea which would have novelty for his untravelled father, he continues, 'We can see France any ordinary day, distant about twenty-one miles'. 'Steam packets cross every day: the eggs which my fair landlady provides for me, are *laid* in that hostile country.'[36] Before the end of October, Carlyle and his party had made the crossing themselves, and were in Paris.

One member of the group in whom Carlyle took a particular interest was Kitty Kirkpatrick, a cousin of Mrs Strachey with a romantic background. She was the daughter of an Indian princess, 'handsome and young and sole mistress of fifty thousand pounds', as he informed his father, but 'meek and unassuming as a child'.[37] Carlyle later thought Mrs Strachey would have 'liked to see "dear Kitty" and myself come together', and even ventured to suggest that Kitty 'might perhaps have been charmed' by the rough Annandale genius who was savouring, as can be seen from his letters, his unexpected social success among these new friends.[38]

As Jane had presented the tragicomedy of Dugald Gilchrist for his delight and torment, so now Carlyle told her the romantic story of Kitty's parentage, making sure that he described her personal charms, if only by way of unkind contrast with poor Isabella Irving's conspicuous lack of beauty:

Good Kitty! It is like pitchy darkness between rosy-fingered morn and tallow candle-light, when I stroll with her, the daughter of Asiatic pomp and dreamy indolence, and the Fife Isabella, skilful in Presbyterian philosophy and the structure of dumplings and worsted hose.[39]

This was written from Dover on 5 October 1824, and produced a satisfyingly petulant response from Jane, with just enough of a hint of the Shakespearian or Jane Austenish young lady about it to suggest ironic self-awareness:

Miss Kitty Kirkpatrick – Lord what an ugly name! 'Good Kitty!' Oh, pretty dear delightful Kitty! I am not a bit jealous of her – not I indeed – Hindoo Princess tho' she be! Only you may as well never let me hear you mention her name again.[40]

If Carlyle was inclined to think this pettish, he would be softened by her turning next to strike a serious note, envisaging a married future with an unnamed man who bears more than a passing resemblance to himself, though it is significant that this imaginary husband has already achieved a comfortable degree of wealth and fame, and moreover has the adjective 'graceful' applied to him:

A fashionable Wife? Oh never will I be anything so heartless! I have pictured for myself a far higher destiny than this – Will it ever be more than a picture? Shall I ever have the wish of my heart fulfilled? a 'sweet home' calmly embosomed in some romantic vale; with wealth enough to realize my ideal of elegant comfort; with books, statues, paintings all things suitable to a tasteful, intellectual manner of life; with the friendship and society of a few, whose conversation would improve the faculties of my head and heart and with *one* to be the polar star of my being – one warmhearted, highminded *dearest* Friend, whose sublime Genius would shed an ennobling influence on all around him; whose graceful and splendid qualities would inspire a love that should be the heart and soul of my life![41]

The letter moves next into knockabout comedy. Mrs Welsh, being perversely and 'extravagantly fond' of the unfortunate Dugald Gilchrist and his sister, has invited the latter to stay for the winter, thus, as Jane says, furnishing 'a continual pretext for her Brother's visits'. 'The only comfort I have', she concludes, 'is a faint hope that Doctor Fyffe may knock Mr Gilchrist's brains out; and be hanged himself for murder – I should thus be quit of two very great plagues at once.'[42]

Carlyle's next letter, dated 28 October, came from Paris:

'Paris?' I hear you exclaim: 'Unhappy soul! what has taken *thee* to Paris? Art thou frantic? Art thou dreaming? Or has the Hindoo Princess actually bewitched thee that thou *hast* brought thy acid visage and most atrabiliar philosophy into this land of fops and pastry-cooks, where vanity and sensuality have set up their chosen shrine, and every one that falls not down to worship them is an alien and an interloper! What hast *thou* to do with Paris?' In truth, my Love, I have very little to do with it; yet here I am, and little less surprised than you are at my journey hither.

The explanation lay in the proximity of France to Dover, which 'had awakened the travelling propensities of the little fidgetty, higgle-haggling, good-hearted, logic-chopping Mr Strachey and of the fair Princess whose name I must *not* mention'.[43]

On a trip of only a week or so with such a group of companions,

Carlyle could do little more than register, with his quick and accurate mind, the external scene and draw some general conclusions. He noticed the 'eating, everlasting eating', 'gambling ad infinitum', and the propensity of Parisians to conduct their lives outdoors. 'Their houses are not homes', he told Jane, 'but places where they sleep and dress; they live in *cafés* and promenades and theatres.'[44] He found time to attend a lecture on comparative anatomy by the famous Baron Cuvier. Reporting to Jack on this, he noted that his brother might do well to think of completing his medical studies in Paris, 'when you have done with Edinburgh'.[45] Parisian scientists had the advantage over their British counterparts of being allowed 'dissection *ad libitum* for the general purposes of anatomy'.[46] Not till 1832, after the notorious affair of Burke and Hare, who murdered vagrants to supply the Edinburgh medical school with corpses for dissection, was the Anatomy Act passed, making dissection legal, though restricting it to the bodies of paupers.

While in Paris, Carlyle introduced himself to Legendre, whose book on geometry he had translated for Brewster.[47] Otherwise, he saw and did little in the French capital, yet, as he recalled in old age, this trip was 'very entertaining for a 10 days, and proved *useful* after[war]ds'.[48] So clearly did he take in the topography and atmosphere of Paris that he could draw disproportionately on his experience when conjuring up the city in his history of the French Revolution more than a decade later.

In writing home he was once more in his stylistic element when describing the eccentricities of people he observed. Mr Strachey's comic attempts at speaking French to waiters were relayed to Jack:

'*C'est bien imposante!*' said he at Beauvais; '*c'est une – une – rascalitie – vous dis-je; vous avez chargé deux fois trop! vous etes &c*'; to all of which they answered with the gravity of judges passing sentence of death: *Monsieur, c'est impossible; on ne vous surfait nullement; on ne &c. 'Où est les chevaux?*' shrieked he at the end of every post: *vont venir, Monsieur*, said they; Kitty and I were like to split with laughing. At length Strachey himself gave up the cause entirely and took to speaking French-English without disguise. When a man asked him for *quelque chose à boire; je vous ai conduit très bien*; Strachey answered without looking at him '*Nong! vous avez drivé devilish slow*', which suited quite as well.[49]

More seriously, he told Jane from Paris that they should 'abide by one another'. 'We have chosen one another', he declared firmly, 'and nothing shall part us.' He added, not without prescience, 'together we may fail to be happy; separate, we can hardly fail to be miserable'. Already displaying an unfortunate propensity to decide what would be best for him and expect her to fall in with the decision, he declared that he was 'meditating to engage with some literary Tradesman for a full translation of all Schiller's works dramatic and philosophical to retire with the necessary apparatus into Annandale'. Would she take a share in the concern?[50]

Jane's response was not encouraging. How could it be, when she longed to see London, and perhaps even Paris, for herself? When Haddington irked her because nothing happened in such a small, sleepy town? She pursued her unsuccessful campaign against his accent – 'at least you will not speak Annandale, surely, after having *travelled*' – and burst out, showing prescience in her turn:

Oh mercy never think of establishing yourself in Annandale! All your faults are the effects of your isolated way of life: if you seclude yourself altogether from your fellows, as sure as fate, you will sink in a year or two, into the most surly, misanthropic, self-opinionative, dreadfully disagreeable person alive.[51]

Back in London by November 1824, Carlyle was still casting about for a long-term prospect. His suggestion to Oliver and Boyd in January 1825 that he translate Schiller's works was 'respectfully declined'.[52] Undaunted, he wrote to Jane on 9 January, formally proposing that they marry and go to Annandale, to a farm in Nithsdale, north-west of Dumfries. He needed to recover his health, and was determined not to 'degenerate into the wretched thing which calls itself an Author in our Capitals, and scribbles for the sake of filthy lucre in the periodicals of the day'.[53] Jane was horrified, especially as her precipitate lover had seized on a 'joke' in her last letter but one. In a foolish moment she had mentioned that the farm she had inherited from her father at Craigenputtoch, sixteen miles north-west of Dumfries, was to let. Quoting Carlyle, she had written, 'If you had Land of your own you would improve it! Suppose you improve mine?'[54]

Jane now expressed her perplexity at his proposal:

I love you – I have told you so a hundred times; and I should be the most ungrateful, and injudicious of mortals if I did not – but I am not *in love* with you – that is to say – my love for you is not a passion which overclouds my judgement.

Here is gratitude again, where passion ought to be. Jane went on to say she would not marry him to live on less money than was 'sufficient for my wants'; nor could she marry 'into a station inferior to my own'. What '*certain* livelihood' could he offer? He assuredly had 'noble gifts', but he had not yet achieved anything with them. As for the idea of the two of them keeping house together at Craigenputtoch, 'I would just as soon think of building myself a nest on the Bass-rock.' He had never seen the solitary place. 'Depend upon it, you could not *exist* there a twelvemonth. For my part I would not spend a month on it with an Angel.' She finished this uncompromising disquisition with the placatory statement that 'at all events I will marry no one else', but declared that she could promise no more than that.[55]

Poor Carlyle. Once more he sensibly took his time in replying. When he did, it was in a letter remarkable for its paradoxical effects. One sees the push and pull of hurt pride and humble submission, of common sense and irrationality, of fatalism and a determination to make his own destiny. In the end, he simply refuses to give up in the face of all obstacles. First, he thanks her for her candour. Her 'resoluteness' does not offend him; his love for her is 'unabated'. Of course she is being sensible and prudent, and he has no wish to ask impossible sacrifices of her. Yet he thinks that 'love which will *not* make sacrifices to its object is no proper love'; surely she is generous enough to agree with that? Not, he swiftly adds, that he has any intention of requiring her to sacrifice all worldly comforts; in a few months he 'might be realizing from literature and other kindred exertions the means of keeping *poverty* at a safe distance'.[56]

Finally, he assures her that she is 'dear to me as the light of life', and suggests that they postpone an ultimate decision until they meet again when he returns to Scotland. As a kind of postscript he adds, with that odd, unnerving, slightly hysterical determination he often showed in extremity:

Is that farm of yours *really* to be let? And where is it, and who has the letting of it? My Brother [Alick] and I have long had a scheme of conjoint farming; and I feel more and more the essentialness of something like it to my recovery. Now why should we not be *your* tenants! It seems to me that I could delve and prune with ten times tenfold pleasure, if I thought my delving and pruning were in any shadow of a sense for *you*.[57]

Jane took stock in her turn. She was not, she told him, seeking 'wealth and rank', merely wishing to see him 'earning a *certain* livelihood, and exercising the profession of a gentleman'. She now thinks 'the most *probable* destiny' for her will be to become his wife. 'How could I *part* from the only living soul that understands me?' Struggling under the weight of knowing that she needs him but does not love him, she accurately intuits what he fails to see, namely the fatal lack in his love for her, despite all his protestations:

Your present situation is miserable; it *must* be altered; but is it with reference to *me* that it must be altered? Is it *I* who have made it miserable? No! you were as unhappy before we met as ever you have been since: the cause of your unhappiness then must lie in other circumstances of your destiny, which I have no connection with – no real connection, however much I may seem to have, from being frequently associated with them in your mind.[58]

There was to be much more of this mutually frank yet oscillating correspondence before they finally married. Once Carlyle was back in Scotland, Mrs Welsh's reiterated objections to his bad temper and social inferiority continued to make meetings between them infrequent, delayed, brief, and awkward. On the other hand, her attempts to sabotage the relationship had the usual result of such parental interference, by enhancing for Jane the prospect, if not of living with Carlyle, at least of getting away from home.

★

Carlyle left London before the end of February 1825, travelling north via Birmingham, where he stopped off at Badams's for a week or two. His family were asked to find a farm to rent near Mainhill, where Alick could try out his skills independently of his father and Carlyle could read, write, and ride about in an attempt to improve his health. The plan was for his mother to keep house for the two brothers; the two youngest sisters, Jean, aged fourteen, and Janet, aged nearly twelve, would join them. Hoddam Hill, a few miles from Mainhill, was taken from Whitsunday 1825.[59]

Mrs Carlyle, whose customary anxiety about her eldest son had increased during his stay in London (reaching a climax when she knew he was travelling to Paris),[60] was thankful he was now on his way home. She had written to him in London on 18 December 1824, full of motherly solicitation and exhortation, not in themselves unusual, but sitting oddly with the rest of her twenty-nine-year-old son's inner and outer life at this time:

It is a long time since we had a sight of each other, nevertheless I am often with you in thought, and I hope we shall meet at a throne of grace where there is free access to all who come in faith. Tell me if thou readest a chapter often. If not, begin; oh, do begin! How do you spend the Sabbath in that tumultuous city? Oh! remember to keep it holy; this you will never repent. I think you will be saying, 'Hold, mother!' but time is short and uncertain. Now, Tom, the best of boys thou art to me! Do not think I am melancholy, though I so speak.[61]

Carlyle did not answer this directly; presumably he could not have done so without either being dishonest or causing her pain. Instead, he asked Alick to 'thank my true Mother for her note: tell her it will not be long till I answer all her queries by word of mouth'.[62] He was back at Mainhill by late March, happy among his adoring family. In *Reminiscences* he was to describe the last stage of his journey home from London:

At Ecclefechan, next day, within two miles or so of my Father's, while the coach was changing horses, I noticed through the window my little Sister Jean earnestly looking up for me; she, with Jenny [Janet], the youngest of us all, was at School in the village; and had come out daily of late to inspect the coach in hope of me; – always in vain till this day: her bonny little blush, and radiance of look, when I let down the window and suddenly disclosed myself, are still present to me.[63]

To Jane, who was showing more impatience about their next meeting than he, Carlyle explained his family's plans, reassuring her that he was still 'altogether yours, to take or reject, according to your will'.[64] She was disposed to take him, though she confessed, after various delays had put off their seeing one another until mid-April, that 'the idea of *meeting* you after all this nonsense is quite terrible to me'.[65] He visited Haddington, but was once more unable to reconcile Mrs Welsh to the idea of him as a son-in-law. 'Try to persuade her that if I were less sick, I should be less disagreeable', he begged Jane on 6 May, after leaving Haddington.[66] For once Jane was the more positive lover. 'Best and Dearest', she replied, 'I love you with all my soul', and she signed herself 'Yours, for ever and ever Jane Welsh'.[67]

Carlyle moved to Hoddam Hill on 26 May, 'set up my Books, and bits of implements', and 'took to doing *German Romance* as my daily work; "ten pages daily" my stint, which, barring some rare accident, I faithfully accomplished'.[68] He had agreed with the Edinburgh publisher William Tait that he would translate a number of German stories and short novels, including *Wilhelm Meister's Travels*. The work, for which he was paid £180, was finally published in four volumes, entitled *Specimens of German Romance*, in January 1827.[69] It was not a particularly stimulating task, but it kept Carlyle quietly busy for the next year. In April he wrote to Henry Crabb Robinson, Germanist and friend of Wordsworth and Coleridge, asking for advice about which stories to choose.[70]

He also asked Crabb Robinson to send a copy of his *Life of Schiller*, just published in London, to Goethe. Carlyle himself had sent a copy of his *Meister* translation the previous summer, expressing the hope that he might 'one day see you, and pour out before you, as before a father, the woes and wanderings of a heart whose mysteries you seemed so thoroughly to comprehend'.[71] The seventy-five-year-old Goethe had replied graciously a few months later in a letter which pleased Carlyle for its 'patriarchal style' and seemed to him 'almost like a message from Fairy Land'.[72]

The quiet routine at Hoddam Hill suited Carlyle. Alick managed the farm, while 'beloved Mother' and one or other of the little sisters saw to his needs. Jack visited often too, having finished his medical degree at Edinburgh. The year spent there until his marriage later seemed to him like a 'russet-coated Idyll'. Financial worries were briefly in abeyance, since he had been paid £90 for *Schiller*.[73] His health improved in the country air, helped also, he thought, by 'long solitary rides' on his wild Irish horse, Barry.[74] Best of all, he recalled in *Reminiscences*, it was during the time at Hoddam Hill that he finally 'conquered all my scepticisms, agonising doubtings, fearful wrestlings with the foul and vile and soul-murdering Mud-gods of my Epoch', these being chiefly the temptations of atheism and philosophical scepticism but also, on the opposing side, the 'Puseyisms, Ritualisms' and other 'cobwebberies' to which some troubled souls clung as their response to religious doubt.[75] Prominent among these 'ritualists' were Irving and his enthusiasts.

During the summer of 1825 Jane, preparing to pay her first visit to Carlyle's family, disburdened herself of her guilty secret with regard to Irving, finally telling Carlyle she had once 'passionately' loved him. The catalyst for her confession was Mrs Montagu, who was keeping up a flattering correspondence with Carlyle and had expressed a wish to correspond with Jane too. This she did, in a flowery style, encouraging the romance with Carlyle, whom she praised to Jane (not seeming to mind his Annandale accent and less than elegant manners), and letting it be known that she knew (from Irving) about the former Irving–Jane relationship.[76] Jane was overwhelmed by Mrs Montagu's minute psychologising – 'Mercy how romantic she is', she exclaimed to Carlyle.[77] She followed the advice of 'the Noble Lady', as she and Carlyle were soon calling their enthusiastic friend, and made her confession to Carlyle on 24 July. He was magnanimous in reply, assuring her that his feelings remained unchanged.[78]

With the air thus cleared, Jane's visit to Mainhill and Hoddam Hill in September was a success. Carlyle had told her his mother was afraid Jane would find the humble household arrangements intolerable, while his father had no fear of her arrival. 'For him, he could open the wattled door of his wigwam, if he dwell in one, and welcome with a serene spirit the monarch of Europe'.[79] Jane charmed them all, especially Jean, with whom she began a sisterly correspondence.[80] She and Carlyle rode about the quiet countryside together. Carlyle fondly remembered that nothing ever went wrong on these excursions, 'my guidance taken as beyond criticism; she ready for any pace, rapid or slow; melodious talk, of course, never wanting'.[81] A russet-coated idyll, indeed, though the romance of riding about with Jane, showing her his home country and introducing her to his family, was partly clouded by his continued despair at being a slave to degrading dyspepsia.[82]

★

In October 1825 Carlyle went to Annan to see Irving, who was visiting his parents there. His baby, also Edward, had died of whooping cough, and 'the poor Orator', whom Carlyle had derided the previous summer for his exaggerated fatherly pride (treating the baby 'as if it were a cherub from on high'), was now 'sallow and care-worn'.[83] Irving told him about the plans for the new University of London (now University College

London), with which he had been involved until he found that 'religion was not cared for'.[84] The university had been the brainchild of Carlyle's despised Scottish poet, Thomas Campbell, who had been impressed by the freedom from religious affiliation he found on a visit to the University of Bonn. It was associated not only with secularism but also with Whig and Radical politics through such patrons and founders as Henry Brougham, James Mill, and Jeremy Bentham.[85]

The non-allegiance of the new foundation to the Church of England did not upset Carlyle, who told Jane he had 'some faint thoughts of looking after some appointment there'.[86] Jane rather hoped he would succeed. She wondered in December what he would do once *German Romance* was off his hands. 'Perhaps you will write a novel, or a tragedy, or become Editor of a literary newspaper at Edin*r*, or Professor of Lord knows what in the University at London.'[87] It was now settled that they would marry when he had finished his translation and realised some money for it, but Jane was naturally keen that something more note-worthy should follow.

They had to decide where they would live. This, too, was the subject of protracted arguments and misunderstandings during the early months of 1826. Once more, Mrs Welsh made it clear that she did not want to see Carlyle, so the couple could not meet to discuss the matter in person. Both blew hot and cold on the merits of a quiet country life versus the job opportunities likely to come Carlyle's way if they settled in or near Edinburgh. Both made disastrous suggestions. Jane proposed that Mrs Welsh should sell the Haddington house and take another in Edinburgh to which Carlyle would come and live 'as her son'. Carlyle was horrified, replying that he had assumed Mrs Welsh would go to live with her father in Dumfriesshire. If she must live under one roof with him and Jane, it would be on condition that she 'consent in the spirit of Christian meekness to make *me* her guardian and director, and be a second *wife* to her daughter's husband!'[88]

So unappealing was this prospect to Mrs Welsh that she decided to go and live at Templand with her father after all.[89] She even wrote graciously to Carlyle, accepting at last that the marriage would go ahead:

May God grant that it may draw us *all* together in the bonds of love and happiness with every good wish for your welfare. Believe me in affection what you wd wish the Mother of your Jane to be, G. Welsh.[90]

Carlyle could hardly have managed things better if he had consciously employed a Machiavellian tactic, though he seems to have genuinely believed that they could all live together as long as he was boss. As for Jane, she seems simply not to have thought at all clearly about life after marriage, or she would never have made the suggestion that the temperamental Mrs Welsh and the irritable genius should occupy the same house.

In May 1826 Mrs Welsh sold her Haddington home (to Dr Fyffe) and took a small, recently built house in the ever-extending New Town of Edinburgh. She and Jane would live here, at 21, Comely Bank, until the marriage, when Carlyle would settle there with Jane and Mrs Welsh move to Templand. Jane described the house as 'quiet and light and dry', with 'a pretty tree before the door' and a view of green fields from the windows.[91] The house still stands in the middle of a gracious, if modest, Georgian terrace, but the green fields have long since been built over.

The Carlyle family was on the move too. The lease at Mainhill was running out, and an argument had arisen with the landlord over the renting of Hoddam Hill, so Alick and his father took a farm large enough for the whole family at Scotsbrig, about five miles from Mainhill.[92] They all moved there in May 1826, Carlyle joining them until his wedding.

That long-deferred event finally took place on 17 October 1826. Both Carlyle and Jane were nervous, as well they might be. It was a whole year since they had last seen one another, when Jane had visited Hoddam Hill and Carlyle had paid a brief visit to Templand to meet Jane's aunt and grandfather.[93] Carlyle complained of poor health and fussed about what to wear. He had expected to receive £200 for *German Romance*, but his publisher had gone to London for a month, so no money was forthcoming. This was a serious setback, as Carlyle had lent most of his savings to his father and brother to make repairs at Scotsbrig. He was, he told Jane on 19 September, splenetic, sick, sleepless, and 'void' of hope, faith, and charity.[94] She kept a cooler head. 'The purgatory will soon be past', she told him, announcing that she would marry in white and finally put off the mourning black she had worn for nearly seven years.[95]

Carlyle later remembered how in August 'Haddington became aware of what was toward; a great enough event there, the loss of its loved and admired "Jeannie Welsh", – "the Flower o' Haddington"'.[96] Much later David Masson recalled a conversation with one of Jane's old Haddington nurses, whom he quoted:

Ah! when she was young, she was a fleein', dancin', light-heartit thing, Jeanie Welsh, that naething would hae dauntit. But she grew grave a' at once. There was Maister Irving, ye ken, that had been her teacher; and he cam aboot her. Then there was Maister – [name not given, but might be Dr Fyffe or Dugald Gilchrist]. Then there was Maister Carlyle himsel'; and *he* cam to finish her off like.[97]

On 1 October 1826 Jane herself wrote a fine letter to the wife of her father's brother George, explaining that though others would say that

Carlyle was poor and would 'indulge in some criticisms scarce flattering, on his birth', they

would not tell you he is among the cleverest men of his day; and not the cleverest only but the most enlightened! that he possesses all the qualities I deem essential in *my* husband, – a warm true heart to love me, a towering intellect to command me, and a spirit of fire to be the guiding star-light of my life . . .

Such then is this future husband of mine; not a *great* man according to the most common sense of the word, but truly great in its natural, proper sense – a scholar, a poet, a philosopher, a wise and noble man, one who holds his patent of nobility from Almighty God, and who's [*sic*] high stature of manhood is not to be measured by the inch-rule of Lilliputs! – Will you like him? no matter whether you do or not – since *I* like him in the deepest part of my soul.[98]

They were married, quietly, as both had wanted, at Jane's grandfather's home, Templand, in the presence of Jane's immediate family and Carlyle's brother John. After the wedding breakfast this combative couple, so intimately known to one another through long years of letter-writing yet still virtual strangers in the flesh, drove off immediately for Comely Bank to begin their married life as Mr and Mrs Carlyle.

PART TWO

MARRIAGE

CHAPTER 4

Edinburgh 1826–1828

Two days after the wedding Carlyle wrote to his mother from the little house in Comely Bank. Knowing she would be anxious to hear from him with particulars of his health, he obliged with a letter in which pathos, gloom, and self-pity predominate, expressed in a pitch peculiar to his letters to his mother, as of a man bravely, if plaintively, putting up with difficulties which only she would understand to be almost impossible to bear. Carlyle always played up to his mother's weaknesses, as we have seen from his responses to her fretful piety. His health was the other subject they lovingly rolled back and forth between them. This being so, his letter of 19 October 1826 is less odd than would otherwise be the case; nevertheless, as a description of Carlyle's state of mind on achieving the goal of marrying Jane, which he had set himself more than five years earlier, it is passing strange.

'I am still dreadfully confused, still far from being at home in my new situation, inviting and hopeful as in all points it appears', he begins. Then:

On the whole I have reason to say that I have been mercifully dealt with . . . The house is a perfect model of a house, furnished with every accommodation that heart could desire; and for my wife I may say in my heart that she is far better than any other wife, and loves me with a devotedness, which it is a mystery to me how I have ever deserved. She is gay and happy as a lark, and looks with such soft cheerfulness into my gloomy countenance that new hope passes over into me every time I meet her eye. You yourself (and that is saying much) could not have nursed and watched over me with kinder affection, wrecked as I am, by my movements, and counter-movements; all my despondency cannot make her despond, she seems happy enough if she can but see me, and minister to me.

For in truth I was very sullen yesterday, sick with sleeplessness, quite nervous, *billus*, splenetic and all the rest of it. Good Jane! I feel that she will be all to me that heart could wish; for she loves me in her soul . . .

You will ask about sleep: fear not for that, my good Mother; I shall sleep better than ever, Scotsbrig or the Hill were not quieter than this, and our bed is, I should think, about *seven feet wide*! Besides she herself (the good soul!) has ordered another bed to be made for me in the adjoining room, to which I may retire whenever I shall see good.[1]

The question of whether the marriage was consummated has often been raised. It is possible that Carlyle used his ill health and insomnia as an

75

excuse to avoid sexual relations which he may well have feared. But the extra bed mentioned in his letter is in itself no more proof of this than the fact that the marriage was childless. All we can say is that no positive proof of consummation survives, but then, apart from pregnancies and children, of what could such proof consist? Jane, for her part, may have been discouraging sexually, since it is clear that she was not physically attracted to Carlyle. Maybe it suited them both to have little or no sexual element in their relationship. No amount of speculation, or reviewing the speculations of others, can take us further into the mystery at the heart of this, as of any other, marriage.

Carlyle wrote again to his mother a month later, describing Jane's love for him, her usefulness, and her willingness to obey his command:

In *every* thing great and little she gives me entirely my own way; asking, as it seems, nothing more whatever of her destiny, but that in any way she could make me happy. Good little girl! Sometimes too we *are* very happy; in our trim quiet house, sitting by our own tea, with a good book in my hand, and a clear fire on the hearth, I feel as if all would be well, and far better than my best expectations. From her I can anticipate no hindrance in any arrangement of my life I may see good to adopt: I firmly believe, in the poorest cottage of Scotland, with me happy beside her, she would be the blithest wife in Scotland too. Courage, therefore, I say to myself: one way or other, it must and shall be ordered for good! Give me a little time to sift it and settle it all, and then to fasten on it with rigid perseverance, and the evils of my lot will at length be beneath my feet! On the whole I ought to be ashamed of complaint: a hundred times in my life I have been far worse in health than I am, and never half so well in all other particulars. In spite of my drugs, I sleep quite passably in our giant bed, and were it not that I am so over-anxious to be *well*, I should not let my *illness* discompose me.[2]

How unrecognisable is this representation of Jane, whose letters reveal her to be a woman with a strong will, accustomed to be courted and flattered, who liked having the freedom to choose whether to give or withhold consent. But she *had* consented, and Carlyle, like many another man supported by history, society, and the law, saw it as his natural right to command and be obeyed by his life's partner. She accepted that right too, though like the little girl magnanimously sacrificing her doll, she found herself repenting and sometimes bewailing her lot.

No clear picture emerges of Jane's feelings immediately after the wedding. Her only surviving letters from this time are loyal postscripts to her mother-in-law, reassuring her that she is hoping to improve Carlyle's health, that they love one another, and are happy. Jane becomes for a time – at least as far as curious posterity is concerned – submerged in Carlyle and the Carlyle family. Old Mrs Carlyle was carefully told that he and Jane attended church and read a sermon on Sundays.[3] Soon John Carlyle was visiting Comely Bank, and he, too, added a postscript informing his mother in December that '*Tom* is much better in every respect since the last letter was written'.[4] (Jane seems never to have described Carlyle as Tom, but always as 'Carlyle'.)

In February 1827 Jane wrote to Carlyle's younger sister Jean, inviting her to come for a visit and bring her mother with her.[5] It took many repetitions of this invitation before Mrs Carlyle was persuaded to leave her Annandale home; she finally came to Edinburgh in December 1827. We do not know if Mrs Welsh and her father and sister were also asked to visit the newly married pair. Nothing survives of the correspondence between Jane and Templand. We do know, however, because Carlyle told his mother so, that Jane was 'the most compliant and best-hearted of wives'.[6]

That Jane was corresponding with the romantic Mrs Montagu is clear from that lady's replies to letters of Jane now lost. Mrs Montagu's admiration of Carlyle may have been one of many determining factors which shook Jane into finally accepting him as a husband, since for a woman who was a close acquaintance of Coleridge and other London luminaries to welcome the rough northern genius as a friend despite his accent, his clumsiness, and his gloom was a strong testimony to his worth. Mrs Montagu sent congratulations on the marriage, encouraging Jane's 'confiding love' for 'this excellent man' whom she nevertheless saw to be pessimistic and difficult, or, as she put it, remembering Carlyle's London sojourn, 'in a mist, wholly bewildered', with 'good-looking eyes' which 'ever more scowled at me with a doubting glance'. In December 1826 she referred to 'your anxiety for your Husband', Jane having presumably told her of Carlyle's continuing battle with ill health.[7]

The Carlyles were short of money, since he had no specific task in hand. *Specimens of German Romance* finally came out early in 1827, having been delayed partly because three other such collections had recently been published and partly because of the spectacular publishing crash of 1826 which had involved Sir Walter Scott's publisher Constable and Carlyle's printer Thomas Ballantyne.[8]

What could Carlyle do next to earn some money? In February he announced to Alick that he had begun a book. This was the never-to-be-finished 'wretched "Didactic Novel"' called 'Wotton Reinfred', a limping preliminary attempt at autobiographical fiction.[9] In March he almost came to an agreement with the London publishers Hunt and Clarke to translate Goethe's memoirs, *Aus meinem Leben: Dichtung und Wahrheit* (*From My Life: Fiction and Truth*). But they were fearful of the risk at such a time, and nothing came of the idea.[10]

Scornful as he had been of London literary men scribbling for magazines, that is precisely what Carlyle now found himself doing. Telling Alick in February that his *German Romance* was 'travelling thro' the

Cuddy-lane of Newspaper criticism, and most of these long-eared quadrupeds seem rather to smell at it with affection', he added – apparently for once not seeing the irony of the situation – that Procter had sent him a letter of introduction to 'Jeffrey of the Edin*r* Review; one of these days I design presenting it, and you shall hear the result'.[11] He lost little time in doing so.

★

It must have taken an effort to subdue the memory of his angry pride at Jeffrey's utter silence when he had last been approached in 1820, but Carlyle needed money. Moreover, he respected Jeffrey, partly in his capacity as Edinburgh's celebrity lawyer, partly as a shrewd critic, and largely because the *Edinburgh Review* was regarded by Carlyle, as by many others, as the most important public journal of the day.

He had first seen Jeffrey pleading cases in court in Edinburgh and had been struck by the eloquence of this small dandyish man. Jeffrey's greatest claim to fame as a lawyer was his defence in 1812 of Helen Kennedy, a girl from Dumfriesshire, on a charge of multiple murder. 'Not a human creature', Carlyle recalled, 'doubted but Nell was the criminal, and would get her doom.' His account in *Reminiscences* demonstrates his ability to conjure up a picture in a passage of breathless yet controlled syntax, with a touch of sly underlying irony:

Assize-time came, Jeffrey there; and Jeffrey, by such a play of Advocacy as was never seen before, bewildered the poor jury into temporary deliquium, or loss of wits (so that the poor foreman, *Scottice* 'chancellor', on whose casting-vote it turned, said at last, with the sweat bursting from his brow, 'Mercy, then, mercy!'), and brought Nell clear off, – home that night, riding gently out of Dumfries in men's clothes to escape the rage of the mob. The jury-chancellor, they say, on awakening next morning, smote his now dry brow, with a gesture of despair, and exclaimed, 'Was I mad?'[12]

Carlyle's admiration of the lawyerly chutzpah of the man is obvious; equally clear is his revulsion at the moral dubiousness necessarily involved in the profession of advocacy, a feeling which may earlier have contributed to his own speedy abandonment of thoughts of the law. 'Advocate morality', he muses in *Reminiscences*, 'was clearly on his side; it is a strange trade, I have often thought, that of advocate: your intellect, your highest heavenly gift, hung up in the shop-window, like a loaded pistol for sale.'[13]

Even as critic and editor, Carlyle thought, Jeffrey was ever the lawyer determined to argue the case to a successful conclusion. His own articles for the *Edinburgh Review* were always subject to dispute with Jeffrey; when the two men dined together at Jeffrey's country house outside Edinburgh, they had 'long discussions, and argumentative parryings and thrustings' well into the night. 'There we went on in brisk logical exercise, with all the rest of the house asleep; and parted usually in good humour, though after a game which was hardly worth the candle.'[14] In Jeffrey Carlyle found an antitype, one against whom he could measure himself, and by contrast to whom he could define his own opinions, in a way which proved fruitful, unlike the brief encounter with Coleridge.

As for Jeffrey the critic, his reputation preceded him here too. He was the scourge of the 'Lake School of Poets' – a term he invented in 1802 in the first number of the *Edinburgh Review*, to describe (and deride) Wordsworth, Coleridge, and Southey – the man who provoked Byron into a satirical attack in *English Bards and Scotch Reviewers* (1809), and the writer of the most famous opening lines of any review article, 'This will never do', said of Wordsworth's long poem, *The Excursion* (1814). In 1825 he had reviewed Carlyle's translation of *Wilhelm Meister's Apprenticeship*, not attacking the translator, but pronouncing his uncompromising British judgement on the work as 'almost from beginning to end, one flagrant offence against every principle of taste, and every just rule of composition'.[15]

Carlyle, who had anticipated such a reaction, was not upset. 'I think the critic very honest', he had told a Dumfriesshire friend, James Johnston, at the time, 'and very seldom unjust in his feeling of individual passages'. Though Jeffrey had no sense of the whole, 'except as a heap of beautiful and ugly fragments', he was 'an honest and clever man, and by far the best of them all'.[16]

Jeffrey had edited the *Edinburgh Review* since its founding in 1802. Though Carlyle did not share the Whig politics of the *Review*, he recognised its value as a serious periodical which rose above party politics in its careful attention to literature. Much later, he annotated his copy of J. C. Hare's 1848 biographical memoir of their mutual friend John Sterling. Treating the book, as he did all his books, as a conversational partner, he responded in the margin to a remark by Hare that reading the *Edinburgh Review* could hardly 'yield less wholesome food for a young mind'. 'Nonsense, Sir!' scribbles Carlyle in robust refutation. 'It was the best, indeed the only Picture of the Actual World he had been born into, that was attainable to him – or to any one!'[17] In Carlyle's mind, the *Edinburgh Review* was an exception in the ephemeral world of reviewing and being reviewed.

When he was sent a letter of introduction to the fascinating and powerful Jeffrey, therefore, he 'went up one evening' in February 1827 and delivered it. 'The little man received me in his kindest style', Carlyle told his mother; 'talked with me for an hour, tho' very busy, on all possible things; and really proved himself by much the most agreeable citizen of Edinburgh that I had ever met with.' More promisingly still, Jeffrey proposed that Carlyle write something for the *Edinburgh*, to which Carlyle replied that 'he must first read the *German Romance* to see what manner of man I was, and then we might determine if I could suit him'.[18]

Carlyle told Mrs Montagu on 7 May that he had seen Jeffrey: 'Me he seemed to look upon as an enthusiast, distracted nearly, but amiable in my distraction.'[19] In early June he visited Jeffrey again, and it was agreed that he should write a short preliminary article.[20] 'The little jewel of Advocates', he told Jack,

was to all appearance anxious that I would undertake the task of Germanizing the public, and ready even to let me do it 'con amore', so I did not treat the whole Earth not yet Germanized as a 'parcel of blockheads'; which surely seemed a fair enough request . . . I engaged as it were for paving the way, to give him in this present publication some little short paper; I think, on the subject of Jean Paul, tho' that is not quite settled with myself yet: and thus, O Jack, thou seest me busily occupied with a *new* trade! . . . certainly Jeffrey is by much the most lovable of all the literary men I have seen; and he seemed ready nay desirous, if time would but permit, to cultivate a further intimacy.[21]

Jean Paul Richter was chosen because he was the German writer, after Goethe, who had most fascinated Carlyle. Two of his whimsical stories, 'Army-chaplain Schmelzle's Journey to Flaetz' and 'Life of Quintus Fixlein', were included in *German Romance*. Richter had a penchant for expansiveness, wild humour, and digression; his works could plausibly be seen as German cousins of *Hudibras* and *Tristram Shandy*, two of Carlyle's favourite books.[22]

In his article for Jeffrey, Carlyle characterises Richter's fiction in terms which might well be applied to his own *Sartor Resartus*:

He has a whole imaginary geography of Europe in his novels; the cities of Flachsenfingen, Haarhaar, Scheerau, and so forth, with their princes, and privy-councillors, and serene highnesses . . . No story proceeds without the most erratic digressions, and voluminous tagrags rolling after it in many a snaky twine . . . It is, indeed, a mighty maze; and often the panting reader toils after him in vain; or, baffled and spent, indignantly stops short, and retires, perhaps forever.[23]

Though Carlyle always acknowledged his close interest in Richter, he later corrected a suggestion by Althaus that his own writing was 'Germanized, Jean-Paulized':

Edward Irving and his admiration of the Old Puritans & Elizabethans . . . played a much more important part than Jean Paul on my poor 'style'; − & the most important part by far was that of Nature, you would perhaps say, had you ever heard my Father speak, or very often heard my Mother & her inborn melodies of heart and of voice![24]

The Richter article 'caused a sensation among the Edinburgh buckrams', as Carlyle recalled in 1866.[25] One can see why. The author, though no longer an inexperienced youth, being now thirty-one, had not yet made his mark in any field of literature. Reviewing was a trade he thought little of, but he solved the problem of its indignity by writing an authoritative essay rather than a review. He boldly dismissed the book ostensibly under review, a biography of Richter by the hapless Heinrich Döring, in favour of a confident biographical-critical account of his own. Carlyle's own interesting mind, expressed in his own style, is displayed. He opens the article with a paragraph full of uncomfortable warnings for practitioners of the art of biography, among whom he could count himself, and rather prophetic of what was to be done with his own life after his death:

Dr Johnson, it is said, when he first heard of Boswell's intention to write a life of him, announced, with decision enough, that, if he thought Boswell really meant to *write his* life, he would prevent it by *taking Boswell's*! That great authors should actually employ this preventive against bad biographers is a thing we would by no means recommend: but the truth is, that, rich as we are in Biography, a well-written Life is almost as rare as a well-spent one; and there are certainly many more men whose history deserves to be recorded, than persons willing and able to record it. But great men, like the old Egyptian kings, must all be tried after death, before they can be embalmed: and what, in truth, are these 'Sketches', 'Anas', 'Conversations', 'Voices', and the like, but the votes and pleadings of so many ill-informed advocates, jurors and judges; from whose conflict, however, we shall in the end have a true verdict? The worst of it is at the first; for weak eyes are precisely the fondest of glittering objects. Accordingly, no sooner does a great man depart, and leave his character as public property, than a crowd of little men rushes towards it.

Döring is held up as an example of how not to do it:

Biographies, according to Döring's method, are a simple business. You first ascertain, from the Leipsic *Conversationslexicon* . . . or other such *Compendium* or *Handbook*, the date and place of the proposed individual's birth, his parentage, trade, appointments, and the titles of his works . . . In this manner a mass of materials is collected, and the building now proceeds apace. Stone is laid on the top of stone, just as it comes to hand; a trowel or two of biographic mortar, if perfectly convenient, being spread in here and there, by way of cement; and so the strangest pile suddenly arises; amorphous, pointing every way but to the zenith, here a block of granite, there a mass of pipeclay; till the whole finishes, when the materials are finished; – and you leave it standing to posterity, like some miniature Stonehenge, a perfect architectural enigma.[26]

Such mechanical book-making is not what we require, so Carlyle puts Döring aside and writes his own account, not disdaining facts, dates, and places, but using them not as ends in themselves but as a context in which to discuss his subject's unusual genius. This he does rather impression-istically, finding an apt metaphor: 'On the whole, Genius has privileges of its own; it selects an orbit for itself; and be this never so eccentric, if it is indeed a celestial orbit, we mere stargazers must at last compose ourselves; must cease to cavil at it, and begin to observe it, and calculate its laws.'

Jeffrey was sufficiently taken by this essay to commission a second article, graciously permitting that too to address a German subject, while at the same time declaring, 'I think your taste vicious in some points, and your opinions of your German idols erroneous.'[27]

This longer article, 'The State of German Literature', was published in the October number of the *Edinburgh*. Compendious and in places vague, it is also detailed and sometimes startling, and everywhere exhibits Carlyle's determination to be the chief exponent and champion of German culture (Coleridge, Henry Crabb Robinson, and De Quincey having more or less stopped writing on German subjects). He tackles two often heard objections to German literature – bad taste and mysticism – and bravely attempts an explanation of the philosophy of Kant and his followers, though he is himself only partially acquainted with their work.[28]

The most original aspect of the article, however, is the foretaste it gives of what would become Carlyle's trademark, namely his ability to look at the larger picture and to offer analyses of contemporary *British* culture by contrasting it with German culture. It is a broad-brush portrait, but it attracted attention because it laid bare and ministered to anxieties about contemporary politics, religion, philosophy, and literature; it characterised, in short, 'the spirit of the age':

The Nineteenth Century stands before us, in all its contradiction and perplexity; barren, mean and baleful, as we have all known it, yet here no longer mean or barren, but enamelled into beauty in the poet's spirit; for its secret significance is laid open, and thus, as it were, the life-giving fire that slumbers in it is called forth, and flowers and foliage, as of old, are springing on its bleakest wildernesses, and overmantling its sternest cliffs. For these men [Goethe, Schiller, and other German writers] have not only the clear eye, but the loving heart. They have penetrated into the mystery of Nature; after long trial they have been initiated; and to unwearied endeavour, Art has at last yielded her secret; and thus can the Spirit of our Age, embodied in fair imaginations, look forth on us, earnest and full of meaning, from their works.[29]

The article was the talk of Edinburgh. Carlyle reported to his mother on 20 October with that offhand pride with which he viewed all his works, that 'the people seem to think that I am a genius perhaps, but of what sort Heaven only knows'.[30] He meant Jeffrey chiefly, though through the article he also came to know other Edinburgh stars at this time, notably John Wilson, with whom he enjoyed one great 'Supper', as he recalled in *Reminiscences*.

Under the pseudonym 'Christopher North', Wilson had been co-editor of *Blackwood's Magazine* in its early days of scurrilous attack on Wordsworth and Coleridge; he was a prodigious drinker and prankster; as a Tory he had been shoehorned into the post of Professor of Moral Philosophy at the University of Edinburgh in 1820 by a Tory town council determined not to appoint the much better qualified Whig, Sir William Hamilton. Recalling the business in a pen-portrait of Wilson written in 1868, Carlyle aims his sharpest thrust not at Wilson, but at corrupt Edinburgh politics and the indifference of Edinburgh academia under which he himself had smarted:

I remember well enough that Tory hoisting process – hoisting of Wilson by main force into the Professorship of 'Moral Philosophy' . . . A pretty Professor 'of *Morals!*' snorted all manner of indignant Editors and speculative men; – and indeed it was a rather high procedure, this of the Tories in respect of Wilson and their Party: but it turned out better than was expected . . . he was a most eloquent, fervid, over-powering kind of man, alive to all high interests and noble objects, especially of the literary or spiritual sort, and prompt to foster any germ of talent or aspiration he might notice in that kind, among his pupils . . . preferable, surely, to the logical frost which would otherwise have been their Academic portion, had Wilson *not* been there.[31]

Despite Carlyle's warm feelings, the friendship did not blossom. Carlyle later thought Wilson avoided him because of their different politics and Wilson's apprehension that Carlyle would disapprove of his drinking. He shrewdly observed the 'forced wedlock of Presbyterian Piety with so much Bluster and Whisky-Punch' in Wilson, in addition to his high Toryism.[32]

Meanwhile, the relationship with Jeffrey continued. He called at Comely Bank, met Jane, discovered they had a mutual distant cousin, and began a flirtatious correspondence with her.[33] 'He was much taken by my little Jeannie' – Carlyle's pet name for Jane – and became 'in a sort, her would-be openly declared friend and quasi-lover', wrote Carlyle in 1866. Though over fifty, Jeffrey was in the habit of flirting with pretty women. The woman who had until lately been the belle of Haddington 'properly understood all that sort of thing, the methods and rules of it', continues Carlyle, himself innocent of all such wiles, 'and could lead her clever little gentleman a very pretty minuet'.[34]

*

Though Carlyle now had an entrée to the *Edinburgh Review* and through it to other periodicals such as the newly founded *Foreign Review*, to which he contributed several German articles over the next couple of years, he was still hoping for a more stable source of income. Two radically different possibilities presented themselves: applying for professorships and moving back to the country to earn a living on a small farm. Edinburgh was proving less hostile to him than in previous years, but because of his health he and Jane gave no dinners and refused all invitations to dine, though Jane held Wednesday evening 'At Homes', when Brewster, Sir William Hamilton, and Jeffrey might drop in.[35]

Already in March 1827 Carlyle was complaining to Alick that town life was 'little to my mind'. He still thought of Craigenputtoch, despite Jane's vehemence about the place. Alick was asked to consider 'pitching your tent there' and managing the farm, should Carlyle and Jane decide to go. It is clear that Carlyle had not yet consulted his wife. 'As for Jane', he wrote complacently, 'I think there is little fear that her tolerance would be less than mine: in good sooth, she is a *true* wife, and would murmur at *no* scene or fortune which she shared along with me.' He conjured up a Carlyle family idyll which must have caused Jane's heart to sink, if he ever revealed it to her. Not only Alick, but also Jack might join the colony, or live nearby:

From all that I have learned there seems to be a fair opening for our Body-curer in Dumfries; nay I think he has a *good* chance to succeed, if he tried it rightly; and then do but think how pleasant to be all planted down within sight of each other; our Father and Mother and all that we cared for in the world, within a half-day's journey![36]

Mrs Welsh, to whom Jane had made over the rent of Craigenputtoch before her marriage, was having trouble with her current tenant; Alick was still looking for a farm to manage; Jack had not yet found a medical practice; Carlyle was worried about his health and did not like Edinburgh life. Putting these elements together, he dismissed (by underestimating) Jane's disinclination, and set about seeing if he and Alick could take over Craigenputtoch from Whitsun, the traditional changeover date for rented land and property. First the brothers rode over to Craigenputtoch in April to inspect it and to quiz the tenant over non-payment of rent. They reported to Jane and her mother that the place had been neglected. Mother and daughter replied in alarm that in that case Carlyle must get the tenant out as soon as possible.

Jane wrote slightly hysterically, saying she missed him and hated being separated from him. She urged him to save Craigenputtoch (which, though loathsome to her as a place to live, was hallowed theoretically by its association with her father), yet suggested mildly that 'we *might* not wish the place for ourselves'.[37]

Carlyle succeeded in negotiating a handover with the unsatisfactory tenant and his brother. He told Mrs Welsh that they had 'parted in fair spirits, and fine fellowship, with cordial shaking of hands: your health was drunk in fiery punch, and I upbraided for my *Whiggism* because I joined not beyond tea-spoonfuls of the noxious beverage'. His spirits were high:

And now, my dear Mother, let me congratulate the whole household on this auspicious result, which I hope in God will be good for us all. To me it gives the fairest chance of recovering health, the *only* thing I want for being the happiest man this sun shines on: my dear wifie's happiness is bound up in mine, and yours in that of us both.

To Jane he wrote, 'O Jeanie! How happy we shall be in this Craig o' Putto!'[38]

What could Jane do? She submitted to her fate. She shared Carlyle's anxieties about his health, and if he was convinced that only at Craigenputtoch – which had the added advantage of being cheap and having Mrs Welsh for its landlord – would he recover, it was difficult for her to gainsay this. She even simulated gaiety in a letter to Mrs Montagu in May, though the jolly tone is undermined by melancholy and doubt, as two opposing voices seem to battle it out in describing Craigenputtoch:

I hope much from a new plan of life we are just arranging, which offers him at least a fair *chance* of recovery. What say you to our quitting Edinr in Spring next, to settle down in the wildest place of all Dumfriesshire, leaving the world to run its own race and bear away its prizes; content might we but *walk* thro' life with unfettered limbs? A tract of the worst land in this country belongs to us, which one of my ancestors (apparently no lover of sweet sounds) has named Craigenputtock! There is a sort of house upon it which, I am told, it *is* in the power of man to make habitable, and trees, – starred belts of scotch fir, and dark melancholy lakes – of moss water. In short it is a place where Thomas Carlyle and I may live in great content, – where most people would die of ennui in a month. A Brother of my Husband's is going thither with us to farm the land; he himself is to study and ride and garden and write books; while I am to ride and study also, work, paint, play, and pet great quantities of live-creatures – There will be nothing of what is generally called pleasure in all this; but there will be *peace* which it is harder to do without, and which, under existing circumstances seems unattainable in any other way.[39]

Alick was to move to Craigenputtoch immediately, in May 1827, to begin farming and to oversee building works in preparation for Thomas and Jane moving in at Whitsun 1828.

There was some inconsistency in Carlyle's planning, however. Despite his conviction that his health would improve only if he lived in the country, he was still open to the possibility of an academic appointment. Sending Henry Crabb Robinson a copy of *German Romance* in May 1827, he took the opportunity to inquire about vacant chairs at 'that "London University" of yours' – Crabb Robinson being a founder member of the Council. Carlyle had heard that the new institution, which was to open formally the following year, had advertised several professorships. He listed his areas of expertise, beginning with moral philosophy and rhetoric. Then: 'I can teach Mathematics also, and Physics . . . , and touches of Metaphysics, the oddest mixture of Scotch and German, Dugald Stewart and Immanuel Kant! But the *fittest* place for me would be that of 'Jack of all Trades', in case they wanted such a hand.'[40]

This recalls Jane's joke in December 1825 about his prospects of becoming 'Professor of Lord knows what in the University at London'; it also looks forward to Carlyle's title for Diogenes Teufelsdröckh in *Sartor* – 'Professor of Things in General'. Carlyle's claim to be competent in half a dozen subjects may seem boastful, but academic expertise was less specialised in the early nineteenth century than it is today, and at least his appointment, should it occur, would not be a purely political one like Wilson's in Edinburgh.

Jane was aware of the inconsistency of believing that for Carlyle's health a move to the country was imperative while at the same time he applied for a job in the metropolis. She tried to explain in her next letter to Mrs Montagu that the matter of economics was almost as pressing as that of health. Her letter of 2 September rehearses arguments she seems to have learned from Carlyle. In the middle, however, she lets slip that she, at least, is as happy in Edinburgh as she would be anywhere else:

Our dear little home here grows more attractive every day; all the conveniences both of town and country lie around it; and we have as good society as the place (indeed perhaps any place) affords. But then to be at the mercy of such people as Booksellers! to be this with a sick body and a high mind! it would render the finest situation under the Sun unbearable. Now whether as a Farmer in the moors of Dunscore, or a Professor in the London university, one should be equally independent as to income: in the one case being placed *below* the necessity of *writing* for bread, in the other raised *above* it. For the rest, the arguments for and against the two projects are so well balanced, that one can hardly tell which to prefer.[41]

Carlyle, meanwhile, was taking the idea of London seriously; if he got the chair in moral philosophy for which he now applied, he could spend the summer vacations at Craigenputtoch.[42] Irving, asked for his opinion, advised proceeding with the application, despite his own disapproval of the university's utilitarian, and in some cases atheist, founders and members. Carlyle quotes his friend with sorrowful amusement: ' "The Lord", he says, blesses him: his Church rejoices in "the Lord"; in fact, the Lord and he seem to be quite hand and glove.'[43]

Carlyle also asked Jeffrey to advise and to write a reference. Jeffrey replied in a rather high tone, weighing up the evidence for and against Carlyle's suitability for the chair of moral philosophy (though a chair of rhetoric was what Carlyle had primarily in mind, until he discovered that no such vacancy existed),[44] and passing down a sentence notable for its even-handedness between praise and censure. He could recommend Carlyle as a man of 'genius and learning', but must be candid:

You are, to say it in one word, a *sectary* in taste and literature, and inspired by some of the zeal by which sectaries are distinguished – a zeal, that is, to magnify the distinguishing doctrines of your sect, and rather to aggravate than reconcile the differences which divide them from the votaries of the Establishment, and I confess I doubt whether the patrons of the new University either *will* or *ought* to appoint such a person to such a charge. The very frankness and sincerity of your character tend to make this objection more formidable. If your admiration of the German models were a mere air of singularity adopted capriciously or to create a sensation it would be easy for you conscientiously to disguise or qualify it, so as not to let it very conspicuously affect your academic instructions. But I very greatly mistake you if this be the case, and indeed can fancy that I see you, as you read the surmise, swelling with all the virtuous indignation of one who would rather submit to martyrdom than renounce any article of his philosophical and critical creed.

After all this, Jeffrey divulges some inside information, namely that Carlyle's old *bête noire*, Thomas Campbell, is likely to be offered the chair, provided 'the disagreements which I am aware have arisen between him and some of the Directors are healed'.[45]

An invitation to Carlyle and Jane to dine with him at Craigcrook, his house outside Edinburgh, followed. Jane gave a very lively account of the evening to her brother-in-law, calling Carlyle 'Sir Thomas' in amused allusion to Goethe's having addressed a brief letter of May 1827 to 'Sir Thomas Carlyle'.[46] In her opinion, he had overcome Jeffrey's objections to his eccentric German taste:

Sir Thomas used all manner of arguments to show him, that there really was no sectarianism or heresy in the case; that he was merely more open to light than others of his craft and that in short the Patrons of the University would do excellently well to make him Professor of Rhetoric.

On discovering that there was no professorship in rhetoric, Jane cheerfully switched her support to her husband's application for the moral philosophy post instead.[47]

By the end of October hopes of that position had faded. Invoking the unlucky hero of Jean Paul's story, Carlyle told Alick, 'I may say with Attila Schmelzle that "the Professorship is taking *another* turn".' Henry Brougham, another Scottish lawyer and founder of the *Edinburgh Review*, and therefore a man whose ear Jeffrey commanded, was chairing the committee set up to appoint these first University of London professors. He was, Carlyle heard, 'for the present little more favourable to me than Schabacker was to that courageous Army-chaplain [Schmelzle]'.[48] The thing fizzled out. As Jeffrey had foreseen, the chair was offered to Campbell, who declined it, upon which it remained empty for the time being. By the end of November 1827 Carlyle had given up hope of hearing news from London.[49]

★

Of necessity, the plan of settling near to Alick was revived. 'We are still bent for Craigenputtoch against Whitsunday', Mrs Montagu was told on 20 November; 'not indeed irrevocably, but with the main current of our purposing'.[50] John Carlyle no longer formed part of the plan, however, having taken up an offer from Baron d'Eichthal to accompany him to Munich as his physician.[51] Carlyle, who was writing an article on the minor German novelist Zacharias Werner for William Fraser's new *Foreign Review* in October, asked his brother about life in Germany, particularly literary life. 'Did you see Schlegel, and find him a "puppy"? Is Schelling at Munich, and accessible?'[52] Jack was soon answering that he had met August Wilhelm Schlegel, the elder of the two famous brothers, a fine critic (especially of Shakespeare), but known for his personal vanity; Jack noticed that he wore a brown wig and took snuff.[53]

While at Munich he also attended Friedrich Schelling's lectures on philosophy, reporting in February 1828 to his elder brother: 'The spirit, geniality, clearness and firm precision with which he states his principles, are not lost for me, and will banish that portion of selfsufficient scepticism, which I have imbibed from the conclusions of Scotch philosophy – about the vanity and uselessness of all speculations of the kind.'[54]

This called forth an interesting reply from Carlyle:

I am glad to find both that you admire Schelling and know that you do not understand him. That is right my dear Greatheart: look into the deeply significant regions of Transcendental Philosophy (as all *Philosophy must* be), and feel that there are wonders and mighty truths hidden in them; but look with your clear grey Scottish eyes and shrewd Scottish understanding, and refuse to be *mystified* even by your admiration.[55]

Carlyle, who saw in Jack a younger version of himself, was in effect describing his own paradoxical position between British, particularly Scottish, empiricism and German transcendentalism. In *Sartor Resartus*, he would separate the two sides of his intellect, giving his German professor, Teufelsdröckh, all the idealism and mysticism and a commonsense British 'editor' all the empiricism and scepticism.

Both his jottings in notebooks during 1827 and the 'State of German Literature' article show Carlyle welcoming the recent German philosophy of Kant, Fichte, and Schelling as an answer to the empiricism of Locke and Hume which, as he wrote in his notebook, 'leads direct to atheism'.[56] He had been through the Humean temptation to unbelief while a student, as we know, and had credited Goethe with saving him from the abyss. He now tackled the transcendental philosophers, especially Kant, who had set out to escape the conclusions drawn by Hume by negotiating a path between scepticism and materialism, on the one hand, and dogmatic idealism, on the other. Kant called his third way 'transcendentalism', or, less bafflingly, 'the critical method', because he sought to avoid the errors of the two main, opposing schools of thought.

The empiricists, arguing from experience, could find no logical way of proving abstractions such as the idea of necessary cause and effect, the existence of God, and the immortality of the soul. For Hume, these abstractions could only be believed by custom, or habit, not by reason. The idealists, such as Descartes and Leibniz, began from the opposite point of view, arguing *from* abstractions *to* concrete experience, but their conclusions were invalidated, in Kant's view, because they depended on unproved absolute assumptions, such as 'God exists', or 'man has innate reason and an immortal soul'. Kant applied a 'critique' to these assumptions, arriving at the conclusion that we cannot know anything except through experience – thus far agreeing with the empiricists – but that, when thinking, we apply categories of understanding which are independent of experience – so avoiding the limitations placed on knowledge by the empirical approach.[57]

Though Carlyle struggled, like many before and after him, to understand Kant, he seized on the Kantian philosophy as an antidote to the atheism he saw as the inevitable result of the empirical method. This is how he represented Kant and his followers in 'The State of German Literature', lining up the transcendental philosophy alongside the works of Goethe and Schiller and the criticism of the Schlegels and other German Romantics, in fact offering recent German culture as a whole as a refutation of the recent British tradition of empiricism in philosophy and utilitarianism in politics.

As had happened ten years earlier, when Coleridge gave an analysis of German philosophy in his *Biographia Literaria* (1817), hardy commonsense British critics cried mysticism! idealism! German moonshine! Jeffrey labelled Carlyle's philosophy 'German Mysticism', while he tried in vain to argue Carlyle back into 'dead Edinburgh Whiggism, Scepticism, and Materialism', as he recalled in *Reminiscences*. It was Carlyle's unique contribution to nineteenth-century thought to merge different disciplines into one in order to identify and seek to rout these dangerous enemies of truth and morality. Though he grappled with philosophical systems, he was not a philosopher, soon giving up, as he said, the business of 'thinking *about thinking*' (a quotation from Goethe, who had also abjured metaphysics).[58]

It pleased Jeffrey, however, to tease Carlyle as a 'German mystic', and Carlyle discovered from his old pupil Charles Buller that 'my German Metaphysics were an unspeakable stone of stumbling' to those with influence in the University of London, 'whereby Buller began to perceive that my chances had diminished to the neighbourhood of zero', as Carlyle reported, cheerfully enough, to Jack in March 1828. Paradoxically, though, his championing of German literature and philosophy in general in his *Edinburgh Review* articles was turning him into 'a sort of newspaper *Literatus* in London', with a critic in the *Courier* declaring that he was 'the supremest German Scholar in the British Empire!'[59]

In Edinburgh, too, 'The State of German Literature' won him friends. 'De Quincey praises it in his Saturday Post', Carlyle told Jack in November 1827. 'Sir W. Hamilton tells me that it is "*cap'tal*"; and Wilson informs John Gordon that it has "done me a *deal* o' good".'[60] Carlyle had recently met De Quincey, who spent most of the time in Edinburgh lodgings with two of his children, 'while his wife with other two resides in Westmoreland, – as a kind of "hostage" to his creditors', as Carlyle explained with horrified sympathy to Mrs Montagu.[61] De Quincey was invited to one of Jane's Wednesday evenings. Carlyle described him to Jack as 'one of the smallest men you ever in your life beheld; but with a most gentle and sensible face, only that the teeth are destroyed by opium'.[62] He once called on De Quincey at his lodgings, and was astonished to find the 'unhappy little opium eater invisible in bed' at two o'clock in the afternoon.[63] He remembered these few encounters with De Quincey with vivid clarity in *Reminiscences*:

One of the smallest man-figures I ever saw; shaped like a pair of tongs; and hardly above five feet in all: when he sat, you would have taken him, by candlelight, for the beautifullest little Child; blue-eyed, blonde-haired, sparkling face, – had there not been a something too, which said, '*Eccovi* [behold], this Child has been in Hell!'[64]

Surprisingly, perhaps, Carlyle did not think of De Quincey when he came to distribute six medals Goethe sent him in January 1828, requesting that two be given to Walter Scott and the rest bestowed on other 'Wohlwollende' [well-wishers] of Carlyle's choosing.[65] A polite and friendly correspondence had sprung up between Carlyle and Goethe when the former sent a copy of his *Life of Schiller* to Weimar in April 1827. In his reply a few months later, Goethe warmly praised the biography of his late friend, and extolled the role of the translator as a mediator 'in this universal spiritual commerce' between nations.[66] Goethe also sent presents for Carlyle (his works in five volumes and a pocket-book) and Jane (a necklace and poems).[67] Carlyle told him in August 1827 that 'this little drawing-room may now be said to be full of you', with Goethe's books and portraits filling the bookcase and the medals lying on the mantelpiece.[68]

In fulfilment of Goethe's request, he wrote to Scott, quoting Goethe's praise of him as 'the first novelist of the century' (Scott had also, in his youth, translated Goethe's early drama *Götz von Berlichingen*), and asking to be allowed to visit him to deliver the medals personally. He sent the letter care of Scott's son-in-law, John Gibson Lockhart, Wilson's erstwhile partner in satire at *Blackwood's Magazine*, now living in London as editor of the *Quarterly Review*, the Tory rival to the *Edinburgh*. Would Lockhart also accept a medal, due to him as a friendly critic of German literature? Carlyle asked.[69] For some reason – perhaps his increasing ill health and hectic activity, as he tried to write his way out of the huge debts which were the consequence of the publishing crash of 1826 – Scott failed to reply. Carlyle wrote again in late May, expressing dignified disappointment and telling Scott he had given the medals to Jeffrey to pass on.[70]

Still no reply came from Scott. These two writers, who shared a passion for story-telling and history, and a love of the border country in which both were brought up, never met. Later, Carlyle's published utterances about Scott were careful but cool; in private, he blamed Scott for a lack of courtesy over Goethe's medals, and expressed a rather sharp opinion of his writings. Carlyle's view, jotted down in his journal soon after Scott's death in 1832, was that he 'understood what *history* meant; this was his chief intellectual merit'. 'As a thinker' Scott was 'strong, rather, and healthy, yet limited, almost mean and *kleinstädtisch* [provincial]'.[71] On 18 April 1828 Carlyle reported to Goethe that he had sent medals to Scott and Lockhart and was meditating (strangely, we may think) giving one to Jeffrey.[72]

Goethe was asked for a testimonial for another attempt to storm the Bastille of academic life. In January 1828 Carlyle applied for the chair of moral philosophy at St Andrews. 'A word from you', he assured Goethe with unwarranted confidence, 'may go farther than many words from another.'[73] Goethe complied graciously, but his reference arrived too late to be used. Perhaps this was just as well, since it consisted of a wide-ranging conspectus of literature and philosophy in general and German literature in particular, with a paragraph of praise for Carlyle's achievement as a mediator of German culture.[74]

Carlyle did not rely solely on Goethe's testimony. Edward Irving, Charles Buller, Bryan Procter, and Basil Montagu were asked to write, while the Edinburgh trio of John Wilson (that well-known expert in moral philosophy), Brewster, and Carlyle's old mathematical professor, John Leslie, offered their warm support. As with the London chairs, however, Jeffrey was his prize referee.[75] All obliged, as Carlyle reported in a letter to his mother which expressed his amusement at the motley character of the people he now mustered to his aid:

These same recommendations are now beginning to come in upon me: I had . . . a most majestic certificate in three pages from Edward Irving. The good orator speaks as from the heart; and truly says, as he has ever done, that he thinks me a most worthy man; not forgetting to mention among my other advantages the 'prayers of religious parents'; a blessing which if I speak less of it I hope I do not feel less than he. On the whole it is a splendid affair this of his; and being tempered by the recommendation of John Leslie a professed infidel and scoffer, may do me much good.[76]

Jeffrey wrote him 'a Testimonial which should get me the best Professorship of the Island in that kind'.[77] He did not tell his family that Jeffrey, who knew everything, had warned him that Dr Nicol, the Principal of St Andrews, 'an active, jobbing, popular man', held the chair in his gift.[78] Carlyle soon heard that Dr Nicol's placeman was sure to be successful. He took the anticipated disappointment stoically, even humorously, telling Jack on 7 March:

An old stager (Cook of Laurencekirk) is to be appointed, at least is applying: he will vote for another old stager succeeding to the Principality, and a young stager will get his Kirk, and so the whole thing be rounded off in the neatest manner possible. In which case what would the certificate of the Angel Gabriel himself avail me? No pin's worth. But the *Deevil* may care.[79]

Less than a week later Carlyle had given up all remaining hope. 'Dr Cook will be Professor there', he told Jack, 'and I — shall be Professor nowhere.'[80]

The only thing to do now was to fall back on the other plan and move to Craigenputtoch. This he and Jane did at Whitsun 1828, though not in the end entirely of their own (or rather Carlyle's) free will. During April Carlyle had gone to stay with his parents in Scotsbrig, making forays to Craigenputtoch to see how Alick was getting on, while Jane was at Templand helping her mother to nurse her aunt. Aunt Jeannie died, leaving Mrs Welsh alone at Templand with her father. While both Carlyles were away from Comely Bank, the landlord, not having heard from them whether they intended to renew the lease for another year, had let it to someone else from Whitsun. 'We might have been tempted to engage it again, and stay here at least another year', Carlyle told Jack, but now Craigenputtoch was the only alternative remaining to them: 'Accordingly Jane is out endeavouring to hire a fit servant; we are choosing paper-specimens; forwarding all plans of repair and adjustment; and six carts come hither in the end of May to transport us hence bag and baggage.'

Carlyle was cheerful, hoping for 'a friendly and rather comfortable arrangement at the Craig; in the midst of which, not in idleness, yet in peace and more self-selected occupations, I may find more health'.[81]

Jane hired Grace Macdonald to accompany them to the Dumfriesshire moors as their servant.[82] In late May they set up home in the solitary moorland, rather against the advice of friends. Irving had written 'a sublime note'[83] a year earlier, praising his heretical friend's 'great gifts', but warning against proud isolation:

I pray God to grant you leisure and composure of soul to occupy the talents which you have. Oh! what you know. And what it is given you to feel. Steer clear of solitariness, my dear friend, I mean of mind and spirit.[84]

If Irving was anxious for Carlyle's soul, the more worldly Jeffrey advised against the move out of concern for the social man (not to mention the social woman in Jane). 'Do not run away into Dumfriesshire', he counselled in December 1827. 'You can be as quiet here as there, when the reading or the studious fit is on you, and you surely may divert yourself as well, and certainly give more pleasure, when you can condescend to be social.'[85] But professorial appointments had not been forthcoming; life would be cheaper at Craigenputtoch, and Edinburgh still felt like hostile ground to Carlyle. To Craigenputtoch he was now determined to go, taking a perhaps silently reluctant Jane with him to this 'wild moorland home'.[86]

CHAPTER 5

Craigenputtoch 1828–1831

When the Carlyles went to Craigenputtoch in May 1828, they had no clear idea of how long they would remain there. Would Carlyle's health improve? Could Alick make a decent living by farming the rather unyielding soil in this high-lying exposed stretch of moorland? Was it possible for Carlyle to combine his beloved country pursuits of walking, riding, and gardening with fruitful study and writing? Could improved health and peace and quiet – or what Jeffrey and Irving called a deliberate cutting himself off from the society of friends and people of influence – provide the right environment for a man who had long ago decided that his vocation was to be a writer but who had yet, at the age of thirty-two, to bring forth a 'proper' book?

He was still writing articles for Jeffrey, and for William Fraser's *Foreign Review*, for about £50 a time. London friends continued to hold out the (slim) chance that he might finally breach the defences of academia. The University of London was about to become two distinct colleges, since the Church and King party had decided that an alternative was needed to the avowedly secular 'godless institution of Gower Street', which had been founded on the principle of religious freedom – no swearing on the Thirty-Nine Articles of the Church of England in order to matriculate or graduate, as was required at Oxford and Cambridge. A new 'King's College' was therefore to be established, 'a thing got up by the Church Nobility and Gentry Commonality and Rascality and Public in general, by way of counteracting Radicalism and Infidelity', as Carlyle succinctly put it in a letter to Jack of 25 August. 'Southey is said to be busy in it, and Duke Wellington, and Bishops this and that.'[1]

If Carlyle had been less than enthusiastic about the Benthamite and atheistic tendencies of some members of the original Gower Street institution – henceforth called University College London to distinguish it from its newly founded rival King's College London – he was positively antagonistic towards this new organ of the establishment. Charles Buller wrote suggesting he might propose to give lectures on German literature and philosophy there, but Carlyle's reply must have been negative, since nothing more was said about it.

Could Jane be happy at Craigenputtoch? We have observed the stark fact that Carlyle considered her happiness as entirely bound up in his, a mistake from which he never fully emerged, even when, in the months after her death in 1866, he went through her letters and journals, learning something of her misery and resentment, and compulsively annotating her writing in his curiously frank yet unself-knowing way. In reviewing the six years they spent at Craigenputtoch we are helped (and hindered) by the survival of a vast amount more in the way of written evidence about Carlyle's experience than about Jane's. Whereas many contemporary letters of his remain, very few of hers do. Her later comments, particularly to female friends in the mid-1850s, leave no room for doubt that she was miserable, though they may be exaggerated, or at least coloured by her deep feeling of disaffection from Carlyle at that time on account of his relationship with Lady Ashburton.

After her death, Carlyle cursed himself for his blindness to Jane's unhappiness, yet he channelled all his guilt into confessing his insensitivity to her *physical* ill health, never really allowing himself to see that she had been for long periods unhappy and unfulfilled. The Craigenputtoch experience is a tangled one for the observer to unravel. Since it was clearly so different for each of the two protagonists, it will perhaps be best to deal with them to some extent separately.

Did Carlyle's health improve? Yes. Complaints about dyspepsia all but disappear. Did Alick make a going concern of the farm? No. By August 1830 Carlyle was telling Jack that Alick could not keep the farm on beyond next Whitsunday, 'finding it a ruinous concern'. It was in general 'but a ticklish business taking farms at present', he thought; 'nothing but loss and embarrassment on all hands. I often calculate that the land is all let some thirty per cent too high.'[2] Looking back in 1866, he acknowledged that in Alick's household, consisting at first of their sister Mary until she married in November 1830 and then of Alick and his wife Janet, whom he married in December of the same year, there were 'faults, short-comings, misgoings; all of a smallish sort, and involuntary all'. But the chief problem, he still believed, was that the rent of £200 a year was too high.[3]

Neither at the time nor later did Carlyle blame Mrs Welsh directly for asking too much in rent. Nor, however, out of loyalty to his brother, did he dwell on Alick's personal problem – drunkenness – which Jane found an added trial during her first three years at Craigenputtoch. Alick gave up the farm in May 1831, then cast around for another. By 1835 he had failed again, and became a shopkeeper first in Annan, then in Ecclefechan. Finally, in 1843, he emigrated with his family to Canada, where he farmed with better success for the rest of his life.[4]

For such an intolerant man, Carlyle showed tremendous patience with his brothers. Not only Alick but also Jack caused him pain and disappointment. Jack had been fortunate in landing a job with Baron d'Eichthal, but was soon chafing at the dependence of this position. For four months in 1828 he failed to write; Carlyle reported to his mother that Jack was afflicted with 'the old demons Pride and Poverty'; his stomach was 'getting highly squeamish' about living off the Baron's gifts, and he was now proposing to leave his employ and wander round Germany trying to teach English for a living. Carlyle, who required for Jack a settled existence of a kind he had not managed for himself, exploded to his mother that his 'foreign jaunt' had 'cost him a round sum of money' but 'not a whit abated his love of vagrancy, or opened his eyes to the necessity of settling down as a quiet professional man'.[5]

By October 1828 Jack had separated from Baron d'Eichthal; he went first to Vienna, then came slowly home by way of Paris. Carlyle had asked William Fraser to commission for the *Foreign Review* an article by Jack on German medical practice; he informed his brother sharply in March 1829 that Fraser was asking 'rather eagerly' about it; 'but this, I suppose, like so much else, is still lying in the inkstand'. Irritated and protective, bossy and encouraging by turns, Carlyle cajoled his undermotivated brother all the way back to Britain, ensuring that when John reached London, his own friends Irving and the Montagus were standing by to receive and help him.[6] For Carlyle's sake these friends, and Badams in Birmingham, passed on news of medical vacancies, but though John went to Warwick in December 1829 to investigate a position, nothing came of it.[7]

John stayed in London, establishing a pattern of dependence on those whom his brother had cultivated. He knew how much he owed Carlyle by way of example and encouragement, as well as money. In 1823 he had written that it would be 'the chief aim of my life to make myself worthy of you'.[8] Unfortunately, he tried to do so by emulating his older brother – learning German, moving among literary people, writing articles, in all of which activities he could be nothing but the palest imitation of Carlyle – rather than forging a way for himself in the profession for which he had trained. Carlyle's own feelings were rather mixed; having failed to fix on a 'proper' profession himself, he was perhaps too keen to prod John, whose heart may not have been in medicine at all.

In 1830 Carlyle was becoming anxious about Jack, advising him not to accept loans offered by Badams and the Montagus to set up in practice. This advice arose, he declared, 'from a deep conviction that the grand thing you want is, not practising in London, or becoming rich, or renowned, but simply feeling that you stand on your own legs'.[9] He wrote revealingly in August 1830 on the don't-do-as-I-do, do-as-I-say principle:

The voice of all Experience seems to be in favour of a Profession: you sail there, as under convoy, in the middle of a fleet, and have a thousandfold chance of reaching port. Neither is it Happy Islands and Halcyon Seas alone that you miss; for Literature is thickly strowed with cold Russian Nova Zemblas, where you shiver and despair in loneliness . . . To my own mind nothing justifies me for having adopted the trade of Literature, except the remembrance that I had no other, except these two that of a schoolmaster or of a Priest, in the one case with the fair prospect of speedy maceration and starvation, in the other, of perjury which is infinitely worse. As it is, I look confidently forward to a life of poverty, toil, and dispiritment, so long as I remain on this Earth, and hope only that God will grant me patience and strength to struggle onwards thro' the midst of it, working out His will, as I best can, in this lonely claypit where I am set to dig . . . let these things be known for my Brother's warning, that he may order his Life better than I could do mine.[10]

*

Jane busied herself with arranging the house and doing domestic tasks with the help of the servant Grace – for, poor though the Carlyles were by middle-class standards, they could afford a live-in servant whose wages consisted mainly of her food and board. If Jane had hopes of becoming a mother, we do not know of them. There is no direct mention of the subject in any of her surviving letters (though once or twice an oblique glance at it occurs), and, unlike other aspects of her marriage, her childlessness seems to have been a matter on which she did not speak or write to close female friends in later life. Given Carlyle's solitary habits – he read, wrote, walked, and rode alone – and the fact that the nearest neighbouring farm was some six miles away, with Dumfries sixteen miles in one direction, while her mother and grandfather at Templand were the same distance in another, she was bound to be left for long periods on her own. Post came once a week, on Wednesdays; she rode over to Templand from time to time to see her mother, and Mrs Welsh occasionally visited at Craigenputtoch. Nonetheless, for an intelligent, sociable young woman of twenty-seven, it was a very quiet life indeed.

The few surviving letters from Craigenputtoch to Eliza Stodart in Edinburgh are positive enough, though one suspects an element of loyal pride and forced cheerfulness in her account in July 1828 of the early days of her new life. 'I have survived my astonishing change', she wrote:

The solitude is not so irksome as one might think. If we are cut off from good society, we are also delivered from bad; the roads are less pleasant to walk on than the pavement of Princes Street but we have horses to ride; and instead of shopping and making calls I have bread to bake and chickens to hatch – I read, and work & talk with my Husband and never weary.[11]

97

To Carlyle she wrote briefly on 19 August from Templand, where she had been obliged to stay longer than expected because of some biliousness which her mother was treating with castor oil and brandy and a proposed visit to the medicinal waters at nearby Moffat. She told Carlyle she loved and missed him, but declared too that she was enjoying being spoilt by her mother.[12] The summer passed quietly till Jeffrey 'with wife and child and maid and lapdog' descended on them for a few days in October 1828. 'And how on earth did Mr Jeffrey get himself amused at Craigenputtoch?' asked Jane in a letter to Eliza in November, answering her own question immediately: 'Why, in the simplest manner: he talked – talked from morning till night, nay till morning again – I never assisted at such a talking since I came into the world; either in respect of quantity or quality.' Since the Jeffreys' departure the house had been once more very still – 'just one servant and not even a cat in addition'.[13] (It is not recorded how Grace Macdonald felt about living in 'the desert' with only Carlyle and Jane for company.) When winter came, Jane found it harder to be cheerful. She asked Eliza in December to do some errands in Edinburgh – 'my tea and sugar are drawing fast to a close' – fearing that a heavy fall of snow would cut them off from luxuries and necessities alike. Would Eliza also get some pens and paper and have them sent by the Dumfries carrier?[14]

The following winter it did snow; Jane wrote to Eliza in February 1830 in a strange mood induced by her isolated circumstances, making one of her few indirect (and perhaps bitter) remarks about having no children:

It is well we have meat and fire *'within ourselves'* . . . otherwise we should live in hourly apprehension of being snowed up, and consequently starved to death without even the mournful alternative of *'eating our own children'*. Oh for a sight of the green fields again or even the black peat-moss – anything rather than this wide waste of blinding snow! The only time when I can endure to look out (*going out* is not to be dreamt of) is by moonlight, when the enclosure before the house is literally filled with hares – and then the scene is really very picturesque – the little dark forms skipping and bounding over the white ground so witch-like![15]

Jane's life at Craigenputtoch, merely glimpsed in these letters, later became concentrated into a story told to three female friends: Geraldine Jewsbury, Mary Smith, and Ellen Twisleton. All three accounts, dating from the difficult mid-1850s, may exaggerate Jane's woes, but though her talent for self-dramatising is evident, so also is the ring of truth to experience as she remembered it.

The most direct account occurs in a letter of January 1857 to Mary Smith, a teacher in Carlisle who had first written to Jane in 1854, explaining that she felt undervalued and discontented and wanted to be a writer.[16] She wrote again three years later, and Jane replied with a kind of uplifting discouragement, quoting one of Carlyle's frequent sayings from Goethe about the importance of doing the duty nearest at hand.

Rather than merely preach resignation, however, Jane reached for an example from her own life at Craigenputtoch. Her story is both extended, as a response to Miss Smith's letter, and condensed, as an account of almost six years of her life and feelings from nearly thirty years before. Jane singles out an illustrative episode, rendering it with vivid recall and giving it the status of a revelation:

I know I was very near mad when I found it out [i.e. the need to do one's nearest duty] for myself (as one has to find out for oneself everything that is to be of any real practical use to one). Shall I tell you how it came into my head? Perhaps it may be of comfort to you in similar moments of fatigue and disgust.

I had gone with my husband to live on a little estate of *peat bog*, that had descended to me, all the way down from John Welsh, the Covenanter, who married a daughter of John Knox. *That* didn't, I'm ashamed to say, make me feel Craigenputtoch a whit less of a peat bog, and most dreary, untoward place to live at. In fact, it was sixteen miles distant on every side from all the conveniences of life – shops, and even post office!

Further, we were very *poor* and, further and worst, being an only child, and brought up to 'great prospects', I was sublimely ignorant of every branch of useful knowledge, though a capital Latin scholar and a very fair mathematician!! It behoved me in these astonishing circumstances to learn – to sew! Husbands, I was shocked to find, wore their stockings into holes! and were always losing buttons! and *I* was expected to 'look to all that'. Also, it behoved me to learn *to cook*! No capable servant choosing to live at 'such an out of the way place', and my husband having 'bad digestion' which complicated my difficulties dreadfully. The *bread* above all, brought from Dumfries, 'soured on his stomach' (oh Heavens!); and it was plainly my duty as a Christian wife to bake at home! So I sent for Cobbett's '*Cottage Economy*' and fell to work at a loaf of bread. But knowing nothing of the process of fermentation or the heat of ovens, it came to pass that my loaf got put into the oven at the time myself ought to have [been] put into bed, and I remained the only person not asleep, in a house in the middle of a desert! One o'clock struck, and then two and then three; and still I was sitting there in an intense solitude, my whole body aching with weariness, my heart aching with a sense of forlornness and *degradation*. 'That I who had been so petted at home, whose comfort had been studied by everybody in the house, who had never been required to *do* anything but *cultivate my mind*, should have to pass all those hours of the night watching *a loaf of bread*! which mightn't turn out bread after all!'

Such thoughts maddened me, till I laid my head on the table and sobbed aloud. It was then that somehow the idea of Benvenuto Cellini's sitting up all night watching his Perseus in the oven, came into my head; and suddenly I asked myself, 'After all, in the sight of the upper powers, what is the mighty difference between a statue of Perseus and a loaf of bread, so that each be the thing one's hand hath found to do? The man's determined will, his energy, his patience, his resource, were the really admirable things, of which the statue of Perseus was the mere chance expression. If he had been a woman living at Craigenputtock, with a dyspeptic husband, sixteen miles from a baker, *and he a bad one*, all these same qualities would have come out most fitting in a *good* loaf of bread!'

I cannot express what consolation this germ of an idea spread over an uncongenial life, during five years we lived at that savage place; where my two immediate predecessors had gone *mad*, and the third had taken to *drink*.[17]

The striking thing about this account to a sympathetic stranger is that Jane's response to events, and her way of remembering them, is so intense, bristling, magnified. The bread-making attracts to itself all sorts of feelings and memories – loneliness, resentment, fear of failure, vivid awareness of better times gone for ever – and Jane found it difficult to let go of any strong emotion, however wasteful of energy or destructive of peace and progress it might be. These character traits were prominent throughout her life; unfortunate in themselves, they were rendered infinitely more so when brought into constant contact with Carlyle's equally difficult temperament. As Frederic Harrison, one of the many later observers of the marriage, said in a review of Froude's biography of Carlyle:

As we read these letters and diaries, these tales of Carlyle and of his wife, on which art has thrown a light so dazzling, and a magnifying power so peculiar, we feel as if we were caught up again into the bewildering realm of Brobdingnag. Husband and wife rail at each other like giants and giantesses in a fairy tale; when they have a tiff, it stuns us like the Tower of Babel.[18]

In her letter to Mary Smith, Jane manages to draw an uplifting moral from her story and stops short of outright criticism of her husband for taking her to live that 'uncongenial life' at Craigenputtoch. She was less restrained with her passionate friend Geraldine, who sympathised so warmly, almost intrusively, with all Jane's troubles, tending to stoke the fires rather than damp them down. Geraldine heard the Benvenuto Cellini story from Jane herself, and in a letter of 1876 to Froude, who was already preparing his biographical materials and had asked for her memories of Jane, she exploited the Cellini analogy in her own analysis of her friend. The focus was on the Craigenputtoch years, but Geraldine begins with a description of her friend's 'clear pitiless common sense' which 'never failed her':

She was not heartless, for her feelings were *real & strong* but she had a genuine *preference* for *herself*. From her earliest girlhood this was her characteristic in all matters where men were in question. She *would* be the *first* person with everybody man or woman whom she cared for enough to wish to subjugate . . . In marrying, she undertook what she felt to be a grand & noble life-task . . . She was to be the companion-friend, help-mate, *her own* gifts were to be cultivated & recognised by him . . . She had gone off into that Desert with him, she had taken up poverty, obscurity, *hardship* even, cheerfully willingly & with an enthusiasm of self-sacrifice – only asking to be allowed to minister to him. The offering was accepted but like the precious things flung by Benvenuto into the furnace when his statue was molten they were all consumed in the fierce flame – & *he* was so intent & occupied by what he was bringing forth that he could take no heed of the individual treasures, they were all swallowed up in the great whole – in her case it was the *living creature* in the midst of the fire which felt & suffered . . . six years she lived there – she had undertaken a task & she *knew* that whether recognised or not, that she *did* help him. Then they came back to the World [i.e. to London] – & the strain told on her then – she did not falter from her purpose of helping & shielding him – but she became *warped*.[19]

Earlier, in the weeks after Jane's death, Geraldine had written down her memories in a notebook which she gave to Carlyle, who in his usual fashion annotated and corrected it in a passage which turned into his own long reminiscence of Jane. Naturally, even Geraldine is more circumspect in her handling of Jane's complaints here than in her later account to Froude, but she gives a lively sense of what Jane had told her about Craigenputtoch life, beginning with the famous bread-making episode. The extraordinary quietness of the place is described. Jane 'used to say that the stillness was almost awful – and that when she walked out she could hear the sheep nibbling the grass and they used to look at her with innocent wonder'.

As for life with Carlyle, Geraldine takes the long view, perceiving that Carlyle was driven, and moreover driven to do great things, which the world now recognised he had eventually been enabled, with Jane's help, to do:

It was undoubtedly a great strain upon her nerves from which she never entirely recovered but she lived in the solitude cheerfully and willingly for six years. It was a much greater trial than it sounds at first, for Mr Carlyle was engrossed in his work, and had to give himself up to it entirely . . . it was his *Life* that his work required, and it was his *Life* that he gave, and she gave her life too which alone made such life possible for him. All those who have been helped and strengthened by Mr Carlyle's written words and they have been Wells of Life to more than have been numbered but they owe to her a debt of gratitude no less than to him . . . Hers was no holiday task of pleasant companionship she had to live beside him in silence that the people in the world might profit by his full strength and receive his message. She lived to see his work completed, and to see *him* recognised in full for what he is and for what he has done.[20]

One or two other stories told by Geraldine, about a heroic bout of house-cleaning (something Jane was famous for at Cheyne Row too), the milking of a cow, and a midnight ride home from Dumfries when she lost her way, Carlyle in his correction to her text describes as exaggerated or even 'mythical'. Nonetheless, he goes on himself to tell of similar exploits of 'my heroic Darling', who 'triumphed' over adversity – a form of words much used by both Carlyles to describe their particular pilgrims' progress through life – and 'made the Desert blossom for herself and me there'. Yet he refused to accept that Jane had been miserable. 'We were not unhappy at Craigenputtoch', he declared, adding defiantly, 'perhaps these were our happiest days'.[21]

His memory, on this point, is at odds with Jane's. In November 1855, a time of deep depression, she poured out a verbal account of the Craigenputtoch years to a young American friend, Ellen Twisleton. Ellen, the daughter of a rich Boston family, had married the Honourable Edward Twisleton, an amateur scholar and archaeologist who sat on various government-appointed commissions and was an admirer and visitor of Carlyle's. After her marriage in 1852, Ellen lived the life of the adored wife of an aristocratic younger son; she was sweet-natured, childless, a semi-invalid (she died in 1862 aged thirty-four), and quickly entered into a warm friendship with Jane. On 23 November 1855 she wrote to her sister Mary: 'I had such a long, interesting talk with Mrs Carlyle the other day, all about their life just after they were married – I couldn't help wishing you were in the wall, – a more miserable story I never heard, – but *never say so*.'[22]

Ellen wrote down the conversation, which reveals Jane at her most bitter, blaming Carlyle and remembering her deep dislike of his brother and sister, for a time their neighbours at Craigenputtoch. Though there are a few factual errors in the memoir – for example, it records Jane as being twenty-two when she was in fact twenty-seven – and though Jane herself undoubtedly accentuated the negative in her conversation with Ellen, the account deserves attention. Several features tally with what we already know. Ellen, given her own leisured, moneyed background, was impressed by Jane's account of the domestic and social deprivation, the dreariness of the place, and the dreadful fate of the farmers' wives before her.

When Ellen innocently asked why Jane went there – 'Did you like the idea of it *before* you went?' – she received a passionate reply, which she set down with an attempt to reproduce Jane's Scottish accent:

Oh no, I *never* liked the idea of it – oh, there's no way of making ye understand what kind of a wretched place it was, – I had seen it only once in my life, when my *grandfather* took me there, when I was quite a little child, & had always remembered it as the most dreadful, lonesome barest of places, – and all thro' my childhood I used to be frightened with it, – it used to be the *threat*, if ye understand, 'if ye behave so badly, ye shall go to Craigenputtoch'; – & I remember once, when I must have been fourteen years old, & was self-willed about something, my Mother telling me that I 'deserved to be sent to Craigenputtoch to live on a hundred a year'; – and to think that I *did* live there *five* years, with not much more than a hundred a year.

Dr Welsh had drained and manured the land, and planted trees 'where possible', but 'there was very little of it that ever could be made into anything but a black peat moss; – have ye ever seen one – if ye have, ye know what an ugly, dreary thing that is, – & of course, they were only the hardiest trees would grow – & so all the plantation there was of Scotch firs, which make a wood fit to *hang* oneself in'.[23]

There follows a passage which agrees entirely with the facts as we have already observed them, namely Carlyle's taking it into his head during their courtship that they should live together at Craigenputtoch, together with Jane's dusty answer about not living there with an angel. Jane adds a sad remark about how much *she* had liked living at Comely Bank, while Carlyle did not, and a bitter recognition that once she had become his wife, there could be no more dusty answers to anything he decided:

And then my Mother took a little jewel of a house for us in Edinboro', & furnished it all for us, so that it was the neatest, prettiest thing – as *pretty* as any picture, & we went into that. But we hadn't been there two months, before Carlyle grew perfectly frantic with it all, & couldn't support it any way, couldn't endure his life at all nor get on with the people that were about us, – but had it all this time fixed in his head that if he were only at Craigenputtoch he should be well, & everything that *was* wrong would grow right; – I might refuse before, but then, you know, it was a different matter; & there was no refusing.[24]

Jane's description of Alick's behaviour differs from Carlyle's protective one. He was 'a man of the most outrageous, coarse, violent temper', and Jane had to suffer in silence, 'for I could never say a word to Carlyle, that would be to drive him perfectly crazy, and "my dear, what *can* I possibly know, or do, about all this!"' Whenever Alick went off to Dumfries on farm business, he would drink whisky or gin, since 'in those days, no bargain was ever concluded in Scotland without the parties *drinking* together' – which we know from Carlyle's amused account of the peaceful expulsion of Mrs Welsh's tenant in 1827 – and would come home 'as drunk as a man could be'. Jane also accuses Alick of being lax about paying rent to her mother, telling of an occasion when she herself seized a cheque which Carlyle had received from London, rode to Dumfries to cash it, and went straight on to Templand to pay her mother the four months' rent Alick owed.[25]

Finally, Jane launches into an attack on the temperament of Carlyle's sister Jean, who spent some time at Craigenputtoch (though not the eighteen months that Ellen records) – 'a coarse, rude girl' with 'such a temper, & such a *tremendous* will as I never met with in any other woman but herself; – a will just like Carlyle's', but without any excuse (such as genius and dyspepsia) which might 'induce ye to put up with it'. This is a harsh depiction of Jean, whom Jane had at first befriended, sending her little gifts during the early days of her marriage, and trying to gentrify her. 'Have you given over saying *a's gan*?' she had asked Jean in September 1827.[26] Her description of both Alick and Jean as 'coarse' suggests she found their social manners too peasant-like, reminding her, perhaps, of her dislike of Carlyle's manners until a combination of her admiration for his genius and the smoothing effect on his social behaviour which his trip to London had perhaps achieved reconciled her to his demeanour.

The Twisleton memoir coincides with Geraldine's statements about Jane's being left alone for long periods. We can sympathise with her, though we may find the litany of complaints unattractive:

Living at Craigenputtoch, it wasn't as if I saw anything of Carlyle; – he went to his own room directly after breakfast, & worked till an hour before dinner, & always rode those two hours. And he rode *alone*, because he only galloped or walked, and it fretted him to have my horse cantering along by his side; so he rode alone and I rode alone; then he came to dinner very much *worked-up*, as bilious people always are by a ride, & he was 'dangerous' you know, & there was no freedom of communication during dinner; then he went to walk for an hour, which wasn't very wholesome, I always thought, right after eating, & to his room till tea; & afterward to his room, until about ten o'clock, & then he'd come in, quite tired out with his work, & say, 'Jane, will ye play me a few of those Scotch tunes' – I would sit down & play Scotch tunes till he went to bed, – oftenest with the tears running down my face, the while I played.[27]

What had happened to Jane's ambition, often expressed during the courtship and encouraged by Carlyle at that time, to write herself? They both knew she was a gifted story-teller and, thanks to both her father and Carlyle, unusually well educated for a young woman of the time. We may wonder why she did not try her hand at something during the long hours when she was not needed to see to the house or play the piano for Carlyle. Probably she got little encouragement from him now that she was his wife and set in *her* claypit with the duty of ministering to him. Still, other women writers, married and unmarried, managed to fulfil their ambitions against the odds; Jane Austen, Fanny Trollope, the Brontës, Elizabeth Barrett, Elizabeth Gaskell, and George Eliot were successful. It seems that Jane lacked the compulsion which drove others to succeed in spite of husbands, children, demanding or forbidding fathers, or sheer poverty and discouragement.

Carlyle did not see Ellen's memoir, of course. His own account of Jane playing the piano for him was a cheerful one.[28] In recalling those days in his 1866 reminiscence, he answered Geraldine's mild suggestion about Jane's loneliness and boredom by seizing on the fighting metaphor he so often used for his own, as well as Jane's, attitude to life. 'The saving charm of her life at Craigenputtock', he wrote all unseeing, 'which to another young Lady of her years, might have been so gloomy and vacant', was that of 'conquering the innumerable Practical Problems that had arisen for her there; – all of which, I think all, she triumphantly mastered'.[29]

He seems never to have wondered how she filled the time *not* spent in heroic household victories. Both he and Jane were fond of taking life as a war against the odds; for her, Craigenputtoch was a battle lost, whereas for Carlyle, it was, eventually, a battle won.

★

The work Carlyle was slowly hatching, the great utterance which was to come forth from his solitary life in the bleak Dunscore region of Dumfriesshire – 'this Dunscore Patmos', as he described it to Jack in August 1830, alluding to the Aegean island where the banished St John had written the Book of Revelation[30] – was *Sartor Resartus*, which he began to write that autumn. He had toyed with other ideas for books, including a life of Goethe and one of Luther, who had begun to occupy his thoughts early in 1829. How attractive this 'son of peasants', who fronted the world and endured imprisonment for his principles, was to a man of Carlyle's own background and temperament is seen from his notebook at this time: 'Is it true that he *did* leave Wittenberg for Worms "with nothing but his Bible and his Flute"? There is no scene in European History so splendid and significant.'[31] William Fraser told him that the publishers Black, Young, and Young would be willing to print such a life of Luther, but Carlyle hesitated, knowing that he would have to visit Germany to do the necessary research and feeling half tempted but half reluctant to make such a journey.[32] Lack of money was a serious consideration, as was Carlyle's concern for his health and his inability to put up with the disagreeable elements of travelling, particularly those related to sleeping and eating.

Even the lure of Goethe at Weimar was not enough to make Carlyle do more than talk about a visit to Germany. Their correspondence, meanwhile, flourished. Carlyle wrote dramatically of his removal to the solitary Scottish moor. He liked Goethe to think of his life as a heroic isolation, physical and cultural, and represented himself as a lone voice crying out in the wilderness to his uncomprehending fellow men. In writing to Goethe, he turned Jeffrey's narrow-minded caricature of him as a 'German mystic' into a positive portrait of the lone champion of German culture.[33]

Goethe was charmed by the idea of Craigenputtoch, requesting a sketch of it for the title page of the German translation of Carlyle's *Life of Schiller* he was seeing through the press. A drawing was done in October

1829 by George Moir, an Edinburgh lawyer and German scholar, who visited Craigenputtoch for the purpose, and the German *Life of Schiller* appeared at Frankfurt am Main in 1830, with Craigenputtoch adorning the title page.[34]

Jane made a 'smart Highland bonnet' for Goethe's daughter-in-law Ottilie in December 1829. It was sent off in a box containing a lock of her own hair and 'a nice little verse of poetry professing to be written by me but in truth I did not write a word of it', as Jane told Carlyle's mother. The four lines are so poor in point of rhyme and rhythm that they could only be by Carlyle (whose cloth ear for poetry had marred his attempts to render the poems in *Wilhelm Meister*):

> Scotland prides her on the 'bonnet blue',
> That it brooks no stain in love or war;
> Be it on Ottilie's head a token true
> Of my Scottish love to kind Weimar.[35]

To Goethe Carlyle confessed in November that he was 'still but an Essayist, and longing more than ever to be a Writer in a far better sense'.[36] He took up the theme again in August 1830, alluding to Goethe's poem 'Symbolum', a celebration of the brotherhood of man, of an ideal freemasonry, which became a favourite source of quotation for Carlyle, not least because of the link between freemasonry and the honest trade of stonemason which his own father had pursued. He was ambitious, he told Goethe, for 'higher honours' than mere literary journalism, for 'till one knows that he *cannot* be a Mason, why should he publickly hire himself as a Hodman!' (Three years earlier Carlyle had privately described Walter Scott as a 'hodman', a useful but unskilled workman, in contrast to the mason, the creative artist.)[37]

Using Goethe as a genial repository of his slowly ripening creative idea, he continued:

When I look at the wonderful Chaos within me, full of natural Supernaturalism, and all manner of Antediluvian fragments, and how the Universe is daily growing more mysterious as well as more august, and the influences from without more heterogeneous and perplexing, I see not well what is to come of it all; and only conjecture from the violence of the fermentation that something strange may come.[38]

'Wonderful Chaos', 'natural Supernaturalism' (which became the title of an important chapter in *Sartor*), 'fragments' and influences 'hetero-geneous and perplexing' – Carlyle could not have described better *Sartor Resartus*, the 'something strange' which was growing in his mind but had not yet (to use the masonic metaphor) been chiselled into an outward form.

Throughout 1829 and 1830 Carlyle was hesitating, working inter-mittently on his 'History of German Literature', which William Fraser had offered to publish. By April 1830 Fraser and his publishing partners were in financial trouble and Carlyle was left with one and a half volumes of a projected four-volume history on his hands. With characteristic proud naivety he offered the work to William Tait, his old Edinburgh publisher, describing the fiasco with Fraser and saying he 'reckoned it an indifferent kind of Book'.[39] Tait unsurprisingly declined to publish, whereupon Carlyle resigned himself to cutting up the material – on early German literature – to print in magazines.[40] He was less inclined than ever to live by writing articles, but poverty forced him to do so for a few more years.

Fraser's financial embarrassment meant delays in Carlyle receiving payment for articles already written. By February 1831 he was close to being penniless. His journal reads, 'I have some £5 to front the world with; and expect no more for months. Jack too is at the neap tide. Hand to the oar!'[41] It is not clear whether he confided fully in Jane over his financial difficulty; she certainly knew they had little money and made it a matter of honour and pride to manage the household cleverly on a shoestring.

A year earlier, in March 1830, Jeffrey had tried to help Carlyle by offering him an annuity of £100, hoping to persuade his proud friend that he himself would have accepted such generosity if their positions had been reversed. He enclosed £50 for Carlyle's immediate use.[42] Carlyle refused all of it. 'I have just sent the meekest, friendliest, but most emphatic refusal, for this and all coming times', he told Jack on 19 March.[43] Meek his letter may have been – it has not survived – but he was worried about the egotism of his refusal, especially as he turned it over in his mind alongside the masonic/Goethean idea of universal brotherhood. In his journal he noted Jeffrey's offer; 'he did it neatly enough, and I had no doubt of his sincerity'. In refusing, 'how separate Pride from the natural necessary feeling of Self?' 'On the whole, I have been somewhat in the wrong about "independence"; man is *not* independent of his brother.'[44]

At the end of May 1830 Carlyle did reluctantly borrow £60 from Jeffrey, but the necessity to do so rankled with him, and he was relieved to be able to pay it back after many more penurious months – together with £43 which Jack owed Jeffrey – in October 1832.[45] When he remembered it in his reminiscence of Jeffrey he was ungenerous in inferring Jeffrey's motive to have been perhaps 'less of godlike pity for a fine fellow and his struggles' than 'of human determination to do a fine action of one's own'. Of his acceptance of the loan – 'my pitiful bits of "Periodical Literature" incomings having gone awry' – he recalls with satisfaction that 'this was all of pecuniary chivalry *we* two ever had between us'.[46]

He still had the awful warning of Coleridge's dependence before him, and more immediately the example of 'poor Hazlitt', to whom John Carlyle was attending in London in September 1830, and who wrote in despair to Jeffrey to say he was dying and to ask for £100. Hazlitt died on 18 September, before Jeffrey's cheque could reach him.[47] Carlyle remembered well enough how he had wished to avoid the fate of a Hazlitt or a De Quincey, scribbling for magazines and hiding from creditors in the 'roaring cauldron of stupid prurient anarchic London', as he put it in *Reminiscences*.[48] It was a strange and unwanted coincidence that his own hard-up brother should have been involved with Hazlitt as he died in poverty and despair, while Carlyle himself was near to insolvency and having to consider borrowing till payment for his own magazine scribblings arrived.

All this might have been enough to push Carlyle into writing a book at last, for he would have liked nothing more than to bid a final farewell to magazine editors. But he and Jane needed to live while he wrote his book, and so he was caught in the usual trap of the unwaged writer. He had to carry on reviewing for the periodicals. The *Edinburgh Review*, the best of them as to income and reputation, was, however, less open to him from 1830 on, Jeffrey having resigned as editor on his appointment as Dean of the Faculty of Advocates in Edinburgh. He was replaced by Macvey Napier, who shared all Jeffrey's distrust of Carlyle's German propensities but none of his admiration of Carlyle's genius or amused tolerance of his style.

Carlyle had already felt angered by Jeffrey's editorial interference, especially his 'cutting up' of an article on Burns in 1828. Jeffrey, finding it too long, and also objecting, as usual, to Carlyle's 'mystical jargon', had rather breezily set about his 'mutilation of your dissertation'.[49] Carlyle submitted reluctantly and not without a fight. His pride was all the more bruised because his heart was involved in the subject as well as his head. Burns had, after all, farmed at Ellisland, near Dumfries; moreover, he was a peasant genius at first unrecognised and unrewarded by others, and – most pertinently for Carlyle – he had preserved a proud, almost prickly, independence even in his poorest days. (He had also, unlike Carlyle, fathered several illegitimate children, and he drank too much.)

Carlyle wrote angrily to Jeffrey in a letter now lost, to which Jeffrey replied on 22 October 1828 with sly humour and infuriating superiority:

How can you be so absurd as to talk of my cancelling that excellent paper of yours on Burns, after it has given both of us so much trouble – or to imagine that I do not set a true value on it, because I was compelled to make it a little shorter – and induced to vary a few phrases that appeared to me to savour of affectation, or at all events of mannerism? . . . I do not think I shall let you have any more proof sheets. It only vexes you, and does no good – for you correct them very badly, leaving half the typographical errors unredressed, and exerting yourself only to replace all the words and phrases, which I, for very good reasons, had taken out.[50]

Carlyle was still smarting from his treatment in January 1829, after his truncated Burns article had appeared in the *Edinburgh*. He told Jack that 'the Duke' – his nickname for the prosperous Jeffrey sitting in his little 'castle' at Craigcrook – had 'maltreated *Burns* till I cannot bear to look on it'.[51] But at least Jeffrey had published his articles and had encouraged him, even if he smiled patronisingly as he snipped away at them. Napier, soon dubbed 'Naso' by Carlyle on account of his long nose, and described variously as 'a solid old-established Edinburgh Whig', 'a dry, fainthearted, wooden kind of man', and – with inspired imagination – a 'hungry *Simulacrum*', was distinctly unenthusiastic, even turning down several of Carlyle's suggestions for articles.[52]

Napier's new star reviewer was Thomas Babington Macaulay, who often wrote on subjects which Carlyle wanted to do; it was Macaulay who succeeded in reviewing Thomas Moore's life of Byron in the *Edinburgh Review* in 1831, though Carlyle had also offered to cover the subject.[53] Napier wrote in a truly offhand manner after Carlyle had sent him an article on the radical poet Ebenezer Elliott's *Corn-Law Rhymes* (in which Carlyle sided with the reformers against the establishment):

I was delayed longer than I expected in London, on my return, a few days ago, from which place, I found your parcel and letter. I sent your art[icle] to press, for a proof, without looking at it, and now send you the proof for correction. I shall not read [it] till I receive the article with your corrections. In my state of utter ignorance I can say nothing about it, but if you could *shorten* it, by withdrawing any part capable of being spared, I should be glad; for I have a large quantity of matter for this No., all of which *must* go into it.[54]

★

Carlyle soon stopped sending suggestions to Napier, though two of his most influential articles, 'Signs of the Times' (June 1829), commissioned by Jeffrey before he resigned as editor, and 'Characteristics' (December 1831), appeared in the *Edinburgh* under Napier's editorship. They, along with a seventy-page article on Voltaire in the *Foreign Review* (April 1829), give evidence of Carlyle's arrival, at last, in the public arena as an original, thoughtful, and important, if as yet anonymous, social commentator.

After a long period of gestation, Carlyle's intellectual activities, seemingly so scattered and tentative, now came together to produce the works for which he became justly famous. It may seem hard to square

Jane's description of Carlyle's strict work routine during their time at Craigenputtoch with the output – a handful of articles, an idea for a Luther biography, an unfinished history of German literature – but those articles are almost books in themselves, being often more than fifty pages long, and covering their subjects in an unusually ambitious way. The essay on Voltaire, for example, is partly a detailed biographical critique of the man and his works and partly nothing less than a panoramic characterisation of the eighteenth century, of which Voltaire was, according to Carlyle, 'the paragon and epitome'.[55] Through his wide reading for these essays, Carlyle was storing in his excellent memory an encyclopædia of knowledge on which he would draw extensively and repeatedly, to the astonishment of his readers, in all his works to come.

The eighteenth century, indeed, was a lifelong obsession; not only would Carlyle write intricate histories of its greatest event – the French Revolution – and its greatest ruler (in Carlyle's opinion, at least) – Frederick the Great of Prussia – but he consistently defined himself and his own age in direct contrast to the preceding one, the age of Reason, Enlightenment, Materialism, Atheism, and Revolution. When he attacked phenomena belonging to his own time, as he frequently did, it was for the tendencies it inherited from the eighteenth century. Like Coleridge, but more starkly, he discerned two main strands surviving into the nineteenth century: the materialist philosophy of Bentham and the Mills, father and son, which carried on the tradition of Hume and the French *philosophes*, and its counterweight, the transcendental or neo-idealist philosophy of the late eighteenth-century German philosophers.

For Carlyle, taking the broad view and disdaining those details which did not support his case, Voltaire's mockery and cynicism were the literary manifestation of the first strand, while Goethe's serenity and humanity constituted the chief example connected with the second. The two tendencies were in conflict, and Carlyle aimed to enlist his readers and followers on the side of the angels. Something of this ambition lay behind all his proselytising for German culture. In 'Signs of the Times', for the first time, he took contemporary British life as his subject, bringing to bear in his confident, unusual style his convictions about recent European history. For the first time, too, he demonstrated his desire to be thought a prophet by his fellow men and women; and in taking on the role of prophet, he relied explicitly on his strong sense of history.

The title of his essay is taken from Matthew 16:3, in which Jesus answers the Pharisees who tempt him to show a sign from heaven: 'O ye hypocrites, ye can discern the face of the sky, but can ye not discern the signs of the times?' Carlyle steps forth to warn his generation that 'the time is sick and out of joint'. Alluding to the creeping political reforms which were coming in slowly and against much opposition – the removal of Catholic disabilities in 1829 after more than twenty years of agitation, and the continuing efforts of the radicals which would inevitably issue in wholesale political reform, as Carlyle correctly perceived – he half threatens his readers with, and half rejoices in, the 'boundless grinding collision of the New and the Old'.

Though he belonged to no political party, indeed scorning all parties as he did all particular church denominations, Carlyle welcomes the radical sweeping away of outmoded privilege and injustice. But political and social reform is in the hands of the Benthamites, and Carlyle warns against their mechanistic view of society, their counting by numbers and concern with the feeding of stomachs rather than souls. There is, he says, 'a science of *Dynamics* as well as of *Mechanics*'. Society is not just a machine; progress must be spiritual as well as material. He concludes the essay in ringing fashion:

To reform a world, to reform a nation, no wise man will undertake; and all but foolish men know, that the only solid, though a far slower reformation, is what each begins and perfects on *himself*.[56]

From his Dunscore wilderness Carlyle had been keeping up with the reform agitation in London. In March 1829 he declared that the Catholic Question must be settled, and ought to have been settled over a century earlier, when John Locke wrote his *Letter concerning Toleration* (1689) – 'but there are some people who require three hundred years to begin to see an absurdity'.[57] He held existing political parties and churches in contempt, but did not want to destroy the essential truths of politics or religion. The outward vestments needed to be stripped off to render visible the underlying body. It was Carlyle's independence of party, his apartness, his loud voice crying from the wilderness, which won him admirers, and, in due course, disciples.

The first stranger to respond to the prophetic Carlyle was Gustave d'Eichthal, nephew of Jack's Munich benefactor and a member of the Parisian communitarian sect founded by the Comte de Saint-Simon. D'Eichthal wrote in April 1830, addressing his letter to the anonymous author of 'Signs of the Times', claiming fellowship and sending some books expounding the views of the Saint-Simonians, which included the abolition of inherited property and the emancipation of women. Carlyle was flattered by the praise though cautious about the sect; he wrote a polite, brotherly reply notable for its public, sage-like tone, with its talk of the eighteenth century as 'a period of Denial, of Irreligion and Destruction', and the need for 'a new period of Affirmation, of Religion', if 'Society is to be reconstituted'.[58]

Carlyle gave his old friend Irving the credit for suggesting the title of his essay, Irving having published a forty-page pamphlet, *The Signs of the Times*, earlier in 1829.[59] Both old friends agreed in distrusting the Utilitarians, or 'Millites', as Carlyle named them for the sake of the pun on James and John Stuart Mill's name, but Carlyle was equally keen to distance himself from the opposite party, the 'Millenarians', to whom, as a religious fanatic, Irving could be said to belong.

Irving's career had now become problematic in the extreme. As Carlyle had feared, his head was turned by his huge success as a preacher. In May 1827 he celebrated the opening of his newly built church in Regent Square by inviting his old mentor Dr Chalmers to come down from Glasgow to perform the ceremony. A disgruntled Dr Chalmers reported afterwards that 'there was a prodigious want of tact in the length of his prayers – forty minutes; and altogether it was an hour and a half from the commencement of the service ere I began'. The congregation, 'in their eagerness to obtain seats, had already been assembled three hours'. Irving had offered to help Chalmers by reading a chapter for him. '*He chose the longest in the Bible*, and went on for an hour and a half', Chalmers complained.[60] In 1828 Irving published three volumes of his sermons, in which he argued for the 'sinfulness of Christ's human nature' – that is, his belief that Christ was *truly* tempted by Satan – which brought down coals of fire on his head from his co-religionists.[61]

Every year, in early summer, Irving visited Scotland, where he preached to enormous crowds; but tragedy as well as farce accompanied him. In June 1828 he was due to preach at his father-in-law's church in Kirkcaldy, when 2,000 people crowded into the building, causing a gallery to collapse on those below. Carlyle told Jack about the disaster, after reading about it in the local Dumfries paper: 'Irving was going to preach there, and the kirk fell and killed eight and twenty persons. "What thinkst *a* he means", said my Father, "gawn up and down the country *tevelling* [raging] and *screaching* like a wild bear?" '[62]

The following May and June he preached again in Scotland, including twice at Dumfries, where he attracted a congregation in the open air of over 13,000. Here he met his old friend Carlyle, and rode back to Craigenputtoch with him. Carlyle told Mrs Montagu of this brief visit: 'He stretched himself out here on the moors, under the free sky, beside me, and was the *same* honest soul as of old.'[63]

Perhaps he was, but Irving was sailing into uncharted waters. Also in the summer of 1829 he prepared another long work for the press. His biographer, Margaret Oliphant, describes its strange combination of biblical prophecy and vehement anti-Reform politics:

This was a work on *Church and State*, founded upon the vision of Daniel, and tracing the line of antique history, the course of the Kings and of the Church, through Nebuchadnezzar, Cyrus, and Alexander, up to fated Rome, in all its grand developments. He himself explains the book to have been an expression of his own indignant sentiments in respect to the late invasions of the British Constitution, which, according to his view, destroyed the standing of the country as a Christian nation: these being specially the abolition of the Test and Corporation Acts, and the repeal of Catholic disabilities.[64]

Irving's book bore the extravagant title *Daniel's Vision of the Four Beasts and of the Son of Man opened, and applied to our Present Crisis in Church and State*. It was dedicated to the male members of the Martin family into which Irving had reluctantly married; the dedication recalls similar ones he had flourished before a startled Montagu and an embarrassed Coleridge a few years earlier:

> To the Reverend SAMUEL MARTIN, D.D.,
> My venerable Grandfather-in-law:
> The Reverend JOHN MARTIN,
> My honoured Father-in-law:
> The Reverend SAMUEL MARTIN,
> My faithful Brother-in-law:
> And to all my Fathers and Brethren,
> The ordained Ministers of the Church of Scotland.

Reverend and well-beloved, the peace of God be with you and with your flocks; the blessing of the great Head of the Church preserve you from all heresy and schism; and the Holy Ghost give you plentiful fruit of your ministries.[65]

Irving wrote, as he spoke, preposterously. Hazlitt, who had included him among the character portraits in *The Spirit of the Age* (1825) – for he saw that Irving was indeed a significant, if extreme, manifestation of the time – wittily summed up the effect of Irving's bellicose sermons. Irving, he wrote, used 'the battering-ram of logic, the grape-shot of rhetoric, and the cross-fire of his double vision' to challenge his flock.[66] The great squinting orator was well on his way to embracing the miracle cures and speaking in tongues which broke out among his congregation in 1831. According to Froude, Jane Carlyle once said, 'There would have been no tongues had Irving married me.'[67] Maybe so, but it is equally likely that she would have had as little softening influence on Irving's peculiarities as she had on Carlyle's; and when one reads Irving's sermons and letters one can hardly imagine how she, with her sharp eye and sharper tongue, would have fared with the inspired juggernaut of Regent Square.

★

At Craigenputtoch various changes were now afoot. Carlyle's quiet sister Margaret died at Dumfries on 22 June 1830 at the age of twenty-six. Carlyle and Alick received the news about midnight and rode together through the shortest night of the year, arriving in Dumfries about four in the morning. 'That solstice night with its singing birds and sad thoughts I shall never forget', he wrote in his journal.[68]

Meanwhile his sister Mary, keeping house for Alick at Craigenputtoch, was ill. Carlyle's letters to his mother, and to Jack in London, show him worried about her and discreetly suggesting the possibility that she might be pregnant. Sure enough, Mary married in November 1830 and gave birth to a daughter in March 1831. Her husband was 'stupid' James Austin, a farm labourer who was given work at Scotsbrig, though the Carlyle family disliked him.[69] Alick married Janet Clow in December 1830, but was struggling, as we have seen, and left Craigenputtoch in May 1831, to be succeeded by a new tenant, 'a peaceable man: able but dull stupid fellow', with whom Jane and Carlyle had little to do.[70]

Two of Jane's rare letters to Eliza Stodart date from December 1830 and January 1831. Both stress the lack of company at Craigenputtoch during the winter months:

We have been very solitary for a long while, our only visitors are now and then a stray pack-man, and the last of these pronounced the place 'altogether *heathenish*' so there is no hope of our being favoured with *his* company another time. Nevertheless I keep up my heart . . . tho' the desert around looks the very head quarters of winter; and our knocker hangs a useless ornament.[71]

On 16 January Jane wrote again, demonstrating her ability to 'make a story about a broom handle and make it entertaining', as Geraldine Jewsbury said:[72]

Notwithstanding my prediction that I should fall off rapidly after twenty, I keep my looks surprisingly well – An old Irish packman met me riding alone the other day, and modestly insinuated that I should buy an almanack of him – 'By no means' – 'But I have travelled all day Lady and got nothing to pay my Lodgings'! 'Well – for God's sake – there's a penny to you' 'Thank you *young* Lady – thank you most kindly – and' – his gratitude and his voice mounting higher and higher till they reached the pitch of enthusiasm 'and the Lord send you a Husband according to your heart!' – 'Amen, friend'! – From which passage one may infer one of two things – either that an Irish packman thought me too youthful looking to be already provided with a Husband; or that he conceived the provision of a Husband incompatible with galloping over the country *alone*.[73]

Such cheerfulness may have been more assumed than felt. By June 1831 even Carlyle had decided that they would 'spend no other winter' at Craigenputtoch.[74]

Carlyle's resolution had another motive apart from consideration for his own or Jane's comfort, however. He was planning to spend the following winter in London looking for a publisher for *Sartor Resartus*, which he had at last begun to write in October 1830. Immediately after another visit from Jeffrey and his family in September 1830, and in a combative mood perhaps induced by his conversational sparring with no-nonsense Jeffrey, he announced in his journal, 'I am going to write – Nonsense. It is on "Clothes". Heaven be my comforter!' A few weeks later he noted, 'Written a strange piece "On clothes": know not what will come of it.'[75] He worked on, not yet calling it *Sartor Resartus*, but sometimes 'Clothes', sometimes 'Teufelsdreck' or 'Teufelsdröckh' – asafoetida, 'Devil's Dung' or 'Devil's Dirt', as the Scots called it.[76]

In January 1831 Carlyle asked Jack in London to 'get my long Paper entitled *Thoughts on Clothes*' back from James Fraser, to whom Carlyle had sent it, hoping it would be published in *Fraser's Magazine*. He had in the meantime decided that *Fraser's* gave 'the most scurvy remuneration of any Periodical extant' and was 'a frothy, washy, punchy, dirty kind of Periodical', not good enough for his piece, which he now planned to extend to book length. 'I can devise', he told Jack, 'a second deeper part, in the same vein, leading thro' Religion and the nature of Society, and Lord knows what.'[77]

At his request Jack showed 'Teufelsdröckh' to Irving, who thought it 'very graphically and humorously drawn' but lacking in action.[78] He suggested that more explanatory material was required to carry the reader along with the strange outpourings of Professor Diogenes Teufelsdröckh in his rhapsodic-sardonic treatise on the worn-out old clothes of society's institutions, as represented by the dandy's outfit (for a superannuated aristocracy) and the bishop's gorgeous robes and shovel hat (for a worldly and stale church doctrine and clergy). Carlyle now thought he should descend on London, as he told Jack on 4 March 1831, 'with my wifekin under my arm', as soon as he had 'finished my prodigal son *Teufelsdreck*, and got fifty pounds in my pocket'. 'With this sum, under the guidance of Heaven, we will visit the great Beehive and Waspnest, and (till it run done) see what is to be seen.'[79]

Another powerful motive was at work in Carlyle, drawing him towards London. It was closely connected with his ambitions for *Sartor*, his first *real* work. All his religious, political, social, and literary thinking went into the book, and Carlyle felt the urge to preach in person his belief that out-moded institutions should be reformed, his secular-cum-spiritual philosophy, his natural supernaturalism according to which everything in the world is a miracle if seen correctly, if only one penetrates through the outer garments to the body beneath. He declared to Jack:

Nay, I have half a mind (but this in deepest secrecy) to start when I come there, if the ground promise well, and deliver a Dozen of Lectures, in my own Annandale accent, with my own God-created brain and heart, to such audience as will gather round me, on some section or aspect of this strange Life in this strange Era; on which my soul like Eliphaz the Temanite's is getting fuller and fuller [Job 4:2]. Does there seem to thee any propriety in a man that has organs of speech and even some semblance of understanding and Sincerity, sitting forever, mute as [a] milestone, while Quacks of every colour are quacking as with lungs of brass? True I have no Pulpit: but as I once said, cannot any man *make* him a pulpit, simply by inverting the nearest Tub? And what are your whigs and Lord Advocates, and Lord Chancellors, and the whole host of unspeakably gabbling Parliamenteers and Pulpiteers and Pamphleteers; – if a man suspect that 'there is fire enough in his belly to burn up' the entire creation of such![80]

He had no quack's pulpit such as Irving had, and no university chair or political appointment, but he would have his say. All his history of careers considered and abandoned came together with his political and social views until 'Providence seems saying to me: Thou wilt never find Pulpit, were it but a Rhetoric chair, provided for thee: invert thy Tub, and speak, if thou have aught to say!'[81] He had now created an *alter ego*, Teufels-dröckh, who did have a chair, albeit of Things in General at the University of Know-Not-Where, and he gave him the first name Diogenes, after the Greek founder of the Cynic sect who believed in training the body to have as few needs as possible and therefore, reputedly, lived in a tub.

His strange creation's strange surname signals Carlyle's desire to have, through his book and perhaps also through his personal contact by lecturing, an emetic effect on the ailing British establishment, to purge it and thus do it good. 'I sometimes think the Book *will* prove a kind of medicinal Assafoetida for the pudding Stomach of England', he told Jack in July, 'and produce new secretions there.'[82] The dyspeptic prophet would channel his disgust at his own bodily (mal)functions into a metaphorical dose of salts for the reading and listening public.

Now was the time, Carlyle knew, not only to spring *Sartor Resartus* on an unsuspecting world, but also to be in London trying to influence events, to 'wander down', as Jeffrey floridly expressed it, 'from your Blasted Paradise, hand in hand with your Blooming Eve, to seek a peaceful shelter in our lower world'.[83] Reform was heavily in the air and London the only place to be. The disreputable (and anti-Reform) George IV had died in June 1830. In November the Duke of Wellington's Tory ministry, riven over the Catholic Question, had resigned and the Whigs came in under Lord Grey, who was determined to put through the Reform Bill. Henry Brougham, now Lord Brougham, was appointed Lord Chancellor, and the new Lord Advocate was none other than Jeffrey. 'O yes, alas, I am Lord Advocate!' wrote Jeffrey to Carlyle on 18

December 1830, sounding like a figure from Gilbert and Sullivan, 'and about to be M.P.' Could he do anything for Carlyle in his new position? he wondered. Carlyle had only to ask.[84]

Carlyle was infected by the excitement of the political changes going forward, in which several of his acquaintances were involved. His old friend and pupil Charles Buller was now an MP voting for radical change. Carlyle was reading with keen interest a series of articles on 'The Spirit of the Age' in the radical newspaper, the *Examiner*, which showed a knowledge of Saint-Simonism. This intrigued Carlyle, who 'hunted out' the anonymous author when he came to London later in 1831 and found him to be the young Utilitarian, John Stuart Mill.[85] In January 1831 he mused to Jack, rebuking him for not writing more often:

You are there in the focus of British activity at a great era in the world's history, at a great era in your own; I am here in the dead silence of peat-moss, yet warmly interested in all that pertains to both these eras; and you take the trouble to tell me very little. Some half hundred things you might throw great light on for me . . . nevertheless you will not so much as fill your paper, no matter what.[86]

There was clearly nothing for it but to plunge back into the great metropolis himself.

The irrepressible Jeffrey teased him when he heard of the plan. 'And are you really coming to this resort and mart of all the Earth', he asked in July, 'with your manuscript in your pocket, like Parson Adams?'[87] He knew, of course, as did Carlyle, that the eccentric Parson Adams in Fielding's *Joseph Andrews* carried his weighty and unsaleable sermons with him in the forlorn hope of finding a willing publisher. Would Carlyle's manuscript meet the same fate?

On 4 August 1831 Carlyle left his Scottish desert to travel to London. He did not carry Jane under his arm, nor yet wander down from his blasted paradise hand in hand with her, but it was agreed that she would follow him to London if he managed to find a publisher for *Sartor Resartus* and get together enough money for them both to spend some time there. At last it seemed that Jane was to see London, while her husband made a second attempt, at the age of nearly thirty-six, to take the citadel by storm.

CHAPTER 6

Closing the First Act 1831–1834

Having paid a brief visit to his parents at Scotsbrig, Carlyle made his way to London, determined to publish his manuscript and also to deliver his personal homily on 'gigmanity'.[1] Carlyle coined the word, along with 'gigmania', with its play on *mania*, to mean a false or shallow respectability. In an article on Jean Paul Richter in the *Foreign Review* in January 1830 he introduced and explained the allusion: during the famous trial for murder of John Thurtell in 1824 a witness had described the suspect as owning a gig – a two-wheeled horse-drawn carriage – and being therefore a respectable person.[2]

Carlyle, amused by this simple association of outward respectability and inner worth, worked the 'gigmanity' reference into many of his writings. There was a close kinship between the term and the many variations in *Sartor Resartus* on the theme of sartorial disguise and the necessity to penetrate misleading appearances. Professor Teufelsdröckh has the gift of seeing – 'as by some enchanter's wand' – the clothes of 'Dukes, Grandees, Bishops, Generals' and other worthies fly off at 'pompous ceremonials', leaving 'every mother's son of them straddling there, not a shirt on them'. It was a Swiftian vision which Teufelsdröckh's creator had himself experienced and noted in his journal in August 1830, shortly before he started writing *Sartor*.[3]

On arrival in London, Carlyle joined Jack in his lodgings (in a house belonging to Edward Irving's brother George), and quickly visited Jeffrey, who gave him a letter of introduction to the great publisher John Murray, 'a tall squinting man' whom Carlyle saw, with some difficulty, in his Albemarle Street office.[4] Murray promised to read the book within a week, but when Carlyle called on 17 August, as agreed, he was at first denied access to Murray, who finally 'showed his broad one-eyed face, and with fair speeches signified that his family were all ill, and he had been called into the country'. 'Teufelsdreck' lay 'still unopened' on his table.[5] Carlyle returned twice more, only to find his manuscript still unread and a note from Murray offering to keep it for a month, after which he would 'be able to say a word, and by God's blessing a favourable one'. Carlyle, desperate for an answer and in need of immediate money or at least the promise of money so that he could decide how long to stay in London, and whether and when to call Jane down to join him, picked up 'my poor Teufelsdreck' and walked off in 'silent fury', as he told Jane.[6]

Carlyle simply could not wait for the great man to pronounce. He went straight to Regent Street and 'looked in upon James Fraser' of *Fraser's Magazine*. 'Honest James' said he would publish the book 'on this principle: if I would give *him* a sum not exceeding £150 sterling!' Whereupon Carlyle set off to try Longman on Paternoster Row, and was promised a reply within two days.[7] The Longmans were prompt to 'decline the article', so he gave it to Jeffrey, who had promised to cajole Murray.[8] More delays followed, but by 4 September Jeffrey had persuaded Murray to 'print a small edition (750 Copies) of *Dreck*, on the half-profits system (that is I getting *nothing*, but also *giving* nothing) after which the sole Copyright of the Book is to be mine'.[9]

Poor Carlyle. He disliked relying so heavily on Jeffrey for favours, and he did not want either Jeffrey or Murray to know how much he depended – financially and psychologically – on arriving at an agreement for his book. Though prepared to accept Murray's cautious offer, Carlyle tried one more publishing house, Colburn and Bentley, in the hope of getting a deal which would put money in his pocket.[10] Predictably enough, Colburn did not make an offer. Showing his naivety in business matters, Carlyle went back to Murray, with whom he had been rather abrupt, being now ready, *faute de mieux*, to accept the half-profits, or no-profits, option. By this time Murray was offended that Carlyle had offered the book to all and sundry, and discouraged by his fellow publishers' refusals; he insisted on getting the manuscript read 'by some literary friend' before he would commit himself.[11] Carlyle wrote a proud reply, denying duplicity and offering to take back his unfortunate manuscript and forget the matter.

Murray had gone so far as to have a specimen page set up in type, of which Carlyle had sent a scrap to Jane on 19 September with premature satisfaction.[12] Four days later he had to let her know that 'Murray's Bargain with me has burst into the air'; he consoled himself with feeling superior to 'poor Murray and all his tribe'.[13] Six week after arriving in London, he still had his manuscript on his hands and no clear prospect of making money from it or anything else.

John Carlyle, meanwhile, fared rather better. Having got down to his last seven shillings in July, he, too, was looking to Jeffrey for help. Jeffrey used his interest to find him a post as travelling physician to the Countess of Clare, who was planning to spend a year in Italy. It was agreed that John should be paid 300 guineas plus expenses, and he set about learning Italian in preparation to leave with his new patron early in October 1831.[14]

Jane received Carlyle's twice-weekly letters, responding excitedly as the prospects for 'Teufelsdreck' and for her trip to London rose and fell during August and September. She was fiercely supportive of the book, reporting on 18 August that she had had a joking letter from Jeffrey:

[He] writes me that you 'look very smart and dandyish – have got your hair cut and a new suit – and are applying various cosmetics to your complexion' – Moreover – that he 'will *do what he can for the book* but fears its extravagance and what will be called its affectation' Let him not tro[u]ble his dear little heart overmuch – Dreck is *done* . . . and no Bookseller or body of booksellers, no discerning public can *undo* him – not the Devil himself can undo him – If they will not publish him – bring him back and I will take care of him and read him and admire him – till we are enabled to publish him on our own account.[15]

On 1 September she repeated her loyal praise of her husband's book. 'My beloved Dreck! my jewel of great price!' she exclaimed. 'The builders despise thee; but thou wilt yet be *brought out with shouting* and I shall live to see thee in thy place.'[16]

She was missing Carlyle; she confessed in her first letter to him after his departure that she had cried herself to sleep and kissed his nightcap. It had been arranged that James, Carlyle's youngest brother, should leave Scotsbrig – where, now aged twenty-five, he helped his father on the farm – and spend a few days at Craigenputtoch, so that she would not feel too lonely. Jane enjoyed his company, telling Carlyle that she was sorry to part with him when he went back to Scotsbrig: 'He is the best of my Brothers in law – in other words he likes *me* best'.[17]

Alick and his wife Jenny, though they no longer farmed at Craigen-puttoch, still visited, but Jane found them difficult to get on with, especially Jenny with her 'unspeakable eye-sorrow, toning forth an occasional "ee-a" and "doost"', which drove the fastidious Jane to distraction.[18] Jenny was heavily pregnant with her first child (a girl, born in early October and named Jane Welsh),[19] and Jane seems to have taken advantage of the situation – perhaps unintentionally – to arouse her jealousy. She told Carlyle of an incident one evening during James's stay:

I thought Alick going out of his wits the last night of Jamies visit – I was playing to them and he broke out in such a strain of lyrical recognition as set us all in astonishment. 'It was heavenly', he said 'it transported him out of this earth into a new world of *celestial delight* – these *strings were like so many little winged spirits speaking to him out of the skies*'! and much more of the same sort till Jenny asked with a deadening and killing look 'What ails thee man?'[20]

A few weeks later, after Jane had paid a visit to her mother at Templand and had brought a friend, Isabella MacTurk, back with her to Craigen-puttoch, she reported another outburst by poor Jenny:

She has been quite insufferable of late with *jealousy* of her husband – whether with

Isabella or me or both I cannot say – but last night I cut Alick's hair and Isabella sat looking on; she was nearly beside herself – cried till bed time and broke out on me with a bur[s]t of impertinence that filled me with weender and amazement.[21]

Geraldine Jewsbury's remark in her memoir of Jane about her having to be the first person with any man or woman she had dealings with seems vindicated by Jane's own account here.

Meanwhile, Jane had fallen out with her mother at Templand, as she usually did when they were under the same roof, and she was angry with Alick for turning up to take her home to Craigenputtoch 'mortal drunk'. Naturally she was mortified that her mother and friends should see him 'making such a deplorable figure'; her description to Carlyle of the journey home with Isabella and a drunken Alick is characteristically dramatic:

Off we went about seven having vainly waited to see if he would sober – and of course drove like Jehu [i.e. furiously, as in 2 Kings 9:20] up hill down dale over stock and stone – making such hairbreadth turns! O mercy – I left Templand with my cheeks burning like a coal and my heart not less – but I was pale enough after.[22]

Alick wrote a note of apology, and Carlyle expressed his anxiety 'when I look into the future and think of my poor brother a Drunkard'.[23]

It is just possible that Jane thought herself pregnant at this time. She told Carlyle on 1 September that she had been fainting. She herself connected this explicitly with her excitement at the prospect of joining him in London – 'Mr Carlyle a's maist ashamed to say it, but a's far too impetuous – my speculative ardor I feel will shorten my life.'[24] However, Carlyle made a strange comment in his letter of 14 September, in which he instructed her on what to bring in the way of books and useful items: 'Take every care of thyself, Wifekin: there is more than thy own that thou carriest with thee.'[25]

This could have the simple meaning that *he* claimed a share in her precious person; on the other hand, the fact that at least one of Jane's letters to him, written about 7 September, is missing has led to some speculation that in it she told him of her suspicions (or hopes) that she might be pregnant. Members of Carlyle's family much later recalled a story handed down about baby clothes being packed to go with her to London and later found in a drawer at Cheyne Row. However, no direct mention is made of a pregnancy or miscarriage in Carlyle's reply to the missing letter or in any subsequent surviving letters. The family tradition, or hearsay, was invoked by Carlyle's nephew, Alexander Carlyle, when he was engaged in a furious war of words with Froude and his supporters over

Carlyle's alleged impotence, and published in order to prove that the marriage was consummated.[26] The whole question must remain open, though the warmth expressed by both Carlyles in their letters during their two-month separation suggests that they had enjoyed some kind of physical relationship at Craigenputtoch.

Jane made her way south, via her uncle and cousins in Liverpool, arriving in London on 1 October. Mrs Montagu had written offering to pay for her journey and to put her up on arrival, but, eager though Jane was to get to London, she was as adamant as Carlyle that she would 'never, God willing, buy myself *pleasure* with another's means'.[27] Though Carlyle was making no headway with finding a publisher for 'Teufelsdreck', he calculated on 22 August that he had £40 in hand and was owed £36 by Napier of the *Edinburgh Review*, with another £25 or so due from John Cochrane, editor of the *Foreign Quarterly Review*, with which William Fraser's *Foreign Review* had recently merged.[28] He was willing to risk bringing Jane down to spend the winter on this £100 or so, if she was prepared to come, which of course she was.[29]

Jane wrote on 11 September, displaying, though rather tentatively, her eagerness to leave Craigenputtoch for the winter at least, even while she acknowledged its usefulness as the cradle of 'Teufelsdreck':

At Craigenputtoch we have always had a secret suspicion that we were quite wrong – removed out of the sphere of human activity fully as much thro' cowardice as superior wisdom – (am I not right in regard to you as well as myself) and thus all our doings are without heart and our sufferings without dignity – With a goal before me I feel I could leap sixbar gates – but how dispiriting tethered on a barren heath – running round and round – Yet let it not be forgotten that at Craigenputtoch you have written Teufe[l]sdreck.

As with Carlyle, so with Jane. Her main dread was of getting into debt, so she added prudently:

Nevertheless I am taking all possible pains to preserve the poor Putta [Craigenputtoch] in habitable order for no more than you would I *renounce* it It is a safe haven (tho but a desert island) in stress of weather.[30]

Having taken the boat from Annan to Liverpool, as Carlyle had done before her, she wrote to him from her uncle's house there, giving an indication of what would be her lifelong suffering during journeys, particularly sea voyages (she never crossed the Channel to Europe, largely for this reason), and her equally lifelong intolerance of other people's domestic arrangements:

I felt quite worn out with my rough passage hither and thought it would be well to take in a new outfit of strength and spirit before starting again – Never did poor young woman miscalculate so egregiously. *Sleep* which is my great want is precisely the thing which cannot be had in this house by any means – I could sleep sounder in the open street – good Heavens how did *you* get on. They would drive *me mad* in another week . . . O my love my love in your arms I shall feel so safe so blessed after all this tossing and tumbling and fretting and raging.[31]

★

After Jane's arrival, the Carlyles moved out of George Irving's rooms into a quieter house at 4, Ampton Street, off Gray's Inn Road and close to Irving's church on Regent Square. The house was owned by a family of 'quiet decent people' who had once been wealthy but were now 'reduced to keeping lodgings, and prettily resigned to it', as Carlyle noted in his reminiscence of Jane. The daughter, Eliza Miles, 'fell in love' with Jane, even offering to join them as their servant in Craigenputtoch when they returned there the following summer.[32] Mrs Montagu was soon writing to Jane to invite her to visit and meet her face to face at last, but warning her to prepare herself for 'an old woman, sallow and severe, like the Abbess of some Nunnery in the old-times, not cold-hearted, but schooled into the suppression of her feelings'.[33] Poor Mrs Montagu had fallen out with her old friend Badams over investments, and her stepsons were all going to rack and ruin. Carlyle had reported to Jane in August that her house was 'like a House of Atreus; a curse seems to rest on it; all things go round and round'.[34] By January 1832 Jane had decided that her friendship with 'the Noble Lady' was 'dying an easy natural death' now that they had met in the flesh.[35]

Of the two acquaintances Jane already had in London, Jeffrey and Irving, the first was invisible for the first six weeks of her stay because he was seriously ill. He wrote her what he himself called 'a foolish, pettish, unreasonable note'; 'I told you not to come when I was in agonies, and you never came at all.' Moreover, 'you live and are occupied with people I cannot care about'.[36] He meant the Montagus and probably also Irving. The 'gift of tongues' had started among the latter's flock; Carlyle had spent an evening with him in August 'in the *animali-parlanti* [talking animals] region of the Supernatural'.[37] Soon after Jane's arrival they both visited Irving, to find the house 'decked out for a "meeting" (that is, a bout of this same "speaking with tongues")', as Carlyle told his mother on 20 October. A shrieking arose on an upper floor of the house, and Irving forced the Carlyles to go upstairs with him to hear a woman 'prophesying', or, as Carlyle described it, '*hooing* and *ha*-ing'. Both were shocked and dismayed; 'poor Jane was on the verge of fainting'. *The Times* had described similar scenes at Irving's church the previous day. Carlyle began a letter to Irving to warn him of his madness, but 'gave it up again as hopeless'.[38] In November Carlyle took courage and spoke to his friend about his 'scandalous delusion'; Irving was 'almost at crying', but remained adamant in his self-belief and belief in his associates.[39]

Carlyle's friend John Badams, now living in Enfield, was introduced to Jane, but he, too, was much reduced from the time, in 1824, when Carlyle had put himself and his dyspepsia in his hands in Birmingham and had envied Badams his settled, organised, eight-day-clock existence. Badams was now financially ruined, suspected of fraud by the Montagus, and an alcoholic.[40] Carlyle and Jane spent five days at his house in November; there they met Badams's neighbour in Enfield, Charles Lamb. The two men got drunk over dinner, Lamb becoming obstreperous and clamouring for gin and water 'with a rude barbarism', as Carlyle told Jack, while Badams sat 'already *dosed*, and asleep'.[41]

Carlyle was repelled by Lamb. (He may not have known about the Lamb family tragedy, the killing of their mother in 1796 by Lamb's sister Mary in a fit of insanity.) The visit to Enfield is described in his reminiscence of Jane:

Charles Lamb and his Sister came daily once or oftener; a very sorry pair of phenomena. Insuperable proclivity to *gin*, in poor old Lamb. His talk contemptibly small, indicating wondrous ignorance and shallowness, even when it was serious and good-mannered, which it seldom was; usually *ill*-mannered (to a degree), screwed into frosty artificialities, ghastly make-believe of wit; – in fact more like 'diluted insanity' (as I defined it) than anything of real jocosity, 'humour', or geniality . . . He was infinitely astonished at my Wife; and her quiet encounter of his too ghastly London wit by cheerful native ditto. Adieu, poor Lamb! He soon after died; as did Badams, much more to the sorrow of us both.[42]

Through Badams Carlyle had also met the seventy-five-year-old William Godwin, father-in-law of Shelley and radical author of the *Enquiry Concerning Political Justice* (1793) and the novel *Caleb Williams* (1794), both of which had been enormously influential on the previous generation in the immediate aftermath of the French Revolution. Carlyle took away a strong impression from the occasion, but, as was usual with him when meeting 'celebrities', by no means a positive one. On 17 August he had sketched Godwin for Jane:

He is a bald, bushy-browed, thick, hoary, hale little figure with spectacles: taciturn enough, and speaking when he does speak with a certain *epigrammatic* spirit; wherein except a little shrewdness there is nothing but the most commonplace character . . . By degrees I hitched myself near him, and was beginning to open him, and open on him, for he had stared twice at me; when suddenly enough began a speaking of French among the Kennys and Badamsinas (for they are all French-English); and presently Godwin was summoned off to – take a hand at whist! *I* had already flatly declined. There did the Philosopher sit, and a swarm of noisy children, chattering women, lounging dilettantes round him; and two women literally crashing hoarse thunder out of a piano (for it was louder than an iron-forge), under pretext of its being music by Rossini. I thought of my own piano, and the far different fingering it got; looked sometimes not without sorrow at the long-nosed whist-player; and in the space of an hour (seeing supper about to be laid in another room) took myself away.[43]

The younger generation of literary and political men whom Carlyle met pleased him better. There was Albany Fonblanque, editor of the radical *Examiner* newspaper, and one of his chief contributors, John Bowring. With the latter Carlyle 'talked copiously, he utterly utilitarian and radical, I utterly mystical and radical'.[44] Reform was the topic of the day; Carlyle attended a debate in the House of Commons in August, and one in the House of Lords in September, in order to hear Jeffrey speak. He revenged himself verbally on Jeffrey's patronage in his account to Jane on 4 September of 'the poor little Darling telling his story like a little King of Elves'.[45]

Later, in his rather intemperate, if funny, reminiscence of his friend, Carlyle recalled that Jeffrey had been 'a Parliamentary failure', 'unadapted to the place'. Reporters complained of his accent, which

was indeed singular, but it was by no means Scotch: at his first going to Oxford (where he did not stay long), he had peremptorily crushed down his Scotch (which he privately had in store, in excellent condition, to the very end of his life, producible with highly ludicrous effect on occasion), and adopted instead a strange swift, sharp-sounding, fitful modulation, part of it pungent, quasi-*latrant* [barking], other parts of it cooing, bantery, lovingly quizzical; which no charm of his fine ringing voice (*metallic* tenor, of sweet tone), and of his vivacious rapid looks and pretty little attitudes and gestures, could altogether reconcile you to; but in which he persisted through good report and bad. Old Braxie (Macqueen, 'Lord *Braxfield*', a sad old cynic, on whom Jeffrey used to set me laughing often enough) was commonly reported to have said, on hearing Jeffrey again after that Oxford sojourn, 'the laddie has clean tint [lost] his Scotch, and found nae English!' – which was an exaggerative reading of the fact, his vowels and syllables being elaborately English (or English and *more*, e.g. 'heppy', 'My Lu'd' etc. etc.), while the *tune* he sang them to was all his own.[46]

Moving among *Edinburgh Review* Whigs and *Examiner* Radicals, Carlyle was soon introduced to Sarah Austin, translator of German works, and her husband the lugubrious John Austin, Professor of Jurisprudence at University College London, 'a lean grayheaded painful-looking man, with large earnest timid eyes, and a clanging metallic voice' who 'set forth Utilitarianism *steeped* in German metaphysics, not dissolved therein'. More attractive than these two was the younger Mill, 'Spirit-of-the-Age' John Stuart Mill. Against the odds, he and Carlyle took to one another immediately.[47]

The young man had famously endured an experimental education at the hands of his father and Jeremy Bentham which consisted of beginning Greek at the age of three and Latin at seven, mastering the dialogues of Plato and the whole of Herodotus before he was ten, followed by a diet of English history and mathematics. The reading of poetry was discouraged in favour of logic (at twelve), with the intention that Mill would grow up to be the perfect calculator and reasoner, the true Utilitarian philosopher who would work out a conclusive theory of society and morals. In 1826, at the age of twenty, Mill had a nervous breakdown when, on asking himself whether, if 'all the changes in institutions and opinions which you are looking forward to, could be completely effected at this very instant', he would be happy, he found the answer to be, as he wrote in his *Autobiography* (1873), in the negative.[48]

Mill slowly made his way out of his despair through reading the poetry of Wordsworth and Coleridge and opening himself to European, specifically German, philosophical and cultural influences. Coleridge's prose writings, so opposite in tendency to the mechanistic empiricism Mill had imbibed as a youth, played their part. So also, as Mill recalled in his *Autobiography*, did 'Carlyle's early articles in the *Edinburgh* and *Foreign* Reviews, though for a long time I saw nothing in these (as my father saw nothing in them to the last) but insane rhapsody'.[49] Carlyle's essays helped to 'enlarge my early narrow creed', though Mill never became a complete disciple of Carlyle's view of the world as a set of symbols to be interpreted by the seeing eye of the prophetic philosopher.

For a time, Carlyle thought he *had* converted the younger man. He described their very first meeting to Jane on 4 September. Mill was 'a slender rather tall and elegant youth' of twenty-five, 'modest, remarkably gifted with precision of utterance'. The two men had 'almost four hours of the best talk I have mingled in for long', and as they walked homewards together from the Austins' house, Mill 'seemed to profess almost as plainly as modesty would allow that he had been converted by the Head of the Mystic School', namely Carlyle.[50]

As soon as Jane arrived and they had set up home in Ampton Street, Carlyle invited Mill to visit. Jane saw how much Mill admired her husband, and told her cousin Helen Welsh on 26 October that she liked him best of 'all the literary people that come about us'.[51] Mill's astute description of Carlyle in a letter to his friend John Sterling is as interesting as Carlyle's of him, giving a good sense of what it was about Carlyle's philosophical and political position that attracted thoughtful people caught between tradition and reform:

He does not seem to me so entirely the reflexion or shadow of the great German writers as I was inclined to consider him; although undoubtedly his mind has derived from their inspiration whatever breath of life is in it. He seems to me as a man who has had his eyes unsealed, and who now looks round him & sees the aspects of things with his own eyes, but by the light supplied by others; not the pure light of day, but another light compounded of the same simple rays but in different proportions. He has by far the largest & widest liberality & tolerance . . . that I have met with in any one; & he differs from most men who see as much as he does into the defects of the age, by a circumstance greatly to his advantage in my estimation, that he looks for a safe landing *before* and not *behind*: he sees that if we could replace things as they once were, we should only retard the final issue, as we should in all human probability go on just as we then did, & arrive again at the very place where we now stand.[52]

Mill added that Carlyle was having no luck with his manuscript; 'no bookseller will publish anything but a political pamphlet in the present state of excitement'. The Reform Bill had been rejected in the Lords, causing unrest among the deprived and unease among the favoured classes. In November Carlyle told his mother of the seething atmosphere in London and elsewhere – riots in Bristol, cholera in many cities – and wrote to Jack (now in Florence) that members of the aristocracy were fortifying their London mansions against expected attacks by disenfranchised mobs.[53] Against this background, he was writing 'Characteristics' for the *Edinburgh Review*, 'a sort of second *Signs of the Times*', as he told Alick on 4 December, his thirty-sixth birthday.[54]

This article, though less surprising and original than its predecessor, attracted the attention of readers who were aware of, and perhaps nervous about, the unstoppable advance of political reform. Once again, Carlyle took no party line, but wrote about the inevitability of change and urged his readers to think about spiritual, as well as material, progress. Trespassing on his own literary ground as mapped out in the perforce unknown 'Teufelsdreck', Carlyle writes of 'worn-out Symbols of the Godlike' and the people who 'keep trimming and trucking between those and Hypocrisy'. Some end in denial, 'and form a theory that there is no theory'. Others 'have dared to say No, and cannot yet say Yea; but feel that in the No they dwell as in a Golgotha, where life enters not, where peace is not appointed them'. One such was Hazlitt, wandering 'on God's verdant earth, like the Unblest on burning deserts; passionately dig[ging] wells, and draw[ing] up only the dry quicksand', wrestling among 'endless Sophisms, doing desperate battle as with spectre-hosts'.[55]

This passage attracted the attention and admiration of the young Robert Louis Stevenson fifty years later, when he read 'Characteristics' in one of the many reprinted editions of Carlyle's *Essays*.[56] Before writing the article Carlyle had been reading Hazlitt's posthumously published *Table Talk*, which he vividly described in his journal in October 1831 as 'an incessant *chew-chewing*, the Nut never cracked, nothing but teeth broken and bleeding gums', the work of a man who 'has thought much; even intently and with vigour: but he has discovered nothing; been able to *believe* nothing. One other sacrifice to the Time!'[57]

Carlyle himself thought 'Characteristics' 'ill written' and feared that no one would understand it.[58] In the event, as was the case with most of his works, he delighted some, disgusted others, and bewildered many. Macaulay, as conscious of Carlyle as the *Edinburgh Review*'s other commanding reviewer as Carlyle was suspiciously aware of him, wrote with dry wit to Macvey Napier on reading the article: 'As to Carlyle, or Carlisle, or whatever his name may be, he might as well write in Irving's unknown tongue at once.'[59] No doubt Napier agreed with him, but he had not found a way of curbing Carlyle. Jeffrey scolded his successor in February 1832, after reading 'Characteristics':

I fear Carlyle will not do, that is, if you do not take the liberties and the pains with him that I did, by striking out freely and writing in occasionally. The misfortune is that he is very obstinate . . . It is a great pity, for he is a man of genius and industry, and with the capacity of being an elegant and impressive writer.[60]

Napier solved the problem by commissioning no more articles from Carlyle after the one on 'Corn-Law Rhymes' which he had already accepted.

Among those who read and admired 'Characteristics' was Leigh Hunt, who sent a little book of his own, *Christianism*, to 'the writer of the article in the Edinburgh Review'. Carlyle invited him to take tea one evening in February 1832; in March he noted in his journal that he found Hunt 'a pleasant, innocent, ingenious man, filled with *Epicurean Philosophy*', but likeable for all that.[61] The two men had no opportunity to take their friendship further, for it had already been decided that the Carlyles would return to Craigenputtoch that spring. Murray had finally rejected 'Teufelsdreck' after receiving a report from his reader, who, though for long thought to have been Lockhart, was in fact another *Quarterly* reviewer, the Reverend Henry Hart Milman. In his report Milman allowed that the work was clever, but he thought it too 'whimsical' for the public and too long for such a *jeu d'esprit*. 'After all', he concluded in comic bewilderment, 'is it a translation or original?'[62]

Two other publishers, Charles Tilt and Charles Wentworth Dilke, looked at the poor scorned manuscript and also turned it down.[63] Charles Buller and John Stuart Mill then read it, at Carlyle's request, neither with much enthusiasm despite their admiration for its author, who at last resigned himself to 'slitting' it up into articles for a magazine, thinking that William Tait might publish them in his new radical journal, *Tait's Edinburgh Magazine*.[64]

Carlyle had made several new acquaintances who were attracted to him, among them Mill, the Austins, Leigh Hunt, Albany Fonblanque, and John Bowring. He was also now sought after by a number of periodical editors. James Fraser 'pestered' him, he wrote in his journal in January, with his 'Dog's meat Cart of a magazine'; he was also being courted by Tait of Edinburgh and Dilke of the *Athenaeum*, 'the bad best of literary Newspaper syllabubs'.[65] With reluctance, but resigned to having little choice but to 'lay out [his] manufacture in one of those Old Clothes shops',[66] he set about writing for them. A paper on a new edition of Boswell's *Life of Samuel Johnson* for Fraser was eventually split into two parts, the first, 'Biography', appearing in *Fraser's Magazine* in April 1832 and the second, on Boswell's *Johnson*, in May.

Fraser also invited him to a literary dinner with a strong Scottish flavour. James Hogg, the 'Ettrick Shepherd', poet and contributor to *Blackwood's Magazine*, had been brought to London in January 1832 by his publisher and was 'walking about the London Streets with a grey Scotch Plaid! The vain goose', as Carlyle told Jack.[67] Fraser held a dinner in his honour, inviting Lockhart, William Fraser, Carlyle, and two other Scottish writers, Allan Cunningham and John Galt. Carlyle noted in his journal that Hogg appeared 'in the mingled character of Zany and raree-show: all bent on bantering him, especially Lockhart' (who had, with Wilson, made unpleasant fun of Hogg for years in the pages of *Blackwood's Magazine*). 'Stupidity, insipidity, even not a little obscenity (in which all save Galt, Fraser and myself seemed to join) was the only outcome of the night.' 'Literary *men*!' he expostulated. 'They are not worthy to be the valets of such.'[68]

Carlyle was not at ease with such people. He hated the puffing and vanity he saw around him. Having been asked by Dilke for 'a scrap of writing with my *name*' for the *Athenaeum*, he had given him a translation of 'Faust's Curse' from Goethe. It appeared in print, with his name, in the window of the *Athenaeum* office in Catherine Street, off the Strand, where Carlyle caught sight of it in passing. He recorded in his journal that he 'hurried on with downcast eyes, as if I had seen myself in the Pillory'.[69] He was also a little ashamed, he confessed to Jack on 16 February, of having consented to a request from James Fraser to 'sit to his Artist'. Daniel Maclise was doing a series of portrait sketches for *Fraser's*. Carlyle went to Regent Street to be drawn 'in foolish attitude, leaning on elbow (it was of his choosing), at full length'.[70] The sketch appeared, making something of a dandy of Carlyle, in *Fraser's* in June 1833.

If Carlyle felt out of his element in these circles, Jane also seems to have been disappointed with her time in London. Very few of her letters survive, but those that do suggest that she was underwhelmed by meeting people such as Lamb, Badams, and the Montagus. She told one of her Liverpool cousins, Mary Welsh, in a letter of December 1831, that she had 'seen most of the Literary people here, and, as Edward Irving said after his first interview with Wordsworth, "I think not of them so highly as I was wont"'. The fierce snowstorms of the last three winters in Craigenputtoch had depressed her and she had succumbed to sore throats and illness; now she found the London winter equally trying: 'one day a ferocious frost; the next a fog, so thick you might put it in your pocket; a dead sea of greencoloured filth under foot; and above an atmosphere like one – of my Uncle's sugar-boilers'.[71]

The 'fine en-thu-si-asm' between her and the romantic Mrs Montagu could not be 'kept alive without more hypocrisy than one of us at least can bring to bear on it', she told Jean Carlyle in January 1832. Fortunately she had a new friendship to hail as a contrast with the old one being discarded. As Mrs Montagu fell away, Sarah Austin rose to fill her place. 'Mrs Austin I have now seen and like infinitely better', she declared. 'If I "swear everlasting friendship" with any woman here it will be with her.'[72]

Jane soon saw, to her delight, that Carlyle was attracting a set of interesting young men to sit at his feet. Charles Buller came up from Cornwall, 'grown a great tower of a fellow, six feet three in height, a yard in breadth', Carlyle told his mother in November 1831. He 'shows great talent, and great natural goodness, which I hope he will by and by turn to notable account'. He came to call, followed by Mill, 'and the two made what Jane called "a pleasant forenoon call of five hours and a half"'.[73] Jane told her mother-in-law that 'enough people come about us to talk, or rather to listen, among whom are several whom I really like'. The chief talker himself was 'in tolerable health and spirits', Mrs Carlyle was told, and had 'abundant prospects of employment'.[74]

The emphasis is meaningful. As both Carlyle and Jane had feared, the prospects turned out to be nothing more than the detested writing for periodicals which Carlyle had already been doing for four years or more, and for which he did not require to be in London. The idea of setting himself up to lecture was abandoned because of the Reform fever and presumably also because of Carlyle's lack of fame beyond the limited circles in which he moved. The plan, therefore, was unchanged from the original cautious one of returning to Scotland in the spring.

★

On 22 January 1832 old James Carlyle died, aged seventy-three. He had written to his son the previous September, anticipating the event:

My dear Son, — I cannot write you a letter, but just tell you that I am a frail old sinner that is very likely never to see you any more in this world. Be that as it may, I could not help telling you that I feel myself gradually drawing towards the hour appointed for all living. And, O God! may that awful change be much at heart with every one of us. May we be daily dying to sin and living to righteousness. And may the God of Jacob be with you and bless you, and keep you in his ways and fear. I add no more, but leave you in his hands and care.

James Carlyle.[75]

News of his father's death reached Carlyle on Tuesday, 24 January. The next day he shut himself away to write a memoir of his father, emerging the following Sunday. The funeral was fixed for Friday, 27 January, giving him no time to travel to Scotsbrig to attend as chief mourner. He told his mother he would see no one until it was over: 'I will be with you in spirit, if not in person.'[76] Jane understood his grief, and helped him through it. He remembered in the days after her own death how tender she had been. A detailed picture arose in his mind of a scene from more than thirty years earlier:

I remember our walk along Holborn forward into the City, and the *bleeding* mood I was in, she wrapping me like the softest of bandages: — in the City somewhere, two Boys fighting with a ring of grinning Blackguards round them; I rushed passionately through, tore the fighters asunder, with some passionate rebuke ('in this world full of death'), she on my arm; and everybody silently complied.[77]

The reminiscence Carlyle wrote of his father is a slightly rambling, utterly spontaneous record of feelings and memories, written with no thoughts of a readership but simply because he was compelled to do it. It became the first in the collection of *Reminiscences* published by Froude immediately after Carlyle's death. Carlyle's memory is of a man who could be frightening to his children and from whom he had felt kept at a distance, but he also expresses his admiration of his proud, honest, pious peasant father. 'I call him a natural man; singularly free from all manner of affectation.'[78] What a contrast existed between this father's life and the lives of those Carlyle was now living among. As he sat in his room in sophisticated, reform-fevered London, he dwelt in spirit once more in the distant villages of Annandale where hard work, poverty, near illiteracy, and strict religious piety had ruled over the simple lives of his family and — until he escaped them — himself.

Carlyle recalled how proud his father had been on his son's last visit to Scotsbrig in August 1831, before embarking for London:

What he had never done the like of before, he said, on hearing me express something which he admired: 'Man, it's surely a pity that thou should sit yonder, with nothing but the Eye of Omniscience to see thee; and thou, with such a gift to speak.' His eyes were sparkling mildly, with a kind of deliberate joy.[79]

The man with the gift to speak had not yet – not quite – found an audience wider than the readership of the *Edinburgh Review*, but this was about to change. A piece of writing Carlyle had agreed to do for *Fraser's Magazine* chimed in with his mood in the weeks following his father's death. On 13 January he noted in his journal that he had spent nearly three weeks reading Boswell's *Life of Samuel Johnson* in a new edition by the *Quarterly* reviewer John Croker. For this review, he intended to 'try whether I cannot get into a more *currente calamo* [with flowing pen] style of writing',[80] knowing that his usual style was found too outlandish by many. By 21 January he was writing the introductory part on biography in general, in which he briefly introduced a German professor, Gottfried Sauerteig (i.e. leaven), to give his opinions on history as 'the essence of innumerable Biographies', and to claim the usefulness of the small life – so long as it is illuminating – alongside the lives of kings and generals. Carlyle uses the word 'environment' in the modern sense (where before him it had meant the act of encircling) to explain what was needed in historical writing,[81] an idea he developed in the companion essay on Croker's Boswell's Johnson.

This second article, written after the death of his father (with his small obscure life), is a quite brilliant piece of writing. Carlyle first brings all his wit to bear against Croker's editing. 'The Editor will punctually explain what is already sun-clear', and will poke unwanted editorial information into the middle of Boswell's text by means of interruptive brackets which 'stitch you in from half a page to twenty or thirty pages of a Hawkins, Tyers, Murphy, Piozzi'. Worse, he strikes in with his mean-minded assumptions that 'Need and Greed' and 'Vainglory' are the only possible human motives, so that, for example, 'when we know that Johnson *loved* his good Wife', Croker opens his 'two closed lips' to tell us that Johnson married her only for convenience.[82]

Having thus disposed of the editor, Carlyle turns to Boswell. He offers a revision of the usual view of Boswell as a 'wine-bibber and gross liver', a 'vain, heedless babbler' with 'much of the sycophant, alternating with the braggadocio, curiously spiced too with an all-pervading dash of the coxcomb'. None of this can be denied, he concedes, then gives vent to a marvellously expressed insight:

And now behold the worthy Bozzy, so prepossessed and held back by nature and by art, fly nevertheless like iron to its magnet, whither his better genius called! You may surround the iron and the magnet with what enclosures and encumbrances you please, – with wood, with rubbish, with brass: it matters not, the two feel each other, they struggle restlessly towards each other, they *will* be together. The iron may be a Scottish squirelet, full of gulosity [gluttony] and 'gigmanity'; the magnet an English plebeian, and moving rag-and-dust mountain, coarse, proud, irascible, imperious: nevertheless, behold how they embrace, and inseparably cleave to one another!

Ideas which are embedded deep and for the moment invisible in the 'Teufelsdreck' manuscript, and which will in due course be embodied in Carlyle's distinctive historical works and his lectures 'On Heroes', have a bright preliminary airing in this article. Boswell is offered as the unlikely example of the 'Loyalty, Discipleship, all that was ever meant by *Hero-worship*' which 'lives perennially in the human bosom, and waits, even in these dead days, only for occasions to unfold it, and inspire all men with it, and again make the world alive!' And because Boswell gives us the man Johnson in his 'whole personal Environment', his biography will live while countless works which 'keep dinning in my ears that a man named George the Third was born and bred up, and a man named George the Second died', 'that debates were held, and infinite jarring and jargoning took place', are consigned to oblivion:

The thing I want to see is not Redbook Lists, and Court Calendars, and Parliamentary Registers, but the LIFE OF MAN in England: what men did, thought, suffered, enjoyed; the form, especially the spirit, of their terrestrial existence, its outward environment, its inward principle; *how* and *what* it was; whence it proceeded, whither it was tending.

And Johnson himself? Having skewered Croker and rehabilitated Boswell, Carlyle turns to the shambling genius, an Ariel 'encased in the coarse hulls of a Caliban', 'a poetic soul' imprisoned in 'an inert, unsightly body', whose life presents an example of the ultimate triumph over adversity. How could Carlyle do other than identify with Johnson's poor, obscure background, his proud silent stoicism when a student at Oxford, so poor that 'the toes of the man are looking through his shoes', his wounded 'retreat into his father's mean home', his ghastly experiment with schoolteaching? Johnson enters London without firing of cannon or flourish of drums and trumpets; he 'creeps into lodgings in Exeter Street, Strand'. He works at his dictionary without patronage or encouragement, writing, when the task is at last finished, to the now interested Lord Chesterfield that his offer of help has come too late: 'Is not a patron, my Lord, one who looks with unconcern on a man struggling for life in the water, and when he has reached ground, encumbers him with help?' Every word of this Carlyle feels with personal force.

He divulges in a footnote that while preparing the article he visited Gough Square (not far from his Ampton Street lodgings) to look at Johnson's house and stand in the very room – a small bedroom – in which Johnson worked, not forgetting also 'the three garret bedrooms where his three copyists sat and wrote'. Though himself on the whole a dutiful son,

Carlyle experiences with Johnson his guilt at having once disobeyed and disobliged his father by refusing to run Michael Johnson's bookstall in Uttoxeter market one day when his father was ill and could not go. Fifty years to the day, Johnson did voluntary penance by visiting Uttoxeter and standing for an hour with his head uncovered on the spot where his father's stall used to be.

Carlyle wrote this article in the weeks after his own father's death, immediately after plunging into his own obscure past. Small wonder that the Boswell essay has such clarity and strength of honest feeling. Though much too good for *Fraser's Magazine*, it had the unexpected but deserved consequence that James Fraser, finding that his readers liked the Johnson article, as well they might, eventually agreed to publish *Sartor Resartus* in monthly parts in his 'scavenger-cart of a Magazine'.[83]

★

The Carlyles left London on 24 March 1832. There was a sad reunion with Carlyle's mother and siblings, then a visit to Mrs Welsh at Templand. The announcement in *The Times* on 2 April of Goethe's death at Weimar prompted Carlyle to write to Alick that he felt as if he had lost a second father.[84] Requests soon came from periodical editors for him to memorialise Goethe. Abraham Hayward, a barrister and translator of *Faust* whom Carlyle had met in London, wrote to him on behalf of Edward Lytton Bulwer, editor of the recently founded *New Monthly Magazine*, who was keen to have a comprehensive account of Goethe's life and influence. 'I told him', wrote Hayward flatteringly, 'that there was no living Englishman but you who could do it as it ought to be done, and [A. W.] Schlegel says the same.'[85]

Carlyle wrote three essays: a brief account to accompany a rather inappropriately caricaturish sketch of Goethe for *Fraser's Magazine*; a slightly longer essay, 'Death of Goethe', for the June number of the *New Monthly Magazine*; and a full-length, somewhat rambling article on 'Goethe's Works' – Carlyle himself described it as a 'desultory, rhapsodic concern of 44 pages' – for Cochrane's *Foreign Quarterly Review*.[86] In all of them, Carlyle invokes Goethe as the great example of the hero as a man of letters, the 'World-Poet' who struggled 'out of darkness into light', wrote works which rehearsed that struggle, and through his art gave hope to others.[87]

In early May he went down to Scotsbrig to read his father's will. 'All was methodical, just, decisive'; the estate of nearly £600 was divided among those children who had 'helped by their toil to earn it', Carlyle having previously dissuaded his father from including himself and Jack on the grounds that they had already received their share in the form of an education.[88] With the will business settled amicably, he returned to Craigenputtoch, where Jane was hiring a new servant and supervising the painting of the house.

Carlyle's main correspondent now was Mill, to whom he wrote self-consciously from 'our Patmos', contrasting the 'whinstone mountains' with 'the life-torrent of Fleet Street', and describing the idyllic summer weather and satisfying outdoor occupations he was enjoying, while at the same time expressing his eagerness to hear all the news from London.[89] The Reform Bill was finally passed on 4 June, enfranchising £10 householders like Carlyle himself, who was moved during the last weeks of the Bill's passage to write introspectively in his notebook:

The only reform is in *thyself*. Know this O Politician, and be moderately political.

For me I have never yet done any one political act; not so much as the signing of a petition. My case is this. I comport myself wholly like an alien; like a man who is not in his own country; whose own country lies perhaps a century or two distant.[90]

Mill could keep him up to date with radicalism, philosophy, and London gossip of all sorts. Though Carlyle found Mill's letters 'too speculative', he reckoned him nevertheless 'an excellent person, and his love to *me* is great!'[91] In July Mill described the 'edification' he had derived from reading Carlyle's articles, particularly 'your paper on Johnson'. He found it useful to define himself by explicit contrast to Carlyle: he was only 'a logical expounder', while his correspondent was that much higher being, 'an artist'. Indeed, Carlyle was 'perhaps the only genuine one now living in this country'. 'The highest destiny of all lies in that direction; for it is the artist alone in whose hands Truth becomes impressive, and a living principle in action.'[92]

This was music to Carlyle's ears, for even the most determined 'alien', if he has a message to deliver, delights in having an appreciative listener. Even as Mill wrote so pleasingly, however, he was letting Carlyle know that he could not be a complete disciple, but would always differ on the spiritual question. That mattered surprisingly little to Carlyle, who relished debating and declaiming in his letters to Mill, taking comfort from the genuine admiration of this honest, intelligent man with a background and training so different from his own. In his *Autobiography* Mill recalled how he had felt that Carlyle

was a poet, and that I was not; that he was a man of intuition, which I was not; and that as such, he not only saw many things long before me, which I could only, when they were pointed out to me, hobble after and prove, but that it was highly probable he could see many things which were not visible to me even after they were pointed out.[93]

It is a neat encapsulation of the difference between the two men; if there is an implied criticism in the concluding remark (i.e. that Carlyle sometimes saw what was not there), there is also a recognition of something positively visionary about him.

While Carlyle worked on his articles, Jane spent the summer relearning how to bake bread and run a house on a shoestring. She wrote cheerfully in June to Eliza Miles at Ampton Street, describing the quiet summer routine into which she and Carlyle had settled, their days beginning with

such a surprising breakfast of home-baked bread, and eggs, etc., etc., as might incite anyone that had breakfasted in London to write a pastoral. Then Carlyle takes to his writing, while I, like Eve, 'studious of the household good' [*Paradise Lost*, IX, 233], inspect my house, my garden, my live stock, gather flowers for my drawingroom, and lapfuls of eggs; and finally betake myself also to writing, or reading, or making or mending, or whatever work seems fittest.[94]

Her 'writing' seems to have been a translation from Goethe; at least that is what Carlyle told Jack on 2 July in the course of an interesting passage:

As to Craigenputtoch, it is, as formerly, the scene of scribble-scribbling. Jane is in a weakly way still, but I think clearly gathering strength. Her Life beside me constantly writing here is but a dull one: however, she seems to desire no other; has, in many things, pronounced the word *Entsagen* [renunciation], and looks with a brave if with no joyful heart into the present and the future. She manages all things: poultry, flowers, bread-loaves; keeps a house still like a bandbox: then reads, or works (as at present) on some Translation from Goethe. I tell her many times there is *much* for her to do, if she were trained to it: her whole Sex to deliver from the bondage of Frivolity Dollhood and Imbecility into the freedom of Valour and Womanhood.[95]

Might the description of Jane's 'brave' but not 'joyful' heart refer obliquely to disappointment that no children had been born to them? A poem which Froude discovered among Jane's papers may suggest as much. The verses probably belong to this summer of 1832. They are written from 'The Desert' – Craigenputtoch – and are wistfully suggestive. Though it is possible that Carlyle wrote them, rather than Jane, they have a relatively easy and regular rhythm, which suggests they are hers:

To a Swallow building under our Eaves

Thou too hast travelled, little fluttering thing –
Hast seen the world, and now thy weary wing
    Thou too must rest.
But much, my little bird, couldst thou but tell,
I'd give to know why here thou lik'st so well
    To build thy nest.

For thou hast passed fair places in thy flight;
A world lay all beneath thee where to light;
   And, strange thy taste,
Of all the varièd scenes that met thine eye –
Of all the spots for building 'neath the sky –
   To choose this waste.

In truth, I rather take it thou hast got
By instinct wise much sense about thy lot,
   And hast small care
Whether an Eden or a desert be
Thy home so thou remain'st alive, and free
   To skim the air.

God speed thee, pretty bird; may thy small nest
With little ones all in good time be blest.
   I love thee much;
For well thou managest that life of thine,
While I! Oh, ask not what I do with mine!
   Would I were such!

The Desert.[96]

The burden of the poem, as also of Carlyle's remarks, is that Jane felt under-occupied. In the absence of children to look after she perhaps thought of doing some sort of writing, in which she seems to have been half encouraged by Carlyle with his grand talk of her freeing her sex from the bondage of frivolity, though what he meant by the phrase 'if she were trained to it' is unclear. In December 1833 Carlyle reported to his mother that Jane was writing – '*what* she will not tell me'; the following February Jane herself told Jack, 'The notebook you gave me is half filled; with such multifarious matter; no Mortal gets a glimpse of it.'[97]

This notebook seems to have disappeared. We cannot know if it contained, as later ones did, stories from her childhood and youth; or did it give an account of her life at Craigenputtoch? Was there even an attempt at a novel, the genre for which Jane's talents seemed best to fit her? Unfortunately, something – her own diffidence or Carlyle's taking up all the available writing space, as it were – prevented her from fulfilling herself intellectually and imaginatively. She fell back on victorious housekeeping, about which Carlyle was complacent, though both would suffer from her ultimate dissatisfaction in that limited role. And of course she wrote her incomparable letters with their miniature dramatic narratives.

★

A sign of Carlyle's self-imposed status as 'alien' appears in his devil-may-care way of bringing unexplained pseudonyms and initials into his periodical writing. Professor Sauerteig, first introduced in 'Biography' in *Fraser's* in April 1832, was to reappear as 'our friend Herr Sauerteig' in the same magazine in July and August 1833 in articles on 'Count Cagliostro', the eighteenth-century adventurer and swindler. Meanwhile, Carlyle invented 'Smelfungus Redivivus' in the *Edinburgh Review* essay on 'Corn-Law Rhymes' (July 1832), using a name borrowed from Sterne's *Sentimental Journey* (1768); and in 'Goethe's Works' in the *Foreign Quarterly Review* for August 1832 he quoted 'a continental Humorist, of deep-piercing, resolute though strangely perverse faculty, whose works are as yet but sparingly if at all cited in English literature'. This turned out to be 'D. Teufelsdröckh', author of '*Die Kleider: ihr Werden und Wirken.* Weissnichtwo Stillschweign'sche Buchhandlung, 1830' (*Clothes: Their Origin and Influence*, Know-not-Where, Silent Publishers), who, as Carlyle almost alone among mortals knew, had no existence outside the pages of his unpublished manuscript, and so was until this moment not at all 'cited in English literature'.[98]

Carlyle revelled in this combination of humour and private revenge, this mystification of an unknowing and perforce uncaring public. He told Jack gleefully in August that he had received a letter from London 'asking *where* Teufelsdreck's great work (*Die Kleider*) was to be fallen in with!' His correspondent was Adolphus Bernays, Professor of German at King's College London, whom Carlyle had met at a dinner and who now asked 'who der Teufel is Teufelsdreck, & where [have you] aufgegabelt [picked up] this odd book of his?'[99]

There was a kind of solitary fun to be had from this kind of thing, but even Carlyle began to pine for congenial company and conversation. Jane wrote frankly to her mother-in-law in September, announcing that they planned to spend part of the winter in Edinburgh: 'Carlyle is going mad for speech – and proposes making a descent on the capital about the beginning of winter and filling it with a whole deluge of articulate sound.' She added with disconcerting sharpness, 'I mean to look about me for a parrot while there, that he may not be so ill off in time coming.'[100]

On 10 October Jane asked Eliza Stodart to look out for 'a little furnished house to contain my husband self and a maid for as many months as we see good to exchange our country life for your town one'. She told Eliza, whom she rebuked for not having written to her for over a year, that she had suffered 'prolonged bad health and worse spirits' before, during, and after the London sojourn. 'A few days before I left London', she added, 'a certain Dr Allan said to Carlyle in a complimentary tone as I left the room – "Mrs Carlyle has the remains of a fine woman!" think of that now! at thirty to pass for a remains!'[101]

The move to Edinburgh was delayed by the illness and death of Jane's grandfather at Templand in November. Jane went to help her mother during his last days, and returned with some anxiety about Mrs Welsh's future. 'Her plans are unknown to me and I believe uncertain to herself', Jane told Eliza.[102] Eliza found the Carlyles some rooms in a house in Stockbridge, not far from Comely Bank, and they moved in on 7 January 1833. Carlyle informed Jack, now in Rome, of their new address, and confided that he did not think he could stay for ever at Craigenputtoch, but would soon choose between Edinburgh and London. He also sent news of the recent election, the first since the Reform Act of June. Jeffrey had been voted in at Edinburgh, and Buller at Liskeard in Cornwall. 'The Whigs prevail everywhere: only some five or six *perfect* Radicals', he wrote, adding cheerfully, 'the Tories may drink hemlock when they please, for they are extinct not to be re-illumed'. He himself had not voted; 'in thought, I am the deepest radical alive in this island, but allow it to rest there, having other to do'.[103]

It soon became clear yet again that Carlyle and Edinburgh did not agree. He told Mill on 12 January that though the city had no fogs – the 'horrid flood of Spartan black-broth one has to inhale in London' – it was irredeemably '*kleinstädtisch*' (provincial) and lacking in stimulating company.[104] 'All is Whiggery here', he wrote in his journal on 1 February, though the Tory town council was still filling university chairs with political appointees; of his old Edinburgh acquaintances, Jeffrey had gone to London to 'join the new Reformed Parliament', Wilson was avoiding him on political grounds, he thought, and De Quincey was now wholly invisible, having gone to ground to avoid debtors' prison.[105] Only the philosopher Sir William Hamilton pleased him; otherwise Edinburgh was 'a wretched *infidel* place', he told Jack in May.[106]

By spring 1833 the Carlyles were back in Dumfriesshire, Jane feeling weak with flu. 'Teufelsdreck', now 'cut into slips', was to come out in *Fraser's Magazine*.[107] Carlyle had been talking of printing it as a book at his own expense if ever he could spare £50 or £60, but that day never came, though Jack had repeatedly offered to pay for publication now that he had received his handsome salary from Lady Clare. In the autumn of 1832 he had sent £135, but Carlyle had refused to use any of it, on the grounds that Jack would need it to set up in medical practice. Poor Jack was not permitted to put his relationship with his older brother on an even footing. He was obliged to remain in Carlyle's debt for all the 'hard-earned money' Carlyle had previously given him to study and further his career.[108]

Carlyle looked forward to his brother's return. 'We will front the world together', he wrote in May 1833, declaring also in a ringing tone: 'Outwardly and inwardly a kind of closing of the First Act goes on with me; the second as yet quite *unopened*.'[109] This probably refers to his decision to leave Craigenputtoch for good, and perhaps to his delayed resolution to publish *Sartor Resartus* – it was now that he began to use that 'whimsical title' for his manuscript, as he told Mill in July.[110] His journal during the early months of 1833 contains several entries in which he scrutinises his spiritual condition. On 13 February he wrote, 'Oh for *Faith!*' and 'I often look on my mother (nearly the only genuine *Believer* I know of) with a kind of sacred admiration. Know the worth of Belief; alas! canst thou acquire none?'[111] The year 1832 had been both publicly and privately a turning point for Carlyle, with the momentous Reform Act and the deaths of his father and Goethe early in the year, followed by those of Bentham in June and Walter Scott in September, events indicative of changing times.

Jack arrived home and stayed at Craigenputtoch for a few weeks in June and July, reading Italian with Jane and telling her that all her headaches and general ill health would be cured if she could find 'some agreeable occupation to fill [her] whole mind', a diagnosis with which at present she was inclined to agree.[112] On 28 July she told Eliza Stodart that her brother-in-law was planning to return to Italy after all, to spend another two years with Lady Clare. Showing a trace of irritation that Carlyle had been prepared to make his next move (and therefore hers too) dependent on his brother's decisions, she added that John's new plan meant 'that our movements will not for the present be determined by *his* choice of a settlement'.[113]

On Sunday, 25 August a rare visitor lifted the usually silent knocker on the Carlyles' door. It was Ralph Waldo Emerson, a thirty-year-old scholar from Boston who had been until recently a Unitarian preacher. Doubts about doctrine had made him resign his post the previous summer; his wife had died; Emerson was ill and depressed. At Christmas 1832 he set off for Europe, visiting Italy and France before making for Britain, where he intended to see as many great men as he could.

'Like most young men of the time', he remembered in his book on England, *English Traits* (1856), 'I was much indebted to the men of the Edinburgh Review, and my narrow and desultory reading had inspired the wish to see the faces of three or four writers, – Coleridge, Wordsworth, Landor, De Quincey, and the latest and strongest contributor to the critical journals, Carlyle . . . If Goethe had been still living, I might have wandered into Germany also.'[114] Emerson's attention had been drawn to Goethe by Carlyle, as is amply demonstrated by his journals for the troubled year 1832, with their frequent references to, and quotations from, Carlyle's essays and his *Life of Schiller*.[115]

Having visited Coleridge at Highgate, and seen other London literary men, Emerson travelled to Edinburgh, where he met Alexander Ireland, who inquired on his behalf after Carlyle's address. Ireland's wife, in her biography of Jane Carlyle, recalled that Emerson 'found his way, after many hindrances, to Craigenputtoch'; 'he had the grand American indifference as to our petty distances', and 'would not be deterred by a score or so of barren miles of moorland'.[116] Emerson had letters of introduction from Gustave d'Eichthal and John Stuart Mill in his pocket; he arrived at dinner time on 25 August and was warmly invited to stay overnight before pursuing his journey to the Lake District on his way to Liverpool to embark for home. Carlyle told various correspondents about the sudden arrival of this unknown American admirer, whom he found 'a most gentle, recommendable, amiable, whole-hearted man'. He stayed 'four and twenty hours; and was thro' the whole Encyclopedia with me in that time'. To his mother Carlyle wrote, 'Jane says, it is the first journey ever since Noah's Deluge undertaken to Craigenputtoch for such a purpose'[117] – which is probably no exaggeration.

Jane summed up the visit for Henry Inglis in November, treating it as the highlight of their lives since their return to Craigenputtoch:

John Mill had to go to France; so we were disappointed of him . . . and were thankful to Providence for the windfall of a stray American, 'come out for to see whatsoever things were wise and of good report' [Philippians 4:8] – from one end of Europe to the other. With such accuracy of investigation did he prosecute this object, that he arrived, by paths unknown, at the door of Craigenpootoch, which was, of course, opened to him with all the pleasure in life. To find the Christian charities inside, and even the Graces seemed to occasion him the most agreeable surprise. Carlyle had been represented to his transatlantic imagination, quite *Teufelsdreckish*, – a man severe – living in complete isolation, and partial barbarism: the Individual before his bodily eyes was shaven and shorn, overflowing with the milk of human kindness, *und mit Weib im Haus* [and with a wife in the house].[118]

For his part, Emerson was captivated by the Carlyles. He told Ireland that he had found Carlyle 'most simple and frank':

He talks finely – seems to love the broad Scotch, and I loved him very much at once. I am afraid he finds his entire solitude tedious, but I could not help congratulating him upon his treasure in his wife & I hope they will not leave the moors. Tis so much better for a man of letters to nurse himself in seclusion than to be filed down to the common level by the compliances & imitations of city society.[119]

If Jane had seen this, she would have recommended Emerson to try living as the wife of a secluded genius and spending a winter at Craigenputtoch.

In the days immediately following this flying visit, as he travelled on to talk to Wordsworth in the Lakes, Emerson filled his notebook with his impressions. Stopping over in Carlisle on 26 August, he noted of Carlyle that he had never seen 'more amiableness than is in his countenance. He speaks broad Scotch with evident relish, "in London yonder", "I liked it well", "aboot it", Ay Ay, &c &c.'[120]

Emerson recollected the visit in *English Traits*. There he gives a full description of Carlyle's appearance – 'tall and gaunt, with a cliff-like brow' – and demeanour – 'self-possessed, holding his extraordinary powers of conversation in easy command'. Emerson had been struck by his propensity to invent nicknames for all sorts of phenomena:

He had names of his own for all the matters familiar to his discourse. 'Blackwood's' [actually *Tait's*] was the 'sand magazine'; 'Fraser's' nearer approach to possibility of life, was the 'mud magazine'; a piece of road near by that marked some failed enterprise was the 'grave of the last sixpence'.

Carlyle on books was also recorded:

Gibbon he called the splendid bridge from the old world to the new. His own reading had been multifarious. Tristram Shandy was one of his first books after Robinson Crusoe, and Robertson's America an early favourite. Rousseau's Confessions had discovered to him that he was not a dunce; and it was now ten years since he had learned German, by the advice of a man who told him he would find in that language what he wanted.[121]

Emerson remembered discussing London with his host:

He was already turning his eyes towards London with a scholar's appreciation. London is the heart of the world, he said, wonderful only from the mass of human beings. He liked the huge machine. Each keeps its own round. The baker's boy brings muffins to the window at a fixed hour every day, and that is all the Londoner knows or wishes to know on the subject. But it turned out good men. He named certain individuals, especially one man of letters, his friend, the best mind he knew [John Stuart Mill], whom London had well served.[122]

Naturally Carlyle's name arose when Emerson visited Wordsworth at his home Rydal Mount after leaving Craigenputtoch. The stately old poet criticised his writing as obscure, though clever. 'Carlyle he thinks insane sometimes. I stoutly defended Carlyle', wrote Emerson.[123] Once back in America, Emerson continued to follow Carlyle's career with interest, talked of him to his friends, and was soon in a position to help find an American audience for the man he had chosen, from all the great men across the Atlantic, as his spiritual mentor.

★

Winter 1833-4 was spent braving the cold winds and rain of Craigenputtoch. For the very last time Carlyle attempted to get an academic post with Jeffrey's help. The failure of the project caused a rift between the two men so deep (on Carlyle's side) that it never completely mended. The position of Professor of Astronomy at Edinburgh was advertised in January 1834; Carlyle asked Jeffrey if he would support an application. The reply was uncompromising: 'My dear Friend – It is best to tell you at once that I dont think there is the least chance of you getting the chair of astronomy – & that it wd be idle to make an application.'

Jeffrey would not presume to judge whether Carlyle had 'the proper *scientific* qualifications for the place', but he was prepared to judge Carlyle's suitability as a teacher. Such a post is 'a useful and noble one', he wrote,

but you cannot actually exercise it, unless you offer to teach what is thought worth learning, and in a way that is thought agreeable – and I am afraid you have not fulfilled either of these conditions. You know I do not myself set much value on the paradoxes & exaggerations in which you delight – and at all events I am quite clear that no man ever did more to obstruct the success of his doctrines by the tone in which he promulgated them.[124]

Carlyle described Jeffrey's letter to Jack as 'a kind of polite Fishwoman-shriek', but took comfort in his mother's remark, 'He canna hinder thee of God's Providence'.[125] It was at last clear to Carlyle that Providence did not intend him to be a professor.

Meanwhile *Sartor Resartus* began its serial publication in *Fraser's* in November 1833, having been heralded in June by Maclise's dandified sketch of Carlyle and an accompanying description of the author by William Maginn, a heavy-handed parody of Carlyle's 'Germanic' style.[126] The book which contained so much of Carlyle's spiritual biography – the bullied schoolboy, the discontented student, the young man whose faith is undermined and re-established – and so much of his hard-won anti-materialism, anti-cant, and anti-sham philosophy crept thus belatedly into print in a middle-of-the-road magazine known more for its pranks than for philosophy.

Sartor Resartus is certainly full of jokes, but they rely on a range of literary and linguistic allusion far beyond the reach of the average magazine reader or critic. Drawing on the satirical tradition of Rabelais, Voltaire, Swift, and Sterne, the prophetic tradition of the Bible (the most quoted text in *Sartor*), and the rhapsodic elements in recent German writers from Goethe to Jean Paul Richter, Carlyle moves between wit and wisdom, fun and philosophy. Teufelsdröckh's treatise on clothes, with its doctrine that the visionary sees through them to the man beneath, is presented in extravagant prose:

Happy he who can look through the Clothes of a Man (the woollen, and fleshly, and official Bank-paper and State-paper Clothes), into the Man himself; and discern, it may be, in this or the other Dread Potentate, a more or less incompetent Digestive-apparatus; yet also an inscrutable venerable Mystery, in the meanest Tinker that sees with eyes![127]

Carlyle and Teufelsdröckh chart their shared path from religious scepticism, 'the Everlasting No', to the embracing of a 'new Mythus', a spirit of religion freed from the 'old clothes' of church dogma and tradition, but freed also from that temporary sojourn in the barren landscape of atheism, 'the vast, gloomy, solitary Golgotha, and Mill of Death'. The spirit of wonder, of recognising the supernatural in nature, is affirmed.[128]

Readers, when they eventually materialised, responded to the uplifting rhetoric, and also to Carlyle's eloquent hatred of hypocrisy and his concern for the poor and disadvantaged. The first main object of his satire is the Church of England with its shovel hats and bishops' aprons, outward signs of the Church's worldliness. Against these Carlyle pits the founding Quaker George Fox, a shoemaker whose break from the complacent Church is symbolised by his going out into the woods to make himself a 'perennial suit of Leather'. 'Stitch away, thou noble Fox', exclaims Teufelsdröckh; 'every prick of that little instrument is pricking into the heart of Slavery, and World-worship, and the Mammon-god.'[129]

The other chief victim of Carlyle's righteous wrath is dandyism, a disgraceful aristocratic fad insulting to the wretched poor. Carlyle resorts to the Swiftian trick of seeming to approve. First he 'quotes' the 'Articles of Faith' from the dandy's 'Bible', Bulwer's fashionable novel, *Pelham* (1828):

1. Coats should have nothing of the triangle about them; at the same time wrinkles behind should be carefully avoided.
2. The collar is a very important point: it should be low behind, and slightly rolled.
3. No licence of fashion can allow a man of delicate taste to adopt the posterial luxuriance of a Hottentot.
4. There is safety in a swallow-tail.
5. The good sense of a gentleman is nowhere more finely developed than in his rings.
6. It is permitted to mankind, under certain restrictions, to wear white waistcoats.
7. The trousers must be exceedingly tight across the hips.

(This is actually a comic pastiche of a set of no less preposterous 'Maxims' set out by Pelham in Bulwer's novel; they include the following: 'There is an indifference to please in a stocking down at heel – but there may be a malevolence in a diamond ring.')[130]

Carlyle continues with *faux* innocence:

In strange contrast with this Dandiacal Body stands another British Sect, originally, as I understand, of Ireland, where its chief seat still is; but known also in the main Island, and indeed everywhere rapidly spreading . . . in England they are generally called the *Drudge* Sect; also, unphilosophically enough, the *White Negroes*; and, chiefly in scorn by those of other communions, the *Ragged-Beggar* Sect. In Scotland, again, I find them entitled *Hallanshakers*, or the *Stook of Duds* Sect; any individual communicant is named *Stook of Duds* (that is, Shock of Rags), in allusion, doubtless, to their professional Costume. While in Ireland, which, as mentioned, is their grand parent hive, they go by a perplexing multiplicity of designations, such as *Bogtrotters, Redshanks, Ribbonmen, Cottiers, Peep-of-Day Boys, Babes of the Wood, Rockites, Poor-Slaves*.

The articles of faith of *this* sect appear to be 'the two Monastic Vows, of Poverty and Obedience', especially the former, which, 'it is said, they observe with great strictness'.[131]

Carlyle's onslaught on Bulwer's novel was in tune with recent attacks in *Fraser's* by Maginn, Thackeray, and others, as Carlyle knew. Indeed, in offering *Sartor* to James Fraser in May 1833, he described it in terms calculated to appeal to the publisher whose magazine he despised but was obliged to court if he wished to get his unlucky manuscript published at all. *Sartor* was, he said, 'a kind of Didactic Novel; but indeed properly *like* nothing yet extant'. It might be called a 'Satirical Extravaganza on Things in General'. The creed promulgated 'is *mine*, and *firmly believed*', but the 'editor' of Teufelsdröckh's treatise has a kind of 'Anti-Quack' character which 'would suit *Fraser* perhaps better than any other Magazine'.[132]

Carlyle had long had Bulwer in his sights. He had offered to make 'a sort of sally on *Fashionable Novels*', particularly Bulwer's, for the *Edinburgh Review* in January 1831, only to be told by Napier that Bulwer was a friend and contributor.[133] Now he took advantage of his free rein in *Sartor* to fix Bulwer and his novels as heartless trash. Tennyson, one of many writers who later entered the fray against Bulwer, picked up the rhetoric of *Sartor* when he described Bulwer to Richard Monckton Milnes in 1837 as sitting 'to all posterity astride upon the nipple of Literary Dandyism'.[134]

It would be a long time before *Sartor* truly entered the nation's consciousness; when it did, the impression was deep and lasting, ranging from the response of an Edinburgh student, Francis Espinasse, who 'lighted' on the book in 1841 and found it 'the *Pilgrim's Progress* of the nineteenth century', to Oscar Wilde, who included *Sartor Resartus* among the books he requested from his prison cell in July 1896.[135]

When *Sartor* began publication in the winter of 1833–4, however, such appreciation lay some way in the future. Meanwhile, both Carlyles were preoccupied with anxieties about their mothers. Mrs Welsh was now alone at Templand; she and Jane seem to have agreed that they could not live together, so there was no question of her moving in with the Carlyles. Nor was it decided that Carlyle's mother should join them when her future residence became a matter of family discussion in late 1833 and early 1834. Both Jean and James were planning to get married, Jean to her cousin James Aitken, a house painter whom the family disliked as much as they did Mary's husband, James Austin. Carlyle, called on by the others to intervene, refused to advise Jean against the marriage, which took place in November 1833. 'He is not worthy of Jean', Carlyle thought, but Jean was resolute. Carlyle and Jane attended the wedding, though Jean had written that she did not mind if they 'would much rather avoid such a thing' – weddings being not very cheerful affairs in the Carlyle family. The youngest brother James was also determined to marry 'that Miss Calvert of his', as Carlyle told Jack disparagingly.[136]

There was much worrying on Carlyle's part about which of the sons and daughters should provide a home for their mother. He seems to have made no suggestion of having her at Craigenputtoch, and a letter from Jack to Mrs Carlyle in February 1834 hints at the impossibility of her and Jane sharing a house:

I should however disapprove much of your trying to live at Craigenputtoch, I am sure it would never do for you, it is so different from all you have been accustomed to. And then it is not as if Tom were settled there. I hope to see him come out of that wilderness ere long were it but to some cottage among civilised men.[137]

Jack did not have to wait long for this eventuality. Mrs Carlyle declared she would be happy to live at Scotsbrig with James and his wife Isabella after their wedding in June 1834, being ready to move on to one of her daughters if that proved uncongenial. The Carlyles were thus relieved of responsibility for their mothers. They finally turned their backs on windswept Dumfriesshire moors and unwelcoming Edinburgh, and decided on London once more. Liking to see Providence taking a hand in the major decisions of his life, Carlyle welcomed the surprise announcement by their servant Grace that she wanted to leave them to go home in May. Carlyle told Jack excitedly on 25 February:

After meditating on it for a few minutes, we said to one another: 'Why not *bolt*, out of all these rocky despicabilities, of . . . peat-moss, and isolation, and exasperation, and confusion, and go at once to London?' *Gedacht, gethan* [no sooner thought than done]! Two days after, we had a Letter on the road to Mrs Austin to look out among the 'Houses to Let' for us, and an advertisement for M'Diarmid to try for the letting of our own. Since then, you may fancy, our heads and hearts have been full enough of this great enterprise; the greatest (small as it is) that I ever knowingly engaged in.

Jane added her twopence-worth at the end of this long letter. 'Here is a new prospect opened up to us with a vengeance!' she exclaimed. 'Am I frightened? not a bit.'[138]

Leigh Hunt, who had written to say he now lived in a delightful house, big enough for his ten children, 'at Chelsea, all wainscotted &c for 30 guineas',[139] was asked to 'fish Chelsea' for a similar one for the Carlyles, while Sarah Austin offered to 'angle in Kensington'.[140] Carlyle travelled alone to London to find a house before summoning Jane to follow with their belongings. He arrived at their old lodgings in Ampton Street on Tuesday, 13 May, recording in his journal that as the coach from Liverpool rolled under Holloway Arch and he caught his first sight of 'huge smoky London', he hummed, 'in a kind of defiance, my mother's tune of "Johnny O'Cox"'.[141]

Carlyle was conscious that the 'First Act' of his life was now well and truly closed, and that he was even now beginning the second. What was true for him was equally true for Jane, as she prepared to come out of the wilderness in which she had been far from happy to see if she could find fulfilment in London.

PART THREE

MR AND MRS CARLYLE AT HOME

CHAPTER 7

Preparing to Astonish the World 1834–1835

Carlyle settled into the familiar rooms in the Miles household in Ampton Street where he and Jane had lodged during the winter of 1831–2. He had preceded Jane to London because he mistakenly thought all house-letting was done at Whitsun, as in Scotland. He discovered his error on his first evening, 13 May 1834, when he visited Sarah Austin in Bayswater. As he told Jane a few days later, he was welcomed 'with a most graceful little kiss', and learned 'in the course of five minutes' that 'Whitsunday is no day at all in London'. Mrs Austin and her friend the writer Anna Jameson – 'a little, hard, proud, redhaired, freckled, fierce-eyed, square-mouthed woman' – took him out next morning on a house-hunting expedition in Kensington, in the course of which they passed through Kensington Gardens. Here suddenly

there starts from a side-seat a black figure, and clutches my hand in both his: it is poor Edward Irving! O what a feeling! The poor friend looks like death rather than life; pale and yet flushed, a flaccid, boiled appearance; and one short peal of his old Annandale laugh went thro' me with the wofullest tone.[1]

After promising to visit Irving at his house in Newman Street – where he now preached to a breakaway group of fanatics, having been evicted from his Regent Square church in May 1832[2] – Carlyle hurried on to look at a succession of unsuitable houses. A day or so later he stepped out with Leigh Hunt to view houses in the Chelsea neighbourhood, after taking tea in Hunt's 'indescribable dreamlike household' of sleeping wife and beautiful dirty children.[3] The excitement of being in London once more rings out in Carlyle's detailed letters to Jane and to his mother and brothers, especially Jack, with whom he was, as always, less guarded than with the other members of his family.

As well as pounding London's streets – which he described to his sister Jean as 'a Newspaper Column of *living* Letters' in the form of Hackney coaches, cabs, omnibuses, butchers' and brewers' and bakers' drays, wheelbarrows, trucks, dogcarts, and an endless stream of pedestrians[4] – Carlyle renewed contact with the Bullers, Mrs Strachey, Mrs Montagu, Mill, and the magazine editors Cochrane and James Fraser. Jeffrey, soon to be Lord Jeffrey, received him in an 'anxiously cordial' manner, showing his consciousness of having written offensively about the astronomy professorship. Carlyle told Jane that his own demeanour at their awkward meeting was one of 'iron gravity'. 'And so ends', he wrote decisively, 'our dealing with bright Jeffreydom; once so sparkling cheerful, now gone out into darkness', at least as far as Carlyle was concerned.[5]

He soon discovered from Sarah Austin – 'a Niagara of gossip'[6] – that Mill had love problems. He told Jane on 21 May what he had heard:

Mrs Austin had a tragical story of his having fallen *desperately in love* with some young ill-*married* philosophic Beauty (yet with the *innocence* of two sucking doves), and being lost to all his friends and to himself, and what not; but I traced *nothing* of this in poor Mill; and even incline to think that what truth there is or was in his adventure may have done him *good*. Buller also spoke of it; but in the comic vein.[7]

It was true. In 1830 Mill had met Harriet Taylor, the ambitious dissatisfied wife of an older man, through her friend the Unitarian minister William J. Fox. As Carlyle later put it in conversation with his American friend Charles Eliot Norton, Harriet wanted an intellectual companion, and Fox thought of Mill, a man who, 'up to that time, had never so much as looked at a female creature, not even a cow, in the face', and now 'found himself opposite those great dark eyes, that were flashing unutterable things' while Mill was discoursing concerning all sorts of 'high topics'.[8] The two embarked on an open friendship, letting it be known that there was no question of adultery, though the husband, John Taylor, was, not unreasonably, unhappy with the situation.

The reason why Mill had travelled to Paris in October 1833 instead of visiting Craigenputtoch as he had promised was that Harriet Taylor had gone to live there for a six-month trial separation from her husband. Mill had felt impelled to follow her.[9] He was besotted, as his letters to Harriet show, but determined not to act dishonourably. She was equally clear that there should be no scandal, no separation; and so a strange triangle developed which endured until Mill and Harriet were enabled to marry in 1851, after the death of the long-suffering John Taylor.

Meanwhile, anyone who hinted at impropriety either to Mill's face or behind his back was instantly cut. One friend, the radical MP John Roebuck, tried talking to him directly about the ridicule he and Harriet aroused, and found his friendship had come to an abrupt end.[10] Carlyle himself, though a favourite of Mill's for some time to come, would in due course be received by him 'like the very incarnation of the East Wind'. He never knew for sure what caused Mill to freeze towards him, but suspected it might have been because he repeated an amusing anecdote told him by the French radical Godefroi Cavaignac about Mill and Mrs Taylor being seen eating grapes together off one bunch, like a pair of lovebirds. Carlyle told the story to Charles Buller, 'a man who was not always to be trusted', and could only assume that Buller had relayed it to Mill.[11]

The first meeting between the Carlyles and Mrs 'Platonica' Taylor, as they were soon calling her, went well enough, as Carlyle told Jack in July:

Our most interesting new friend is a Mrs Taylor (thro' Mill, who is said to be in love with her, – in platonic love, *versteht sich* [naturally]), who came here for the first time yesterday, and staid long: she is a living romance-heroine, of the clearest insight, of the royallest volition, very interesting, of questionable destiny, not above twenty-five: Jane is to go and pass a day with her soon (about the Regent's Park), being greatly taken with her.[12]

Jane had arrived in London, with Chico the canary, on 4 June. She had viewed Carlyle's first choice of house, 5, Cheyne Row, just round the corner from the indolent but welcoming Hunts, and had agreed that they should take it. The removal took place on 10 June, and the couple embarked on their life in their £35-a-year house in Chelsea, with the words of Jane's uncle John Welsh ringing in their ears. He had written to Jane's mother saying he fully expected Carlyle to do 'something to astonish the world'; 'he has it in him if he would only let it escape in a tangible shape'.[13]

Neither regretted leaving Craigenputtoch. Jane was partly sorry to have travelled so far away from her mother, but as before she and Mrs Welsh had found they grated on one another. Jane told Carlyle on 22 May, shortly before leaving Scotland, that her mother had helped her pack and clear up at Craigenputtoch; she 'worked like a Turk', but was 'pettish' and 'annoying with contradictory advice'.[14] A few days later Jane wrote that Mrs Welsh was 'in the most gracious *bountiful* mood – giving me gowns &c &c'. 'What a mercy for you Dearest that I have not *her* turn for managing the finance department – we should soon sit rent free in the Kings bench.'[15] As Carlyle later noted, Jane's mother was 'right kind, generous, affectionate, in many points right *noble*', and 'much loved' by Jane, but 'not quite easy to live with in detail!'[16]

Jane was soon describing to her distant correspondent Eliza Stodart what everyday life in London was like. One letter takes in Mrs Montagu, the noises of London, a description of the house and garden at 5, Cheyne Row, and a surprise visitor. She begins with an elaborate discourse on the old subject of the infrequency of their letters, in which Mrs Montagu is amusingly invoked:

Mrs Montagu who has made '*the fine arts*' her peculiar study has a pretty and original way of knitting up a ravelled correspondence – Instead of outraging the already outraged with a lengthened apology, she commences with a lively attack 'is astonished that you have not written to inquire the reason of her silence' – 'thinks it strange that you should adopt with her the formal letter for letter system'

– 'Is hurt', 'is angry' is every thing but what you expected namely ashamed of herself – and you find yourself suddenly much to your surprise transformed into the offending party and thankful for the kind forgiveness with which she ends – This beats out and out our old simple fashion of making confessions of indolence &c &c or telling lies about excessive occupation and so forth. But having let you into the secret I need not play it off upon you this time, only I let you see what I might do if I liked – and I give you instead of a useless apology a useful hint which you may find your account in against enraged correspondents.[17]

Next Jane asks, as she had done on first moving to Craigenputtoch six years earlier, 'Well! is it not very strange that I am here?'

sitting in my own hired house by the side of the Thames as if nothing had happened; with fragments of Haddington, of Comely Bank, of Craigenputtoch interweaved with *cockneycalities* into a very habitable whole? Is it not strange that I should have an everlasting sound in my ears, of men, women, children, omni-buses, carriages glass coaches, streetcoaches, waggons, carts, dog-carts, steeple bells, doorbells, Gentlemen-raps, twopenny-post-raps, footmen-showers-of raps, of the whole devil to pay, as if plague pestilence, famine, battle, murder sudden death and wee Eppie Daidle [a child in Scott's *Heart of Midlothian*] were broken loose to make me diversion. – And where is the stillness, the eternal sameness, of the last six years – ? Echo answers at Craigenputtoch! . . . this stirring life is more to my mind, and has besides a beneficial effect on my bowels. Seriously I have almost entirely discontinued drugs, and look twenty percent better, every one says, and 'what every one says must be true'.

From this it seems that Jane had been borrowing Carlyle's medicines to deal with a troublesome digestive problem of her own.

Number 5, Cheyne Row, she tells Eliza, is 'of most antique physio-gnomy, quite to our humour', 'all wainscoted carved and queer-looking; roomy, substantial, commodious, with closets to satisfy any Bluebeard'. The garden – 'so called in the language of flattery' – is in poor order, except for two vines which have produced two bunches of grapes and a walnut tree which has yielded 'almost sixpence-worth of walnuts'. All this is theirs at a rent only two or three pounds a year more than they had paid at Comely Bank. 'This comes of our noble contempt for fashion – Chelsea being highly unfashionable.'

Their surprise visitor was George Rennie, a sculptor and one of Jane's suitors in the days before Carlyle 'came about her'. 'I was within an ace of fainting and he looked like one of his own marbles', not, she added, out of mutual lingering tenderness, but rather 'mere queaziness from the intense sensation of the flight of time which such a meeting occasioned one – fifteen years!' She is able to report that Rennie 'lives in the wretchedest atmosphere of "*gigmanity*" – his wife is a perfect fool'.[18]

Jane and Carlyle had annoyed Mrs Montagu by hiring as their servant Bessy Barnett, the daughter of Badams's old housekeeper in Birmingham.

Even before they left Craigenputtoch, they had been in correspondence with Bessy about her joining them, and she now came down from Birmingham, to be treated, as Carlyle told his mother on 12 June, 'not as a servant but as a friend'.[19] Carlyle divulged to Jack less than a week later 'a new trait of Montaguedom and the Noble Lady' at 25, Bedford Square:

The night before Bessy was to arrive, Jane went to drink tea there; at her answer to the question, Have you got a servant? great eyes were made; and then the direfullest narration opened, of Bessy having been Badams' kept mistress 'for years and years', and the artfullest, wretchedest, wickedest creature on Earth; as a whole sheaf of Letters in the hand of Montague and two others (agents in B's affairs) would prove to the blind: which Agents Mr Carlyle would of course instantly go to, and so put far from him the accursed thing: *otherwise* consequences without end would ensue; for example, being *cut* by all respectable women, especially by the respectable women of No 25! My good Dame was much shocked and staggered: for my own share, I confess I was struck with a kind of horror at the *infernal* temper of these poor persons, persecuting beyond the very Grave; . . . at any rate, not being minded to *wed* Bessy, but only to *hire* her, [we] have almost *nothing* to do with it: respectable women take servants out of the Magdalen Asylum [for penitent prostitutes]; and are still visited by respectable women . . . But Oh, from that spirit of Hatred and horrid Cruelty good Lord deliver us![20]

This shows a refreshing tolerance on the question of sexual mores, though the Carlyles were not entirely consistent in their attitude. Carlyle was always inclined to tolerate sexual licence in scamps and rogues by whom he was fascinated, or in whom he valued some other trait very highly – Boswell and Burns, for example, and among his personal acquaintances the Buller brothers, and Leigh Hunt, who may not have practised such licence, but openly preached it. Besides, the spirit of contradiction flared up in the case of Bessy; if Mrs Montagu, whose own household (at least the male part of it) had its none-too-hidden skeletons, sought to dictate how he should act, he would show her that he was his own master in such matters.

He and Jane had been less understanding when one of their Craigenputtoch maids, Betty Smail, had become pregnant in 1832 (a year after Carlyle's sister Mary had been pregnant at her wedding to James Austin). To his mother Carlyle wrote then with unpleasant moral emphasis about the 'total and peremptory dismissal for ever and a day of our servant Betty', the 'wretched Adulteress'. He also wrote in his journal that Betty, 'a much-favoured creature, long with us, proves to be sinking Hellward'.[21] This was harsh, though if Betty's misdemeanour was indeed adultery, it probably caused more damage and distress than mere out-of-wedlock pregnancy.

The Carlyles were not much different from their fellow human beings in their varying response to sexual (mis)conduct. Personal liking for the people involved, as well as circumstances which might be construed as extenuating, could incline them to tolerance, as could their genuine sense of fairness, the desire to give the benefit of the doubt in cases – such as Mill's – where the only people who could know for sure whether their relationship was adulterous were the two principals.

Separation was difficult for many couples for financial reasons and also because it caused scandal and gossip, and was particularly unpleasant for the children of the marriage – the Taylors had three – who might become social outcasts. Divorce was almost impossible except where a clear case of adultery and cruelty (or insanity) could be proved. It was also expensive and therefore beyond the reach of most pockets, especially female pockets, which in most cases had been legally picked by their husbands, as the wife's property became by law her husband's on marriage. Still, John Taylor was as much a victim of the law as was his wife. He had little choice in the three-cornered arrangement, given his fondness for Harriet and the children and his disinclination to insist on a permanent separation.

The Carlyles soon found themselves making the acquaintance, through Mill, of a group of people who were involved – some openly – in extra-marital arrangements. The ascetic Mill's chief (perhaps only) confidant in the Harriet Taylor affair was the man who had introduced them, W. J. Fox, the Unitarian minister. Fox's own household was an unorthodox one, consisting of his wife and children, and two young sisters and members of his congregation, Sarah and Eliza Flower. By 1832 Mrs Fox had retired to the upstairs part of the house in order to separate herself from Fox's affair with Eliza Flower. She wrote to him, formally asking for a separation, to which he replied that he could not afford to support two establishments, and she must put up with the current arrangement.

Mrs Fox took her complaint to Fox's South Place congregation in July 1834, soon after the Carlyles' arrival in London; a full-scale scandal followed, with members of the congregation taking sides. Fox was loath to resign from his pulpit in case it looked like an admission of guilt, but on 15 August he did finally offer his resignation. In September he was acquitted by a majority of his congregation of the adultery charge (though it was true). The matter was complicated by the fact that Fox had expressed 'advanced' views on divorce in the Unitarian periodical, the *Monthly Repository*, which he edited. He seems to have decided that his actions were in accordance with his principles. Mill, who owed his acquaintance with Harriet Taylor to Fox, supported him.[22]

Though all this was going on just as the Carlyles met Fox, they did not know the whole story at first. Carlyle wrote to Jack on 15 August giving his customary pen sketch of this new set of acquaintances:

We dined with Mrs (Platonica) Taylor and the Unitarian Fox (of the *Repos[i]tory*, if you know it), one day: Mill also was of the party, and the Husband, an obtuse most joyous-natured man, the pink of social hospitality. Fox is a little thickset bushy-locked man of five-and-forty, with bright sympathetic-thoughtful eyes ... with a tendency to pot-belly, and *snuffiness*: from these hints you can construe him; the best *Socinian Philosophist* going, but not a whit more. I shall like well enough to meet the man again; but I doubt he will not me: he professed to be unwell (as I too was) and rather 'sang small'.[23]

Fox may well have felt 'unwell', since his scandal was in full swing. Carlyle had a further reason to doubt that he and Fox would get on. Mill let him know at this time that he – Carlyle – was not to be offered the editorship of a new radical periodical, the *London Review*, which was being set up by Mill and his rich friend, the radical MP Sir William Molesworth. Instead Fox, 'who has just quitted his Preachership, and will like myself be out on the world', as Carlyle noted, was expected to get it.[24]

A couple of months later Carlyle, having caught up with the gossip, reported to Jack on the doings of these 'friends of the species', as he dubbed the Taylors and the Foxes and all who in theory or practice denied the indissolubility of marriage:

Round her [Mrs Taylor] come Fox the Socinian, and a flight of really wretched-looking 'friends of the species', who (in writing and deed) struggle not in favour of Duty being *done*, but against Duty of any sort almost being *required*. A singular creed this; but I can assure you a very observable one here in these days ... Jane and I often say: 'Before all mortals, beware of a friend of the species!' Most of these people are very indignant at marriage and the like; and frequently indeed are obliged to divorce their own wives, or be divorced: for tho' the *world* is already blooming (or is one day to do it) in everlasting 'happiness of the greatest number', these people's own *houses* (I always find) are little Hells of improvidence, discord, unreason. Mill is far above all that, and I think will not sink in it; however, I do wish him fairly far from it, and tho' I cannot speak of it directly would *fain* help him out: he is one of the best people I ever saw, and – surprisingly attached to *me*, which is another merit.[25]

Though not entirely unsympathetic to these 'friends of the species' – Mrs Taylor, for example, and Mill as an associate 'friend' – Carlyle could not help relishing the ironic and euphonious Unitarian-Utilitarian connection he was able to make by reference to the cornerstone of the Utilitarian philosophy, its desire to bring about 'the greatest happiness of the greatest number', and the liberal theology of the Unitarian (or Socinian) church. He told Jack that Sarah Austin 'mourned' and 'feared' for these friends of hers, unaware that poor Mrs Austin, married to a stiff, neurotic, hypochondriac husband, was engaged even then in a passionate, sexually suggestive correspondence with the German adventurer Prince Hermann Pückler-Muskau. She had recently translated his *Tour of a*

German Prince, the narration of his journeys to France, England, and Ireland in search of a rich wife to get him out of his financial difficulties. By February 1834 the strain of her guilty correspondence had brought her to the brink of a nervous breakdown. She feared, with some reason, that Pückler-Muskau, who collected lovers and love letters for recycling in his semi-fictional, semi-autobiographical writings, would publicly expose the frank, though entirely epistolary, passion between them.[26]

Sarah Austin's friend Anna Jameson, to whom Carlyle had taken an instant dislike, was also an unhappy wife, estranged from her husband and earning her living by writing books about women in art, in literature, and in history. When Anna's husband, Robert Jameson, summoned her the following year to join him in Canada, Sarah's advice was that she should acquiesce, but only because she had no choice. She might get a crumb of comfort, or even 'the everlasting satisfaction', of being able to say 'at least I have done my part'. But Sarah's opinion, born of her arid life with a depressive who was so often incapacitated that he could not earn enough to keep her and their daughter Lucy – Sarah was for several years the breadwinner of the family through her translating and reviewing – was a bitter one:

I have done with wondering at the injustice of men – at what they exact, in proportion to what they are prepared to give or to do. To make any impression on them, armed as they are with power, backed by opinion and absorbed in interests of ambition or of business, is hopeless.[27]

Leigh Hunt was also a 'friend of the species', being open about his Shelleyan view of love as something to be freely given and freely withdrawn, regardless of marriage vows, though his own practice was more heroic, since he remained with his alcoholic wife Marianne. Carlyle wrote of Hunt in his résumé to Jack in October, 'we make an exception of him; tho' nowise of the Doctrine as held by him'. Hunt had written colourfully to Carlyle in May 1833 of marriage as 'an experiment which I should hardly think can be said to have succeeded in the world, even in this chaste & hypocritical & Mamma-sacrificing country of England', where 'a sixth part of the poor female sex' (prostitutes) are sacrificed 'for the convenience of prudential young gentlemen & the preservation of chastity in the five remaining classes of shrews & scolds, & women good & bad, & wives happy, unhappy, & crimcon-ical'.[28]

Anticipating Dickens's caricature of Hunt as Harold Skimpole, the irresponsible man-child in *Bleak House* (1852–3), Carlyle continued in his letter to Jack: 'I never in my whole life met with a more innocent childlike man; transparent, many-glancing, really beautiful, were this Lubberland or Elysium, and not Earth and England. His family also are innocent, tho' wholly fools and donothings.'[29]

Jane had soon discovered that Mrs Hunt was an assiduous borrower, as well as showing an amusing metropolitan amazement at Jane's pursuits. Carlyle's mother was regaled in September with an illustrative story:

Our little household has been set up again, at a quite moderate expense of money and trouble (wherein I cannot help thinking with a *chastened vanity*, that the superior shiftiness and thriftiness of the Scotch character has strikingly manifested itself). The English women turn up the whites of their eyes and call on the 'good Heavens' at the bare idea of enterprises which seem to me in the most ordinary course of human affairs – I told Mrs Hunt one day I had been very busy *painting*: 'What?' she asked is it a portrait? 'O No', I told her 'something of more importance; a large wardrobe' – She could not imagine she said 'how I could have patience for such things' – And so having no patience for them herself what is the result? she is every other day reduced to borrow my tumblers, my teacups, even – a cupful of porridge, a few spoonfuls of tea are begged of me, because 'Missus has got company and happens to be out of the article' – in plain unadorned English because 'Missus is the most wretched of Managers and is often at the point of having not a copper in her purse'.[30]

In November Jane wrote again with news of Marianne:

Mrs Hunt I shall soon be quite terminated with I foresee. She torments my life out with borrowing – She actually borrowed the brass fenders the other day and I had difficulty in getting it out of her hands – irons, glasses tea-cups silver spoons are in constant requisition – and when one sends for them the whole number can never be found.[31]

In the same letter Jane gives an interesting insight into fashion and the ingenuity of London servants: 'The diameter of the fashionable Ladies at present is about three yards; their *bustles* (false bottoms) are the size of an ordinary sheep's fleece – The very servant girls wear bustles – Eliza Miles told me a maid of theirs went out one Sunday with *three* kitchen dusters pinned on as a substitute.'[32]

Though we know Jane could make a comic anecdote out of a broom handle even in the lonely wilds of Craigenputtoch, her joy at having so much to observe, to describe, and to criticise in London shines out of her letters.

The Carlyles' Scottish habit of eating porridge in the evening, at which Lamb had injudiciously scoffed in Enfield, was noticed by many visitors. Leigh Hunt joined in with delight, as Carlyle told Alick soon after receiving a supply of 'Annandale oatmeal' from him:

He comes in some once a week . . ., takes a cup of tea, and sits discoursing, in his brisk fanciful way, till supper-time, and then cheerfully *eats* a cup of porridge (to sugar only), which he praises to the skies, and vows he will make his supper of at home.[33]

Both Carlyles reported back to Scotland on the inferiority of the milk (to which water and chalk were often added), the cost of potatoes, the joy at finding a Scottish baker, the excellence of the beer, and the peculiarity of the English in spending money on fruit – 'for no use but to give people a cholic', as Jane put it severely, inadvertently offering an insight into one of the probable reasons for the Carlyles' digestive problems.[34]

★

On 25 July 1834 Coleridge died at James Gillman's house in Highgate. Carlyle reported to John Bradfute in Edinburgh that 'carriages in long files, as I hear, were rushing all round Highgate when the old man [Coleridge was sixty-one] lay near to die'. 'Foolish carriages!' he added. 'Not one of them would roll near him (except to splash him with their mud) while he lived.'[35] This was an exaggeratedly gloomy view of Coleridge's career – though it is true that he never made a living out of his writing, and for much of his life was ridiculed in the periodical press, not least by Jeffrey.[36]

Carlyle's own mood was despairing. The day after Coleridge's death, he complained in his journal about his lack of a 'practical friend' or confidant. 'No periodical editor wants me: no man will give me money for my work.' 'Bad health' of an unspecified kind adds to his gloom, as do 'despicablest fears of coming to absolute beggary'. All this outweighs the friendship of Mill and 'the Unitarian-philosophic fraternity' around Harriet Taylor, which 'bodes little'. 'Poor me!' he exclaims.[37]

Coleridge still loomed as a warning example of a poor genius who had become financially dependent on others and lost his pride. Carlyle and Jane had recently picked up a phrase which seemed to sum up this aspect of Coleridge's life. Telling Alick that Jane had created a comfortable home at Cheyne Row, Carlyle echoed Coleridge: 'I sit quite snug, and "far better than I deserve"'; this became a catchphrase for both Carlyles, with the addition of the explanatory part, 'as Coleridge said of his cold tea'.[38]

Carlyle described to his mother how Coleridge had been supported by the Gillmans for many years, his wife and children having to 'shift else-where as they could'. 'He could earn no money, could set himself steadfastly to no painful task.' 'A better faculty has not often been worse wasted', he wrote. 'Yet withal he was a devout man, and did something, both by writing and speech. Among the London Literaries he has not left his like or second.'[39] We can see Carlyle here identifying with one half of the picture – the giftedness, the doing something, the difficulty of earning money – while he dissociates himself from the other half – the dependence, the abandonment of his family, the lack of steadfast application to a task.

Carlyle had not seen Coleridge since his visit to Highgate with Irving in 1824. During his second stay in London in 1831 he had been on the point of going once more with Irving to listen to the 'Dodona Oracle', but was prevented by a downpour, and had not had an opportunity to go again.[40] Irving himself was now ill, and had not much longer to live. After being greeted by his ghostly figure in Kensington Gardens on his first full day in London, Carlyle had tried four times to call on him, but was not admitted. Hearing that Irving's health was deteriorating, he went back to Newman Street on 14 August. The sad encounter was described the following day to Jack, Carlyle venting his anger at Isabella Irving's refusal to let him talk privately with his old friend:

Yesterday I went again with an insuppressible indignation mixed with my pity: after some shying, I was admitted! Poor Irving! he lay there on a sofa, begged my pardon for not rising; his Wife, who also did not and probably could not well rise, sat at his feet, and watched all the time I was there, miserable haggard, like a watchful Hysperides [sic] dragon. I was civil to her, but could not be more: I never in my time was concerned in another such despicability as I was forced to suspect her of. Irving once lovingly ordered her away; but she lovingly excused herself, and sat still. He complains of biliousness, of a pain at his right short-rib; has a short thick cough which comes on at the smallest irritation. Poor fellow! I brought a short gleam of old Scottish laughter into his face into his voice, and that too set him coughing. He said it was the Lord's will; looked weak, dispirited, partly embarrassed. He continues toiling daily, tho' the Doctor (Darling) says, rest only can cure him. Is it not mournful, hyper-tragical? There are moments when I determine on sweeping in upon all Tongue-work and Martindoms and accursed choking Cobwebberies, and snatching away my old best Friend, to save him from Death and the Grave! It seems too likely he will die there.[41]

A few weeks later Carlyle was discussing Irving with their old friend William Graham. Graham wrote that the elders in Irving's breakaway group, which called itself the 'Catholic Apostolic Church', had become, instead of his followers, 'his imperious taskmasters; he is sunk under their proud control', the 'degraded slave of these bloated, inflated, deceiving, self-deceived, &c., &c'.[42] Irving was soon sent off on doctor's orders to Wales, the North of England, and Scotland. Before he left, he paid one visit to Cheyne Row, as Carlyle remembered in 1866:

Edward Irving rode to the door one ev[enin]g, came in and staid with us some 20 minutes; the one call we ever had of him here, – his farewell call before setting out to ride towards Glasgow, as the Doctors, helpless otherwise, had ordered. He was very friendly, calm and affectionate; spoke chivalrously courteous to [Jane] (as I remember), 'Ah, yes', looking round the room; 'you are like an Eve, make every place you live in beautiful!' He was not sad in manner; but was at heart, as you cd notice, serious, even solemn. Darkness at hand, & the weather damp, he cd not loiter. I saw him mount at the door; watched till he turned the first corner (close by the Rector's garden-door), – and had vanished from us altogr.[43]

Irving died at Glasgow on 7 December 1834, aged forty-two. Carlyle thought London – 'this mad City' – had killed him, as he told a Glasgow acquaintance David Hope, who had asked him to write an obituary for a Glasgow newspaper.[44] In the article he did write, for *Fraser's Magazine* (January 1835), Carlyle sketched a man of large gifts 'sent forth a Herculean man' from Scotland, only to be 'worn and wasted' by 'our mad Babylon'. He treated his friend in the same way in which he often confronted (or avoided confronting) his own difficulties and failures, by describing him as a victim of external forces: 'By a fatal chance, Fashion cast her eye on him', and he was lost. After a while,

Fashion went her idle way, to gaze on Egyptian Crocodiles, Iroquois Hunters, or what else there might be; forgot this man, – who unhappily could not in his turn forget. The intoxicating poison had been swallowed; no force of natural health could cast it out.[45]

It was generous of Carlyle to wish to exculpate Irving; he wanted to pay his due to his first and best friend. He ends the *Fraser's* essay with words of gratitude: 'But for Irving, I had never known what the communication of man with man means. His was the freest, brotherliest, bravest human soul mine ever came in contact with.'

Carlyle's impulse is to praise and not to blame in this farewell to his former friend. His linguistic facility in the passage just quoted about 'Fashion' dancing attendance on Irving and then abandoning him is capable of dazzling sufficiently to blind readers to an abdication of responsibility on the part of the praised or exonerated subject, in this case Irving, but in subsequent examples in Carlyle's writings the subject might be an unscrupulous 'great man' such as Napoleon, Cromwell, or Frederick the Great.

Irving was an extraordinary phenomenon, as Carlyle well knew; he was also vain and obsessed to the point of madness. Though his heart was 'filled with trust in Heaven's goodness', as Carlyle noted in his reminiscence,[46] he was alarmingly and self-flatteringly certain. Irving's speech in his own defence to the London Presbytery in March 1832 shortly before his expulsion is an example of his self-belief. It is one long turning of the tables on his accusers. They are wrong in their interpretation of scripture, not he; this is the burden of his flowing, obsessive speech:

Jesus is the Head of the congregation, not I; I am only His deputy, and the prophets are His voice. You are very ignorant of the Old Testament, if you know not that the prophet is the voice of God to kings and to princes; he is the voice of Jesus to His Church; and if I be speaking anything contrary to the mind of

Jesus, shall not He, the Head of the Church, have liberty by His prophets to tell the congregation so, and guard them from error?

And so on for pages and pages in its published version.[47]

The trouble was, if Irving could have seen it, that any such intervention by Christ or his 'prophets' could only be a matter of interpretation; thus the speaking with tongues which went on among his congregation in the last few years of his life was a tangled business, subject to disagreement and rivalry among the 'gifted'. How was one to tell whether it was the Lord or Satan speaking through the medium? How discern who *was* gifted? One female member of Irving's church wrote to him in May 1832, 'It was revealed to me that our breaches could not be healed until we received the gift of discernment of spirits',[48] thus opening up an abyss of difficulty – to whom is the gift vouchsafed of 'discerning' the gift vouchsafed to a speaker in tongues?

The gifted, many of whom were women, often sought to discredit one another. Carlyle had foreseen such mass madness, and Hazlitt had hinted at the dangers of Irving's attractiveness, especially to women, as he stood in the pulpit, handsome and eloquent, in his first days in London. Henry Crabb Robinson noted in his diary in May 1825 – in shorthand to ensure secrecy – that there was gossip abroad about Irving's lack of 'personal holiness'; in other words, he was suspected of sexual lapses.[49] Crabb Robinson did not believe it; nor would Carlyle have believed it. But Irving's attractiveness did hasten his downfall, inasmuch as the group gathered round him used the idea of the gift of speech to jostle for position and constantly came to him to adjudicate between them.

It was a sorry affair. Carlyle knew he could never write the biography of Irving for which he was in so many ways fitted. How could he bear to get into that '*bottomless* element'?[50] He contented himself with a long private account in his 1866 reminiscence, which he summed up appropriately: 'What a falling of the curtain; upon what a Drama!'[51]

★

Carlyle felt Irving's death was the end of an era, though he had long ceased to have much direct contact with him. He had come to London hoping to get a foothold on the literary life, and on 1 September 1834 he began to write the book which would at last bring him fame, *The French Revolution*.

He had been reading concentratedly on the 'subject of subjects' since October 1833, when he had been given access to a large private library, the Barjarg Library, in Dumfriesshire, and after his arrival in London Mill lent him books by the 'barrowful'.[52] There was still a huge amount of reading to do – for Carlyle never skimped, but always saturated his subject – and what were he and Jane to live on while he toiled? The best he could do in the way of a contract was an offer of half-profits, 'that is *zero*', from James Fraser in June 1834.[53] Mindful of the misunderstandings with Murray and others over *Sartor Resartus*, and aware how unsaleable his books appeared to be, he was prepared to accept this time, but it left him financially vulnerable until the book was done and published.

Carlyle therefore had good reason to fear 'absolute beggary', as he noted in his journal immediately after Coleridge's death. Yet in the same entry of 26 July he was able to balance the negative with something positive:

In the midst of innumerable discouragements, all men indifferent or finding fault, let me mention two small circumstances that are comfortable. The first is a letter from some nameless Irishman in Cork to another here (Fraser read it to me without names), actually containing a *true* and one of the friendliest possible recognitions of me. One mortal then says I am *not* utterly wrong. Blessings on him for it. The second is a letter I got to-day from Emerson, of Boston in America; sincere, not baseless, of most exaggerated estimation. Precious is man to man.[54]

Both the Irishman, whom Carlyle later found to be a priest named Father O'Shea, and Emerson were responding to *Sartor Resartus* as it proceeded monthly in *Fraser's Magazine*. For once Carlyle did not exaggerate when he said, now and later, that the only voices raised in favour of the work were O'Shea's and Emerson's and Jane's. He remembered it all clearly in a conversation with Charles Eliot Norton in 1873, when he related how *Sartor* was 'beset on all sides with vehement protests against such damned stuff, mere jargon and extravaganza'.[55] Carlyle had been given a gloomy picture of the initial reception of *Sartor* when he called on Fraser on first arriving in London in May 1834 and was told that 'an oldest subscriber came in and said, "If there is any more of that d——d stuff, I will &c"; on the other hand, an order from America (Boston or Philadelphia) to send a copy of the Magazine *so long* as there was anything of Carlyle's in it'.[56]

The order came from Emerson, as Carlyle discovered when he received the letter in July praising him for casting a 'new eye' on the 'mouldy forms' of society, politics, and religion, and for making 'a brave stand for Spiritualism'.[57] Carlyle wrote back gratefully on 12 August, sending Emerson four copies of *Sartor* in the form of 'a stitched Pamphlet' – bound sheets given him by Fraser.[58] He later remembered having sent six of these pamphlets to 'six Edinburgh Literary Friends' (unnamed, but likely to have included John Wilson, De Quincey, and Sir William Hamilton, as well as Jeffrey, now Lord Jeffrey and a Scottish judge), 'from not one of whom did I get the smallest whisper even of receipt', with the result that he rarely sent any of his other books to anyone in Edinburgh.[59] He gave copies to his London friends, including Mill and Mrs Taylor, and several more went to his Dumfriesshire friends and family.

The response from unliterary Dumfriesshire was astute and bracing. William Graham, the Ecclefechan correspondent with whom Carlyle was exchanging news of Irving at the end of 1834, quoted the opinion of friends and acquaintances around Carlyle's birthplace:

Menzies says that no other man but just your *very sel'* could have wrote the *Sartor*, that it abounds with original, profound ideas, with Attic salt of your own manufacture . . . My sister got hold of it and read a whole day most vigorously. Hear her criticism: 'I kent [knew] it was Thomas Carlyle's, for it just gangs on like a "mill shillin"'!! [the stream of husked grain flowing from the mill]. Mr Clow of Land was in raptures with it; but Currie says, 'What's ta use on't? nobody can tell what he would be at'.[60]

Carlyle was amused and heartened, picking up Currie's pithy comment – 'What's ta use on't?' – and adding it to his and Jane's store of coterie phrases for future use.[61]

Meanwhile, mainly pessimistic but with gleams of humour and pleasure at this mixed, though limited, reception of *Sartor*, Carlyle went on tirelessly with his work on the French Revolution, which was to be, as he told Jack, an attempt at 'an artistic Picture'. It was also to be the first publication of Carlyle's to carry his name on the title-page. By July 1834 he was visiting the British Museum to consult the (largely uncatalogued) pamphlets on the subject held there, as well as books and pictures.[62] He told William Graham in September that his journey of about four miles from Chelsea to the Museum took him past 'the palaces of Belgrave Square' (built in 1825 close to Chelsea) at one end and 'the squalid dens of St Giles' near the British Museum (cleared in the 1840s with the building of New Oxford Street) at the other – 'the extremes of Life'.[63]

By the end of October Carlyle had finished the first three chapters and was making a pause for a day or two before launching into 'The Taking of the Bastille'. He told Jack:

I feel at every sentence that the work will be strange; that it either must be so, or be nothing but another of the thousand-and-one 'Histories', which are so many 'dead thistles for Pedant-chaffinches to peck at and fill their crops with'; a kind of thing I for one wish to have no hand in. Jane rather thinks 'it will do'.[64]

As well as giving Carlyle precious encouragement, Jane was pursuing her friendship with Sarah Austin, and, more cautiously, with Harriet Taylor. Her already soured relations with Mrs Montagu worsened when, having offended her by taking on Bessy Barnett, she replaced her – Bessy having become homesick and returned to her mother in Birmingham in October – with a servant who had been sacked by Mrs Montagu's daughter-in-law. Jane was philosophical in a letter to Carlyle's mother in November about the loss of this 'whimsical' friend.[65]

Reporting to John in January 1835 that she had been confined to the house for five weeks after an accident in which the maid poured boiling water over her foot, Jane added that Mrs Montagu had sent 'a sentimental effusion' '*threatening*' to come and see her, but never appeared; Mrs Austin 'sends me occasional "*threepennies*", overflowing with "*dearests*" and all that', but could not offer sincere friendship. The most promising woman was Harriet Taylor, but 'she is a dangerous-looking woman and engrossed with a dangerous passion and no useful relation can spring up between us'.[66]

The general election of January 1835, for which Peel wrote the famous Tamworth Manifesto defining modern, post-Reform Bill Conservatism, resulted in an increase in Radical representation, and in April Lord Melbourne's Whig Government came in with the support of the Radicals. Carlyle exclaimed to William Graham on 10 January that his own interest in politics was 'as *zero*',[67] but he had attended a Radical meeting in November 1834 for Charles Buller's sake, since 'Charlie' was to speak, hoping 'to make himself notable as the most decisive of Radicals'.[68] Charles, however, failed to be given a position in Melbourne's Whig–Radical administration.[69]

Carlyle saw himself as a sceptical observer of the politics of the reformed Parliament. His sympathies were with the poor and disenfranchised, but he did not identify with any party and could offer no solutions to the problems he perceived so clearly. He knew from his correspondence with his brothers and brothers-in-law how difficult it was to make a living out of agriculture and related pursuits; the theme of emigration to the United States or Canada began to sound in the family letters in 1835, as advertisements appeared in the Dumfriesshire press for the sale of plots of land for farming in North America.[70]

On his way south in May 1834 Carlyle had seen in Staffordshire 'a long Trades' Union in procession' protesting about the transportation of the 'Tolpuddle Martyrs', labourers found guilty of administering illegal oaths in those early days of the Trade Union movement.[71] When the Houses of Parliament burned down on 16 October 1834, Carlyle saw the flames from 'our back top-windows' and went out to watch the blaze for a couple of hours.[72] He observed the crowd with amusement, noting how they greeted the fire as a punishment for the privileged existence of the House of Lords and for the unpopular New Poor Law, which many, including Dickens, thought too severe.[73] In his journal Carlyle quoted the shouts of pleasure, as people encouraged the wind: 'There's for the House of Lords!' 'A judgment for the Poor Law Bill!' 'There go their *Hacts*!'[74]

Carlyle's contribution to political debate was to increase as his reputation and influence grew, but was always extra-parliamentary, though he did try during 1835 to become directly involved in the movement for national education. In February he wrote a few pages on the subject, 'a kind of Prospectus of an *Educational Association*' which he would like to see established, on which he consulted Mill. The main thrust of the draft pamphlet was that education should be taken out of the hands of the different religious sects, though it should include general religious teaching. Carlyle wished to see universal education (which was not enshrined in law until the Act of 1870), thinking it scandalous that out of twelve 'grown-up persons in England' only one could read and write, and that so many were therefore 'shut out from participating in the common inheritance of mankind'.[75] In June Carlyle applied to Mill to see if he could get appointed to a committee set up by Parliament to inquire into education. Mill's friends the radical MPs Roebuck, Molesworth, and George Grote were members of the committee. Carlyle was not invited to join; nor did the committee succeed in bringing about any legislation on the subject.[76]

If nobody at home seemed to want to learn from Carlyle, either in his own person or in that of his visionary (and distinctly un-parliamentary) 'Professor' Teufelsdröckh, the response among Emerson's American circle in Boston was heartening, almost to the point of persuading Carlyle to try his luck in America. Emerson wrote encouragingly in November 1834: 'Come & found a new Academy that shall be church & school & parnassus', and 'read literary lectures'. He wrote again the following spring, outlining in detail the cost of living and the likely financial rewards of lecturing. He offered his own hospitality – he was soon to marry for the second time – and that of several enthusiastic friends, and suggested that Carlyle arrange for another 'fifty or a hundred copies of the *Sartor*' to be sent for Emerson to sell and use as the basis of a new edition. At the very least, he wrote, 'you might see Niagara, get a new stock of health, and pay all your expenses by printing in England a book of travels in America',[77] as Fanny Trollope had done with great success in 1832 with *Domestic Manners of the Americans*, and Harriet Martineau, on a visit to Philadelphia when Emerson wrote in April 1835, would do with *Society in America* (1837).

Carlyle was tempted. He noted in his journal on 7 February that he had not earned a penny for twenty-three months; a few weeks earlier he had told Jack that he and Jane still had 'some £230', enough, he thought, to last just twelve months; he boasted that his London friends considered him 'a very heroic man, – that must understand the art (to them unhappily unknown) of *living upon nothing!*'[78]

Though fame and fortune still eluded him at home, Carlyle was not without reasons to stay in London. Mill was still a good friend, though dry. 'One esteems him exceedingly: but to love *him*? It were like loving the 47th of Euclid'.[79] A new acquaintance promised better. This was John Sterling, a friend of Mill and Sarah Austin, a Coleridgean enthusiast, who had been ordained deacon in the Church of England in 1834 and until recently was curate to Julius Charles Hare at Herstmonceux in Sussex. Ill health, along with doubts about the Thirty-Nine Articles fostered by Carlyle's writings, forced him to resign and bring his family to London, where he met Carlyle in February 1835.[80] Sterling's father, Edward Sterling, a regular writer in *The Times*, was known, like the paper itself, as the 'Thunderer' for his vehement leading articles; Jane and Carlyle soon nicknamed him 'Senior Hurricane'. Jane swore 'everlasting friendship' with John Sterling's mother Hester, and became a favourite of the whole Sterling family.[81]

Here was a most promising new friendship for both Carlyles. John Sterling sent a thirteen-page appreciation-cum-critique of *Sartor Resartus* which Carlyle took as evidence of true discipleship, though, in his reply on 4 June 1835, he corrected Sterling's impression that Teufelsdröckh (and therefore Carlyle) had no belief in a personal God, and resisted his objections to the 'peculiarities' of the style.[82] In his journal Carlyle expressed irritation that even his admirers – Mill, Emerson, and now Sterling – found fault with his style: 'The poor people seem to think a style can be put off or put on, not like a skin, but like a coat.'[83]

Sterling was becoming indispensable to Carlyle, as Irving had once been and Mill had for a while looked likely to be. The two men walked and talked together, discussing religion, Coleridge with his 'Church of England cobwebs', and a recent pamphlet on the Thirty-Nine Articles by Sterling's clergyman friend, F. D. Maurice, one of the exponents of the Coleridge-influenced liberal wing of the Church of England, known as the Broad Church Movement.[84]

For her part, Jane sensed that she too could attach Sterling to her by the force of her personality. Writing on the same day as Carlyle, 4 June, she thanked him for sending a separate note 'all to myself'. She makes the first of many pleas – light-hearted and joking here – for attention:

For in spite of the honestest efforts to annihilate my *I-ety*, or merge it in what the world doubtless considers my better half; I still find myself a self-subsisting and alas! selfseeking *Me*. Little Felix, in the Wanderjahre [*Wilhelm Meister's Travels*], when, in the midst of an animated scene between Wilhelm and Theresa, he pulls Theresa's gown, and calls out, '*Mama Theresa I too am here!*' only speaks out with the charming trustfulness of a child, what I am perpetually feeling, tho too sophisticated to pull peoples skirts, or exclaim in so many words; Mr Sterling, '*I too am here.*'[85]

Jane also takes the opportunity to defend *Sartor* against Sterling's doubts about its religion: 'I am loth to believe that I have married a Pagan'; but in any case, 'I care almost nothing about what a man believes, in comparison with *how* he believes.' 'Thus you see', she concludes cleverly, 'I am capable of appreciating your fervour in behalf of the thirtynine articles, without being afflicted because my Husband is accused of contumacy against them.'[86]

Her strong sense of self, often threatened in her relationship with Carlyle, achieves witty and charming expression in her relations with interesting young men like Sterling, though it could issue forth in sharper, more negative tones with people she liked less. Jean Aitken, for example, received a brisk rebuke in August 1835 for not writing directly to her but only adding in letters to Carlyle 'remember us to Mrs Carlyle', or, worse, 'remember us to *your Lady*'. 'I have told you often', she writes, 'that it afflicts me to be always, in the matter of correspondence with you, obliged like the Annandale man to thank God "for the blessings made to pass *over my head*"',[87] demonstrating the very intellectual and temperamental qualities that made Jean, with her uncertain spelling and ordinary diction, reluctant to write to her clever sister-in-law.

★

On the evening of Friday, 6 March 1835 'Mill's rap was heard at the door: he entered pale, unable to speak; gasped out to my wife to go down and speak with Mrs Taylor; and came forward (led by my hand, and astonished looks) the very picture of desperation.' Thus Carlyle in his journal the following day.[88] The cause of Mill's anguish was not, as Jane confessed she had for a moment imagined, that he and 'his Platonic inamorata' had run off together and wanted to take solemn leave of the Carlyles before 'setting out for the Devil', as Carlyle put it colourfully to Jack,[89] but something much worse, at least for the occupants of Cheyne Row. Carlyle's journal account continues:

After various inarticulate and articulate utterances to merely the same effect, he informs me that my *First Volume* (left out by him in too careless a manner, after or while reading it) was, except four or five bits of leaves, *irrevocably* ANNIHILATED! I remembered and can still remember less of it than anything I ever wrote with such toil: *it* is gone . . . Mill very injudiciously staid with us till late; and I had to make an effort and speak as if indifferently about other common matters; he left us however in a *relapsed* state; one of the pitiablest. – My dear wife

169

has been very kind, and become dearer to me. The night has been full of emotion; occasionally sharp pain (something cutting or hard – grasping me round the heart) occasionally with sweet consolations . . . This morning I have determined so far that I *can* write a Book on the F[rench] R[evolution], and will do it. Nay, our money will still suffice.[90]

Carlyle's response was heroic. He told his publisher Fraser about the disaster – as luck would have it Fraser had just announced as forthcoming '*The French Revolution*, A History in Three Books, By Thomas Carlyle' in the March number of his magazine[91] – and also his mother and brothers, and later Emerson. He named Mill only in the letters to his own family, and in all his remarks on the subject this master of the exaggerated response understated the heaviness of the blow. To his mother he wrote that he had 'some occasion lately for a portion of your faith', but assured her that he had got over the shock and was carrying on: 'Be of good cheer, therefore.'[92]

The exact fate of the manuscript of volume one of 'The French Revolution' was never fully known. In the weeks after the catastrophe Carlyle wrote in his journal and letters of its being left out carelessly by Mill and 'destroyed', 'annihilated', 'torn up for waste paper' by 'some people' in Mill's house.[93] Years later Carlyle was reported to have said that a maid had lit the fire with it. He recalled after Mill's death in 1873 that he had the 'impression' that 'some trifling neglect' at Mrs Taylor's house was the cause, 'but in fact, to prevent him almost perishing with excess of misery, we had to forbear all questioning on the subject'.[94] This was written to Mill's sister with perhaps diplomatic vagueness. Carlyle's American friend Charles Eliot Norton recorded Carlyle as saying less equivocally on 9 May 1873, just after hearing of Mill's death, that Mill had taken the manuscript to 'that woman' in her country house, where 'the housemaid had lighted the fire with it, and it was gone'.[95]

This seems the most likely scenario, but Carlyle and Jane were discreet, determined to keep the catastrophe quiet and not feed the flames of rumour and gossip. It took a very different kind of writer, though a surprisingly admiring one, to draw a comic conclusion over sixty years later. Oscar Wilde, who as a young man could quote long passages from *The French Revolution* by heart, asked a friend, Wilfred Hugh Chesson, in 1898 if he knew who had destroyed the manuscript. 'Mill's servant', came the reply. 'It was finer than that', returned Wilde:

It was Mrs Mill [then Mrs Taylor]. She read it and saw at once that, if it was published, the first name in nineteenth-century English literature could not be John Stuart Mill. It would be Carlyle . . . But her heroism was wasted. She had not reckoned on Carlyle's marvellous memory. How great he was! He made history a song for the first time in our language. He was our English Tacitus.[96]

The day after Mill's appearance, 'pale as Hector's ghost',[97] Carlyle wrote reassuring him and recognising that 'your sorrow must be far sharper than mine; yours bound to be a *passive* one'.[98] Mill, knowing Carlyle was living off slender savings, sent £200 to cover Carlyle's expenses as he set about rewriting the volume. Carlyle worked out that the five months he had spent writing the first draft had cost nearer £100 than £200, and sent £100 back. He did, however, accept from Mill the gift of a *Biographie Universelle* to help him in his task. With that, he sat down to start again, though it took him two or three weeks to get properly into his subject once more.[99]

The summer of 1835 was spent thus retracing his steps. As Carlyle wrote, Jane went to music parties with the Sterlings and began having Italian lessons with a contessa from Bologna, Clementina degli Antoni, whom she invited to tea with the exiled Italian nationalist, Count Carlo Pepoli, and John Sterling.[100] By 10 September Carlyle was reporting considerately to a no doubt relieved Mill that he had nearly finished his rewriting and expected soon to be 'one of the joyfullest of creatures – for some hours!'[101] Exhausted by his efforts and desperate to get away from the city, he set off to see his family after finishing volume one on 21 September. Mrs Welsh had come on a visit to Cheyne Row at the end of August, whereupon Jane, not for the first or last time, had succumbed to illness in due time to be nursed by her mother. Carlyle left the two women together, travelling by sea to Dumfriesshire, having 'a kind of passion to see green fields again', as he told William Graham.[102]

The Carlyles' correspondence during his absence set a pattern for later years, as did his going alone to visit his family. In 1835 the reasons were probably as much practical and financial as they were temperamental. Money was scarce; Carlyle needed a break after his Herculean efforts; and Jane had her mother with her. In later years he and Jane appeared to need to get away from one another as well as London, so they often holidayed separately. Their letters, however, show already in 1835 that Carlyle was a gloomy and difficult companion – though he had some reason, at least after the accident with his manuscript – not so heroic at the breakfast or dinner table as he was towards Mill, and that Jane's sharp wit was more often directed at him than Carlyle liked.

Carlyle's first letter to his 'dear little Wifie' on 6 October was friendly and loving. He gave details of his journey and an account of his brothers and sisters – Alick was still unable to scrape a living and talked of emigrating – and announced that he had 'all but hired you a Scotch Servant, to come home *with* me'.[103] Jane, having received at first no letter but just a newspaper with a stroke indicating his safe arrival (to avoid the postage levied on letters), wrote tartly, 'A newspaper is very pleasant when

171

one is expecting nothing at all, but when it comes in place of a letter it is a positive insult to one's feelings.' As she would always do, she relented in the course of the letter, showing her restored good humour by telling anecdotes – here of Mrs Hunt at a tea party looking 'devilish' and being 'drunkish', while Leigh Hunt lowered himself in her estimation by responding to the flattery of Jane's friend Susan Hunter and kissing her as she left. 'If he had kissed me it would have been intelligible, but Susan Hunter of all people!'[104] (Hunt published his famous poem 'Jenny kissed me' in the *Monthly Chronicle* in 1838; the Jenny who kissed him was Jane Carlyle:

> Jenny kissed me when we met,
> Jumping from the chair she sat in;
> Time, you thief, who love to get
> Sweets into your list, put that in:
> Say I'm weary, say I'm sad,
> Say that health and wealth have missed me,
> Say I'm growing old, but add
> Jenny kissed me.)[105]

If Leigh Hunt 'talked like a pengun' (a toy air-gun made from a quill) at the kissing tea party, Jane could report of Mill only that she had been 'privileged with two notes and one visit – He tried evidently to yawn as little as possible and stayed till the usual hour lest, I suppose, he should seem to have missed your conversation'.[106] Always alert to slights and conscious of her 'I-ety', Jane was torn between pleasure at her husband's ability to attract admiring friends and sheer jealousy. She makes sure that she tells Carlyle how 'wonderfully' John Sterling's wife 'takes to me' along with the rest of that devoted family.

Carlyle let her know, as he had done once or twice during their courtship, that he did not like her fits of pique. 'Understand', he wrote on 19 October, 'if the little vein of satiric humour have again come into play, that *this* is literally the first post, by which any letter could have come that was worth sending.' Later in the letter, full as always of (belittling) endearments – Goody, dear little Wifie – Carlyle exclaims, part-apologetically, part-accusingly, and part-fatalistically, 'O Jeannie dear, *do* the best thou canst with me! It is actually no easy task thou hast. God will order it; His Will and our (we hope *honest*) wills.'[107]

Jane's response was to write in Italian to show off her precocity. 'Caro e rispettabile il mio Marito', she begins, before launching into another complaint about his 'long silences' and 'long absence', but softened and made acceptable by being in a foreign language. She also alludes wittily to Penelope waiting for the return of Odysseus, beset by suitors: 'In vain do worthy gentlemen come in great numbers to court me!', the most assiduous being old Edward Sterling, the 'Stimabile'('estimable one' in Italian), as she and Carlyle sometimes called him.[108] Jane's need to be constantly winning small battles could not be satisfied by mere house-keeping conquests; she had to win battles of wit with her husband. She could not do so face to face; all the more, then, was she ready in letters to wield the pen in warlike and strategic fashion.

Carlyle replied – as he would do more and more – with obstinacy and pathos. 'Dear Bairn', he wrote on 2 November, 'I could say with Job of old: Have pity upon me, have *pity* upon me, O my friends!':

And thou, my poor Goody, depending on cheerful looks of *mine* for thy cheerfulness! For God's sake, do not; or do so as little as possible How I love thee, what I think of thee, it is not probable that thou or any mortal will know; but cheerful looks, when the heart feels slowly dying in floods of confusion and obstruction, are not the thing I have to give.[109]

With that far from consoling message Carlyle returned at the end of November, bringing his lack of cheerfulness with him but also a new servant, Ann Cook, who, he told Jean on 4 December (his fortieth birthday), 'goes on rattlingly, a brisk uncomplaining, unhesitating lass' who 'astonish[es] the natives with her pure Annandale *breadth* of utterance'.[110] Jane was amused by Ann too, telling her mother-in-law on 23 December of her 'perfect incomprehension of every thing like ceremony', and her sudden change of attitude towards the handsome Count Pepoli. 'Instead of calling him "a *fleysome* [frightful] *body*" any longer she is of opinion that he is "a real fine man and nain that comes can ever [be] named in ae day wi him"', Jane reported.[111]

And so ended the year 1835, when Carlyle turned forty and when he should have been 'astonishing the world' with the first volume of his history. Instead, he astonished the small world of his close acquaintances with his fortitude and determination to rewrite the lost volume, while Jane was obliged to live with the bad temper which was the by-product of his intense intellectual labours.

CHAPTER 8

Changed Times 1836–1838

Financially, times were hard for the Carlyles at the beginning of 1836. Carlyle was toying with the idea of applying for '*another* Astronomy Professorship', this time in Glasgow, because he 'would go anywhither on Earth for an honest quietude of employment that would give me honest bread', as he told Jack on 26 January. In the next breath he was fulminating against Basil Montagu's recent offer of employment – 'a Clerkship under him at the rate of £200 a-year' – which he turned down 'with grave thanks', though with savage feelings. Imagine Montagu 'wishing *me* for his Clerk', he exclaimed; 'thinking the Polar Bear, reduced to a state of dyspeptic dejection, might be safely trusted tending Rabbits!'[1]

He was almost halfway through writing *The French Revolution*, having just finished the chapter on the death of Mirabeau, but was earning nothing. Jane announced in a postscript to the letter that she had 'lately with unheard of effort accomplished a piece of translation which may possibly bring me some two or three guineas'.[2] This was 'a short French Translation I got for her to do', as Carlyle told his mother.[3] Nothing more was heard of it.

A month later Jane told Jack that Carlyle had been offered the editorship of a radical newspaper in Lichfield through Mill, who 'in his usual business style dropt us a *threepenny*; and Carlyle in another three-penny has answered *no* by no means, and so the whole affair is ended almost as soon as begun'. Jane expressed her relief that they were not to settle in 'a little provincial English town'. 'Where would one be better than here? to be sure, one is threatened with starvation; but for the rest "*tout va bien*"!'[4]

Mill asked Carlyle to contribute to the new *London and Westminster Review* which was to be established in April by merging the *Westminster* and the *London* Reviews. He sent an essay on the 'Diamond Necklace' affair, a complicated business a few years before the outbreak of the French Revolution, involving Marie Antoinette and a cast of characters ranging from cardinals to criminals.[5] Since Mill wanted him to make changes, Carlyle turned to James Fraser, who offered £50 for it in October, and 'The Diamond Necklace' appeared in two parts in *Fraser's Magazine* in January and February 1837.[6] Two other offshoots from the research on the

French Revolution appeared in the *London and Westminster Review*, though not until 1837; these were 'Memoirs of Mirabeau' and 'Parliamentary History of the French Revolution'.

As Carlyle went on with his writing, Jane made the most of her opportunities among the Sterling family and her Italian friends. She wrote to Eliza Stodart in a rather subdued key, all the more striking for being an attempt to pick up her old tone of outrageousness:

I have set myself very seriously to the business of loving since I came here – conscious that my long sojourn in the wilderness had developed certain misanthropical tendencies in me that were leading me rather devilward, – into the region of hatred and all uncharitableness! With a good deal of effort I have got up a sentiment for several men and women which has a good right to go by the name of friendship in these days. I have even executed two or three *innocent flirtations* with good effect, and on the whole live in great amity with my fellow creatures. They call me 'sweet', and 'gentle'; and some of the men go the length of calling me 'ENDEARING' and I laugh in my sleeve and think oh Lord! if you but knew what a brimstone of a creature I am behind all this beautiful amiability![7]

Some light is shed on her low spirits by an entry in Carlyle's journal in March, in which he complains of ill health holding back his work and recognises his own 'gloomy silence of rebellion against myself and all the arrangements of my existence'. 'I shudder sometimes at the abysses I discern in myself, the acrid hunger, the shivering sensitiveness, the *wickedness* (and yet can I say at this moment that I think myself rightly *wicked?*)'[8] His words probably relate to his bad temper, which he sometimes realised was a cause of misery and illness in Jane.[9] Her health was often poor; she caught flu each winter, and suffered from debilitating headaches; in June 1836 Carlyle told Jack that 'her ailment is being *sick* far too often (I mean as women are sick)'[10] – presumably a reference to an irregular menstrual cycle. Moreover, though she talked boldly about not fearing poverty and starvation, she dreaded penury as much as Carlyle.

John Sterling, beloved of both Carlyles, was also ill, spitting blood; Carlyle told Jack in March that the doctors, 'trusting in *stethoscope*' (a fairly recent and still controversial invention), had told him not to spend another winter in England. 'They speak of Madeira; of the West Indies, where he has property: I am very sad about it, for I love this man.' Sterling, with his 'radiant, lambent all-hoping brotherly' temperament, reminded Carlyle of 'my poor Irving'. Mill, too, was 'wasted thin'; 'the hair of his head is fast falling out'. Carlyle blamed the 'Taylor-Platonica affair mainly' and the illness of Mill's stern, feared, but respected father.[11] James Mill died in June, after which his son suffered a second breakdown.

John Carlyle was at last coming home. Jane confided in April to her Liverpool cousin Helen Welsh that he would not be successful among the

London fashionables who 'fill up' their spare time 'with vapours and something that goes by the name of *"checked perspiration"* '. 'I am afraid he is not a Man for grappling in a cunning manner with *"checked perspiration"*, and accordingly that there is small hope of his getting into profitable employment here as a Dr.'[12]

Jack spent a month 'flying about', as Carlyle told his mother; he talked of 'doing all things under the Moon and above it', but never actually did anything. Lady Clare wanted his services again for the winter, after which Jack thought he might stay on in Rome and try to maintain a practice there.[13] In August, when John was awaiting the summons back to Rome, Carlyle was sorry but also relieved that his brother would no longer be on hand with his 'whimsicalities and littlenesses, offensive and self-offensive'.[14] John certainly offended Jane in July, when he apparently told her again that her illness might be cured if she would only find something to do.[15]

In July Jane left for Templand and her mother, stopping at her uncle's house in Liverpool, but first in Manchester, where she stayed with Carlyle's youngest sister Jenny, who had recently married Robert Hanning, a former farm labourer at Scotsbrig now engaged 'in some small kind of trade in Manchester'.[16] Jane took her first ever journey by train, travelling from Manchester to Liverpool, at first 'dreadfully frightened', fearing she might faint and not be able to get 'the horrible thing stopt', but finding it felt no faster or more alarming than the coach she had travelled in from London.[17]

With the Carlyles, absence always made the heart grow fonder, apart from sulks and tiffs over missed posts and continuations of arguments begun before they parted. Jane wrote from her mother's house on 30 July, opening surprisingly, 'Dearest of friends – I write the thanks which I cannot speak', which Carlyle, in his note on the letter, identifies as one of Mrs Montagu's 'too stately preludes' which had amused Jane. Life with her mother and three Welsh cousins who were staying at Templand did not suit her. Breakfast was at 10 a.m., and there was no peace anywhere except in one's locked bedroom. Her mother drove her mad: 'You know my Mothers way – she will give you every thing on earth except the thing you *want* – will do anything for you except what you *ask* her to do.'[18] Carlyle was sympathetic in reply: 'O my poor Lassie, what a life thou hast had: and I could not make it other; it was to be *that* and not another!'[19]

It being August, London had emptied. Mill had gone abroad, ill, with two younger brothers, and was to join Mrs Taylor and her children; John Sterling had also left, not to return for many months; and the Austins were getting ready to go to Malta, where Mr Austin was to prepare a report on the administration. Carlyle saw that 'the appointment ought to cure poor Austin, but will not: a twanging, iracund, incompatible painful man'. As for Sarah Austin, what was she but a *'femme alors célèbre – ach Gott!'*[20]

In Jane's absence Carlyle was being sociable, going to dinners and 'routs' at the Bullers', where he met, but kept his distance from, Bulwer and 'seven "Persian Princes"', with scimitars, turbans and long greenish gowns'. *'Ach Gott!'* again.[21] At another Buller party Carlyle observed the French exile Cavaignac being introduced to Harriet Grote, wife of the Radical MP and historian of Greece, George Grote. He recounted the experience to Jane:

Charles Buller led C away to introduce him to a large lady, whom I afterwards perceived to be Mrs Grote: C went, without struggling, tho' verily like a sheep led to the slaughter; the presentation performed, he made I think *five* successive low bows to Mrs Grote (a very shower of rapid bows); then without uttering a word, like a sheep *from* the slaughter (or a *calf*, for you know how he *goes*), and landing in a very elegant attitude, stood, five paces off, with his hat behind his back, looking out into space and the general movement of the Rout, – *this* whole Introduction, Acquaintance, Friendship being begun, carried on, finished and abolished with such incredible brevity as I describe! . . . That, I think, is the best method I have ever seen of being introduced to the large Mrs Grote.[22]

By early September Jane was back at Cheyne Row, describing to her cousin Mary Welsh how she had missed Carlyle at the coach terminus and had boarded a Chelsea omnibus to get home:

By and by however, the omnibus stopt, and amid cries of *'no room Sir'* – *'Cant get in'* – Carlyle's face beautifully set off by a broad-brimmed white hat gazed in at the door, – like the Peri who *'at the gate of heaven stood disconsolate'* [in Thomas Moore's *Lallah Rookh*, 1817] – in hurrying along the Strand pretty sure of being too late, – amidst all the imaginable and unimaginable phenomena which that immense thorough fare of a street presents; his eye (heaven bless the mark) had lighted on *my trunk* perched on the top of the omnibus and had recognised it! This seems to me one of the most indubitable proofs of *genius* which he ever manifested.[23]

Mill and Mrs Taylor, meanwhile, were causing tongues to wag as news arrived that they had left Mill's young brothers and Mrs Taylor's children with a nurse in Switzerland while they went on to Nice and Italy. Carlyle relayed the gossip to Jack, now in Geneva with Lady Clare. Mill 'is on with the wa[ter]-witch or Land-witch!'[24] To Sterling, who was in Bordeaux, he told the same story, demonstrating his ability to be simultaneously broad-minded and critical, though comically so:

Is it not very strange, this pining away into desiccation and nonentity, of our poor Mill, if it be so, as his friends all say, that this Charmer is the cause of it? I have not seen any riddle of human life which I could so ill form a theory of. They are innocent, says Charity; they are guilty, says Scandal: then why in the name of wonder are they dying broken-hearted?[25]

★

In April 1836 Emerson had sent Carlyle a copy of his friend Dr Channing's anti-slavery pamphlet and, momentously, a copy of 'our American reprint of the Sartor'. 'Five hundred copies only make the edition, at $1.00 a copy. About 150 copies are subscribed for.'[26] Emerson and his friends had found a Boston publisher to undertake the reprint, which appeared in 1836 with a short anonymous introduction by Emerson himself. It was the first edition of Carlyle's long-nurtured book – indeed his first published book altogether – and when reprinted the following year, sold 1,166 copies in America, making a profit for James Munroe, the publisher.[27] Munroe was not obliged to pay the author a single cent, since there was no copyright agreement between Britain and the United States, much to the annoyance of British authors, notably Dickens, who famously courted American displeasure by making the scandalous piracy of American publishers the theme of his after-dinner speeches when he visited the United States in 1842.

Emerson's efforts (and those of his associates Charles Stearns Wheeler and Le Baron Russell) brought Carlyle's work to an appreciative American intellectual audience. Longfellow, Oliver Wendell Holmes, and James Russell Lowell owned early copies.[28]

Carlyle was encouraged by Emerson's news of his book's progress in America, but because of his precarious financial position he could not afford to redeem the package Emerson had sent. He was amused at the fate of Sartor, lying 'dormant, very singularly again, waiting his new destinies; never to be liberated by me'. Finally John Carlyle struck a bargain with the Post Office and collected the unlucky book.[29]

Emerson again pressed him to come over to America and lecture when he wrote in September announcing that the first 500 copies of Sartor had been sold.[30] But Carlyle was in no more of a position to accept the invitation than he had been the previous year. However, some friends in London had begun to think he should lecture at home, and by December 1836 they were investigating lecture halls and preparing to print prospectuses and drum up subscribers for a series of six lectures on German literature.[31] The leading light was Harriet Martineau, who was also soon doing a 'thriving trade' in American copies of Sartor which she had brought with her from America in August 1836, later importing more and selling them 'at fifty percent!', as Jane informed Carlyle in July 1837, 'the profits (I understand) being considered as pertaining to you'.[32]

In late November Harriet Martineau called on the Carlyles with her friend Jane Wilson. Carlyle described Harriet to Jack:

She is not half so ill-favoured as they represented her; indeed not ill-favoured at all; but a rather interesting woman: very shrewd, and very good; of the Unitarian friend of humanity species. She is deaf as a Post, but carries an ear trumpet, and manages quite handsomely.[33]

Harriet and Carlyle took to one another, rather surprisingly given the propensity of both to be hypercitical of other people. Harriet set down her thoughts about her contemporaries in her *Autobiography*, written in 1855 when she thought she was dying and had long since withdrawn to the Lake District to act out, as if in a play – as Carlyle recalled in *Reminiscences* – *'Life in the Sick-room'*.[34] According to Harriet, Macaulay was vain, Brougham 'play[ed] the fool among silly women', and Jeffrey (the source of the Carlyles' information that she was 'excessively ugly')[35] flirted 'with clever women, in long succession'. Bulwer sat on a sofa, 'sparkling and languishing among a set of female votaries, – he and they dizened out, perfumed, and presenting the nearest picture to a seraglio to be seen on British ground'. The list went on: 'Poor Campbell, the poet, obtruding his sentimentalities', and the women – Lady Sydney Morgan, Mrs Austin, Mrs Jameson with their 'gross and palpable vanities'[36] – her gallery is nearly as clever as Carlyle's own pen-portraits.

Amidst all this sharpness comes the long appreciative portrait of Carlyle – the only contemporary whom she remembered warmly, except for the scientists Lyell and Darwin:

No kind of evening was more delightful to me than those which were spent with the Carlyles. About once a fortnight, a mutual friend of theirs and mine [Jane Wilson] drove me over to Chelsea, to the early tea table at number five, Cheyne Row . . . I like the house for no other reason than that I spent many very pleasant evenings in it: but it has now become completely associated with the marvellous talk of both husband and wife.[37]

About Carlyle specifically, with his 'rugged face, steeped in genius', Harriet was remarkably astute. She remembered that he would come down from his writing to take tea with his visitors looking 'as if he was on the rack' until conversation got fairly under way, when he became animated, though 'as variable as possible in mood'. She continued with a passage of genuine insight:

I have seen Carlyle's face under all aspects, from the deepest gloom to the most reckless or most genial mirth; and it seemed to me that each mood would make a totally different portrait. The sympathetic is by far the finest, in my eyes. His excess of sympathy has been, I believe, the master-pain of his life. He does not know what to do with it, and with its bitterness, seeing that human life is full of pain to those who look out for it: and the savageness which has come to be a main characteristic of this singular man is, in my opinion, a mere expression of his intolerable sympathy with the suffering. He cannot express his love and pity in natural acts, like other people; and it shows itself too often in unnatural speech. But to those who understand his eyes, his shy manner, his changing colour, his sigh, and the constitutional *pudeur* which renders him silent about every thing that he feels the most deeply, his wild speech and abrupt manner are perfectly intelligible.[38]

Jane and Harriet also liked one another; in February Jane regaled Sterling with an account of Carlyle's new-found success with women, including Harriet: 'You cannot fancy what way he is making with the fair Intellectuals here! There is Harriet Martineau presents him her ear-trumpet with a pretty blushing air of coquetry.'[39] Harriet and Jane Wilson, with the help of Henry Taylor, a civil servant and minor poet and dramatist who was later, with Carlyle, a favoured guest at Lady Ashburton's house parties, set about organising Carlyle's six lectures, which were delivered in Willis's Rooms on King Street, St James's, in May 1837. Harriet Martineau recalled simply: 'He had matter to utter; and there were many who wished to hear him; and in those days, before his works had reached their remunerative point of sale, the earnings by his lectures could not be unacceptable.'[40]

All the preparation was taken out of Carlyle's hands; he only had to turn up at 3 p.m. on Mondays and Fridays in May to deliver them, which he did, trembling. When in February Jane Wilson gave him a 'list of Ladyships and honourable women' who had paid their guinea subscription, Carlyle confessed to feeling 'a kind of terror'.[41] He did not want to lecture, but he was persuaded by his friends that it was 'a sure financial card', and since 'there was no other card in my hand at all', he agreed.[42] The lectures had to be given without notes, as he was busy correcting proofs of *The French Revolution* – finished in January 1837 – right up to the end of April.

A number of recent acquaintances rallied to the cause. James Spedding, who spent his life on an edition of Bacon's works, wrote to the writer, politician, and dilettante Richard Monckton Milnes (later Lord Houghton) on 4 April:

The list of subscribers is at present not large, and you are just the man to make it grow. As it is Carlyle's first essay in this kind, it is important that there should be a respectable muster of hearers . . . Learning, taste, and nobility are represented by Hallam, Rogers, and Lord Lansdowne. H. Taylor has provided a large proportion of family, wit, and beauty, and I have assisted them to a little Apostlehood [members of an exclusive brotherhood from their Cambridge University days]. We want your name to represent the great body of Tories, Roman Catholics, High Churchmen, metaphysicians, poets, and Savage Landor.[43]

*room where I was born; to the middle of that Arch was my father's House, village of Ec--clefechan, 4 Dec. 1795. —T. Carlyle (Chelsea, 5 ju--ly, 1871)—

Thomas Carlyle's birthplace
at Ecclefechan.

Jane Carlyle's birthplace
at Haddington.

Carlyle's parents, James and Margaret Carlyle, silhouettes by Jane Carlyle.

Jane Carlyle's parents, Dr John Welsh and Grace Welsh.

Carlyle's first Edinburgh lodgings.

Edward Irving, pencil sketch
by Joseph Slater, 1825.

Jane Welsh, miniature by
Kenneth Macleay, 1826.

Comely Bank, Edinburgh.

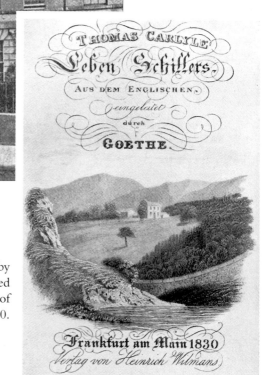

Craigenputtoch, drawing by
George Moir reproduced
in the German edition of
Carlyle's *Life of Schiller*, 1830.

Carlyle, sketch by Daniel Maclise, *Fraser's Magazine*, June 1833.

Charles Dickens, by Daniel Maclise, 1839.

'The Fraserians', sketch by Daniel Maclise, *Fraser's Magazine*, January 1835.
CENTRE BACK: Maginn, with Procter seated on left, Irving on right. LEFT: Hogg with tartan, Coleridge with stick, Thackeray behind with eyeglass. RIGHT: Fraser, centre, talking to Lockhart, Carlyle in back row, second from right, with shock of hair.

Carlyle, drawing by Alfred,
Count d'Orsay, 1839.

Jane Carlyle, by Samuel Laurence, *c.* 1838.

5, Cheyne Row, Chelsea.

Carlyle's mother, by Maxwell, 1842.

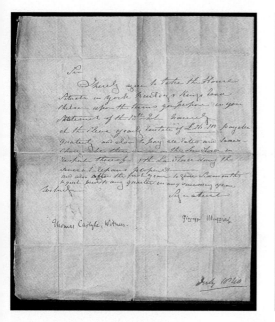

(*Above*) Copy of Mazzini's lease, witnessed by Carlyle, 1840.

(*Above right*) Thackeray rope-dancing, sketch by himself, May 1851.

(*Right*) 'Hero worship reduced to "faute de mieux"', Carlyle's trousers being exhibited to admirers, sketch by Elizabeth Paulet, 1843.

(*Below right*) 'Notre Dame de Chelsea', sketch by Elizabeth Paulet, 1844.

Jane Carlyle, by Samuel Laurence, 1849, copied by Elizabeth Paulet.

Rumour had it that Lord Brougham was planning to attend, as Carlyle told Alick a week before he was due to begin. 'I contemplate the withered *kippered* countenance of that Ex-Chancellor twitching and jerking there on me (as its wont is) with a strange mixture of a shudder and a laugh on my part.'[44] Alick, who had written apologetically about the £200 or more he had long owed his brother but was still unable to repay, must have felt a twinge of anxiety on Carlyle's behalf. But Carlyle, always magnanimous where either money or family or both were concerned, told him not to worry about the debt.[45]

In addition to his exhaustion from writing *The French Revolution* and his anxiety about the lectures there was Jane's persistent illness, which became so worrying that Carlyle asked Mrs Welsh to come and nurse her. He reported to Jean that Jane's mother 'made no dallying; but put herself into the mail' as soon as she received his letter.[46] By the end of April Carlyle had called in the Sterlings' doctor, James Morrah, who, 'I saw, dreaded consumption', but decided that there was 'nothing organic gone wrong'.[47] Looking back in November, Carlyle confided in his journal that he had been 'terrified' by the seriousness of Jane's illness.[48]

Somehow he got through the lectures, earning £135, enough to live on for the next year, he thought. He found the experience less dreadful than he had feared, though he did recall how he had 'stood wriggling in my agony of incipiency' before beginning, while Jane Wilson whispered reassuringly to Jane that 'people like it; the more of that, the better does the Lecture prove!'[49] People did like it, on the whole, though Harriet Martineau found that, as organiser and prime mover, she was herself unnerved by Carlyle's 'unconcealable nervousness', as he stood, 'yellow as a guinea, with downcast eyes, broken speech at the beginning, and fingers which nervously picked at the desk before him'.[50] Henry Taylor, who also had a stake in the success of the venture, reported that Carlyle's nerves were alarming, but that he was saved by his very naivety and by 'occasional outbreaks of his genius and spirit'.[51]

Another new friend, Fanny Wedgwood, wife of Hensleigh Wedgwood, commented, 'We were agreeably surprised to see the room very decently full & a very good audience'. Samuel Rogers, Sir Humphry Davy, and Lord and Lady Lansdowne were there, '& the audience looked altogether fashionable & Eras says Mr C talks of making £150 by these lectures which we all thought wd have been such a failure'.[52] 'Eras' was Erasmus Darwin, cousin of the Wedgwoods; he had been 'hovering' round the Carlyles for some months, as Carlyle told Jack in February 1837.[53]

It is a testimony to the attraction Carlyle exercised on his growing number of acquaintances and well-wishers that they were so concerned about the success of his lectures. Over 200 people attended, and though Carlyle certainly did not enjoy the experience, he saw that he could do it, and that he could earn a useful amount of money in a short time; by the end of the year he was telling his mother that he was preparing to lecture again in 1838 to earn another year's bread.[54]

★

By December 1837 Carlyle had become famous. Not the lectures, though they did spread his name among literary people, but the publication of *The French Revolution*, on 9 May 1837, was the cause. Its eruption into the world after such an extraordinary and prolonged labour was remarkable. Carlyle was no longer an unknown writer; his translations, and even more his essays, had attracted attention, anonymous though they were. He was already known personally to a range of influential people, but that range was about to expand exponentially, until the Carlyle 'circle' became one of the phenomena of the age.

The French Revolution begins with the death of Louis XV in 1774. Carlyle sketches the conditions from which the Revolution arose — aristocratic luxury and selfishness, mismanagement of the country's finances, and the plight of France's neglected poor. Carlyle does not write like other historians; there is no measured, authoritative tone, past tense narrative, or logical setting out of cause and effect. He writes the whole history in the vivid present tense; addresses many of the huge cast of characters directly, from kings and queens and ministers to humble members of the National Guard and even the blacksmith who fashions the pikes for the storming of the Bastille; and treats the whole complex event as a vast panorama enacted before 'the eye of History'.[55]

Carlyle's comments and conclusions are also delivered in the present tense; in the second chapter he sketches a member of the nobility and lets him do duty for the whole class, then turns in the next paragraph to the crimes of that class against the poor:

Such are the shepherds of the people: and now how fares it with the flock? With the flock, as is inevitable, it fares ill, and ever worse. They are not tended, they are only regularly shorn. They are sent for, to do statute-labour, to pay statute-taxes; to fatten battlefields (named 'bed of honour') with their bodies, in quarrels that are not theirs; their hand and toil is in every possession of man; but for themselves they have little or no possession.[56]

Such mingled irony, anger, and sympathy is sustained throughout; the tone transforms the usual ironic mode, in which a cool distance is assumed in the service of moral outrage, into one in which the outrage is visible and audible *through* the apparent disinterest. Like readers of a Scott novel,

affording view over something

invited to share some vantage point with the narrator – a hill overlooking the scene of the Battle of Prestonpans in *Waverley* (1814), for example[57] – we perch with Carlyle in 'some coign of vantage', watching the National Assembly meeting in May 1789 and using our foresight (which is actually hindsight) to predict or question the outcome: 'Destiny has work for that swart burly-headed Mirabeau', and 'That greenish-coloured (*verdâtre*) individual is an Advocate of Arras; his name is *Maximilien Robespierre*.'[58]

The narrative method is more flexible than one might imagine. A few pages on from the vignettes of Mirabeau and Robespierre, Carlyle can turn his attention to an important actor in the drama who is *absent* from this Assembly:

And worthy *Doctor Guillotin*, whom we hoped to behold one other time? If not here, the Doctor should be here, and we see him with the eye of prophecy: for indeed the Parisian Deputies are all a little late. Singular Guillotin, respectable practitioner; doomed by a satiric destiny to the strangest immortal glory that ever kept obscure mortal from the resting-place, the bosom of oblivion! . . . Unfortunate Doctor! For two-and-twenty years, unguillotined, shall hear nothing but guillotine, see nothing but guillotine; then dying, shall through long centuries wander, as it were, a disconsolate ghost, on the wrong side of Styx and Lethe; his name like to outlive Caesar's.[59]

The storming of the Bastille occupies the most celebrated passage, the one which, more than any other, impressed Dickens, whose narrative technique in *A Tale of Two Cities* (1859) consciously recalls Carlyle's in 'that wonderful book', which Dickens claimed in a letter of 1851 to be reading 'for the 500th time'.[60] In the Preface to his novel, Dickens repeated in public his private praise, saying he hoped 'to add something to the popular and picturesque means of understanding that terrible time, though no one can hope to add anything to the philosophy of Mr Carlyle's wonderful book'.[61]

In Carlyle, the philosophy and the picture are one. As early as September 1834, when he was writing 'The Diamond Necklace', Carlyle told Jack, 'It shall be such a Book! Quite an Epic Poem of the Revolution: an Apotheosis of Sansculottism!' adding, 'Here, as in so many other respects, I am alone: without models, without *limits*.'[62] This is no exaggeration. Carlyle read all the French histories of the Revolution; he even gave them scrupulous mention in his footnotes. But what he wrote was *sui generis*.

His 'I am a camera' technique, though tiresome from time to time, is fully vindicated when he describes the events of 14 July 1789:

All morning, since nine, there has been a cry everywhere: To the Bastille! Repeated 'deputations of citizens' have been here, passionate for arms; whom De Launay has got dismissed by soft speeches through port-holes. Towards noon,

Elector Thuriot de la Rosière gains admittance; finds De Launay indisposed for surrender; nay disposed for blowing up the place rather. Thuriot mounts with him to the battlements: heaps of paving-stones, old iron and missiles lie piled; cannon all duly levelled; in every embrasure a cannon, – only drawn back a little! But outwards, behold, O Thuriot, how the multitude flows on, welling through every street: tocsin furiously pealing, all drums beating the *générale*: the Suburb Sainte-Antoine rolling hitherward wholly, as one man!

In the middle of the excitement, Carlyle pauses briefly to note the ordinariness, as well as the extraordinariness, of time passing: 'How the great Bastille Clock ticks (inaudible) in its Inner Court there, at its ease, hour after hour; as if nothing special, for it or the world, were passing! It tolled One when the firing began; and is now pointing towards Five, and still the firing slakes not.'

He unleashes the climax in a surprisingly short space of narrative time, for, with all his expansive rhetoric, Carlyle uses his present tense method in a deliberately breathless way, as if the prose were trying heroically to keep up with events as they succeed one another with bewildering speed:

For four hours now has the World-Bedlam roared: call it the World-Chimera, blowing fire! The poor Invalides have sunk under their battlements, or rise only with reversed muskets: they have made a white flag of napkins: go beating the *chamade*, or seeming to beat, for one can hear nothing. The very Swiss at the Portcullis look weary of firing; disheartened in the fire-deluge: a porthole at the drawbridge is opened, as by one that would speak. See Huissier Maillard, the shifty man! On his plank, swinging over the abyss of that stone Ditch; plank resting on parapet, balanced by weight of Patriots, – he hovers perilous: such a Dove towards such an Ark! Deftly, thou shifty Usher: one man already fell; and lies smashed, far down there, against the masonry! Usher Maillard falls not: deftly, unerring he walks, with outspread palm. The Swiss holds a paper through his porthole; the shifty Usher snatches it, and returns. Terms of surrender: Pardon, immunity to all! Are they accepted? – '*Foi d'officier*, On the word of an officer', answers half-pay Hulin, – or half-pay Elie, for men do not agree on it, 'they are!' Sinks the drawbridge, – Usher Maillard bolting it when down; rushes-in the living deluge: the Bastille is fallen! *Victoire! la Bastille est prise!*'[63]

It is characteristic that Carlyle should find a moment in this pell-mell account to give scrupulous attention to the disagreement among witnesses and historians about which half-pay officer, Hulin or Elie, gave the vital 'word of an officer'.

This is, as Dickens said, a wonderful book. Others pointed out that Carlyle's strength lies in the first and third parts, 'The Bastille' and 'The Guillotine', rather than in the second, 'The Constitution'. Mill wrote in his wide-ranging review of the work in the *London and Westminster Review* that Carlyle went 'much too far in his distrust of analysis and generalisation' and 'set too low a value on what constitutions and forms of government can do'.[64] And Frederic Harrison, reading the book while a student at Oxford in 1852, distinguished between the marvellous pictures – like scenes in a Shakespeare play – and the incomplete hold on constitutional issues, exacerbated by a too-great disdain, or as Harrison called it a 'Rabelaisian' sneering, towards the eighteenth century in general.[65]

Carlyle's opinion of the Revolution was a simple one. It was, he thought, the inevitable result of a long build-up of corruption at state, church, and local level, undermining the people's faith in monarchy, aristocratic rule, and Catholic Christianity. The whole edifice was rotten, and had to fall. To that extent, Carlyle welcomes the Revolution, supporting with his exhortative prose the masses who finally took up arms against oppression. If things went too far, and too much blood was shed for no permanent gain, that was a regrettable but also inevitable irony. As with the sorcerer's apprentice in Goethe's story, the spell had been cast and the work begun, and no command to stop could hope to be heeded.

The earliest review to appear, by Lady Sydney Morgan, the fashionable Irish novelist, in the *Athenaeum* on 20 May, was not heartening. 'Originality of thought is unquestionably the best excuse for writing a book; originality of style is a rare and a refreshing merit', runs the momentarily encouraging opening sentence, which, however, ends, 'but it is paying rather dear for one's whistle, to qualify for obtaining it in the university of Bedlam'. Carlyle is charged with 'quaintness, neologism and a whimsical coxcombry', faults which become intolerable when sustained through 'three long volumes of misplaced persiflage and flippant pseudo-philosophy'. The only crust thrown to Carlyle is an admission that there are, 'amidst an all-pervading absurdity of mannerism', passages 'of great power'.[66]

Carlyle was not upset by this unpromising start. 'Some condemn me, as is very natural, for "affectation"', he told Jack on 30 May. 'Others are hearty, even passionate (as Mill) in their estimation':

On the whole it strikes me as not unlikely that the Book may take some hold of the English People, and do them and itself a little good. Jeffrey writes me a very brisk Letter about it last week; full of good augury, of praise and blame, and how I shall infallibly be much praised and much blamed, and on the whole carry my point.[67]

Mill wanted to atone for the destruction of the manuscript by writing a long and – if he found it possible conscientiously to do so – admiring review. He had hoped to be the first into print on the subject, asking Carlyle as early as February if he could read the proof-sheets as they were produced.[68] In the event, his review appeared in the *London and*

Westminster Review in July. Mill explained to a correspondent three years later that he had been determined to review the work early because it was

> a book so strange & incomprehensible to the greater part of the public, that whether it should succeed or fail seemed to depend upon the turn of a die – but I got the first word, blew the trumpet before it at its first coming out & by claiming for it the honours of the highest genius frightened the small fry of critics from pronouncing a hasty condemnation, got fair play for it & then its success was sure.[69]

Mill's review is a fine appreciation of a work written in a style quite the opposite of his own. Like Lady Morgan, he lodges objections against the repetitions, the 'quaintnesses of manner', and the German phraseology. But he introduces these criticisms in order to sweep them aside with the force of his appreciation. 'This is not so much a history, as an epic poem', he begins, and, reversing the movement of the *Athenaeum*'s opening sentence, he adds, 'and notwithstanding, or even in consequence of this, the truest of histories': 'It is the history of the French Revolution, and the poetry of it, both in one; and on the whole no work of greater genius, either historical or poetical, has been produced in this country for many years.'[70]

If Carlyle's style is peculiar, it is so by contrast with 'the jog-trot characterless uniformity which distinguishes the English style of this age of Periodicals'. Even when compared to great historians like Hume and Gibbon, Carlyle takes the palm, because, like Shakespeare, he brings you amongst human beings rather than abstractions. 'There is, as Mr Carlyle has said, the fifth act of a tragedy in every peasant's death-bed'; it is Carlyle's special achievement to have placed such living pictures before us that we see the 'human interest', whether epic, tragic, elegiac, or comic and farcical. Though Mill rejects Carlyle's disdain for institutions and constitutions in general, he agrees with his underlying view that the Revolution 'was the breaking down of a great Imposture', the tyranny of the few over the twenty-five million.[71]

Mill ends by placing Carlyle among the very great names in the history of English literature:

> When we consider that Wordsworth, Coleridge, and others of their time, whose deviation from the beaten track was but a stone's throw compared with Mr Carlyle, were ignominiously hooted out of court by the wise tribunals which in those days dispensed justice in such matters, and had to wait for a second generation before the sentence could be reversed, and their names placed among the great names of our literature, we might well imagine that the same or a worse fate awaits Mr Carlyle; did we not believe that those very writers, aided by circumstances, have made straight the way for Mr Carlyle and for much else . . . The book before us needs to be read with catholic spirit; if we read it captiously,

we shall never have done finding fault. But no true poet, writing sincerely and following the promptings of his own genius, can fail to be contemptible to any who desire to find him so; and if even Milton's 'Areopagitica', of which now, it would seem, no one dares speak with only moderate praise, were now first to issue from the press, it would be turned from with contempt by every one who will think or speak disparagingly of this work of Mr Carlyle.[72]

This review set the tone for the subsequent response. Thackeray praised the work in *The Times* on 3 August, complaining mildly of the 'Germanisms and Latinisms, strange epithets, and choking double words', but excusing them as mere details like the 'quaint carvings' on a Gothic cathedral. He quotes from the storming of the Bastille, agreeing that 'this is prose run mad' but perceiving that there is method in the madness, and marvelling at the 'breathless interest' Carlyle has managed to instil into 'this hundred-times told tale'. Above all, the book 'has no CANT' and 'possesses genius, if any book ever did'.[73]

Jane read Thackeray's review in proof before it appeared, presumably through Edward Sterling. She told Carlyle, who was recovering from his exertions at Scotsbrig, that 'as Tommy Burns said of Eliza Stodart's leg – "it's nae great tings"!' but would do the book no harm.[74] Carlyle had seen Thackeray at the Bullers' and the Sterlings' houses; 'his article is rather like him, and I suppose calculated to do the Book good', he told Jack on 12 August. He gives a succinct *curriculum vitae* of Thackeray: 'a half-monstrous Cornish giant; kind of painter, Cambridge man, and Paris Newspaper Correspondent, who is now writing for life in London'.[75] Thackeray, not yet a famous novelist but still a young journalist and caricaturist, was well disposed towards Carlyle. He was a friend of Charles Buller, with whom he had been at Cambridge; he had helped Buller get elected for Liskeard in 1832 by canvassing for him; and he had noted in his diary in that year that Buller was lucky to have had Carlyle as a tutor. While in Liskeard, he read Carlyle's *Wilhelm Meister* translation and *German Romance*.[76] The two men became personally acquainted some months after his well-meaning review of *The French Revolution*; Thackeray remained a genuine, if often perplexed, admirer of the older man.

★

Worn out from writing and lecturing and worrying, Carlyle had gone to Scotsbrig towards the end of June; he stayed there until the middle of September, leaving Jane, with her health somewhat improved, still being looked after by Mrs Welsh. Before he went he told Jack that 'Jane and her Mother *cannot* live together'. 'Poor Mrs Welsh', though full of good intentions, was impossible to live with unless you disregarded altogether the 'whims emotions caprices and conclusions she takes up chameleon-like by the thousand daily' – which Jane could not do.[77] By the time Mrs Welsh returned to Templand at the end of July, Jane had reached the same conclusion. 'I shall never more flatter myself with the notion of being able to live *reasonably* beside her', she told Carlyle on 3 August.[78]

The couple exchanged warm letters; Jane told funny stories about social encounters and Carlyle replied lovingly. He sent gloomy news about his siblings and their spouses, none of whom was doing well financially. Alick was a particular source of anxiety because of his poverty, bitterness, and drinking, and his mother was querulous in her fear that he would emigrate.[79] When writing his 'Reminiscences', Carlyle recalled this summer as one of exhaustion and jangling nerves. He writes of a moment during his return home in a way which has affinities with Wordsworth's description in *The Prelude* (1850) of 'spots of time', those moments in which flashes of backward- and forward-looking insight occur in an outdoor landscape familiar to the traveller from childhood:

I well remember that ten-minutes' survey I had of Annan and its vicinity, the forenoon after my landing there: Brother Alick must have met me at the Steamboat Harbour, I suppose; at any rate we were walking towards Scotsbrig together, and at Mount-Annan Gate, bottom of Landheads Hamlet, he had left me for a moment till he called somewhere; I stood leaning against a stone or milestone, face towards Annan, of which with the two miles of variegated cheerful green slope that intervened, and then the Solway Firth far and wide, from Gretna to St Bees Head, and beyond it, of the grand and lovely Cumberland mountains, with Helvellyn and even with Ingleborough in the rearward, there was magnificent view well known to me. Stone itself was well known to me: this had been my road to Annan School from my tenth year onward; right sharp was my knowledge of every item in this scene, thousandfold my memories connected with it, and mournful and painful, rather than joyful, too many of them! And now here it was again; and here was I again. Words cannot utter the wild and ghastly expressiveness of that scene to me; it seemed as if Hades itself and the gloomy Realms of Death and Eternity were looking out on me through those poor old familiar objects; as if no miracle could be more miraculous than this same bit of Space and bit of Time spread out before me . . . for seven or more weeks after, I rode often down and up this same road, silent, solitary, weird of mood, to bathe in the Solway; and not even my dear Mother's love and cheery helpfulness (for she was then still strong for her age) could raise my spirits out of utter grimness, and fixed contemptuous disbelief in the future. Hope of having succeeded, of ever succeeding, I had not the faintest, – was not even at the pains to wish it; said only in a dim mute way, 'Very well, then; be it just so, then!'[80]

Of the progress of *The French Revolution* Jane reported with proprietorial pride from Cheyne Row on 3 August: '*The Metropolis* is entirely occupied with our work'. She, meanwhile, was about to set off with the elder Sterlings in 'the handsomest carriage in all London' on a tour to Oxford,

Worcester, and Malvern, the 'eminent watering-place, where of course people eat monstrous breakfasts' and suffer from ennui.[81] From Malvern she wrote again a week later, commenting sardonically on her hosts and travelling companions:

We have private rooms like the rest of the *great* people, and are served with excellent food, and Mrs S sews at her worsted work, and I work at your purse and the [Stimabile] exclaims '*By Jove Hester this tranquillity is – delicious*', but from the fierce tone he begins in, tho' sinking into dieaway softness at the close, I am always expecting the '*delicious*' will come out a '*damnable*' – and when there is no more to be done 'we go about worship' and so to bed where I for one, tho' quiet enough, sleep no better than at Chelsea . . . and in short tout va bien – so far. How long it will go so well is another question – He talks of being absent a month. But I guess that either he will return sooner, or I will separate myself from the Great Balloon and alight in a parachute, before that time.[82]

Soon Jane was entertaining Carlyle from Clifton, near Bristol, with a tart account of the imminent breaking up of the travelling threesome. Riding with Mr Sterling on donkeys at Malvern, she had made a sharp remark about stubbornness and Conservatives, to be told by 'his Whirlwindship' (hitting near the mark): 'Do you know Mrs Carlyle you would be a vast deal more amiable if you were not so *damnably* clever!'[83] As well as regaling Carlyle with her witty, self-mocking anecdotes, Jane responded kindly to his evident depression, but she also acknowledged that when they were together she often found it impossible to cope with his moods:

I wanted to kiss you into something like cheerfulness and the length of a kingdom was betwixt us – and if it had not – the probabilities are that *with the best intentions* I should have quarrelled with you rather. Poor men and women! what a time they have in this world – by destiny and their own deserving – But as Mr Bradfute used to say 'tell us something we do not know'.[84]

Back in Chelsea by the end of September, Carlyle wrote to Jack, without apparent pleasure, that he was now 'to be considered as a kind of successful man', though still having to worry about money. He had agreed to write an article on Scott (a review of Lockhart's seven-volume biography of his father-in-law) for the *London and Westminster Review*, in order to put 'a few pounds into my pocket'.[85] It is a cautious essay, polite to Lockhart and grudgingly fair to Scott as a 'noted and even notable man', though whether he was a 'great man' was 'still a question with some'. Carlyle seesaws between disapproval of Scott's worldliness and a lukewarm endorsement of his genuineness, between warmth towards Scott's Scottishness and disdain for the flummery of his 'Scotch' novels.

Scott's great fame and enormous fortune, before he lost it in the great publishing crash of 1826, are handled with subdued irony. Carlyle makes no attempt at a detailed critique of the novels, saying 'the great fact about them is, that they were faster written and better paid for than any other books in the world'.[86] The whole review, which was published in January 1838, though demonstrating flashes of insight into the writing of novels, history, and biography, shows signs of the restraint, even constraint, Carlyle imposed on himself not to attack a writer with whom he could be compared in many respects, and of whom it might be thought that he was jealous.

John Forster reviewed *The French Revolution* positively in the *Examiner* in September; Forster was, Carlyle told Jack, 'a blustering bubbly-jockish [turkey-like] kind of man, from *whom* surely I expected not praise'.[87] He wrote to his mother, too, about his book's success, grateful that she had been 'toiling' through it during the summer, finding the French names 'a sad clog', but getting further than any of the rest of his family.[88] He humorously describes how 'everybody is astonished at every other bodys being pleased with this wonderful performance!'[89]

In October the actor-manager William Charles Macready sent him a free ticket for the season to Covent Garden Theatre. Macready had just taken over the management, and was trying to restore the respectability of the theatre by putting on serious plays and clearing the auditorium of prostitutes. He sent free tickets to people who were distinguished in science, the arts, and literature.[90] Carlyle began attending about once a week to see 'some Shakespeare notability or the like'. 'Last night we had Macbeth', he told Jack on 7 November, 'deeply impressive in some parts, totally distracted in others'. 'I skip the Farce [which followed the main drama] and get home about eleven.'[91]

Carlyle was somewhat surprised at the approaches from eminent people who admired *The French Revolution*. The most unexpected praise came from Southey, poet laureate, Tory, and *Quarterly* reviewer, though an ex-firebrand and revolutionary enthusiast in his young days in the 1790s. The two men had first met in February 1835 at Henry Taylor's house, where Carlyle had formed a more positive impression of Southey than of Wordsworth, whom he met at the same time.[92] Southey astonished him by his height and leanness – like a pair of tongs, Carlyle said – and also by his propensity to vehement anger. In his short reminiscence, written in 1867, he recalled how Southey would blush beautifully like a girl 'when you touched genially the pleasant theme', but was covered by a 'serpent-like flash of *blue* or black blush' as soon as 'you struck upon the opposite'.[93] When the two men met again in April 1838, 'fancy my surprise at finding Southey full of sympathy, assent, and recognition of the amplest kind, for my poor new Book!'[94]

Carlyle had sent a copy to Emerson, who wrote in September 1837 calling it 'wonderful', though 'too Gothically efflorescent' in style. He had noted in his journal in August his feelings on seeing Carlyle's handwriting in the post office window:

How noble it seems to me that his words should run out of Nithsdale or London over land & sea, to Weimar, to Rome, to America, to Watertown, to Concord, to Louisville, that they should cheer & delight & invigorate me . . . How noble that alone & unpraised he should still write for he knew not who, & find at last his readers in the valley of the Mississippi.

Emerson, who had seen Carlyle in his dignified poverty in the isolation of Craigenputtoch, gives due expression here to the extraordinariness of Carlyle's achievement; in the process, he provides an insight into the darker side of Carlyle's character and career, the side which we have seen in his journals and letters – his terrible grimness and the utter conviction that he was alone and misunderstood which persisted long after he had been recognised and admired. Emerson also wrote to Carlyle of his shame as an American 'that you should educate our young men & that we should pirate your books'.[95]

A couple of months later, Emerson took steps to prevent the same thing happening with *The French Revolution* as had happened with *Sartor*. He told Carlyle in November that he had negotiated with a Boston publisher to bring out Carlyle's history officially. Carlyle would receive 76 cents for each copy sold.[96] Emerson was able to send £50 (or $242) in July as the first instalment of payment due.[97]

At last Britain seemed disposed to catch up with America in its appreciation. In December 1837 Carlyle told his mother that James Fraser had actually proposed to reprint *Sartor* and his collected essays. 'The wind is changed there at any rate! The last time he heard of Teufelsdröckh and the proposal to print it, he shrieked at the very notion.' 'Changed times!' as Carlyle wrote in his journal.[98]

After some hesitation on Fraser's part about financial details, *Sartor Resartus* finally appeared in July 1838 in its first English edition, not with Fraser but with Saunders and Otley of Conduit Street. *Critical and Miscellaneous Essays*, in four volumes, was published in September 1839 by Fraser, but in an edition imported from Emerson's American printing.[99]

Harriet Martineau almost became involved when she offered to correct proofs of the *Essays*, supposing, as she recalled in her *Autobiography*, 'that the pieces were to be simply reprinted' from their originals in the periodicals. She intended to save Carlyle from himself, since 'the sight of his proofs had more than once really alarmed me, – so irresolute, as well as fastidious, did he seem to be as to the expression of his plainest thoughts. Almost every other word was altered; and revise followed upon revise.'

Carlyle would not let Harriet undertake the task. She remembered his visiting her one day while the printing was going on:

In came Carlyle, laughing loud. He had been laughing in that manner all the way from the printing-office in Charing Cross. As soon as he could, he told me what it was about. He had been to the office to urge on the printer: and the man said, 'Why, Sir, you really are so very hard upon us with your corrections! They take so much time, you see!' After some remonstrance, Carlyle observed that he had been accustomed to this sort of thing, – that he had got works printed in Scotland, and . . . 'Yes, indeed, Sir,' interrupted the printer. 'We are aware of that. We have a man here from Edinburgh; and when he took up a bit of your copy, he dropped it as if it had burnt his fingers, and cried out, "Lord have mercy; have you got that man to print for? Lord knows when we shall get done, – with all his corrections!"' Carlyle could not reply for laughing, and he came to tell me that I was not singular in my opinion about his method of revising.[100]

The ghosts of disagreements with Tait over *German Romance*, and perhaps also his spat with Jeffrey over the proofs of the Burns article, had no doubt returned to haunt him through this comic encounter.

Though Harriet and Jane had liked one another at first, the more Harriet visited Cheyne Row, the less she liked Jane. 'She is so coquettish', she wrote to Fanny Wedgwood on 20 February 1838, 'so different when she & I are alone, & when others are by; & she breaks in with little jokes & wanting notice when we are talking.'[101] Perhaps Jane was jealous of Harriet Martineau, an independent writer to whom Carlyle talked as he would to a man, and one to whom Carlyle was obliged for her enterprise in selling American copies of *Sartor* to British friends. Harriet recalled in her *Autobiography* that when she gave Carlyle money from the sale of the first batch, he was uncomfortable, and spent it on a pair of signet rings, one for Jane and one for Harriet herself; so the next time she sold a bundle of *Sartors*, in February 1838, she and Erasmus Darwin brought four bottles of brandy instead of cash.[102]

The question arises: why did Jane not help Carlyle with his proofs? She was proud of his writings, which she sometimes called 'ours', and she was Carlyle's first and most loyal reader. Was it that she and Carlyle could not co-operate? Did she feel that if she undertook any sort of intellectual work, it should be her own – something original, or at least a translation such as the one she had begun in January 1836? Why then had she not finished that? Carlyle's dark hints in his journals about his temper, depression, loneliness, and 'wickedness' suggest that he excluded her from the things that mattered to him; if so, she responded by being a super-wife in the sense of creating domestic comfort – Eve making everything beautiful on a shoestring – but also by sniping at him in letters and, increasingly, also at home when visitors came, as they now did in numbers, to listen to the Sage of Chelsea. Many acquaintances commented on her self-appointed role, apparently complacently tolerated by Carlyle, of mockingbird and put-upon wife of genius presiding over the tea table. She was not happy in the role, which could not satisfy her any more than mere housekeeping for two (with the help of a servant) did, but she appears to have been unable to create a more fulfilling one for herself.

★

In February 1838 Carlyle began to discuss with Henry Taylor the subject of his next set of lectures, which was to be the history of European literature, beginning with the Greeks.[103] He was dining out quite often, accompanied by Jane when she was well, seeing the Sterlings, Erasmus Darwin, and Harriet Martineau, but very little of Mill, who had withdrawn more and more from friends outside the Taylor–Fox circle. At the Sterlings' Carlyle met F. D. Maurice, the liberal Church of England clergyman – now John Sterling's brother-in-law – who was becoming famous as the leader of the Broad Church Movement and an advocate of workers' education.

Though Maurice admired Carlyle, the feeling was not mutual. Carlyle found him 'one of the most entirely uninteresting men of genius that I can meet with in society'.[104] He was never more than lukewarm in his opinion of Maurice, though the pair were to be linked in the famous picture by Ford Madox Brown – *Work*, begun in 1852 and finished in 1863 – which showed the two men of letters looking on approvingly as a group of muscular labourers dig up a road in Hampstead.

Carlyle was cooling towards Sterling, whom he found 'argumentative, *babblative*, and on the whole unpleasant and unprofitable to me'. He made a memo to himself: 'Keep out of his way till he mend a little.' Sterling's wife was, he wrote sourly, 'a heap of euphuistic affectations'.[105] Richard Monckton Milnes kept asking Carlyle to dinner and to his famous miscellaneous breakfasts; Milnes bought a copy of *Sartor* from Harriet Martineau, attended Carlyle's lectures, and began to jot down his conversation in a commonplace book. Carlyle 'talks as graphically as his "French Revolution"', he wrote in 1838; 'his personality is most attractive'.[106] Milnes was an incorrigible wit and practical joker like his friend Charles Buller; his career in Parliament was held back by distrust of his reputation for flippancy and epicureanism. (He collected a huge library of licentious and erotic literature after inheriting his father's property in 1858.)[107]

Carlyle rather liked Milnes, though like everyone else he did not take him seriously. Years later the story was told that Carlyle 'who, when some ecclesiastic gloomily inquired in his presence "What would happen if Jesus Christ returned to earth *now*?" retorted – "*Happen*! why Dickie Milnes would ask him to dinner, to be sure, and would ask Pontius Pilate to meet him." '[108]

Whether he liked it or not, and for the most part he did not, Carlyle was beginning to move in more elevated circles. In February 1838 he was invited to an evening party given by the Chancellor of the Exchequer in Melbourne's government, Thomas Spring Rice. He described the occasion in a letter to his mother, sharing with her his lively sense of the sharp contrast in fortune between host and guest:

The invitation being now on my table, I think I will send it you, as a strange thing enough. I could not help thinking, Here is the man that disposes annually of the whole revenue of England; and here is another man who has hardly enough of cash to buy potatoes and onions for himself: Fortune has for the time made these two tenants of one drawing-room. The case, I believe, is this: Miss Spring Rice, the Chancellor of the Exchequer's eldest daughter, a very beautiful and rather intelligent young woman, was one of my German hearers last year and took a fancy for my notability; so her mother the Lady Theodosia was obliged to be 'at home' for me. The people were very kind; Spring Rice himself a substantial goodhumoured shifty-looking man of fifty: the rooms were genial with heat, and light as the sun at noon; there were high dames and 'distinguished males', simmering about like people in the press of a June-Fair: the whole thing went off very well; and I returned about one in the morning with a headache that served me for more than a day after. 'It will help with your Lectures', Jane said. May be so: but in the meantime it has quite *hindered* my natural sleep and composure.[109]

Carlyle took trouble here to make his descriptions accessible to his mother by drawing analogies with things and places she knew, the June-Fairs, or livestock markets in Dumfriesshire; he did so again on 12 April when telling her of the 'dinnering and *partying*' that went on in London at that season. He also described his glimpse of the Queen the day before, when she passed in an open carriage on her way to Windsor. Victoria had succeeded William IV in June 1837, aged only eighteen. Carlyle felt sorry for her:

It seemed to me the poor little Queen was a bit modest nice sonsy [cheerful] little lassie; blue eyes, light hair, fine white skin; of extremely small stature: she looked timid, anxious, almost frightened; for the people looked at her in perfect silence; one old liveryman alone touched his hat to her: I was heartily sorry for the poor bairn, – tho' perhaps she might have said as Parson Swan did, '*Greet* [weep] not for me brethren; for verily yea verily I greet not for myself.'[110]

In a rare surviving letter from this time Jane told Fanny Wedgwood about preparations for the new lectures:

This time he positively set his face against *fire-eating* in Willis's Rooms, amidst

Harp-players and Dancing Masters and such like; whereupon Mr Darwin has found him a less *fashionable* quarter (near Portman Square) where he expects to feel less like a Mountebank.[111]

The *Examiner* carried a paragraph on 22 April describing the forthcoming lecture topics as 'the four great periods of Paganism, Christianity, Scepticism, and what, in deference to Mr Carlyle's predilections, we suppose we are to call Germanism or *Goetheism*'.[112] The writer was probably Leigh Hunt, who reviewed all twelve lectures as they were delivered during May and the first half of June.

Hunt had visited his friends less often during the past year or two; Carlyle thought as early as October 1834 that he was put off by Carlyle's 'Cameronian rigour'. Then in 1835 Hunt had been embarrassed by his son John's petitioning the Carlyles for 'a few shillings' after being excluded from his father's house, an affair which Carlyle handled with sympathy for the young man and tact towards his father, who was himself an inveterate, if imaginative, borrower of shillings.[113] Carlyle observed in his journal on 15 May 1838 that Hunt's criticism of his lectures so far was 'no longer *friendly*, not so in spirit, tho' still in letter; a shade of spleen in it'. He put it down to jealousy – 'he finds me grown to be *something* now' – and commented drily on Hunt's taking him to task for praising Roman thrift in the third lecture: 'He expresses himself afflicted with my eulogy of *thrift*, and two days ago he had, *multa gemens* [groaning mightily], to borrow two sovereigns from me!'[114]

The lectures earned Carlyle £260. Thackeray reviewed the first one favourably in *The Times*, and Jane was able to give a cheerful account to Jean Aitken after attending it, which she did Lazarus-fashion. 'I in a manner "took up my bed and walked" to hear him', she wrote on 1 May, 'for I was hardly up after several days of tugging on with Influenza like a fly among treacle when the arrival of a Gentleman [Erasmus Darwin] with a close carriage to take me, was a temptation not to be resisted'. Jane thought Carlyle's demeanour much improved on the previous year:

I can assume his nerves were a vast deal stiffer than last year – I took one glimpse at him (just one) when he came on the stage – and to be sure he was as white as a pocket handkerchief – but he made no gasping and spluttering as I found him doing last year at *the fourth* lecture. By and by when the rate he was getting on at, told me I might look with safety he had recovered all that 'bonny red in his cheeks' which Miss Corson of Craigenputtoch so highly admired – and having a very fine light from above shining down on him he really looked a surprisingly beautiful man.[115]

One new acquaintance during this year, Charles Darwin, took immediately to Carlyle, as his cousin, soon to be his wife, Emma Wedgwood, also did. Emma dined with Carlyle at her brother

Hensleigh's house in June, and found he had 'the most straightforward manner in the world'. Charles, visiting Cheyne Row for the first time with his brother Erasmus in November, came away convinced that 'one must always like Thomas', but he was not favourably impressed by Jane: 'It is high treason, but I cannot think that Jenny is either quite natural or lady-like'.[116] In Jane's defence it must be said that Darwin's ideal of a wife, as written under the column headed 'Marry' opposite the one headed 'Not Marry' in his notes weighing up his options, was summed up as follows: 'Only picture to yourself a nice soft wife on a sofa with good fire, and books and music perhaps.'[117]

Not only was Carlyle now showered with invitations, but he began to be asked to sit for his portrait. In July 1838 Jane told Jean that 'an artist of *genius*' – Samuel Laurence, who did portraits of all the great Victorians – was to do Carlyle's. Laurence's sketch was delivered to her in September, when Carlyle had once more escaped to Scotland, and she got the artist to promise to do a bigger one in oils when he returned from a trip to Italy.[118]

Macready sent another year's complimentary theatre ticket in October. Carlyle was now indubitably, at the age of nearly forty-three, a successful man, though he was still poor and still plagued by depression and dyspepsia. He scribbled a poem at this time, 'Poor Thomas Cairel', in which he castigates himself as the 'foolishest of men' and bemoans the fact that though he has published his book on the French Revolution – 'Book without its like' – and though '*Sartor* called *Resartus*' has also finally appeared, there has come 'not a coin of money in', which was no more than the melancholy truth.[119] In his journal on 3 December he berated himself in guilt-ridden, though opaque, terms:

I seem to myself more a monster than a man. O the detestable irrepressible beastly ideas I have of myself and of man and men! How could Swift laugh at such things and write them down. They are things to be shuddered over, and kept in profoundest concealment. – For one thing, I am always in the despicablest state of health: *that* is the main source of them I believe.[120]

It is impossible to tell whether Carlyle refers here to matters sexual or excremental or both. He was a troubled man with an unfulfilled wife. Yet times *had* changed for both of them. After twelve years of marriage and many more of financial difficulties and the struggle for recognition, he was a force to be reckoned with. He and Jane together in their little Chelsea house represented a Mecca for young men and women who came from far and wide to seek them out.

CHAPTER 9

Rising into Fame 1839–1840

Late in 1838 Carlyle had begun the research for a book on Cromwell. He hoped to obtain permission to use a private room at the British Museum for his studies, since he found the public reading room noisy and distracting. F. D. Maurice was asked to investigate this, while Carlyle also arranged to borrow books from the Cambridge University Library.[1] With Spedding, Milnes, John Forster, and others, he was campaigning for a new London Library, from which books could be borrowed, a luxury not available to readers of books in the British Museum. Spedding wrote a prospectus, which Carlyle sent to Forster in January 1839, asking for his support. Carlyle and Spedding already had the historian Henry Hallam, the poet and giver of literary breakfasts Samuel Rogers, Lord Lansdowne, and the Marquess of Northampton as subscribers and guarantors.[2]

On 27 January Forster published in the *Examiner*, of which he was then editor, 'a fierce blast' by Carlyle, 'Appeal for London Library':

> To all readers the buzz and bustle of a public room is an importunate distraction; to this waste of faculty add waste of time in coming and going; waste of patience in waiting; add discomfort, perturbation, headache, waste of health . . . There does not exist here any library whatever, worthy of the name of library, from which a reader can borrow books.[3]

The group continued to hold meetings at intervals, to draw up prospective rules for the library, and to write to the press, until the London Library was finally opened in May 1841, proving an immediate success.

Carlyle's new-found fame made him a natural magnet for those who were proposing or agitating for reform in various areas of social policy. He had already agreed to support Henry Cole's petition to Parliament for universal penny postage, a cause close to his heart. As he put it in a statement he drafted for Cole, 'a tax on Letter-writing is a tax on deliberate Speaking, – on the deepest want and most indefeasible right of man; a tax, as it were, on the act of living'.[4] Cole's reform replaced payment by the recipient, according to weight, with a penny stamp paid for by the sender.

The measure was finally passed, coming into effect on 10 January 1840 – 'a most blessed result', as Carlyle declared to his sister Jean on New

Year's Day, though by 15 February he was complaining that 'the Penny arrangement brings in so many [letters], it eats in upon one's morning not a little'.[5] He had become a desirable correspondent for friends and strangers alike just at the time when letter-writing was rendered easier for all.

Another petition in which Carlyle could not fail to take an interest was Thomas Noon Talfourd's bill to extend authors' copyright to sixty years from the date of publication. Wordsworth, Southey, and his old acquaintance David Brewster were among the supporters, and Carlyle told Forster in February 1839 that he would add his weight too.[6] True to his word, he wrote a petition which Talfourd presented to the House of Commons on 7 April 1839, and which Forster published in the *Examiner* on the same day. The assembled MPs were surely startled by the novelty of Carlyle's aggressive-defensive self-presentation:

To the Honourable the Commons of England in Parliament assembled, the Petition of Thomas Carlyle, a Writer of Books,
    Humbly sheweth,
That your petitioner has written certain books . . .
That your petitioner had not the happiness to receive from Mr Thomas Tegg [publisher of cheap reprints and opposer of the copyright campaign], or any Publisher, Republisher, Printer, Bookseller, or Book-buyer, or other the like man or body of men, any encouragement or countenance in writing of said books, or to discern any chance of receiving such; but wrote them by effort of his own and the favour of Heaven.
That all useful labour is worthy of recompense; that all honest labour is worthy of the chance of recompense . . .
May it therefore please your Honourable House to protect him . . . and (by passing your Copyright Bill) forbid all Thomas Teggs and other extraneous persons, entirely unconcerned in this adventure of his, to steal from him his small winnings, for a space of sixty years at shortest. After sixty years, unless your Honourable House provide otherwise, they may begin to steal.[7]

Thus spoke the author of the much-rejected *Sartor Resartus* and the critically successful but financially unrewarded *French Revolution*. He may have had those proud ironic words of Samuel Johnson to his belated would-be patron again in mind. For once a piece of Carlyle's writing pleased Wordsworth, who, as another writer whose works had made very little money, was a keen petitioner for reform. Wordsworth wrote to Talfourd on 8 April, 'Carlyle's petition is like all he does and is, quite *racy*.'[8] A compromise bill extending copyright to include the author's life plus seven years, or forty-two years from publication, whichever was longer, was finally passed by Parliament in July 1842.

Carlyle had been reminded of his own position by the recent arrival of bills of exchange from Emerson for the American editions of his books –

£50 sent in July 1838 for the first two volumes of *Essays* and £100 in January 1839 for *The French Revolution*.[9] Carlyle announced his American earnings to Jack on 4 February: 'A hundred and fifty pounds from beyond the salt sea, while not a sixpence could be realised here in one's own country by the thing!'[10] He took the bills to show James Fraser, 'and told him I hoped he would blush very deep. The poor creature did blush: but what could that serve?' Fraser had sold almost the whole edition of *The French Revolution*, and had raised, Carlyle told Jean, more than £1,000 from it, 'but none of it seems to belong to the writer'.[11] Fraser's affairs were mysterious, not to say chaotic, and Carlyle was no man of business himself. In March Fraser talked of Carlyle receiving some money, and in April he paid £110 and negotiated to print a second edition of 1,500 copies of *The French Revolution*.[12]

The Carlyles' circle of acquaintance was widening. In March Carlyle met Forster, with whom he was collaborating over copyright and the London Library. Forster, later Dickens's close friend and biographer, was a non-practising lawyer, an energetic journalist and miscellaneous writer, a taker up of causes, a sociable, well-meaning, but opinionated and 'noisy' man, as Carlyle told Sterling in 1841. He was nicknamed 'Fuz' in 1839 by his amused (and sometimes exasperated) friends, after Bulwer's estranged wife Rosina caricatured him in a novel attacking her husband, now Sir Edward Lytton Bulwer. In *Cheveley; or, the Man of Honour*, Forster is 'Mr Fuzboz', 'a sort of lick-dust . . . to Mr anybody, and everybody else of celebrity to whom he could get access'.[13] Dickens, for whom Forster acted as literary agent and legal adviser over the years, could not resist representing his friend as the dogmatic, pompous, 'too, too smiling' Mr Podsnap 'with a fatal freshness on him', in *Our Mutual Friend* (1864-5).[14]

Soon the Carlyles were experiencing Forster's managerial demeanour at first hand. Mrs Welsh was staying at Cheyne Row, and as Carlyle told Jack on 11 March, 'the whole three of us' had set out the previous Saturday evening to see Macready act in Bulwer's play *Richelieu; or the Conspiracy*, which had just opened at Covent Garden. They went

under escort of one Foster [*sic*] the Examiner Critic who had volunteered to serve on the occasion, to see a new tragedy of Bulwers, from the orchestra box! . . . Foster is a noisy inflated mortal, full of goodwill to me, not wise overmuch, but trained to civility and the rules of life. We had the best theatrical place imaginable, nay a little drawing room and fire behind us when we liked. The Tragedy pretended to be applauded, drew from *us* peals of laughter more than once; as perfect a dud I venture to say as has been written lately; but Macready acted Richelieu the old Cardinal very well . . . After the play [Forster] *insisted* on taking me round to Macready; I went unwilling thro' a chaos of scenery and machinery, found Macready, a very fine fellow, pulling off his beard, extremely civil at sight of me; and standing by him, a high dressed, longfaced, flaccid, yellow-eyed, goose-looking, incoherent figure, with lean body and gaping expression of countenance, whom they presented me to as to – Sir Lytton Bulwer! Our interview needed to be brief; but I shall never forget Bulwer in this world. A mad world, my masters! We got home from farce and all, soon after midnight; nearly frozen (I feared, for the cold was bitter, St James's Pond is frozen, near to skating if this weather hold), but otherwise no worse for our expedition hitherto.[15]

Jane was, as usual during the winter, often unable to go out. She also wrote few letters – or at least few survive – and is once more visible only in snatches from Carlyle's letters. She did hold one soirée at the end of February, which Carlyle defined for his mother as 'a Party of Persons who have little to do except wander thro' a room or rooms, and hustle and simmer about, all talking to one another as best they can'.[16] A month later Jane gave a dinner, to which she invited three Frenchmen from opposite political parties, the exiled republicans Godefroi Cavaignac and Louis Latrade and a new arrival, Alexis François Rio, a royalist and art historian, introduced to the Carlyles by Monckton Milnes.[17]

Jane recounted the evening to her mother on 7 April:

The dinner, however, could hardly be called a 'successful one'. Rio appeared on the scene at half-past three, as if he could not have enough of it. Latrade came as the clock struck four. But Cavaignac – alas! Two of his friends were on terms about blowing each other's brains out, and Cavaignac was gone to bring them to reason; and not till they were brought to reason would he arrive to eat his dinner. Now, whether the men would be brought to reason before the dinner was quite spoiled, was a delicate question that Latrade himself could not answer. So, one half hour being gone, and still no appearance of him, I was on the point of suggesting that we should wait no longer, when a carriage drove up and deposited Mrs Macready and Macready's Sister. Was ever beefsteak pie in such a cruel predicament! There was no help, however, but to do the amiable, which was not ill to do even in these trying circumstances, the visitors were such attractive sort of people. Mrs Macready asked me how I liked Harriet's Book [Harriet Martineau's novel, *Deerbrook*]. I answered 'how do *you* like it?' She made wide eyes at me and drew her little mouth together into a button. We both burst out a-laughing, and that is the way to get fast friends. An hour and a half after the dinner had been all ready we proceeded to eat it, – Rio, Latrade and we. And when it was just going off the table cold, Cavaignac came, his hands full of papers and his head full of the Devil knows what; but not one reasonable word would he speak the whole night. Rio said nothing to his dispraise, but I am sure he thought in his own mind 'Good Gracious! I had better never be in the same room with him again!'[18]

In fact Rio recorded this dinner of 1 April in his journal, allowing that Cavaignac had 'something of a lion in his face and his look', but declaring that he was 'much less interesting to me than my hosts by whom I was more and more enchanted'.[19] The previous day, Easter Sunday, 31 March, Rio described his evening call on the Carlyles, when he had met Jane for the first time and received the surprise invitation to dine with Cavaignac. Jane must have been in a soft and cheerful mood, or Rio's understanding of English somewhat lacking, or perhaps her tone hard to decipher, for he came away with a pleasant impression from Jane of her life at Craigenputtoch:

[Carlyle's] wife has the most beautiful gaze possible. When I arrived, it was she who received me; her husband had not yet returned from his walk. She told me charming details of their six years of solitude, in Dumfriesshire in Scotland, immediately after their marriage, and little by little the conversation became so spirited and so intimate, that I strongly regretted not having arranged a way of passing more time with this interesting couple already so attractive to me; unhappily I was promised elsewhere, and I had to leave Elysium for Limbo.[20]

For good measure, Rio recounted in his journal on 8 April, after his last visit to the Carlyles before leaving London, what he had heard of the 'romantic' history of their marriage. The story was a mangled version of Carlyle's relation to the Bullers and Irving's to the Welshes: 'It seems that Carlyle was private tutor at her father's house and that their union was strongly opposed by maternal authority.'[21]

In the same letter to her mother in which she described the republican–royalist dinner, Jane told of another French visitor, who had caused the Carlyles' maid, Helen Mitchell of Kirkcaldy, to burst out with expressions of admiration:

To-day gone a week the sound of a whirlwind rushed thro' the street, and there stopt with a prancing of steeds and footman thunder at this door, an equipage, all resplendent with skye-blue and silver, discoverable thro' the blinds, like a piece of the Coronation Procession, from whence emanated Count D'Orsay! ushered in by the small Chorley [Henry Chorley, literature and music critic of the *Athenaeum*]. Chorley looked 'so much alarmed that he was quite alarming'; his face was all the colours of the rainbow, the under-jaw of him went zig-zag; indeed, from head to foot he was all over one universal quaver, partly, I suppose, from the soul-bewildering honour of having been borne hither in that chariot of the sun; partly from apprehensions of the effect which his man of Genius and his man of Fashion were about to produce on one another . . . Carlyle in his grey plaid suit, and his tub-chair, looking blandly at the Prince of Dandies; and the Prince of Dandies on an opposite chair, all resplendent as a diamond-beetle, looking blandly at *him*. D'Orsay is a really handsome man, after one has heard him speak and found that he has both wit and sense; but at first sight his beauty is of that rather disgusting sort which seems to be like genius, 'of no sex'. And this impression is greatly helped by the fantastical finery of his dress: sky-blue satin cravat, yards of gold chain, white French gloves, light drab great-coat lined with velvet of the same colour, invisible inexpressibles, skin-coloured and fitting like a glove, etc., etc. . . . He was no sooner gone than Helen burst into the room to condole with me that Mrs Welsh had not seen him – such a '*most* beautiful man and most beautiful carriage! The Queen's was no show i' the worl' compared wi' that! Everything was so grand and so preceese! But it will be something for next time.'[22]

Carlyle, too, was amused at the sudden arrival in Cheyne Row of the 'Phoebus Apollo of Dandyism' who was known to be living with Lady Blessington, stepmother of his estranged wife.[23] In May Carlyle actually 'dined at D'Orsaydom, or Blessingtondom one day, with W. Savage Landor', on which occasion D'Orsay 'drew a fine portrait of me in the drawing-room, really very like'.[24] That D'Orsay's sketch was published as a lithograph by J. Mitchell of Old Bond Street in June 1839 gives eloquent proof of the interest Carlyle now generated, helped no doubt by the notoriety of the artist.[25]

If the assorted French visitors were enchanted with the Carlyles, so were two Scottish friends, George Lillie Craik and the Edinburgh lawyer John Hunter, who was visiting London in March 1839. Hunter thought Carlyle 'one of the most wonderful men of his day', 'a very extraordinary personage, full of originality and genius', though without the 'plastic power' of Coleridge. He noticed on a visit to Cheyne Row – when he found Carlyle 'at his siesta in a *house* dress of striped plaid from head to foot, the surcoat being in the form of a long dressing gown' (exactly as in *A Chelsea Interior*) – that he was 'not happy'. He concluded shrewdly that Carlyle's 'immortal longings and high aspirations are dashed and thwarted by the vain struggle he is always making to solve the riddle of the world'. He also noted the paradox in Carlyle's manner. With all his gloom he would intermingle 'bursts of laughter which made his lungs crow like Chanticleer'.[26]

Hunter's friend Leigh Hunt 'joined us about nine o'clock and gave a livelier and happier tone to the conversation', though it touched on the macabre too:

A horrible fact as to Bentham was mentioned, of wch I had not before heard. It seems he left special instructions in his will that his body should . . . be preserved & *dried* by some method . . . that it shd then be dressed in a particular suit wch he had been in use to wear . . . Mrs Carlyle mentioned one horribly ludicrous part of the affair – that he had himself selected the *eyes* that were to be put in this fearful mummy.[27]

(The fearful mummy – Bentham's body bequeathed to science and to his followers – still sits in his everyday clothes in a glass box in University College London.) Hunter observed that Jane Carlyle 'joined in *con amore* in all our conversations & took her own views often combating those of her husband'.[28]

In March 1839 Carlyle first talked tête-à-tête with Lady Harriet Baring, wife of William Bingham Baring, who became Lord Ashburton on the death of his father in 1848. He was invited to dinner at Bath House, Piccadilly, along with Chevalier Bunsen, the Prussian diplomat and scholar. Lady Harriet was in the habit of commanding the presence and conversation of clever men like Milnes and Henry Taylor, and she now called on Carlyle to 'sit and talk' with her 'specially for a long long while', as he told his mother on 8 March.[29] To Jack he wrote more freely, beginning with a sketch of Bunsen, whom he had first met a few weeks before at one of Milnes's breakfasts:

Others were there; and the great hero Bunsen with red face large as the shield of Fingal; not a bad fellow, nor without talent; full of speech, Protestantism, Prussian Toryism, who zealously inquired my address, and walked with me into Pimlico, but has not called yet. I saw him since, the hero of a dinner at Bingham Baring's, of whose wife the proud Lady Harriet ('a cleva Devil', as Taylor calls her) there was mention above . . . The dinner was after 8, and ruined me for a week after. Bunsen did not shine there; the Lady hardly hid from him that she feared he was a *bore*; she kept me talking an hour or more up stairs, 'a cleva devil', *belle-laide*, full of wit, and the most like a dame of quality of all I have yet seen.[30]

Though he routinely complained about the effect of dining out on his head and his digestion, Carlyle relished the opportunities he now had to go into society and meet people prominent in literature, science, and politics, if only because he could collect his impressions of these specimens of the age. His main subject of study at this time was the seventeenth, rather than the nineteenth, century, but his greatest urge was to comment on the 'condition of England' in the present day.

At a dinner given by Erasmus Darwin in the spring of 1839 Carlyle came up against two rival conversationalists, Charles Babbage, the mathematician and inventor of a famous calculating machine (called 'the Difference Engine'), and Charles Lyell, the geologist. According to Charles Darwin, who was also there, Carlyle's talk 'was very racy and interesting, just like his writings', but he sometimes went on for too long on the same subject. On this occasion he 'silenced every one by haranguing during the whole dinner on the advantages of silence. After dinner Babbage, in his grimmest manner, thanked Carlyle for his very interesting lecture on silence.'[31] Carlyle, for his part, reported to Jack that Babbage was 'a mixture of craven terror and venomous-looking vehemence; with no chin too', 'forever loud on the "wrongs of literary men" tho' he has his £20,000 snug!'[32] Babbage was one of the great eccentrics, inventor of innumerable machines and gadgets, including one-way glass, a stomach pump, and a design for a tunnel under the Thames, as well as his great machine which could calculate all the prime numbers between 0 and 10,000,000. He had scant success in getting government support during the 1820s and 1830s; bureaucracy held up the process of patenting in the fashion satirised by Dickens with his Circumlocution Office in *Little Dorrit* (1855–7).[33]

★

The lecturing season saw Carlyle deliver six lectures on the Revolutions of Modern Europe – two on the Reformation, two on the English Revolution, and two on the French Revolution – beginning on 1 May 1839. For the first time, as Carlyle observed to his sister Jean at the end of March, he was 'not driven by absolute poverty'. In April he told Emerson that he was 'richer than I have been for ten years', but had thought it wise to lecture again to be sure of an income.[34] He was even contemplating hiring a horse for regular riding, since he had so enjoyed a 'canter round by Hampstead' with John Sterling. But the expense put him off – 'one ride I find would cost me, with ostlers, messengers and other trash, 8 shillings of money!'[35]

The audience for his lectures was more fashionable than ever. Jane treated Mrs Carlyle to a description of the fine carriages which blocked the street, though she also gave a graphic picture of the state of Carlyle's nerves and digestion at the second lecture on 4 May:

He had neglected to take a pill the day before, had neglected to get himself a ride, and was out of spirits at the beginning – even I who consider myself a perfectly unprejudiced judge, did not think he was talking his best or anything like his best, but the '*splendids*' '*devilish-fines*', '*most trues*' and all that which I heard heartily ejaculated on all sides, showed that it was a sort of mercy in him to come with bowels in a state of derangement, since if his faculties had had full play, the people must have been all sent home in a state of excitement bordering on phrenzy.[36]

Leigh Hunt reviewed the series in the *Examiner*. He was struck by the effect of the lecturer's opinions and style on his hearers, especially when he dealt with Protestantism and his heroes Luther and Knox in the second lecture:

There is frequently a noble homeliness, a passionate simplicity and familiarity of speech in the language of Mr Carlyle, which gives startling effect to his sincerity . . . The effect of hearty convictions like these, uttered in such simple, truthful words, and with the flavour of a Scottish accent (as if some Puritan had come to life again, liberalized by German philosophy and his own intense reflections and experience), can be duly appreciated only by those who see it. Every manly face among the audience seems to knit its lips, out of a severity of sympathy, whether it would or no; and all the pretty church-and-state bonnets seem to thrill through all their ribbons.[37]

Hunt noticed, however, that Carlyle came to some dubious conclusions, 'as when he pronounces a victory in battle to be a "judgment of

God" ' and, in his third lecture (on Cromwell and Puritanism), 'hampered himself with denouncing falsehood in Charles I, and allowing it in his successful adversary – Cromwell'.[38] This is an early recognition of Carlyle's propensity, which increased with the years, to argue for the rightness of might.

As in previous years, Carlyle suffered tortures of anxiety and thought the lectures poor. He declared to Emerson on 29 May, when the course was safely behind him, that there was 'but one moderately good Lecture, the last, – on Sansculottism, to an audience mostly Tory, and rustling with the beautifullest quality silks'.[39] Jane, who had suffered from his nerves and temper while he was engaged in the task, proudly told her mother-in-law that the last lecture 'was the most splendid he ever delivered – and the People were all in a heart-fever over it'. 'In short we left the concern in a sort of whirlwind of "*glory*".' She also related the poignant fact that she saw 'poor Mrs Edward Irving sitting opposite me in her weeds and looking as ugly as sin': 'I thought of her lot and all the things that must be passing thro her heart to see her husbands old friend there carrying on the glory in his turn, while *hers*! – what was it all come to.'[40]

Jane was eager for glory too, though it came in the form of domestic victories, such as the one described humorously to Carlyle's mother:

Perhaps I am a genius too as well as my Husband – indeed I really begin to think so – especially since yesterday I *wrote down* a parrot! which was driving us quite desperate with its screaching. Some new neighbours that came a month or two ago brought with them an accumulation of all the things to be guarded against in a London neighbourhood – viz a pianoforte, a lap-dog and a Parrot – the two first can be born[e] with as they carry on the glory within doors but the Parrot since the fine weather has been holding forth in the Garden under our open windows – Yesterday it was more than usually obstreperous – so that Carlyle at last fairly sprang to his feet declaring he could 'neither think nor live' – Now it was absolutely necessary that he should do both – so, forthwith, on the inspiration of conjugal sympathy I wrote a note to the Parrot's mistress (name unknown) and in five minutes after Pretty Polly was carried within and is now screaching from some subterranean depth whence she is hardly audible – Now if you will please to recollect, that at Comely Bank I also *wrote down* an Old Maid's house-dog and an only son's pet-bantamcock you will admit I think that my writings have not been in vain.[41]

In June a wealthy Yorkshire manufacturer, John Marshall, one of Carlyle's 'constant Lecture-auditors', gave him the free use of a horse, which Carlyle called 'Citoyenne'. 'This is a good man; and I believe has £80,000 a year', Carlyle told his mother. He became very fond of the 'beautiful quadruped', which he lodged for the summer in a nearby stable and rode at will.[42]

Jane and Carlyle set off for Scotland at the beginning of July, travelling together for once. They went first to Liverpool, then to Templand, and in August Jane and Mrs Welsh had a holiday by the sea in Ayr while Carlyle went to Scotsbrig. He wrote to Emerson on 4 September, putting an end to any lingering hopes Emerson might have of seeing his friends in America. 'My wife sends a thousand regards', he wrote; '*she* will never get across the ocean, you must come to her; she was almost *dead*, crossing from Liverpool hither, and declares she will never go to sea for any purpose whatsoever again.'[43] The Carlyles travelled home together, taking the recently opened railways from Preston to Birmingham and from Birmingham to London. It was Carlyle's first train journey – 'like a Faust's flight on the Devil's mantle', he told Jack.[44]

Their Kirkcaldy friend Elizabeth Fergus had married the young exile Count Pepoli while they were away, having earlier taken refuge with them to avoid her brother's anger at this match, which he – and the Carlyles – thought was a clear case of fortune-hunting on the part of Pepoli.[45] Jane reported to Helen Welsh on 22 September:

Miss Fergus had become 'La contessa Pepoli' two days before our arrival, and is now domesticated with her angelic Conte within a quarter of an hour's walk of me. They both look well content; if the romance of the thing could but hold out! She will be an acquisition to *me*, and I hope her bold step (not to say rash) may be justified by a better fortune than onlookers predict for her. Old Sterling, who had been to see her, said to me to-day 'Heavenly Father! what a wreck she is! She is fifty by jove!' But love has no arithmetic. Cavaignac says 'Voilà un homme condamné à rendre sa femme heureuse! J'espère qu'il se donnera cette justification!' I hope so too. Mr Darwin says '*Ah!*' – and perhaps that is the best that can be said of the matter.[46]

In October 1839 Carlyle's stalwart supporter Sterling went into print, not without trepidation, with an assessment of Carlyle's works in Mill's *London and Westminster Review*. The trepidation was because he openly appreciated Carlyle's anti-sectarian religious position, and therefore implicitly endorsed his attacks on the Church of England, of which Sterling was still an ordained member, though unable to preach for health reasons. He had been reading David Friedrich Strauss's critical analysis of the New Testament, *Das Leben Jesu, kritisch bearbeitet* (1835–6), which interpreted the events as told in the Gospels as mythical. Orthodox Christians were alarmed at Strauss's rejection of miracles, but Sterling thought a fresh view of Christian evidences should herald an effort to revitalise the Church rather than cause it to put its head in the sand. His article on Carlyle was an attempt, as he told his clergyman friend R. C. Trench, 'to free one's own soul from the intolerable burden, the fiery load, of struggling utterance'.[47] Carlyle was touched by Sterling's review, which he called 'the most magnanimous eulogy I ever knew one man utter of another man whom he knew face to face, and saw go grumbling about there, in coat and breeches, as a poor concrete reality'.[48]

With fame and appreciation had come – though not proportionately – money, enough for the frugal Carlyles to live on. A journal entry of 23 October 1839 expresses Carlyle's relief: 'This last year, it is very strange, I have for the first time these twelve years – I may say in some measure the first time in my life – been free, almost as free as other men perhaps are, from the bewildering terror of coming to actual want of money.'[49]

But if he himself was able to say farewell to poverty, he was only too aware of the increasing distress among the country's poor, particularly in agricultural districts. In February 1839 he had agreed with the struggling Alick about the need to repeal the 'iniquitous Corn-Laws', which restricted the import of cheap foreign corn.[50] The Anti-Corn Law League, led by Richard Cobden and John Bright, had been established in 1838 and was finally successful in 1846, when Peel repealed the Corn Laws. The cold winter of 1838–9 had exacerbated the distress, and working-class protests and petitions for 'The People's Charter' increased during 1839. Carlyle expressed his sympathy in a letter to Jack of 11 March, and two days later he was discussing with Alick parliamentary initiatives to assist emigration to Australia for the distressed poor.[51]

He had no sooner finished his last lecture (on Sansculottism) than he wrote, rather surprisingly, to John Gibson Lockhart, offering to write an article for the *Quarterly Review* on '*the condition of the lower classes* in this country', explaining his choice of the Tory quarterly as follows:

My notions on this subject differ intensely from those of the speculating radicals, intensely from those of the Whigs; it seems to me the better class of the Conservatives were on the whole the persons to whom it were hopefullest and in many ways fittest to address myself.[52]

Lockhart prevaricated, but Carlyle set about writing his essay in October, after he had observed at first hand the hardship of the agricultural labourers in Annandale in the summer; he was convinced that, in their case at least, it could not be ascribed to idleness or mismanagement.[53] The piece was called 'Chartism', though it dealt only indirectly with the Chartists' calls for universal (male) suffrage, annual parliaments, paid MPs, and secret ballots. It is not one of Carlyle's best works, being often vague and taking that distant satirical tone towards current events which he had adopted, with more justification, towards the French Revolution:

These Chartisms, Radicalisms, Reform Bill, Tithe Bill, and infinite other discrepancy, and acrid argument and jargon that there is yet to be, are *our* French Revolution: God grant that we, with our better methods, may be able to transact it by argument alone![54]

Carlyle's satire embraces the *laissez-faire* establishment, the Church, the aristocracy, but also the Radicals, reformers, and agitators, none of whom was able, in his view, to solve the 'Condition-of-England Question', though the second group at least saw that 'something ought to be done'. Not that Carlyle had any solutions. His chief merit was to give striking expression to the problem, for example when he described post-feudal society as existing on '*Cash Payment*' as 'the universal sole nexus of man to man',[55] a phrase he repeated in *Past and Present* (1843), where it caught the attention of two German readers, Karl Marx and Friedrich Engels. In the ninth and penultimate chapter, 'Parliamentary Radicalism', he famously characterised Parliament as the 'National Palaver', of which Dickens undoubtedly took note for future reference – for example in *Bleak House* and other novels in which he satirised the establishment in scornful terms. In his own arresting rhetoric Carlyle demonstrated his solidarity with the poor and his understanding of their agitations and protests:

Not that Chartism now exists should provoke wonder; but that the invited hungry people should have sat eight years at such a table of the Barmecide [an imaginary meal in the *Arabian Nights*], patiently expecting somewhat from the Name of a Reform Ministry, and not till after eight years have grown hopeless, this is the respectable side of the miracle.[56]

No one could express scorn for the neglected ills of society like Carlyle, as Mill, for one, saw. 'It is a glorious piece of work', he told Carlyle early in December, having read the essay in manuscript, though he criticised (rightly) the introduction of a historical disquisition by Carlyle's old friend Professor Sauerteig as not pertinent to the subject and serving only to make the conclusion 'comparatively flat'.[57] Carlyle ignored Mill's advice to drop Sauerteig. Finding that 'no Tory dare print' the piece, he turned to the amiable James Fraser, who brought it out as an anonymous pamphlet on the old half-profits system.[58]

★

Carlyle was amused to find that the *Morning Chronicle*, noticing *Chartism*, accounted him 'a kind of *Tory*'. He told Sterling on 6 January 1840 that the author of the review, W. J. Fox, and other Radicals 'give tongue, vituperative-astonished' at his criticism of the Chartists. 'Yesterday', he added, 'I read on some Newspaper Placard in big letters "Carlyle's Cant on Chartism"; my brother was for stepping in to buy the Newspaper, but I decisively said NO.'[59] A shrewd piece of private criticism, unseen by Carlyle, was Harriet Martineau's comment to Fanny Wedgwood. 'There is a fine sympathy with many at bottom', she wrote on 17 January, 'but it is stuck thro' with prejudices and bits of injustice, as thick as tipsy cake with almonds.'[60]

Much of Carlyle's time was now taken in replying to letters from strangers. Mindful of his own feelings of despondency and rejection as a young man diffidently approaching Jeffrey, he was generous in answering requests for advice and expressions of admiration, especially when they came from students on matters of faith or career difficulties, or from uneducated working men. He was *almost* tempted, he told his mother on 17 January, to say yes to 'an innocent blithe wise-looking Scotch lad' who called on him to ask him to lecture 'on any or on all sorts of things to certain young Booksellers' shopmen' in the City.[61] And when a 'poor Paisley weaver' wrote thanking him for his writings, Carlyle asked his friend the lawyer and religious writer Thomas Erskine of Linlathen personally to seek him out.[62]

Erskine was a religious enthusiast with a faithful following, whose letters to both Carlyles were full of pious urgings; they both liked him for his sincerity and genuine kindness. In April 1838 he had written to Jane suggesting she try homoeopathy for her ailments and expressing his concern about her lack of religious faith:

I shall hope to meet with you at some other stage of the road, & finally at the end of the road, in the Kingdom of our Father – purged of our dross . . . May the blessing of God rest on you – & may you learn to open your heart wide to let it all in, – whatever shape it may come in.[63]

Another Paisley weaver, now a writer, Thomas Ballantyne, sent Carlyle his statistical study of the Corn Laws, for which Carlyle thanked him at generous length on 24 January.[64] He also found himself answering an admiring letter from the celebrated Dr Thomas Arnold of Rugby School, who described *The French Revolution* as 'a Treasure' and invited Carlyle to visit Rugby. While adroitly turning down the invitation – 'unhappily I am the worst of travellers' – Carlyle gave Arnold an account of his political concern for the poor, his lack of hope that the aristocracy and Church would do anything, and his fear that if nothing was done, disturbances such as John ('Jack') Frost's Chartist uprising at Newport in November 1839 would become more frequent and more violent.[65]

As he prepared to lecture one more time in May – this time on heroes and hero-worship – Carlyle dined out often during the spring months, though he complained about the endless invitations and refused as many as he decently could. Jane nursed her winter colds and went out infrequently, but she was happy to receive an increasing number of visitors at Cheyne Row, some for tea or just an evening chat, and a few favoured friends for dinner, which the Carlyles always ate unfashionably early in the evening. One such visitor, the exiled Italian patriot Giuseppe Mazzini, soon built up a special relationship with Jane, though it was Carlyle's reputation which had first drawn him to Chelsea. Mazzini spent most of his time gathering together English sympathisers with his cause – to free Italy from Austrian control and establish a national republic – while complaining repeatedly in his regular letters to his mother in Genoa about the waste of time involved in all the visiting and dining out he was forced to do to keep Italy in people's minds.

Harriet Taylor's husband had first brought Mazzini to meet the Carlyles in November 1837; he told his mother then that Carlyle's *French Revolution* had 'made a great noise here in England'.[66] It was not until late 1839, however, that he began to visit regularly. He lived a chaotic existence, based at various addresses in London, often travelling incognito in Europe since he had been sentenced to death in his absence in Italy in 1833; when staying in London he was dependent on money sent by his adoring mother, with which he supported various near-destitute friends, including his co-conspirators the brothers Giovanni and Agostino Ruffini.[67]

His impression of Carlyle, whose *French Revolution* (in its second edition of 1839) he reviewed in the *Monthly Chronicle* in January 1840, was of a man 'of heart, of conscience, and of genius', though two-thirds of his opinions differed from Mazzini's own, and he could see that neither would ever convert the other. As for Jane, she was intelligent and 'very kind'.[68] By March 1840 Mazzini was giving his view of the Carlyles and their marriage to the Ruffinis' mother. He told her he had met 'a Scotsman of substance and intellect', the first Briton with whom he found himself in sympathy. 'We differ in almost all our opinions; but his are so sincere and disinterested that I respect them.' Carlyle 'has a wife of talent, of generous spirit, but sickly; they have no children. They live outside the city and I go to see them now and again. They don't have the usual insular prejudices, or anything else that irks me.'[69]

Mazzini began to visit at least once a week, complaining in his weekly letter to his mother of the time it took, particularly as he lived five miles away and often had to walk for economy's sake, but also telling her of the kindness of the couple, especially Jane, 'the only woman here who knows and understands me'. At the same time, in April 1840, he wrote in English to his friend Eliza Fletcher, demonstrating the approximate grasp of the language which so amused the Carlyles: 'The flower of the souls of us exiles is faded, but, thanks to God, the perfume has remained.'[70] Mazzini was a keen attender at the lectures on heroes in May, impressed by Carlyle's speaking extempore rather than reading aloud. He and Jane went out and about seeing the sights of London together, visiting St Paul's Cathedral in June, for example.

Encouraged and helped by the Carlyles, Mazzini and Giovanni Ruffini found lodgings in the King's Road, just two streets away from Cheyne Row, into which they moved in August.[71] Both Jane and Carlyle had written references to Edinburgh acquaintances for Agostino Ruffini, who settled there as a teacher of Italian.[72] In September Jane was trying out her Italian in spirited short letters to Mazzini's mother, who became a little alarmed by her son's enthusiasm for a married woman. She was assured that Jane's affection for him was 'that of a sister', but Mazzini had to allay her anxiety in further letters in which he described Jane's appearance to his curious correspondent. She was 'still young', 'neither beautiful nor ugly', with black hair and eyes, slim, lively, but in poor health and liable to severe headaches. He loved her, he insisted, as a sister.[73] His friend Giovanni Ruffini, however, observed his demeanour with Jane and concluded in November 1840 not only that the Carlyles were not happy together, though they wished one another well, but that Jane loved Mazzini 'with womanly intensity'. Ruffini blamed Mazzini for exercising his charm on her and then protesting that he had not encouraged her feelings.[74]

It is hard to know whether Jane really had romantic feelings for Mazzini, or whether it was Ruffini who was romancing. She certainly enjoyed Mazzini's company at home and in jaunts round London, and she later confided her feelings about her mother's death and about her marriage in letters to him (now lost), but her comments on him – like her comments on most people – are routinely ironic as well as sympathetic.

Carlyle liked Mazzini too, and was very willing to write letters of introduction for him, such as one to Henry Cole in April describing him as a 'brave and gifted man'.[75] But he had little sympathy with Mazzini's republican and socialist idealism – 'smoke, smoke, and talk about *progrès*' was his shorthand version to Jack of a visit from Mazzini in March.[76] In his reminiscence of Jane he neatly summed up the course of their acquaintance with this exotic man, who brought a whiff of conspiracy and excitement into the drawing rooms of London:

Recognisably a most valiant, faithful, considerably gifted and noble soul; but hopelessly given up to his republicanisms, his 'Progress', and other Rousseau fanaticism, for which I had at no time the least credence, or any considerable respect amid my pity. We soon tired of one another, Mazzini and I; and he fell mainly to *her* share; off and on for a good many years, yielding her the charm of a sincere mutual esteem, and withal a good deal of occasional amusement from his curious bits of Exile London-and-Foreign life, and his singular *Italian*-English modes of locution now and then. For example, – Petrucci having quenched his own fiery chimney one day, and escaped the fine (as he hoped), 'there *came to pass* a Sweep', with finer nose in the solitary street, who involved him again.[77]

Carlyle remembered that he had felt more personal liking for Godefroi Cavaignac, also a republican, but less fanatical than Mazzini. Cavaignac had been helpful in 'elucidating many little points to me' during the writing of volumes two and three of *The French Revolution*, and was in the habit of giving Jane some 'frugal but elegant' gift on her birthday. He had left England for Paris rather suddenly later in the year, and Carlyle was not in London when Cavaignac visited again a few times before his death in 1845.[78] Carlyle had complained to Jack at the time, in October 1840, that his manner of departing was 'what they call "French leave", a cold scrawl of a Note sent hither some days *after* he was gone'. He mused that he had never clearly seen 'the force of that phrase before'.[79]

Apart from political exiles, there were friends old and new with whom Carlyle mixed during the spring social season. Thackeray had paid his first visit to Cheyne Row in January, enthusing to his mother in Paris that he had never met 'pleasanter more high-minded poeple'.[80] Carlyle told his own mother in February about his meeting with Bulwer once more, a man 'dressed in the extremest style of dandyism; an uneasy incoherent-looking man: − poor fellow, he has parted from his wife, who is writing books against him'.[81] Perhaps Bulwer looked uneasy because he was talking to the author of *Sartor Resartus*, in which his fashionable *Pelham* had been so mercilessly ridiculed.

In March Carlyle dined − protesting − at the house of Edward Stanley, a Cheshire MP who later became Baron Stanley, to meet 'wonderfully "high people", among the highest in the land', who 'wanted to see *me*, it appeared!' as he told his mother half in mockery. These included the great Whig socialites Lord and Lady Holland, the husband a nephew of the famous statesman Charles James Fox, and the wife the 'queen of lions'; there were 'Lords and Ladies as thick as blackberries'.[82] It was at this dinner that Carlyle first met Dickens, celebrated for *Pickwick Papers* (1837), and also, to Carlyle's sharp eye, a dandy, though less repulsively so than Bulwer:

He is a fine little fellow, Boz, as I think; clear blue intelligent eyes, eyebrows that he arches amazingly, large protrusive rather loose mouth, − a face of the most extreme *mobility*, that he shuttles about, eyebrows, eyes, mouth and all, in a very singular manner while speaking.[83]

Jane had her usual winter and spring colds. We catch sight of her through Harriet Martineau, who marvelled at the 'very kind and entertaining letters' (now lost) she received from Jane, but who also disliked her scepticism, particularly 'the scepticism she *strives to manifest*, while I fully believe there is some sound faith at the bottom of her soul'.[84] By the middle of April Jane was feeling better; she told her mother-in-law that she meant to go out riding, which she did a few days later, accompanied by John Forster. Carlyle described on 1 May how Jane was improving 'with the progress of the sun'.[85]

Once more Carlyle's preparations for lecturing involved bad temper and complaints, which Jane disliked, though she turned her annoyance to wit for Mrs Carlyle on 5 May, immediately after he had given the first lecture:

He has been very tormented for several days back, but to-day when it was to come to the point, he held his peace, and *behaved so well*, that I was almost frightened, and would like to have heard him growling again, to be sure it was himself, it reminded me of my mother's consternation once on hearing her only child tumble downstairs, and roar never a bit!, she had been lecturing me on the propriety of taking such accidents quietly, and so I bit my lips and was as quiet as a lamb, whereupon she ran to me in the greatest terror – told me *that the next time I fell that I might as well give some sign of life at least?!*[86]

The six lectures on heroes – beginning with 'The Hero as Divinity' (on Scandinavian mythology), and moving through 'The Hero as Prophet' (Mahomet), 'The Hero as Poet' (Dante and Shakespeare), 'The Hero as Priest' (Luther and Knox), 'The Hero as a Man of Letters' (Johnson, Rousseau, and Burns), to 'The Hero as King' (Carlyle's odd term for Cromwell and Napoleon) – were the last Carlyle was to deliver and the only ones to be written up for publication, appearing as a book in 1841. He had discussed many of these subjects before in essays and previous lectures; here they were strung together on the common thread of the heroic, or visionary, great man. Carlyle worked with a broad brush, seeking out the valour and virtues he could find in each, and ignoring their failings and all problematic issues. He showed, in short, as the *Globe* critic noted on 9 May of the first two, a strange 'tenderness' towards some 'mighty great ruffians'.[87] As usual, however, his sincerity and freshness of utterance carried the day.

A cluster of new hearers recorded their impressions. Robert Browning attended some of the lectures, meeting the Macreadys there. 'Carlyle is lecturing with éclat', he told a friend.[88] Macready was 'charmed, carried away' by the lecture on Mahomet on 8 May, delivered, he recorded in his diary, with 'fervour and eloquence'. He was less enamoured of the Dante and Shakespeare one, finding it unoriginal (which it was, being not much more than a general overview); moreover, Macready's not inconsiderable vanity was offended by Carlyle speaking 'of managers of playhouses being the most insignificant of human beings, which made me smile, but sent the blood into my face', he declared on 12 May, 'as I fancied the thoughts of many present would revert to myself'.[89]

An appreciative new listener was Caroline Fox, a member of the

Quaker Fox family of Falmouth, who had become fast friends with Mill and Sterling, especially the latter when he moved to Falmouth for his health. Sterling had told Caroline in March that Jane Carlyle was 'the most brilliant letter-writer he has met with', and had paraphrased one of her notes to him:

Mrs Carlyle's letter was to this effect: – 'Do come and see us! Here are many estimable families – JC.' She plays all manner of tricks on her husband, telling wonderful stories of him in his presence, founded almost solely on her bright imagination; he, poor man, panting for an opportunity to stuff in a negation, but all to no purpose; having cut him up sufficiently, she would clear the course.[90]

Caroline's excitement at being in London in time to attend the fifth lecture on the hero as a man of letters on 19 May is recorded in her journal for that day. She makes it seem as if the very air was full of Carlyle, as it certainly was in the circle in which she moved:

We had heard much of Thomas Carlyle from enthusiastic admirers, and his book on Chartism had not lessened the excitement with which I anticipated seeing and hearing him . . . The audience, amongst whom we discovered Whewell, Samuel Wilberforce and his beautiful wife, was very thoughtful and earnest in appearance . . . Carlyle soon appeared, and looked as if he felt a well-dressed London crowd scarcely the arena for him to figure in as popular lecturer. He is a tall, robust-looking man; rugged simplicity and indomitable strength are in his face, and such a glow of genius in it – not always smouldering there, but flashing from his beautiful grey eyes, from the remoteness of their deep setting under the massive brow. His manner is very quiet, but he speaks like one tremendously convinced of what he utters, and who had much – very much – in him that was quite unutterable, quite unfit to be uttered to the uninitiated ear; and when the Englishman's sense of beauty or truth exhibited itself in vociferous cheers, he would impatiently, almost contemptuously, wave his hand, as if that were not the sort of homage which Truth demanded. He began in a rather low nervous voice, with a broad Scotch accent, but it soon grew firm, and shrank not abashed from its great task . . .
    Returned with Harriet Mill from Carlyle's lecture to their house in Kensington Square, where we were most lovingly received by all the family . . . A good deal of talk about Carlyle and his lectures: he never can get over the feeling that people have given money to hear him, and are possibly calculating whether what they hear is worth the price they paid for it . . . [Mill] read us that striking passage in 'Sartor Resartus' on George Fox making to himself a suit of leather. How his voice trembled with excitement as he read, 'Stitch away, thou noble Fox' &c.[91]

Mill invited the Carlyles on 3 June to meet Caroline, who soaked up Carlyle's talk about the desperate state of the poor, especially in Ireland. She also overheard Jane doing 'some brilliant female portraiture, but all in caricature'. When back in Cornwall in August, Caroline called on

Coleridge's younger son, Derwent, at Helston. Again the talk was – as it seemed to be wherever Caroline went – of Carlyle.[92]

★

Carlyle spent the summer writing up *On Heroes, Hero-Worship, & the Heroic in History*, finishing in September. The book was published by Fraser early in 1841, priced 10s. 6d.[93] In August he took a short break, riding his horse to Herstmonceux in Sussex to spend a few days with Sterling's mentor, the Reverend Julius Charles Hare, seeing the site of the Battle of Hastings, among other things. He played up the eccentricity of his 'rural ride' in a letter to Hare describing his projected travel arrangements, calling himself Quixote and exclaiming, 'I hope you have no Ladies!' since he was bringing no smart clothes with him.[94] Jane went nowhere, enjoying London in the heat as much as Carlyle hated it. 'She likes this Oven-Babylon', he told Jean on 25 August, when everyone had left town and 'a universal painting, papering and plastering' was going on.[95]

The London Library scheme was coming to completion. A public meeting was held at the Freemasons' Tavern on 24 June, at which Carlyle spoke ringingly of London's needs, following this up with a letter to *The Times* on 27 June in which he made a startling point about there being 'in the wretched fishy village of Reykiavik, a Public Lending Library, free to all Icelanders, very decidedly better than any such that exists in London'.[96] By the end of the year enough subscribers had been found to warrant setting down the rules and the cost of the annual subscription (£2 a year after an initial charge of £5), as well as beginning the tasks of appointing a Librarian and starting a collection of books. Carlyle was helped in these arrangements by a young lawyer, William Dougal Christie.[97]

A new correspondent wrote from Manchester, declaring that Carlyle's works had inspired her with hope 'of there being some means of escaping from the paralyzing influence of *Materialism*' under which she had feared falling since losing her faith. The writer was Geraldine Jewsbury, critic and later novelist, who was soon to become Jane's closest female friend. With characteristic directness, she refused to apologise for writing to ask Carlyle what the source of his spiritual certainty was, saying, 'if you had not in some sort assumed the attitude of an *Instructor*, I wd not have intruded on you'.[98] Carlyle replied kindly, saying he had 'triumphed' over the same difficulties which she described, and recommending that she read Goethe and *Sartor Resartus*.[99] Geraldine wrote again in the same vein in June; Carlyle replied again, and when Geraldine came to London in 1841 after the death of her father she made straight for Cheyne Row, where she reinvigorated the tired old metaphor by sitting – literally – at Carlyle's feet and giving Jane much matter for sardonic comment.

In September 1840 'the Poet Tennison' visited, 'a fine large-featured, dim-eyed, bronze-coloured, shaggy-headed man', as Carlyle told Jack; 'dusty, smoky, free-and-easy: who swims, outwardly and inwardly, with great composure in an inarticulate element as of tranquil chaos and tobacco-smoke'.[100] Though always languid and untidy, Tennyson was not, as the Carlyles found when they got to know him better, as free and easy or composed as he seemed. The son of a drunken, bitter, depressed Lincolnshire clergyman, he was himself subject to fits of depression and alcoholism, and, with one brother insane, another an alcoholic, and a third an opium addict, he feared insanity in himself. For some years he had been engaged, on and off and with no encouragement from her family, to Emily Sellwood, whom he finally married in 1850, the year of *In Memoriam*, when he was nearly forty-one and Emily four years younger.[101] The Carlyles knew little or nothing of this when they first met him; indeed, over the next few years they gossiped and speculated about finding him a suitable wife.

Carlyle thought little of Tennyson's poetry to date, two collections of poems, published in 1830 and 1832, of romantic-nostalgic sentiment and myth exquisitely measured and rhymed – poems such as 'Mariana', 'The Lady of Shalott', and 'The Lotos-Eaters'. He commented unpoetically to Milnes about 'Mariana':

If Alfred Tennyson could only make that long wail, like the winter wind, about Mariana in the Moated Grange, and could not get her to throw herself into the ditch, or could not bring her another man to help her ennui, he had much better have left her alone altogether.[102]

Carlyle's poor ear and almost philistine lack of appreciation of poetry *as poetry*, and his dislike of sentiment, were noticed by John Hunter, in London again in April 1840, where he met Leigh Hunt and Carlyle once more at Craik's house. The conversation on this occasion turned to Petrarch, whom Carlyle 'crushed to a sapless nothing in his grasp', declaring he had 'no sympathy with his weak, washy twaddle about another man's wife'. However, when challenged by Hunter about his lack of imaginative understanding, he made the revealing remark that he was perhaps 'shut out' from certain pleasures and feelings experienced by others.[103]

Some American poetry came Carlyle's way in December in the form of Henry Wadsworth Longfellow's first volume of poetry. Longfellow, a Harvard professor and friend of Emerson who had called on the Carlyles during a visit to London in 1835, had been one of those who acquired

Sartor Resartus in the original edition of fifty-eight copies bound together from *Fraser's Magazine*.[104] Carlyle thanked Longfellow, finding a novel way of indicating his appreciation for the collection, which he had not yet read: 'It now beckons to me from one of my shelves, asking always, When wilt thou have a cheerful vacant day?'[105]

The year 1840 marks a high point in Carlyle's career, yet his end-of-year account in his journal is as pathologically gloomy as ever. 'For a famous man', he wrote on 26 December, 'my bookseller's economics seem singular enough', but that did not worry him particularly: 'I happily do not need cash at present.' In spite of the interesting company he could command in London, his thoughts turned to Craigenputtoch again: 'I often long to be in the country again; at Puttock again, that I might work and nothing else but work. Had not my wife opposed, I should probably have returned hither before now.' We can only imagine the conversation between them, and Jane's horror at the idea. Carlyle hints at problems in his marriage and at his desire for death:

My one hope and thought for most part is that very shortly it will be over, my very sore existence ended in the bosom of the Giver of it – at rest somehow. Things might be written here which it is considerably better not to write. As I live, and have long lived, death and Hades differ little to me from the earth and life.[106]

Something of Carlyle's constitutional depression communicated itself to Sterling, who reported to Mill on 9 December that he had received a letter (now lost) from Carlyle, 'who is as usual cordial, earnest, & gloomy, his subjectivity being a fiery Dragon which he is perpetually killing & never can rid himself of the carcass, which is always reviving again'.[107]

Jane complained to Mrs Carlyle in October 1840 that he was 'reading voraciously great folios preparatory to writing a new book – for the rest he growls away much in the old style'.[108] She was having problems with the servant Helen, who had recently got drunk, obliging the Carlyles to struggle to get her to bed at three in the morning.[109] 'I feel as if I had adopted a child', Jane told her mother-in-law. She also delivered a sharp little lecture to the Carlyle clan and their wives on the subject of children:

What do I do with my time you wonder? with such '*a right easy seat of it*' one might fancy I should be glad to write a letter now and then just to keep the devil from my elbow – But Alicks Jenny and all of you were never more mistaken than when you imagine a woman needs half a dozen squeeling children to keep her uneasy – she can manage to keep herself uneasy in a hundred ways without *that*.[110]

All was clearly not well for Carlyle and Jane. Though together they were attracting the admiring attention of the world, they could not, it seems, enjoy life together, and yet they remained close and sometimes quite loving in spite of their mutual intolerance and temperamental differences.

CHAPTER 10

Lion and Lion's Wife 1841–1843

On 1 January 1841 the Carlyles were 'first-footed' by Mazzini, as he told his mother a few days later, explaining the Scottish custom of treating the first visitor of the New Year as an omen for the year to follow. Jane had indicated that she would like Mazzini to fulfil the role, presumably because, according to the superstition, a dark handsome man was thought to bring the greatest luck. Whether he brought the traditional lump of coal to presage domestic wealth and comfort, he did not say.[1]

The Carlyles could now face the future free from money worries, though they were by no means well off. Carlyle's brother Alick was still struggling as a small shopkeeper, and his youngest brother James, wanting to buy a new farm but unable to afford it, was hoping for a loan from Jack, who was by now rather wealthy, having taken on another well-paid, if difficult, job looking after a mentally ill patient, William Ogilby. Carlyle wrote to James on 24 March, mediating between his two brothers, defending Jack against the charge of stinginess and telling James that if he showed himself more businesslike, Jack might 'venture £200'.[2]

Poverty was as dire and widespread in London as it was in the country-side. Jane was kept busy helping starving beggars who came to the door, offering them gifts of old clothes and sometimes practical help in finding jobs.[3] Carlyle's keen sense of injustice was aroused afresh when he reluctantly accepted an invitation to dine with the Reverend Henry Hart Milman, Rector of St Margaret's Church, Westminster, and, though he did not know it, the puzzled reader who had reported for John Murray on 'Teufelsdröckh' ten years earlier. Carlyle told Jack on 5 February that acceptance of the invitation was the price Milman had demanded for voting in favour of his preferred candidate for Librarian of the London Library, J. G. Cochrane. Carlyle described without enthusiasm Milman's 'shrewd Oxford wit' and the 'highdressed women beautiful and not' who attended the soirée which followed the dinner amid the 'antique sumptuosities in the Cloisters of Westminster'.[4] Later in the year, when the whole country was in the grip of an even colder winter than the previous one, he referred scornfully to the Bishop of London's reported remark about clerical salaries, that 'unless Truth have four thousand five hundred a-year in its pocket' it 'has no chance for victory', that being the amount Bishop Blomfield apparently thought was required to keep a bishop.[5]

In early March, after Cochrane's appointment, the London Library Committee met to finalise arrangements. Prince Albert agreed to be patron. Milnes reported cheerfully to Carlyle that the Prince 'is to take the German department into his own hands, & begs to know whether your works are to be classed as German or English. Pray let him know.'[6] Carlyle replied in similar vein:

Pray make my compliments, and say, It were hard to determine under what rubric the Writings in question are to be brought; but if he arrange them either as German or English, or even as Annandale-Teutonic, or altogether of doubtful gender, it will do well enough.[7]

Though he was to be long associated with the London Library, he told Jack with relief after the appointment of Cochrane that he could now 'formally resign my shadow of Secretaryship' and 'let the whole matter sink or swim'.[8] The matter swam most successfully; Carlyle kept out of the business, except as a borrower, until a dispute arose in 1852 about the appointment of a successor to Cochrane, when he entered the lists swiftly and vigorously against Gladstone, who was trying to have a protégé elected.

Meanwhile Carlyle struggled on with the preparation for his work on Cromwell, reading 'the dullest Books ever written by any mortal' and declaring that 'no human writers had ever a more perfect talent of *killing* whatsoever they wrote upon than those Historians and Memoirists of the Seventeenth Century in Britain!'[9] – a view he was to modify only when he began in the 1850s to read German histories of the life and times of Frederick the Great. His temper was not improved by the summons to sit on a jury in February 1841 to decide a controversy between two Manchester men over the invention rights to 'Patent India-rubber cotton-cards'. In the jury room Carlyle suffered 'two endless days' of deliberation, by the end of which 'we were eleven for the Plaintiff, and *one* the other way who would not yield!' Carlyle told his mother on 18 February how the matter was resolved:

The refractory man, a thickset flathead *sack*, erected himself in his chair; said, 'I am one of the firmest-minded men in England. I know this room pretty well; I have starved out three juries here already!' – Reasoning, demonstration was of no use at all . . . 'Do not argue with him', I said; 'flatter him' . . . I set to work upon him, we all set to work; and in about an hour after our 'withdrawal' – the hash (I pulling him by the arm) was got scind [removed] from his chair . . . and then, in few instants more, we were all rejoicing on the road home! In my life I have seen nothing more absurd. I reflected, however, that really *I* had perhaps contributed to get justice done to some poor unknown Manchester man; that had I not been there, it was very possible they would have quarrelled with this 'firmest-minded man in England', and cost somebody another £10,000![10]

Carlyle may have been the soul of tact in the jury room, but he later remembered with remorse his behaviour at home – 'intolerable suffering, rage, almost despair (and resolut[io]n to quit London)' – which Jane handled, as she had by now begun regularly to do, by turning the story into a comic one told at Carlyle's expense in her letters and in conversation with visitors. After her death Carlyle recalled that she 'used to narrate' this episode 'in an incomparable manner'.[11] She also told it to Sterling in a letter in early March, almost transforming the jury experience into her own by means of a narrative of cause and effect which ends, satisfactorily, with her:

My poor Man of Genius had to sit on a Jury two days – to the ruin of his whole being physical, moral, and intellectual – and ever since he has been *reacting* against the administration of British Justice to a degree that has finally mounted into Influenza – while I poverina [poor thing] have been reacting against his reaction – till that malady called by Cocknies 'mental worry' fairly *took me by the throat* – and threw me on my bed for a good many days – and now I am but recovering – as *white* as the paper I write upon, and carrying my head as one who had been making a failed attempt at suicide – for in the ardour of my medical practice I flayed the whole neck of me with a blister.[12]

The pride Carlyle took in Jane's witty way of avenging herself on his temper was part of his way of atoning, as was noticed by, among others, David Masson, who recalled in 1885 how Carlyle would 'listen benignantly and admiringly to those caricatures of his ways, and illustrations of his recent misbehaviours' as Jane recited them to the amusement of her friends and the bewilderment of his worshippers.[13]

However complacent Carlyle may have been on these occasions, he was not always disposed to be amused at Jane's sharpness, and she was not always able to channel her frustration into biting humour, but sometimes wept or sulked instead. Increasingly this became the Carlyles' *modus vivendi*; Jane was licensed to criticise Carlyle in front of others, Carlyle's concession being to tolerate the criticism – easier than reforming his behaviour, no doubt – and so a kind of serio-comic double act grew up alongside Carlyle's solo performances.

Jane described to her friend Susan Hunter, now Mrs Stirling, at the beginning of 1841, how 'in my character of *Lion*'s wife here I have enough to *do*':

Applications from young Ladies for autographs, *passionate* invitations to dine, announcements of inexpressible longings to drink tea with me – all that sort of thing which as a provincial girl I should have regarded perhaps as the highest promotion, but which at this time of day I regard as very silly and tiresome work.[14]

She was proud of her 'man of genius' husband, and pleased and excited to be courted by famous men, exotic exiles, and eager girls, but she was constantly aware of the high price she paid in sick nerves, headaches, and unpleasant exchanges of temper. She was already exhibiting something of that despairing self-satisfaction captured by Tait sixteen years later in *A Chelsea Interior*.

In late March Jane declared to a Haddington friend, Mary Scot, that Carlyle was 'one of the most popular London sights at present'.[15] His fame brought visitors, admirers, petitioners, and painters to Cheyne Row. Samuel Laurence turned up again in March to begin an oil painting of Carlyle, which he exhibited at the Royal Academy in May.[16] Carlyle was enthusiastic at first, but told Sterling in August that it was 'frightful', 'a compound of the head of a Demon and of a Flayed Horse'.[17] In November an Italian acquaintance of Emerson's, Spiridione Gambardella, arrived in London hoping to draw Carlyle.[18] Meanwhile the D'Orsay sketch was doing the rounds in Richard Monckton Milnes's circle. The Reverend W. H. Brookfield, with whom Carlyle coincided in future years when both were guests of the Ashburtons, wrote to his fiancée on 2 April 1841, seeking to impress her with a description of his first meeting with the famous Carlyle:

Yesterday was rather eventful with me. I was off duty (being 1st of the month) and was at Milnes' with my legs over the arm of a chair reading aloud while he breakfasted when in stepped impromptu: The Prince? . . . Alfred Tennyson? – Archbishop ditto? No, No, No: Father Gerard solid in his thick shoes? – nearer – Carlyle! The form of his face is like that portrait of Count D'Orsay's you have seen. But complexion very coarse – and general appearance 'solid in thick shoes'. As tall as I about – and certainly no less ungainly – a hearty laugher with discoloured teeth – very broad Scotch – talks not unlike his writing – unreserved – unaffected, of course – a leetle shy and awkward – but very likeable.[19]

Milnes invited Carlyle to spend a few days over Easter at his father's country house, Fryston, near Leeds. Carlyle was glad to go, as he and Jane were getting on badly. He wrote from Derby on 5 April, *en route* for Fryston, saying Jane's look when he left had haunted him all the way. 'O Jeannie', he exclaimed, 'would thou wert happier; would I could make thee happy!' And, two days later, from his destination: 'Think not hardly of me, dear Jeannie: in the mutual misery we often are in we do not know how dear we are to one another.'[20] If his way of apologising was to express pathos and endearments, Jane's was initially to dispense with endearments altogether, but to write herself into good, or better, humour in the course of the letter itself. She never addressed him as Tom or Thomas, but when not angry with him she called him 'dear' and 'dearest'. Now, though, she began aggressively, and in quotations marks – '*Unresting One*' – told him about her various visitors (the older Sterlings, Erasmus Darwin, Elizabeth Pepoli, Giovanni Ruffini) in dashing style, then deigned to sympathise with his sleeplessness, until she could finish magnanimously with 'God bless you' and 'Yours affectionately'.[21]

Carlyle and Milnes got on well together, though the latter insisted on showing off his guest to the local notables – 'I am his trump card at present' – and Carlyle found he was expected to attend church on Easter Sunday, about which he had scruples.[22] He relished the opportunity to observe 'English Squirearchical life'; a valet waited on him 'like a silent-assiduous minister', doing everything for him, and he slept in a bed eight foot square with a ladder to get him into it, as he told his mother. Such a 'life without work' was, he thought, contemptible.[23] From Fryston Carlyle went on to Leeds to visit James Marshall, son of the wealthy manufacturer who had provided him with the horse Citoyenne, and from there he travelled, on impulse, to visit his family in Annandale. He had heard that his mother was unwell, and wanted to see her. Jane responded to the surprise news of his whereabouts not angrily, but with implicit criticism: 'I *believe* your Mother will be less unwell than you think, at all events that the sight of her pet-child will quite set her up again . . . at all times you have a tendency to exaggerate your *Mother*'s ailments.'[24]

His attitude towards her own illnesses was quite different. So also was John Carlyle's, who visited her while Carlyle was away and showed no interest in anything except 'his own personality'. Jane reported to Carlyle with evident relish that Jack had consulted a phrenologist (probably James Deville of the Strand, the most celebrated practitioner of this fashionable 'science' of reading character by feeling the contours of the head), to be told what no doubt the Carlyles could have told him for nothing, namely that he was '*capable of anything*, but not capable of turning his capability to account!'[25]

On 15 April Jane told Carlyle she had received 'a prodigiously long letter from Geraldine containing a philosophical desertation [*sic*] on the passion of *Love* as it differs in Men from Women!! She is far too *anatomical* for me.'[26] Carlyle's admiring Manchester correspondent had made her first visit to Cheyne Row in March, when Carlyle found her 'a most heroic-looking damsel'.[27] Now Geraldine began a gushing, passionate, frank, and rather wearing correspondence with Jane, opening her first letter with the ominous words, 'You will think I am possessed by as great a mania for letter-writing as any of Richardson's heroines'.[28]

Over the years Geraldine adored and quarrelled with and was

patronised by Jane, while also throwing herself at a succession of alarmed or indifferent men. Jane came to rely on Geraldine's devotion, clinging and irritating though it was; already in these early letters Geraldine demonstrated an unfortunate tendency to magnify Jane's sufferings and feelings of neglect. By July she was addressing Jane in the language of passionate female friendship: 'carissima mia', 'my darling'. She was 'crazy with delight' at the prospect of seeing Jane in Manchester later in the summer, and she wrote injudiciously and at length about her friend's exceptional sufferings and self-sacrifice for her genius of a husband.[29]

Having assured himself that his mother was not dangerously ill, and looked longingly at some cottages, raising once more, though tentatively, the possibility of living for part of the year at Craigenputtoch or nearby, Carlyle returned home in May.[30] He was still having more problems with his Cromwell studies than he had experienced with any of his other books, all of which had caused him anguish. He confided to Sterling that 'Oliver Cromwell lies inaccessible, ever more inaccessible (like a Tower far up among granite chasms), the nearer I get to him'.[31] On 17 September he addressed Cromwell in despair:

O Oliver, my hero, can I by no alchemy extricate thee from the dim cave, where buried under Presbyterian, Royalist and other obsolete rubbish thou liest unintelligible, all defaced, unrecognisable! Thou art become a most gaunt, spectral nondescript; little other than a ghastly chimera.[32]

The problem he faced – how to give a vivid, clear picture of the man in his environment – seemed insuperable in Cromwell's case, partly because of the partisan and often unreliable nature of previous accounts of Cromwell's career, and perhaps also because Carlyle was afraid he might swamp or obscure Cromwell in the course of clarifying the complex political, religious, and social context in which he lived. The method he had found of subduing the equally dense thicket of material involved in telling the story of the French Revolution would not quite suit here, since the focus had to be on one man, not on the succession, as in a moving panorama, of heroes and villains and 'men of the hour' who played their part in the storming of the Bastille, the National Assembly, and the Terror. Carlyle's lack of progress with Cromwell put a strain on him and on the marriage during the summer of 1841, when he and Jane tried the mistaken experiment of spending several weeks alone together on holiday.

Before they set off, they showed how kind they could be to a friend in distress. Thackeray had asked Carlyle for a letter of introduction to Godefroi Cavaignac in Paris, where he had taken his wife Isabella after she had become insane following the birth of her second surviving daughter in the summer of 1840. In November 1840 he had placed Isabella in a *maison de santé* in Paris, the expense of which made him desperate to earn money. His *Comic Tales and Sketches*, including 'The Yellowplush Papers', were due to be published in April 1841, and Thackeray wrote to friends asking for their help in getting the book noticed. Jane Carlyle was one of his preferred correspondents. He addressed her with brave humour, thanking her and Carlyle for their sympathy and laughing at Carlyle's 'outrageous' letter of introduction to Cavaignac with its extravagant praise of him. 'I left Carlyle's monstrous puff at Cavaignac's', he wrote to Jane in February 1841, going on to plead for help in getting puffs of a different kind:

Now you have that within you Madam wch surpasses money: viz. You can incite Sterling to get me a great puff of the reprint of the Y Plush in the Times. 2 vols. are fast coming out with illustrations . . . puffs puffs are what I desire.[33]

Thackeray followed this with another letter of thanks and news in March, telling Jane it would be 'a long long while I fear ere [Isabella] be restored to me'.[34] Carlyle, who was prepared to take real trouble to help a friend, wrote to Jane from Fryston when he heard Thackeray's news, urging her to write a line to Cavaignac 'about calling on Thackeray'.[35]

When Thackeray returned to London in the summer, leaving his wife in care in France, he turned to the Carlyles for support. Carlyle interrupted a letter to his mother on 16 June to tell his friend's story:

Alas, here is a poor man, by name Thackeray, just come in from Paris; where his poor wife is left, having fallen *insane* on his hands some six or eight months ago! I believe he is not well off for cash either, poor Thackeray (tho' *born* a rich man); he is very clever with pen and pencil; an honest man, in no inconsiderable distress! He seems as if he had no better place, of all the great places he once knew, than our poor house to take shelter in![36]

Thackeray had been born of wealthy parents in India, educated expensively and unhappily at one of the great public schools, Charterhouse (or Slaughterhouse, as he renamed it in stories), and had lost his fortune of £1,500 through gambling while a student at Cambridge. Both Carlyles responded warmly to Thackeray's need for support, and Jane in particular enjoyed his whimsical letters with their little caricatures to illustrate his text.

A few days after describing Thackeray to his mother, Carlyle was writing to Robert Browning, who had sent him, 'many months ago', his long poem *Sordello* and, more recently, *Pippa Passes*. Browning had attended Carlyle's 'Heroes' lectures, and the two men had met at literary parties. Carlyle reported to Sterling that Browning 'dwells in an element of Charles Lamb-ism, British Museum Classicality and other Cockney encumbrance', out of which he might, 'not without a great effort', struggle eventually.[37] This lukewarm appraisal was not much altered by *Pippa Passes*, about which Carlyle wrote to the author on 21 June. He carefully praised Browning's 'rare spiritual gift, practical, pictorial, intellectual', while suggesting that a battle lay ahead for him. 'Fight on', he wrote encouragingly, though he followed this advice with the devastating suggestion that Browning's next work should be 'written in prose!'[38] Browning might have been dashed by this if he had not seen these early works of his utterly reviled by reviewers. He was actually grateful for Carlyle's response, remembering after Carlyle's death 'the goodness and sympathy which began so long ago' and continued all Carlyle's life. 'His love', Browning told Charles Eliot Norton in 1885, 'was altogether a free gift, and how much it has *enriched* my life I shall hardly attempt to say.'[39]

When Browning was, as he thought, about to be introduced to the invalid Elizabeth Barrett on her sofa in Wimpole Street, it was Carlyle's (modest) praise of his work which predisposed her to like and admire him. A self-confessed 'adorer of Carlyle', she told her brother George in March 1842 about Browning's expected, but in the end long postponed, visit:

Mr Kenyon proposed also to introduce to my sofa-side . . . Mr Browning the poet . . . who was so honour-giving as to wish something of the sort! I was pleased at the thought of his wishing it . . . Mr Kenyon says that he is a little discouraged by his reception with the public – the populace, he shd. have said. 'Poor Browning', said Mr Kenyon. 'And why poor Browning?' – 'Because nobody reads him.' – 'Rather then, poor readers!' Mr Carlyle is his friend – a good substitute for a crowd's shouting![40]

The famous correspondence between Elizabeth Barrett and Browning which followed their eventual meeting in May 1845 has for one of its main subjects the writer whom both admired above any other – Carlyle.

★

Carlyle was the first to escape the London heat, setting off ahead of Jane for Dumfriesshire. He left on 30 June, staying briefly with James at Scotsbrig, where he took note of the general election in early July, caused by Lord Melbourne's resignation over the defeat of his proposal to repeal the Corn Laws and bring in limited free trade. Robert Peel's Tories were voted into office, a result which Carlyle deplored.[41] He rented a 'lonely-standing' house at Newby for four weeks, pleased that he would have a horse and 'sea-bathing of a sort' in the tidal waters of the Solway Firth.[42]

It was a bad misjudgement, and followed several attempts to find and describe houses to let in the area. Jane, still in Chelsea, treated John Forster on 10 July to one of her exasperated and amused put-downs of her husband, who had sent her three letters with pages of 'infinitesimal details about houses issuing like one of our friend Oliver's parliamentary speeches in simple *zero*! "And now", he says, "comes the practical question what are YOU to do?" God knows! unless I set about getting a divorce, and marry again, some man with *common sense* instead of *Genius*!'[43] Her horror at having to spend four weeks in the utterly deserted 'grotesque' location of Newby with no neighbours, no milk, cracked mirrors, wild cats and kittens, 'industrious fleas', and the sea 'moan-moaning under ones window', made her feel, as she exploded to Fanny Wedgwood when she had finally escaped, quite *'vicious'*.[44]

Even Carlyle, though he enjoyed bathing naked in the sea and minded the solitude much less than Jane, wrote sombrely to Milnes and Emerson about the wildness and remoteness of the spot on the one hand, and its relative nearness, on the other, to Annan, which he was reminded was the place 'where I very miserably learned Latin (in the *Hinterschlag Gymnasium*)', and to the 'drab coloured waters' of the Solway in which he had nearly drowned as a boy in 1806.[45] When not bathing, Carlyle was reading French novels by Balzac and George Sand, which he had borrowed from the London Library. He had offered to do an essay for Macvey Napier of the *Edinburgh Review* on 'that notable Phenomenon, consisting of George Sand, Abbé Lamennais &c with their writings; what Goethe well names the "Literature of Desperation"':

I find enormous temporary mischief and even a radical perversion, falsity and delirium in it, yet withal the struggle towards an indispensable ulterior good. The taste for it, among Radical men, especially among Radical women, is spreading everywhere.[46]

The essay did not, however, get written.

By the end of August both Carlyle and Jane had left their desolate cottage for Jane's mother's house at Templand, where Jane promptly conformed to her usual pathology by falling ill for two days. She told Fanny Wedgwood of the 'indescribable comfort' of feeling herself 'once more in the region of white sheets, and pretty chintzy curtains and soft carpets and green waving trees! – and to have one's *clean* nice-looking mother bringing one little seductive-looking *white*-napkined trays, which one had the firmest, most consolatory assurance would *not* contain – a flounder!'[47]

Carlyle, by contrast, disliked being at Templand, where three of Jane's cousins were also staying, and so he got up early one morning and set off for 'his barbarous Annandale', as Jane told Forster. His family was in disarray over Jenny's separation from her 'blockhead' of a husband, Rob Hanning.[48] Some stupidity, or perhaps even criminal behaviour, on

Hanning's part led him to emigrate to America, without Jenny and the children, in mid-September.[49]

After he had helped sort things out for his troubled family, Carlyle took advantage of an invitation from Thomas Spedding to visit him at Keswick. He declined to visit Wordsworth, Dr Arnold, and Coleridge's son Hartley, but accepted an invitation from the Marshalls, who had a house on Ullswater. He told Jane on 2 September that on the way to Spedding's house he passed Greta Hall, where Coleridge's family had lived with Southey's (the two being brothers-in-law), and where Southey now lived with his new wife, having become insane in the years after the death of his first wife Edith, who had also lost her mind. Carlyle was touched to see 'the light of [Southey's] candle visibly shining, the light of his own soul gone out into darkness forever!'[50]

While visiting the Marshalls Carlyle attended 'a grand Mechanics-Institute soiree' where 'Whewell the huge Cantab' lectured 'to the rustics on astronomy'.[51] William Whewell, Cambridge philosopher and scientist, had read and disapproved of Carlyle's *Chartism*, and had written a verse pastiche, turning selected passages into hexameters.[52] Carlyle himself had seen a copy in April 1840, describing it to Alick as 'a strange printed quiz of a thing – the cream of my *Chartism* done up into Classical verse (the same verse as Homer's) by a certain Cambridge Professor of eminence; a thing one could laugh at for moments'.[53]

In his *Reminiscences*, Carlyle recalled how Erasmus Darwin, seeing Whewell 'sit all ear (not all *assent*)' at the lectures on Heroes in May 1840, had dubbed him 'the Harmonious Blacksmith', a nickname which Carlyle and Jane used for Whewell thereafter. Carlyle, free-associating in his reminiscence of Jane in 1866, ranged over the connections between Whewell and the fabulously rich Marshalls, whose daughter Cordelia he married in 1841:

It is well known the Marshall daughters were all married off (each of them had £50,000) and what intricate *inter*marrying with the Spring-Rices there was. – 'Dowager Lady Monteagle' that now is, being at this day Quasi-*Mother-in-Law* of James Marshall her own Brother's *Wife* etc. etc.! 'Family so used up!' as old Rogers used to snuffle and say. – My Jeannie quarrelled with nothing in Marshalldom; quite the contrary, formed a kind of friendship (*conquest* I believe it was on her side) with *Cordelia* Marshall, a prim, affectionate, but rather puling weak and sentimental elderly young Lady, who became, shortly after, Wife *first* Wife of the late big Whewell, and aided his position and advance towards Mastership of Trinity, etc. I recollect seeing them both here, and Cordelia's adoration of her 'Harmonious Blacksmith', with friendly enough assent, and some amusement, from us two.[54]

Carlyle joined Jane again, and together they visited Harriet Martineau in Tynemouth, Northumberland, on their way south. They were home by the end of September 1841, both relieved to have put their disastrous holiday behind them, and both taking stock. Carlyle did his accounts, and found that he had only £145 in hand, with little prospect of more until he finished Cromwell.[55] His incompetent publisher James Fraser died in October – aged about thirty-five, Carlyle thought – after a long illness.[56] In due course Forster helped Carlyle move to Dickens's publishers, Chapman and Hall, who reprinted *On Heroes* in 1842 and published all Carlyle's subsequent works. As for Jane, in a rare moment of confession, she described her stay at Templand to Irving's old patron Thomas Chalmers:

My dear Mother, thank God is still spared to me, and enjoying tolerable health. I spent a month in Dumfriesshire with her this summer – after a separation of two years. I often think, because perhaps, having no children of my own, I am interested in finding reasons for not regretting it – how little good poor Mothers get of their married daughters, whom they have had such a world of plague in bearing, and nursing up, and training, and teaching, until they could shift for themselves![57]

Both mothers, Mrs Welsh and Mrs Carlyle, had to be hastily written to in December, after rumours had begun to appear in Scottish newspapers that Carlyle was to return to Scotland to take up a chair in history at Edinburgh University. He had been approached by two students, Francis Espinasse and Henry Dunipace, for permission to nominate him. Carlyle was not tempted; not only did the chair carry no stipend, but, as he told the students in a gracious reply, 'Ten years ago such an invitation might perhaps have been decisive of much for me; but it is too late now.'[58] Carlyle forestalled his mother's disappointment by telling her it was an impossible idea because of the lack of salary, and Jane characteristically went further, informing Mrs Welsh frankly:

No, no, we are done with Edinburgh. He owes it no gratitude for any recognition he ever found there. It is only now when London and the world have discovered his talent that they are fain to admit it. As for me, I would as soon go back to Craigenputtock as to that poor, proud, formal, 'highly respectable' City.[59]

★

It was as well that Jane had seen her mother in the summer, for in February 1842 Grace Welsh died suddenly of a stroke. Her doctor and friendly neighbour, James Russell, wrote to tell Jane she was ill. Jane left as soon as she received his letter, on Monday, 28 February. When she arrived in Liverpool the next morning, her cousins told her Mrs Welsh had died on the Friday evening. Jane's health collapsed, and she remained in Liverpool, while Carlyle set off to see her, then went on to Templand. He missed the funeral, but stayed for two months in Dumfriesshire, supervising the sale of the house and its contents. He responded well to the crisis, in a sombre way enjoying the solitude and the enforced removal from London (and Cromwell), seeing his mother again, and getting on well, as always, with Mrs Welsh's Liverpool brother John, who also spent some time at Templand.[60]

Jane sinks into invisibility, first in Liverpool, then in Chelsea, where she returned, bringing her cousin Jeannie Welsh for a prolonged stay, since her letters from this time of grief and self-reproach have disappeared. On the whole, Carlyle showed her the sympathy he genuinely felt and understood about the loss of a parent. However, hard as he worked at disposing of Mrs Welsh's property according to Jane's wishes, he made some serious errors of judgement. He brought up yet again the possibility of their taking on Craigenputtoch, only to backtrack with alarm on receiving what we can guess was an anguished letter from Jane. He was apologetic, but let her know that her response was excessive. 'Know well always', he wrote on 27 March, 'that I cannot deliberately mean anything that is harmful to you, unjust or painful to you, — indeliberately I do enough of such things without meaning them.'[61]

A week later he wrote that he was thinking of giving her grandfather's (and father's) writing desk to Alick; she must have exploded, reminding Carlyle of her embarrassment when Alick had turned up drunk at Templand to collect her, for Carlyle replied immediately, giving in to her 'very natural' feelings about Alick, yet indicating that he himself, as executor, would do something for Alick, the only one of his family who was not remembered in Mrs Welsh's will: 'He shall have nothing that was hers; I can make the poor man a gift in some other way.'[62] Family pride speaks out here, as it does again in his letter of 16 April describing the sale of Mrs Welsh's possessions, at which, he is careful to point out, Alick *bought* a cow for £7 8s. Carlyle had the patriarchal desk, with some chairs and other items, brought to Cheyne Row, where it became his own work desk.[63]

One short letter of Jane's survives. She wrote to her uncle John Welsh on 8 April, calling herself a 'poor *only* child', 'left so lonely on this earth'.[64] She appears to have confided in Mazzini, who reported her feelings to his mother:

Madame Carlyle is very sad, firstly, as is natural, at the loss of her mother; then because she remains alone, alone in the world: she has no children; her husband is good, but like all such writers, he lives only in ideas, in his own books, in short in the brain more than in the heart. She is a woman of intense feeling, even a little excitable: she has neither brothers nor sisters: she is alone, and feels herself alone in the world.[65]

Jane must have complained to Carlyle too about her loneliness and lack of a role in life, apart from the haphazard self-appointed task of dispensing aid to a motley crew of indigent refugees and Chelsea beggars, for he replied rather harshly on 9 April, provoked to criticise *her* criticism of her life and the blame, implicit or explicit, which she put on him:

No wonder, my dear Wife, you feel disheartened and sick about all work, and weary of the world generally. 'Benevolence', I also agree with you, is no trade, – altogether or nearly altogether a futility when followed as a *trade*. Yet work does still remain to be done; and the Highest Law does order us all to work. My prayer is and has always been that you would rouse up the fine faculties that *are* yours into some course of real true work, which you felt to be worthy of them and you! Your life would not then be happy; but it would cease to be miserable, it would become noble and clear, with a kind of sacredness shining thro' it . . . The deepest difficulty, which also presses on us *all*, is the sick Sentimentalism we suck in with our whole nourishment, and get engrained into the very blood of us, in these miserable ages! I actually do think it the deepest. It is this that makes me so impatient of George Sand, Mazzini and all that set of Prophets, – impatient, so as often to be unjust to what of truth and genuine propriety of aim is in them. Alas, how often have I provokingly argued with you about all that! I actually will endeavour not to do so any more. It is not by *arguing* that I can ever hope to do you any service on that side. But I will never give up the hope to see you adequately *busy* with your whole mind; discovering as *all* human beings may do, that in the grimmest rocky wildernesses of existence there are blessed well-springs, there is an everlasting guiding-star. Courage, my poor Jeannie – ah me, had *I* been other, for you too it might have been all easier: – but I was not other, I was even *this*. In such solemn seasons, let us both cry for help to be better for each other, and for all duties, in time coming! Articulate *prayer* is for me not possible; but the equivalent of it remains forever in the heart and life of man: I say, let us pray, God look down upon us; guide us not happily but *well* thro' life, unite us well with our Buried Ones according to His will! – Amen.[66]

No doubt Jane was irritated further not only by this continuation of arguments they had had about 'sentimentalism', but also by Carlyle's posture of helplessness, particularly when the subject was his own shortcomings, and by the very vagueness of his wish that she should find something to do. Unlike G. H. Lewes, who was to be so impressed by Marian Evans's narrative wit in her *Westminster Review* articles in the mid-1850s that he positively encouraged his diffident partner to try her hand at fiction, and so helped create 'George Eliot', Carlyle could dispense only general praise to Jane – 'fine faculties' – and even more general advice – 'some course of real true work'.

It was a low point in the marriage. Carlyle is quite explicit in recognising Jane's unhappiness and in candidly, if infuriatingly, expressing his belief that nothing could be done to make her happy. Both had sour feelings towards one another and about marriage in general. When Jane suggested that John Carlyle had romantic leanings towards Jeannie Welsh, who was keeping Jane company in Chelsea, Carlyle was sceptical. 'If John did fall in love with Jeannie', he wrote, 'the first question that arises is: Would Jeannie fall in love with him? If I were in her pumps, I think I should perhaps demur considerably there!'[67] As Jane undoubtedly would too.

Carlyle returned home in early May, stopping on the way at Manchester, where he noticed the eerie lack of smoke from the factories, many of which were closed.[68] The cotton and weaving trades were in difficulties; a few months earlier, in October 1841, Carlyle had described a 'pallid Paisley weaver' with his 'famishing children round him', and had taken note of a trial, at Stockport in Cheshire, 'of a human father and human mother, for poisoning three of their children to gain successively some £3.8s. from a Burial Society for each of them', so desperate was their condition.[69]

These things were working in Carlyle to make him burst forth with a book on the condition of England, though he did not yet know it. Still hoping to complete the book on Cromwell, he took up Dr Arnold's earlier invitation to visit Rugby, stopping off there on his way home so that he could view the nearby site of Cromwell's great Battle of Naseby. He and Arnold went over the battlefield together; Carlyle plucked some wild flowers from the 'burial heaps of the slain' and cried 'Honour to Oliver!'[70]

Times were so hard that in March Peel brought in, for the first time since 1816 (when revenue was needed in the aftermath of the Napoleonic Wars), income tax at the rate of seven pence in the pound on incomes over £150. Carlyle rejoiced that the rich would be made to pay it.[71] 'These are bad times for Kings and Queens', he told his mother on 4 June, when the Queen had been shot at by John Francis, a young man '*not* mad at all' but 'in great want'. Another youth 'presented his pistol at the Majesty of England' on 3 July, as Carlyle again reported to his mother.[72] Carlyle sympathised with the desperate young men, while his attitude towards the Queen was much the one he had adopted towards Marie Antoinette in *The French Revolution* – an ironic sorrowfulness. Caroline Fox visited Cheyne Row on 6 June and noted down Carlyle's conversation:

'Tis an odd thing this about Queen Victoria. After having had a champion to say before the world assembly of them [at her coronation], 'O Queen, live for ever!' a little insignificant fellow comes up, points his pistol at her, and says, 'Chimera!

die this minute!' Poor Little Queen! I have some loyalty about me, and have no wish to see her shot; but as for having any right to hold the reins of government if she could not manage them, all the cart-loads of dirty parchment can't make that clear.[73]

Caroline Fox noticed, as others such as Mazzini and Sterling did, that Jane was still suffering from the loss of her mother – 'her health and spirits are deeply depressed by what she has gone through'.[74] Carlyle did his best after his fashion. Jane told her cousin Maggie Welsh on 15 July, the day after her forty-first birthday, that it had been a sad occasion, though relieved by Carlyle's having given her a birthday present for the first time, 'he who never attends to such *nonsenses* as birthdays – and who dislikes nothing in the world so much as going into a shop to buy anything – even his own trowsers and coats':

Well he actually risked himself in a Jewlers shop and bought me a very nice smelling-bottle! . . . in *great* matters he is always kind and considerate, but all these *little* attentions which we women attach so much importance to he was never in the habit of rendering to any one – his up-bringing and the severe turn of mind he has from nature had alike indisposed him towards them – and now the desire to replace to me the irreplaceable makes him as good in *little* things as he used to be in great.[75]

In summer 1842 one of Emerson's friends, Bronson Alcott, came to call. Carlyle and Emerson were corresponding cordially as ever, but less frequently and with an increasing reserve. They liked one another's work less and less; Jane's frank comment to Sterling on Emerson's essays, a copy of which had arrived in April 1841, was that they were 'a bad imitation of Carlyle's most Carlylish *translations* of Goethe's most Goetheish passages!'[76] Carlyle, who had benefited so richly from Emerson's warm introductions, returned the favour by writing a brief preface to the English edition of Emerson's *Essays*, but he gave only grudging praise, which appears to have annoyed Emerson, though he thanked Carlyle politely for 'the good word of one whose word is fame'.[77]

Alcott (father of Louisa May Alcott, later celebrated as the author of *Little Women*) came to visit the Carlyles in June 1842. A transcendentalist, communitarian, and zealous vegetarian, Alcott had been one of those early American admirers of Carlyle, reading *Sartor Resartus* as it came out in *Fraser's Magazine* and, as he remembered years later, absorbing with 'zest' the essays on Burns, Johnson, and Goethe. 'Mine', he wrote in 1881, 'like Emerson's, was a less muscular type of mysticism than his'; he recognised that when he met Carlyle at Cheyne Row in 1842 he presented himself as 'a tempting butt of the giant's ridicule – a sentimentalist, as he saw me, and speechless in his presence'.[78] His visits to Carlyle in late June and early

July were spectacularly unsuccessful. Alcott thought Carlyle's conversation 'cynical' and 'trivial': 'His wit was sombre as it was pitiless; his merriment had madness in it; his humor tragical even to tears'; moreover, he was 'faithless in all social reforms', as Alcott noted sorrowfully after his first visit on 25 June.[79]

Carlyle was certainly scornful of Alcott's brand of social idealism. 'You made a real escape in the case of Brownson Alcott', he told Sterling on 23 July:

He is an ingenious, honest-hearted kind of Quixote, – a long lean man, very like the Don even in figure, who drawls terribly, and 'guesses', and has a kind of rustic dignity and loveability about him: but the second time, discerning my hopeless unbelief in vegetables he expressed real affliction; and tho' we kept him all night, and fed him with Scotch porridge . . . he refused to be comforted, and has not come again.[80]

Alcott did return towards the end of July, when he found that Carlyle was not the only British scoffer. As Carlyle laughingly told Sterling,

Little Paracelsus Browning, a dainty Leigh-Huntish kind of fellow, with much ingenuity, vivacity and Co[c]kney gracefulness, happened to be here: and answered his solemn drawling recommendations of vegetable diet with light Cockney banter and logic; whereupon Alcot[t], at parting, told me 'he would never come to me again!' No absurder Yankee Quixote has come to me of late; and yet a truly honest-hearted man; – like the Quaker who, getting to Rome and to the Pope, ordered his Holiness to forsake idolatries, and assume the broadbrim there & then.[81]

Browning himself described to a friend how 'my outrageous laughters have made him ponder seriously of the hopelessness of England'.[82] Even Mazzini, of whose 'sentimentalism' Carlyle was almost as wary as he was of Alcott's, told his mother that Alcott had come to London to convince 'Carlyle and me that the true way of regenerating the human race is by proscribing meat and eating nothing but vegetables and drinking water'.[83] In August Carlyle reported to Emerson his regret that he and Alcott had got on so badly; Emerson replied soothingly, absolving Carlyle of blame and expressing his vexation with Alcott, whom he described as a man with 'more than a prophet's egotism' and without compensatory 'reconciling talents'.[84]

Jane and Carlyle avoided repeating their holiday mistake of the previous year. While he went on a brief sea journey to the Low Countries with Stephen Spring Rice in early August, Jane set off for Suffolk with the elder Bullers to stay with the youngest Buller son, Reginald, who was Rector of Troston. Carlyle remembered him as 'an airy, pen-drawing, skipping clever enough little creature' in the Edinburgh days when he had tutored the two older brothers; Reginald had now turned into an 'utterly stupid somnolent "Reverend Incumbent"'.[85] Jane regaled Carlyle and Jeannie Welsh – still in Chelsea – with amusing letters about life in the country with the Buller clan.

She showed herself broad-minded on sexual matters, at the same time managing a hit against Carlyle's prejudice against George Sand, when she described the Bullers' arrangements with Theresa or 'Tizzy' Revis, daughter of the woman (also Theresa Revis) who had been until recently Arthur Buller's mistress. Braving the disapproval of her female friends, Mrs Buller senior had 'adopted' Tizzy a few years earlier, though it seems she was not Arthur's child but the legitimate daughter of his mistress and her estranged husband.[86] Now Tizzy had gone to join her consumptive mother in the south of France, and Jane reported Mrs Buller's sorrow at parting with the child: 'The Mother is a most amiable and unfortunate woman Mrs Buller says and she seems to have been on the most intimate terms with her – But Mrs Buller reads George Sand – like me.'[87]

Carlyle was also treated to a mock-horrified description of a church service Jane attended, when her (ex)Presbyterian experience of extempore prayers and sermons led her to feel shocked by Anglican laxity. Reginald, she wrote, 'ascended the pulpit in his white *vestment*, and in a loud, sonorous, perfectly church-of-England-like tone gave out the psalm'. The service 'went off quite respectably – it is wonderful how little faculty is needed for saying prayers *perfectly well*!' or rattling off a sermon written by someone else.[88]

On 26 August Carlyle was able to tell Jane a funny story of his own. He had been visited one day by a man in white trousers whom the maid, Helen Mitchell, announced as 'Oedipus knows what, some mere mumble'. The stranger said he came recommended by Caroline Fox, and sat down,

disclos[ing] himself as a man of huge coarse head, with projecting brow and chin (like a cheese in the *last* quarter), with a pair of large protrusive glittering eyes, which he did not direct to me or to anybody, but sat staring with, into the blue vague! . . . I thought to myself Good Heavens can this be some vagrant Yankee; Lion-hunting Insipidity, – biped perhaps escaped from Bedlam; coming in on me by stealth? He talked a minute longer; he proved to be Owen the Geological Anatomist, a man of real faculty, whom I had wished to see; my recognition of him issued in peals of laughter, and I got two hours of excellent talk out of him . . . After his departure I asked Helen what she had called him? 'She did not know, but was sure it was his right name at any rate!' – what an assistant this little damsel would have been to Adam, when *names* were just beginning![89]

Two days later Carlyle called on Richard Owen at the Hunterian Museum of the Royal College of Surgeons, where he was Professor of Comparative Anatomy and Physiology. Owen was an expert on fossils, birds, and dinosaurs – he coined the word in 1841. It was he who created the models of prehistoric animals for the grounds of the Crystal Palace when it moved to its home in Sydenham in 1853. He was also the chief founder of the Natural History Museum, which was finally opened in South Kensington in 1881.[90] Though he and Carlyle hit it off, Owen was often poisonous in his relations with fellow scientists like Darwin and Huxley. Huxley later remembered that Jane Carlyle disliked Owen, remarking that his sweetness 'reminded her of sugar of lead'; Darwin thought the phrase 'capital' when he heard it, and henceforth adopted it as his nickname for Owen.[91]

At the end of August Carlyle joined Jane and the Bullers in Suffolk, where he embarrassed Jane by delaying dinner one day when he was walking about looking at places connected with Cromwell; he 'overset all our household arrangements here as he oversets all household arrange-ments wherever he goes'.[92] He undertook a riding tour, taking in Sidney Sussex, Cromwell's Cambridge college, Hinchinbrook, where his ancestors had lived, St Ives, where he had farmed, and Ely, where he was the elected MP. On his visit to Ely Cathedral Carlyle 'thought vividly of Cromwell stepping up these floors, with his sword by his side, bidding the Priest (who would not obey his *first* order, but continued reading his liturgies), "Cease your fooling and come out, Sir." '[93]

Carlyle returned to Chelsea, leaving Jane with the Bullers. She little knew what lay ahead for herself when she told her cousin Jeannie about the family's excitement, with 'slaying of the fatted calf', at the expectation of Charles Buller's arrival from London, and their repeated disappoint-ment at his non-appearance, which had for its chief cause the attraction of Lady Harriet Baring:

He was to have come when Parliament rose, and he went instead to 'Lady Harriet's' – As if he had not flirted with *her* the whole season thro'! – Then he went to Havre 'to be near the sea'! – what on earth could be the benefit of *the sea* to a political town-wit and *diner-out* like Mr C Buller? Then he would surely come at last! – but no – not yet – off to the Lady Harriet's again – then he finally fixed Tuesday – then some Thompson or Johnson asked him to dinner and he changed the day to Wednesday; and of his Wednesday's appointment *this* was the result!

Charles finally arrived at midnight, so that 'today all faces have a look of sunshiny gladness', though Jane herself kept in her room 'in a sort of spirit of reaction against the extravagant homage which he is used to receive from all people, especially women'. In her next letter she had to confess that he was so pleasant that, after 'a sublime effort of *grumpiness*', she had been won over by his fun and charm.[94]

Carlyle's fieldwork had helped him to get an imaginative purchase on

Cromwell; this was now enhanced by the chance discovery that the shy poet and translator Edward FitzGerald owned the land on which the Battle of Naseby had been fought. Carlyle met FitzGerald on 15 September, when the painter Samuel Laurence brought him to Cheyne Row, and he immediately began to ask for FitzGerald's help with maps, facts, and artefacts to do with Cromwell's battle. Carlyle was a charming and usually successful pleader, complimenting his correspondent by assuming on his part a degree of knowledge and interest in the subject equal to his own as demonstrated in his detailed questioning.

FitzGerald was able to point out that Carlyle and Dr Arnold had been mistaken about the centre ground of the battle when they visited the site; nevertheless, he was impressed by Carlyle's 'great sagacity in guessing at the localities from the vague descriptions of contemporaries: and his short *pasticcio* of the battle is the best I have seen'. But, he added, 'he will spoil all by making a demigod of Cromwell, who certainly was so far from wise that he brought about the very thing he fought to prevent – the restoration of an unrestricted monarchy'.[95] FitzGerald set about finding mementoes of the battle – teeth, bones, and bullets – to send to Carlyle, as well as doing some detailed sketches as requested. Despite this unexpected extra support, however, Carlyle still despaired of getting the Cromwell book written, feeling that he lay buried beneath a whole 'Continent of Earth' which he had to 'heave up with me from the bottom of the sea'. In the privacy of his journal for 25 October he tortured himself with accusations of 'sinful disgraceful sloth'.[96]

By October 1842 Jeannie Welsh had gone home to Liverpool after her long visit. Jane's letters to her from now on contain the most confidential remarks, with Carlyle very often the subject of unflattering comment. On 19 October Jane recounted the unexpected visit of a second cousin, Adam Hunter, a successful doctor, who told Carlyle he ought to take Jane abroad, 'and use *any means under Heaven in the way of gratifying her wishes*', in order to improve her health. 'No wonder he was a well employed Dr among the women at least if this be the sort of advice he deals in!' she added, before turning her wickedness away from cousin Adam and towards Carlyle: 'C had looked monstrous glum at the speech about gratifying my wishes.'[97] Jeannie was the recipient of another confidence ten days later. 'His Wisdom', Jane wrote, 'kicked up a rumpus' about her 'George-Sandish excess of humanity' towards Mrs Revis (the elder Theresa). He told her that her 'doctrine' was infamous, and also her practice 'in making myself the advocate of W[hore]s'. Jane had been unable to treat Carlyle's vehemence jokingly; she 'cried like a simpleton and so made bad worse'.[98]

It is impossible to know whether Carlyle's invectives against 'George

Sandism', his usual shorthand for the literature, and practice, of sexual freedom, had any special significance. He had long complained about the phenomenon, but had not written it out of his system in the article he once contemplated doing for Macvey Napier of the *Edinburgh Review*. His excessive anger on the subject may have been a chance deflection from his intolerable misery and guilt about the continuing lack of progress with Cromwell. Jane, always thin-skinned and ailing, was intensely so in these months following her mother's death, and so may have exaggerated his reaction. The marriage had long been strained, and may never have been easy in the physical sense. Now Jane, aged forty-one, had lost her youthful looks and relied increasingly on her witty but cutting tongue to attract admiration, while Carlyle, who turned forty-seven in December 1842, was on the verge of becoming infatuated with the formidably flirtatious Lady Harriet Baring.

★

During December 1842 and January 1843 Jane was at her most discontented, both with herself and with Carlyle. She was, as usual in winter, ill, but this time in addition to colds and flu she was suffering from a pain in her side. John Carlyle was called in, but Jane had no faith in either his diagnostic powers or his bedside manner.[99] On 8 January she disclosed to Jeannie that she had married Carlyle because he was 'the least unlikable man in the place', and because she was unwilling to do without him in the way she could not do without her slippers or her bonnet. In this letter, as in the next, Jane gave full rein to her all-consuming bitter feelings, which embraced not just Carlyle and his brother, but also other friends who irritated her.

Geraldine Jewsbury was one object of scorn. She had been writing, with her Liverpool friend Elizabeth Paulet, a 'daring' George-Sandish novel, and had sent the manuscript to Jane for comment. Jane's moral scruples in her reply were met by 'a whole *pamphlet* of witty, devil-may-care objections to my objections', as she reported to Jeannie.[100] At Carlyle's urging, Geraldine was invited to visit, but Jane was not disposed to enjoy the company of her enthusiastic friend, and by 24 February, when Geraldine had been at Cheyne Row for 'three most uncomfortable weeks', Jane was 'weary of her' and unable to pretend otherwise. Carlyle ignored her, and other friends, notably Erasmus Darwin and Mazzini, demonstrated 'a sort of *sacred horror* of her'. Geraldine was, Jane wrote tartly, 'wheedling John Carlyle at a great rate pretending all the while to have the greatest dislike to him – every Sunday and on no other day – she makes a *grande toilette* – comes down in the forenoon with a *bare neck* – and a black satin gown – or coloured silk! – all wasted I assure you.'[101]

Carlyle said after she had gone what a relief it was 'to be able to sit here in peace without having that dreadful young woman *gazing* at me', as Jeannie was told on 12 March. Jane added: 'To be sure she did *gaze* at him – and try all sorts of *seductions* on him . . . but the poor man proved absolutely *unseducable* – Even when she took the strong measure of stretching herself on the hearth rug at his feet and sleeping there.'[102]

Unseducable by the insistent and rather ridiculous Geraldine, yes. Jane had actually expressed to Jeannie a slight anxiety about bringing Geraldine into the house:

Tho I am not jealous of my husband (pray read all this into yourself and burn the letter) tho I have not only his *habit* of preference for me over all other women (and *habits* are much stronger in him than *passions*) but also his indifference to *all* women *as women* to secure me against jealousy – still young women who have in them, as Geraldine has, with all her good and great qualities, a born *spirit of intrigue* are perilous sort of inmates for a married pair to invite.[103]

This was an astute enough remark, but Jane could not reckon with the rather different attractions, for someone of Carlyle's make-up, of Lady Harriet Baring. Rich, ailing, childless (her only child having died), adored by her husband, she invited all the clever men of the age, commanding their presence in the way Jane had recently noticed in the case of Charles Buller. She had set her sights on winning Carlyle as a regular recruit to her soirées in London and weekend parties at her country houses, Addiscombe, near Croydon in Surrey, and later the Grange in Hampshire.

In the same letter in which she showed a half-dismissed anxiety about Geraldine's stay, Jane joked about Carlyle's 'having received a *seductive* letter from the *Lady Harriet*'. Carlyle had accepted an invitation for a night when Jane wanted to attend 'a corn law lecture in the Strand' by W. J. Fox. Jane tells her story with her usual zest, all unaware of the painful feelings she would soon suffer:

Lady Harriet writes to my husband that she is ill – that she dines at four o'clock and is allowed to go nowhere in the evenings – to do nothing but speak – that 'there is nobody – (she may really say almost nobody in the world) she likes so well to speak with as him' – Pray mark the fine truth-giving effect of the modifying parenthesis! – 'So he sees what a work of *charity* and *piety* is cut out for him'! When a handsome, clever, and reputedly *most haughty* woman appeals to the *charity* and *piety* of a simple man like Carlyle you may be sure she will not appeal in vain – So he writes to her engaging to visit her on Thursday evening – and *forgets* to tell *me* he has done so – Then comes a ticket of admission for one gentleman and one Lady – to Mr Fox's lecture for the same Thursday evening – and he asks me would I like to go? The Devil puts it in my head to answer unexpectedly 'yes' – In fact I have been long wanting to hear this Fox lecture – for I understand him to be a first rate speaker – and observing that his place was this time on the straight line of the Omnibus I thought I could never have so good a chance – 'Very well says he rather perplexedly – but *I* cannot go with you – I promised to go to Lady Harriet tomorrow evening – Can you get another man? – Mazzini is the never failing man in every case of need but I would not propose him – for young Italy has been horribly out of favour [with Carlyle] this long while – seeing that I remained silent he himself however proposed him – As *he* was going *his* road he felt the fairness of allowing *me* to go *mine*.[104]

That Lady Harriet possessed a great deal of charm is clear from the way in which several men wrote of her and to her. Charles Buller's letters are courteous and playfully idolatrous, as are Milnes's; Thackeray's show him trying to resist her imperiousness, quarrelling with her, and humbly if wittily making up; while Mill's reveal him unbending from the cool, rational style of his correspondence with all but his 'inamorata', Mrs Taylor.[105] One note from Mill, written probably in 1843, gives a tantalising glimpse of Lady Harriet's ability to overturn men's common sense:

Dear Lady Harriet – I entreat you to burn, & if possible forget, an insane rhapsody that I wrote to you a few days ago. I must have been, & I believe I was, actually out of my right mind when I wrote & sent it – & nothing else could excuse it in the smallest degree. I am in my senses again now & I beseech you to consider that wretched farrago as cancelled & unwritten & when you write again let it be as if it had never reached you – would to God it had not! J.S.M.[106]

Fortunately for Mill, Lady Harriet appears to have acted on his request. Carlyle's rhapsodies, by contrast, have survived, though Lady Harriet's side of the correspondence has not, thus rendering her extremely elusive. Carlyle's expressions of homage and fealty look odd and silly, though they differ from those of Lady Harriet's other courtiers only in degree, exhibiting the same vehemence and intensity which are the hallmark of his writing generally. He writes to her with old-fashioned courtliness in these early days of the relationship. He also reveals that her attraction for him precisely at this moment has to do with her class as well as with her beguiling person.

By February 1843 Carlyle was finishing a book – not *Cromwell*, with which he had been wrestling for so many months, but *Past and Present*, his direct response to the distress of the poor he had witnessed in town and country over the past year. He told his mother in January that he felt he should hold his peace no longer on the subject.[107] He had begun writing this new book the previous November – it was the quickest piece of writing he would ever do – when his concern for the present condition of the country came together in his imagination with his interest in the past: not in this case Cromwell's seventeeth century, but the twelfth century.

In October 1842 he had borrowed from the London Library a Latin chronicle published by the Camden Society, by Jocelin de Brakelonda, a monk at Bury St Edmunds.[108] It detailed the heroic career of Abbot Samson, on whom Carlyle seized as the type of the wise governor taking over a community at a difficult time in its history. Carlyle saw that by selective attention to detail he could exploit the contrast between a small, homogeneous religious community in medieval times and the hetero-geneous, fractured society of a rapidly industrialised and troubled nineteenth-century Britain. 'I think of calling it "Past and Present", or some such title', Carlyle told James Marshall on 1 February; 'A "Tract for the Times" full of the most portentous Speculative-Radicalism ever uttered in Governess English, or even in *Carlylese* as they call it!'[109]

Carlyle's 'radicalism' in the book consists of a famously sustained attack on a 'do-nothing' aristocracy, and herein lies one element of Lady Harriet's fascination. Her husband had been appointed Secretary to the Board of Control by Peel in 1841. She was ambitious for him, and enter-tained widely for his sake. They moved in the highest circles, and both admired Carlyle. He might perhaps, through them, exercise an influence on government itself, by encouraging this pair of willing aristocrats to do something for those who shared none of their wealth, privilege, or position. He wished both to study them and to influence them. In the middle of February 1843 he wrote to Lady Harriet, accepting an invitation and telling her with coy humour about his new book:

I am just finishing a dreadful *Book* on these Times and Aristocracies, which (tho' we by no means will have *you* killed in this general Twilight of the Gods) will most likely deprive me of your friendship for evermore: – wherefore I must make the best of my few opportunites that remain![110]

The friendship flourished. Carlyle adopted the tone of a petitioner and adorer, writing on 21 April, just as *Past and Present* was being published by Chapman and Hall, that he was thinking of 'pilgriming on foot to a certain Shrine; the name of it is Addiscombe'. 'I shall arrive all dusty, weary, woebegone; but if the light of your looks fall on me', he continued, 'I shall become quite cheerful again.'[111] The tone he struck with Lady Harriet contrasts strangely not only with that of his letters to all other corres-pondents (even Jane in her days of pseudo-mastery before the marriage), but also with the confident rhetoric of *Past and Present*, one of his most characteristic utterances and the book which represents him at the very height of his powers and influence.

PART FOUR

THE HEIGHT OF FAME

CHAPTER II

Fascinations and Flirtations 1843–1845

Past and Present, published in April 1843, begins as follows:

The condition of England, on which many pamphlets are now in the course of publication, and many thoughts unpublished are going on in every reflective head, is justly regarded as one of the most ominous, and withal one of the strangest, ever seen in this world. England is full of wealth, of multifarious produce, supply for human want in every kind; yet England is dying of inanition. With unabated bounty the land of England blooms and grows; waving with yellow harvests; thick-studded with workshops, industrial implements, with fifteen millions of workers, understood to be the strongest, the cunningest and the willingest our Earth ever had; these men are here; the work they have done, the fruit they have realised is here, abundant, exuberant on every hand of us: and behold, some baleful fiat as of Enchantment has gone forth, saying, 'Touch it not, ye workers, ye master-workers, ye master-idlers; none of you can touch it, no man of you shall be the better for it; this is enchanted fruit!'[1]

This opening chapter bears the title 'Midas'; it continues in a sustained flight of outraged rhetoric to lay before the reader's eyes the paradoxical state of Britain in the present day, 1843. Carlyle mingles far-fetched metaphor – the idea of everyone sitting paralysed under an evil spell – with observations gleaned from his own recent journeys to Scotland and to Cromwell country, and also from official reports by Poor Law Commissioners and other bodies set up in a well-meaning attempt to collect statistics and assess for the first time in detail the state of the poor, of manufacturing, of agricultural districts, of education, of health – in short, the state of the nation.

The facts Carlyle adduces are shocking enough. Though no political economist himself – he was to coin the term 'Dismal Science' for political economy in 1849[2] – Carlyle gives in *Past and Present* the first striking description of the economic problems associated with capitalism and an industrialised society, of which Britain was the leading example. If his book disappoints in terms of serious analysis of the problems or attempts to provide solutions, it brilliantly employs emotional rhetoric to describe the human cost of those problems in such examples as the broken figures in the workhouse of St Ives, a version of Dante's Hell, and the 'scenes of woe and destitution and desolation' in 'thrifty Scotland'.

The Stockport child-poisoning case Carlyle had noted in letters of October 1841 is brought to the reader's attention as a terrible sign of the times:

At Stockport Assizes . . . a Mother and a Father are arraigned and found guilty of poisoning three of their children, to defraud a 'burial-society' of some 3*l.*8*s.* due on the death of each child: they are arraigned, found guilty; and the official authorities, it is whispered, hint that perhaps the case is not solitary, that perhaps you had better not probe farther into that department of things . . . a human Mother and Father had said to themselves, What shall we do to escape starvation? We are deep sunk here, in our dark cellar; and help is far. – Yes, in the Ugolino Hunger-tower stern things happen; best-loved little Gaddo fallen dead on his Father's knees! – The Stockport Mother and Father think and hint: Our poor little starveling Tom, who cries all day for victuals, who will see only evil and not good in this world: if he were out of misery at once; he well dead, and the rest of us perhaps kept alive? It is thought, and hinted; at last it is done. And now Tom being killed, and all spent and eaten, Is it poor little starveling Jack that must go, or poor little starveling Will? – What a committee of ways and means![3]

How did this come about? And what is to be done? It came about, according to Carlyle, because those who should have been governing, an ideal group which if it existed would be called 'the Aristocracy of Talent', have been absent while actual governments made up variously of 'Benthamee' Radicals singing 'the gospel of Enlightened Selfishness', uncaring capitalists with their 'gospel of Mammonism', and an unworking, game-preserving, partridge-shooting aristocracy intoning 'the gospel of Dilettantism', have been allowing the country to go to ruin in the name of their different vested interests.[4] Peel, Prime Minister since the summer of 1841, is bluntly attacked as Sir Jabesh Windbag, a leader no better than any of his predecessors – Mr Facing-both-ways, Viscount Mealymouth, or the Earl of Windlestraw – in his lack of commitment to the repeal of the Corn Laws which might relieve the distress of the poor.[5] As to what is to be done in the longer term, Carlyle suggests, drawing on his favourite themes of the strong leader or hero and the rediscovery of a true (as opposed to sham) religious and political will, that we look to the past and find there an example which might be adaptable to modern conditions.

This is where Jocelin's twelfth-century chronicle, detailing the revival of the moribund community of monks at Bury St Edmunds by the strong leader Abbot Samson, comes in. With grandiose selectiveness Carlyle describes the election and successful reign of the wise Samson, contrasting this scornfully with ballot boxes and other modern reform measures. 'A heroic people chooses heroes, and is happy; a valet or flunky people chooses sham-heroes, what are called quacks, thinking them heroes, and

244

is not happy', he declares, without explaining what can possibly be meant by a heroic people, or how such a body can be secured.[6]

When dealing with the past Carlyle makes a virtue out of vagueness, demanding that we admire a feudal set-up which he himself could not have borne, as one of his reviewers, William Henry Smith, quickly pointed out in *Blackwood's Magazine*: 'He and the monk would be intolerable to each other.' Carlyle, with the Protestant's deep dislike of Catholic doctrine and ritual, ignores everything that makes medieval Catholicism distinctive except the one thing he wants to hold up as a positive contrast to the present, namely its 'religious spirit'.[7]

If the evocation of an idealised past community gave Carlyle a structure of a sort, and allowed him, however quixotically, to attack the evils of the present by means of contrast, it was his extraordinary exposure of the ills of his own age which gave the book its quality and influence. Though no supporter of Chartism or direct action such as the recent 'Manchester Insurrection' – a protest by 'a million hungry operative men' – Carlyle is unequivocal in his belief in the rightness of their cause: ' "A fair day's-wages for a fair day's-work" is as just a demand as Governed men ever made of Governing. It is the everlasting right of man.'[8]

No one could better him in his scornful attack on the 'National Palaver' (Parliament) or so-called Government which had allowed supply and demand in the manufacturing industries to get grievously out of balance:

But what will reflective readers say of a governing Class, such as ours, addressing its Workers with an indictment of 'Over-production'! Over-production: runs it not so? 'Ye miscellaneous, ignoble manufacturing individuals, ye have produced too much! We accuse you of making above two-hundred thousand shirts for the bare backs of mankind. Your trousers too, which you have made, of fustian, of cassimere, of Scotch-plaid, of jane, nankeen and woollen broadcloth, are they not manifold? Of hats for the human head, of shoes for the human foot, of stools to sit on, spoons to eat with – Nay, what say we hats or shoes? You produce gold-watches, jewelries, silver-forks, and epergnes, commodes, chiffoniers, stuffed sofas – Heavens, the Commercial Bazaar and multitudinous Howel-and-Jameses cannot contain you. You have produced, produced; – he that seeks your indictment, let him look around. Millions of shirts, and empty pairs of breeches, hang there in judgment against you. We accuse you of over-producing: you are criminally guilty of producing shirts, breeches, hats, shoes and commodities, in frightful over-abundance. And now there is a glut, and your operatives cannot be fed!'[9]

The rhetorical force of this, with its battering-ram of repetition, its dogged amassing of detail, its shifting point of view, is unmatched except perhaps by Dickens, so much Carlyle's admirer, in his great 'social problem' novels, especially *Bleak House*. Both writers are adept at the rhetoric of scorn and surprise; both mingle and exchange the abstract with the concrete; both create striking images which are made to do duty for the general malaise. That Dickens had at his command a wide repertoire of voices, and so had no need to imitate Carlyle or any other writer, is indisputable. Nevertheless, his public voice of contemporary observation may well have owed something to Carlyle's, as his public voice of history avowedly did when he came to write *A Tale of Two Cities* with *The French Revolution* ringing inside his head.

In fact, the whole generation of British novelists who were writing their 'condition-of-England' novels in the years following *Past and Present* expressed homage to Carlyle's influence. Elizabeth Gaskell quotes from Carlyle on the title-page of her Manchester novel of industrial poverty, *Mary Barton* (1848). Charles Kingsley in *Yeast* (1848) and *Alton Locke* (1850) quotes frequently from *Chartism* and *Past and Present*; in the latter novel he introduces an intemperate but good-hearted Scot, Sandy Mackaye, as mentor to the impoverished tailor and poet Alton Locke. Mackaye, like his real-life model, specialises in seeing through shams. Disraeli, in *Sybil: or The Two Nations* (1845), though espousing a Young England Conservatism remote from Carlyle's position, echoes the latter's rhetoric of the gulf between rich and poor. Dickens's *Hard Times* (1854) was dedicated, like *A Tale of Two Cities*, to Carlyle. Even Thackeray, though suspicious of forceful rhetoric of the Carlylean kind, and a satirist of a different sort, gave at least a nod towards his friend's example in his exposure of quackery of all kinds in *Vanity Fair* (1848).

In an inspired piece of naming and characterising in *Past and Present*, Carlyle famously described the proffered solutions to the condition of England – Reform Bills, ballot boxes, five-point charters – as so many quack cures, or 'Morrison's Pills', his (misspelt) allusion to James Morison's Vegetable Universal Pills, claimed to be effective against fevers, smallpox, consumption, senility, and Carlyle's familiar enemy, constipation.[10] Like so many of his sounding phrases, this one was universally taken up.

Past and Present was reviewed critically by friends and foes; its repetitions, vagueness, occasional ranting, and signal lack of practical solutions to the problems so searingly described were taken to task even by admirers like Mazzini (in the *British and Foreign Review*) and Emerson (in the *Dial*). But its great power was recognised too. F. D. Maurice, Sterling's brother-in-law and a troubled but loyal Church of England clergyman, defended Carlyle's attacks on modern 'sham religion' in a letter to the *Christian Remembrancer*, saying it was salutary for the Church to be woken up and put on its mettle by such a conscientious opponent.[11]

One review ensured that his influence spread into the fledgling movement for international socialism. The twenty-three-year-old Friedrich Engels, representing his father's cotton firm of Engels and Ermen in

Manchester, reviewed *Past and Present* in the *Deutsch-Französische Jahrbücher*, a Paris-based German periodical edited by his friend Karl Marx. The article was entitled 'The Condition of England' ('Die Lage Englands'); at the end, Engels promised a series of articles which would expand on this important subject. The result was his book, published in German in 1845, *Die Lage der arbeitenden Klasse in England* (*The Condition of the Working Class in England*).

Engels praises Carlyle's descriptions of urban misery, quoting many of the most striking passages. He endorses the diagnosis of the condition of England, while dissenting absolutely from Carlyle's anti-democratic, hero-worshipping, neo-feudalist stance and his regret that religion has become a sham. Engels, following the German philosopher and advocate of the 'religion of humanity', Ludwig Feuerbach, believes that traditional religion has exhausted its usefulness; he positively rejoices in its woeful position, looking forward cheerfully to a fairer post-Christian society in which *human* relations will be at the centre of spiritual life.[12]

For all his dissent from Carlyle's conclusions, Engels in his own book, with its graphic accounts of Manchester wealth sitting alongside Manchester poverty, owes his inspiration to *Past and Present*. He and Marx were also prompted by some of Carlyle's leading ideas and terms when they came to write *The Communist Manifesto* early in 1848. In *Past and Present* Carlyle uses two now famous phrases, 'Captains of Industry', and 'cash payment', to denote respectively the factory owners, the industrial new rich or 'working aristocracy', and their relation with their workers, that of 'cash payment' and short-term contracts. Carlyle expresses the wish that these so-called captains would become 'real captains' over 'a firm regimented mass' of workers.[13] In *The Communist Manifesto*, which Marx wrote using Engels's notes as well as his own, Carlyle's phrase 'cash payment', described as the only 'nexus between man and man', is seized on as the outward and visible sign of the alienation of the worker from the fruits of his labour, which is, according to Marx and Engels, the inevitable result of the capitalist system.

Of course their conclusions are diametrically opposed to Carlyle's, but the rhetoric is similar. Where in *Past and Present* Carlyle apostrophises the workers whom he truly pities but wants to see better led rather than in revolt – 'Awake, ye noble Workers, warriors in the one true war' – Marx and Engels proclaim at the end of *The Communist Manifesto* (in which they too employ the metaphor of enchantment and paralysis) a war between the classes, which the workers will win:

Let the ruling classes tremble at a Communistic revolution. The proletarians have nothing to lose but their chains. They have a world to win.
WORKING MEN OF ALL COUNTRIES,
UNITE![14]

Carlyle's established friends and admirers welcomed *Past and Present*. 'Wondrous' was Caroline Fox's word when she finished reading it in August 1843.[15] Elizabeth Barrett wrote in May 1843 to Richard Hengist Horne, with whom she was about to collaborate on an essay on Carlyle for *A New Spirit of the Age* (1844), that there was 'nothing new' in *Past and Present*, 'but almost everything true − I am a devotee of Carlyle'.[16]

Young men and women of the new generation, some of whom would become famous in their turn, responded equally to the book. Carlyle had described the forthcoming *Past and Present* in February 1843 as a 'Tract for the Times',[17] an allusion to the series of essays under that title which had been written by a number of Oxford dons and clerics, including John Henry Newman, Edward Pusey, and John Keble. Collectively known as the Oxford Movement, these men urged in their writings a return to a traditional, ritualist, truly 'Catholic' Church of England as a bulwark against evolutionary science and the so-called 'Higher Criticism' of the Bible, especially Strauss's *Life of Jesus* with its conclusions that the Gospel accounts of Christ's life were mythical. The last of the *Tracts for the Times*, Tract XC, published in 1841, had caused an outcry among orthodox Anglicans. Written by Newman, it argued that the Thirty-Nine Articles of the established Church of England shared more with Roman Catholic doctrine than had been generally allowed.

Though Newman did not convert to Rome until 1845, his influence on the theology of young men still in the Anglican Church was both magnetic and troubling. J. A. Froude and A. H. Clough were among those who came under that influence as students and fellows at Oxford; instead of confirming their faith, Newman's arguments had the contrary effect of shaking it. By the end of the 1840s both found it impossible to subscribe to the Articles and consequently resigned their fellowships. Froude later remembered that the antidote to Newman's 'siren song'[18] had been his discovery about 1843 of Carlyle's works, particularly *The French Revolution*, *Heroes*, and *Past and Present*. Carlyle's natural supernaturalism, his anti-materialism and anti-atheism, and at the same time his freedom from the dogma of any church faction, saved Froude in the hothouse atmosphere of Oxford in the early 1840s:

Amidst the controversies, the arguments, the doubts, the crowding uncertainties of forty years ago, Carlyle's voice was to the young generation of Englishmen like the sound of 'ten thousand trumpets' in their ears, as the Knight of Grange said of John Knox.[19]

The same was true of Clough, who, having 'passed under Carlyle's influence',[20] resigned his fellowship in 1848, and left Oxford for a rather unsettled career as poet and teacher.

Others who testified to Carlyle's importance in their youthful lives were T. H. Huxley and George Eliot. Huxley, born in 1825 the son of a struggling schoolmaster, began at fifteen to keep a journal, in which he noted down quotations from Carlyle's essays, especially those relating to German literature, and from the translation of *Wilhelm Meister*. Much later he recalled that his debt to Carlyle consisted half in his being led to learn German, which was to prove useful for his biological studies, and half in his imbibing an intense hatred of 'cant and shams of all sorts'.[21] At sixteen Huxley became assistant to his brother-in-law, a doctor in the poor east London district of Rotherhithe, as a prelude to beginning his own medical studies, and so saw for himself 'something of the way the poor live'. Two years later, therefore, when *Past and Present* came out, its 'advocacy of the cause of the poor appealed very strongly' to the young Huxley.[22]

George Eliot, or Marian Evans, born in 1819, also experienced the reading of Carlyle's works in her early twenties as revelatory. For her, *Past and Present* was 'that thrilling book';[23] along with *Sartor* it was the work chiefly in her mind when she wrote a brief but thoughtful essay on Carlyle in October 1855. She writes perceptively about Carlyle's place in British intellectual life at mid-century, giving expression to the feelings of so many of her generation:

It is an idle question to ask whether his books will be read a century hence: if they were all burnt as the grandest of Suttees on his funeral pile, it would only be like cutting down an oak after its acorns have sown a forest. For there is hardly a superior or active mind of this generation that has not been modified by Carlyle's writings; there has hardly been an English book written for the last ten or twelve years that would not have been different if Carlyle had not lived. The character of his influence is best seen in the fact that many of the men who have the least agreement with his opinions are those to whom the reading of *Sartor Resartus* was an epoch in the history of their minds.[24]

Though, as George Eliot seemed almost to predict, Carlyle's direct influence was to wane dramatically by the beginning of the twentieth century, with the change in literary taste and the growing horror at German militarism and later Fascism, he had irrevocably affected life, thought, and language in the experience of a whole generation, many of whom, like George Eliot and Huxley, did not share his political views, let alone those of later extremists who claimed him as a precursor. The 'modification' of minds described by George Eliot was diffusive, all-pervasive.

★

Carlyle did not yet know of any of these young admirers, but he did know that he was a celebrity, and that his influence was great. Though his income had increased, he and Jane continued to live unostentatiously, even frugally. Success, and the freedom from financial anxiety, brought Carlyle little pleasure and no peace. He resumed work on Cromwell, with all the woes associated with that book of difficult birth, and he complained as usual about ill health, lack of sleep, and neighbourly noise and distractions. His family caused him pain, with Jack 'roving about' London 'like a blazing torch all day', then coming back to Cheyne Row to sleep, as Carlyle complained in April 1843.[25] Jane was vitriolic about Jack's selfishness, aborted plans, and refusals of jobs as not good enough for him, as well as his indifference to her ailments. He was happy, she told Jeannie Welsh, to '*eat the dinners which Carlyle declines*', instead of practising his profession.[26]

Jack came and went over the next couple of years, always restless and always idle. Though he did eventually publish his translation of Dante's *Inferno* in 1849, he was as dilatory about this literary task as he was about finding medical work. He wrote defensively from Leamington in August 1845 that he was once more looking out for a medical position, telling Carlyle he need not reply with 'any of the old scorn; for I sincerely want some wholesome work'.[27] Alick, too, was a source of anxiety. He finally emigrated to Canada in June 1843, despite his mother's pleadings. Carlyle wrote encouragingly, and gave him £250 to help him get started. He hoped to go to Liverpool to see his brother off, but Alick had already gone before such a meeting could be arranged.[28] They continued to correspond until Alick's death in Canada in 1876, but never saw one another again.

In July Carlyle made his escape from the London heat. He spent ten days in South Wales with an 'infatuated' and 'wearisome' admirer, Charles Redwood, followed by a few days with Connop Thirlwall, Bishop of St David's, expressing his amusement at the fact that he was a guest in the very bishop's palace where Archbishop Laud – Oliver Cromwell's antagonist – had once lived.[29] He then went on to Annandale. Jane was as always happy to be left in London in summer, overseeing house decorations and alterations and being visited by her clutch of loyal admirers, chiefly Mazzini, old Mr Sterling, and Erasmus Darwin. She commented humorously to Carlyle on Mazzini's joining the ranks of Lady Harriet Baring's courtiers. Lady Harriet had sought him out to ask for private Italian lessons; he was impressed by her tolerance of his republicanism, as he told his mother after their first meeting in July.[30] Mazzini seems to have gone straight round to Cheyne Row to report on the occasion to Jane, who immediately reported it in turn to Carlyle: 'Mazzini's visit to Lady Baring (as he calls her) went off wonderfully well. I am afraid my dear this Lady Baring of yours and his and John Mill's and everybody's is an arch coquette – she seems to have played her cards with Mazzini really too well.'

Lady Harriet, she continued, 'talked to [Mazzini] with the highest commendations of George Sand', and surprised him by indulging in some confidential conversation, which he thought unusual in an English lady. According to Mazzini, Mill 'appeared to be *loving* her very much',[31] an observation which is supported by that surviving frantic note to Lady Harriet about this time apologising for a previous indiscreet letter.

While Carlyle was away, Jane regaled him with stories of old Edward Sterling's temper tantrums and Mazzini's plans for an Italian uprising. 'HE a conspirator *chief*!' she exclaimed of the latter on 27 August:

I should make an infinitely better one myself – what for instance can be more out of the *role* of Conspirator than his telling *me* all his secret operations even to the *names of places* when conspiracy is breaking out and *the names of the people* who are organizing it? – *me* who do not even ever ask him a question on such matters.[32]

She had by now collected round her a number of European exiles, political and non-political, for whom she tried to find accommodation or positions, as she had done for the Ruffini brothers and for Mazzini, who told George Sand in a letter of September 1844 that 'Madame Carlyle' was the woman he esteemed most in England.[33] An uneasy, and unequal, friendship grew up between Jane and Amely Bölte, a persistent visitor at Cheyne Row, who became a practised observer of the Carlyle marriage, sending regular gossip to her Berlin correspondent Varnhagen von Ense. Jane found a succession of governess posts for Amely, several short-lived because of Amely's religious unorthodoxy. She told Carlyle in August that she was arranging for Amely to join the Bullers as governess to Theresa Revis, adding: 'Certainly to goodness I have "unconsciously" opened a bureau for destitute young women!'[34]

And not only for destitute young women. Among the German fraternity in London she had befriended two men who showed frequent symptoms of insanity, often when alone in her company, as she delighted to tell friends. She now gave Carlyle the latest news of both. One, Joseph Garnier, was later described by Carlyle as

a revolutionary Exile, filled to the brim with mutinous confus[io]n of the usual kind, and with its usual consequences: a black-eyed, tall stalwart-looking mass of a man, face all cut with scars (of duels in his student time), but expressive still of frankness, honesty, ingenuity, and good humour; *dirty* for most part, yet as it were *heroically* so; few men had more experience of poverty and squalor here, or took it more proudly.

Carlyle helped to get Garnier a clerkship under Henry Cole, but later heard that when the European revolutions of 1848 broke out, he 'had rushed into German Whirlpool, and fighting in Baden [where Engels also fought in the unsuccessful revolutionary army], had perished'.[35]

The other mad German was Richard Plattnauer, whom Jane was to rescue from a lunatic asylum the following summer, bringing him home to Cheyne Row for a few weeks until arrangements could be made to get him to Switzerland for treatment.[36] Carlyle's note on Plattnauer, written when he was going through Jane's letters after her death, confirms that, though always willing to do a kindness to anyone in distress, he was less enamoured of such figures than Jane, who derived not only a sense of usefulness but also a *frisson* of excitement from supporting them. 'On the whole', Carlyle mused, 'one rapidly enough perceived that the Foreign-Exile element was *not* the recommendable one, and, except for *her* picturesque aesthetic, &c interest in it, *wd* have been *brief* with it here.'[37]

In these notes to Jane's letters Carlyle underestimated her neediness. Her letters describing Plattnauer and the others demonstrate much more than a merely aesthetic interest. She wanted to be needed, and she needed to be adored. Though her correspondence with Carlyle during these summer months of 1843 was peaceful and affectionate, the nearest he came to expressing adoration was to address her in his usual fashion as the thrifty little housewife – 'my Goody', 'dear Bairn', 'my little Dear', 'poor lassie', 'dear little Wife'.[38] Much of her letter-writing genius was put to work in amusing him with dramatised versions of domestic events. Magnifying problems with servants, decorators, smoking chimneys, neighbours' pets, pianos, and so on helped to make her feel useful, but she required the whiff of the exotic which her male admirers, her exiles, and her 'mads', as Mazzini called them, added to her daily experience.

When Carlyle returned home in October he expressed himself pleased at first with her efforts during his absence to rearrange the house so that he could study undisturbed by the piano-playing ladies next door, but she was soon describing to Jeannie Welsh and other friends his renewed outbursts about the impossibility of working and sleeping. Jeannie was treated to a running commentary on 25 October:

There were wanderings about during the night – fires kindled with his own hands, bread and butter eaten in the china-closet! – all sorts of what shall I say – strange things upon my honour done [Mazzini's phrases] – and I all the while lying awake listening with a bouncing heart but *afraid* to meddle with him – even to offer any assistance – then the sort of days sure to follow that sort of nights![39]

Geraldine Jewsbury ill-advisedly stoked the fire. She told Jane on 17 October that she was 'horribly uneasy about you, for though you laugh and make witty speeches, I know the state you are in'. 'You have no one who has any consideration for you', she continued; 'my dear child you ought to know your value better.'[40]

Meanwhile Carlyle, apparently unaware that his bad temper was having quite such an impact on Jane, expressed in his journal his rage that Richard Hengist Horne intended to write a biographical essay on him 'in some beggarly *spirit of the age* or other rubbish-basket he is about editing'. 'The world', he wrote, 'has no business with my Life; the world will never know my Life, if it should write and read a hundred "biographies" of me.'[41]

His own biographical work was driving him mad once more. He could not easily get at the kind of detailed statistical material he needed; the papers relating to Cromwell were scattered, uncollected, uncatalogued. Henry Cole of the Public Record Office was asked for help and thanked, on 25 October, for 'the ray of light you have thrown over that dreary labyrinth of a mouldering Necropolis, named *Record Office*, – a true City of the Dead, and not yet properly Buried!'[42]

Jane only seldom expressed sympathy with Carlyle's authorial purgatory. She did tell Susan Stirling in November, in the midst of relating a fuss about his newly prepared study, that 'the thing he has got to write – his long projected life of Cromwell – is no joke – and no sort of *room* can make it easy'.[43] Her intermittent understanding is demonstrated in one interesting letter of December 1843 to Amely Bölte, in which her skill at following an amusing stream of consciousness wherever it might lead is as evident as her pity and self-pity:

He came into this room the other morning when I was sitting peaceably darning his stockings, and laid a great bundle of papers on my fire, enough to have kindled the chimney if it had not been, providentially, swept quite lately – the kindling of a chimney (as you in your German ignorance may perhaps not be aware) subjecting one here in London to the awful visitation of *three* fire engines! besides a fine of *five pounds*! I fancied it the contents of his waste-paper-basket that he was ridding himself of by this summary process – but happening to look up at his face, I saw in its grim concentrated self-complacency the astounding truth, that it was all his labour since he returned from Scotland that had been there sent up the vent, in smoke! . . . To tell you a secret, I begin to be seriously afraid that his *Life of Cromwell* is going to have the same strange fate as the child of a certain French-marchioness that I once read of – which never could *get itself born*, tho' carried about in her for *twenty years* till she died! – a wit is said to have once asked this poor woman if 'Madame was not thinking of swallowing a tutor for her son?' So one might ask Carlyle if he is not thinking of swallowing a publisher for his book? – only that he is too miserable poor fellow without the addition of being laughed at In lamenting his slow progress, or rather no-progress, he said to me one day with a naivete altogether touching 'Well! they may *twaddle* as they like about the miseries of a bad conscience: but I should like to know whether Judas Escariot was *more* miserable than Thomas Carlyle, who never did anything *criminal; so far as he remembers!*' – Ah my dear! this is all very amusing to *write about*; but to TRANSACT? – god help us well thro' it! and, as the Kilmarnock weaver prayed 'give us all a good *conceit* of ourselves', for this is what is chiefly wanted here at present! If my husband had half the *conceit of himself*, which shines so conspicuous in some writers I could name, he would 'take it *aisy*' and regenerate the world with rose-water (*twaddle*), as *they* do – instead of ruining his digestive organs in the manufacture of *oil of vitriol* for that purpose![44]

Jane never wavered in her pride in Carlyle, and yet there is scarcely a comment in her letters about the quality of his individual works. We know that she read them as they were being produced, but she and Carlyle were not in the habit of writing to one another about the works themselves. Probably they talked about work in progress, but it seems unlikely that Jane made many suggestions or criticisms. He wrote his books *more suo*, and she simply took them – when they finally saw the light after all the agonies of being 'transacted' – for granted.

★

The fun-loving, if spoilt, only daughter in Jane enjoyed a rare treat on Boxing Day 1843 when she attended a birthday party for the Macreadys' daughter Nina. Jeannie Welsh received her lively account of Dickens's amazing conjuring of plum puddings and live guinea pigs out of hats and boxes and Forster's seizing her round the waist and making her dance like a person on a treadmill. Jane not only describes with excitement the pleasures of the occasion; she also shows some self-knowledge in the matter of her winter illnesses. She tells Jeannie that she had been on the brink of sending an apology '*as usual*':

When voila – on the morning of the appointed day arrives a note from Mrs Macready *imploring* me almost with tears in its eyes not to disappoint her and her 'poor little daughter' by sending an apology! – that a well aired BED was prepared for me &c &c – this forestalling of my cruel purpose was successful – I felt that I *must* go *for once* . . . – 'My dear' says Carlyle 'I think I never saw you look more bilious your face is *green* and your eyes all *blood-shot!*' fine comfort when one was about to make – public appearance! 'the first time this season' – In fact I was very ill – had been *off* my sleep for a week and felt as if this night must almost *finish* me – But little does one know in this world *what* will *finish* them or what will *set them up* again. I question if a long course of mercury would have acted so beneficially on my liver as this party which I had gone to with a sacred shudder! But then it was the *very* most agreeable party that ever I was at in London.

The description of the conjuring and capering follows – 'the thing was rising into something not unlike the *rape of the Sabines*' – and Jane's conclusion is: 'Well and the result? – Why the result my dear was, that I went to bed on my return and – slept like a top!!! Plainly proving that *excitement* is *my rest*!'[45]

Ten days later Jane wrote again, showing a comic horror of misplaced religious philanthropy to rival Dickens's with his Chadbands, Mrs Jellybys, and Mrs Pardiggles (all in *Bleak House*). A religious Mrs Reid had been at the party, but fortunately had left before the demonic dancing. Jane had observed her, as she reported to Jeannie,

trying to *indoctrinate* one of Dickens's small children with *Socinian benevolence* – the child about the size of a quartern loaf was sitting on a low chair gazing in awestruck delight at the reeking plum-pudding which its Father had just produced out of 'a gentleman's hat' – Mrs Reid leaning *tenderly* over her (as benevolent gentlewomen understand how to lean over youth) said in a soft voice – *professedly* for *its* ear but loud enough for mine and everybody elses within three yards distance – '*Would* not you like that there was such a nice pudding as that in every house in London tonight? I am sure *I* would!' – The shrinking uncomprehending look which the little blowzy face cast up to her was inimitable – a whole page of protest against twaddle! if she could but have read it![46]

Dickens himself wrote to Jane on 27 January 1844, showing that a rapport had been speedily established between them, particularly in relation to their dislike of religious humbug:

The Guinea Pig is dead! He left it in his will that he believed conjuring had done it; but that he forgave his enemies, and died (he was a very small Pig you know) believing in the whole Bench of Bishops.[47]

Carlyle and Dickens, though not close friends, had met in society over the last few years, and in 1842, when Dickens was in America making speeches to shame American pirate publishers and agitate for international copyright, he had been grateful to Carlyle for writing a letter of support full of 'plain and manly Truth'.[48] Carlyle's letter was characteristically robust about the commandment 'Thou Shalt not Steal'.[49] In the summer of 1844 Dickens was once more all admiration for Carlyle's trenchant intervention in another matter of natural justice – the opening of Mazzini's letters by the Post Office.

A few months before, Carlyle and Jane took an interest in the 'criminal conversation' case brought by William Fraser against his wife. The case was dismissed, but it filled the newspapers in February 1844, and Mrs Fraser, whom Jane supported by visiting her after the verdict, was stigmatised by being 'dragged before the public', Jane thought.[50] The Carlyles had heard about the proceedings from John Carlyle, who was called as a medical witness. Much play was made in court of the testimonies of servants about the familiar behaviour of Mrs Fraser with her husband's friend Bagley, who had been asked by Fraser himself to support her in his absence.

Jane saw immediately that the circumstantial evidence – such as Mrs Fraser's being heard to address Mr Bagley as 'my dear' – could apply as well to her own demeanour with her male friends. Indeed, she had described to Jeannie only a few weeks before the Fraser case came to court how she and Mazzini had been sitting tête-à-tête when Elizabeth Pepoli came in:

The fact was, Mazzini and I had just been regaling ourselves with wine *figs* and gingerbread, and when the rap came to the door I bade him put away the glasses and he put them into – *my writing desk!* so that when she opened the room door we both presented an unusual appearance of discomposure – which Elizabeth whose head is always running on 'what shall I say – strange things upon my honour' – interpreted doubtless into 'a delicate embarrassment' – Elizabeth to have been always *virtuous*, as I am sure she has been has really a curious incapacity of comprehending the simplest *liaison* between man and woman.[51]

Her own familiarity with Mazzini, and with Erasmus Darwin too, was no doubt in her mind when she ruminated, again to Jeannie, on the 'criminalities' she had 'walked over the top of without knowing it'. She had been determined to visit Mrs Fraser to show her support:

'So soon as it *is* decided' I said to Darwin 'I will go and nobody shall prevent me' – 'whichever way it goes?' said Darwin – 'Yes' said I 'and all the faster if it goes against her' – 'Bravo!' said he – with a benignant smile – 'Oh' said Carlyle 'the woman is not that sort of woman at all – if you knew her you could not for a moment believe her to have done anything beyond *imprudences* – such as calling people *my Dear* and all that' (looking significantly at poor me) – 'Ah! – for my share' says Darwin 'I cannot even see the *imprudences!*' 'Thank you for that' exclaimed I with *effusion!*[52]

Jane did go several times to see Mrs Fraser, whose case had become the subject of public tittle-tattle. They were selling prints of Fraser in the streets, wrote Jane, 'under the name of *the handsome Husband*'.[53] She was much taken by the affair, telling Forster more than a year later, 'I have never been entirely my own woman since', and repeating the alarming fact that the calling of a man not one's husband 'my dear' had very nearly caused an innocent woman to be scandalously divorced.[54]

Of course she herself continued to risk her reputation, as she liked to imagine, since flirtatious friendships with men added spice to her life. Jeannie was given an amusing description in April 1844 of Plattnauer's astonishment when he coincided at Cheyne Row with Jane's old admirer Jeffrey, who kissed her '*plump on my lips!*' and called her 'my dear Love', which made Plattnauer stare, blush, and 'reel' out of the room. 'I have since heard', Jane wrote gleefully, 'that he went from here to Elizabeth [Pepoli] to compliment her on the extraordinary character of *Scotch Salutations* as illustrated in the meeting he had just witnessed between Lord Jeffrey and Mrs Carlyle'.[55]

A week or two later Jeannie was hearing how Jane's life 'for some days back has been "as good as a play" (to use *Mrs Macready's* favourite simile)'. First Garnier came in with his shirt open 'disclosing "what shall I say? strange things upon *my* honour"', rolling his eyes, and saying that he had discovered a nest of murderers in the court where he lived. Mazzini arrived just after the departure of the mad Garnier, as did Edward Sterling, who thought something was going on between her and Mazzini and 'permitted himself to utter *an impertinence*, whereupon my humour being already jarred I told him that he was an old fool and had better get about his business'.[56]

Thus was Jane kept amused, flattered, and diverted. All the while Geraldine was writing from Manchester in lover-like tones, though she also talked of matrimonial possibilities for herself as they came and inevitably went. 'I am as jealous as a Turk', she declared in June 1844, and in September, 'I think of you much more than if you were my lover'.[57]

On 18 June 1844 Carlyle wrote his celebrated letter to *The Times*, protesting about the opening of Mazzini's correspondence by the Post Office on the orders of the Home Secretary, Sir James Graham. It was done at the request of the Austrian and Neapolitan authorities, who rightly suspected that Mazzini was plotting with friends in Italy to rebel against Austria and set up an independent Italy. Mazzini discovered his post was being tampered with, and found an MP, Thomas Duncombe (who had taken up the cause of imprisoned Chartists in 1840), to present a petition to Parliament complaining of this breach of his rights. Carlyle's letter turned the thing into a *cause célèbre* and swung the country behind Mazzini in outrage, and even in some cases in approval of his undoubtedly subversive plans to overthrow a foreign despot on foreign soil.

This 'glorious letter', as Jane proudly called it,[58] declared 'sealed letters in an English post-office' to be 'things sacred', and the opening of them 'a practice near of kin to picking men's pockets'.[59] After it was published on 19 June, questions were asked in the Commons and the Lords chiefly because, as Mazzini jubilantly told his mother, Carlyle was such a power in the land, celebrated for his honesty and genius.[60] Sir James Graham instigated an inquiry into his own actions, which found that he had not exceeded his legal powers, but his credibility was diminished by the affair, while Mazzini's cause was enhanced. Dickens, in a gesture of solidarity with Carlyle, took to writing on the flap of his envelopes a message to the letter-opening Home Secretary: 'It is particularly requested that if Sir James Graham should open this, he will not trouble himself to seal it again.'[61]

Two comic codas were added to what was universally known as the Mazzini affair. One was that Amely Bölte, who had recently become governess in none other than Sir James Graham's family on Jane's recommendation (via Mrs Buller), was now dismissed, the reason given being, as Carlyle noted, that 'when the children asked her, "What the Holy Ghost was like?" she said with all circumspection, she could not tell!'[62] The other was that Lady Harriet Baring, excited by the Carlyle–Mazzini–*Times* business, once more invited Mazzini to visit her, a rather daring act given that her husband was then Secretary to the Board of Control. Mazzini related to his mother in September 1844 how her father-in-law, Lord Ashburton, had reprimanded her for fraternising with revolutionaries and how her husband had been reproved by Peel's ministers. 'In short', he concluded, 'a real comedy' ('una vera Commedia').[63]

Jane observed with close interest Lady Harriet's attempts to attract Mazzini into her circle. On 26 July she told Jeannie that her 'making new advances to him' was, 'for a Tory woman of *her* distinction connected with the enemy as she is', very much to her credit. Mazzini had been invited for the previous evening to meet 'divers persons in authority'; 'Carlyle was there OF COURSE'. Mazzini failed to turn up, which Jane took as evidence of his admirable ability to resist 'that siren', though in fact Mazzini had set out for her house and got lost on the way.[64] On 1 August Jane conceded to Jeannie that Mazzini had probably been caught in Lady Harriet's snare after all:

Carlyle is to dine with Lady Harriet again to day – and this time poor Mazzini *must* go – I begin to have a real *admiration* for that woman – her *fascination* of Carlyle proves her to be the most masterly coquette of Modern Times![65]

Relations between Jane and Carlyle this summer were not good. The beginnings of Jane's real jealousy (as opposed to joke-jealousy) of Lady Harriet's influence on Carlyle are evident. They quarrelled about other things too. Jane wanted to spend some time with her Liverpool cousins and at nearby Seaforth with Geraldine's friend, Elizabeth Paulet. Carlyle objected, partly on grounds of cost. Jane dug in her heels against this 'Reign of Terror' and proposed to finance the trip out of her own savings.[66] After going off at the end of June, without having reconciled Carlyle fully to her trip, she jested uneasily in a letter written from her uncle's house:

I am always wondering since I came here how I can ever in my angriest moods talk about leaving you for good and all – for to be sure if I *were* to leave you today *on that principle* I should need absolutely to go back tomorrow *to see how you were taking it!*[67]

If she had slipped deep into the habit of complaining to Jeannie of life with Carlyle, she now launched into a set of complaints about Jeannie and her family to him. Jeannie had been '*deteriorating*', becoming 'painfully indolent, and *young-ladyish*', while her brother Alick's Toryism was 'perfectly insupportable'. As for the girls, the 'unwearying earnestness with which they all dress themselves *three times a day* is a continual miracle for me combined as it is with total want of earnestness about every thing else in Heaven or earth!' With a flash of self-criticism she added, 'How grateful I ought to be to you Dear for having rescued ME out of the young-Lady-sphere!'[68]

Such moments of insight and marital warmth were hard to sustain when she returned to life at Cheyne Row. On 26 July she resumed complaining to her young-ladyish cousin; Carlyle had been pleased to have her back at first, but had already 'relapsed into his usual indifference', while hurrying off at every opportunity to see Lady Harriet, 'OF COURSE'.[69]

★

In September 1844 John Sterling died of tuberculosis. He had suffered the deaths of his mother on 16 April 1843 and his wife two days later from complications arising from the birth of their sixth child.[70] His own health had been wretched for years, and he had recently moved to the Isle of Wight, where he approached his own end, at the age of thirty-eight, with quiet courage. Carlyle told his mother on 14 August 1844 that Sterling, one of his first admirers, had written to say he was dying. 'He is one of the cleverest and best men I have ever known', wrote Carlyle.[71] Sterling's farewell letter touched on the religious question. He who had turned away from the ministry because of struggles from which he felt Carlyle had in part delivered him, by his writings and his companionship, told his mentor that he had no fear and much hope:

Certainty indeed I have none. With regard to You & Me I cannot begin to write having nothing for it but to keep shut the lid of those secrets with all the iron weights that are in my power. Towards ME it is still more true than towards England – that no one has Been & Done like you.[72]

It was a fine tribute, to which Carlyle wrote a moving reply, praising his friend and showing that he shared Sterling's faith in a personal God and a probable afterlife:

My Friend, my brave Sterling! A right valiant man; very beautiful, very dear to me; whose like I shall not see again in this world!

We are journeying towards the Grand Silence; what lies beyond it earthly man has never known, nor will know: but all brave men have known that it was Godlike, that it was right GOOD, – that the name of it was GOD. *Wir heissen euch hoffen* [We bid you hope].[73]

To Carlyle's offer to go and see him one last time Sterling replied, via his brother Anthony, that he was unfit to see his friend: 'His letter was too much for me. A kinder & better one was never penned by man.'[74]

Sterling died on 18 September, after arranging for books to be sent to Carlyle and jewellery to Jane, and composing a poem 'To Thomas Carlyle', which begins by saluting Carlyle's public role as prophet, then moves to the personal. He, Sterling, is one

> To whom Laugh groan & maddest flight
> More than the Sage the Man commend.[75]

In September Carlyle paid his first visit to the Grange, the country mansion in Hampshire belonging to Lord and Lady Ashburton, later to be the centre of their daughter-in-law Lady Harriet's social life, when her husband succeeded to his father's title. Carlyle spent a week there, leaving Jane to manage Plattnauer, whom she had plucked from the Wandsworth Lunatic Asylum with the help of Erasmus Darwin.[76] He found the company less than brilliant; 'nay if it were not for the Lady Harriet and myself we should almost be definable as a dull commonplace one', he told Jane with more honesty than modesty.[77]

Among the guests, he reported, was Henry Fleming, a civil servant and friend of Charles Buller, known for his gossip and for wearing make-up. One of Lady Harriet's more durable witticisms as reported by friends was her remark, on hearing that burglars had entered his house, that 'it was hard on him, for he could not move, having unfortunately left his backbone on the dressing-table'.[78] Jane and Carlyle soon added to the general nickname for Fleming – 'the Flea' – a frank one of their own, 'Jenkins's hen', a Scottish name for a hen that never knew a cock.[79] Another visitor was Charles Greville, the copious diarist and friend of politicians of all parties. Carlyle described him as 'an old English hack of quality who runs race-horses'. 'He has Court gossip, Political gossip &c, and is civil to all persons, careless about all persons; – equal nearly to zero.'[80]

Carlyle liked his hosts, and enjoyed riding in the grounds and environs of the 'Grecian Temple' – the Grange was designed in 1809 by William Wilkins, architect of the National Gallery and University College London, and built on the site of an older house designed by Inigo Jones.[81] But he was not at ease with such idle, vapid members of the dandy or non-working aristocratic species as Fleming and Greville. The only conclusion to be drawn about his willingness to spend even a few days in their company was the one drawn by Jane. She told Jeannie that Lady Harriet 'like the Queen must have her Court' and so had 'summoned' Carlyle, 'and *he* – *never* by any chance refuses a wish of *hers* – the clever woman that she is!'[82] When Carlyle returned to Chelsea towards the end of September, Jane's feelings were sour. 'Plainly he had been straining his nerves quite preposterously to please the Lady Harriet', she told Helen Welsh, *living on his capital* in the article of *agreeableness* – So now I shall have but an indifferent time with him for weeks to come!'[83]

Lady Harriet was soon on her way abroad. As in previous years, she escaped to the south of France for the winter, her husband and Charles Buller accompanying her, with the elder Bullers and Theresa Revis also among the company. Charles acted as a kind of assistant and supporter to Bingham Baring, encouraging the latter's diffident efforts to further his career in government, travelling abroad with him, and writing courtly, semi-intimate letters to Lady Harriet, whom he addressed as 'Wisest of friends'.[84] Jane, who was no doubt relieved at Lady Harriet's departure, predicted that there would be trouble with 'the Child Theresa', who would probably 'run off with some mustachioed count before long', so tremendous was her 'premature Genius for *flirtation*'.[85]

Amely Bölte went with the party as Theresa's governess; in December she was ill with a fever and was left alone by the Bullers in a hotel in Nice (where by coincidence the mad Plattnauer also turned up). Lady Harriet stepped in to help, eventually bringing Amely back to England with her. Jane heard from 'Jenkins's hen' that Amely felt neglected, and that young Theresa had told lies about her in order to have her dismissed.[86] Carlyle wrote ingratiatingly to Lady Harriet herself, thanking her for 'interposing as a goddess' to help 'poor Bölte'. He continued in the embarrassed and embarrassing chivalric tone which characterises his letters to Lady Harriet from now on:

Very pleasant it has been to me, Ma Dame, to figure you all along as a Beam of Light in that miserable element of Darkness; spreading round you what of order, settlement, good sense and nobleness was possible there.[87]

As for Amely, her gratitude was no more than lukewarm. A prickly woman who hated her anomalous, powerless position as a governess, she told Varnhagen von Ense that Lady Harriet's gesture smacked of pity, 'a fruit for which I have no taste at all'.[88] Carlyle had got the measure of Amely, describing her to Lady Harriet as decisive and nimble, but inclined to hysteria, as had been borne out when he and Jane observed her being successfully mesmerised at Mrs Buller's house. He had also noticed 'a certain want of reticence' in her, a characteristic which came to light when, having returned to Germany, she published in 1860 Varnhagen's replies to her detailed accounts of marital life at 5, Cheyne Row, causing another member of the Carlyle circle, Charlotte Williams Wynn, to describe her as 'neither more nor less than a Household Spy'.[89]

In December 1844 Jane described the mesmerising scene at the Bullers' to her uncle. Mesmerism was sweeping the country, partly as a party trick in private houses, partly as a method of treating otherwise incurable conditions, physical and mental. By late 1844 it had been given the seal of approval by Harriet Martineau, who had thought she was dying of a tumour, but now believed she had been cured by mesmerism, and announced her belief in a series of articles published in the *Athenaeum* in November and December 1844.[90] Jane read the articles with a scepticism slightly modified by her observation of the experiment on Amely Bölte, when she was 'stiffened' and rendered immune to the pain of having her hand pricked by the point of a penknife. Jane, believing that the practitioner's success depended on the susceptibility of the subject, and that Amely '*wished* to be magnetized', had challenged him to try his skills on her. As she told her uncle, she successfully resisted coming fully under his influence, but she had felt a flash of something akin to galvanism when he passed his hands over hers, though she had been careful not to let him see this.[91]

Just as Jane was becoming seriously jealous of Carlyle's relations with Lady Harriet, she herself was fixed on by two jealous wives of her acquaintance. It was one thing for her to flirt with old married men like Jeffrey and Edward Sterling, or even with younger unmarried foreigners like Mazzini and Plattnauer. With them Jane could control the situation and enjoy, without guilt, the feeling of triumph so important to her sense of self-worth. She was delighted to be able to report to Jeannie in May 1844 that Plattnauer had told Elizabeth Pepoli that one Count Krasinski, a Polish exile living in London, was 'preposterously fond of Mrs Carlyle', to which Elizabeth had replied drily, 'Oh all THE MEN are *that!*'[92]

The case was somewhat different when in November 1844 Anthony Sterling's wife Charlotte had a mental breakdown as a result of her fixed idea that her husband, son of old Edward Sterling and brother of John, was in love with Jane. The latter showed scant sympathy, apparently making no connection between Charlotte's mad jealousy of her and her own growing feelings about Lady Harriet. She told Helen Welsh rather coolly: 'Happily I never liked her much, so that I can bear her misfortune *like a christian.*' Carlyle, meanwhile, was 'making himself merry at what he calls "*the judgement* come upon me" and calls me oftener than "Jane" or "my Dear" "*Destroyer of the peace of families!*" '[93]

She knew well enough that she fascinated Anthony. In a letter to Jeannie a few years later she mused:

I wonder what strange attraction lies in me for all of the blood of Sterling – For Father and Mother and *both* sons I have been more than any other woman – not married to them – There is no understanding these things – I am sure I have taken a hundred times more pains to please some others who never took to me at all.[94]

No doubt she felt superior to such jealous wives as Mrs Sterling and the wife of the writer and civil servant Arthur Helps, whom Jane did attempt to appease by discouraging Helps from visiting Cheyne Row.[95] She knew that she felt nothing for their husbands, though she also knew they were infatuated with her; somehow she expected the wives to accept the state of affairs with an equanimity which she could not even approach herself. Carlyle certainly was infatuated by Lady Harriet, as Jane saw. She does not seem to have believed that Lady Harriet returned his feelings, but she nevertheless resented that clever woman's complacent acceptance of her husband's homage.

The essay on Carlyle in *A New Spirit of the Age*, written by Elizabeth Barrett, with editorial additions by Horne, was published in March 1844. The authors assess Carlyle's influence, noting the idiosyncrasies of his language and opinions, but declaring that these form 'part of his truth'. 'Let no man say that we recommend Carlylisms'; nevertheless, Carlyle 'has knocked out his window in the wall of his century'; 'he tells us what we know, but had forgotten, or refused to remember; and his reiterations startle and astonish us like informations'.[96]

Elizabeth Barrett plucked up courage to send Carlyle a copy of her *Poems* in August, declaring that she held his genius and teaching in high respect, and hoping that he would think her poems 'true enough, not to disgrace the truth with which I am one of the most grateful of his readers'. Carlyle's reply, now lost, was described by her as kind and touching, though she told her friend Mary Russell Mitford that he had counselled her to 'use "speech" rather than "song" in these days of crisis'.[97] When her delayed acquaintance with Browning began early the next year, she asked him if he too had been told to give up poetry in favour of prose, which of course he had.[98] Browning was helping Carlyle at this time, acting as an intermediary between him and Henry Field, a descendant of Cromwell's son Henry and the possessor of some Oliver Cromwell letters, about which Field was being elusive and obtuse.[99]

The Cromwell book was at last nearing completion. Early in 1845 Carlyle finally decided on the form this troublesome work should take; it would be an annotated edition of Cromwell's letters and speeches. He had given up the idea of a full biography, largely because of the mass of propaganda and misinformation, perpetrated mainly by royalists after the restoration of Charles II, which made it impossible to recover the truth sufficiently for a sustained narrative of the life. When his book was published in two volumes by Chapman and Hall in November 1845, it sold quickly and earned Carlyle about £1,000.[100] He soon found he had changed the general perception of Cromwell from that of a schemer and religious hypocrite – a view which had persisted since the Restoration, even among the Whigs, who disliked his fanatical Puritanism – to that of an honest man inspired by true national and religious zeal. John Forster, who had written a critical *Life* of Cromwell in 1839, had his view sufficiently challenged by Carlyle's advocacy to publish a much revised version of his own work in the 1860s.[101]

There were those, among them FitzGerald, Richard Monckton Milnes, and G. H. Lewes, who disliked Carlyle's hero-worship of Cromwell, and especially his defence of Cromwell's cruelty in Ireland, but even these dissenters accepted that Carlyle had righted (if over-righted) a wrong to Cromwell's reputation. Milnes, writing shortly before the book was published and seeming to know (presumably from Carlyle's conversation) what it would contain, predicted that it would 'bring down infinite censure' on Carlyle's head, though he thought it 'ingenious' of Carlyle to give all his 'ultra' expressions as quotations from another 'laborious and thoughtful writer' – the old method, used by Carlyle since the *Edinburgh Review* essays and *Sartor*, of putting some of his own views into the mouths of fictional editors and professors. Lewes, writing, like Milnes, to Varnhagen von Ense in Berlin, objected to Carlyle's 'deification of the Past', especially the Puritan past, an attitude which he described as 'easy moralizing'.[102]

Oddly enough – and it is striking testimony to Carlyle's influence over a younger generation with a wide range of political opinion – Carlyle's pro-Cromwellian stance on Ireland at this time of terrible poverty did not prevent the leading agitators of the nationalist Young Ireland movement from seeking him out at Cheyne Row along with the rest of the world. Jane described one visit in her notebook on 27 April 1845:

Last night we had a novelty in the way of society, a sort of Irish *rigg*. Mr L[ucas] came in before tea with a tail consisting of three stranger Irishmen – real hot and hot live Irishmen, such as I have never before sat at meat with or met 'in flow of soul', newly imported, with the brogue 'rather exquisite' . . . They came to adore Carlyle, and also remonstrate with him, almost with tears in their eyes, on his opinion, as stated in his 'Chartism', that 'a finer people than the Irish never lived; only they have two faults; they do lie and they do steal'. The poor fellows got into a quite epic strain over this most calumnious exaggeration. (Pity but my husband would pay some regard to the sensibilities of 'others', and exaggerate less!)

The youngest one – Mr Pigot – a handsome youth of the romantic cast, pale-faced, with dark eyes and hair, and an 'Emancipation of the Species' melancholy spread over him – told my husband, after having looked at and listened to him in comparative silence for the first hour, with 'How to observe' written in every lineament, that now he (Mr Pigot) felt assured he (my husband) was not in heart so unjust towards Ireland as his writings led one to suppose, and so he would confess, for the purpose of retracting it, the strong feeling of repulsion with which he had come to him that night. 'Why, in the name of goodness, then, *did* you come?' I could not help asking, thereby producing a rather awkward result. Several awkward results were produced in this 'nicht wi' Paddy'. They were speaking of the Scotch intolerance towards Catholics, and Carlyle as usual took up the cudgels for intolerance.[103]

Of the three Irishmen – John Edward Pigot, John O'Hagan, and Charles Gavan Duffy – it was Duffy who went on to have the closest relations with Carlyle. He was imprisoned in 1844 and again in 1848–9, when he was acquitted of treason, after which, disillusioned with the results of the Young Ireland movement at home, he emigrated to Australia, where in due course he demonstrated his admiration of Carlyle by founding the Carlyle Township in New South Wales in 1858.

Two of Jane's cousins came into contact with the Carlyles in June 1845. James Welsh, the son of her father's brother Robert, came to visit in June, outstaying his welcome and irritating both Carlyles with his 'Edinburgh Logic'. Jane described him to Jeannie as 'argumentative and self-complacent beyond anything that one can conceive out of Edin[burgh]'. James dared to contradict and interrupt not only Carlyle – 'with no more respect for his superior years and wisdom than if himself were the Archangel Michael' – but also Lady Harriet, 'who unhappily had come to tea'.[104] The other cousin was the reduced dandy, James Baillie, who came up to Jane in the street while she was window-shopping and insisted that she stop to speak to him:

'Come – it is not *my* fault if I am out of Bedlam, and scandalizing sensible people like you' – And so he rattled on . . . I could not but see that the passers by all stared at us, in wonder what such a decent looking woman as myself could have to say to a member of the Swell-mob [respectably dressed pickpockets] – for decidedly that is the style of man he is grown into – the shabbiest of done up Dandies![105]

Carlyle made no objections this summer to Jane's plan to visit Liverpool. She told him of the large doses of medicine (mainly mercury) she had been taking against her usual ailments, and of her deep depression, and he was alarmed into letting her go, though she had to agree first to accompany Lady Harriet to Addiscombe for 'four mortal days!'[106] From Liverpool she complained again of Jeannie, who was, much to Jane's annoyance, in a 'lukewarm' and 'tacit' engagement with a Glasgow acquaintance, Andrew Chrystal, and whose worship of new clothes contrasted unpleasantly with her 'apathetic' reception of Jane.[107]

Carlyle's endearments in his letters grated on her until she rounded on him:

Always my 'bits of letters' and 'bits of letters' as if I were some nice little Child writing in half-text on ruled paper to its Godpapa! . . . a woman of my invention can always find legitimate means of revenging herself on those who do not 'treat her with the respect due to Genius' – who put her off with a pat on the head or a chuck under the chin, when she addresses them in all the full-grown gravity of five feet-five-inches-and-three-quarters – without her shoes![108]

When she returned to London Carlyle set off in his turn for Annandale, where he received on 23 September an account of her evening at the theatre seeing Ben Jonson's *Every Man in his Humour* performed by Dickens and his amateur acting company:

Forster as Kitely and Dickens as Captain Bobadil were much on a par – but Forster preserved his identity even thro his loftiest flights of *Macready-ism*, while poor little Dickens all painted in black and red, and affecting the voice of a man of six feet, would have been unrecognisable for the Mother that bore him![109]

At the end of September, while Carlyle was still at Scotsbrig, Jane told him how Lady Harriet had sent round a servant with a brougham to take her to visit, but instead of dropping her at the Barings' house in Great Stanhope Street, it deposited her at 'a great unknown House', where she felt she had entered a fairy tale. This was Bath House on Piccadilly, the London home of the elder Ashburtons, a house Jane would come to hate when the Barings took it over as their London headquarters in 1848. 'She was very gracious and agreeable', Jane wrote, 'and I dare say in spite of Mrs Buller's predictions we shall get on very well together – altho I can see that the Lady has a genius for *ruling* – whilst I have a genius for – not being ruled!'[110] To Jeannie she was less circumspect, saying Lady Harriet had insisted on Jane's agreeing to spend the whole winter with her at the Barings' Hampshire home, Bay House at Alverstoke, 'and yet I have an unconquerable persuasion that she does not and never can like me!'[111]

Carlyle, uneasy and inept as he had always been when Jane indulged in her peculiar kind of sharp playfulness, and particularly keen to promote a friendship between the two women, replied on a false note to her description of herself and Lady Harriet:

The Lady Harriet has a genius for ruling? Well, I don't know but she may . . . I know a Lady – But I will say nothing, lest I bring mischief about my ears. Nay, she is very obedient too, that little Lady I allude to, and *has* a genius for being ruled withal. Heaven bless her always! Not a bad little Dame at all.[112]

To which Jane wisely did not allude at all in her reply.

Jane and Carlyle both spent six weeks in November and December 1845 in Hampshire with Lady Harriet and various other house guests. They returned to Chelsea on 26 December to find that *Cromwell* had already sold nearly the whole of its print run of 1,200 and was to be reissued in a fresh edition.[113] Jane described to her mother's friend Mary Russell her six weeks of doing 'absolutely nothing but playing at battledore and shuttlecock – chess – talking nonsense' with Lady Harriet, 'the very cleverest woman – out of sight – that I ever saw in my life'.[114] A relationship of sorts had begun between these two clever, childless, professionless women.

CHAPTER 12

Revolutions Domestic and Foreign
1846–1849

Early in 1846 Carlyle reluctantly set about preparing a second edition of *Cromwell*. 'A good many *new* Letters &c' had turned up as a consequence of the first edition.[1] Among the surprises about the reception of *Cromwell* was a largely favourable notice by Young Ireland's John Mitchel in the Dublin nationalist paper, *The Nation*. It began with high praise for Carlyle, 'the greatest writer, and profoundest philosopher, now living upon English soil, with eloquence, the like of which has not uttered itself in English speech since John Milton's time'. Mitchel approved of Carlyle's account except as it related to Cromwell's actions in Ireland. He described himself as 'a determined Repealer and Irish Nationalist' who owed a huge debt to Carlyle; 'yet Carlyle considers Repeal an insane dream, and Ireland (God forgive him!) a nation of very poor creatures'.[2]

Ireland – with its succession of bad harvests and potato blights between 1845 and 1849, during which time more than a million died and a similar number of desperate people emigrated to Britain, America, and Australia – was to be the chief topic of political concern over the next few years, and one which caused Carlyle to consider, albeit briefly, attempting to enter Parliament. 'All Reform-Bills are a small matter to this of the Potatoe', he wrote to Lady Harriet in March 1847, adding dramatically, 'Shall I set up a weekly Newspaper? Shall I squeeze into Parlt itself, and there *speak* Pamphlets, hot and hot, right from the heart, – and burn up the *World-Humbug*!'[3]

Lady Harriet was receiving ever more extravagant letters, in which she was cast as the sun and stars illuminating the world in general, and Carlyle in particular; he was a 'dark man' in need of her shining on him. He apostrophised her in February 1846 as 'my Beneficent', 'daughter of the Sun', 'my sovereign Lady'.[4] For her part, Lady Harriet made a bid for Jane's friendship, though on her own imperious terms. She occasionally sent a carriage in the evening to collect Jane for a couple of hours of talking, reading, and playing chess. Carlyle was naively pleased to think of the two women getting on together, the small dark one and the large fair one, the one whose rightful 'master' he felt he was and the one whom he had voluntarily adopted as 'mistress' to his chivalrous slave or knight. Jane, of course, saw things differently, though she admitted to Jeannie in March that she was intrigued by Lady Harriet, a 'very *large* bit of fascination', and to Jane an insoluble psychological puzzle.[5]

Jane spent a month with Lady Harriet at Addiscombe, commenting to Helen Welsh on the 'imposed *do-nothingism*' of Lady Harriet's social position, and wondering how, with the 'largest intellect' of any woman Jane had met, she reconciled herself to a life 'which is after all a mere dramatic representation'.[6] Jane also confessed to Jeannie in May that her own life was dangerously empty. Telling her cousin that Mrs Macready was expecting another child, she was moved to consider her own domestic lot: 'I wish I could find some hard work I *could* do – and saw any sense in doing – If I do not soon it will be the worse for me'.[7]

Communication broke down between the Carlyles in the summer, undoubtedly because of Carlyle's continued devotion to Lady Harriet. Jane at first did not write from Seaforth House near Liverpool, where she was staying with the Paulets. When she did, on 6 July, she indulged in indirect criticism of him by praising her hosts, who granted her 'the amplest tolerance to be as ugly and stupid and disagreeable as ever I please'. 'For *you*', she added, 'you must feel as if a millstone had been taken off your breast.'[8] Carlyle kept writing to her, with his usual mixture of self-pity, semi-reproach, and patronising encouragement. He remembered to send her a birthday letter and present, assuring her that, 'in spite of the chimeras and delusions', she was 'dearer to me than any earthly creature'.[9]

Some of Jane's letters to him have been lost; that they were seriously morbid and disaffected is clear from his alarmed replies, which he fired off almost every day. Whether Jane confided in the Paulets is unclear, though she probably did in Geraldine Jewsbury, who came over from Manchester to help nurse her. Geraldine wrote a long letter to Amely Bölte, explaining that Jane was unfit to write and implying that Amely's letters were an irritant. However, Jane did write to Amely on her birthday, 14 July, thanking her for remembering the day. Her tone was almost hysterical; she had not yet received Carlyle's letter and present when she wrote, and she told Amely that she felt herself utterly neglected on 'the sorry occasion'.[10]

One person to whom she wrote openly, and despairingly, was Mazzini. Her letters, which have not survived, brought forth earnest replies from him, counselling a religious faith which he sees she lacks, and suggesting that she try to find some satisfaction in dutifulness. The message Mazzini preached must have been wormwood to Jane, though her fondness for him and gratitude for his concern may have helped her through this crisis. Perhaps she even smiled at his curious English. He wrote on 10 July, urging her to 'send back to nothingness the ghosts and phantoms that you have been conjuring up' and to do life's duties in an 'earnest, sacred and resigned' mood, with 'due reverence to your immortal soul'. 'But', he added, 'I would make you frown or scorn: we have a different conception of Life, and are condemned here down to walk on two parallels.' He compared his own difficult lot, claiming, 'I have mustered up, thanks God, strength enough to go on'. Then:

Your life proves an empty thing, you say? Empty! do not blaspheme; have you never done good? have you never loved? Think of your mother and do good. Let the rest to Providence. It is not as a mere piece of irony that God has placed us here . . . Can't you trust him a little longer?[11]

This is astute on Mazzini's part, for it had become an ingrained habit in Jane to view life ironically, a defensive mechanism which afforded her some intellectual satisfaction but no happiness. He wrote again five days later, encouraging her to believe in God and the afterlife, to commune with her dead parents and derive strength to carry on, and to 'get up and work' rather than cut herself off from her friends.[12] It is noticeable that Mazzini makes no mention of Carlyle, a fact which suggests either that Jane was uncharacteristically oblique in her expressions of unhappiness or that Mazzini saw there was little hope of Jane finding happiness in her relationship with Carlyle and therefore stressed the importance of friends and faith in God as a substitute.

That Jane was contemplating suicide is made clear in one of her surviving letters to Carlyle this summer. On 15 July she wrote:

I am weary weary to such a point of moral exhaustion that *any* anchorage were welcome even the stillest coldest where the wicked should cease from troubling and the weary be at rest, understanding both by the *wicked* and the weary – *myself.*

Even here, however, her ironic wit finds expression, her target being the ludicrous lengths to which Edinburgh scepticism can go – 'Nobody out of Bedlam even *educated in Edinr* can continue to doubt of *Death*'.[13] Carlyle's reply, shot off the next day, reminds her that *life* is 'our present concern', not death. His pity for her is expressed in his opening words, 'Still very unwell, my poor Goody'.[14]

And so the summer passed, with Carlyle assiduous and prompt at writing, assuring Jane again and again that she had no reason to be cross or morbid, while at the same time he was sending notes to Lady Harriet in which he addressed her as 'Daughter of Adam most beautiful', 'Lady mine, – *mine* yes, and yet forever no!'[15] He spent a few days with Jane at Seaforth at the end of July, then went on alone to Scotsbrig. They had quarrelled again, and once more Jane did not write. He had arranged to meet the Barings, who were also holidaying in Scotland; this being the bone of contention between them, he hastened to request Jane's pity by describing his few days with them as 'unsuccessful' in point of pleasure, since it rained non-stop, he could not sleep, and Lady Harriet was ill. 'O my Goody, my Goody, what a *daft* creature art thou in thy sick imaginations!' he wrote on 20 August. He also assured her that Lady Harriet herself had written to Jane.[16]

Indeed she had. It is one of the very few surviving letters and it gives an insight into the impossibility of these two women ever becoming friends. Lady Harriet scolds Jane roundly:

You are very, very foolish to go on without some trial, at least, of advice and remedies. I *am sure* your headaches could be very much mitigated; and cough and all kinds of derangement will come upon neglect. Whatever one's own belief and feelings in the matter, it is a thing one owes to those who are anxious and careful, to neglect no reasonable care for one's health and life. And you are really trifling with the first. Nevertheless, against my harsh strictures, I will set the hope that you are really bettering ere this; and that we shall improve and take still further care of you in November at Alverstoke.[17]

While Lady Harriet's male protégés – Mill, Buller, Milnes, Fleming, Carlyle, and even the slightly more resistant Tennyson and Thackeray – were generally happy to be bossed by her, secure in the knowledge that they could reclaim their individual freedom when they returned to their normal lives as writers and politicians, a woman like Jane Carlyle, with a strong sense of identity and self-worth but no profession and a constant fear that she was viewed only as the 'worser half to a "celebrated author"',[18] could not stand to be patronised by another woman. She resented being to Lady Harriet what Geraldine, her cousins, and Amely were (willingly, for the most part) to her – women on whom she felt licensed to practise her sharp and sometimes unkind wit and wisdom and yet still be attended and adored.

In the unhappy triangle that was forming between Carlyle, Jane, and Lady Harriet, each was to blame in some degree. Carlyle was selfish and acted, for such an honest man, in self-deceiving bad faith. Jane was excessively sensitive and excessively punitive. And Lady Harriet was either surprisingly insensitive or actually malicious. Without her letters to Carlyle, we cannot tell whether she encouraged his slavish homage or merely neglected to discourage it. She certainly treated Jane with a superior kindness which she must have noticed was galling to its recipient. The wives of her other courtiers may not have suffered as Jane did, since most of them had children to occupy them and none had either the pretensions to intellectual superiority that Jane had or her nervous, irritable temperament with its habit of going out to meet a perceived slight halfway.

There is some evidence that Lady Harriet could be difficult in her overwhelming desire to rule. She seems to have had a free rein with her doting husband. Their correspondence shows her playfully imperious during their courtship – 'down upon your marrowbones and bless my condescension', wrote the then Lady Harriet Montagu in one letter of 1822 – and frankly critical during the marriage, when she hoped Bingham Baring would achieve high office but feared that Peel would abandon him in favour of Lord Clarendon:

I want you to be *cautious, & moderate – & cool –* and not allow yrself to be *excited* – for that is yr weak point . . . Clarendon is yr extreme opposite – no opinions – no chivalry, – no earnestness in any cause – but as the necessary consequence, mild, conciliating, persuasive.[19]

Baring wrote loving, unrancorous, companionable letters in return.

With relations still not restored between him and Jane, Carlyle set off from Scotland at the beginning of September to Ireland, determined to see something of the country and its miseries at first hand. He was escorted by Duffy 'and other young Repealers', and remembered years later how 'every here and there' the air was poisoned with the 'fateful smell' of the rotten potato crops. In Dublin he heard the activist Daniel O'Connell – 'this Demosthenes of blarney' – speak out against England to an audience of poor people. But he got on well with Duffy, Mitchel, and other young associates, who were seduced, he later thought, 'by the Big Beggar-man' into seditious actions which nearly ruined their lives.[20]

Carlyle was back in Cheyne Row by the end of September. Jane was still resentful, but acknowledged to Helen Welsh that the problem was that she and Carlyle were in some respects too alike, 'and so we aggravate one anothers tendencies to *despair!*'[21] Helen Mitchell, her loyal servant, left them at this time to join her brother in Ireland. Scottish friends sent her a replacement in the form of an Edinburgh girl who turned out to be an enthusiast for the Free Church. Jane joked to her mother's friend Mary Russell in December that the girl seemed to have more pretensions to 'free grace' than to 'any "works" she was capable of'; she was quickly dismissed.[22]

At the end of October 1846 the Carlyles were guests of Lady Harriet Baring's parents-in-law, Lord and Lady Ashburton, at the Grange. The old poet Samuel Rogers was also there, along with a selection of lordships and ladyships, as Jane told Jeannie, adding that though the elder Ashburtons were 'excellent people – very *homely*', she knew Carlyle was visiting only because of Lady Harriet. Jane felt herself 'in *a false position*', consoled only by the thought that no one except Carlyle knew how she felt among these 'sumptuous, selfpossessed, brilliant people' in the opulent house with its painted ceilings, 'some dozen public rooms on the ground floor all hung with magnificent paintings – and fitted up like rooms in an Arabian nights entertainment'. Jane describes the household arrangements:

Lord A reads prayers every morning to a numerous congregation consisting of men and women-servants ranged on opposite sides and his own wife and daughters kneeling beside him – the *effect* as seen from the *gallery above* is very pretty!! but I did not meddle with it personally further than looking over the balustrade – and I saw old Rogers this morning doing the same. They are very good in the religious sense of the word – the whole family of them – except of course Lady Harriet – who *goes* upon nothing of that sort – but they are not bigotted and let one hold ones own opinions.[23]

Carlyle gave Jack a glimpse of life at the Grange, describing Rogers, now eighty-three, as 'a most sorrowful distressing distracted old phenomenon; hovering over the rim of deep Eternities with nothing but light babble, fatuity, vanity, and the frostiest London wit in his mouth'. Lady Harriet, a free spirit even in the home of her parents-in-law, kept 'mostly to her own apartments, dined at another hour than we; and except at breakfast and tea did not much appear'.[24]

★

In January 1847 Jane reluctantly allowed Carlyle to take her to visit the Barings at Bay House. She was ill and resentful, though Lady Harriet was at first kind, bringing her doctor to see Jane. After a week or so 'the Lady' never came near her, and 'the housemaids do not find it *in their department* to look after sick visitors'.[25] By mid-February Jane was fit to go home, still wondering about the aristocratic enigma; 'I do not pretend to *understand* her any better than heretofore', Helen Welsh was told on 17 February. Jane relished recounting an awkward moment arising from one of her fellow guests being the daughter of Lady Palmerston by a lover. She liked showing that she was no admirer of the sexual mores of certain members of the upper class while being no prude either.[26]

A 'strange *rusty* old Yarmouth gentleman', one William Squire, now wrote to Carlyle saying he possessed 'certain papers relating to the time of the troubles written by one who rode with Oliver'. Though Carlyle was intrigued, his curiosity and generally scrupulous attitude towards research were overcome by a disinclination to add to the work he had already done on Cromwell and a strong dislike of travelling and attempting to sleep in strange beds and digest strange dinners. He rather cavalierly passed the Norfolk man on to Edward FitzGerald, who lived in Suffolk and had already helped with the Cromwell research: 'On the whole, as he lies in your district, and you are partly concerned in the business, I will hand him over to your care, in the first instance.'[27] FitzGerald was to interview the man and inspect the papers for authenticity.

Carlyle and FitzGerald eventually decided on dubious evidence that the new letters were genuine; Carlyle published them in *Fraser's Magazine* in December 1847 and included them in an appendix to the third edition of *Cromwell* in 1850. He was severely criticised for taking the Squire forgeries for the real thing, and, more specifically, for refusing to step out of his study to meet Squire and inspect the papers for himself. The *Athenaeum* critic accused him of 'supineness' in the matter.[28]

Oddly, Carlyle persisted in his public expressions of belief in the Squire Papers, though he half realised that the arguments for their being a forgery were compelling. His comment in the third edition of *Cromwell* was quintessentially and quixotically Carlylean. He had been urged by friends 'who believe, like myself, in the fundamental authenticity of Squire' to include the new letters, and had decided that even disbelievers would wish to see them 'under the head of the semi-romantic or Doubtful Documents of Oliver's History'. Finally, whatever his readers thought of the papers, they 'will please to excuse me from farther function in the matter; my duty in respect of them being now, to the last fraction of it, done; my knowledge of them being wholly communicated; and my care about them remaining, what it always was, close neighbour to nothing'.[29] With this novel piece of metahistorical rhetoric, Carlyle turned his back on the Squire affair.

Irksome though he found the unexpected aftermath of his Cromwell venture, Carlyle noted with pleasure that he had brought his neglected hero to wider public attention. In April 1849 he learned that a committee had been formed in St Ives to erect a statue to the town's famous son.[30] By this time Carlyle had taken to calling Lady Harriet 'Daughter of an Ironside', having discovered that her ancestor, the first Earl of Sandwich, was a captain in Cromwell's famous army.[31]

The sore throat Jane had nursed at Alverstoke early in 1847 became severe in the summer; she told Helen Welsh in June that John Carlyle had diagnosed a throat tumour, which she kept secret from Carlyle.[32] She was dosing herself, on recommendations from various doctors, with tartar and opium, confiding in Caroline Fox in May that, as Caroline noted, the opium caused her 'not beautiful dreams and visions, but a miserable feeling of turning to marble herself and lying on marble', her 'whole person petrifying and adhering to the marble slab on which she lay'. In one such dream she recognised the location as her mother's grave.[33]

Carlyle went to Scotland late in the summer, after carefully refusing an invitation from Browning, now married to Elizabeth Barrett and living in Florence. Browning had written on 14 May, expressing quasi-filial feelings towards Carlyle:

We determined that whenever I wrote to you, as I meant to do for the last six or seven months, it would be wiser to leave unsaid, unattempted to be said, my feelings of love and gratitude for the intercourse you permitted since a good many years now – but go on and tell you what an easy thing it would be for you to come to Italy'... and let us have the happiness, – the entire happiness of remembering that we got ready the prophet's-chamber in the wall, with bed and candlestick, according to scripture precedent [an allusion to 1 Kings 4:7, in which each of the district governors of Israel is commanded to provide supplies for King Solomon for a month].[34]

The modern Solomon's reply, which Elizabeth Barrett Browning described as 'delightful' and 'full of kindness', expressed his hearty rejoicing on hearing of the marriage and assured Browning that Italy would be the very place to tempt him to travel, if he had any love of travel left to tempt, which, alas, he had not.[35]

Carlyle played host in June to Karl Alexander, son of the Duke of Saxe-Weimar and 'grandson of Goethe's Duke'.[36] Jane, with her own reasons for not wishing to bow down before aristocracy – a disinclination, as she said, to being 'invited down to my own sitting room, as an ineffable condescension' – left the house for the duration, going to spend the afternoon at Mrs Buller's.[37] In August both Carlyles, following the fashion, visited the spa at Matlock in Derbyshire, drinking the waters and swimming in them, and concluding, as Carlyle told Jack cheerfully, that they were 'probably not worth twopence for any complaint in the Nosology, except as the imagination may be solaced by them a little'.[38]

They joined W. E. Forster, a young philanthropic wool trader from Bradford who took an interest in Irish affairs and was later to be the politician responsible for the Education Act of 1870. Together the threesome explored the pretty town of Buxton, where they encountered at the table d'hôte of a first-class hotel 'old maids, and worn-out half-pay roués, and peaked-up parsons, a species of walking white neck-cloths, altogether a race of men the most opposite to Carlylean that can be conceived', as Forster reported to a friend. Carlyle got into an argument about Ireland with a parson, and began to declaim. 'How they did stare', wrote Forster with relish; some were aghast and others admiring. 'We remained incog. the whole time, spite of all the schemes of the guests, and the entreaties of the waiter to book our names, and my proposal to Mrs C to save our expenses by showing him at so much a head.'[39]

Jane, now in her mid-forties, and Forster, not quite thirty, got on famously first in Derbyshire and then in Yorkshire, where the Carlyles spent a few weeks in Forster's house. Forster described Jane as being 'like a girl in her delight at new scenes and situations', and when she was back in Chelsea in October she reported to Carlyle (in Scotsbrig) that she had received 'a long letter from William Edward', marked 'Private' inside and out, 'and stopping in the midst besides, to beg that it might be *burnt* the moment I had finished it'. In it Forster confided the details of his love of a young woman, telling Jane that 'nothing but the Magnet-power of sympathy' she possessed could have 'so beguiled him into laying open the secrets of his heart'.[40] She responded warmly, writing on 28 October:

Verily I feel quite SCHWESTERLICH [sisterly] towards you. That journey into Yorkshire was a modern version of Saul going out to meet his Father's asses & finding a Kingdom. I went to seek the *picturesque* & found *you* – & catch me losing you again! – Dear Wm Edwd you are worth a cartload of Emersons & so God bless you with *calm* & all good things.[41]

Emerson is invoked here because he had just arrived at Cheyne Row. This was his first visit to Britain since his trip in 1833, when as a young man uncertain of his vocation he had determinedly penetrated to the wilds of Dumfriesshire to see the *Edinburgh Review* essayist he so admired. In the fourteen intervening years both men had become famous as social prophets, one known as the critical conscience of Victorian Britain, the other as the chief philosopher of America. Their correspondence had remained cordial, though they differed on several points, with Emerson more positive about democracy than his fiery mentor, and also inclined to cling rather more closely to his original religious beliefs. By the time they met again now, when Emerson stayed as a guest at Cheyne Row at the end of October 1847, each had lost sympathy with the other's opinions and rhetoric, though they were pleasant to one another for old times' sake, with Jane looking on, sceptical.

Emerson's first impression on knocking on the door at ten o'clock in the evening of 25 October was that both Carlyles had changed very little. He found, as before, that 'the floodgates of Carlyle's discourse are very quickly opened, & the river is a great & constant stream', as he reported to his wife. 'We had a large communication that night until nearly one o'clock and at breakfast next morning it begun again.'[42] Carlyle's description to his sister Jean was brief:

Emerson the American Friend came upon us last night, and is now here, – nothing but talkee talkee; – for the rest, a very fine fellow, whom it is pleasant to talk with. He stays 'till next week', I dimly apprehend; then goes to Lancashire &c to *lecture* to all manner of Mechanics Institutes and the like.[43]

As the week went on, Jane noticed that Carlyle was disappointed in his old friend, though, as she told Lady Harriet, he was 'under the restraining grace of Hospitality', and so no explosions had occurred. Jane took pleasure in her rare advantage over Lady Harriet, who had not yet met the distinguished American:

I hardly know what to think of him, or whether I like him or not. The man has *two* faces to begin with which are continually changing into one another like '*dissolving views*', the one young, refined, almost beautiful, radiant with – what shall I say? – '*virtue its own reward*'! the other decidedly old, hatchet-like, crotchety, inconclusive – like an incarnation of one of his own *poems*! In his speech he is not dogmatical the least in the world, nor anything like so *fantastical* as his letters give one to suppose; in fact, except for a few phrases consisting chiefly of odd applications, of the words '*beauty*' and '*child*' he speaks simply and clearly, but without any eloquence or warmth – What I should say he failed in is what the Yorkshire wool-cleaner called 'natur' – He is *genial*, but it seems to be with his head rather than his *heart* – a sort of theoretic geniality that (as Mazzini would say) 'leaves me *cold*'. He is perhaps the most *elevated* man I ever saw – but it is the elevation of a *reed* – run all to h[e]ight without taking breadth along with it. You will not I think dislike him as you expected, but neither will you like him.[44]

For his part, Emerson wrote to his wife on 27 October that 'Carlyle and his wife live on beautiful terms: Nothing can be more engaging than their ways, and in her book case all his books are inscribed to her.'[45] With that, he went off on a tour of Britain, meeting some of the younger generation of Carlyle's admirers, including Clough in Oxford, Marian Evans in Coventry, and Geraldine Jewsbury and Francis Espinasse in Manchester. Clough, who had invited Emerson to lecture in Oxford, reported to a friend in January 1848 that, according to rumour, 'Carlyle and he talked for three days and nights and then Carlyle is said to have called him "a sham", but that is probably an exaggeration.'[46]

In September 1847 Geraldine had sent Jane the manuscript of her second novel, *The Half Sisters*, asking for her comments. In November Jane was correcting the proofs. She had been instrumental in getting Carlyle's publishers, Chapman and Hall, to publish Geraldine's previous novel, *Zoe*, in 1845, but now Carlyle 'has got some furious objection to my meddling' with the proofs of the new novel, she told John Forster in November. He 'even declares that I "do not know bad grammar when I see it any better than *she* does" – that "if I HAD any faculty I might find better employment for it" &c &c'. She added with that clever bitterness which could be taken as a joke by the recipient, 'I do think there is much truth in the *young german* idea that Marriage is *a shockingly immoral Institution* as well as an extremely disagreeable one.'[47] Jane's knowledge of Young Germany, a political movement modelled to some extent on Mazzini's Young Italy, came from Amely Bölte, who had just returned from a visit to Germany 'all agog with *something* that she calls "*the new ideas*" – above all quite rabid against *marriage*', as Jane told Helen Welsh.[48]

There was another fuss in February 1848 when Geraldine wanted to dedicate her new novel to Jane; the latter once more consulted Forster, who acted as reader for Chapman and Hall:

Knowing [Carlyle's] dislike to be connected in people's minds, by even the slightest spider-thread, with what he calls 'George Sandism and all that accursed sort of thing' I was not at all sure that the *half-toleration* he gave when asked about it would not be changed into *prohibition* if he found it likely to be acted upon – At the time I *sounded* his feelings; the Book, I was able to assure him, contained nothing *questionable* – Can I say so now?[49]

Geraldine's novels air the same concerns which form a large part of the subject matter of her letters to Jane: women's role in society, questions of equality in marriage, and the desirability of female education and work opportunities. In general she takes an 'emancipated' line, even allowing a certain amount of sexual freedom into her plots, though not as much as appears in the works of the notoriously free-living and free-writing Frenchwoman George Sand. The debate about women's rights which had been rather submerged since Mary Wollstonecraft's brave efforts in the years immediately following the French Revolution – *A Vindication of the Rights of Woman* (1792) and her unfinished novel, published in 1798 after her death, *The Wrongs of Women* – was about to break out in a serious and sustained form, coinciding with another political revolution in February 1848.

Caroline Norton's claim for custody of her children after the collapse in 1836 of her husband's adultery suit against her, and the various unsuccessful bills put before Parliament on her behalf, had highlighted the difficulties faced by women who took on their husbands in the law courts. Agitation grew for more liberal divorce laws. But the argument for female education and for opening the professions to women was at least as important as reform of the marriage laws, since access to wage-earning independence would offer a third alternative to the two existing choices for most women – entering a perhaps loveless marriage and enduring poverty-stricken spinsterhood.

In October 1847 a new novel was published under the title *Jane Eyre: An Autobiography edited by Currer Bell*. Jane Carlyle read the three volumes of this extraordinary plea for clever womanhood as soon as they came out.[50] Like everyone else, she was eager to know who 'Currer Bell' was. In January she passed on to Carlyle the latest gossip as told to her by Charlotte Williams Wynn – 'the town is all full of news that "Jane Eyre has been written by Mr Thackey's *mistress*" '.[51] Charlotte Brontë had dedicated the second edition of her novel to Thackeray, not knowing that he had an insane wife; parallels were quickly drawn, by those who did know, between Thackeray's situation and that of Mr Rochester with his mad wife, Bertha, kept in the attic in *Jane Eyre*.

Carlyle objected mainly to sensualism in fiction – hence the phrase he often used, 'George Sandism' – though he seems not to have read many novels right through. As early as 1832, in his *Fraser's* essay 'Biography', he had delivered a passing denunciation of 'the Fashionable Novel', by which he meant chiefly Bulwer's novels about aristocratic dandies. In his letters he often referred to the latest Dickens novel, always fleetingly and usually dismissively, with no detailed discussion to show he had done much more than glance at the volumes as Jane read them. Friendly as he was with Dickens and Thackeray, Carlyle viewed their works half seriously as one of the many gloomy signs of the times. He noticed the tremendous increase in novel-writing which took place in the 1840s and 1850s – much of it in response to his own social writings – and shook his head over the phenomenon in the manner now expected of his sageship. Writing to Browning in June 1847, he summed up the news from England:

Dickens writes a *Dombey & Son*, Thackeray a *Vanity Fair*, not *reapers* they, either of them! In fact the business of rope-dancing goes to a great height; and d'Israeli's *Tancred* (readable to the end of the first volume), a kind of transcendent spiritual Houndsditch [an area of East London populated by Jewish dealers in old clothes], marks an epoch in the history of this poor country.[52]

The rope-dancing metaphor may have been repeated by Carlyle to Thackeray himself, for in an undated note to the Carlyles he drew a caricature of himself walking a tightrope, and signed himself 'W M Thackeray/ Equilibrist and Tightrope dancer in ordinary to the nobility & the Literati'.[53] He sent a copy of *Vanity Fair* to Jane in December 1848. Among the many sketches he included in the first printing of the novel, as it came out in monthly parts in 1847–8, was one of the novelist wearing an ass's ears, a direct visual reference to one of Carlyle's verbal insults in his 'Biography' essay – an allusion to 'long-eared moralists', a term Thackeray also echoes in his own text.[54] Both he and Dickens accepted with good humour Carlyle's exaggerated antagonism towards their profession.

Elizabeth Gaskell was luckier. When she sent Carlyle a copy of her first novel, *Mary Barton: A Tale of Manchester Life*, published anonymously by Chapman and Hall in October 1848, he not only read it but wrote kindly to the author, whom he guessed to be a woman. Perhaps recognising its indebtedness to his own *Past and Present*, and certainly sympathising with Mrs Gaskell's obvious concern for the conditions of the urban poor, he praised its 'beautiful, cheerfully pious, social, clear and observant character'.[55]

There is, of course, no 'George Sandism' about *Mary Barton*. G. H. Lewes's two novels, *Ranthorpe* (1847) and *Rose, Blanche, and Violet* (1848), on the other hand, have more than a touch of that quality, especially the second, the very title of which echoes that of an early novel co-written by

George Sand and her then lover Jules Sandeau, *Rose et Blanche* (1831). Lewes gave Jane Carlyle copies of both his novels, inscribing *Ranthorpe* 'To Madame Jane Carlyle. Souvenir d'une vraie Amitié'.[56] Perhaps he wrote in French because he knew of Jane's enthusiasm for George Sand, despite her husband and the general disapproval in Britain of the French writer. In 1843 she had borrowed *Rose et Blanche* from the London Library, entering her name in the ledger, as she boasted to her cousin Jeannie, as '*Erasmus Darwin*! to the wonderment of the bookkeeper doubtless, who must have thought me an odd sort of Erasmus!' The impersonation, she explained, was done in the name of '*decency*'.[57]

Jane's opinion of *Ranthorpe*, a kind of London *Wilhelm Meister*, is not recorded, but when Lewes presented her with *Rose, Blanche, and Violet* in April 1848, she told Carlyle that it was 'execrable'. 'I could not have suspected even the Ape [the Carlyles' nickname for Lewes] of writing anything so silly.' Lady Harriet, who had also been reading it, pronounced it 'too *vulgar* to go on with', Jane reported.[58] Carlyle, rather surprisingly, read both of Lewes's novels. He liked the younger man's energy, talent, and unpretentiousness, and was willing to help with Lewes's research for his biography of Goethe. But he did not like the novels, perceiving not only that Lewes had little gift for the imaginative creation of character, but also that what he called 'Phallus Worship' had crossed the Channel from France and got into recent English novels, including Lewes's. His marginal comments on both novels relate mainly to scenes between the sexes, and though mainly comic – 'Gott im Himmel!' 'Sorrow on you!' 'What beggarly nonsense is this!' – they indicate Carlyle's disgust and alarm at the tendency of modern literature to concentrate on the physical nature of romantic love.[59]

A long journal entry on 9 February 1848 gives some insight into Carlyle's vehement feelings. Having noted the state of his finances – now very comfortable indeed, at about £1,500 – Carlyle went on to review himself:

For above two years now I have been as good as totally idle, composedly lying *fallow*. It is frightful to think of! . . . I am wearied and near heartbroken. Nobody on the whole '*believes* my report'. The friendliest reviewers, I can see, regard me as a wonderful athlete, a ropedancer whose perilous somersets it is worth sixpence (paid into the Circulating Library) to *see*; or at most I seem to them a desperate half mad, if usefullish fireman, rushing along the ridge tiles in a frightful manner to quench the burning chimney.[60]

Carlyle saw the extent of his influence; yet he knew that he was viewed as a kind of raree-show, an exotic figure to be admired and cherished, but not, in the end, to be taken seriously, and certainly not to be heeded by those in a position to have a practical effect on political and social conditions. His dismissal of the 'rope-dancing' of novelists makes sense in the light of his analysis of the frivolous reception of his own writings. This troubled him, as did the increasing amount of time he was spending in idle aristocratic circles. In the same journal entry he recalls his stay at Alverstoke in January and his observation of 'the higher ranks' there. His conclusion is that 'our aristocracy' is 'the best, or as good as any class we have; but their position is fatally awry'; even the well-meaning members of the class seem not to produce any positive results. As for Emerson, at present lecturing to Mechanics' Institutes in the north of England, what can he achieve? Emerson is 'very *exotic*', differing greatly from Carlyle himself – 'as a gymnosophist sitting idle on a flowery bank may do from a wearied worker and wrestler passing that way with many of his bones broken'.[61]

Carlyle sketches four 'schemes of books to be now set about'. One is to be called 'Exodus from Houndsditch', to encourage thinking people to come out of the Church of England and other outworn institutions. The second is to be a book on Ireland, though Carlyle feels he knows too little about the country to set about this task quite yet. Then there should be a 'Life of John Sterling', 'some picture of a gifted soul whom I knew, and who was my friend. Might not many things withal be *taught* in the course of such a delineation?' And finally, 'The Scavenger's Age', prompted by the sight Carlyle was met with daily at this time of engineers sent by the sanitary reformer Edwin Chadwick to survey for a new system of sewers from the top of St Luke's Church, Chelsea: 'Our age is really up to nothing better than the sweeping *out the gutter*. Might it but do that well! It is the indispensable beginning of all.'[62]

An unfinished and unpublished essay Carlyle wrote around this time returns to the subject of 'Phallus Worship', relating it rather recklessly to a whole parcel of signs of so-called 'progress', political, social, and religious, in the wake of the new revolutionary outbreaks in Paris and other European cities in the spring of 1848:

These universal suffrages, national workshops, reigns of fraternity, and generally red or white republics with their fraternities and phenomena are to me very mainly a George-Sand Novel come forth from the land of dreams, intending to enact itself as a fact under this sun. If the laws of the universe be as the melodious Anti-virgin reads them, this fact will stand and prosper. Most excellent Phallophilos, you do not sufficiently consider how paramount 'religion' is, after all.

The New Sand religion is not yet developed into articles; creeds, and bodies of divinity; far from that. Much lies yet undeveloped, inarticulately slumbering in it, and huge world-wide mythologies, little suspected of being mythic, struggle to unfold themselves: an Egg of Eros swimming on the dark immensities; still albuminous, requiring to be *hatched* . . .[63]

Carlyle was wise not to publish these remarks. Yet, as he grew older, he was increasingly willing to make sweeping rhetorical gestures, linking complex phenomena merely by the whimsical force of his vocabulary and syntax, without pausing to test his logic or question his assumptions. His next published work, *Latter-Day Pamphlets* (1850), was as unrestrained as this manuscript in its attacks on all forms of 'progress', including, in an echo of this piece, a dire warning about a 'strange new religion, named of Universal Love, with Sacraments, mainly of *Divorce*, with Balzac, Sue and Company for Evangelists, and Madam Sand for Virgin'.[64] Though he anticipated that the more violent his rhetoric became, the less seriously he would be taken by those he hoped to influence, he was impelled to express in pungent language the strong feelings so evident in his troubled private journal.

★

Towards the end of February 1848, revolution broke out in Paris following the banning of a political banquet planned by reformers. The seventy-four-year-old Louis Philippe fled to England under the name 'William Smith', arriving at Newhaven in the early hours of 3 March. He was settled by Queen Victoria at Claremont, the Surrey house owned by her uncle, King Leopold of the Belgians. 'No encouragement should be given by your Majesty', the Prime Minister warned the Queen on 29 February, 'to any notion that your Majesty would assist them to recover the Crown.' Public opinion, he assured her, would not approve of her offering more than the asylum which 'the sacred duties of hospitality' would require to be given to 'persons of all opinions'.[65]

Lord John Russell showed himself a shrewd judge of public feeling, which was over-whelmingly against foreign monarchies and dictatorships, though disinclined to follow the example set by Paris and quickly emulated in Berlin, Vienna, and other cities across Europe. Dickens, who celebrated events in Paris by signing his letters 'Citoyen Charles Dickens', told a French friend that the news from France was causing a sensation in London:

There was hardly room to stand in the Athenaeum last night among the bishops priests and deacons, lords, artists, authors, members of Parliament, and genteel tag rag and bobtail, who were busily discussing it. The aristocratic feeling of England is against it, of course. All the intelligence and liberality, I should say, are with it, tooth and nail. If the Queen should be marked in her attention to old Papa Philippe, I think there will be great discontent and dissatisfaction expressed throughout the country. Meantime we are in a queer position ourselves, with great distress in the manufacturing towns.[66]

The Times, which responded to the public interest by issuing its largest print run to date on 1 March (54,000 as opposed to the normal 35,000), disapproved of the revolution.[67] But other newspapers rejoiced, as did various dissenting and reforming groups, notably the Chartists. One of them, Thomas Frost, described in his memoirs the excitement at a meeting of the Association of Fraternal Democrats he was attending when the news of the Paris uprising arrived. He and his fellow democrats rushed out of their meeting, and, 'with linked arms and colours flying', marched to Dean Street, Soho, where the Westminster Chartists were holding their own meeting. 'There another enthusiastic fraternisation took place, and great was the clinking of glasses that night in and around Soho and Leicester Square.'[68]

Carlyle, too, rejoiced, telling Emerson, who was lecturing in Scotland, that everyone was in 'a sort of joy-dance over the new French Republic, which has descended suddenly (or shall we say *ascended*, alas?) out of the Immensities upon us; shewing once again that the righteous Gods do yet live and reign! It is long years since I have felt any such deep-seated pious satisfaction at a public event.'[69]

His pleasure related entirely to the ejection of the 'Sham-King' Louis Philippe and not at all to the attempt (soon defeated) to set up a constitutional government in France, as he made clear in letters to friends like Emerson and John Forster.[70] The latter went 'almost down on his knees to me' for an article on Louis Philippe for the *Examiner*, Carlyle told his sister Jean.[71] A short piece appeared in the paper on 4 March, attributing the fleeing of 'Sophist Guizot, sham-King Louis-Philippe, and the host of quacks, of obscene spectral nightmares under which France lay writhing' to 'a divine Nemesis'. Slotting at once into the tone of his history of the 1789 Revolution, Carlyle wrote: 'Louis-Philippe one could pity as well as blame, were not all one's pity concentrated upon the millions who have suffered by his sins.' He stopped short of expressing predictions or hopes for the future.[72]

His words were read and echoed by Marian Evans in a letter of 8 March:

I have little patience with people who can find time to pity Louis Philippe and his moustachioed sons . . . Let them sit on soft cushions and have their dinner regularly, but for heaven's sake preserve me from sentimentalizing over a pampered old man when the earth has its millions of unfed souls and bodies.

Shrewdly, she saw that in Britain there was both less need and less likelihood of an uprising than in France and her neighbours, since 'our little humbug of a queen is more endurable than the rest of her race because she calls forth a chivalrous feeling', and 'there is nothing in our constitution to obstruct the slow progress of *political* reform'. Ireland, already restive with poverty and calls for independence, might erupt, though she predicted that it would not. Recent riots by unemployed workers in Glasgow were more serious, 'but one cannot believe in a Scotch Reign of Terror in these days'. 'I should not be sorry to hear that the Italians had risen en masse and chased the odious Austrians out of beautiful Lombardy', she continued, foreseeing what was to occur only ten days later, when Austria's troops were ejected from Milan.[73]

Jane Carlyle followed events in Italy with particular interest on account of Mazzini, who made for Paris as soon as Louis Philippe 'decamped', in order to gather resources for his own return to Italy in April to lead the struggle there.[74] Several of the Carlyles' friends were soon travelling to Paris to see things for themselves. Geraldine Jewsbury, the Paulets, and W. E. Forster left together on 1 May. When they got to Paris, they found Milnes, Emerson, and Clough already there. Carlyle told his mother that they had all spent the time 'larking' as if 'out upon the *ploy*', finding the fighting between socialist and republican members of the post-revolutionary National Assembly, 'as all Paris was finding it, comical rather than tragical'.[75]

These English liberals and self-styled radicals could afford to take the European upheavals so lightly only because British radicalism was not inclined to follow suit. This had been amply proved on 10 April, when a huge Chartist rally on Kennington Common, south of the Thames, was followed by a procession to Parliament with a petition of over five million signatures. The Government, fearing an insurrection, swore in around 100,000 'special constables' for the day – any 'gentleman in London' qualified for the task – but the event passed peacefully, helped by the cold and rain, which dampened any enthusiasm for trouble-making. Dickens wrote amusedly to his friend Bulwer, now known as Bulwer-Lytton, on the day itself: 'I have not been special constable-ing, myself, today. Thinking there was rather an epidemic in that wise abroad, I walked out and looked at the preparations, without any luggage of staff, warrant, or affidavit.'[76]

Carlyle also went out to see for himself, reporting to Jane, who was staying at Addiscombe: 'How can I tell you of the "revolution", in these circumstances? I did go out earlier than usual, to see it; or at least all buttoned up, and decided to walk myself into a glow of heat: but – but the venomous cold wind began unexpectedly, in Cadogan place, to spit rain, and I had no umbrella!' He tells of the rain beginning to pour and of his taking refuge in the Burlington Arcade on Piccadilly, where he saw various cartoons of Louis Philippe as a pear (which is how *Punch* regularly represented him), and struck up a conversation with another shelterer. He then went home to Chelsea by way of the royal parks and the environs of Buckingham Palace, noting the precautions that had been taken along the route. He concluded that

there is *no* revolution, nor any like to be for some months or years yet; that the City of London is as safe and quiet as the Farm of Addiscombe; and that empty rumour, and '150,000' oaths of special constables, is hitherto the sole amount of this adventure for us. Piccadilly itself, however, told us how frightened the people were; directly at Hyde Park Corner one could see that there was something in the wind. Wellington had his iron blinds all accurately down [at Apsley House, the Duke's London home at Hyde Park Corner]; the Green Park was altogether shut, even the footpaths of it . . . For the rest not a single fashionable carriage was on the street: not a private vehicle, but I think two surgeons' broughams, all the way to the Egyptian Hall omnibuses running, a few street cabs, and even a *mud*-cart or two; but nothing else. The flag-pavements also nearly vacant; not a fifth of their usual population there, and those also of the strictly business kind; not a *gentleman* to be seen: hardly one or two of the sort called *gents*.[77]

Emerson had returned to London by this time, and Carlyle added his signature to a letter drafted by Dickens and John Forster inviting him to lecture in London and offering to make the arrangements. Emerson delivered six lectures on 'The Mind and Manners of the Nineteenth Century' in June to an audience of the literati and the cultured aristocracy, including Lady Harriet.[78] In the meantime Forster gave a dinner on 15 April, to which Emerson, Dickens, and Carlyle were invited. Emerson reported to his wife that it 'seemed the habit of the set to pet Carlyle a good deal, and draw out the mountainous mirth'.[79]

Carlyle's preoccupation with political and so-called social and sexual 'progress', as expressed in his notes on phallus worship, found an outlet in the conversation at this all-male dinner party, according to Emerson's jottings in a notebook:

Forster, who has an obstreperous cordiality, received Carlyle with loud salutation, 'My Prophet!' Forster called Carlyle's passion, Musket-worship. There were only gentlemen present, & the conversation turned on the shameful lewdness of London streets at night. (Carlyle said, & the others agreed, that chastity for men was as good as given up in Europe.) 'I hear it', he said, 'I hear whoredom in the House of Commons. Disraeli betrays whoredom, & the whole H. of Commons universal incontinence, in every word they say.' I said, that, when I came to Liverpool, I inquired whether the prostitution was always as gross in that city, as it then appeared? . . . C. & D. replied, that chastity in the male sex was as good as gone in our times; &, in England, was so rare, that they could name all the exceptions.[80]

It sounds as though Carlyle and Dickens were exaggerating in order to shock the famously serene Emerson, just as Carlyle was supposed, according to a story George Eliot was told a few years later, to have got angry with Emerson 'for not believing in a devil', and so 'to convert him took him amongst all the horrors of London – the gin shops etc. and finally to the House of Commons plying him at every turn with the question "Do you believe in a devil noo?" '[81]

For all his innocence in this interesting discussion of life in London in 1848, Emerson was a shrewd judge of Carlyle. His notes show him quite aware of his friend's intolerance. He partly admired Carlyle's vehemence: 'His talk will often remind you of what was said [by Oliver Goldsmith] of Dr Johnson, "If his pistol misses fire, he will knock you down with the butt-end." ' But he observed that Carlyle's influence on the younger generation, though still immense, was on the point of falling off on account of the outrageousness of his views and his temperament:

The young men are eager to see him . . . Carlyle is a vivacious aggressive temperament, & unimpressionable. The literary, the fashionable, & the political man, each fresh from triumphs in his own sphere, comes eagerly to see this man, whose fun they have so heartily enjoyed, – sure of a welcome, – and are struck with despair at the first onset. His firm, victorious, cutting, scoffing, vituperative declamation strikes them with chill & hesitation.[82]

The Carlyles attended Emerson's lectures, by which they were not impressed. Jane, perhaps a little jealous on Carlyle's behalf, told Lady Harriet – now Lady Ashburton, since her husband's father had died in May – that the third lecture, delivered at Portman Square on 10 June, had charmed the audience, 'so beautiful it all *sounded*, so profound, and lofty, and prophetic!', but that if you asked what it was about, no one would be able to say.[83] Carlyle told his mother that Emerson had 'something excellent in him tho' he is a little "moon shiny" '. He announced also that he and Emerson were off to spend a few days together visiting Stonehenge.[84] This they did in early July, after which Emerson travelled to Liverpool once more to embark for home.

Although 10 April had passed peacefully, Carlyle was still concerned, as was the Government, about the condition of Ireland, so ripe for armed protest on its own account, and vulnerable also to influence from France. He published four newspaper articles on Ireland, two in the *Examiner* on 29 April and 13 May, and two in the *Spectator*, both published on 13 May. Everyone read these short pieces, and most people dissented from them for one reason or another. In the first Carlyle robustly rejects calls for repeal of the Union on the grounds that 'the stern Destinies have laid upon England a terrible job of labour in these centuries', namely the job of governing and regulating the country 'lodged in her back-parlour'. As ever, he offers no alternative solution, but only vehement feelings, particularly on the need for a strong, wise governor. These feelings are expressed by way of satirical comment on 'the gentry of Ireland', the absentee or uncaring landlords 'drinking punch, fortune-hunting, or playing roulette at Brighton, Leamington, or other places of resort'.[85]

Though Carlyle shows pity for the 'governable *un*governed millions' in Ireland 'living the hunger-life, in degradation below that of dogs', he also manages to be alarmist, drawing on his observation of Irish incomers, navvies involved in the construction of railways, seen on his journeys to Scotland over the last few summers, and beggars on the streets of London and other cities. He paints a picture of 'our land overrun with hordes of hungry white savages, covered with dirt and rags, full of noise, falsity, and turbulence, deranging every relation between rich and poor, feeding the gibbets all along our western coasts, submerging our populations into the depths of dirt, savagery, and human degradation'.[86]

This was too much for John Stuart Mill, long estranged from Carlyle personally because of Harriet Taylor, and increasingly estranged politically and philosophically since his days of discipleship nearly twenty years before. He replied to Carlyle's article in one of his own, 'England and Ireland', printed in the *Examiner* on 13 May. Mill had long been urging land reform for Ireland in the *Morning Chronicle*, and he now repudiated Carlyle's simple repetition of the need for strong and wise governance by England. What Ireland needed was self-government, Mill argued; Carlyle's idea of England's 'messiahship' was both naive and dangerous, encouraging John Bull's already over-full conceit and self-satisfaction in a case where self-criticism was required.[87]

Carlyle was also the object of private criticism among his friends. Thackeray's opinion, expressed in a letter to FitzGerald, was that

Gurlyle is immensely grand and savage now. He had a Cromwellian letter against the Irish in this weeks Examiner I declare it seems like insanity almost his contempt for all mankind, and the way in wh he shirks from the argument when called upon to préciser his own remedies for the state of things.[88]

The ever-observant Amely Bölte told Varnhagen von Ense on 7 May that Carlyle had published a 'forceful article' on Ireland. 'It is noticeable', she continued, 'how few people now come to see him! They call him "such a bore" because he declares opinions which no-one shares, and insists on sticking to them.'[89] Amely exaggerated the falling off of friends, but her remarks, along with those of Thackeray and Emerson, and of Carlyle himself in his journal ruminatings, do catch the moment when Carlyle's always mixed and paradoxical figure began to look to others more negative than positive in its effect.

And yet Carlyle could still surprise with his generosity and humanity. On 26 May he wrote to the new Lord-Lieutenant of Ireland, Lord Clarendon, pleading on behalf of John Mitchel, whose trial for sedition (he had incited rebellion in his new breakaway newspaper, *The United Irishman*) was then taking place. Sentence was due to be delivered the next day, and Carlyle sought to mitigate the punishment on the grounds of Mitchel's honesty, blaming his excesses on the influence of the 'loud False-Prophet' O'Connell. Clarendon was polite but disbelieving in reply, and Mitchel was sentenced to fourteen years' transportation.[90] Duffy too was arrested, in July, and wrote to Carlyle from prison in October, while awaiting trial on a charge of high treason. He expressed his appreciation of Carlyle's friendship, but called his *Examiner* remarks 'most cruel and unjust'. Once more he asked Carlyle to use his influence with Clarendon (an influence which flowed through Milnes and the Ashburtons) to procure a favourable or at least merciful verdict.[91]

That summer Chopin visited London. The Carlyles heard him play; even Carlyle, whose musical taste seems to have been restricted more or less to Scottish ballads, thought him 'a wonderful Musician'.[92] Jane told Helen Welsh in mid-July that she had heard Chopin twice, and that he had visited Cheyne Row. In the same letter she described a busy social round, including a dinner at Mrs Norton's and one at Macready's, 'where was Count D'Orsay! and old Lady Morgan "naked as robins" half way down – age seventy five!'[93] In August Jeannie came to visit. Carlyle described her to John Forster as 'a cheery bright little girl', 'the only specimen I know or ever saw of the ancient Scottish *golden hair*', 'hair the colour of a new guinea'. Forster took them all to the opera to hear the famous Swedish soprano Jenny Lind sing in Bellini's *La Sonnambula*, 'a chosen bit of nonsense from beginning to end', according to Carlyle:

'Depend upon it', I said to Fuz, 'the Devil is busy *here* tonight, wherever he may be idle!' – Old Wellington had come staggering in to attend the thing. Thackeray was there; d'Orsay, Lady Blessington, to all of whom (Well*n* excepted!) I had to be presented, and grin some kind of foolery.[94]

Since Jane and Carlyle did not part this summer, we have none of the usual exchange of letters to indicate how well, or badly, they were getting on. Amely Bölte told Varnhagen of a scene which she had witnessed which suggests that relations were not particularly good, though managed by the pair as a sort of marital *modus vivendi*:

There was a comical scene recently. He, she, and I were sitting alone at tea. He asked for her advice over something, and she replied that he ought not to do it, because people would take him for 'goodhearted', an epithet which hardly suited him. He looked straight ahead, visibly struggling with unpleasant feelings ... Then he looked up, pinched his lips together, and answered, 'Well! my dear, then we are remarkably well suited for each other; for you were never accused of being good-natured either.' She laughingly admitted he was right.[95]

At the beginning of September the Carlyles were at the Grange. Carlyle had some hopes that the amiable William Bingham Baring, now Lord Ashburton, with his 'real desire' to do good, might use some of his immense wealth – £60,000 a year, Carlyle reckoned – on social and political initiatives.[96] Carlyle did not specify what he had in mind, but a few years later Lord Ashburton was active in trying to reform the education system, an effort in which he enlisted Carlyle's advice. The visit to the Grange lasted a month; even Jane appears to have enjoyed it. Charles Buller and Lady Ashburton's formidable mother, Lady Sandwich, were among the guests. Carlyle explained to his mother that Lady Sandwich used to live entirely in Paris, but was 'driven hence by the late Revolutions'; Jane told Jeannie that she found the old woman '*very* agreeable', noting that 'her daughter can hardly endure her'.[97]

Life at the Grange was one of '*total idleness*'. Breakfast was at half-past nine, 'where are infinite flunkies, cates, condiments, very superfluous to me, with much "making of wits" (as Bölte calls it), and not always a very great allowance of grave reason', Carlyle grumbled. He enjoyed riding around with Lord Ashburton, accompanying him one day to a meeting of the Petty Sessions to grant publicans their licences and try a 'case of bastardy'. Buller exasperated him as always: 'When I get him alone, [he] is worth talking to, but in company he goes wholly upon "wit", and merely makes one laugh.'[98] He and Jane differed in their opinion of two new guests who arrived halfway through the month, the minor writers Henry Taylor and Aubrey de Vere, 'the two *greatest* bores', Carlyle told Jack:

De Vere I could rather like if by himself; for he is a serious, tho' very soft, Puseyish and theoretic young Irish gentleman; but Taylor and he, with their mutual admiration, much aggravate one another; and, in brief, my best resource is to keep considerably out of their way! 'Making of wits' is, as you say, a wretched trade; and except the Lady A herself and C Buller, none here do it, even it, tolerably well.[99]

Jane's account of meeting the 'Puseyish' de Vere – by which Carlyle meant an adherent of the Oxford Movement, with its revival of High Church ritual – is more positive. She told Jeannie that her relationship with him might deepen into 'a real friendship':

The name is romantic enough Aubrey de Vere – and the man who bears it is romantic enough – very handsome – young, *religious* – to the extent even of eating fish on Fridays and fasting in Lent – A Poet – highly accomplished every way despising '*wits*' (wonderfulest of all) and in short a rare mortal as men go.[100]

De Vere was equally fascinated by Jane, writing to her on 30 September to express his gratitude for her 'unreserve' on 'subjects which are too often shunned'. He meant religion, and spent thirteen pages describing his own faith and diffidently offering to help her with her scarcely existent religious belief.[101]

In November Charles Buller had a minor operation to remove a fistula. To everyone's shock and surprise, he died from a typhus fever which set in after the operation. Carlyle commiserated with Lady Ashburton on the loss of this 'blithe' man of forty-two who, like Sterling, had died before he could show what he was really capable of achieving. As Froude put it somewhat callously in his *Life* of Carlyle, 'The House of Commons likes to be amused, but does not raise its jesters into Cabinets.'[102] Knowing how fond Lady Ashburton was of her bachelor courtier, Carlyle tried to console her. Jane, he said, had gone straight to Mrs Buller, who had lost her husband earlier in the year and now her beloved son.[103]

The *Examiner* of 2 December 1848 carried a warm tribute by Carlyle to the 'very beautiful soul' who had died, 'one of the clearest intellects and most aerial activities in England', 'a man long kept under by the peculiarities of his endowment and position, but rising rapidly into importance of late years', and one whose wit and 'natural gaiety of character', though often taken for levity, went along with 'intrinsic higher qualities'.[104] In his journal Carlyle recalled first walking with the boy Charles 'six and twenty years ago round the root of Salisbury Crags at Edinburgh'.[105]

A few weeks later Carlyle was once more musing in his journal on life and death, this time his own:

[Erasmus] Darwin said to Jane, the other day, in his quizzing-serious manner, 'Who will write Carlyle's Life?' – The word, reported to me, set me thinking how impossible it was, and would forever remain, for any creature to write my 'Life'; the *chief* elements of my little destiny have all along lain deep below view of surmise, and never will or can be known to any Son of Adam. I would say to my Biographer, if any fool undertook such a task, 'Forbear, poor fool; let no Life of *me* be written; let me and my bewildered wrestlings be buried here, and be forgotten swiftly of all the world. If thou write, it will be mere delusions and hallucinations.'[106]

As time went on, Carlyle realised that he would inevitably be the subject of biography, however much he hated the idea. He preserved a huge mass of materials, thus making himself, paradoxically, probably the most co-operative biographical subject in history. Not that this makes his 'bewildered wrestlings' a simple matter to record and analyse; his 'little destiny' retains its mysteries and impenetrable elements as much as any life, however poorly documented in comparison.

★

If 1848 was the year of revolution, 1849 was the year of fallout from revolution. In December 1848 Louis Napoleon, nephew of Napoleon Bonaparte, was elected President of France, defeating the more radical General Cavaignac, brother of Godefroi, of whom Jane had been so fond. Various socialist members of the provisional government, including their leader Louis Blanc, fled to England, and in due course turned up at Cheyne Row.[107] In February 1849 Mazzini became one of a triumvirate which declared a Roman Republic – the other two were Aurelio Saffi and Carlo Armellini – the Pope having fled to Naples. Their triumph over the papacy and Austria was short-lived. By July they had been evicted from Rome by a French force pledged by Louis Napoleon to restore the Pope. Jane followed Mazzini's rise and fall eagerly: 'Poor dear Mazzini – all my affection for him has waked up since I knew him in jeopardy and so gallantly fulfilling his destiny', she wrote to Jeannie on 17 May.[108]

In April Clough set off for Rome to witness the new Republic, as he had gone to Paris the previous year. His most famous poetical work, *Amours de Voyage*, published later in the year, drew on his experiences. He carried with him a cigar case for Mazzini from the Carlyles. Before he left, he told Carlyle about his friend and fellow Oxford doubter, J. A. Froude. 'This heretic F', Carlyle reported to Jane, had recently escaped to Devon to stay with his friend Charles Kingsley.[109] Froude, whom Carlyle met for the first time in June, had caused a furore at Oxford by publishing, in February, *The Nemesis of Faith*, a painfully autobiographical novel about the loss of belief in the Thirty-Nine Articles by a young man on the brink of taking orders.

Being written by a fellow of Exeter College, the book was bound to cause a fuss in Oxford and church circles because of its honest expression of religious doubt, or at least doubt about the doctrines of the Anglican Church. Since Froude also borrowed an adulterous plot involving the neglect and death of a child directly from Goethe's novel *Elective Affinities* (*Die Wahlverwandtschaften*, 1809), the scandal was complete. 'Oxford grows rapidly too hot for me', Froude told Clough on 28 February. 'I have *resigned*. I was *preached* against Sunday in Chapel, denounced in Hall, and yesterday *burnt* publicly.'[110] (That is, his book was burnt by the college authorities.)

Froude fled to Devon before he could be dismissed. The burning of the book was the talk of Oxford and beyond.[111] Kingsley, his robust clerical friend, thought Froude foolish to publish:

There are spiritual as well as physical diarrhoeas. And a man is better after them – having got rid of so much wh did his intestines no good. Nevertheless, if he chooses to have the diarrhoea in public, as Froude had – he must take the consequences of so offending the public nose.[112]

Carlyle, who seems to have read the novel, or at least heard enough about it to express an opinion, also responded in terms of bodily functions when writing to John Forster on 4 April:

Froude's Book is not, – except for wretched people, strangling in white neckcloths, and Semitic thrums [loose threads], – worth its paper and ink. What on Earth is the use of a wretched mortal's vomiting up all his interior crudities, dubitations, and spiritual agonising belly-aches, into the view of the Public, and howling tragically, 'See!' Let him, in the Devil's name, pass them, by the downward or other methods, in his own water-closet, and say nothing whatever![113]

In his biography Froude expressed his gratitude to Carlyle for having saved him, by his writings, 'from Positivism, or Romanism, or Atheism, or any other of the creeds or no creeds which in those years were whirling us about in Oxford like leaves in an autumn storm'. He also recalled, though without going into detail, the episode of *The Nemesis of Faith*, which changed the course of his life, and the first face-to-face meeting with Carlyle which followed soon after its publication:

I had written something, not wisely, in which heterodoxy was flavoured with the sentimentalism [i.e. sensualism] which he so intensely detested. He had said of me that I ought to burn my own smoke, and not trouble other people's nostrils with it. Nevertheless, he was willing to see what I was like. James Spedding [Froude's cousin] took me down to Cheyne Row one evening in the middle of June. We found him sitting after dinner, with his pipe, in the small flagged court between the house and the garden.[114]

Froude remembered the impression made on him by this first sight of Carlyle:

He was then fifty-four; tall (about five feet eleven), thin, but at that time upright, with no signs of the later stoop. His body was angular, his face beardless . . . His head was extremely long, with the chin thrust forward; the neck was thin; the mouth firmly closed, the under lip slightly projecting; the hair grizzled and thick and bushy. His eyes, which grew lighter with age, were then of a deep violet, with fire burning at the bottom of them, which flashed out at the least excitement. The face was altogether more striking, most impressive every way. And I did not admire him the less because he treated me – I cannot say unkindly, but shortly and sternly. I saw then what I saw ever after – that no one need look for conventional politeness from Carlyle – he would hear the exact truth from him, and nothing else.

As for Jane:

Her features were not regular, but I thought I had never seen a more interesting-looking woman. Her hair was raven black, her eyes dark, soft, sad, with dangerous light in them. Carlyle's talk was rich, full, and scornful; hers delicately mocking. She was fond of Spedding, and kept up a quick, sparkling conversation with him, telling stories at her husband's expense, at which he laughed himself as heartily as we did.[115]

Both Froude and Clough had now resigned their fellowships and left Oxford because of their religious difficulties. On 19 April Carlyle linked them to his old friend John Sterling when he summed up the signs of the times for Emerson:

Clough has gone to Italy; I have seen him twice, – could not manage his *hexameters*, tho' I like the man himself, and hope much of him. 'Infidelity' has broken out in Oxford itself, – immense emotion in certain quarters in consequence, virulent outcries about a certain 'Sterling Club', altogether a *secular* Society![116]

The Club had been founded in Sterling's lifetime; Sterling's clerical friends J. C. Hare, F. D. Maurice, R. C. Trench, and others met to dine and to discuss religious and philosophical subjects. In 1848 Hare, now Archdeacon of Lewes in Sussex, had published Sterling's *Essays and Tales* with an introductory biographical memoir, in which he regretted Sterling's reading of German biblical criticism and coming under intellectual influences which undermined his faith and turned him away from his vocation. Despite the orthodoxy of Hare's position, his memoir and the activities of the Club attracted the disapproval of several religious newspapers, which attacked the sympathetic commemoration of an 'infidel'. Mill wrote to Harriet Taylor that his own name and Carlyle's had been dragged into the controversy as mentors who were 'strongly suspected of being no better than infidels themselves'. What the furore showed, Mill thought, was that it 'required some courage in a church dignitary to write about a heretic even in the guarded way that Hare did'.[117]

Carlyle, who was, with Hare, Sterling's literary executor, had been too busy with *Cromwell* to discuss with him how best to present Sterling's life and work to the public. He now began to be persuaded, partly by his conscience, partly by Hare's memoir, and partly by the Sterling Club controversy, that he should write something himself. Early in 1851 he finally began work on a full biography of his friend.

Relations with Sterling's brother Anthony were renewed at this time. Jane told Jeannie in January 1849 that his monomaniacal wife had got into a 'horrid state in Rome and *exposed her person* before the male servants', and that Anthony now wished to live with his children in a separate establishment from her. 'You may fancy the little domestic *hell* of all this! – a little of "the new ideas" might really be introduced into English life with benefit', she added, alluding to the divorce laws and Amely Bölte's enthusiasm for the comparative freedom of divorce in Germany.[118] A week or so later Jane reported that Mrs Sterling had visited her with 'meek and brave words of apology' for her jealousy, a gesture much admired by Jane, who wished she could reconcile the Sterlings, though their case seemed hopeless – 'Anthony and she grate on each other like a couple of files'.[119]

Jane's relations with her own husband appear to have been quiet and not unharmonious during the spring round of socialising. They dined at the Ashburtons' London home, and on 12 May they attended a large dinner party at Dickens's house to meet Mrs Gaskell, who was on a visit to London. Jane describes the opulence of the event:

The dinner was served up in the new fashion – not placed on the table at all – but handed round – only the des[s]ert on the table and quantities of *artificial* flowers, but such an overloaded des[s]ert! – pyramids of figs raisins oranges – ach! – At the Ashburton dinner served on that principle there were just *four cowslips* in china-pots – four silver shells containing sweets, and a silver filigree temple in the middle! but here the very candles rose each out of an artificial rose! Good God![120]

Jane liked Mrs Gaskell, thinking her a 'natural unassuming woman, whom they have been doing their best to spoil by making a *lioness* of her'. Elizabeth Gaskell's own account of the Dickens dinner lists the guests, who included Forster, Thackeray, and Samuel Rogers – 'the old poet, who is 86, and looked very unfit to be in such a large party' – and speaks of Jane telling amusing stories about her servant. This was not, as might be expected, the redoubtable Helen Mitchell, who had returned from Ireland and been re-engaged by Jane, only to be dismissed in February 1849 after answering the door drunk and looking like 'a very ill got up stage-ghost'.[121] The servant in question was Ann Cook, who had been hired in 1835 and fired in 1837, but had amused her master and mistress in between with her broad Scots accent and inability to stand on ceremony. Mrs Gaskell retells Jane's story:

I sat next to Mrs Carlyle, who amused me very much with her account of their only servant who comes from Annandale in Scotland, and had never been accustomed to announce titles; so when Count Pepoli called she announced him as Mr Compilloly; Lord Jeffrey as Lorcherfield; and simply repeated it louder & louder each time; till at last Mrs Carlyle said 'What is it – man, woman, or beast?' to which the servant answered 'a little wee gentleman, Ma'am'.[122]

Old Rogers, unfit though he appeared to Mrs Gaskell, was lively (and spiteful) enough to cause Jane annoyance and embarrassment at Dickens's party, as she told Jeannie:

[He] said to me pointing to a chair beside him, 'sit down my Dear – I want to ask you; is your Husband as much infatuated as ever with Lady Ashburton?' – 'Oh of course – I said *laughing*, 'why shouldn't he?' – 'Now – do *you* like her – tell me honestly is she kind to *you* – as kind as she is to your husband?' – 'Why you know it is impossible for *me* to know *how* kind she is to my husband – but I *can* say she is extremely kind to *me* and I should be stupid and ungrateful if I did *not* like her' – 'Humph! (disappointedly) Well! it is very good of you to like her when she takes away all your husbands company from you – he is always there isn't he?' – 'Oh good gracious no! (still laughing *admirably*) he writes and reads a great deal in his own study' – 'But he spends all his evenings with her I am told?' – 'No – not all – for example you see he is *here* this evening.' – 'Yes he said in a tone of vexation I *see* he is here *this* evening – and *hear* him too – for he has done nothing but talk across the room since he came in' – Very devilish old man! but he got no satisfaction to his devilishness out of *me*.[123]

Good for Jane, we may think, while noting that, over-sensitive as she undoubtedly was, Carlyle's 'infatuation' with Lady Ashburton was now a matter of gossip.

Though she was proud of having kept up appearances on this occasion, Jane was still a prey to the misery of jealousy, as well as terrible headaches; she was swallowing large numbers of quinine powders, as she told Jeannie on 15 June, on the grounds that it was worth trying '*any thing* to stop that horrid sensation of dying always'.[124] It is impossible to know for sure whether Jane took reckless amounts of medicines, or whether indeed she was even addicted to opium in some form, as has been suggested.[125] Certainly her symptoms are compatible with addiction and withdrawal, mechanisms not fully understood in the mid-nineteenth century, when doctors still prescribed opiates freely. When Caroline Fox visited Cheyne Row at this time, Jane 'talked in rather a melancholy way of herself and of life in general', and described dosing herself with morphine.[126]

★

Jane was preparing herself mentally for her first visit to Scotland since her mother's death in 1842, finally deciding at the end of June that she would go, travelling alone and by stages, stopping off at Haddington, then going on to Kirkcaldy, where her cousin Walter Welsh was now a minister, and where Jeannie was already on a visit.[127] She had just finished sitting to two portrait painters, Amely Bölte's friend Carl Hartmann, and Samuel Laurence, whom Anthony Sterling had secretly commissioned, not daring to tell either Jane or his wife that he was the instigator, though Jane guessed: 'I think I know *who* is fool enough to be up to giving fifteen guineas for a sketch of my faded *charms*'.[128] Lady Ashburton pronounced the Laurence picture 'the horridest thing she had ever seen', just like 'a poor old starved *rabbit!*' – which piece of honest malice Jane reported without comment to Carlyle, who had gone to Dublin on a second Irish visit.[129]

Off she went on her adventure. She wrote from Nottingham, where she was staying with a German admirer of Carlyle, Joseph Neuberg, to John Carlyle, towards whom she felt warmer than usual, since he was taking her headaches seriously. 'Dearest John', she wrote, teasing him about Neuberg's sister, whom she intended that he should marry, a theme she pursued in her letters to him during her journey, fearing that he would 'dawdle' and 'squander away Miss Neuberg like all the other young women you have cast a practical eye on'.[130] Her next stop was with W. E. Forster in Yorkshire, where the Paulets were also staying. Jane told Carlyle with comic petulance that Mrs Paulet was flirting very obviously with the desirable Forster. 'William Edward', she wrote, 'is no longer the devoted *Squire of Dames* he was; but *the Squire of ONE Dame* and that *one* is not *me*'.[131]

She eagerly attended a meeting held in Bradford to press for 'Roman Liberty', at which Forster spoke against papal misgovernance and the interference of France in Mazzini's fledgling Republic. Jane gave her name and address to a working man who spoke from the platform. She told Carlyle that the man, on looking at the name, squeezed her hand and said, 'Mr Carlyle has been my teacher and Master – I have owed everything to him for years and years!' Upon which she comments meaningfully, 'I *felt* it a credit to you really to have had a hand in *turning out* this man – was prouder of that heart-tribute to your genius than of any amount of Reviewer praises or of aristocratic invitations to dinner'.[132] Thus she wrapped an undoubtedly genuine compliment round a core of resentment at Carlyle's fondness for accepting invitations from one member of the aristocracy in particular.

On 25 July Jane arrived in her home town of Haddington, staying incognito at the George Inn. It had taken her fancy, as she explained to John Carlyle, to play the part of 'Stranger at the Inn', and to walk out to see her old house, the school where she had been top of the class, the church, and her father's grave in the churchyard.[133] She also wrote, for her own benefit, an account of her brief stay as a ghost, or 'mystery lady', which she entitled 'Much ado about Nothing', and about which Carlyle knew nothing until he found it when going through her papers in August 1866, a few months after her death. While revisiting her old haunts she came across an old man who recognised her and confirmed her as the worthy heroine of her own story by saying, 'The minute I set eyes on ye at the *George*, I *jaloosed* [suspected] it was *her* we all looked after whenever she went up or down.' A local shopkeeper told her that Dr Welsh's death was 'the sorest loss ever cam to the Place', and that his daughter 'went away into England and – died there!' He added, as she notes, 'a handsome enough tribute to my memory'. She picked up where her old tomboy self had left off forty years before by climbing over the seven-foot-high wall of the locked churchyard to see her father's grave.[134] And one last encounter found her disclosing her identity to a shopkeeper, who asked how many children she had: 'None, I told him. "None!" (in a tone of astonishment, verging on horror) "None at all! then what on the Earth had I been *doing* all this time?" "Amusing myself", I told him.'[135]

While Jane was undertaking her emotionally important Scottish journey, Carlyle was renewing his acquaintance with Ireland, visiting Lord Clarendon's residence out of politeness, but glad of an excuse to refuse a dinner invitation which Clarendon had issued reluctantly, as he made clear in a letter to Lord John Russell towards the end of Carlyle's visit:

Duffy accompanied by that double-barrelled coxcomb Carlyle has been perambulating the provinces collecting abuses and I believe has met with considerable success which proves that the apprehensions about [Duffy's] pestilent paper are not unfounded.[136]

Carlyle told Jane that he was being 'killed with "attentions" here' (in Dublin), and that he had nearly wept on seeing the skull of Esther Johnson, Swift's 'Stella', which was preserved in the University Museum.[137] He wrote politely to Clarendon – whom he hoped to influence but only succeeded in irritating – telling him frankly that Ireland 'painfully represents itself to me as a country scourged by angry gods', and urging Clarendon to do something to save the situation.[138] He then set off with Duffy on his month's 'perambulations', spending some time with Edward FitzGerald's brother in County Kildare and noticing everywhere he went 'winged flights of migratory beggars'.[139] In Cork he was visited by Father O'Shea, the early admirer of *Sartor*.[140]

Having spent a month 'roam[ing] extensively over this unfortunate Ireland', Carlyle wrote honestly, if naively, to Clarendon, suggesting a new diversity in crop-growing to avert the total catastrophe caused by potato blight, and assuring him that Duffy was a man of 'intrinsic worth' whose opinions and popularity could be of use to Clarendon (who was all the while manoeuvring to neutralise Duffy's influence).[141] Carlyle met one Irish landlord of whom he could approve, Lord George Hill, in whose family Jane's friend and protégé Plattnauer was employed as tutor. Lord George was 'courteous as an ancient chevalier', and benevolent in a paternalistic way towards the tenants of his estate.[142]

Carlyle crossed from Ireland to Glasgow, joining Jane in Kirkcaldy after a quick visit to his seventy-eight-year-old mother at Scotsbrig. The couple were soon arguing again over Carlyle's determination to travel on to the Highlands, where the Ashburtons were on holiday. Jane refused to accompany him, going home to Chelsea instead. As he had done three years before, Carlyle took refuge from Jane's withering anger and his own conscience by telling her how miserable he was when he got there. His strategy – which never worked – was to seek her sympathy with his torn nerves and sleeplessness, and to complain of the incessant rain, the enforced idleness, the other guests, and the sheer folly of Lord Ashburton in paying £500 for two months at such a 'wretched' establishment as the one he had rented in Kingussie.[143]

Once more Jane responded first by silence, then in a letter without salutation at beginning or end, in which she emphasised the kindness and sympathy she had received from her old Haddington servant Betty Braid, now living in Edinburgh.[144] Carlyle continued stubbornly to report his doings. By the end of September they were together again in Cheyne Row, Jane taking large doses of morphine to combat sleeplessness.[145]

Dickens's *David Copperfield* was appearing serially throughout 1849. Both Carlyles read the numbers as they came out, and Carlyle was later reported to have pleased Dickens at the dinner party in May by replying to questions about his health in the words of Mrs Gummidge from the third chapter of the novel; he was, he said, 'a lone lorn creetur and everythink goes contrary with me'.[146] This was gracious, but Carlyle's indifference to the fictional genius of his contemporaries was in evidence in a letter to Jack in October, in which he described a recent number of *David Copperfield* – Dickens's 'present series of funambulisms', as he called it – as 'innocent wateriest twaddle with a *suspicion* of geniality'. For good measure he added that 'poor Thackeray' had been dangerously ill, reportedly from 'too diligent a course of dinners', and had had to suspend his current serialisation, 'his *Pendennis* nonsense', which, according to Carlyle, 'everybody says he had better give up, the total, and even tiresome inanity of it being palpable to all creatures'.[147]

The great spate of novels continued, regardless of Carlyle's gloomy disapprobation. In November Jane was 'wholly occupied' in reading Charlotte Brontë's *Shirley*, which she had borrowed from the London Library. 'You see', she explained comically to Jeannie, 'I get the credit with certain CRITICS IN STYLE of writing these Jane Eyre books myself – and I was curious to know whether the new one was up to my reputation!' Not only that, but Anthony Sterling had told her that the heroine 'was so ridiculously like myself that the Author must have drawn it from me feature by feature – I was curious to know what he thought ridiculously like "me" – and have reason to be satisfied! especially with the *age* of my likeness'.[148] Shirley Keeldar is a spirited, independent-minded young heiress, with whom Jane might well like to see herself compared. She asked John Forster if he knew the real name of the mysterious 'Currer Bell'.[149]

On 13 November Dickens and Forster attended the double hanging of Frederick and Maria Manning, whose trial for murder and mutual incriminations had held the country spellbound since August. Dickens wrote to *The Times* describing his horror at the disgraceful behaviour of the crowd and pleading for the discontinuation of public hangings.[150] The Carlyles followed the case in the newspapers along with everyone else. Jane collected illustrations of the murderous couple, telling Jeannie on 2 December that Londoners had talked of nothing else for months, and 'even now that they are got well hanged out of the road, "additional particulars" are turning up daily'. She added a particular of her own: 'I will send you their pictures. *Maria* has a strange likeness to (never tell it) – Lady Ashburton!'[151]

Fired by his visit to Ireland, Carlyle was again writing on social issues. His *Latter-Day Pamphlets* were to appear in eight numbers between February and August 1850, on the serialisation method borrowed from the novelists. He had been reading Henry Mayhew's celebrated articles on London labour and the London poor as they came out in the *Morning Chronicle*, and Carlyle drew from the horrors of Mayhew's investigations proof for his own distrust of so-called political economy and the free trade and *laissez-faire* views of such writers as Richard Cobden and John McCulloch. 'Last night I read *five* old *Chronicle* Newspapers', he told John Forster on 28 November. They dealt with 'prostitute Needlewomen, Miners &c &c – terrible proof to me once more that the Gospel according to Macculloch' and 'the sublime doctrine of Salvation by Freetrade *with* Nihilism and Laissez-fai[re] have been weighed in the balance and found *wanting*'.[152]

These new writings of Carlyle's marked a dip in his popularity and in the respect in which he was held by his peers. The reason can be found partly in the fact that his own example had helped to bring forth other labourers in the vineyard, serious commentators like Mayhew as well as socially concerned novelists such as Dickens, Disraeli, Mrs Gaskell, and Kingsley. In addition, though, his satire had become excessively scornful and his prophecy increasingly doom-laden. His novelty now had an air of *déjà vu*; he had become for the reading public a caricature of himself.

At home, Jane found some relief in the arrival of a new companion. A young Greek acquaintance in Manchester, Stavros Dilberoglue, sent her a little mongrel dog, whom she called Nero. She told John Carlyle on 10 December that he followed her about like a shadow and slept at the foot of her bed without disturbing her; it was 'a comfort to have something alive and cheery and fond of me always there'. To John Forster, with whom she was always somewhat confessional, she marvelled at Nero's success with Carlyle:

Mr C has accepted it with an amiability! – to be sure when he comes down gloomy in the mornings, or comes in wearied from his walk the infatuated little beast dances round him on its hind legs as *I* ought to do and can't, and he feels flattered and surprised by such unwonted capers to his honour and glory.[153]

CHAPTER 13

Courting Controversy 1850–1852

As a 'small Pilot Engine' to the *Latter-Day Pamphlets*, Carlyle published an essay, 'Occasional Discourse on the Negro Question', in *Fraser's Magazine* in December 1849.[1] It caused an outcry, not at all to Carlyle's surprise. 'All and sundry are astonished, enraged &c, which really is the only thing one could expect or even wish', he told his brother James on 20 January 1850.[2] The essay, which Carlyle reprinted, with additions, as a sixpenny pamphlet in 1853,[3] is an intemperate attack addressed to 'my Philanthropic Friends' the members of the 'Universal Abolition-of-Pain Association', who are 'sunk' so deep in 'froth-oceans' of 'Benevolence', 'Emancipation-principle', 'Christian Philanthropy', and a general 'rose-pink Sentimentalism', that they concern themselves with 'the Negro Question' at the expense of looking at poverty and injustice at home and in neighbouring Ireland.[4]

The sugar plantations of the West Indies had employed 'free' labour since the abolition of slavery there, while Cuba and Brazil were still slave states. Agitators were calling for abolition in the latter countries, and also pointing out the economic unfreedom of those in the West Indies who were nominally no longer slaves, a claim which Carlyle ignored. His point about abuses at home is a fair one, picked up by Dickens in *Bleak House*, in which Mrs Jellyby is the prime example of 'telescopic philanthropy', so intent is she on helping 'the natives of Borrioboola-Gha, on the left bank of the Niger', that she criminally neglects her own children in an over-crowded district at the heart of London.[5] However, Carlyle's rhetoric, unlike Dickens's, is not confined to the home end of what both men felt was misplaced benevolence. His description of the freed black sugar-workers is unpleasant: 'Our beautiful Black darlings are at last happy; with little labour except to the teeth, *which* surely, in those excellent horse-jaws of theirs, will not fail!' He pictures them 'sitting yonder with their beautiful muzzles up to the ears in pumpkins', too lazy to work and letting the sugar crops 'rot round them'. The indignation on behalf of the British and Irish poor, so movingly expressed in *Past and Present*, is now yoked in a repetitive contrast of 'there' and 'here' – 'beautiful Blacks sitting there up to the ears in pumpkins, and doleful Whites sitting here without potatoes to eat'.[6]

There follows a rant about 'the gods' decreeing that the black man's chief 'right' is the 'indisputable and perpetual *right* to be compelled' by white landowners to 'do competent work for his living'. Exploiting his gift for naming, Carlyle employs the already widely used generic name 'Quashee' for his typical idle, brutish black man, claiming that it is right and proper for 'Quashee' to be 'hired for life'.[7] Though Carlyle's language, so rich, strange, and vehement, marks him out among nineteenth-century observers and students of race and civilisation, his frankly racist attitude was by no means unique. His view that different races are nearly equivalent to different species, and his belief in the moral and intellectual superiority of certain races over others, was shared by large numbers of his contemporaries.

Chief among these was Robert Knox, the Edinburgh surgeon of Burke and Hare fame, known to have dissected bodies brought to him by the murderers before they were arrested and punished in 1829, and widely suspected of being complicit in the murders –

> Burke's the butcher, Hare's the thief,
> Knox the boy that buys the beef

as a popular ballad of the early 1830s crudely put it.[8] Knox had lectured in various British cities on 'The Races of Men'; in 1850 he published a paper of the same title, reprinting it with additional chapters in 1862 as *The Races of Men: A Philosophical Enquiry into the Influence of Race over the Destinies of Nations*. By then Darwin's *Origin of Species* (1859) had encouraged Knox to consider different races as different species, though Darwin himself draws no such conclusion.

The Ethnological Society, founded in 1843, was full of scientists and travellers whose study of primitivism, cannibalism, and miscegenation – a term for the mixture of races, particularly white with 'Negro', or Afro-Caribbean, which seems to have been first used in 1864[9] – started from the view, generally accepted by a confident imperialist nation, that white people, especially the British, were demonstrably superior to black.[10] Carlyle's views on race, although politically controversial, were widely shared. When in October 1865 the Governor of Jamaica put down a native insurrection with hundreds of summary hangings and floggings, opinion at home was polarised. Mill, supported by liberals and progressive scientists such as Darwin, Huxley, Lewes, and Herbert Spencer, led the attempt to have Governor Eyre prosecuted, while Carlyle was joined on the Eyre Defence Committee by Kingsley and Ruskin, with support from their fellow 'romantic authoritarians' Tennyson and Dickens.[11]

Carlyle's ferocity on the subject of race was only one expression of his fierce mood in 1850. An insight into his state of mind is given by a comment to his sister Jean in January on the article's reception – a 'universal barking' from 'all the dogs of the Parish', especially the 'poor scraggy critics of the "benevolent" school'. He prophesied that the *Latter-Day Pamphlets*, the first of which was about to appear, would add to the uproar, and he felt defiant:

All the twaddling *sects* of the country, from Swedenborgians to Jesuits, have for the last ten years been laying claim to 'T. Carlyle' each for itself and now they will all find that the said 'T.' belongs to a sect of his own, which is worthy of instant damnation.[12]

Carlyle's bad-tempered outburst may well have been an expression of his realisation that he had not really had much practical influence on public and political affairs, despite being so widely known and respected. Froude recalled that Carlyle later told him he had thought of standing for Parliament at the time of *Latter-Day Pamphlets*.[13] If so, he soon saw that he had not the health, the temperament, or the power base for it. His role, carved out by himself with such difficulty and determination against early poverty and obscurity, had been, and was to remain, that of the warning, prophetic voice of his age. Though he knew his *Latter-Day Pamphlets* would offend, he pressed ahead with the one mode he knew of influencing his contemporaries.

His supplementary role, that of conversational pugilist, was also continued at full tilt. Thackeray told James Spedding on 5 January 1850 how he had coincided with Carlyle at a dinner party two weeks earlier, at which Henry Reeve, Sarah Austin's nephew and a diplomat and miscellaneous writer, was a fellow guest:

[Carlyle] fell foul of Reeve, who had a stiff white neckcloth, wh. probably offended the Seer. He tossed Reeve and gored yea as a bull he chased and horned him: for an hour or more he pitched about him ripping open his bowels and plunging his muzzle into Reeves smoking entrails.[14]

To Lady Ashburton Thackeray reported on the same occasion, and also on Carlyle's amusing comments at a dinner Thackeray himself gave on Christmas Day 1849:

At my house he said that Genius was universal & could be anything if it had a mind to, & when I asked whether he could dance like Taglioni or sing ravishingly or paint like Landseer upon the whole he was rather inclined to think that he could – about wh. some people may have their doubts. But the very errors and vagaries of Men of Genius are rich and instructive.[15]

The very first attack on the 'Occasional Discourse' came from Carlyle's former friend and disciple Mill, who replied in *Fraser's* in January 1850 that slavery was to be deplored on grounds not of 'rosepink Sentimentalism' but of plain justice. Carlyle expressed surprise that this 'most shrill, thin, poor and insignificant' attack was by Mill, telling himself in his journal that Mill's withdrawal from 'reverent discipleship' to take on 'the function of getting up to contradict whatever I say' was without visible cause.[16]

Undaunted, Carlyle proceeded to publish his *Pamphlets* monthly between February and August. The first, 'The Present Time', analyses the contemporary situation, treating the 1848 revolutions as an important cleansing of the Augean stables of Europe, leading to the welcome (if temporary in some cases) removal of 'Sham-Kings'. But if monarchism has become a parody of itself, democracy, according to Carlyle, is a dangerous chimera. He is withering about the democratic solution offered by 'all the world':

All the world answers me, 'Count heads; ask Universal Suffrage, by the ballot-boxes, and that will tell.' Universal suffrage? ballotboxes, count of heads? Well – I perceive we have got into strange spiritual latitudes indeed. Within the last century or so, either the Universe or else the heads of men must have altered very much.

Moreover, if anyone should 'brag to me of America, and its model institutions and constitutions', that person should 'cease' immediately. What use is there in men sitting 'idly *caucusing* and ballotboxing on the graves of their heroic ancestors'? What have they achieved? 'They have begotten', replies his old *alter ego* Smelfungus, 'with a rapidity beyond recorded example, Eighteen Millions of the greatest *bores* ever seen in this world before'.[17] This last knockabout insult in an essay full of burlesque and loose satire brought down on Carlyle – whose patience had been sorely tried by not millions, but certainly dozens, of American visitors who came to stare at him – retribution from more than one outraged American critic.[18]

This pamphlet sets the tone for the other seven, 'Model Prisons', 'Downing Street', 'The New Downing Street', 'Stump-Orator', 'Parliaments', 'Hudson's Statue', and 'Jesuitism'. They contain the familiar call for a wise and great governor, the usual distrust of democracy, the ridicule of socialist or revolutionary solutions, the warnings against new sham 'kings' like George Hudson, the millionaire speculator in railway shares who had been proved a fraud – all expressed in the utterly Carlylean rhetoric of comic disdain. Phallus-Worship reappears, as does the 'Gospel according to George Sand'. Where in *Past and Present* he had used Morison's Pill as the type of the illusory panacea, in 'The New Downing Street' Carlyle introduces 'Godfrey's Cordial', a solution of opium and treacle given to children, in a similar role. The whole series ends with a mock catechism, 'Pig Philosophy', in which Carlyle indicts contemporary

Christianity by collapsing it into one with his (and its) old enemy Utilitarianism, the philosophy of the 'greatest happiness of the greatest number'. The 'articles' of the pig creed include the following:

Moral evil is unattainability of Pig's-wash; moral good attainability of ditto . . . It is the mission of universal Pighood, and the duty of all Pigs, at all times, to diminish the quantity of unattainable and increase that of attainable.[19]

There are some fine moments in this least attractive of Carlyle's works, as when he refers to the Foreign Secretary, Palmerston, as 'Hercules-Harlequin, the Attorney Triumphant, the World's Busybody', and characterises parliamentary government as 'a settlement effected between the Honourable Mr This and the Honourable Mr That, as to their respective pretensions to ride the high horse'.[20] Carlyle draws on a huge range of reference, from the Bible to topical gossip, from Plato to Goethe, yet, as Emerson justly observed when summing up the *Pamphlets*, 'tis curious the magnificence of his genius & the poverty of his aims'.[21]

The falling off was noticed by friends and critics alike. FitzGerald wrote to Frederick Tennyson in April:

Do you see Carlyle's 'Latter-Day Pamphlets'? They make the world laugh, and his friends rather sorry for him. But that is because people will still look for practical measures from him: one must be content with him as a great satirist who can make us feel when we are wrong though he cannot set us right.[22]

Thomas Spedding wrote thoughtfully to Carlyle himself in May, agreeing that 'men are mostly blockheads', but asking:

1st with respect to the world, if it is God's world and not the Devil's, why should it be thought to be going always towards the Devil?
And 2dly, with respect to Government, why should the government of the wisest be held indispensable in the world, when throughout the world's history it has in point of fact never been the rule, but only the exception?

Carlyle replied amicably but implacably, and with no attempt to answer Spedding's questions:

I find Zion, this Zion of ours, a most delectable Devil's Dungheap built as high as the very stars over all of us, which calls on every son of Heaven to fire redhot shot thro' it, according to ability! With or without shot, I see it shaking towards rapid destruction now, and believe the *Abyss* will get it in one form or other before many years, – and carry Russell along with it: that is my comfort.[23]

On 12 April Lord John Russell, butt of a Carlylean joke in 'Downing Street', made a wry reference to the pamphlet in a House of Commons debate. He defended official salaries against the criticisms of 'a very clever but whimsical writer of the day', according to whom 'the public offices were an Augean stable which required a Hercules to cleanse out'.[24]

Russell's administration was struggling in spring 1850, and Peel was ready to come in with a new Tory government. Carlyle had changed his view of Peel since caricaturing him as 'Sir Jabesh Windbag' in *Past and Present*; in 'The New Downing Street', published on 15 April, he went so far as to express the hope that Peel would soon come to power.[25] On 25 May he sat next to Peel at a dinner at Bath House, commenting in his journal that he had found him 'fresh and hearty' and 'a kindly man'.[26]

When Peel died unexpectedly on 2 July after falling from his horse on Constitution Hill, Carlyle was moved to sorrow, and also to the realisation that any slight hope he himself might have harboured of gaining public office – through Lord Ashburton, a close colleague of Peel – was now well and truly dashed. He mused in his journal the day after Peel's death:

I myself have said nothing: hardly know what to think – feel only in general that I have now no hope of peaceable improvement for this country; that the one statesman we had, or the least similitude of a statesman so far as I know or can guess, is suddenly snatched away from us.[27]

Meanwhile the public response to the first few *Pamphlets* was mainly hostile, though often also polite and even indulgent because of Carlyle's earlier writings and reputation. *Punch* carried a mock 'trial' at the court of Mr Punch on 16 March, at which Carlyle was charged with 'being unable to take care of his own literary reputation – a very first-rate reputation until a few months past', but now, 'in consequence of the reckless and alarming conduct of the accused, in a most dangerous condition'. This decline was first to be seen when Carlyle was detected 'running wildly up and down the pages of *Fraser's Magazine*, pelting all sorts of gibberish at the heads of Jamaica niggers', and was now observable in the 'barking and froth' of the *Latter-Day Pamphlets*. *Punch* concluded that Carlyle should no longer be trusted with 'such dangerous weapons' as pen and ink. A few weeks later, on 6 April, after the publication of 'Downing Street', *Punch* produced a cartoon captioned 'A "Latter-Day" Nightmare, brought on by Reading Thomas Carlyle his Pamphlets'. It shows Carlyle, with staring eye and jutting lower lip, pointing gloomily at a tiny Lord John Russell and an elaborately curled Disraeli, with Carlylean phrases like 'Supreme Quack', 'Solemn Sham', and 'Phantasm Captain' strewn around, and 'Quashee' playing a banjo in the background.[28]

'Model Prisons', published in March, was the *Pamphlet* which attracted most attention. Carlyle describes the comfort and cleanliness of prisoners in one of the new model prisons, Tothill Fields in Westminster, which he had visited in February 1849 with Jane and Forster.[29] There he had seen 'notable murderesses' and others living a life free from 'the world and its cares', while outside the law-abiding poor struggled in squalor. He regrets the passing of the treadmill, and interprets the will of 'the gods', namely that the 'abject ape, wolf, ox, imp and other diabolic-animal specimens of humanity' should have 'a collar round the neck, and a cartwhip flourished over the back', treatment which would put them on a par, in fact, with the wretched ex-slaves of the West Indies.[30]

Carlyle's excesses here – 'barking and froth', in *Punch*'s words – called forth expressions of disappointment, though several commentators agreed with his main point about the injustice of 'coddling' criminals while neglecting the plight of the virtuous poor. Dickens responded directly to this point at the end of *David Copperfield*, the last number of which was published in November 1850. The hero visits a new model prison, built at 'vast expense' on the principle that 'there was nothing in the world to be legitimately taken into account but the supreme comfort of prisoners, at any expense, and nothing on the wide earth to be done outside prison-doors'.[31] Dickens gave further public expression to his agreement with Carlyle about the prison system in his own weekly newspaper, *Household Words*, begun in March 1850 to air social and political subjects. One of the early numbers, on 27 April, carried an article called 'Pet Prisoners', attacking the expense and comparative luxury of model prisons.[32]

Another new Saturday paper, the *Leader*, was begun at the same time, edited by G. H. Lewes and his friend Thornton Hunt, son of Leigh Hunt. More radical than *Household Words* in politics, it covered many of the same subjects. The first issue, on 30 March, included in the back half, under the heading 'Literature', Lewes's review of the third *Pamphlet*, just out, 'Downing Street'. The *Pamphlets*, he says, are '*the* talk of the day', and though many deplore them, all admire Carlyle as 'a fierce worshipper of truth'. He is, writes Lewes, 'the Cicero of 1850'.[33]

Carlyle, who had made a rare visit to the theatre in February to see Lewes's tragedy, *The Noble Heart*, at the Olympic Theatre,[34] welcomed the *Leader*. As he explained to his sister Jean on 26 April:

The Paper has a *socialist* tendency (it is understood) but they keep that under hatches pretty well. Leigh Hunt's eldest son, a really clever, little brown-skinned man, and true as steel in his way, is Editor, he and a certain *dramatic* G. H. Lewes, an *airy* loose-tongued merry hearted being, with more sail than ballast – they, on the funds of a certain heterodox Lincolnshire Parson, whom I have seen [Edmund Larken], 'carry on the work of the day'.[35]

Both the *Leader* and *Household Words* added significantly to public comment on social issues at this time. While other European countries were occupied with the aftermath of revolution, in Britain a kind of steady social reformation was going on. London, in particular, was being cleaned up, thanks mainly to the efforts of Edwin Chadwick, architect of the New Poor Law of 1834, indefatigable member of royal commissions of inquiry into the police and the employment of children in factories, and author of the important *Report on the Sanitary Condition of the Labouring Population of Great Britain* in 1842. His Public Health Act was passed in 1848; later that same year a serious cholera outbreak galvanised the authorities into following Chadwick's advice about improving sanitation through the better removal of sewage, and reducing overcrowding in slums. A series of reforms followed, including the Metropolitan Interments Act of August 1850, prohibiting burials in London, and the removal of Smithfield cattle market out of the centre of London in 1852. These pieces of legislation were supported by both Dickens and Carlyle.[36]

The population census of 1851 was the first to include marital status in its statistics; it was discovered that there was a surplus of women, and much discussion followed about the dangers of prostitution, the need to encourage female emigration, and – among women like Harriet Martineau, Bessie Rayner Parkes, and Barbara Leigh Smith – the necessity to extend education and employment for women.[37] The first Ladies' College was founded in Bedford Square in 1849 by Elisabeth Jesser Reid.

★

Amely Bölte introduced her friend, the Austrian exile Moritz Hartmann, at Cheyne Row in April 1850, noting that Jane 'was ill, looked like a shadow, and spoke hardly a word'.[38] Jane found Nero a comfort; she was soon using the dog as a channel of communication with Carlyle. Nero 'wrote' to Carlyle when the latter was at the Grange in January, telling him how an old gentleman in the omnibus had commented on how 'sharp' he was and fed him a biscuit. 'I was quite sorry to part from him', writes Nero, 'he was such a good judge of Dogs'.[39] When Jane herself was at Addiscombe with Lady Ashburton in March, she wrote to Nero, addressing him as her 'poor orphan' and sending a kiss for Carlyle from 'your loving Agrippina' – Lady Ashburton's name for Jane now that she was 'mother' to Nero.[40]

One of Jane's old admirers, Jeffrey, had died in January. Carlyle had called on him during his last trip to Scotland in September 1849, but had not otherwise heard from his old sparring partner since Jeffrey had sent his usual budget of praise and blame on the publication of *Oliver Cromwell* in 1846. 'Poor little Duke!' Carlyle had written to Jane at the time, adding, 'he begins always anew where we left him, like the people in *Sleeping Beauty*'.[41]

Another admirer whom Jane had not seen for some time was Mazzini, who suddenly appeared at the end of May after spending months in hiding following the failure of his Roman Republic the previous year. Jane joyfully reported to Helen Welsh Mazzini's own descriptions of his doings in the two years since he had left London:

He looks much better than I expected and is in excellent spirits[;] he has a greyish *beard* – which is altogether a new feature – as before he wore only black mustachios – but this beard he 'begged me to believe was no *efflorescence of Republicanism* but *necessitated* in the first instance and then persevered in because found so convenient – for you must recollect, my Dear, that in the old times I needed always to have a barber to shave me – and in the camp with Garibaldi, and flying for my life, I could not of course take everywhere with me a barber! – and so my beard had to grow and now and then be cut with *a scissor*.'

Mazzini had stayed in a madhouse at Marseilles while waiting for a false passport, thinking 'they would not seek him amongst *Mads*, decidedly'.[42] Jane's fondness for Mazzini is obvious from this letter; it was shown in her conduct, too, according to Moritz Hartmann, who witnessed Mazzini's unexpected arrival. Jane, he remembered, was stirred as if by an electric shock when she heard Mazzini's voice in the hall, and when he came in she caressed his beard, trembling and exclaiming with tears in her eyes how grey it had grown.[43]

One other old friend renewed contact with the Carlyles this summer. Their old neighbour and borrower of sovereigns, Leigh Hunt, sent a copy of his newly published *Autobiography*, in which he praised Carlyle's honesty and eloquence, though regretting his 'habit of denouncing'. Carlyle thanked him graciously on 17 June, which emboldened Hunt to suggest he might visit Cheyne Row and 'take my good old North-British supper with you'. He duly came on 25 June and had a plate of porridge.[44]

Later in the year Hunt started up his long-defunct *London Journal* once more, soliciting an article from Carlyle. One appeared over four numbers with the title, 'Two Hundred and Fifty Years Ago. (From a Waste-Paper Bag of T. Carlyle's)'.[45] The journal folded again in June 1851, and Carlyle did not receive payment. Hunt apologised in the crafty-ingenuous style Dickens was soon to pillory in *Bleak House* in the person of Harold Skimpole, the child-man on whom responsibility can get no firm hold. 'O how vexed & mortified I was, on finding the condition in which you . . . were to be left!' wrote Hunt, adding, 'not that I supposed you cared anything for such poor profits as might have accrued. Indeed it was clear you did not.'[46]

Geraldine Jewsbury came to London in June, as did the German novelist Fanny Lewald, who visited Cheyne Row, where Lewes was invited to speak German to her, as neither her English nor Carlyle's spoken German was up to the occasion. By the beginning of July Jane was telling Helen Welsh that Geraldine had 'sworn friendship' with Fanny Lewald and was spending less time than usual at Cheyne Row. Jane also met, at Thackeray's house on 12 June, 'Jane Eyre', 'a less figure than Geraldine and extremely unimpressive to *look* at'.[47] Charlotte Brontë had been persuaded to come to London by her publisher George Smith. Her shyness made Thackeray's dinner party in her honour a gloomy affair, as his daughter Annie later remembered. Charlotte Brontë was 'a tiny, delicate, serious, little lady, pale, with fair straight hair, and steady eyes'; she scarcely came up to Thackeray's elbow. We can only assume that Carlyle was as out of sorts that evening as Thackeray himself, for, according to Annie, 'everyone waited for the brilliant conversation which never began at all', much to Thackeray's dismay.[48]

Much more successful was Lady Ashburton's grand ball at Bath House on 24 June, where the Carlyles joined some 500 or more of the 'select aristocracy', as Carlyle noted in his journal the next day; 'the whole thing worth having seen for a couple of hours'.[49] Carlyle had insisted on going, much against Jane's wishes – and her sense of decency – though, as so often happened, she was invigorated by the experience. Her description to Helen Welsh points up the difference in dress code between the aristocracy and the middle class; there was no 'Victorian' buttoning up to the neck for upper-class women in 1850:

The Bath House Ball threw me into a perfect fever for one week – as I had no dress for it; not understanding that I was to go – but Mr C was 'quite determined for once in his life to see an aristocratic Ball and if I chose to be so peevish and ungracious as to stay away there was no help for me' – I pleaded the want of a dress – he 'would pay for any dress I chose to get'; and then I fell back on the horror of *stripping* myself, of 'being bare' – at my age after being muffled up so many years! and that if I didn't I should be like no one else – to which he told me angrily – 'true propriety consisted in conforming to other peoples fashions!!! and that Eve he supposed had as much sense of decency as I had and *she* wore no clothes at all!!!'

After this surprising piece of casuistry on Carlyle's part, Jane submitted:

So I got a white silk dress – which first was made high and longsleeved – and then on the very day of the ball was sent back to be cut down to the due pitch of indecency! – I could have gone into *fits* of crying when I began to put it on – but I looked so astonishingly well in it *by candle light*, and when I got into the fine rooms amongst the universally *bare* people I felt so much in *keeping*, that I forgot my neck and arms almost immediately – I was glad *after* that I went – not for any pleasure I had at the time being past dancing, and knowing but few people – but it is an additional idea for life, to have seen such a party – all the Duchesses one ever heard tell of blazing in diamonds, all the young beauties of the season, all the distinguished Statesmen &c &c were to be seen among the six or seven hundred people present – and the rooms all hung with artificial roses looked like an Arabian Nights entertainment – what pleased me best was the good look I got *into the eyes* of the old Duke of Wellington – one has no notion, seeing him on the streets what a dear kind face he has – Lady Ashburton receiving all these people with her grand-Lady airs was also a sight worth seeing.[50]

On finishing the last *Pamphlet* in July, Carlyle set off to stay with Charles Redwood in Wales as a prelude to visiting Scotsbrig, while Jane got on with house-cleaning. She told Carlyle on 4 August of a visit from Lewes's wife Agnes, who had given birth in April to a 'very brown' child whose father was not Lewes, but his friend and collaborator on the *Leader*, Thornton Hunt. Agnes appears to have been perfectly frank about her open marriage; Jane described to Carlyle her 'calm self-approving manner, and radiant face – radiant as with conscious virtue'. Agnes told Jane that Lewes was 'perfectly happy' in what seemed to Jane his 'monstrous' position; as if to prove it, when Lewes came to collect his wife he kissed her and called her 'darling' – 'a more comfortable *welldoing*-like pair one would not wish to see!'[51] Jane also brought Carlyle up to date with Mazzini's activities; he had rushed off to Paris to warn of the undemocratic intentions of the President, Louis Napoleon, but had returned to announce to Jane that the new revolution was 'postponed for the moment' and to arrange one of his fund-raising concerts for London's Italian refugees.[52]

By the end of August Carlyle was in Scotsbrig, employed in an act of diplomacy among his siblings. Jean, living the life of 'a galley-slave with those heaps of noisy children', was opposing her younger sister Jenny's growing inclination to join her husband Rob Hanning in Canada. Carlyle's mother, too, was querulous at the prospect of her daughter's emigration. Once more Carlyle proved how patient he could be with his family. In April 1851, when Jenny had finally decided she would take her two daughters and try a new life with her husband in Ontario, Jane wrote with words of encouragement, while Carlyle contributed to the costs of her travel and smoothed things over with the rather harsh Jean and with old Mrs Carlyle.[53] Years later, in 1895, Janet Hanning told Carlyle's biographer David Alec Wilson that everyone had been against her going, but she had been determined, 'and strange to tell, before I went away, which was in 1851, Mrs Tom wrote to me, – "Go in God's name, and God be with you, my dear little Jennie" ', by which Jenny knew she had Carlyle's blessing too.[54]

Jane was persuaded to visit the Grange towards the end of September, while Carlyle was still in Scotland. She wrote quite cheerfully to him about the other guests, who included Lady William Russell, sister-in-law of Lord John Russell, Henry Taylor – poet and co-organiser with Harriet Martineau of Carlyle's first set of lectures in 1837 – and his wife, and – eventually – Thackeray, who had upset Taylor by a remark in an article in *Punch* and was at first put off coming by Lady Ashburton. He then wrote an apology to Taylor and was permitted to join the party, where a reconciliation was effected, observed by Jane: 'Henry Taylor and Thackeray have *fraternized* finally . . . like *men and Brothers*! – I lie by and observe them with a *certain* interest: it is "as good as a play".'[55]

Thackeray wrote from the Grange to his confidante Mrs Brookfield, with whom he was in love rather as Mill was with Harriet Taylor, puzzling about his enigmatic hostess: 'How is it that I find myself humbling before her, and taking a certain parasitical air as all the rest do? There's something commanding in the woman . . . and I see we all bow down before her.'[56]

Thackeray had struggled against his subjection, telling Lady Ashburton in the autumn of 1849 that he had been ill and could not accept her hospitality at the Grange, adding, with comic allusion to his huge appetite and her well-known abstinence, that he had been warned 'that henceforth my life is to be that of an anchorite: and that the magnificent appetite with wh. Nature has endowed me for 38 happy years, is to be hung up in the hall as a thing of no further use to me'.[57]

Lady Ashburton became ill, and, since Lord Ashburton was abroad, Jane offered to stay with her after the other guests had left. By the third day, as she told her cousins, Lady Ashburton had 'absolutely nothing to say to me! I dont know whether she is always so when *alone* with women – but the longer we know one another and the more we are intimate to outward appearance the less we have to say to one another *alone*.'[58]

Though Jane did not quarrel with Carlyle over Lady Ashburton this time, she appears to have written a desperate letter to Harriet Martineau, much to the latter's surprise. 'She pours out such a quantity of woe', Harriet told Fanny Wedgwood, adding:

She assigns no cause for her misery, but calls it her 'inveterate malheur', and beseeches me to tell her how to be happier. It is true, she goes off into a burlesque account of bad servants: but the greater part of the letter is serious enough: and the wretchedness must be real enough to make her thus confess herself to *me*.

Intrigued, Harriet invited Jane to visit her at Ambleside, but received no reply. 'What a queer little body she is', Harriet concluded.[59]

In November Jane suffered 'a *wrench* and a *crush* all in one on the ribs under my right breast', a hurt which did not heal with the application of mustard plasters. She feared she might have breast cancer, like two of her aunts, and became very low-spirited.[60] Carlyle fell far short of the sympathy Jane needed. She wrote wretchedly to Helen Welsh on 6 December:

I feel as if it would be a sort of sin not to tell you at once how grateful I feel for your and Jeanies letters containing such kind and also – oh how rare in this world!

such *judicious* sympathy . . . Oh God forbid that I should die a *lingering* death, trying the patience of those about me; beside a Husband who *could* not avoid letting me see how little patience his own ailments have left him for any body else's – should *such a thing* come upon me in reality, I should go away from here, I think, and ask *one of you* to tend me and care for me in some little place of my own – even my low spirits about the thing which in the first days I *could* not conceal from him – nor in fact did I think there was any obligation on me to *keep up appearances* with *him* [–] brought down on me *such* a tempest of *scornful* and wrathful words, such charges of 'impatience' 'cowardliness', '*impiety*', 'contemptibility', that I shut myself up altogether and nothing should ever again wring from me another expression of suffering – to HIM.[61]

'I hear nothing lately of her *hurt*', wrote the unsuspecting Carlyle to his mother a few days later, 'and believe it is getting well.'[62] He went on to comment on the agitation in London about the recent restoration of a Roman Catholic hierarchy in England, with Cardinal Wiseman at its head. As Carlyle told Jack on 23 November, there was 'great noise here still about Wiseman and the Pope's Mountebankeries'. 'Speech enough in Parl*t* there will be about it! The flagstones and walls are all chalked "No Popery!" "Burn the Pope"; "Kick the Pope's bottom" &c &c.'[63]

Carlyle half realised that he was making Jane unhappy, but even in his journal he displaced his guilt, writing in an almost biblical way about the marriage relation:

It is man's part to deal with Destiny, who is *known* to be inexorable. It is the woman's more to deal with the man, whom, even in impossible cases, she always thinks capable of being moved by human means; in this respect a harder, at least a less dignified, lot for her.[64]

Marriage was often on his mind at the moment. He had recently met Tennyson and his new wife. Tennyson, named Poet Laureate in November in succession to Wordsworth, had finally published his long poem, *In Memoriam*, this year and at the same time married Emily Sellwood. Both the poem and the courtship had taken nearly twenty years to complete. In December Carlyle described another young couple, Ruskin and his wife Effie. Carlyle summed up Ruskin as 'a small but rather dainty dainty dilettante soul, of the Scotch-Cockney breed', celebrated for his *Seven Lamps of Architecture* (1849).[65]

At the same time Carlyle was being appealed to by one half of the disastrously paired Bulwer-Lyttons. Rosina wrote asking for Carlyle's help in finding a publisher for her novel, *Miriam Sedley, or, The Tares and the Wheat: A Tale of Real Life*, in which she described her husband's cruelty towards her. Carlyle was sympathetic, recording in his journal in December 1850 that Rosina, 'poor lady', had called on him with her request – 'a most melancholy interview of her seeking'. He replied kindly, saying he would do what he could for her novel, but advising her to 'restrain your grievous sorrow within your own heart', advice which fell on deaf ears.[66]

Thackeray, who was approached on Rosina's behalf a few months later, told Jane that he was keeping out of the 'squabble', while Dickens, a friend of Bulwer-Lytton who was putting on a performance at the Duke of Devonshire's house of Lytton's play *Not So Bad As We Seem* in May 1851, was horrified to receive letters from Rosina threatening to attend the performance 'as an Orange girl'. She planned to distribute a parodic advertisement among the audience for a play called *Even Worse than we Seem, or the Real Side of our Characters*. The advertisement read:

The New Farce is from the pen of Sir Liar-Coward Bulwer-Lytton . . . , a Gentleman (?) with a gutta percha [i.e. flexible] rental of £10,000 for his acquaintance, which conveniently shrinks into as many hundreds whenever he is applied to to give his wife enough to live on.[67]

Jane responded even more strongly than Carlyle to the wrongs done to Lady Bulwer-Lytton. She wrote congratulating her on fighting the 'diabolical' treatment she was suffering from 'that man', treatment which Jane likened to 'a bad dream, or a Balzac novel'.[68] Geraldine performed her self-appointed function of spokesperson for Jane's own sense of grievance by expostulating on 7 February, 'Do make [Rosina] feel that she is not the only ill-used woman in the world.'[69]

Young Theresa Revis, or 'Tizzy', of whom Jane had prophesied dark things, made a sudden appearance in January 1851, landing on the Carlyles like 'a young Heroine of Romance' with 'a quantity of trunks and a Lady's maid', as Jane told her uncle John Welsh. Tizzy had been driving her guardians to despair since the death of Mrs Buller by creating 'the most extraordinary *furor* at Calcutta', where she had received innumerable offers of marriage, all turned down, and had now engaged herself to 'a Capt. Neale (from Ayrshire) who came home in the ship with her and seems a most devoted lover – SHE "does not love *him* a bit" she told me'. After turning Cheyne Row upside down for a few days, she and her lover and luggage moved on. Jane told her uncle that the scheming Blanche Amory in *Pendennis*, which Thackeray had finished serialising in December 1850, was modelled on Tizzy, whom Thackeray detested (and who was supposed by some also to be the model of Becky Sharp in *Vanity Fair*, a creation about whom Thackeray's feelings were rather more ambivalent).[70]

More weddings were being contemplated. Milnes was about to marry, and a notice in *The Times* in April told the Carlyles that John Stuart Mill had at last married his 'Platonica'. Harriet Taylor's husband had died in

July 1849, and now Mill and Harriet became man and wife. True to his belief in the equality of the sexes, Mill abjured all rights to his wife's property; indeed he agitated from now on, in his writings and in Parliament when he became MP for Westminster in 1865, for a Married Women's Property Act, which finally became law in 1870. He also took up the cause of women's suffrage, but that had to wait more than seventy years before finding success.

So clear-sighted in his public writings and actions, Mill was, by contrast, unable to see straight in his private life. He and Harriet secluded themselves even more after their marriage than before; Mill quarrelled with his adoring mother and sisters because they did not seem to him to do sufficient homage to Harriet. When Lord Ashburton wrote to congratulate the couple and asked permission to call, he was rebuffed. 'We are resolved', wrote Mill icily on 30 May, 'not to visit at all.'[71]

Further news of marrying came in May, when Jeannie Welsh, from whom Jane already felt partially alienated, announced she was to marry her Glasgow acquaintance Andrew Chrystal. Jane could not hide her dismay, both because she disliked Jeannie's fiancé and because her own experience of marriage was less than blissful:

How I wish it had not been your idea to pitch your tent in the 'valley of the shadow of *marriage*' – it is a very *relaxing air* I am sure and peculiarly unsuitable to *your* constitution – But certainly I am not the best authorized person to tell people how they should manage their lives under that head of method having made such a mess of my own life – God help me![72]

★

1851 was the year of the Great Exhibition, Prince Albert's great, though controversial, idea, for which Joseph Paxton designed the Crystal Palace. Carlyle commented on the structure as it went up in Hyde Park; he took a sceptical yet also admiring view of this 'monster of a *Gigantic Birdcage*', telling Jack on 12 January that it was now nearly glazed in and that it covered twenty-two acres between Rotten Row and the Knightsbridge Barracks:

Never in the world's annals, I believe, was there a *building* of such extent finished in ten times the *time* by hand of men; – and here Paxton (whose ingenuity is the soul of it, and *enables* him to employ tens of thousands upon it at once) has got it all but ready as per contract; and once its use is over, he can build it again into two streets of dwellinghouses, into a village of iron cottages, or a world of garden greenhouses, without losing a pound of the substance employed (putty excepted). That I call clever; the rest is like to be all fudge and boisterous ostentation.[73]

At the end of March Carlyle noted that the Crystal Palace, due to open on 1 May, was 'taking in floods of rain' and that the 'thousands of sparrows' flying about in it would have to be 'ejected by poison'. Moreover, 'bearded foreign people are already beginning to encumber the streets', all drawn to London to see the 'Works of Industry of All Nations' in this amazing structure.[74] The venture was greeted by the usual discordant chorus on such occasions. Some deplored the expense and ambition; *The Times* and certain politicians were worried about the likely activities of some of the bearded foreigners Carlyle mentions – how many of them were exiled revolutionaries who might use such a large public space, expected to be visited by several heads of state after its opening by Victoria and Albert, to attempt assassination or riot? *Punch* and *Household Words* derided such fears, with Dickens painting a deliberately exaggerated picture of conspiracies in the coffee shops and cigar shops of Soho only days before the Exhibition opened.[75]

In the event, the Crystal Palace was a resounding success: 25,000 people visited it on the first day, with thousands more lining the route from Buckingham Palace. There were more than 100,000 exhibits from all parts of the world, and by the time the Exhibition closed in October it was agreed on all hands to have been worthwhile. In 1852 the building was dismantled and re-erected, not in the ways Carlyle anticipated, but in the same glasshouse form, in Sydenham in south-east London, where in due course it gave its name to the district.

Carlyle visited the Exhibition at least once. Describing it to his mother on 11 June 1851, he fell into the deprecatory tone he often adopted in letters to her. It was 'a very *braw* place indeed; the finest *house* ever seen in the world, – with three huge growing *trees*, with fountains &c &c, in the inside of it', but 'unhappily there was no *result* visible to any rational eye in the whole of it; with Sandy Corrie one asked bitterly, "What's ta use on't?"'[76]

He and Jane were attending Thackeray's lectures on 'English Humourists of the Eighteenth Century'. Jane told Helen Welsh on 5 June that 'between you and me' they 'are no great things – as *Lectures* – but it is the fashion to find them "so amusing"! and the *Audience* is the most brilliant I ever saw in one room – unless in Bath House drawingrooms'.[77] Amely Bölte went with Jane and Mazzini to one of the lectures, where she spotted Milnes and the Leweses among the audience. Thackeray was a nervous speaker, reading the lectures in a 'rather dry manner', according to Caroline Fox, who attended on 12 June, seeing Jane Carlyle and Dickens there.[78]

Nervous though he was, Thackeray stirred controversy in his last lecture on 3 July, when he spoke for more than ninety minutes, 'having seen fit', as Jane reported to Helen, 'to give a long rigmarole about the dignity of the Literary profession *into the bargain!*' Jane found it both undignified and boring, and Carlyle 'could hardly sit still and hold his tongue, and dashed off the instant he ceased speaking, down a side door that nobody found out before, I following and the whole thing was vexatious'.[79]

The reason for Carlyle's displeasure was that Thackeray had attacked the new Guild of Literature and Art, an association founded by Dickens, Forster, and Bulwer-Lytton to gain greater recognition for the literary profession and to help struggling writers and artists. Thackeray, with his old-fashioned 'gentleman's' snobbery, objected to the professionalising of literature. He knew the Carlyles had been offended, writing both pugnaciously and submissively to Jane on 9 July:

Dont you understand that there are a set of men who will be martyrs, who are painting their faces and asking for your money, who want to make literature a chronic beggary under the name of the Guild of &c? . . .

Dont you think it was very kind of you to come to the lectures? I do: and I was a coming to shake hands & thank you: but I heard that you weren't pleased; and I thought I wouldn't like to be scolded: but that it wd. be best to wait a bit and be yours and Carlyle's always gratefully, W M T.[80]

In July Carlyle was invited by Dr James Gully to try his water cure at Malvern in Worcestershire. He and Jane were to be his guests in the famous establishment where Gully and his partner, Dr James Wilson, had been practising hydropathy for the last nine years, promoting the universal benefits of the natural spring water of the region. Gully knew of Carlyle's 'dyspeptic miseries', and expressed the flattering hope that he could do 'something for your stomach of what you have done for my brain – purging it of depressing stuff & elevating its tone'.[81] The Carlyles spent the whole of August in Malvern, Carlyle gamely trying the cure, which began with being 'packed' in wet sheets at 6.30 a.m. and continued with cold baths, brisk walks, plain dinners, and much drinking of Malvern water.[82] Jane merely observed the treatment and the other guests. One of these was Macaulay, who avoided Carlyle, his view being that Gully and Carlyle, doctor and patient, were 'quacks alike'. Carlyle, too, was disposed to 'shun' his rival historian and conversationalist. While his opinion of Gully was more charitable than Macaulay's, he was by no means converted to the water cure.[83]

After Malvern, where they had a misunderstanding over Carlyle keeping a cigar in his mouth when Jane came for a parting kiss, she went to Manchester to stay with Geraldine, while he visited Scotsbrig. Once more their exchange of letters is strained, and once more Carlyle wrote adoring letters to Lady Ashburton, who had invited him to join her and

Lord Ashburton in Paris in October. He replied from Scotsbrig on 13 September that he hoped to be able to come, even if only for a few days, for 'in Paris there will simply be one human soul whom I want to be in sight of'.[84] Before he could go to Paris, he explained, he was due to meet Jane in Manchester, then both were to pay a quick visit to the Stanleys in Cheshire. Edward Stanley, soon to inherit his father's title of Baron Stanley of Alderley, had long been an admirer of Carlyle. Jane had befriended the Stanley daughters, one of whom, Blanche, was about to marry Lord Airlie. This was another match viewed with gloom by Jane, whom Blanche had chosen as her chief confidante. Jane told Helen that Blanche did not 'care a rush' for her boring Scottish nobleman, but was desperate to 'escape her Mother's eternal reproaches that [at twenty-one] she should be still "on her hands"'.[85]

Back in Chelsea by 20 September, Carlyle was delighted to find that the Brownings were also setting off for Paris a few days later. He quickly decided to go with them, letting Browning make all the arrangements. On his arrival in Paris he reported to Jane that they all – Carlyle, Browning, Elizabeth, their son Pen, and their maid – 'did extremely well together'. Browning, though 'a little loudish and talkative beyond need now and then', made up for this by '*courier*[ing] in the most perfect style all the way to Paris, and I had not the least thing to do'.[86]

The Brownings enjoyed Carlyle's company. Elizabeth had met him at the end of July, when she and Browning returned to London for the first time since their marriage. She told a friend proudly that she had 'passed an evening with Carlyle (one of the great sights in England, to my mind)'. Now she wrote from Paris on 22 October:

I was not disappointed at all in what I saw of writers of books in London: no, not at all. Carlyle, for instance, I liked infinitely more in his personality than I expected to like him, and I saw a great deal of him, for he travelled with us to Paris and spent several evenings with us, we three together. He is one of the most interesting men I could imagine even, deeply interesting to me.

In her opinion his scorn was 'only sensibility' and his bitterness only melancholy, an assessment strikingly similar to Harriet Martineau's in her *Autobiography*.[87]

Carlyle wrote a lively account on his return from his French trip: 'Excursion (Futile Enough) to Paris; Autumn 1851: Thrown on Paper, Pen Galloping, from Saturday to Tuesday, October 4–7, 1851'. On landing at Dieppe on 25 September he had gone for a walk, noticing 'streets of fair cleanness, water flowing in the gutters. Beards abundant.' After much haggling and weighing of luggage – all negotiated by Browning while Carlyle 'sat out of doors at my ease, and smoked' – they took the train to Paris. Having let Browning fight 'about nothing at all' with various porters on arrival in Paris, Carlyle got himself taken to the Hôtel Meurice, where the Ashburtons had their suite.[88]

That evening he accompanied the Ashburtons to the Théâtre Français, where 'Lord Normanby has been pleased to furnish us his box':

Play was called *La Gageure Imprévue* [*The Unexpected Wager*], or some such name; worthless racket and cackle (of mistaken jealousy, &c, in a country château of the old régime); actors rather *good*; to me a very wearisome affair.

After this Lady Ashburton left to visit her mother, who was living in Paris once more, while Carlyle and Lord Ashburton stayed on to see the second offering, *Maison de Saint-Cyr*. This play brought out all Carlyle's loathing of 'phallus-worship':

Two roués of Louis XIV time, engaged in seducing two Maintenon boarding-school girls, find the door of Saint-Cyr *locked* as they attempt to get out; find at the window an Exempt '*de par le roi*', are carried to the Bastille, and obliged to marry the girls: their wretched mockeries upon marriage, their canine libertinage and soulless grinning over all that is beautiful and pious in human relations were profoundly saddening to me; and I proposed emphatically an adjournment for tea; which was acceded to, and ended my concern with the French theatre for this bout.[89]

This diary and his letters to Jane recount his usual complaints when away 'enjoying himself' with the Ashburtons: wretched nights, upset stomach, noise, and the annoyance of having to consort with other people, in this case the politician and friend of the Ashburtons, Louis Thiers, who 'talked *immense* quantities of watery enough matter', and the equally talkative 'Man of Letters' Prosper Mérimée. '*Nichts zu bedeuten* [of no consequence]', was Carlyle's summing up for Jane.[90] If Thiers was exhausting company, he was preferable to Guizot, another ex-minister from the time of Louis Philippe. 'I find him a solemn *intriguant*', wrote Carlyle, 'an Inquisitor-Tartuffe, gaunt, hollow, resting on the everlasting No, with a haggard consciousness that it ought to be the everlasting Yea.'[91]

Since Lady Ashburton was unwell, Carlyle went out with Lord Ashburton in his carriage, jumping down at the Temple to talk to a policeman who had 'never heard of Louis XVI or his imprisonment here'. An old concièrge who did know her revolutionary history showed Marie Antoinette's private chapel and 'the place of Cléry's scene of adieu' to the British historian of her city's great Revolution. While Lord Ashburton shopped for bronzes, Carlyle bought a glass of *vin ordinaire* for himself and one for the coachman, to the latter's astonishment and delight.[92] Carlyle's only purchases were a 'collar and string' for Nero and some cigars. Finding the Ashburtons disposed to stay on until Lady Ashburton felt better, Carlyle reluctantly managed the return journey alone, arriving in Chelsea at midnight on 2 October.[93]

★

On 10 October Carlyle wrote to Alick in Canada announcing that another book was about to be published. This was his *Life of John Sterling*, which he had begun in March, feeling that a fairer account was needed of his friend's life, particularly with regard to his troubles with the Church of England, than that achieved by Archdeacon Hare in his 1848 memoir. Of his own work Carlyle wrote modestly to Alick, 'Some tell me it is very readable; but in fact it cannot amount to much importance whether readable or not. The best part of the job, as usual, is that *I* am done with it.'[94]

The *Life of Sterling* was warmly received. After the intellectual and stylistic excesses of *Latter-Day Pamphlets*, this new book shows a Carlyle purged, at least temporarily, of all anger and bile. He writes simply and movingly about his gifted but unfulfilled friend, of whom he says with perfect honesty that his life was one 'which cannot challenge the world's attention; yet which does modestly solicit it, and perhaps on clear study will be found to reward it'. For Sterling, though a half-renegade as a cleric and a rather unsuccessful writer, had shown personal heroism in his life of chronic illness, and, more importantly, had asked, with 'every nerve' and 'drop of blood' in him, the question: 'What is the chief end of man? Behold, I too would live and work as beseems a denizen of this Universe, a child of the Highest God. By what means is a noble life still possible for me here? Ye Heavens and thou Earth, oh, how?'[95]

Carlyle's aim is to correct the view given by Hare that Sterling was tragically deflected from his Church of England vocation first by reading German biblical criticism and *Sartor Resartus*, and then by his illness; Carlyle concentrates, though by no means stridently, on Sterling as son, brother, husband, father, and friend. Though he candidly confesses that Sterling's stories and poems are not great literature, he honours his friend's attempts to find a vocation in an age when, as he says, of the three learned professions – the Church, law, and medicine – none was right for him. In a quietly understated way, Sterling's dilemma is represented as characteristic of the nineteenth century, a salient sign of the times. Carlyle describes without pomp his own role in Sterling's life; prints without comment Sterling's dying letter to him, but withholds the stanzas addressed to him, 'written as if in star-fire and immortal tears; which are among my sacred possessions, to be kept for myself alone'.[96]

The most striking part of the book is the famous chapter on Coleridge, in which Carlyle wickedly satirises the ageing genius whom Sterling had revered and whom he himself had visited as a young man. The pen-portrait, like those of Jeffrey and others in the *Reminiscences*, is rich and animating, spiced with the salt of exaggeration. Coleridge 'sat on the brow of Highgate Hill' looking down on London like 'a sage escaped from the inanity of life's battle'. A kind of magus, he was thought – 'he alone in England' – to hold the key to German transcendentalism; in 'a plaintive snuffle and singsong' he talked of the Kantian 'om-m-mject' and 'sum-m-mject' for hours on end while the listener – at any rate one particular listener – felt like a 'passive bucket' being 'pumped into'. Carlyle remembers the tone in which he had heard Coleridge snuffle his pious remark to Mrs Gillman about his cold tea being 'better than I deserve', a phrase which had gone straight into the Carlyles' stock of quotations.[97]

Reviewers quoted from this chapter with delight; they also, except for the clerical or orthodox ones among them, admired Carlyle's warm tribute to Sterling, while recognising the irony that the biographer is far more gifted and interesting than his subject. This view was given its liveliest expression by Marian Evans in the January 1852 number of the *Westminster Review*, the first number she edited, incognito, for its new owner, John Chapman. She had moved to London the previous year to pursue a career as a journalist, and was living in the liberal and radical circles inhabited by Chapman, Lewes, and Herbert Spencer.

As the author of an anonymous translation of Strauss's *Life of Jesus*, published by Chapman in 1846, she rejoiced in Carlyle's defence of Sterling's decision not to take the final step towards the ministry. In a witty analogy worthy of Carlyle himself, she likened Hare's stance to that of Dr Arnold's friend John Keble, 'who recommended a curacy as the best means of clearing up Trinitarian difficulties', as if full orders were 'a sort of spiritual backboard, which, by dint of obliging a man to look as if he were strait, end by making him so'.[98]

Carlyle's friends were relieved and delighted. Geraldine told Jane on 4 November 1851 that she felt, on reading the book, that she had 'at once gained and lost a personal friend'. For Emerson the *Life of Sterling* was 'the kindest, sanest' work Carlyle had written for a long time; Thackeray thought it 'delightful'.[99] The latter's confession to Lady Ashburton about his feelings towards Carlyle is an interesting example of the power of Carlyle's personality to outlast compatibility of opinions:

I am so glad when I can read and like something writ by the great Master of Craigenputtoch. It feels like a reconciliation; and having admired and believed as a lad, and revolted and doubted as a man, I feel guilty and as it were treacherous towards him. I have written a little notice in the Leader – not about the book –

321

but about the feelings with wh. one reads it, and recals the friends of dear youth.[100]

His *Leader* piece, published on 25 October, compares the tragic early deaths of three friends from Cambridge days – Sterling, Buller, and the subject of *In Memoriam*, Arthur Hallam – before praising Carlyle for speaking 'out of his own fond and faithful heart':

When the universal biographer comes to inquire, What manner of man [Carlyle] was? this public Accuser, this Executioner of Shams, this Hudson-Statue Smasher, and ruthless trampler on windbags – he (the Biographer) will doubtless turn to the life of John Sterling, and will find herein recorded with what a true and simple, and most kind and loving nature said Carlyle, Thomas, was endowed.[101]

When the Ashburtons returned from Paris to London a couple of days after Carlyle, Jane felt herself slighted by Lady Ashburton, whom Carlyle was so eager to see that he set off 'thro' a pouring rain' to Bath House.[102] 'We are in a very dark state here', Carlyle was soon writing to Lady Ashburton, urging her not to reply, the implication being that Jane would cause a scene if she thought they were corresponding.[103] At the beginning of December Jane went, more resentful than ever, to the Grange, to help Lady Ashburton prepare for Christmas.

While there, she heard of Louis Napoleon's *coup d'état* on 2 December. Thiers and other members of the National Assembly had been arrested; Jane observed that Lady Ashburton's letters from Thiers 'enable *her* to appear at breakfast, as triumphant in the news-line as she is in *all* other lines'.[104] Thiers was now on his way to exile in London. Carlyle arrived at the Grange in the middle of the month, as did Macaulay, whom Jane described to her correspondent, John Sterling's daughter Julia, as 'flowing on like a mill-dam within three feet of my ear', while 'the second and third greatest talkers of the age' (Carlyle and Lady Ashburton) 'are trying to get in an occasional sentence'.[105] On 19 December Palmerston was forced to resign as Foreign Secretary because he had welcomed the *coup* in Paris against the wishes of the Queen and the Cabinet. The company at the Grange, which now included Earl Grey and other government ministers, was naturally engrossed in these political developments.[106]

★

Carlyle held himself ever more aloof from the many European exiles who now lived in London, but Jane had contact with them through Mazzini. Carlyle told Lady Ashburton on 10 February 1852 that Mazzini was to hold 'a grand soirée, or Lecture with Coffee (price 2/6) for behoof of his

Italian Society, tomorrow ev[enin]g, in the Freemasons Tavern, – at which I shall have the pleasure of not assisting'.

Jane went, and Carlyle reported once more to Lady Ashburton:

Mazzini's Soirée, which my Wife attended, along with Clough and some other male and female disciples of good figure, was 'perfectly successful' . . . Ledru Rollin was believed to be present: but he has now, ever since the *coup d'état* shaved off his moustaches and is not distinguishable from common French citizens. Nay he refused to go with Louis Blanc and put himself at the head of two 'disaffected regiments' . . . in consequence of which he is, it seems, 'politically annihilated', which is perhaps just as well for him and us. Jane also saw, with Plattnauer a half-mad friend of hers, the *ci-devant* 'Minister of Public Instruction' in Rome, – a wretched little yellow moth-eaten-looking man, smoking an extremely bad cigar with poor Plattnauer, to whom he is now teacher of Italian. O heaven, what a mad farce-tragedy of a world this is.[107]

Though Carlyle was thus dismissive of the miscellaneous and rivalrous foreigners in London, there was in general much sympathy for these victims of foreign despots. *Household Words* and the *Leader* paid a good deal of attention to their meetings and clubs. When the Hungarian patriot Lajos Kossuth visited England in October 1851 he was welcomed by thousands, including Palmerston, to the disgust of Queen Victoria, who naturally felt sensitive about homage done to republicans, even foreign ones. Carlyle met on the street, as he told his sister Jean on 11 October, 'a joyful little man (Lewes of the *Leader*)', who was full of the exciting news that Kossuth was coming.[108]

Another arrival in 1851 whose fame preceded him was the Bonn Professor of Art History, Gottfried Kinkel, who made a miraculous escape from the fortress prison of Spandau, in which he had been imprisoned for life after taking part, with Engels, in the Baden uprising of 1849. He came to London much heralded by the British press, and became the hated rival of Marx, much as Louis Blanc and Ledru-Rollin were disputing the right to lead the French exile community.[109] In 1852 the Russian patriot Alexander Herzen joined the throng of European exiles in London; one of the first things he did, like so many of the others, was to pay a visit to Cheyne Row.

Herzen, like Carlyle, recognised the 'mad farce-tragedy' of the exile life. Though he was drawn into the petty squabbles and jostlings for position, he also viewed them with vivid humour and intelligence. In his memoirs, *My Past and Thoughts*, Herzen sketched both the individual and the national characteristics of his fellow refugees. He noted, as Carlyle also did, the huge vanity of the two would-be French leaders, one, Louis Blanc, 'like a man concentrated, reduced to the smallest size', the other, Ledru-Rollin, 'like a swollen child, like a dwarf of huge dimensions, or seen through a magnifying glass'. They might both, Herzen thought, 'play a part marvellously in *Gulliver's Travels*'.[110]

Meanwhile, British political life was itself in turmoil. Not only had Palmerston resigned, but in February 1852 Lord John Russell was defeated in his attempt to put through a militia bill. The Tories took office under Lord Derby, with Disraeli as Chancellor of the Exchequer, an appointment which brought forth cries in Carlyle's letters about Houndsditch and old clothes.[111] He made no public comments on politics, however, confining his activities and pronouncements at this time to matters concerning the London Library and the book trade. He lobbied to stop Gladstone's protégé, the Italian-born James Lacaita, from being appointed Librarian of the London Library. When the election was held on 12 June, Carlyle was relieved to find that Lacaita, 'the Signor of merit', was defeated by William Bodham Donne, a friend of James Spedding.[112]

While the London Library business was going on, Carlyle's support was also requested by John Chapman, bookseller, publisher of 'free-thinking' books, and new owner of the *Westminster Review*, who was taking on the large price-fixing cartel, the Booksellers' Association, which prevented Chapman and other small publishers from offering discounts of more than 10 per cent of the published price of books. Chapman organised a protest meeting at his shop on the Strand on 4 May, at which Dickens took the chair. Carlyle was unable to attend, but he sent a supportive letter, which was read out along with others from Cobden, Mill, Leigh Hunt, and Gladstone. The meeting was widely reported in the press, and in the end the Booksellers' Association had to climb down.

Early in the year, Carlyle had begun reading in earnest about Frederick the Great, a figure he had long thought of writing about, believing that his modernisation and militarisation of Prussia was, after the French Revolution, the most important phenomenon of the eighteenth century. He now began work on a task that would take thirteen years to complete. From the start he was more than usually gloomy, even ambivalent, about his subject, as his comment to Lady Ashburton on 16 February demonstrates:

I continue reading about *Frederic*; ordering maps, running after books &c to see what I am to order. The thing seems to myself very idle: what have I, here where I am, to say about the 'lean drill-serjeant of the world'? I do not even grow to love him better: a really *mediocre* intellect, a hard withered soul: great only in his invincible courage, in his constant unconscious loyalty to truth and fact: the last and only *King* I know of in Europe since Cromwell.[113]

He rationalised Frederick's many acts of dishonesty into an 'unconscious loyalty to truth', encouraging himself in his half-repugnant task by bringing in the comparison with Cromwell. Part of his reluctance, too, as is clear, stems from his being in London and needing to visit Germany, an adventure he had always managed to avoid and now truly feared. His letters during 1852 are full of pitiful remarks about the necessity to travel, his dread of it, and his hopes that Jane will go with him, though since she had sworn she would never again set foot on board ship, there was no chance of her doing so. In fact she seized on the excuse that the house needed major structural changes to stay behind and supervise the work, and Carlyle finally went off alone, having first secured the services of the willing Joseph Neuberg, who met him at Bonn and accompanied him on his tour.

Though Carlyle could hardly help discovering things of interest in the country of his two great heroes, Goethe and Luther, this German journey was disappointing for both him and his acquaintances in Germany. The inconveniences of travel, strange food, and uncomfortable lodgings, combined with the usual internal suffering, produced a desperate journal summing up of his German trip at its end:

It was a journey done as in some shirt of Nessus; misery and dyspeptic degradation, inflammation, and insomnia tracking every step of me. Not till all these vile showers, fallen into viler ashes now, have once been winnowed quite away, shall I see what 'additions to my spiritual picture gallery', or other conquests from the business I have actually brought back with me. Neuberg, I ought to record here and everywhere, was the kindest, best-tempered, most assiduous of friends and helpers, 'worth ten couriers to me', as I often defined him.[114]

Carlyle was most moved by his visit to Eisenach, especially, as he told his mother on 19 September, the Wartburg, 'where Luther lay concealed translating the Bible'. Surely he had his own parents in mind, and meant his mother to know it, when he gave her details of Luther's room with its oak table and the Cranach portraits of his father and mother hanging on the wall:

Excellent old Portraits, the Father with a dash of thrift, contention and worldly wisdom in his old judicious peasant countenance, the mother particularly pious, kind, true and mother[ly], a noble old peasant woman.

His description of Lucas Cranach's portrait of Luther sounds like an idealised version of Carlyle himself: 'A bold, effectual-looking rustic man, with brown eyes and skin, with a dash of peaceable self-consciousness and healthy defiance in the look of him.'[115]

Jane received Carlyle's account of his brief stay in Weimar, where Goethe's house was opened specially for him. Carlyle was moved on seeing 'the last Book I ever sent Goethe', William Taylor's *Historic Survey of German Poetry*, with a piece of paper 'torn from some scroll of my own (*Johnson*, as I conjectured) still sticking in it after 20 years!' Though he had hoped to avoid being lionised, the Grand Duchess of Weimar, on hearing of his arrival, invited him to dinner, at which he endured 'a singularly *empty* intellectual colloquy, in French (chiefly), in English and in German; the Lady being half deaf withal'.[116]

There followed Dresden, Berlin, and flying visits to some of Frederick's battlefields. 'At Dresden we found Bölte and other Sages and Dilettanti English and Foreign', wrote Carlyle to Jack on 3 October. And in Berlin he met his long-time correspondent Varnhagen von Ense, 'a lively-talking, pleasant, *official* kind of man' with 'a dash of dandy, soldier-citizen and sage'.[117] Amely Bölte and Varnhagen were as disenchanted with Carlyle as he was with their country. The former told the latter on 5 November that Carlyle had been impatient through lack of sleep, and had offended his hosts by dismissing a famous painting in Dresden's picture gallery as 'stinking fish'. She was sorry that he had not thought it necessary to be more polite. For his part, Varnhagen recorded in his diary how Carlyle was full of complaints in his broken but fluent enough German.[118]

While Carlyle was on his tour, Jane encouraged her infuriating brother-in-law in his latest attempt at 'love making' – 'you put so little *emphasis* into it', she scolded him on 30 August. To the surprise of both Carlyles, Jack persevered. On 2 November he married Phoebe Watts, a wealthy widow with four sons whom he had known for fifteen years. 'Jack is suddenly a paterfamilias and rich man in his generation', wrote Carlyle to Neuberg. 'Poor Brother! may it prosper well with him!'[119] When the married couple called at Cheyne Row a few days later, Carlyle found his brother happy in his 'new unexpected position'; he himself took to 'Mrs John' immediately, he told his mother.[120]

In November 1852 Jane wrote her short semi-autobiographical, semi-fictional tale, 'The simple Story of my own first Love', describing the precociousness of her eyelashes, her dancing, and her Latin. The opening of the story reveals that she had been provoked by a harsh comment from Carlyle on Thackeray's latest novel, *The History of Henry Esmond* (1852), in which the three main characters are drawn in some measure from himself and the Brookfields. Thackeray turns his bitterness at the recent break with his friends into fictional wish-fulfilment: Henry Esmond eventually marries Lady Castlewood, the Jane Brookfield figure. The Carlyles knew that William Brookfield had broken off relations with Thackeray and that the Ashburtons had made an unsuccessful attempt to reconcile them in October 1851.[121]

For Jane Carlyle, here was another unhappy marriage to contemplate. She responded vigorously to Thackeray's novel and to Carlyle's scornful attitude towards it. Her story opens:

What the 'greatest Philosopher of our day' execrates loudest in Thackeray's new novel – finds, indeed, 'altogether false and damnable in it', is that 'Love is represented as spreading itself over one's whole existence, and constituting the one grand interest of existence; whereas Love, – *the thing people call Love*, is confined to a very few years of man's Life, – to, in fact, a quite insignificant fraction of it; and even then is but one thing to be attended to, among many infinitely more important things'.

Jane's response to Carlyle's scepticism is passionate – 'my whole inner woman revolts against his view' – and racy:

'At what age, your grace, does a young woman leave off being in Love?' a young Impertinent once asked the late Duchess of Devonshire, then *seventy* . . . 'You must inquire of a woman older than I am', was the spirited reply.[122]

She then tells her story of puppy love, ending with the rueful remark: 'On the whole my first love wasn't the smart piece of work to have been predicted of such a smart little girl, – a girl so renowned for her eyelashes, her Latin and her wit.'

There follows a general conclusion drawn from Jane's own experience of marriage as well as from her memories of suitors from long ago and her interested observation of other marriages and of the romantic affairs of her young female friends and her not-so-young brother-in-law:

But nothing is so baffling for human foresight as to predict of other people's loves; it is hard enough to make head or tail of them in *completion* – Indeed, logically considered the whole 'Thing people call love', like the Power of God, 'passeth all understanding'!

Her last word is that if she reflects any further on the subject, she might be tempted to write a 'whole pamphlet' on 'the *Marriage-question*', a work which would be 'too much in advance of the Century for being committed to writing'.[123]

In October Jane had written to Carlyle, then in Berlin, describing how during the rearrangements to the house she had discovered among her papers an unopened letter 'addressed to Mrs Carlyle in my Mothers handwriting'. Her hopes that it might prove to be a last letter written just before Mrs Welsh's death were disappointed; it was a note about the property rights to Craigenputtoch. But alongside it was 'a long long letter' by Jane herself, 'most sad to read – about my marriage', as well as some copies of letters in her father's writing. She says no more, not explaining why her letter was 'sad to read' or why she talks about 'my' marriage in this letter addressed to her husband. What is certain is that love and marriage, and the wide discrepancies and deep disappointments which were her own experience in this domain, were much on her mind.

In November the Duke of Wellington died; his funeral was an elaborate affair, his body having lain in state in Chelsea Hospital for a few days before. Jane told Helen Welsh on 14 November that 'this end of London' was in confusion:

Thousands and Thousands of people thronging to see him and trampling one another to death! I went yesterday along Paradise row meaning to see the thing myself if it were practicable but when I saw the sea of human beings swaying to and fro I made off fast enough.

Over 46,000 paid their respects on 13 November alone, and two women were indeed killed in the crush.[124]

Carlyle was offered a seat at the funeral by Henry Hart Milman, now Dean of St Paul's, where the service was to be held. He replied with a mixture of graciousness and roughness:

You are very kind to remember [me] in your day of bounty, and I am much obliged. On Thursday I am elsewhere engaged for that affair; and indeed could not, in any case, have ventured on St Paul's, for such a length of time as they predict, and thro' such deluges of hard-elbowed human Stupidity and Irreverence as I see too well there will certainly be. – Chelsea, even to us who lie on the *lee* side of it, is nearly uninhabitable in these days. The utmost that Fallen Humanity can do to desecrate one of the most sacred things that can happen in the world, is now being done! In cities that contain a *canaille* approaching to the cipher of 2,000,000, it strikes me there ought to be no more Public Funerals transacted on these terms.[125]

It was the Ashburtons who had 'engaged' Carlyle to watch the funeral procession as it passed along Piccadilly on its way from Chelsea to St Paul's.

In December Carlyle rejoiced at the fall of the short-lived Tory ministry of Lord Derby, 'our scandalous Protection Ministry', as he called it. A coalition government of Whigs and Peelites – Tories in favour of free trade – came in under Lord Aberdeen.[126] The year thus ended in change and uncertainty in national politics. Domestically, too, all was not well. Carlyle had returned from Germany distraught and gloomy, to find Jane 'worn to a shadow' by superintending the renovations to the house, with which he soon expressed himself dissatisfied. His journal on 9 November describes 'silent weak rage, remorse even (which is not common with me)', though whether about his work or his temper he does not say.[127]

Most probably, though he appears never to have admitted this fully to himself, his remorse arose from his continued adoration of Lady Ashburton, to whom he was writing the day after this journal entry:

Dear Lady, – A word from me, in these black days, can only be a voice *de Profundis*; and to you, the noblest of all the human souls I have still on my list in this world, it is perhaps better, for many reasons, that I *say* nothing whatever . . .

Alas, care and sorrow lie coiled round the horizon of every soul. But I love you for your noble cheerfulness of heart, for your frank courage and ready gracious sense, – in fact I love you for several things, and have a confidence that the gods will not desert you, not altogether, at any time![128]

He loved her, in short, for qualities which neither Jane nor he possessed. While he was scribbling his praise of Lady Ashburton, Jane, who certainly could not count cheerfulness among her characteristics, was displaying her bitter yet entertaining wit about matters at Cheyne Row in a letter of 14 November to Helen Welsh:

You seem to be in Cimerian darkness as to the *condition-of-5 Cheyne-Row question*, dont even know if Mr C be returned – We here have known of his return only too well I can tell you; for he came home (a month ago) in such a state of what he calls 'bilious misery', that I really saw no more suitable winding up of the whole thing, than Cavaignac's Tale of *L'Homme de Bien* – *L'homme de Rien* viz: that he and I should step out into the garden, and joining hands, each holding a loaded pistol in the other, calmly, and resolutely – blow each, his own brains out! I had such a capital pair of pistols too, all ready at half-cock![129]

The surprising Jane had acquired the pistols from Captain Anthony Sterling after the house had been burgled one night while Carlyle was in Germany; she had gone to spend the night in a hotel because of the uninhabitable state of the house under its building works. As she told Anthony's niece Kate Sterling in a lively letter of 23 October, 'the thieves finally walked in – at one of my open windows – and stole – several things some six pounds worth – extremely moderate, considering the facilities afforded them'. After this she had slept at home, until Carlyle's return, with the borrowed pistols beside her bed.[130]

She and Carlyle continued, in their obstinate and self-absorbed way, in the renovated house, Carlyle groaning and struggling over his new writing task and Jane exhausted but unsatisfied by her household heroics.

PART FIVE

MODUS VIVENDI

CHAPTER 14

In the Valley of the Shadow of Marriage
1853–1854

On 6 January 1853 Carlyle wrote one of his occasional letters to Alick in Canada, summing up the doings of the previous year. He described the repairs to the house which had been undertaken after he had bought the remaining lease of thirty-one years. He had long thought of moving, pining as ever for a life in the country, but he could no longer contemplate making his home north of the border. 'Scotland, when I go back to it, is little other than a place of graves to me; I wander there like a ghost among the living.' Moreover, 'my wife was always silently against giving up our advantages here'.[1] Jane felt even more like a ghost in her native land than Carlyle did, and she needed the company London could offer. Cheyne Row was therefore to remain their domicile for life. The rebuilding of number 5 was not yet over, drastic measures becoming necessary only a few months after Carlyle wrote this letter.

It was a particularly cold winter, with a frost hard enough in late February 1853 to allow skating on the Serpentine; earlier in the same month Londoners experienced a spectacular fog, which Carlyle described to his mother, who had never seen the phenomenon:

On Tuesday Afternoon we had our *Fog*; a right '*London* Fog', the first this season, and fairly the *blackest* I ever saw. Jane and I had to go up to the Ashburtons' (who were incidentally here) that night – 2½ miles off us: – the omnibuses and every vehicle had ceased; no team could go except at a snail's pace, and with blazing torches at the head of it, 'Hoh-ho-ing' as it went on: you could *not* see one street-lamp from another . . . various persons asking us, 'Have the goodness to tell me *where I am!*' My new shirt was quite *black* in the inside of the collar when I took it up next morning. – There is no sort of 'danger' whatsoever, for a foot passenger, on such occasions: the police are everywhere, with blazing *lamps* on their breasts, with skilful polite directions to every one that asks it; and all the people maintain the most exemplary good humour, everybody indeed seeming to be partly amused by the *new* state of the world and its atmosphere. This '*London* Fog' is simply a common heavy *mist*, with the *smoke* of 2½ million people's fires superadded, which of course makes it black enough if there be no *wind* and a half-*frost* in the air.[2]

To accommodate the two and a half million, a number constantly growing, London was 'building as never City did', as Carlyle told Alick on 8 April. This letter was accompanied by a 'Talbotype' of himself and one of Jane, done by Anthony Sterling, 'a man rich and idle', who had begun to amuse himself with this latest method of taking likenesses.[3] Using the process devised by William Henry Fox Talbot of making a number of positive prints from a negative, Sterling produced several copies of Samuel Laurence's portraits.[4] Another of photography's early practitioners, Robert Tait, made his first visit to the Carlyles at this time. Carlyle described him to Jack as 'a coarse-looking sensible Scotch man and Painter'.[5]

Part of the building work in London, in addition to new pavements and new railway stations, was Edwin Chadwick's project of laying sewers to 'drain our impurities down into the river', as Carlyle told his mother on 6 May. Cheyne Row itself was having a sewer dug:

Nothing but great ugly mounds of gravel dug out, and puddles of bricklayers, poles, bricks, and roman-cement going like street-mud. For the sewer is truly a work of art here. A big cut (I think almost 20 feet deep, at the lower end) is made first, then in the bottom of this is built, with all precautions, a complete *barrel* (or *double* arch, arch both in the bottom and top) of strong brickwork, where the water is to run; after which, – with infinite rammings &c, they fill it up, and go their ways.[6]

The system was intended to improve sanitary arrangements; at present people mainly used chamber pots, which were emptied into cesspools in a backyard 'privy', with 'nightsoil men' coming at regular intervals to collect the waste. In the Carlyles' case this had to be taken through the house, as there was no side entrance.[7] Better sewage disposal would supplement the other improvements made to number 5 during the works of the previous summer, which had included the introduction of gaslight and mains water via cisterns and a tap in the kitchen sink.[8] While the sewer work was going on, all was mud, dirt, and noise. Not till July did the 'Cloaca-Maxima confusions' finally disappear from Cheyne Row.[9]

Carlyle's letters began to be filled with groans about the cloacal nature of the German works he was reading on Frederick the Great – those 'dungheaps'. To John Forster he wrote especially graphically in April that he was 'up to the lips in German literary dung'.[10] From Teufelsdröckh to Frederick, the defecatory metaphor for book-making was Carlyle's favourite; he used it not only as a form of verbal abuse of others, but also as the linguistic vehicle for the unpleasant but necessary, and in the end relief-giving, process he himself went through when writing.

Carlyle employed the more usual metaphor of giving birth when briefly addressing his and Jane's childlessness in the months after her death, writing in *Reminiscences* that 'no daughter or son of *hers* was to sit' on her little childhood chair from Haddington ('so it had been appointed us'), and adding: 'I have no Book thousandth-part so beautiful as Thou; but these were *our* only "Children" '.[11] His overwhelming feelings about the writing process, however, were those of someone straining to expel a natural yet somehow disgraceful burden of waste matter. His throwaway comments about his books once they were done, and his relative lack of curiosity about their reception, are consistent with these feelings.

In his researcher's despair, Carlyle wrote in April to the ill-disposed librarian at the British Museum, Anthony Panizzi, politely asking if he might study in a 'private room or quiet convenient corner'. Recognising that it might be impossible, he added graciously, 'if you are obliged to refuse me, I shall know it was with regret'. To which Panizzi replied, without any evident regret at all, that all readers were treated alike, that the library was a public place, and that all public places were likely to be noisy.[12]

On 13 April, the day after Panizzi's refusal to make special arrangements for him, Carlyle confided his forlornness to his journal, recording his sense that he had lost the admiration of the world: 'Though no one hates me, I think nearly *everybody* of late takes me on the wrong side, and proves unconsciously unjust to me.'[13] Writing of this period in his reminiscence of Jane, he pointed to the *Latter-Day Pamphlets* as the initial reason why 'everybody' had fallen away from him 'into terror and surprise', John Forster being the particular friend he recalls having done so.[14] Now in 1853 he compounded his descent into relative unpopularity by reissuing as a pamphlet his *Fraser's Magazine* contribution, retitled *Occasional Discourse on the Nigger Question* and published by Thomas Bosworth in the summer.[15] He had chosen to enlarge and reprint his 'Discourse' as a deliberate response to the 'rampant *Uncletommery*' which had overtaken Britain since the publication the previous year of *Uncle Tom's Cabin*.[16]

Harriet Beecher Stowe's anti-slavery novel was the great hit of the year. 'We have got *black* dolls, now, thanks to *Uncle Tom's Cabin*', Carlyle had told Clough, then in America, at the end of December 1852.[17] In May 1853 the author was being lionised in London's liberal circles. Of course Carlyle stayed away or was not invited, and he informed Clough (again with waste matter in mind) that the 'Beecher-Stowe concern' was 'tumbling along like the carcass of a big ass in a dunghill tank which many men are stirring with long poles'.[18] Harriet Beecher Stowe dined and made speeches with the Earl of Shaftesbury and other leading anti-slavery campaigners, while Carlyle half lamented, half gloried in his own quiet life of ex-lion in Chelsea.

Yet he knew very well that his was still a voice that was listened to. Chapman and Hall petitioned him in May to allow some of his essays to be reprinted in their new shilling 'Reading for Travellers' series to be sold at railway stations. He nominated 'Johnson' as the first, whereupon Chapman and Hall printed 3,000 copies. 'Burns' followed early in 1854.[19] The Ashburtons still valued Carlyle too. Lady Ashburton wrote to Jane Brookfield at the beginning of the year, complaining that she had few real friends among her many acquaintances, but taking solace in 'my dear old Prophet Carlyle' and asking, 'has one any right to more than one such friend in a life time?' In April William Brookfield noted in his diary that it was 'pleasing to hear how affectionately [Lady Ashburton] talked of Carlyle. "There is nobody like him", meaning not like him in resemblance – but like him in equality.' Brookfield told her what everyone observed, namely that she was the only person in the world who dared to put a ring through Carlyle's nose.[20]

Lord Ashburton showed his abiding respect for Carlyle by securing his election to the Athenaeum Club in March, handsomely managing to pay Carlyle's subscription without offending his pride. Carlyle expressed his thanks graciously, allowing Lord Ashburton to take him to dinner to introduce him to his fellow club members. 'I do not much believe I shall go *often*', he told Jack. He saw Darwin, Richard Owen, and the ancient Henry Crabb Robinson on this visit, along with 'plenty of loungers, if one wanted lounging!'[21]

At the same time as he was reaping the rewards of his fame in this way, Carlyle was joining forces with Dickens once more in a good cause, that of supporting an application for financial help from the Royal Literary Fund for his young Scottish acquaintance William Maccall. Carlyle wrote a long and generous letter; he might have been talking about himself as a young man when he described Maccall's 'continuous silently indignant struggle' to find an audience for his philosophical articles, his thin skin and shyness, his being 'steeped in poverty and ill-success, and yet with a pride in him' equal to that of 'emperors'.[22] In May Maccall gave a set of lectures, which Jane attended. She also encouraged friends to swell the painfully small numbers, and got notices of them put in the *Examiner* and the *Leader*.[23]

Carlyle was also helping Clough to find a government position – using Lady Ashburton's influence – as an examiner, so that he could return from America and marry his fiancée Blanche Smith. Blanche had recently met the Carlyles, and reported her impressions of them to Clough. She liked Carlyle, in spite of his rumbling talk 'from the bottom of the table' about Mrs Beecher Stowe. Jane she found 'very flighty sharp; nothing whatever gentle and female about her'. She acted, Blanche thought, 'like a spoiled child'. Clough agreed, adding in mitigation, 'however she is very *good* minded at bottom – and would do a great deal for people, and is not very happy'.[24]

Clough's remark about her being unhappy is echoed by many friends and observers of the Carlyles from now on. Jane's appearance, judging from the photographs taken by Robert Tait in 1854 and making full allowance for the stiff pose and the indistinct, grainy quality, is that of a sickly and dejected woman looking every one of her fifty-odd years. Her sharp tongue became sharper than ever; Froude, writing to Amely Bölte after Carlyle's death, remembered that it was 'like a *cat's*'; it 'would take the skin off with a touch'.[25] Jane also wrote fairly openly about her unhappiness to several female friends, including Blanche Airlie and her new young American acquaintance Ellen Twisleton.

If Blanche Smith was repelled by Jane's sharpness, Ellen, who had come over to Britain the previous summer as the new bride of Edward Twisleton, took to Jane immediately. On first visiting Cheyne Row in June 1852, she had thought Jane ugly and had been struck by the broad Scottish accents of both husband and wife; nevertheless she found them rewarding company, 'overflowing with intelligence and stores of agreeable conversation'. This wealthy young woman from Boston's élite noticed the Carlyles' relative poverty. 'They live in Chelsea, in the most ordinary house and style', she told her sisters back home. 'Real poverty it is – and the most wretched neighborhood', but nonetheless pleasing to visit after days among the country aristocracy and gentry, relations and acquaintances of her husband: 'It had a wonderful effect upon my sensations, after passing so many days among extra well-bred, inoffensive, negative people, to come into such an atmosphere.'[26]

Ellen was soon introduced to Lady Ashburton; on 1 July 1853 she described the summer ball at Bath House, which she had attended 'under Mrs Carlyle's tuition', being shown the famous beauties Lady Canning, Mrs Sidney Herbert, and the notorious Caroline Norton, who was about to be in the news again when she took her husband to court for failing to pay her allowance. *The Times* carried vituperative letters from both parties in August and September, and Caroline was soon publishing pamphlets and open letters to the Queen about the law as it treated women. Carlyle called her a 'poor luckless beautiful and clever Lady', who unfortunately, like Lady Bulwer-Lytton, had not the English 'talent of silence' under her wrongs.[27]

As a newcomer, Ellen with her fresh eye is a useful observer of Jane – 'extremely kind to me' and 'a real friend' – and Lady Ashburton – 'a tall, large woman, with a sensible, forcible expression', and 'not at all handsome'.[28] With Blanche Stanley now married to Lord Airlie and living in a Scottish castle, Jeannie Welsh married (on 28 April) to her Glasgow husband, and the Sterling girls seldom in London, Jane was glad to have a new young woman with whom to exchange confidences. She became very fond of Ellen, and Ellen of her, over the next few years.

Young women now formed the group round Jane, replacing the older women (Anna Montagu, Sarah Austin) who had taken her up on her first arrival, the families (the Bullers and the Sterlings) who had made a fuss of her, and the exotic foreign exiles who had kissed her hand, if not her feet. These older friendships had been broken by disinclination, distance, and death. The refugees had scattered, and her favourite Mazzini, even when he did visit London in the interludes between his machinations and manoeuvres in Europe, was to be found being 'worshipped', as Carlyle noted in June, in the circle surrounding William Ashurst, a radical lawyer, and his four enthusiastic daughters.[29] Mazzini had written in his usual way to Jane on New Year's Day, after calling, presumably to first-foot her as of old, but finding her out:

I am going [to Switzerland] and have so much to do that I shall not be able to come again. Should you pass by my street, step in just one minute to shake hands. If not God bless you as I do. I shall write. Your affectionate Jos. Mazzini.[30]

From Geneva Mazzini wrote to Aurelio Saffi in London, first in March, when he enclosed a note for Jane, then again in April, when he encouraged Saffi to ask her for a supporting letter in his efforts to help Italians in England find work.[31] Very few of Jane's letters survive from 1853, so we cannot know whether she did call on Mazzini before he left. But both she and Carlyle noticed that he now went mainly to the Ashursts, who unequivocally supported his republican activities, which the Carlyles could not do.

★

'This morning at ten o'clock I put poor Jane into the Train at Euston Square', Carlyle wrote to Jack on 1 July.[32] He was staying behind with the house painters while Jane, with Nero for company, went to Liverpool, where both her uncle and her cousin Helen were ill; she would also see Geraldine, who came over from Manchester.

The Carlyles' plan, agreed before she left, was that after resting with her relations in Liverpool, Jane would travel to Scotland to stay with John and Phoebe Carlyle in Moffat, from where she would visit Scotsbrig and report to Carlyle on his mother's state of health. It was a risky venture all round. Would Jane be able to keep from strangling her complacent brother-in-law? Would she take to Phoebe? Would she and Jean Aitken, who was sharing the nursing of old Mrs Carlyle with James and Isabella, manage to be civil with one another? Could Carlyle's proud, anxious, unlettered family make the queenly Jane comfortable in their modest homes, and would she contain the disdain, even antipathy, she felt towards some members of her husband's family?

Carlyle was well aware that his mother might die at any moment. He was assiduous in writing lovingly to her and encouragingly to the siblings who were caring for her, but he did not propose to visit her himself this summer, having been so comprehensively demoralised by his last bout of travelling that he felt unable to move from London and his study. He felt anxious and guilty. On 8 July he wrote in a depressed state to Jane, alluding to another coolness between them before she had left Cheyne Row:

Oh Jeannie, Jeannie, you know nothing about me just now: with all the clearness of vision you have, your lynx eyes do not reach into the inner region of me at all, and know not *what* is in my heart, what (on the whole) was always, and will always be there: I wish you did, I wish you did![33]

The next day he wrote again, regretting having sent the first letter. 'Poor little Jeannie: but what could I do? Fly for shelter to my Mammy, like a poor infant with its finger cut, – complain, in my distress, to the one heart that used to be open to me!'[34] For the next few weeks Jane wrote as encouragingly as she could about Carlyle's mother, though she could not resist complaining about Phoebe – 'so formal and cold' – and John, who 'talks talks about his own insight and his unheard of exertions in [his mother's] behalf'. She also told Carlyle of disagreements between his brothers, taking James's side against John.[35] 'Burn this letter and all I write at present', she added, but Carlyle could not destroy them, noting later when collecting Jane's letters that he would keep these letters from Scotsbrig as 'the last clear views' he had of his 'nobly human mother'.[36]

Carlyle worked hard at soothing her, reassuring her that she was 'right well liked' at Scotsbrig. He also wrote to James's wife Isabella expressing his gratitude for her kindness to Jane and his encouragement in the face of what he probably feared would be some sharpness on Jane's part. 'She is always well at Scotsbrig', he wrote, 'and you are always good to her'. 'Pray keep her as long as seems at all convenient for all parties.'[37] He showed himself once more capable of intelligent tact and strenuous efforts where his family were concerned. And it is to his credit that, despite provocation, he never complained about Jane or criticised her to his correspondents.

Nonetheless, what he feared did come about. Having seen Mrs Carlyle and made herself useful by carrying letters between James, Jean, and Mary Austin, Jane left them all rather abruptly to return to Liverpool, telling Carlyle on 21 July that his mother was comfortable and that it was time for her to leave. John's 'hovering about' and Jean's 'rubbing everything up the wrong way of the hair' had persuaded her to go.[38]

While Jane was away, Carlyle came to the conclusion that the 'summer noises' of carriages, dogs, cocks, road diggings, and organ grinders trying to make a living had reached such a pitch that extreme measures were required. He brought in John Chorley, an admirer of his who had been a railway official, to advise on his new plan to add a room to the top of the house and have it sound-proofed.[39] With Chorley in charge of surveying and overseeing the workmen, the job began in August, by which time Jane was home again. In the middle of the month she was describing to Kate Sterling the progress towards achieving the 'silent apartment' in the roof. The workmen 'go up the outside of the house by ladders thank God'; 'things go on like fire'; and if the house becomes uninhabitable at any time, 'there is Addiscombe standing empty with one Maid in it – which Lady Ashburton with her usual practical kindness puts at our service'.[40]

The building proceeded at breakneck speed – almost literally so, as Kate Sterling heard towards the end of August:

My darling I could not leave home just now without the chance of finding Mr C in the Prison on my return for having killed an Irish bricklayer because he had fallen thro the ceiling!! . . .

God bless you dear pray that the next man who falls in maynt fall on my head and break my neck – one fell yesterday within a yard of the spot I was standing on.[41]

Not to be outdone, Carlyle told his sister Jean a couple of days later that three Irishmen, 'unacquainted probably with the nature of lath and plaster, have been successively down upon my poor bedroom', the first two putting 'only their hoofs thro', while on the third occasion there appeared '*half* the person of a gentleman of that Nation, who hastily saved himself up again by the arms!'[42]

Both Carlyles seem to have remained cheerful in spite of such disruptions, retaining their sense of humour even when their servant Fanny ran off with the 'last of the Bricklayers' in September.[43] Alas, as Carlyle later noted, when the work was done he soon found he had 'a room, large, well ventilated, but by far the noisiest in the house', in defiance of all Chorley's efforts.[44]

In the middle of September, when the builders were ready to make the new staircase to the new illusory 'silent room', Jane and Carlyle did escape gratefully to Addiscombe for a few days.[45] The Ashburtons were holidaying in the far north of Scotland, where they received a long document from Carlyle on 8 September setting out the reasons why a National Portrait Gallery, or as he called it, a '*Gallery of true Historic Portraits*', would be a benefit to the nation. Carlyle argued from his experience as a biographer and historian. 'One seeks a Portrait, I say, as a first condition of success in all Biography.' Moreover, historical notices accompanying portraits would enlighten visitors about 'our Historic Heroes', and the whole venture would be an ideal 'patriotic enterprise'. He asked Lord Ashburton to try to interest Prince Albert in 'this important and neglected Enterprise'. The Queen herself could be asked to contribute some family portraits, after which 'Majesty's example would of course work on the Nobility'.[46]

Nothing came of Carlyle's idea immediately, the country and Parliament becoming absorbed in foreign affairs from the end of 1853, when it was clear that Britain would soon be involved in a war with Russia. However, when the National Portrait Gallery was eventually founded in 1856, its main proposer in the House of Lords, Earl Stanhope, used Carlyle's arguments and his name, appealing to 'the testimony of one of the most thoughtful and eloquent writers of the present age'.[47]

That Carlyle was still much appreciated in important quarters is evident from the secret he imparted to Jean on 18 November 1853, telling her to share it only with their mother. Prince Albert had proposed him to the Prime Minister, Lord Aberdeen, for a pension. That he was not fully acceptable to the establishment was made clear when Aberdeen, 'a douce, smallheaded, sleek and feeble old gentleman', shook his 'canny head, and thought my "heterodoxy" on some points might be objectionable'. 'And so it stands', he concluded, happy enough to recognise the intended honour but also content to retain his independence of anything that smacked of patronage.[48] That Lady Ashburton also knew of the offer (indeed she may have had something to do with it) is established by Carlyle's reference to it, and to Aberdeen's objection, in a letter to her the following day.[49]

Carlyle's letters report a larger number of visitors to Cheyne Row during November than for several months past. Thomas Spedding and Harriet Martineau both came up to London from the Lake District, the latter 'very wearisome', as Carlyle told Jack, but 'victorious still over all ills and infirmities that beset other mortals', and translating Comte, 'or some windy French Prophet of the New Epoch; – for the rest, grown fat and old'.[50] Her abbreviated translation of Auguste Comte's *Positive Philosophy*, with its division of history into epochs of belief, the present age being characterised as a humanist, post-Christian one, was published by John Chapman at the end of the year.

John Sterling's brother-in-law F. D. Maurice also came to call, looking 'fidgety, alarmed, and unhappy'. He had recently been dismissed from his theological professorship at King's College London for expressing the view that eternal punishment, prescribed by Article XVIII of the Church of England for all who are not professed or baptised Christians, was

PART FIVE: MODUS VIVENDI

inconsistent with the idea of Christian love.[51] On the same day, 28 November, 'heretic Froude came in', newly arrived in London from Wales to look for a house, and planning to write a history of Queen Elizabeth and to 'stand by his heterod[ox]ies'.[52] Froude's *alter ego* in *The Nemesis of Faith* had struggled with the same Article which now stuck in Maurice's throat.[53]

Then there was Miss Delia Bacon, a fanatical American whom Emerson had sent, somewhat shamefacedly, promising not to 'send you any more people without good reason'.[54] She was obsessed with persuading people that 'the old booth-keeper' Shakespeare could never have written the plays known as his; she preferred to believe they were written by her (unrelated) namesake Francis Bacon. She visited the Carlyles several times, was not in the least perturbed by Carlyle's obstinate 'clinging' to the idea that Shakespeare did write the plays, and was dealt with most patiently by Carlyle, though he told Lady Ashburton rather wickedly on 3 November that he intended that 'she shall a[bsorb] Neuberg next visit' so that they could 'annihilate one another'.[55]

The Carlyles were invited to spend most of December at the Grange. The day before they went Carlyle wrote to his mother. It was his fifty-eighth birthday, 4 December. Sensing that it would be his last birthday letter, and perhaps his last letter of all to her, he put all his love and gratitude into it, deliberately writing, as he used to do as a young man, as piously as he could without compromising himself. 'Surely God is Good; surely we ought to trust in Him', he wrote, before telling her that she had been 'a noble mother' to him. There follows that fine tribute to this unlettered, querulous woman, who had lived a narrow existence, and yet had raised and encouraged this unusual son, made sacrifices so that he could attend university, kept faith during his directionless years, and learned to write so that she could communicate with him when he left for London. Her voice had spoken through his writings, he said; everything she and his father had taught him had found expression in 'all I spoke and wrote'.[56]

From the Grange he wrote anxiously to Jean and Jack, asking if he ought to come to see his mother. He placed more reliance on Jean's opinion than on his brother's, 'for I cannot make much of John's hurried letters'.[57] Distracted and undecided as he was, Carlyle was still Lady Ashburton's trump card when it came to conversational sparring. Brookfield, who was among the guests, noted in his diary on 6 December that he and Lady Ashburton 'made the wits', as Amely Bölte would say, at breakfast, Carlyle claiming not to dislike Samuel Wilberforce, the Bishop of Oxford, who was due to arrive on the 8th, but to believe that he had got where he was by 'pure soapiness, suppleness, and sycophancy'.

Carlyle was soon trouncing 'soapy Sam' in after-dinner conversation.[58] The Bishop also recorded his conversational jousting with Carlyle, concluding in his own journal on 10 December that Carlyle, with whom he had gone out for a ride in the local countryside, was 'full of unconnected and inconsistent utterances' and 'a heap of discordant ideas. Yet a good deal of manhood, and of looking to some better state of being. Poor man, a strange enigma!'[59]

Carlyle and Brookfield accompanied Lord Ashburton on a visit to a local school, for which he was offering to set up a scheme of examinations and prizes. Brookfield recorded his amusement at Carlyle's contribution: 'Carlyle put in a few questions of examination here and there in his odd way. "Queen Elizabeth – at what time was she alive in this world, and what did she do?" It was amusing how he liked to put in his oar.'[60]

Yet Carlyle's heart was not in it. Encouraged by Jane, he decided to leave the Christmas preparations at the Grange and go to Scotsbrig. By 19 December Jane had returned to Cheyne Row to sort out the noise problem with their neighbour at number 6, a laundryman called Ronca who kept hens. Jane told her triumphant story to Carlyle's Welsh admirer Charles Redwood on Christmas Day:

Last Monday I was despatched to London about certain – Cocks! and a Macaw! which you have perhaps heard of – 'the first great Cause least understood' of that 'Silent apartment' which Mr C built this summer at an outlay of some 200£ The Silent Apartment having proved a complete failure having proved in fact the apartment most accessible to sound in the whole house (no wonder! having 14 air-holes in frank and free communication with the before and behind!) it became imperative, that unless we were both to be landed in Bedlam *he* thro' these Demon-birds and I thro their effects on *him* – some thing else should be done of real efficacy . . . The fine people at the Grange, were greatly *amused* as well as astonished to see a Wife sent off from the midst of Xmas festivities to consult with house agents and house owners – But Mr C was quite right in insisting 'She can do it better than I'.

She gave Ronca £5 to get rid of the fowls and got him legally bound not to keep 'any birds *or other nuisance* under penalty of 10£ and a notice to quit'.[61]

Jane also told Redwood that she had urged Carlyle, now that he had finally decided to go north, not to delay any longer:

I was very urgent to hurry him off, since he WAS going; for fear of his finding his Mother no more – I know what *that* is! – dashing along a railway in agonies of impatience and uncertainty to be told at the end 'your Mother is dead' – I have had a few lines from him to say he had found her still alive and glad to see him – tho in the last stage of weakness.[62]

Old Mrs Carlyle died that very Christmas Day. Carlyle later

remembered his journey and arrival at Kirtlebridge Station on Friday morning, 23 December, when he walked over the frozen ground the two miles to Scotsbrig, not knowing if she was alive. To his relief, he found her 'resembl[ing] her old self as the last departing moon-sickle does the moon itself'.[63] He wrote to Jane just after she died, telling her of his mother's last words to him the night before: 'John said, "Here is Tom come to bid you good night." She nodded assent; whispered audibly to me, "I'm mickle obliged to thee!" '[64] He was grateful to Jane for urging him to hurry home, knowing that he had been indecisive and that if he had heard of her death while at the Grange, 'it would have driven me half-distracted, and been a remorse to me till the end of existence'.[65]

Jane understood:

Your grief for your Mother must be altogether sweet and soft. For you must feel that you have always been a good son to her, that you have always appreciated her as she deserved, and that she knew this, and loved you to the last moment . . . Oh what I would have given for last words; to keep in my innermost heart all the rest of my Life – but the words that awaited me were; 'your Mother is DEAD'! – And I deserved it should so end – I was not the dutiful child to my Mother that you have been to yours.[66]

This glimpse of Jane's burden of guilt about her mother was poignantly supplemented for Carlyle after her own death when he found that she had kept two wax candles her mother had bought when on a visit to Cheyne Row in February 1839. Jane had invited guests; Mrs Welsh bought candles and confectionery and set the table for her daughter, who was angry at what she considered ostentatiousness. 'People would say she was extravagant and would ruin her husband.' Mrs Welsh had been upset, and Jane felt so guilty that she wrapped up the candles and told her last housekeeper, Mrs Warren, to light them on her own death.[67]

Carlyle wrote the sad news about his mother to Alick and Jenny in Canada, organised the funeral and the amicable sharing of her few possessions – a picture, a mirror, a clock, some prints.[68] Jane, meanwhile, now heard of the death of her cousin Helen Welsh, whose father, her favourite Uncle John, had died in October. Like Carlyle, she was relieved not to have been at the Grange when the news arrived.[69] It was a melancholy end to the year. Carlyle, who always seems to have found it easier to be generous and loving in letters than in person, closed his grateful letter to Jane of 27 December with a statement of good intentions. 'Let us both try to be *better* by these stern sorrows.'[70]

★

Carlyle was much preoccupied by his mother's death in the early months of 1854. His thoughts, waking and dreaming, naturally went back to his childhood, so different in every way from the life he now lived in London. For not only had the political, social, and economic changes in Britain been enormous in that time – from the war with France to the passing of the Reform Act in 1832 and the spread of the railway network in the 1830s and 1840s, even as far as Annandale – but his own evolution and translation, from lanky eldest son of unlettered peasants to celebrated writer, one of the most influential men of the century, the famous sage of Chelsea, was at least as astonishing. A sense of these great changes is expressed in his journal entry for 28 February 1854, with its echoes of the Bible and *The Tempest*, though it is noticeable that he takes no pleasurable pride in his success:

Sunday morning last, there came into my mind a vision of the old Sunday mornings I had seen at Mainhill, &c. Poor old mother, father, and the rest of us bustling about to get dressed in time and down to the meeting-house at Ecclefechan. Inexpressibly sad to me, and full of meaning. They are gone now, vanished all; their poor bits of thrifty clothes, more precious to me than Queen's or King's expensive trappings, their pious struggling effort, their 'little life', it is all away. It has all melted into the still sea; it was 'rounded with a sleep'. So with all things. Nature and this big universe in all corners of it show nothing else. Time! Death! All-devouring Time! This thought, '*Exeunt omnes*', and how the generations are like crops of grass, *temporary*, very, and all *vanishes*, as it were an apparition and a ghost: these things, though half a century old in me, possess my mind as they never did before. On the whole I have a strange interior *tomb* life, and dwell in secret among scenes and contemplations which I do not speak of to anybody. My mother! my good heavy-laden dear and brave and now lost mother! The thought that I shall never see her more with these eyes gives a strange painful flash into me many times when I look at that poor portrait I have of her. 'Like Ulysses', as I say, I converse with the shade of my mother and sink out of all company and light common talk into that grand element of sorrow and eternal stillness.[71]

Writing to Jean, he declared that he would keep his mother's 'poor old Letters', being unable to destroy them, though afraid of what 'stupid "posterity"' might make of them.[72] His habitual gloom was intensified, and he had horrible dreams, 'the fruit', he thought, 'of incurable biliousness', as well as grief for his mother and depression about *Frederick*. The journal records the scenery of these dreams in April; interestingly, it evokes Craigenputtoch:

Waste scenes of solitary desolation, gathered from Craigenputtock, as I now perceive, but tenfold *intensified*; endless uplands of scraggy moors, with gnarls of lichened crag of a stern ugliness, for always I am quite a *hermit* there too – fit to go into Dante's 'Inferno'.[73]

Lady Ashburton, his forbidden muse, received a letter written on 11

January on the black-edged paper of mourning. He had no news to tell her, but sent

this poor symbol that you are still in my thoughts; like a bright presence walking thro' gloomy caverns and sepulchral halls, willing to cheer the poor inhabitant . . . A little free speech with you, I often think, speech at which no god or man could take offence if they understood it, might be a great solacement to me: but that is not to be had, owing to confused impediments, nor perhaps ever will . . . Adieu, O beautiful Friend, beautiful and good.[74]

Jane, though so understanding in her letters about his grief, had resumed her position of bitter resentment about Lady Ashburton, as Carlyle had resumed his own position of ardent worshipper at the throne. Undoubtedly Jane was the impediment he mentions, though her name does not appear in the letter, or indeed in most of his letters to Lady Ashburton.

People still came to visit, but Carlyle could take no pleasure in them. He wrote without restraint to Jack on 10 February of one such evening:

The other night, Henry Inglis, by volunteer appoint[men]t, came to us; brought one Ricardo (more than half-drunk) in his train, and one Duff, an innocent ingenuous *babe*, in red hair and beard, member for the Elgin burroughs. Ricardo, also and sure conspicuously member for something, is a Jew of the deepest Type, *black* hooknosed Jew, with the mouth of a shark; coarse, savage, infidel, hungry, – and with considerable *strength* of heart, head and jaw. *He* went early away; the rest (to whom Ape Lewes, and an unknown Natural Philosopher sometimes seen here with him, had accidentally joined themselves) staid long. *Nichts zu bedeuten* [of no significance].[75]

Lewes, who was a favourite with both Carlyles, was always referred to as 'the Ape'; his philosopher friend may have been Herbert Spencer, his colleague on the *Leader*. John Lewis Ricardo was the nephew of the famous political economist David Ricardo. He was also MP for Stoke-on-Trent and chairman of the Electric Telegraph Company, which he had founded in 1846.[76]

Distasteful as Carlyle's rhetoric about Ricardo's Jewishness is, it belongs in the context of a general careless superiority towards Jews in nineteenth-century Britain. Dickens, Thackeray, and Trollope are as casually contemptuous as Carlyle, though with less vehemence – but then Carlyle's vehemence extends to all subjects and all sorts and conditions of men and women, of whom Jews are but one category. If he was unpleasant about people he disliked who happened to be Jewish, he was, according to his lights and the general attitude of the time, as fair as he could be to those whom he liked who happened to be Jewish. One such person was Joseph Neuberg, his admirer and helper in gathering materials for *Frederick*, and his companion in Germany in 1852 and again in 1858. Carlyle wrote a sketch of Neuberg after the latter's death in 1867, in which he described him as a 'Jew of the *better* type', 'a man of perfect integrity, of serious reflective temper, of fine strong faculties (able to *understand* anything presented to him), and of many high aspirations'.[77] What strikes us now as an attitude veering between the prejudiced and the patronising was common in Carlyle's time. Much later than this, in 1876, George Eliot bravely attempted, in *Daniel Deronda*, to 'widen the English vision a little', to combat, if she could, the 'disgusting' intellectual narrowness of British culture in its stupid attitude towards Jews and Jewishness.[78]

Early in 1854 William Brookfield and Lord Ashburton were busy writing pamphlets and making schemes on the subject of education, taking a special interest in the children who lived on and around the Ashburton estate in Hampshire, and suggesting that prizes be offered for teaching practical knowledge such as the laws of ordinary household economics and the use of tools. There should be no cramming of children.[79] Carlyle responded warmly to Lord Ashburton's writings on the subject in March, harking back to Goethe, who had so influenced the thoughts of his young manhood. He advised Lord Ashburton to read *Wilhelm Meister's Travels*:

You will find that no man was ever more completely filled with your notion [of teaching practical wisdom] than Goethe, tho perhaps he says little of it in express terms; and that his whole scheme of Education is a beautiful (and truly unrivalled) symbolical preaching of the same.[80]

Though for the next couple of years Lord Ashburton went on with his educational planning in a rather vague way, and Carlyle encouraged him in an equally vague way, nothing much seems to have come of it.

Carlyle's fierceness was increasingly commented on by friends. Emerson wrote one of his rare letters on 11 March, condoling with Carlyle on the loss of his mother, which he had learned from the newspapers, and giving a belated, careful, ruminative response to *Latter-Day Pamphlets*, which he disliked, though still finding much to admire. He had been reading 'Jesuitism':

I think you have cleared your skirts; it is a pretty good minority of one; enunciating with brilliant malice what shall be the universal opinion of the next edition of mankind . . . It required courage . . . , this writing Rabelais in 1850. And to do this alone! You must even pitch your tune to suit yourself . . . I have not ceased to think of the great warm heart that sends [the pamphlets] forth, & which I, with others, sometimes tax with satire, & with not being warm enough – for this poor world.[81]

At this same time Thackeray was thinking about Carlyle when he wrote to Lady Ashburton from Naples, playfully recounting that a fellow visitor, Lord Gainsborough, had given him with a view to my personal salvation an odious book called The Eclipse of Faith or a Visit to a religious Skipjack [i.e. 'sceptic']. Have you read it. On the other side of the hedge sits Mrs Craven and pointing to her Mother Church, says Come enter into the 'venerable bosom'. I have made acquaintance with a dozen of converts and like, and am interested by, some of them very much. But the old Church. Ah me! He of Chelsea is not farther removed from it than I am (I thought of Him of Chelsea – because I wrote ah me).[82]

Carlyle had seen little of Thackeray since his return in 1853 from several months of lecturing and being lionised in America. Writing to Emerson in September 1853, he summed Thackeray up with acuteness and sympathy. He delicately forbore to mention to Emerson that Thackeray's devotion to Mrs Brookfield had begun to raise eyebrows, and that Mr Brookfield had broken off relations, despite the best efforts of the Ashburtons. Carlyle characterised Thackeray's emotional frustration:

He is a big fellow, soul and body; of many gifts and qualities (particularly in the Hogarth line, with a dash of Sterne superadded), of enormous *appetite* withal, and very uncertain and chaotic in all points, except his *outer breeding*, which is fixed enough, and *perfect* according to the modern English style. I rather dread explosions in his history. A *big*, fierce, weeping, hungry man; not a strong one. *Ay de mi*! [ah me!][83]

In March 1854 Britain and France declared war on Russia. The Crimean War was begun over a dispute about shrines in the Holy Land and about which nation, Russia or France, should protect the rights of Christians in Turkey. Britain, it was later agreed by all parties, had no need to enter the dispute, and the new alliance formed with Louis Napoleon, now ruling as Napoleon III since his *coup* in December 1851, disgusted Carlyle, among others.[84] He wrote in his journal soon after the declaration:

Russian war; soldiers marching off, &c. Never such enthusiasm seen among the population. Cold I as a very stone to all that; seems to me privately I have hardly seen a madder business . . . A lazy, ugly, sensual, dark fanatic, that Turk, whom we have now had for 400 years . . . Then as to Russian increase of strength, &c. Really, I would wait till Russia meddled with me before I drew *sword* to stop his increase of strength. It is the idle population of editors, &c., that have done all this in England. One perceives clearly the ministers go forward in it against their will.[85]

This was prescient, though even Carlyle could not foresee the horrors of cold and disease which awaited the soldiers now on their way to the Crimea. It was the first modern war in the sense that newspaper reporters accompanied the troops – the pioneer being William Howard Russell of *The Times* – and sent back reports at great speed, aided by the electric telegraph. By the end of the year the press and public had lost their war fever, and Florence Nightingale had gone out to establish a field hospital at Scutari. *The Times* reported on 23 December that 40,000 out of an army of 54,000 had died. Moreover:

Incompetency, lethargy, aristocratic hauteur, official indifference, favour, routine perverseness and stupidity reign, revel and riot in the camp before Sebastopol, in the harbour of Balaklava, in the hospitals of Scutari, and how much nearer home we do not venture to say.[86]

Carlyle had coined the term 'the unspeakable Turk' in a little-known essay on the *Nibelungenlied* in the *Westminster Review* of July 1831, and was to make it famous by repeating it in a letter to *The Times* in 1876, when he recalled this Crimean fiasco, that 'mad war in defence of the Turk' which cost 'a hundred millions of money and above sixty thousand lives'.[87]

While staying for a weekend with the Ashburtons at Addiscombe, Carlyle accompanied them to nearby Sydenham to see the newly re-erected Crystal Palace,

a monstrous mountain of a glass building on the top of Sydenham Hill (very conspicuous from Cheyne Walk here), innumerable 'objects of art' in it, whole acres of Egyptian monsters, and many really good copies of classical and modern sculpture, which well deserve examination one day. The living visitors, not very numerous in so large an edifice (probably not above 200, sparsely scattered up and down) were almost all *Jews*; outside were as many thousands of the Christian persuasion, or rather Christian Cockney, unable to get in: the whole matter seemed to me the very highest flight of transcendental Cockneyism yet known among mankind.[88]

Alongside the unidentified group of Jewish visitors, the Ashburtons and Carlyle were enjoying a preview, since the Crystal Palace was not formally reopened by the Queen until 10 June. Richard Owen had been the chief organiser of the move, and had commissioned a sculptor to make models of prehistoric monsters to adorn the grounds. On 31 December 1853 Owen rather quaintly presided over a celebratory dinner inside one of these models, an iguanodon.[89]

*

While Carlyle was preoccupied with his outward-facing despair about the Crimea and other 'signs of the times', his inner anxieties were all to do with *Frederick* and with his intense relationships with three women: his mother, his wife, and his lady. Jane, meanwhile, returned in her correspondence again and again to the subject of woman's position. In her reply in January 1854 to the first letter she received from Mary Smith, the

Carlisle schoolteacher who wanted to become a writer, she alluded indirectly to her old ambition to be a writer herself, claiming to have 'seen, and *seen thro*', all you are now longing after'. 'Literary society' cannot, she was sure, nourish 'an aspiring soul' of itself. One must look for 'clear ideas' and 'broad knowledge' wherever one can find them, even in schoolteaching.[90]

Jane had not succeeded in her literary aspirations; nor was she satisfied by her marriage. All the more, therefore, did she look at other people's marriages with feelings of sympathy, jealously, or scorn, depending on the circumstances. All three emotions were expressed in April, when she imparted some gossip to John Carlyle about Mrs Paulet's sister-in-law, Mrs Newton, who had separated from her husband and was trying to support herself by working in a maternity hospital in London. Jane thought she might be considered 'fairly afloat – If only the Husband dont come back and swamp her'. From Mrs Newton and her forceful husband she moved on to her cousin Jeannie Chrystal:

I had a long meandering letter from Jeannie the other week – talking pleasedly of her visit to you – But 'Oh *my*' . . . into what a hebetated state of *conjugal felicity* Jeannie seems to have fallen! – Her letter is all full of her happiness as Andrews wife – her *comforts*, her beautiful house, &c &c . . . Her letter left me in the same sort of silent rage I used to feel when Graham of Burnswark dilated to me when I first became indigestive – on his pleasures of stomach – or how he 'en-jo-yed his breakfast'.[91]

In July she complained even more directly to Mary Russell. Jeannie's letters were those of a '*much-made-of married woman*', a status Jane, though previously a 'much made of' only child, had never enjoyed.[92] At least, her husband was not accustomed to make much of her, and others seemed to pay attention to her only because she was Carlyle's wife, as she complained – though lightly – in a letter to Neuberg of June 1854, thanking him for a present:

I kept *it* in my hands for some five minutes unopened, and *pinched* it, and guessed about it, and finally decided it was *worsted stockings*!! – Upon my honour, I never *can* understand why you are so good to me? – Do you understand it yourself? Sometimes I think it is because I am 'Mr Carlyle's Wife' – and then I feel tempted to gather together all the things you have *given* me and fling them at your head. I am so dreadfully tired of being '*made of*' on *that* principle![93]

On 9 May an interesting convergence occurs in another letter from Jane to Jack, to whom she could write as if they were the best of friends, though she could scarcely bear his company for more than a few hours. She tells him of an encounter with, of all people, Mrs Montagu, the 'Noble Lady' who had undertaken to help along Jane's slow courtship after meeting Carlyle on his first trip to London in 1824. The Carlyles had not seen her since 1834, when the two women fell out over Jane's hiring Bessy Barnett as her servant.[94] Jane describes Mrs Montagu in 1854, sitting alone in a room at the top of her son-in-law Procter's house, 'not a line of her figure, not a fold of her dress changed since we knew her first, 20 years ago and more!' Mrs Montagu 'began to speak of Edward Irving and long ago as if it were last year – last month!'

From this plunge into her own past loves and regrets, Jane moves on in the letter to the latest news, the separation of the Ruskins which led to Effie Ruskin's successful suit for annulment of her marriage on the grounds of non-consummation. Jane shows herself unshocked by the affair, making a shrewd point about the problem in the Ruskin marriage:

There is a great deal of talking about the Ruskins here at present. *Mrs* Ruskin has been taken to Scotland by *her* parents – and Ruskin is gone to Switzerland with *his* – and the separation is understood to be permanent there is even a rumour that *Mrs* Ruskin is to sue for a divorce – I know nothing about it, except that I have always pitied *Mrs* Ruskin while people here generally blame her – for love of dress and company and flirtation – She was too young and pretty to be so left to her own devices as she was by her husband who seemed to wish nothing more of her but the credit of having a pretty well dressed wife.[95]

The case was widely discussed. On the same day that Jane was writing about it to Jack, Clough – himself at last on the verge of marrying his long-time fiancée Blanche Smith – wrote to his American friend Charles Eliot Norton with the news. 'There is a great scandal about Ruskin & his wife – who are separated, & it is said there will be a divorce.' Ruskin was, he explained, 'profoundly indifferent' to Effie.[96] The divorce went ahead quickly, since Ruskin did not contest the case. As Effie had told her father in a letter of 7 March which precipitated the separation proceedings, 'I do not think I am John Ruskin's Wife at all – and I entreat you to assist me to get released from the unnatural position in which I stand to Him.'[97] In July 1855 Effie married the painter John Everett Millais, who had been a constant companion and painter of both Ruskins.

Jane commented at length on the Ruskin marriage and its aftermath in a winning letter in 1856 to a new young admirer of Carlyle's, William Allingham. The tendency of her remarks is critical of both parties, but mostly of Ruskin's oddity and selfishness, and she ends by giving a sardonic hint about her own marriage, which, as so often with her, can be taken both as a joke and as containing a core of serious truth:

What you say of Ruskin's book [*Modern Painters*, vol. III] is excellent. 'Claret and buttermilk' till one don't know which is which! But what *could* be expected from a man who goes to sleep with every night a different Turner's picture on a chair opposite his bed 'that he may have something beautiful to look at on first opening his eyes of a morning' (so his Mother told me). Mrs Ruskin I suppose was not beautiful *enough* to open one's eyes on the first thing; and, *hinc illae lachrymae!* [hence those tears!] You see Millais (I dont know how to spell him) and she have married . . . As for Ruskin, I never saw a man so improved by the loss of his wife! He is amiable and gay, and full of hope and faith in – one doesn't know exactly *what* – but of course *he* does. Twice last summer he drove Mr C and me and *Nero* out to his place at Denmark Hill, and gave us a dinner like what one reads of in the *Arabian Nights*, and strawberries and cream on the lawn; . . . and I returned each time more satisfied that Mrs Ruskin must have been hard to please. One feels always one could manage other women's husbands so much better than they do – and so much better than one manages one's own husband![98]

Carlyle liked Ruskin and thought that in general wives should stay with their husbands if they could; if they could not – as in the cases of Caroline Norton and Lady Bulwer-Lytton – they should at least preserve silence about their husbands' shortcomings. He seems to have written only briefly about the Ruskin affair, in a letter to Jack in November 1855, noting, as Jane did in her letter to Allingham, that Ruskin was 'as cheerful as if there had been no marriage invented among mankind'.[99]

The letters of Jane's new confidante Ellen Twisleton to her sisters in Boston are full of references to the Carlyles. They describe her elevated social round, both in the country and in London, where she was presented to the Queen in June 1853,[100] but at the heart of all her letters is her admiration for the quiet, simple lives of the Carlyles. As a young foreigner, she was grateful for the kind attentions of Jane, who had taken her to meet Elizabeth Barrett Browning one afternoon soon after her first arrival in London. Jane had also straight away let Ellen know that she liked her, 'which, as Edward [Twisleton] is particularly fond of her, is a mercy, and I am uncommonly grateful for it', Ellen wrote in July 1852.[101]

Because of Ellen's weak health she and her husband spent most winters in France and Italy. Every time they returned to England for the summer months she visited Jane. As the wife of a liberal and intellectual member of the aristocracy, she was soon invited by the Ashburtons too. At Bath House, Addiscombe, and the Grange she observed the fraught relationship between Jane and Lady Ashburton. Already on her first acquaintance with Jane, before she was introduced to Lady Ashburton, she noticed that her new friend was 'not in such a sunlight of prosperity and a little love would be a gift to her'.[102] She seems to have set out to supply it.

Reporting home on her first weekend at Addiscombe in July 1853, Ellen describes Lady Ashburton's demeanour with a touch of critical wit: 'It might have been about 5 o'clock when we arrived – Lady Ashburton was in the garden, but came in with a great poke-bonnet on, and an old grey shawl, looking as if she had defied London with a vengeance.' Many of the usual guests were there, though not the Carlyles; Ellen met James Spedding, the Brookfields, Thackeray's friend George Venables, Milnes, and an aged socialite, 'Poodle' Byng, 'now hard upon 70, – excellent manners and altogether an ideal specimen of that well-known individual "The man about town"', whose role at Addiscombe seemed to Ellen to be that of chief butt to Lady Ashburton, 'who played off all her witticisms upon him'.[103]

As everyone else did, Ellen took immediately to Lord Ashburton, 'liked all his manners to everyone, and thought him a thorough gentleman'. 'He is tall, dark and thin'. And, as everyone else also did, Ellen soon moved on from the uncomplicated husband to try to solve the puzzle of the complicated wife:

Lady Ashburton is tall, stout and plain, with an agreeable voice and an enunciation which makes it agreeable to listen to her, she is completely *la femme du grand monde*, accomplished in all the arts of attack and defence, a woman whose life is in society, and with whom conversation is an art and an occupation. She is a grand reader, a thoroughly educated and travelled and cultivated person, and with her fortune, position and talents, commands whatever she wishes in the way of society. She knows all the most distinguished people in England, in all lines, and ranks certainly with the very cleverest women I have ever known as to natural capacity. She likes to talk to five or six gentlemen at once, and for an endless length of time; in fact, if they are entertaining people, I should think she was never tired of it. She seems very fond of her husband – tho' not in the least a demonstrative person – and he evidently enjoys her jokes amazingly.[104]

And yet:

It seems to me I have known characters of a much higher stamp, and no such artificial thing as Lady Ashburton ever delights me . . . She was very polite to me without being painstakingly so, if you understand, but a person who couldn't do an ill-bred thing, any more than she could mis-spell. Moreover she has exquisite good taste and nothing can be prettier than the manner in which she has arranged her house. There is not an ugly thing in it, and all the colours and materials and style of decoration bespeak the taste of the mistress and the fortune of 40,000 pounds a year, and this not joined with formality and insipidity, but with talent and cultivation.

There was 'one thing wanting in this elaborate composition', a heart, something which in Lady Ashburton's orbit 'is so very unfashionable and all feeling a thing so utterly out of the question'.[105] Ellen then makes a direct comparison between the two new women of her acquaintance who have made the strongest impression on her. 'I consider myself slightly fortunate that neither Mrs Carlyle nor Lady Ashburton should have taken an aversion to me', she wrote; 'and Mrs Carlyle I am really fond of, she has a heart and is not fashionable'.[106]

Having left for the continent in mid-August 1853, the Twisletons returned to England in June 1854, when, among other things, they drove out to Sydenham to see the Crystal Palace, along with 'about 12,000' other people.[107] They also renewed their visits to Cheyne Row, meeting there on 10 July John Carlyle and his wife, who had recently set up home in London.[108]

Jane had not had a best friend for some time – Geraldine Jewsbury having rather forfeited the position both by differences of temperament and by distance – and Ellen, though more than twenty years younger than Jane, seems to have slipped naturally into the role. On being asked in March 1859 by the young Annie Thackeray 'who was her greatest friend', Jane named Ellen, who 'looked delighted' when Annie told her.[109] As it happened, Geraldine was even now, in summer 1854, planning to leave her brother Frank's house in Manchester to settle in London and pursue her novelistic and journalistic career. On 13 July Jane told Mary Russell that Geraldine, 'the most *intimate* friend I have in the world', had decided 'to come and live near me for good'.[110] Jane found lodgings for her in Oakley Street, just round the corner from Cheyne Row.[111]

Though it was pleasant for Jane to have her old friend so close, particularly while Carlyle was closeted for such long hours in his noisy sound-proofed study, it did not, as she herself realised, do anything to sweeten the sourness of her marriage. Rather the opposite, in fact. She had complained humorously to Blanche Airlie in December 1851 of a habit of Geraldine's in which she had just caught herself while responding to some sadness in the tone of Blanche's last letter to her:

But I am stupid to be answering your letter *to the same mood it was written in* – How often has Geraldine Jewsbury, the only person I ever write Jeremiads to, driven me wild with a long letter of consolations, or good advice only applicable to a momentary humour, forgotten by myself while *she* had been remembering it too well and bringing all her forces of sympathy and sense to bear on it.[112]

If her letters to Geraldine, almost all of which Geraldine destroyed, were, as she suggests here, more bitter even than those to Jeannie and Helen Welsh and, as the years went on, to Mary Russell, they must indeed have seemed to Geraldine to require large amounts of soothing balm, though she had the knack rather of assisting in sharpening Jane's anger and grief. Jane was nothing if not an exacting friend, critically alert to what she perceived as a lack of sympathy, but equally so to what she deemed an excess of it. With that sharp self-critical faculty of hers, she was soon calling Geraldine 'my *Electra*' in a letter of December to Joseph Neuberg, suggesting that Geraldine saw herself as the avenger of Jane's wrongs.[113] As had always happened in circles with Jane at the centre, her two friends,

Geraldine and Ellen, old and new, clashed. In May 1855, for example, Ellen, describing a visit to Cheyne Row, observed glumly, 'The unfailing Miss Jewsbury was there.'[114]

★

In July 1854 Dickens wrote to ask if Carlyle would allow him to dedicate his new novel, *Hard Times*, to him. He hoped the book, with its denunciation of Utilitarianism in education and of industrial confrontation between factory owner and factory hands – a direct allusion to a strike and lockout of textile workers in Preston – would 'shake some people', and was sure it 'contains nothing in which you do not think with me, for no man knows your books better than I'.[115]

That Dickens was not simply flattering Carlyle is evident from a letter written two months previously to John Forster in which he explains with admirable clarity where he differs from Carlyle, paying him a fine tribute in the process:

Now do let me (and you know that it is impossible for any one to admire him as a great original genius and a most admirable writer, more than I do) remind you that the extraordinary peculiarity of his mind always is a respect for power when it is exercised by a determined man. Some years ago when I was not familiarly acquainted with his writings, I said to you, after meeting him one night in your rooms with Emerson [in April 1848], that it was an anomaly I could not get out of my mind, to hear him immensely lauding even the present Emperor of Russia. You know how the same curious distortion, if I may call it so, in one I so much respect – pervades everything he does . . . I hold that in these things Death and Time should make no manner of difference. A Tyrant is always a detestable creature, publicly, however virtuous privately, and is always a creature to give no quarter to. Spare him two hundred years after he is dead, and you don't know what you do towards the birth of his successor next year.[116]

In July Robert Tait took some excellent photographs of Carlyle, notable because they were the last likenesses of the sage before he grew the beard so familiar from later portraits and photographs, particularly those taken by Julia Margaret Cameron in his old age. One of Tait's photographs shows Carlyle sitting side-on to the camera, his familiar wideawake hat on his knee, looking determined, with his mouth tight shut and his lower lip jutting out, but still handsome and relatively young for a man of fifty-eight. He has a lean, upright body and a fine head of thick dark hair, silvering here and there, and though the eyes are cast to the side, there is a suggestion of the brightness and beauty described by so many of his contemporaries. It is hard to reconcile this youthful-looking man with the broken voice·of the journals, or even the forceful but too often negative voice of the letters.

355

By stark and poignant contrast, Tait's photographs of Jane taken at the same time, when she was fifty-three, show a woman looking much older than her years. Hers is the thinness of ill health; her face looks shrunken and shrivelled, and her eyes heavy with sleeplessness and morphine.[117] On looking at these photographs, one wonders how it was that Carlyle saw so little of her physical and psychological state. Browning's memory of her years later, as having good sparkling eyes and fine black hair, but an excessively turned-up nose and a complexion like 'pickled walnuts', though cruel and reflecting the mutual dislike between him and Jane, was, on the evidence of these photographs, hardly exaggerated.[118]

Tait went off to Germany immediately after photographing the Carlyles, arriving in Weimar where, as he recalled,

I was somewhat surprised, as well as interested, to hear that Mr G. H. Lewes and Miss Evans, so distinguished in literature as George Eliot, had arrived in Weimar about a week previously, and had established themselves in lodgings there, coming usually for lunch and dinner to the Erbprinz Hotel, where I stayed for some 3 weeks. Both of them were previously known to me in London.

One day Mr Lewes and I made an excursion to Eisenach and then on foot to the famous old castle of the Wartburg in which Luther was sheltered and protected – imprisoned some said – for a year after his heroic defiance of the powers of the Papacy at Worms.

Among the objects on display were the two small Cranach oil paintings of Luther's parents which had so moved Carlyle on his visit to the Wartburg in September 1852. Having heard Carlyle talk of these pictures, Tait now 'spent three days in the Luther-Zimmer [Luther's room] at the Castle making copies of them'. He put the copies into 'old-fashioned gilt frames' and sent them to Carlyle. 'They shall hang on my walls here; in daily sight of me', Carlyle wrote on Tait's return, asking for a photograph of any copy he might make of Cranach's portrait of Luther himself, should he return to Eisenach.[119]

Tait's surprise at meeting with Lewes and Marian Evans, Chapman's 'Able Editor' of the *Westminster Review*, together at Weimar was as nothing to the shock their liaison caused at home. Marriage in England was surely in a strange state when one well-known couple – the Ruskins – were divorcing from a blank marriage while another were setting up a 'married' establishment, exposing themselves, but especially the woman, to scandal and social exclusion because the law refused Lewes permission to divorce his wife Agnes on the grounds that, by registering as his own the children she had borne to his friend Thornton Hunt, he had condoned her adultery, thereby forfeiting his right to seek a divorce.

Well might Marian Evans's feminist friend Barbara Leigh Smith publish a pamphlet in this same year entitled *A Brief Summary in Plain Language of the Most Important Laws concerning Women.* Marian Evans soon discovered that her closest family and friends were willing to cut her off, and her proud and in some ways conventional nature suffered from the injustice of her position, though her relationship with Lewes brought her enduring emotional happiness, and he encouraged her, against her own diffidence and fear of failure, to write the celebrated novels which were published from 1859 under the pseudonym George Eliot.[120]

Partly to escape London's wagging tongues, and partly because Lewes needed to visit Germany to complete the research for his *Life of Goethe*, the couple chose to bring their relationship into the open with this trip, which began with their arrival in Weimar on 2 August. Carlyle had written a generous letter of introduction to James Marshall in Weimar, describing Lewes as 'an ingenious brilliant, entertaining, highly gifted and accomplished man and writer', already 'far advanced' in his Goethe researches.[121] Carlyle was one of two valued friends, the other being Arthur Helps, to whom Lewes wrote on 11 October, explaining his position and assuring him that his marriage had been irretrievably broken for some time. His letter is lost, as is Carlyle's reply, but Lewes's second letter of 19 October shows that Carlyle had responded warmly. Lewes thanked him for this, and for his intellectual influence too:

My heart yearned towards you as I read [your letter]. I sat at your feet when my mind was first awakening; I have honoured and loved you ever since both as teacher and friend, and *now* to find that you judge me rightly, and are not estranged by what has estranged so many from me, gives me strength to bear what yet must be borne.[122]

Carlyle did support Lewes at first, knowing about Agnes's complacency on the birth of the first Hunt child, Edmund, in 1850. (By 1854 there were three; a fourth was born in 1857.) Edward FitzGerald received a fairly open-minded account from Carlyle, written on 19 October:

Have you heard about poor Lewes, 'hairy Lewes' as we sometimes call him? He has put away his Wife at last, and for right good cause; but the rest of the rumour about him I believe to be, in brief, *lies*. He is a good soul in several respects in spite of his hair.[123]

When Lewes's second letter of explanation arrived, denying some scurrilous gossip about Miss Evans, including the alleged writing of a letter to Harriet Martineau, but confirming that he was living with her, Carlyle's severity came into play. He noted on Lewes's letter:

Alas, alas! – I had (at his request) approved unequivocally of parting *such a marriage*; and advised to contradict, if he could, on his word of honour, the bad rumours circulating about a certain 'strong minded woman' and him. He assures me, on his word of honour, the strong minded did not *write* etc.: as well assure me her stockings are both of one colour; that is a very insignificant point! – No answer to this second letter.[124]

After the couple's return to London in spring 1855, Carlyle continued to see Lewes, even helping him with the *Life of Goethe*, but he and Jane were not among the few progressive thinkers to invite, and accept invitations from, both Lewes and Marian. Much later Carlyle's Irish friend Duffy recorded a conversation at the Carlyles' which turned first to Carlyle's old *bête noire*, George Sand, and then to Lewes and the by now famous George Eliot. Duffy reports Jane as saying, in caustic mood, that 'when one was first told that the strong woman of the *Westminster Review* had gone off with a man whom we all knew, it was as startling an announcement as if one heard that a woman of your acquaintance had gone off with the strong man at Astley's [the famous equestrian theatre]'.[125]

By November 1854 the Leweses were in Berlin, where they met Varnhagen von Ense. Marian told her Coventry friend Charles Bray that Varnhagen had been 'terribly disappointed when he came to know [Carlyle] in the flesh' in 1852, after corresponding with him for years:

Varnhagen is a courtier, wears an order round his neck and carries a gold headed cane, so you may imagine that Carlyle's roughness and petulance were rather shocking to him. Withal this Varnhagen is a theoretical democrat, and thinks 'Past and Present' Carlyle's greatest work, while to his dismay he found that Carlyle talked the fiercest despotism etc. etc.[126]

In August Carlyle heard that Bulwer-Lytton had made a publishing deal with 'certain Booksellers conjointly' which amounted to £10,000 'for the liberty to print and publish *ad libitum* in railway shilling volumes and all manner of other forms the "works" (so-called) of the said Bulwer'. His informant had added that the sales were not fulfilling expectations.[127] Bulwer-Lytton had been paid not £10,000, but £20,000, by Routledge for the shilling reprint rights to all his novels; at that time it was the largest single deal in the history of British publishing.[128] (Carlyle's own venture into shilling volumes in Chapman and Hall's railway series seems to have run into the sand. Only 'Johnson' and 'Burns' were issued in this form, though other essays had been advertised as forthcoming.)[129]

Carlyle soon had a family tragedy to drive all jealous and scornful thoughts about Bulwer-Lytton out of his mind. His brother John's wife Phoebe, eight months pregnant, had given birth prematurely to a dead child, and had herself survived only a few hours more. John and Phoebe had been in a slight railway accident a few days before, and the shock seems to have brought on the deaths. Carlyle told Alick the sad story on 6 September:

Poor Phoebe, a very cheerful quiet and good lady, with whom it was easy to live pleasantly, used to come often down in the summer evenings with John: they ran about at a great rate thro' the day, 'looking for houses', also 'seeing sights', for she was of a travelling roaming turn like her husband, and they did not seem in any haste to fix upon a house, – tho', as she was five or six months gone with child, we always silently thought it altogether desirable they should be *fixed* . . . We all thought this coming child, and this good and prudent and cheerful Wife might prove the most marked advantage to all parties concerned; and now it has suddenly all vanished; and our poor Brother is mournfully thrown loose, and his poor Life-partner crushed down in that overwhelming manner.[130]

Writing to Isabella Carlyle, Jane exclaims:

Oh if they had only been poor people, with no time or money for racketting about, she might have born[e] him a living son and they might have been very happy over it. He is in a strange, stupefied state – indeed we are all quite stunned . . . I suppose the Dr will be about here for some time settling their affairs. What he will do after I cant think – thrown all at sea again, without so much as a house of his own for a fixed point.[131]

The great change in Carlyle's appearance came about this autumn. A letter of 30 September to Lord Ashburton, who was holidaying in the Highlands, explains how and why he began to grow a beard at a time when facial hair was not very common – hence Carlyle's references to 'hairy Lewes' and 'Ape Lewes' on account of his friend's long hair, sideburns, and lavish moustache. Carlyle writes in high good humour:

But what shall I say of the grand question, the Beard? Certainly I am, and have ever been, a fixed enemy of shaving; a tyrannous product of mere use and wont; fantastic, without a shadow of reason to shew for itself . . . Sure enough you are to be envied, and I envy you, for that noble free flowing beard, of which I hear so much. And if you do really mean to front St James's with it – but I always think your heart will fail at sight of St James's, and you are only joking all this while? Well, if you dare absolutely risk a stroke, for deliverance of yourself and of mankind, in that manner, I am mindful of my promise, and even my wife assents; the razor shall be thrown away, and a second beard appear on the streets, too happy to get out under such backing! Really the Beard-movement does proceed, I perceive. Leigh Hunt I heard not long since, had produced a copious beard, white or nearly so; he complained that there were two drawbacks 1st the little boys laughed at him; 2d the beard abolished an uncommonly sweet smile he was understood to have. That latter evil will not apply to me. Nor do I think practically that little boys will much interfere. Moustaches are already very abundant; and one young gent (of the *gent* species) carries a beard in these streets, black, immense, sticking out from the chin of him like a kitchen kettle.[132]

A pact had been made, as Carlyle explained on 13 October to Jack (by now back in Moffat), when Lord Ashburton appeared unexpectedly one morning early in October – 'hot from the Highlands' and due to return there immediately. 'He wore a respectable really rather handsome *beard*: once, in a careless way, I had said, last year, if *he* adopted a beard, I wd follow: he now claimed my promise, Jane and he combining.' They had gone to Carlyle's bedroom and taken away his razors, and now Carlyle had been four days without shaving, 'and in very questionable mood about it', though pleased to be saving half an hour a day.[133]

Carlyle's beard may not have excited the laughter of little boys, but until it reached its full magnificence, friends were sceptical. Thackeray told Lady Stanley in December: 'Ashburton has grown a beard I hear & Tom Carlyle has a scrubby one.' When Ellen Twisleton saw Carlyle again in April 1855 after wintering abroad, she described to her sisters the 'grand, grizzled and grisly conglomeration' of Carlyle's beard and whiskers. He 'looks hideous', she declared.[134]

Carlyle, Lord Ashburton, and Leigh Hunt were a year or so ahead of fashion. Beards became ubiquitous with the return in 1856 of the soldiers from the Crimean War. They had found, as Mazzini had done when fighting for a Roman Republic, that shaving was a luxury not appropriate in camp conditions, particularly where death, injuries, and cholera prevailed. Already by the end of 1854 it had become abundantly clear that the Anglo-French adventure in the Crimea was a disaster. The infamous 'Charge of the Light Brigade' took place at Balaclava on 25 October. Tennyson's brilliant poem on the subject picked up a comment in the ever-vigilant *Times* about 'some hideous blunder' by those in command. Published in John Forster's *Examiner* on 9 December, the poem caught the confusion and stupidity of the generals, while paying homage to the bravery of the 'six hundred' who lost their lives. The famous second verse expresses the pathos of the situation:

'Forward, the Light Brigade!'
Was there a man dismay'd?
Not tho the soldier knew
    Someone had blunder'd:
Theirs not to make reply,
Theirs not to reason why,
Theirs but to do and die:
Into the valley of Death
    Rode the six hundred.

Jane was 'haunted day and night', she told Mary Russell on 7 November,

with the thought of all the women over England Scotland and Ireland who must be in agonies of suspense about their nearest and dearest. Thank God I have no husband or brother or father or son in that horrible War. I have some few acqaintances however, and one intimate friend Colonel Sterling [Anthony, now promoted from Captain] . . . and I read the list of killed and wounded always with a sick dread of finding *his* name.[135]

All the newspapers, led by *The Times*, were sharply critical of the British command and the British Government. Dickens managed to extract a little fun from the dismal business at the expense of his bossy, self-regarding friend Forster, who was editorialising in the *Examiner*. In a letter of 1 November to Macready Dickens wrote:

Forster is getting a little too fat, but appears to be troubled by the great responsibility of directing the whole War [in his editorials]. He doesn't seem to me, to be quite clear that he has got the ships into the exact order he intended, on the sea-point of attack at Sebastopol.[136]

On 8 November it was arranged through Lady Ashburton that Carlyle should visit Windsor Castle to see the portraits of Frederick the Great contained in the royal art collection. He told her about his day there:

Towards 4 o'clock there came a light footstep to the door: I still busy among 100 Frederick Portraits did not look up, till Glover said, 'Prince Albert!' – and there in fact was his Royal Highness, come for a sight of the monster before he went; – bowing very graciously, and not advancing till I bowed. Truly a handsome flourishing man and Prince; extremely polite (in the English way too): – and with a far better pair of *eyes* than I had given him credit for in the distance. We had a very pretty little dialogue: about Frederick's Portraits first (and your despised Picture now turned to the wall at Bath House, the original of which is well known to H.R.H, came in among other things) . . . That is the history of my day; which I thought good to lay at your Ladyship's feet, that you may see how 'the pleasure of the Lord prospers in your hand', when you do kindnesses to your friends.[137]

This letter shows Carlyle attempting to write in a more positive vein to Lady Ashburton. He had been sending plaintive notes about his solitude and his misery over *Frederick*; she must have taxed him with excessive gloom, for he wrote on 4 November, quoting her phrases back at her: 'Your beneficent message, couched in satirical terms, came duly; and was duly welcomed, satire and all.' But alas, he continues, he cannot acquire what she wants for him – 'a temperate frame of mind, and good digestion'. Indeed, she might as well wish him a pair of wings. Moving on to more light-hearted matters, he reports that his beard is 'the horror of surrounding parishes!' 'I do not think really it will ever do; for it grows daily *more* ugly withal.'[138]

Though invited to the Grange for Christmas, Carlyle declined; 'it was too sad an anniversary for me', he told Emerson some months later, thinking of his mother's death on Christmas Day the previous year.[139] Jane was suffering from one of her colds, as she told Mary Russell on 30

December, so she, too, declined her invitation to the Grange.[140] In one of his guilt-induced notes after Jane's death, Carlyle recalled that at this time she was 'in poor fluctuating health', while he was 'in dismal continual wrestle with *Friedrich* the *unexecutable book*'. His days were 'black and spiritually muddy; hers, too, very weak and dreamy, tho' *uncom-plaining*'.[141] In fact Jane was now approaching a crisis in her feelings about him; towards the end of 1855 she took to writing her bitterness in a journal which she kept secret from him.

CHAPTER 15
Breakdown 1855–1857

Lord Aberdeen had blocked Prince Albert's suggestion that Carlyle be offered a pension on grounds of his heterodoxy; at the end of 1854 some Glasgow University students found that his name was distrusted in Scottish orthodox circles too. The leader of the student Liberal Association, John Nichol, nominated Carlyle, without his knowledge, as a candidate for the vacant Lord Rectorship in opposition to the Conservative Club's candidate, Disraeli. The Scottish newspapers made an outcry about Carlyle's 'hostility to the religion of the Bible' as exhibited in the *Life of Sterling*, and his name was dropped, as was Disraeli's, who was also too controversial a figure to command widespread support.

On hearing this from Nichol, Carlyle replied that he was sorry to learn 'what angry nonsense some of my countrymen see good to write of me', but felt honoured by 'your noble enthusiasm (which reminds me of my own young years)'. He was unable to resist a bit of Carlylean rhetoric about electoral systems:

'Elections' are not a thing transacted by the gods, in general; and I have known very unbeautiful creatures 'elected' to be kings, chief-priests, railway kings, etc., by the 'most sweet voices', and the spiritual virtue that inspires these, in our time![1]

Ruskin, now free from his marriage mistake, sought out Carlyle in January 1855, writing that he had been 'rendered desperate' by the thought that he had not seen him for three years, and showing elaborate anxiety that Carlyle might consider him insufficiently dutiful as a disciple: 'People are continually accusing me of borrowing other men's thoughts, & not confessing the obligation.' He went on to 'entreat' Carlyle not to think that he was 'mean enough to borrow from you knowingly, & without acknowledgment'. Anticipating what Marian Evans was to say in her article on Carlyle in October of this year about his influence being that of an oak which sows acorns far and wide, Ruskin continued: 'How much your general influence has told upon me, I know not – but I always confess it – or rather boast of it.'[2] Carlyle replied warmly, inviting Ruskin to come any day after half-past three, when he generally took some respite from his work on *Frederick*.[3]

The two men were to become firm friends. Carlyle was sympathetic towards Ruskin's later impossible love for the child Rose La Touche and his increasing madness in the late 1860s and 1870s; Ruskin took to addressing Carlyle as 'Master' and 'Dearest Papa'.[4] His observations on the Carlyle marriage, while hardly those of an expert on the subject, are interesting in that they look back to 1855, just when the Carlyles were approaching a crisis. He told Charles Eliot Norton in 1885 that he 'used to see the two constantly together – and there was never the slightest look of right affection. She always called him Carlyle, never Tom – and he – rarely attended to a word she said.'[5]

In February 1855 Jane took radical measures to make Carlyle listen to her. The subject was her housekeeping allowance; she couched her complaint in terms both detailed and humorous. Carlyle was greeted on 12 February by the 'Budget of a Femme Incomprise', which he read with delight at the cleverness of the 'unappreciated woman' who had written it. The piece, which is incidentally full of useful information for historians of the daily life of the period, begins resentfully:

I don't choose to *speak* again on the *Money question*! The 'replies' from the Noble Lord are unfair and unkind, and little to the purpose. When you tell me 'I pester your life out about money' – that 'your soul is sick with hearing about it', that 'I had better make the money I *have* serve, at all rates – hang it! let *you* alone of it'; all that I call perfectly unfair, the reverse of kind, and tending to nothing – but disagreement.

If I were greedy, or extravagant, or a bad manager; you would be justified in 'staving me off' with loud words: but you cannot say *that* of me (whatever else) cannot *think* it of me! At least I am sure that I never 'asked for more' to myself from you or anyone – not even from my own Mother in all my life; and that, thro' six and twenty years, I have kept house for you, at more or less cost according to given circumstances, but always on *less* than it costs the generality of People, living in the same style.

Jane warms to the subject, asking only that he '*keep his temper*' while she explains how costs began to rise when the house was improved in the summer of 1853. 'I will show the Noble Lord, with his permission, what the new current expenses *are* and to what they *amount per annum*. ("Hear!" "hear!" and cries of "be brief!")'[6] There follows an inventory of increased expenses, including £16 a year for the current servant Ann, where runaway bride Fanny had cost only £13. 'We have now gas and water "laid on", both producing admirable results', Jane goes on, but

betwixt 'water laid on' at *one pound sixteen shillings* per annum, with *shilling* to Turncock, and water carried at fourpence a week [from a well to the house], there is a yearly difference of nineteen shillings and four pence; and betwixt *gas* all the year round and a few sixpenny-boxes of *lights* in the winter, the difference may be computed at *fifteen shillings*.

Moreover, taxes have gone up, ten shillings a year having been added to the Lighting, Pavement, and Improvement Rate, a pound to the Poor Rate, ten shillings to the Sewer Rate, and the recent doubling of income tax – to finance the Crimean War – all adding up to an extra £7 16s. 8d. on a previous total tax rate of £17 12s. 8d.[7]

The cost of provisions – bread, butter, meat, coal, candles, bacon, soap, potatoes – had risen, she works out, by about £12 a year. In all, the necessary costs outlined so far are £29 10s. 8d. more than in previous years. What follows shows that she and Carlyle had argued unpleasantly over money:

You asked me at last money-row, with 'withering sarcasm', 'had I the *slightest* idea what amount of money would *satisfy me*? Was I wanting *fifty* pounds more? or *forty*? or thirty? Was there any conceivable sum of money that could put an end to my eternal botheration?' I will answer the question as if it had been asked practically and kindly.

Yes! I have the *strongest* idea what amount of money would 'satisfy' me. I have computed it often enough as I lay awake at nights . . . The above-named sum, 29£, divided into quarterly payments would *satisfy* me.[8]

Lest Carlyle think that she merely expects him to hand over the extra money, she offers to make do with a smaller personal allowance. She had been receiving £25 a year, and assures him:

I can 'keep up my dignity' and my wardrobe, on a less sum – on 15£ a year. A silk *dress*, a 'splendid dressing gown', a Milliner's bonnet the less! what signifies that at my age? – Nothing! – Besides I have had so many 'gowns' *given* me, that they may serve for two or three years. By then God knows if I shall be *needing gowns* at all![9]

Jane's fierce pride does battle with her comic sense as she continues:

There only remains to disclose the actual state of the Exchequer. It is empty *as a drum*. ('Sensation'!) If I consider 29 more pounds indispensable (things remaining as they are) for the coming year, beginning from the 22d of March; – it is just because I have found it so in the year that is gone. And I commenced *that*, as already stated with *ten pounds* of arrears. Now, you 'assisted' me with 15 pounds, and I have 'assisted' *myself* with *ten* pounds *five* last August which I took from the *Savings Bank*, and the *five* you gave me at newyear, which I threw into the coal account. (Don't suppose, 'if thou's i' the habit o' *supposing*' that I tell you this in the *undevout* imagination of being *repaid*; by all that's sacred for me – *the memory of my father and mother* – what else can an 'irreligious creature' like me *swear* by?)[10]

Finally:

If I were a man, I might 'fling the gauntlet to Society, join with a few brave fellows, and rob a Diligence'. But my sex 'kind of' debars me from *that*! – Mercy! to think there are women, your friend Lady Ashburton for example ('*rumeur*' and 'sensation') I say, *for example*; who spend not merely the 'additamental' pounds, I must make such pother about, but *four times my whole income* in the *Ball* of *one* night! and none the worse for it, nor anyone the better! – It is – 'what shall I say?' – *curious*, 'upon *my* honour!'

After this direct thrust, the aggression mitigated a little by the companionable sharing of the odd servant phrase and Mazzini-ism, Jane signs off, 'your Obedient humble Servant, Jane Welsh Carlyle'.[11]

Carlyle, whose picture is painted in no flattering tones here, replied immediately in admiring, if somewhat patronising, acquiescence:

Excellent, my dear clever Goody, – thriftiest, wittiest, and cleverest of women! I will set thee up again to a certainty, and thy £30 more shall be granted, thy bits of debts paid, and thy will *done*!

On re-reading the petition much later, Carlyle recorded that 'the Piece is so clever, that I cannot, just yet, find in my heart to burn it, as perhaps I ought to do'.[12] And, despite the unfavourable light cast on him, he never did.

A serious clash was thus averted on this occasion by Jane's authorial tactics. When Ellen Twisleton came home from Paris in March, she visited Jane, and was treated to her wit and also to her bitterness, which was reaching pathological proportions. Ellen recounted a visit on 29 April, when she and her husband found Jane 'sitting alone with a frightful cold in the head'. On seeing them she

started up when we came in and said, 'Well, it's quite fearful – I was at that moment thinking of ye, when the servant said Mr. and Mrs. Edward Twisleton – I was thinking if ye had grown treacherous too, like the rest of the world – I thought about yer husband, and then I thought of yer clear, black eyes, and I said, "is it possible!"' so we agreed that that was very fearful, indeed, and scolded her, thoroughly, – and after making her a visit, E. went up to see Carlyle in his hole at the top of the house, and I waited, part of the time while other people were there, and part of the time with her alone, and I wish I could write out her conversation for you. Her fun is fun beyond any, though it is sometimes rather bitter, and if you could hear the stories about London life which she and Georgy [Edward's cousin] tell, two people so different, yet agreeing so thoroughly in this, you would think 'Vanity Fair' and Becky Sharp were mild under-statements of the truth.[13]

Later in the year Ellen did 'write out her conversation', the sustained complaint about Craigenputtoch.

The war in the Crimea continued to go badly. Aberdeen's government had fallen early in 1855, and Palmerston had taken his place. A committee of inquiry into the mishandling of the war had been set up under the radical MP John Roebuck; Lord Raglan, the commander of operations, came under strong criticism. Carlyle professed his astonishment that

Britain's despicable ally Louis Napoleon was not shot at when he paid a visit to London at this time. He told Jack on 20 April that he had been in an omnibus on Piccadilly just before Napoleon and his Empress arrived, from which he saw 'two thin and *thinnest* rows of the most abject looking human wretches' drawn up 'from St James's Street to Hyde Park Corner to receive the August Pair'.[14]

Only a few days later a certain J. Studholme Brownrigg wrote to Carlyle from 'Light Division, Camp before Sebastopol', saying he wished he 'could give a cheering report of our doings here but in fact we are doing nothing'.[15] He added that the Russians were 'astute fellows', an opinion shared by Anthony Sterling, who came home on leave in December, complaining in a 'surly' fashion about the prosecution of the war. 'Russian Officers alone know anything about War', 'Russians able to scheme and manoeuvre', the newly bearded Anthony – with 'beard as big as a moderate corn-sheaf' – told Carlyle, who reported the conversation to Lady Ashburton.[16]

Carlyle's thoughts about Russia, which had caused Dickens to demur, were engaged in April 1855 by Alexander Herzen, who sent him a pamphlet in French on the 'Development of Revolutionary Ideas in Russia'. Carlyle replied in a 'rather long letter', as Herzen told Aurelio Saffi,[17] of pure Carlylese:

For my own share I confess I never had, and have now (if it were possible) less than ever, the least hope in 'Universal Suffrage' under any of its modifications: and, if it were not that in certain deadly maladies of the body politic, a burning crisis may be considered as beneficent, I should much prefer Tsarism itself, or Grand-Turkism itself, to the sheer Anarchy (as I reckon it sadly to be) which is got by 'Parliamentary Eloquence', Free Press and counting of heads. 'Ach! Mein lieber Sulzer, Er kennt nicht diese verdammte Race!' [Ah, my dear Sulzer, you don't know this damned race!] said Frederick of Prussia once; and it is a sad truth he expresses there. In your vast country – which I have always respected as a huge dark 'Birth of Providence', the meanings of which are not known – there is evident, down to this time, one talent in which it has the pre-eminence, giving it potency far beyond any other Nation: the talent (indispensable to all Nations and all creatures, and inexorably required of them all under penalties), *the talent of obeying* – which is much out of vogue in other quarters just now![18]

To which Herzen replied, in French, showing wit and independence of spirit, though also respect, that he was not an enthusiast of universal suffrage either, but that socialism as he advocated it 'tries to discover the laws for the most natural organisation of society'. As for the 'talent of obeying':

The ability to submit in agreement with our conscience is a *virtue*; but the ability to resist when one is being forced to obey against one's conviction – that is also a virtue . . . Without the talent of resisting, the world would be in the state Japan is in. No history, no development . . . You are too much of a philosopher not to forgive me for defending my opinions, fully conscious as I am of the inferiority of my powers.[19]

★

In July Jane felt that Carlyle was neglecting her birthday; she complained to her pious old Scottish friend Thomas Erskine about having to spend the day by herself. As Lady Ashburton was in Paris, it is likely that Jane's self-pity on this occasion was due to Carlyle's obsession with his work. Erskine wrote consolingly that he would have liked to spend the day with her, '& to have taken the father's place & part as well as I could', giving her the 'loving care and interest' she craved. There followed his reminiscence of the sweet child at Haddington and his then hopes for a bright future for her, with several pages of flowing expressions about the love of God which, though wasted on her, did not annoy her, since he was so evidently sincere.[20]

The Carlyles ventured out a little during July. They visited Ruskin at Denmark Hill early in the month, to be treated to those strawberries and cream on the lawn and that dinner out of *Arabian Nights* which Jane later described to William Allingham.[21] She had expressed the wish that the treat could have been on her birthday, 14 July, and Ruskin seems to have offered to have them out again on that day, judging by her witty-defiant comment to him:

If 'virtue is ever its own reward', (which 'may be *strongly* doubted', as we say in Edinr) decidedly the same cannot be said of *discretion*! How long might I have been discreet, 'silent', and all that sort of thing, without accomplishing any such good for myself, as in blurting out that foolish little thought; 'I wish *this* had been the 14th.'[22]

Whatever she did or did not do on her birthday, Carlyle continued to be a disagreeable companion. Elizabeth Barrett Browning told Anna Jameson that summer that she and Browning had seen Carlyle at Forster's house, 'and found him in great force, particularly in the damnatory clauses'.[23] The relationship between the Brownings and the Carlyles did not flourish. Though Jane thought Elizabeth '*true* and *good*', she could not believe Browning to be more than a 'fluff of feathers', as she had told John Carlyle in July 1852.[24] Her opinion of him had hardened, if anything, since then, till in July 1856 she described another visit to Mrs Montagu, where she found Browning. He 'dropt on one knee and kissed her hand with a fervour! And I have heard Browning speak slightingly of Mrs

Montagu.' Then 'he kissed *my* hand too with a fervour; and I wouldn't give sixpence for his regard for me.'[25]

This was written in Jane's private journal on 4 July 1856, when she was in the blackest of moods; nevertheless, she was right about Browning's dislike of her. He was later reported to have called her 'a hard, unlovable woman' and to have recalled in 1883 that Carlyle had spoken of her 'as if she had stepped down from the stars to marry him'. 'What was she, after all? The daughter of a small Scotch doctor in an obscure country village.' Browning was one of those who were uncomfortable with Jane's conversational sarcasm at Carlyle's expense: 'She encouraged all Carlyle's whims and fancies, adopted all his ideas and opinions and exaggerated them; but ridiculed them to other people.'[26]

For his part, Carlyle liked Browning, though he was by no means uncritical. You have to 'let him haggle and wriggle thro' the strange jungle of loud speech (loud *soliloquy*, you would say, rather than dialogue)', he told Jack in September 1855, adding that Browning had 'a good talent' but was unluckily stuck in 'the valley of the shadow of man George-Sandism, Mazzini-ism, Leigh Huntism'.[27]

When Browning was in Paris at the end of the year, Carlyle wrote asking him to find out some information about Voltaire, whose relationship with Frederick he had been investigating for the past year. He wrote winningly to others, too, for help with books on Voltaire, petitioning Harriet Grote in February 1855, when he spoke feelingly of Voltaire as 'not a Hero of mine', but as one of the best men in 'his utterly rotten 18th Century'; in fact, he told Mrs Grote, Voltaire and Frederick were 'nearly all I can find of worthy or perennial in said sordid forgettable dungheap of a century'.[28] He found time in August to do a favour for G. H. Lewes, now returned from Germany and finishing his *Life of Goethe*, which was published in November 1855, dedicated to Carlyle, 'who first taught England to appreciate Goethe'. While Lewes took his sons on a week's holiday in Ramsgate, Carlyle read the proofs for him, writing encouragingly that the book 'promises to be a very good bit of Biography'.[29]

The latter part of the summer was one of painful misunderstandings between the Carlyles. After much hesitating, Carlyle went down to Suffolk to spend ten days with Edward FitzGerald, who spelt out details of train and coach and anxiously asked 'dear Mrs Carlyle' to let him know 'what C. is "To Eat – Drink – and Avoid"'[30] Carlyle dreaded the 'shrieking, mad, (and to me quite horrible) rail operations' of getting to Ipswich, as he told his host on 7 August; he was coming down the next day, bringing plenty of books. He assured FitzGerald that he would appreciate 'being left well alone' for much of the time, though he was also prepared to walk, drive about, and swim in the sea sometimes.[31]

Jane planned to go to Scotland while Carlyle was away, but changed her mind on finding that the third-class carriage to Edinburgh was nothing but 'a black hole of Calcutta on wheels! closely roofed in, windows like pigeon holes'. (Why was she planning to go third class? Was she making a point about Carlyle's recent accusations of extravagance?) The second-class carriages were scarcely better, and she declined to spend money on a first-class compartment, 'so *that* project was felled on the spot', she told him on 11 August.[32]

Instead she went to Brighton to look for a holiday cottage that they might share – though not, one supposes, at the same time – with Robert Tait, who had become a frequent visitor, endearing himself to Carlyle by taking photographs of the portrait Carlyle now owned of his mother, so that Carlyle could send copies to all his brothers and sisters. Tait also painted Carlyle during 1855, finishing the picture in time for the Royal Academy's summer exhibition in 1856.[33] Jane reported cheerfully to Carlyle on 14 August: 'Positively I fancy I have found *the Coming cottage*', a little house on the sea front at Rottingdean, four miles from Brighton, a distance which she walked, announcing triumphantly – once again perhaps wishing to remind him of his parsimony and her sound economic sense – that 'the travelling expenses to one of the quietest sea villages in England is just per boat & third class train 3/10*d*.!'[34] She had almost agreed to take the house on the spot for £12 a year, but was afraid he might not like it. 'You must just go and look.'

She had lain on the cliff for an hour or more looking out at the beautiful sea, 'blue as the Firth of Forth', 'which was such a *doing* of the picturesque as I have not been up to for years'.[35] Carlyle, who had always hankered after a seaside summer home, ought to have been infected by her enthusiasm, especially since she stressed the solitude as an attraction – 'as if the Brighton people were all enchanted not to pass beyond their pier' – but he put a dampener on the plan. On 17 August Jane was telling Mrs Brookfield that he was 'resolved against it', and she punished Carlyle in the usual way, by not writing to him, as he noted plaintively in a letter to her from Suffolk.[36] 'The Brighton Cottage has gone to smoke', he told Jack on 28 August; 'by my own movement, that, for Tait and Jane were both very lively about it'.[37]

Now back in Chelsea, Carlyle wrote to Alick in Canada, telling him the family news. Jack was making 'a *business* out of guardianing' Phoebe's sons. Carlyle felt sorry for the waste of a superior intellect, but saw that Jack was 'capable of finding interest for himself, out of next to nothing' and was 'far the *happiest* of the family'. 'He and I never have any cross word now; for I have long since recognised that rebuking him is of no use.' The Ashburtons had offered Addiscombe again, and he and Jane, with a borrowed horse for him, were off there the next day, 30 August.[38]

Relations between them were still sour. Jane stayed only three nights, then left abruptly for home before Carlyle got up on the morning of 2 September. He wrote that night in pathetic-reproachful vein:

My poor little Jeannie is away! You may fancy (or rather perhaps in your spleen you will not fancy) what a dreary *wae* sight it was to me this morning when I sallied out, stupid and sad, and found your door *open*, the *one* cup downstairs, teapot washed out: 'Mrs Carlyle gone at 8, Sir; don't know whither; had not slept at all.'[39]

Carlyle stayed on at Addiscombe till nearly the end of the month, solitary except for the odd visit from Jane 'to give the requisite directions' to Addiscombe's 'austerely punctual housemaid, who does her function, like an eight day clock, generally without bidding', as Carlyle told FitzGerald on 15 September.[40] He and Jane were communicating, but under strain. She reported on 12 September that on her journey back to Chelsea that day she heard 'such a row of bells as we got near London!' The news had come through that the allies had at last taken Sebastopol on 8 September. Jane told Carlyle, 'I had the pleasure of reading on a placard, "Hurrah! hurrah! hurrah! Glorious news! Sebastopol in possession of the allies!" Don't they wish they may keep it?'[41]

The long siege of Sebastopol had provided a spectacle for Londoners in August in the form of a display set up in Cremorne Gardens, a pleasure resort close to Cheyne Row and long one of the chief sources of summer noise and nuisance to Carlyle. It had been since the 1830s the scene of various attractions – balloon ascents, parachute descents, firework displays, rope-dancing, mock elections, and trapeze acts by the famous Léotard. On 13 August the scaffolding erected for the attack on Sebastopol collapsed, leading to some twenty-five 'soldiers' being taken off to hospital with broken legs and bayonet wounds.[42] Jane witnessed the aftermath of the accident, as she told Carlyle on 14 August:

And last night the results of Cremorne in the King's Road were what shall I say? – *strange* upon my honour! First I heard a measured tread; and then out of the darkness advanced on me eight soldiers carrying high over their heads a bier! on which lay a figure covered with a black cloth all but the white white face! and before I had recovered from the shock of that – some twenty yards further on behold precisely the same thing over again! I asked a working man what had happened. 'It was a great night at Cremorne – storming of Sebastopol – 30 or forty soldiers were *storming*, when the scaffolding broke, and they all fell in on *their own* bayonets! The two who had passed were killed they said and all the others hurt.' But a sergeant, whom I accosted after, told me there were none killed and only three hurt badly.[43]

On 21 September, while Jane was on one of her housekeeping visits to

Carlyle at Addiscombe, they walked the few miles to Sydenham so that Carlyle could show her the Crystal Palace – still 'the Apotheosis of Mercantile Cockneyism', as he told Lady Ashburton on 23 September. 'Curious-looking beings, bearded Germans, &c, were in great plenty'. Carlyle consoled himself for Jane's coldness by indulging in romantic sentiments about his solitary time in Lady Ashburton's house:

24 of the strangest beneficent Days, here in your domain, shut out from all the world; eight-and-forty times (only think of that) I must have made tea for myself in your little fairy teapot (the red tile-china saucy little teapot) . . . I have had such rides too, most memorable and beneficial . . . I am in fact rather *better*, both in body and mind for my Quasi-Moslem *Ramadhan* out here; and shall hope to do a little better amid my insoluble imbroglios than has lately been the doom of me, when I get back. Take thanks, therefore, O Royal Lady.[44]

★

On 21 October 1855 Jane began to keep a journal, into which she poured all her resentment about her 'Noble Lord' and his 'Royal Lady'. She recognised in the very first entry that 'your journal all about feelings [Lady Ashburton's disapproving phrase] aggravates whatever is factitious and morbid in you'; she therefore aimed to note only 'what Mr Carlyle calls "the fact of things" '. But 'it is very bleak and barren, this fact of things, as I now see it – very'. The next day she went straight to the heart of her misery:

I was cut short in my introduction last night by Mr C's return from Bath House. That eternal Bath House. I wonder how many thousand miles Mr C has walked between there and here, putting it all together; setting up always another milestone and another betwixt himself and me. Oh, good gracious! when I first noticed that heavy yellow house without knowing, or caring to know, who it belonged to, how far I was from dreaming that through years and years I should carry every stone's weight of it on my heart.

Then, seeing the funny side of her predicament, she pulls herself up – 'About feelings already!'[45]

And so it began. As Carlyle groaned upstairs over *Frederick* and created 'storms within doors' whenever he emerged from his study, Jane filled her journals with her despair. 'Life', she wrote on 23 October, looked like 'a sort of kaleidoscope' to her, with 'black predominating'. She escaped for long walks when it was 'blowing a devil of a gale' indoors. She mended Carlyle's trousers, petulantly exclaiming that 'being an only child', she had 'never "wished" to sew men's trowsers – no never!'[46] And she took to putting down childhood rhymes, and to invoking her mother, in her

To. Jane W. Carlyle
Jos. Mazzini

(*Above*)
Joseph Mazzini, *carte de visite*.

(*Above right*)
J.A. Froude, *carte de visite*.

(*Right*)
John Forster, *carte de visite*,
endorsed by Carlyle:
'John Forster (Man of Letters,
&c, &c), – very like'.

John Forster (Man of Letters, &c &c), – very like

Lady Harriet Ashburton,
lithograph by Francis Holl

The Grange, Hampshire.

Geraldine Jewsbury, photograph, 1855.

Ellen Twisleton.

'A "Latter-Day Nightmare" brought on by reading Thomas Carlyle his Pamphlets',
Punch, April 1850. Carlyle is on the left, with a tiny Lord John Russell at this shoulder.
A curled Disraeli is on the right, and the self-satisfied figure in the centre, facing Carlyle,
seems to be an allusion to Dickens's arch hypocrite Mr Pecksniff, in *Martin Chuzzlewitt*
(1843-4) as drawn by 'Phiz'.

(*Above left*) Jane Carlyle with Nero, photograph, July 1854.

(*Above right*) Carlyle, photograph, July 1854.

(*Left*) Carlyle in back garden at Cheyne Row, photograph, 1857.

Carlyle, portrait by Robert Tait, 1856.

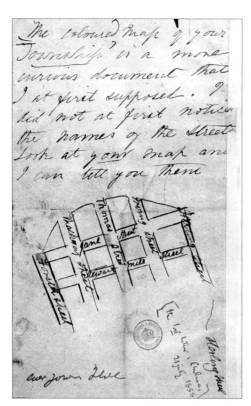

(*Above*) Carlyle on Fritz in Hyde Park, photograph, August 1861.

(*Left*) Carlyle township, New South Wales, sketch by Charles Gavan Duffy, 1858, copied by Jane Carlyle.

Work, by Ford Madox Brown, 1852–63.
Carlyle is second from the right, standing with F. D. Maurice.

Carlyle's handwriting (to John Carlyle, 25 September 1855).

Jane Carlyle's handwriting (to Mary Russell, 30 December 1858).

Carlyle and Lord Ashburton, photograph, Vernon Heath, October 1862.

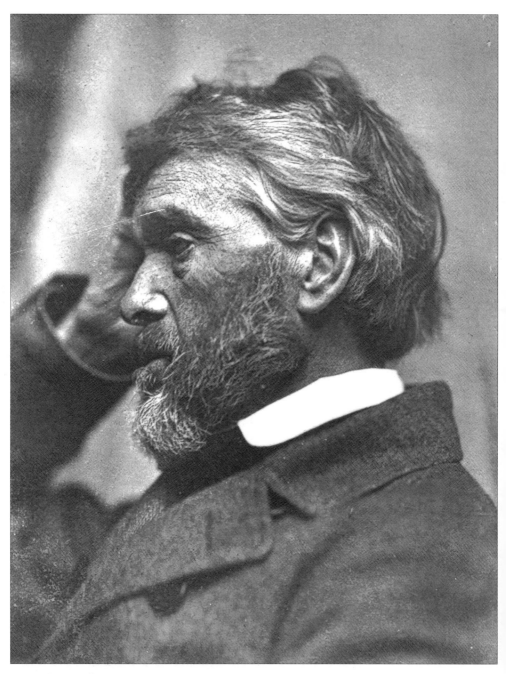

Carlyle, photograph, Elliot and Fry, 1865.

attempts to express what she knew were childish feelings, but ones she was powerless to suppress:

November 5. – Alone this evening. Lady A in town again; and Mr C of course at Bath House.

> When I think of what I is
> And what I used to was,
> I gin to think I've sold myself
> For very little cas.

November 6. Mended Mr C's dressing-gown. My most constant and pressing anxiety is to keep out of Bedlam!

November 7. Dear, dear! What a sick day this has been with me. Oh, my mother! nobody sees when I am suffering now; and I have learnt to suffer 'all to myself'. From 'only childness' to that, is a far and a rough road to travel.

> Oh, little did my mother think,
> The day she cradled me,
> The lands I was to travel in,
> The death I was to dee.[47]

Though Jane seems to have written few letters at this time, she did go out into company, especially on visits to her favourite Ellen Twisleton, who had brought her sister Elizabeth (Lizzie) Dwight over from Boston to spend a year in England. Lizzie was dazzled by Jane, writing home on 8 November:

She seemed to me the most entertaining person I ever heard talk, in her style, which is story-telling. She could write a modern Arabian Nights. – Her talk was almost entirely about people, mostly those that I didn't know, & if she had sketched them on the wall they could not have been more graphically represented than in her broad Scotch accent.

The fashion-conscious girl from Boston adds that Jane was 'dressed in a black silk gown evidently made ten years ago, fastening behind & no basque, & her bonnet was trimmed with a happy mixture of white-watered silk and black velvet'.[48] A week later she reported that Mrs Carlyle 'was as entertaining as one of Thackeray's novels & much in the same style'.[49]

Lady Ashburton sent the usual invitation to the Carlyles to stay at the Grange over Christmas. Jane and Carlyle were unable to communicate about it, Carlyle writing helplessly to Lady Ashburton on 13 November, 'Your Letter to Jane lay on the table when I came down this morning, late for breakfast: thank you heartily for that same. I know not whether she has answered it, or what she has said.' Jane, he continued, had gone out to a lecture to be given by Lord John Russell at Exeter Hall, accompanying the Wedgwoods to hear 'the little dear'. For his part, he was more than willing to accept the invitation to the Grange, despite the 'fond mothers and loud children' who also congregated there at Christmas, for 'there is One always at The Grange, the sight of whom is of the nature of happiness to me'.[50]

Jane answered the invitation the next day, not troubling to hide her irritation with both Lady Ashburton and Carlyle. 'Indeed, indeed, dear Lady', she began, ' "There is no chance of our coming to the Grange?" *Isn't* there!!' 'I dont think Mr C's staying sulking at home last winter turned out so well for him, body or soul, that he should ever again "take that line" (your phrase) as long as he lives.' Then Jane moves on to safer topics, aiming to impress Lady Ashburton with an animated account of the previous evening's lecture at Exeter Hall:

Certainly if Lord John ain't particular about the *quality* of praise he must have had quantity last night to his heart's content – Thousands of young shopmen and shop-women frantically beating with their hands and feet – till their faces were wet with the exertion – I missed much of the lecture, being far off, and Lord John's voice of the feeblest; but what I did hear was only remarkable for its insipidity – good gracious! – if Mr C had been there, I am confident he would have shied something at the little man, when *he* was putting down Dr Johnson, for saying 'The Magistrate had a right to persecute and the holder of truth a right to suffer' – It was more of a sermon than a lecture – but what I found most curious, every time his Lordship named 'Christ', which was very often, the House thundered applause so loud and long and obstreperous that I expected it always to end in '*hip hip hurrah*'! – Was it surprise and admiration that a *Lord* should have heard of Christ? Or what was it that set their hands a clapping and their feet thumping at that name? One time Lord John had said something very complimentary to Christ, and the applause began – but I heard one man cry 'order' – 'order' – and another 'no!' 'no!'[51]

Jane's wits were much needed a week later when, despite her inner turmoil, she turned up to give evidence on Carlyle's behalf to the Tax Commissioners at Kensington. As she had done when confronting the neighbour about his cocks two years earlier, she chose to put herself through the ordeal rather than see Carlyle do it. She dreaded it, as she confided in her journal on 20 November, but reasoned that if Carlyle were to go himself, 'he would run his head against some post in his impatience; and besides, for me, when it is over it will be over, whereas he would not get the better of it for twelve months – if ever at all'.[52]

So on 21 November, after a sleepless night, she got up, had a cup of coffee, and set off, 'feeling like the ghost of a dead dog', for Kensington. The journal received the full story that evening:

Mr C said 'the voice of honour seemed to call on him to go himself'. But either it did not call loud enough, or he would not listen to that charmer. I went in a cab, to save all my breath for appealing. Set down at 30 Hornton Street, I found a dirty private-like house, only with Tax Office painted on the door . . . There were already some half-score of men assembled in the waiting-room, among whom I saw the man who cleans our clocks, and a young apothecary of Cheyne Walk. All the others, to look at them, could not have been suspected for an instant, I should have said, of making a hundred a year.

Eventually Jane was called:

'First-come lady', called the clerk, opening a small side-door, and I stept forward into a *grand peut-être*. There was an instant of darkness while the one door was shut behind and the other opened in front; and there I stood in a dim room where three men sat round a large table spread with papers. One held a pen ready over an open ledger; another was taking snuff, and had taken still worse in his time, to judge by his shaky, clayed appearance. The third, who was plainly the cock of that dungheap, was sitting for Rhadamanthus – a Rhadamanthus without justice. 'Name', said the horned-owl-looking individual holding the pen. 'Carlyle'. 'What?' 'Car-lyle'. Seeing he still looked dubious, I spelt it for him. 'Ha!' cried Rhadamanthus, a big, bloodless-faced, insolent-looking fellow. 'What is this? why is Mr Carlyle not come himself? Didn't he get a letter ordering him to appear? Mr Carlyle wrote some nonsense about being exempted from coming, and I desired an answer to be sent that he must come, must do as other people.' 'Then, sir', I said, 'your desire has been neglected, it would seem, my husband having received no such letter; and I was told by one of your fellow Commissioners that Mr Carlyle's personal appearance was not indispensable.' 'Huffgh! Huffgh! what does Mr Carlyle mean by saying he has no income from his writings, when he himself fixed it in the beginning at a hundred and fifty?' 'It means, sir, that in ceasing to write, one ceases to be paid for writing, and Mr Carlyle has published nothing for several years.' 'Huffgh! Huffgh! I understand nothing about that.' 'I do', whispered the snuff-taking Commissioner at my ear. 'I can quite understand a literary man does not always make money. I would take it off, for my share, but (sinking his voice still lower) I am only one voice here, and not the most important.' 'There', said I, handing to Rhadamanthus Chapman and Hall's account; 'that will prove Mr Carlyle's statement' . . . 'Then what has Mr Carlyle to live upon? You don't mean to tell me he lives on that?' pointing to the document. 'Heaven forbid, sir! but I am not here to explain what Mr Carlyle has to live on, only to declare his income from literature during the last three years.' 'True! true!' mumbled the not-most-important voice at my elbow. 'Mr Carlyle, I believe, has landed income.' 'Of which', said I haughtily, for my spirit was up, 'I have fortunately no account to render in this kingdom and to this board.' 'Take off fifty pounds, say a hundred – take off a hundred pounds', said Rhadamanthus to the horned owl.

After this account, worthy of a Dickens or a Lewis Carroll, Jane miserably concludes her otherwise triumphant journal entry: 'Went back to spend the evening with Geraldine when Mr C set forth for Bath House.'[53] It was at this very time that she poured out to Ellen Twisleton the long story of Craigenputtoch.

Ellen knew Jane was jealous of Lady Ashburton, and she sympathised.

It was to her that Jane offloaded a little of her despair in a spoof letter from Nero the dog, who 'wrote' to Ellen on 30 November in an agony of jealousy:

Stranger Lady!
Please do not think it presuming, that one who is only a Dog, and a very little one, should write to you, out of his own head. I am not wanting in modesty, I do assure you; from earliest puppyhood, it has been inculcated on me that presumption is as insufferable in dogs as in men. Even my Master, tho' calling me '*miserable chimera*' – '*Poor hairy Phantom*' – and other uncouth names, admits that I have 'a quadruped sense of propriety' and am 'very easily repressed'. And if he says that of me; you may think –!

The fact is, Madam, I am in 'a state of mind' – in one of those moments which French Dogs call *suprême*, and in which one does and may do – anything! Oh Madam, unless I *open* my heart to someone, I shall go mad – and *bite*! . . .

For seven years my Mistress and I had been one anothers 'first object'. Not even the little female Dog at *No 10*, tho' I own to having shown her some unmeaning gallantries, ever came seriously between us. And now comes this – *Duck* – this creature without heart or bowels; and off goes my mistress into raptures with her – has no eyes but for *her*! It is *she* who gets shown off to visitors – she who is the new favourite – while I unnoticed unpraised look gloomily on – foaming at the mouth with rage!

Madam! it is easier to destroy the peace of Families than to patch it up . . . Inferior animal tho I am, I can perceive you have 'talents to drive the Genii to despair'; turn them to recovering my still dear Mistress from her infatuation – and making her see the infamy of setting up new favourites at the age she is – and the cruelty of – of – Oh I can write no more – my heart! my heart! – Wo-o-of Wo-o-o-o-f Who o o oho o o h!

The unfortunate *Nero*.[54]

Only temporary relief could be derived from such flights of fancy. As the time drew near for going to the Grange, Jane dreaded it. Carlyle, meanwhile, was looking forward to the visit. 'We are coming on Monday', he wrote to Lady Ashburton on Saturday, 15 December; 'I promise to be, all that is in me, a good Boy.'[55] They went, and Jane's journal entries cease until March 1856.

★

The Brookfields and Lizzie Dwight, the latter invited to the Grange along with the Twisletons, have left accounts of the large party which gathered there for Christmas and the New Year, new guests arriving as some left during the holiday weeks. Lizzie took a particular interest in Mrs Brookfield, having heard that she was Thackeray's ideal woman and the model for Becky Sharp's goody-goody opposite, Amelia Sedley, in *Vanity Fair*. 'She does not speak above a breath', Lizzie observed, 'and comes "the startled fawn" perpetually.' 'The gentlemen admire her and the ladies want to "set a dog on her".'[56]

Mrs Brookfield herself made sharp enough comments on Jane, who, she thought, 'expected and was conceded a certain prominence amongst the many other visitors of more or less distinction in that delightful and hospitable house'. Jane's instinct to take the lead in conversation led to difficulties because of Lady Ashburton's brilliance, and for Mrs Brookfield's taste, Jane's famous story-telling was tiresome, 'with her Scotch accent and her perseverance in finishing off every detail'.[57] This Christmas Lady Ashburton consulted Mrs Brookfield on a present for Jane to be hung from the tree; they decided on a silk dress, by which Jane felt her pride insulted.[58]

William Brookfield reported to Lord Lyttelton on 5 January 1856 on the group still at the Grange. There was Tennyson (the 'dusty Laureate'), Henry Taylor, James Spedding, George Venables, old Lady Sandwich, 'Dr Taylor, analytical chemist', and the Carlyles – 'an atrabilious prophet and perplexed and not too happy wife'.[59] On 2 January Tennyson read his new poem *Maud* aloud to the company; according to Mrs Brookfield Carlyle was too impatient to join the audience, and went for a walk instead.[60] Jane did attend the reading; she noticed that Tennyson was 'much made of by all the large party assembled there', and that he 'seemed strangely excited about *Maud* – as sensitive to criticisms on it, as if they were imputations on his honour'.[61] Perhaps Tennyson was put out by hearing Lady Ashburton read out loud from Browning's new collection of poetry, *Men and Women*. Carlyle told Browning that her 'superlatively well-done' readings were the high point of his Grange visit.[62]

On 6 January, according to Mr Brookfield's diary, the company played the game 'Earth, Air, and Water, in which each person had to assume the name of one inhabitant of Earth'. In answer to the question 'What fish will you be, what quadruped – what bird?' Lady Ashburton replied 'very characteristically' (but not perhaps very aptly) 'a dab, a lamb, a dove'. Carlyle declared, 'with inexpressible humour, self scorn, and scorn of all creation – not without a sense of sympathy with the most despised part of it, "I am an Ass"', and proceeded to play the part to the full.[63] It is not recorded whether Jane joined in the game.

A new visitor on 11 January was Carlyle's admirer John Tyndall, since 1853 Professor of Natural Philosophy at the Royal Institution. He wrote to a friend describing the home-made entertainments. He was captivated by the lavish yet free-and-easy hospitality at the Grange, where 'each seems to do just as he likes; wanders where he pleases through the magnificent rooms; reads, talks, or admires the pictures just as it strikes his fancy'. Such freedom of movement suited Carlyle, and Tyndall was pleasantly surprised to find him the life and soul of the party, even at the breakfast table: 'What I have seen of Carlyle makes me revere the old brute more than ever. Nobody seems to agree with him, but he pushes his way through it all, dealing out doom and praise.'

They discussed homoeopathy, the nature of life – Carlyle refusing to accept Tyndall's theory of molecular force and insisting on the 'incomprehensibility' of life – and Goethe, whose Mephistopheles Carlyle likened to Beau Brummell, of whom he told a racy anecdote; Brummell was said to have replied to a friend's inquiry after his health one morning, 'Suffering from cold. I have been sleeping with a damp woman all night!'[64]

The Carlyles were home by the middle of January. Carlyle wrote on consecutive days to Lord and Lady Ashburton. On 18 January he thanked Lord Ashburton for diplomatically procuring the offer of the loan of a book from Prince Albert.[65] The following day he was complaining of his misery to Lady Ashburton, asking her not to 'cheat me out of a sight of you, as you sometimes tyrannously do', and exclaiming, 'Oh, it is not for me to complain of your stripes: – I am a sinful son of Adam.' In February he expressed his fear that he might have lost her, and 'the light of your countenance' might be turned away. What then? 'I see nobody; I sit here, in grim task work, slaving what I can, day after day.'[66]

Carlyle makes no mention of Jane, who was suffering from a sore throat exacerbated by what she humorously called, in a lively letter to her Edinburgh friend Major David Davidson, an 'involuntary' attempt on her own life:

During my stay at the Grange, the house Dr (the Ashburtons keep a Dr all to themselves, a questionable luxury I think) ordered me an embrocation for my throat, and I DRANK it every drop! supposing that England expected me! A revolution of three days in my 'interior' (as Mr Carlyle calls it) was the unexpectedly unimportant result of this mistake.[67]

She had also, since her return to Cheyne Row, taken 'a flying leap in the dark(!)' and hurt her right side. Again, as she told Mary Russell on 8 February, she had made things worse by over-zealously applying a mustard plaster which had taken off her skin.[68]

On Sunday, 30 March the sound of cannon and bells announced the end, at last, of the Crimean War. All Carlyle could muster by way of welcome was a wan 'Peace come, ah yes, *their* Peace' to Lady Ashburton.[69] Jane had resumed her despairing journal. 'Dear Geraldine' brought her violets on 26 March, but Jane was in a worse way than ever. She who was famous for her religious scepticism wrote, 'Have mercy upon me O Lord' and 'O save me for thy mercies' sake.' On 11 April she noted a visit to 'my Lady', who had come up to London for the season. 'She was perfectly civil, for a wonder.'[70] Jane longed for death, and even thought she might be dying – 'very feeble and ailing' and full of 'dark apprehensions', she noted on 15 April.[71]

Despite feeling so wretched, on 14 April Jane dressed up 'very fine' and was driven to Bath House to a dinner party.[72] She recognised that her illness was partly psychological; on meeting her old suitor George Rennie on 25 April, she 'sprang' into his arms, feeling immediately conjured back into her 'bright, whole hearted, impulsive youth'. 'I am a different woman this evening', she told her journal. When she was invited to dinner by Rennie and his wife, she 'went after' a new dress 'with alacrity'. 'George should see that the smart girl of his Province wasn't become a *dowdy* among London women of "a certain age".' On 1 May she could even joke in this journal of death wishes: 'Last week I was all for dying; this week, all for Ball dresses.'[73]

She and Carlyle went to dinner at the Rennies' on 7 May, then on to a party at Bath House, taking Ruskin with them to meet the Ashburtons. Carlyle had persuaded Ruskin to go, telling him that Lady Ashburton was 'a very high lady both extrinsically and intrinsically' and describing the fine pictures in Bath House, including some Dürers and Murillos.[74] Jane reported proudly to Kate Sterling that she had shown 'a certain force of mind in taking Ruskin's arm to go in', defying those who were inclined to 'stare' at Ruskin since his divorce.[75] On 17 May she recorded in her journal that it was Kate's wedding day; she was marrying a clergyman called Ross, whom Jane disliked.[76] To Kate herself she had written on 14 May, unable to express optimism about the momentous change about to take place, but saying 'God bless you'. She would not, she wrote, attempt to give Kate any advice:

After all, I have never found the least good, myself, in what others *say to us*, either for comfort or edification! One must *work out for oneself* every lesson of Life, or it is merely like a mathematical proposition learnt by rote – turn the figure upside down, or change the letters, and you stand confounded in your pretentious ignorance! Ah Heaven Yes! Haven't I, for example been privileged for the last quarter of a century, to hear 'the Greatest Thinker of the age' denouncing the sins and shortcomings of the World, the first thing in the morning and the last thing at night, and have I hated and despised the world's ways a bit the more for all that – ? 'quite the contrary'; I turn sorry for the poor bad world, and every feeling of mercy and generosity in me is roused to take its part! *that* is the effect of exhortation on *me*, – being of a contradictory turn.[77]

Jane could feel no joy at the thought of anyone marrying. Her journal expresses her fascination with the trial of William Palmer, who was convicted at the end of May, 'after a horridly interesting Trial lasting twelve days', of poisoning his wife to benefit from her life insurance, a conclusion which caused Jane to comment on the unhappiness brought about not by the institution of marriage itself, but by 'the demoralisation' of it.[78] In her more cheerful moments, she could see the funny side of her own marriage, as when a significant mistake was made by a new acquaintance, a wealthy Welsh novelist and friend of Geraldine's, Madame de Winton, who came to lunch on Sunday, 18 May, when Carlyle was at Addiscombe for the day. On looking at the picture of Lady Ashburton which hung on one side of the mantelpiece in the sitting room at Cheyne Row, and at Carlyle's, which hung on the other, Madame de Winton had asked if they were man and wife. Since it was Carlyle who told this story to Lady Ashburton, he must have heard it from Jane when he got back from Addiscombe in the evening.[79]

'Dear little diamond-eyed Mrs Twisleton came to say good-bye for the season' on 19 June, saying 'beautiful things' to Jane, 'but no flatteries *stick* just now. It is as much as I can do to let alone answering like Mr C's Father, short and grim, "*I don't believe thee!*" '[80] On 26 June a passage in Jane's journal – later cut out, though not by Carlyle – reads: 'The chief interest of today expressed in blue marks on my wrists.'[81] Geraldine Jewsbury, with whom Jane spent the following day on an outing to Hampstead – 'preferring to be broiled on a Heath to being broiled in Cheyne Row'[82] – years later recalled, when asked by Froude, that Jane had told her Carlyle had grasped her wrists during a quarrel.[83] The question, much debated by biographers and editors from Froude onwards, of whether Carlyle was seriously violent with her on this occasion is impossible to answer in the absence of a specific charge by Jane. It seems entirely likely, given the state of mind of both partners at this time, that they quarrelled; Carlyle may have handled her roughly enough to cause bruises on the wrists of a woman who was, though he was the last to see it, physically as well as psychologically frail. His chief culpability lies surely in his dogged obtuseness about her distress. They had reached a very low point, as Carlyle accepted when he discovered these journals after Jane's death. Instead of destroying them – which must have been tempting, given the poor light they cast on his behaviour – he incorporated them into his own notebook reminiscence of her, noting that they were 'a very sad record' of 'the *nadir* of my poor Wife's sufferings'.[84]

One subject which occupied Carlyle's attention was the House of Lords debate about a National Portrait Gallery on 4 March 1856, in which his own proposal was quoted in support of the motion. When the National Portrait Gallery was opened in 1857, Carlyle was made one of the Trustees, in recognition of his contribution to the debate leading up to its founding.[85]

Carlyle was now busy arranging for the first collected edition of his works. Since he was so tied up with his work on *Frederick*, he sought the help of others to correct the texts and compile the indexes for the sixteen-volume Uniform Edition which was now agreed with Chapman and Hall. The volumes were to cost six shillings each and to be published at monthly intervals during 1857 and 1858. Two thousand copies of each volume were printed, and Carlyle was paid £1,000, in instalments, for the first ten volumes.[86] It is a measure of the hold Carlyle still had over young men's minds that three new admirers offered their assistance with the edition.

One was Alexander Gilchrist, who had trained as a barrister but practised literary and art criticism rather than the law. He sent Carlyle a copy of his biography of the painter William Etty and was invited to Cheyne Row, where he listened to Carlyle 'pouring himself out', looking in his 'long brown indoors coat' like 'a veritable Prophet, mourning in sackcloth and ashes the sins of the world'.[87] When the house next door became vacant during the course of 1856, Carlyle suggested that the Gilchrists take it, which they did in the autumn.[88]

When Gilchrist's brother was drowned in December, he had to withdraw his assistance in order to settle his family's affairs, at which point another new admirer, Vernon Lushington, stepped in as helper. Lushington, also a young barrister, had been writing a series of articles on Carlyle in the *Oxford and Cambridge Magazine* during 1856, full of admiration for the early works and giving a personal memory of being a Cambridge undergraduate a few years before, strolling into a friend's rooms, finding his friend out, and beginning to read *On Heroes*, which lay on the table. He met Carlyle at the end of the year and made his 'loyal and generous' offer of help just when Gilchrist had to give up. Carlyle accepted with alacrity.[89]

A third assistant on the project was another neighbour, Henry Larkin, a cashier for the Chelsea Steamer Company and partner in an engineering business, who, as Carlyle noted in his reminiscence of Jane, was 'assiduous to serve us in all things (did *maps, indexes,* even *joinerings* etc. etc.)'.[90]

Even Dickens became involved. He wrote to Carlyle from Boulogne on 20 July 1856 to 'present to you my printers and old friends, Messrs. Bradbury and Evans. They desire to have the honor of seeing their imprint attached to the proposed collected Edition of your works.'[91] Bradbury and Evans now became Carlyle's printers. A couple of weeks before writing to Carlyle, Dickens had been thinking of Jane when he told Washington Irving a 'half-sad, half-ludicrous story' about her old adversary Samuel Rogers, who had died in 1855:

You know, I daresay, that for a year or so before his death he wandered, and lost himself like one of the Children in the Wood, grown up there and grown down again. He had Mrs Procter and Mrs Carlyle to breakfast with him one morning –

only those two. Both excessively talkative, very quick and clever, bent on entertaining him. When Mrs Carlyle had flashed and shone before him for about three-quarters of an hour on one subject, he turned his poor old eyes on Mrs Procter, and pointing to the brilliant discourser with his poor old finger, said (indignantly), 'Who is *she*?' Upon this, Mrs Procter, cutting in, delivered (it is her own story) a neat oration on the life and writings of Carlyle, and enlightened him in her happiest and airiest manner; all of which he heard, staring in the dreariest silence, and then said (indignantly, as before), 'And who are *you*?'[92]

The Carlyles went north during July, but peace did not break out between them. Unusually, they travelled together, though not by the usual means of transport. Lady Ashburton had hired 'the great big Railway-carriage called "*the Queen's Saloon*"' to take her to Edinburgh, as Jane told Mary Russell, and having room to spare, she offered to take the Carlyles with her, 'free of all trouble and expense'.[93] The journey was fraught, however, and not just because Jane resented having to accept Lady Ashburton's bounty. Carlyle described the journey 'in her Sacred Majesty's own Apparatus' to Jack on 30 July, and recounted it again in mock-heroic fashion in his reminiscence of Jane. At Peterborough the '*ne-plus-ultra*' of railway carriages 'was found to have its axletree *on fire*':

At every station afterwards *buckets* were copiously dashed and poured (the magnanimous Lady saying never a syllable to it); and at Newcastle-on-Tyne, they flung the humbug *Ne-plus* away altogether, and our whole party into common carriages.[94]

The company parted at Edinburgh, the Ashburtons proceeding to Kinloch-Luichart, a hunting estate in the Highlands, while Carlyle went to stay with his sister Mary Austin on her Dumfriesshire farm, the Gill, and Jane went on to Kirkcaldy to her cousin Walter Welsh at Auchtertool Manse. Jane's letters to Carlyle from here, and later from her aunts' house in Edinburgh and from a brief stay with her old friends the Donaldsons in Haddington, are frosty. She gives no greetings and includes no endearments, signing her letters 'Faithfully yours', and keeping them strictly factual except for deliberately placed exclamations about the kindness of her various hosts.[95]

Carlyle stayed quietly at the Gill, but he hoped to be able to go on to join the Ashburtons. 'And will I come to the Highlands, I myself?' he wrote to Lady Ashburton on 7 August. 'Bright Lady, believe me, if it stood with me, the answer were not difficult. But it stands with so many persons, and with so many things and laws, I dare not yet answer at all.'[96] It stood, of course, with Jane, who also received an invitation from Lady Ashburton, but who used a cold as a reason to refuse. She wrote to Carlyle on 30 August that he could continue his own programme free from 'any *tagrag[g]ery* of uncertainties depending on me'. She outlined her own plans, then added a bitter final sentence about going home ' "to take up the threads of" – what? – Nero! – Poor Dear *he* at least will be glad! If no one else is!'[97]

Carlyle accordingly went north in September, while Jane moved to Scotsbrig to stay with James and Isabella, the most congenial of Carlyle's family. From there she replied to letters from Carlyle complaining, as he always did, of the discomforts of travelling and staying with other people. Jane briefly dropped the *froideur* of her letter-writing tone to burst out hotly at his complaints, which, though intended to assuage her, always – as he ought to have known by now – incensed her:

For the rest – in spite of all objections 'for the occasion got up', I dare say you are pretty comfortable. Why not? – When *you* go to any house, one knows it is because you *choose* to go; and when you stay it is because you *choose* to stay – You dont, as weakly amiable people do, *sacrifice* yourself for the pleasure of '*others*' – So pray do not think it necessary to be *wishing yourself at home*, and 'all that sort of thing' on paper. 'I don't believe thee!'[98]

With this appropriation of old Mr Carlyle's phrase, she ended her outburst, but she had not finished rebuking her husband. Carlyle had relayed an offer from Lady Ashburton to take Jane home. Her response is tart:

Pray make her my thanks for the offer – But though a very little Herring I have a born liking to '*hang by* my own head'. And when it is a question simply of paying my own way or having it paid for me – I prefer 'lashing down' my four or five sovereigns *on the table all at once*! If there were any *companionship* in the matter it would be different – and if *you* go back with the Ashburtons it would be different, as then I should be going merely as part of your luggage – without self responsibility. Settle it as you like; it will be all one to me – meeting you at Scotsbrig, or in Edinr – or going home by myself from Thornhill.[99]

Carlyle rebuked her in turn, reminding her that Lady Ashburton's offer was an entirely kind one, and reasoning: 'What pleasure or profit *they* could get from it, is not apparent. But, any way, we have to stand by the above decision; which I think, and see that you think, the best for various reasons.'[100]

Jane spent a few days with the Russells at Thornhill, near her mother's old home, then prepared for her return to Chelsea, while Carlyle left the Highlands for a brief stay in Scotsbrig, visiting his mother's grave, next to his father's and his sister Margaret's in Ecclefechan Churchyard. From Scotsbrig he wrote rather disingenuously on 3 October to Alick in Canada that he had had 'unwillingly to take a long journey into the Highlands' to visit the deer-hunting Ashburtons in countryside 'thrice as wild as Craigenputtoch' and not beautiful at all to his way of thinking. 'But such things have a charm for idle English people with more money than enough!'[101]

The Carlyles travelled home together, Jane carrying two canaries as a souvenir of her Scottish visit. She complained to Mary Russell on her return early in October that Carlyle had met her at Scotsbrig 'in what the people here call "a state of mind"'.[102] Her cold had got worse as a result of Carlyle insisting on her 'sitting in a violent draught all the journey'. On 10 October she sketched the scene in Cheyne Row:

Figure *this*! – (*Scene* – a room where everything is enveloped in dark yellow London *fog*! – for air to breathe a sort of *liquid* soot! – breakfast on the table – 'adulterated coffee' 'adulterated bread' 'adulterated cream' and 'adulterated water'!) Mr C at one end of the table, looking remarkably bilious – Mrs C at the other looking half dead! Mr C: '*My dear*', – 'I have to inform you that my bed is full of *bugs* or fleas or some sort of animals that crawl over me all night!' . . . I answered with merely a sarcastic shrug, that was no doubt very ill timed – *under the circumstances* and which drew on me no end of what the Germans call *kraftsprüche* [forceful utterances]! – But clearly the practical thing to be done was to go and examine his bed – and I am practical – *moi*! So instead of getting into a controversy that had no basis, I proceeded to toss over his blankets and pillows – with a certain sense of injury! But on a sudden I paused in my operations – I stooped to look at something the size of a pin point – A cold shudder ran over me, as sure as I lived it was an *infant bug*! – and oh heaven that bug, little as it was, must have parents – grandfathers and grandmothers, perhaps! I went on looking *then*, with phrenzied minuteness – and saw – enough to make me put on my bonnet and rush out wildly, in the black rain, to hunt up a certain trustworthy carpenter to come and take down the bed – The next three days I seemed to be in the thick of a domestic Balaklava – which is now even not subsided – only subsiding.[103]

This is much more like the old Jane, cheering up when faced with a challenge which she could first exert herself to meet, and then describe with verve in a letter to her friend. The Russells had been worried about the amount of morphine she had been taking for her headaches and sleeplessness, and Dr Russell had read her a lecture about it at Thornhill; she assured Mary Russell that she was trying to take less, but a 'fearful pain in my left side' had made her reach for the medicine again.[104] It is difficult to know how much Jane took, or how often, during these years, or how her mood was affected, but it is reasonable to suppose that drugs contributed to her health problems at least as much as they alleviated them.

She subsided once more into anxiety about her health, but with that streak of perverseness so prominent in her character she told Mary Russell on 28 November that Geraldine Jewsbury was making even more of a drama about her illness than she could do herself. 'You can't think what difficulty I have had to keep Geraldine from firing off Letters at you every two or three days, with the most alarming accounts of my bodily state!' Jane blamed her friend's 'trade as Novelist' for aggravating her 'besetting weakness', namely 'the *desire of feeling and producing violent emotions*'.[105]

Fortunately for Jane, Ellen Twisleton stayed in London this winter. Her sister Lizzie had gone home, and Ellen told her the latest news at the end of October. Lady Ashburton had departed for Nice, and a group of her courtiers were to follow. Ellen was scathing:

Mrs Brookfield is to follow, with the children, this week, her husband told Edward. Did you ever see anything so odd & English, as going to Nice & taking all the troupe with her, Brookfield, Venables, etcetera? Aren't you glad E & E [Edward and Ellen] are not going, but stand in their own parlour at 3 Rutland Gate? I feel vicious, & imagine what Mrs Carlyle will be.[106]

In December Ellen reported that she herself had been ill and was taking morphine, but had paid a visit to the Carlyles, talking to Jane for an hour while her husband went for a walk with Carlyle:

Of course, the everlasting Jewsbury was there, & after sitting & looking gloomy about ten minutes, got up & went away – & as it is the *third time* this process has been performed, lately, I felt bound to make a sort of apology, both to her & to Mrs C wh. to my amazement produced a burst of feeling from the latter on the subject, to the tune that she was very glad when she did go, & that it would be very hard if she couldn't see me alone when I came, etc. Evidently, 'the best friend' has no sort of self-control, & knows nothing about illness, cries over Mrs Carlyle, spills her jellies, knocks over the coal-pail, kisses her, & writes a letter of fourteen pages, sent in before breakfast, to complain of 'coldness' & 'diminished interest in her internal & external life', &c.[107]

Ellen knew how to spoil Jane without smothering her. In November she took Jane a chair her sister Lizzie had made as a present before returning to America. Jane wrote Lizzie an elaborate letter of thanks on 19 December. 'Mr Carlyle's friends "The Destinies", "The Immortal Gods", "The Superior Powers"', could not have managed better timing for such a gift, she wrote, explaining that she was 'in a crisis of disordered nerves'. Moreover, 'was it not "the gloomy month of November in which", as the Frenchman began his novel, "the People of England hang and drown themselves"? Into *this* state of things your sister introduced *the chair!*'[108]

In the same letter Jane told Lizzie that Carlyle had recently acquired 'a *horse*, and a *secretary* (German) – and the German Secretary is going to prove invaluable to me, I rather think, as a Lightning Conductor'. The horse, which cost Carlyle 50 guineas, was named Fritz after Frederick the Great; from now on Carlyle rode every day for exercise. In 1866 he reckoned he had ridden 'some 35,000 miles', mainly on Fritz, 'during those ten years of *Friedrich*'.[109] Jane told Emily Tennyson in January 1857 that she could not accept an invitation to the Tennysons' home on the Isle of Wight, though she would have liked to if she had been fit, and if 'that man would leave his eternal *Frederick* and come along!':

He goes nowhere, sees nobody, only for two hours a day he rides like the wild German hunter on a horse he has bought, and which seems to like that sort of thing. Such a horse! he (not the horse) never wearies in the intervals of *Frederick* of celebrating the creature's 'good sense, courage and sensibility!' 'Not once', he says 'has the creature shown the slightest disagreement from *him* in *any question of Intellect*' (more than can be said of most living Bipeds!)[110]

Carlyle talked in rather less positive terms about his new secretary, Frederick Martin, 'a desolate little German with a good hand of writing', as he told Lord Ashburton in December.[111] Martin was willing and industrious, though 'a weak helpless creature', but in March 1857 Carlyle dismissed him for incompetence. He explained to Jack that he had been driven mad by Martin's 'hysterical futilities', accompanied by an annoying 'whistling thro' the nose' in cold weather, for which he and Jane christened him 'Peesweep' (peewit), a bird he resembled in sound and general behaviour.[112]

With his usual kindness, Carlyle took some trouble to help Martin to a new position, writing a reference for a post of copyist at the British Museum, but telling Martin in firm terms that he could not recommend him as a translator or editor. 'For *annotating*, rectifying and elucidating', he wrote in June 1857, 'you appear to me to be (rather *eminently*) destitute of the indispensable qualifications.'[113] Carlyle appears not to have suspected Martin of dishonesty, though the secretary actually stole some of his manuscripts, including 'Wotton Reinfred', as was discovered after Carlyle's death.[114]

On 10 December Ellen took Jane out for a drive. 'She is very pale, & has had a horrid attack' (of headache), so that 'it almost kills her to write', Ellen wrote to Lizzie the following day. Jane had told Ellen the latest gossip about Lady Ashburton and her entourage: 'She was full of a story of Lady Sandwich's saying that it made her "*crawl all over* to have Mrs Brookfield sit down & talk to her".'[115]

There was no Grange Christmas this year. In France, both Ashburtons had been ill and news about Lady Ashburton's health came in the form of letters and visitors from Nice. Carlyle must have received an uncharacteristically despondent letter from Lady Ashburton herself, for he wrote to her on 14 January in almost valedictory terms:

Among the many fine things I have loved in you, the bright frank *courage* of your mind, the healthy promptitude with which you shook away annoyances, and walked on as if *incompatible* with 'mud' (in which I may be said to dwell) was always one. Be not 'discouraged'; no![116]

On 23 February he wrote again. 'My heart is dark about you, and very sad.' But he still believed she would recover, and he talked about his own ill health. He and Jane were both weak, but Jane had been 'a model of patience all winter'.[117] On 29 March Carlyle noted in his journal that he had a hernia and was to consult a surgeon.[118]

Jane turned her own miserable health to good account in a letter to Mary Russell on 20 April. The subject is Robert Tait's picture *Susannah*, to be exhibited at the Royal Academy in May:

Only think! my little dog is to have his picture in the Exhibition this year! A friend of ours went into an artist's studio the other day, and saw a picture he was just finishing to send; 'Why, said he, that is *Nero*?' 'Yes said the Artist (the man who did your photographs) but he did not sit for it, I painted him from his photograph.' And if he had painted only *him* in the picture, I should have been well pleased; but the poor little dog has been *used* up as an accessory to the figure of a *stark-naked Woman*! just stepping into a Bath! Now I dont like this at all for as my dog has a very extensive acquaintance, and the portrait of him, I am told, is recognizable at any distance, and the dog was never seen but in my company I am in horror lest the naked figure should be taken for *me*!! – The only comfort is, the naked women in pictures are always *plump* – and I am but two degrees removed from a skeleton at present.[119]

Meanwhile, Lady Ashburton's health was the chief topic of correspondence. 'Just imagine', wrote Ellen on 5 February, 'Lady Ashburton has sent for [Dr] Locock from London to Nice & that he went – to stay 24 hours there, – for a fee of a *thousand pounds*!' 'Of course all London is gossipping about it, and of course *Mrs Carlyle* says it is all owing to *Mrs Brookfield*, who, as she is going to be confined, wishes to see Dr Locock!' Another of Lady Ashburton's doctors, Dr Rous, had written to Lady Sandwich that her daughter was suffering from 'distention of the womb, accompanied by Hysteria'.[120]

Jane expressed some sympathy, tempered by criticism, for the woman she had allowed to cause her such misery, as she passed on the latest news to Mary Russell in March:

[Lord Ashburton] is very ill content with Lady A's progress – but the Doctors say, he writes, she is going on very favourably. They are meaning to come to Paris in the middle of the month and to remain there till the middle of May. Poor woman! this sick life must be a sorer trial to her than to any of us. She has been so used to have everything bend to her will. Her life looked to me always like a *Triumph*! A person so admired, and so prosperous is apt to slight those sympathies and affections which make one's consolation in times of sickness, or of sorrow. And so she will hardly admit anyone to see her now – and those she chooses to see are almost solely *clever men*!!

Worse than this, thinks Jane – no doubt with her own relationship with Mrs Welsh in mind – is the fact that Lady Ashburton has a Mother *living* whom she *would rather not see*! A clever warmhearted woman is the old Countess of Sandwich, and her heart is broken with accounts of her only daughter's illness – but – that Mother and daughter have lived like so many other Mothers and daughters in Fashionable life – always fenced around with ceremonies – and durst no more enter one another's sick room, without leave asked and obtained, or take any kind freedom with one another, than a pair of entire strangers![121]

Lady Ashburton died in Paris on 4 May, presumably of the disease of the uterus diagnosed by Dr Rous. Carlyle told his brother John a few weeks later that he had been hoping for a recovery and was shocked by the news. 'I have indeed lost such a friend as I never had.'[122] Jane, though not triumphalist, was naturally less dejected. She told her chief confidante Mary Russell of her feelings:

I was shocked, and dispirited, and feeling *silence* best. *But* you could *not* guess the *outward* disturbance consequent on this event! The letters and calls of inquiry and condolence that have been eating up my days for the last two weeks! distressingly and irritatingly – For it does not require any particular acuteness to detect, in this fussy display of feeling, more impertinent curiosity than genuine sympathy . . . the greater number of these *condolers* have come to ask particulars of her death (which we were likely to know) and to see how we, especially *Mr Carlyle*, were taking her loss! . . .

Last Tuesday Mr C went to the Grange to be present at her funeral. It was conducted with a sort of royal state, and all the men, who used to compose a sort of *Court* for her, were there; *in tears*![123]

One of them, William Brookfield, noted the occasion in his diary:

12th. At the Grange. Stood beside Carlyle at the Grave. There were present, besides ourselves, Lords Clanricarde, Granville, Grey, Sidney, Sandwich, Stanley of Alderley, Ashburton, Bath, Hinchingbrooke, Dufferin, Venables, H. Taylor, Thackeray, Humphrey Mildmay, F. Byng, Ellice, Dean of Westminster.[124]

While Carlyle attended the funeral, Ellen called on Jane, who 'looked so unhappy, I dreaded to leave her to herself'. Though Ellen knew how sharp and unforgiving Jane could be, she saw the vulnerable side of her on this occasion; she also perceived a contrast between the Carlyles and the Brookfields:

It was so strange, that as I drove thro' Eaton Square in going, who should I see but Mrs Brookfield; it was the day of Lady Ashburton's funeral & I shrunk back in the carriage, feeling as if it were too much to *bow* to her even, – when she bent forward – gave me a bow, with such a broad smile as if we had met at a dinner! – & in all my life I never saw her with a more cheerful & serene expression. And two hours after, I left Mrs Carlyle – so pale & so wretched, hardly able to speak without crying; – & there were the two friends, (the true and the false as Edward said curtly) & poor Lady Ashburton had not the gift to see them as they were. I couldn't *be* convinced after that that Mrs B has a heart, except for her own interests. I do pity the Carlyles.[125]

The Times carried an obituary of Lady Ashburton on 7 May. She had died in her fifty-second year, well known for her 'remarkable qualities' as a hostess, and 'if her wit and the brightness of her raillery sometimes astonished a society accustomed to a vapid and colourless conversation', these characteristics were 'all the more attractive to graver minds which comprehended with how much reflection and with what just perception they were accompanied'.[126] One such mind – the one most likely to miss this mysterious woman – was resigned to suffer the blow quietly. In his reminiscence of Jane in 1866 Carlyle confronted for a moment the problem of Jane's relations with Lady Ashburton, then turned away, merely saying, '*Ay de mi*: it is a mingled yarn, all that of our "Aristocratic" History; and I need not enter on it here.'[127]

CHAPTER 16

A Chelsea Interior 1857–1860

While Carlyle sat in Chelsea reading proofs of the first two volumes of *Frederick*, which were at last being printed, Jane went to Scotland early in July 1857, dividing her time between the Donaldson sisters in Haddington, her Edinburgh aunts, and Walter Welsh at Auchtertool. The letters between the couple during this summer are friendly. Jane asked Carlyle to thank Lord Ashburton on her behalf: 'I couldn't *say* anything about his kindness in giving me those things which she had been in the habit of *wearing*'; 'I felt so sick and so like to cry, that I am afraid I seemed quite stupid and ungrateful to him.'[1] The 'things' were a gold chain and bracelets of Lady Ashburton's, which Lord Ashburton had given her just before she left Chelsea. Jane explained to Blanche Airlie that Lady Ashburton had been wearing them on the unsuccessful royal train journey of the previous summer.[2]

Carlyle kept Jane informed about the welfare of Nero and the canaries, and he told her what gossip he could glean. Thackeray was a parliamentary candidate at Oxford – 'extremely foolish', Carlyle thought. (Thackeray lost, as Carlyle reported on 26 July.) While out riding on Fritz, Carlyle had passed 'Dizzy and his old wife' in Hyde Park, 'out taking an after dinner drive; they looked content, "peacefully sated with revenge and food", and were not speaking one word'. Robert Tait was frequently in the house, painting 'incessantly' but seeming to Carlyle to 'make no progress at all' on the picture which would be exhibited the following year as *A Chelsea Interior*. Tait had also brought his 'malodorous Photographing Apparatus; was fluffing about, all Saturday [25 July] with it, and getting views which will certainly "please Mrs Carlyle"'.[3]

Jane's letters, too, were quite cheerful and informative. She enjoyed recounting to Carlyle a chance meeting with an old flame on the journey from Edinburgh to Auchtertool at the end of July. A large man sitting opposite her on the omnibus, looking 'rather *gentleman-farmerly*' with his whiskers and ample girth, turned out to be Robert MacTurk. 'It was very uncomfortable to have been staring at his belly for five minutes and then to find in him an old lover.'[4] In Walter Welsh's house she soon found matter for grumbling: 'Ever since I came here I have been passing out of one silent rage into another at *the things in general* of this House'; 'the maximum of bother to arrive at the minimum of comfort', she exclaimed on 3 August.[5]

A week later Jeannie Chrystal arrived from Glasgow with a baby 'about three finger lengths long' and two nurses 'nearly six feet each', preceded by five packing cases sent by carrier, and bringing as many more bags with them in the carriage. This was a signal to Jane to escape back to her Edinburgh aunts, 'into the region of Common Sense'.[6] After she had returned to Chelsea, Jane vented the viciousness she had long felt towards her cousin to Mary Russell, the friend who had filled the position of chief epistolary confidante vacated by Jeannie herself: 'Such an affected bedizzened, caricature of a *fine Lady* I never came across. I could hardly keep my hands off her.'[7]

Better though the household management was at her aunts' Edinburgh home, the fastidious Jane had to contend there with excessive religious observance. 'I was so preached to (at the rate of *five* sermons a–day!) and prayed for morning and noon and night, "before *meat*" and "after meat" that I got quite bewildered and stupified', she told Blanche.[8]

While Jane was in Edinburgh Carlyle sent her the first proofs of *Frederick* to read, and despite her resentment of his neglect and bad temper during the past few years of Frederick-related research, she responded spontaneously to the literary genius which had excited her and persuaded her to marry him, against all doubts and counter-arguments, thirty years before. 'Oh, my dear!' she wrote on 24 August, 'What a magnificent Book *this* is going to be! The best of all your Books. *I* say so who *never flatter*, as you are too well aware.' She found it 'forcible and vivid, and sparkling as *The French Revolution*, with the geniality, and composure, and finish of *Cromwell* – a wonderful combination of merits!' Then, reaching for an apt quotation from that fertile source, Helen Mitchell, the Kirkcaldy maid who had served them long and faithfully until alcohol got the better of her:

Really one may say of these first two Books at least, what Helen said of the letters of her sister who died – you remember? – 'So *splendidly* put together; one would have thought that *hand* couldn't have written them!'[9]

Carlyle was delighted. 'Well, you are an excellt *encouraging* Goody', he wrote on 25 August; 'it wd be worth while to write Books if mankind wd read them as you do.'[10]

In 1856 the newspapers had been full of the trial of the poisoner William Palmer; this summer's crime sensation was the alleged arsenic poisoning by Madeleine Smith, daughter of a Glasgow architect, of her French lover Émile L'Angelier, in March 1857. The trial was held in Edinburgh in July. Interest was enormous, partly because of the sexual nature of much of the evidence. The jury returned a majority verdict on 9 July of 'Not Proven', the option available in Scottish law to a jury not convinced of either the innocence or the guilt of the defendant. Madeleine Smith walked free, but with her reputation as a murderess imprinted on the public mind.[11] A London publisher, George Vickers, immediately brought out an account of the trial, with engravings of the proceedings and the scenes outside the court, *Glasgow Poisoning Case: Unabridged Report of the Evidence in this Extraordinary Trial with All the Passionate Love Letters Written by the Prisoner to the Deceased, and Numerous Illustrations, including Portrait of Madeleine Smith* (1857).

Jane passed on some 'inside' information gleaned from an old admirer of hers, Charles Terrot, Bishop of Edinburgh:

Well, never mind – As Miss Madeline Smith said to old Dr Simpson, who attended her during a short illness in Prison, and begged to use 'the privilege of an old man, and speak to her seriously at parting' – 'My dear Doctor! it is so good of you! But I won't let you trouble yourself to give me advice; for I assure you I have quite made up my mind *to turn over a new leaf*!!!' That is a fact! Simpson told it to Terrot who told *me*.

So interesting was the sexually adventurous Madeleine that, as Jane reports, some Glasgow merchants were raising a subscription – which had already reached £9,000 – 'to testify their sympathy for her'.[12]

The other news of the summer was the Indian Mutiny, about which Carlyle said little, though deploring 'the horrors that were done on the English by these mutinous hyenas'.[13] To Varnhagen he wrote in October that the mutiny, a protest by the Bengal native army against British rule, was 'an ominous rebuke' to the British, who would, he was sure, soon 'get it beaten down again'.[14] Jane wrote to Mary Russell in the autumn, commenting on what she had read in the newspapers:

The only comfort I have had in reading about these Indian affairs is in the letters of some of the *women*. The men's letters are detestable generally – mess-room slang and affected *pococurantism* are shockingly out of place in these circumstances – if they ever *are* in place in *any* circumstances. But some of the *women*, afterwards murdered, write, in presence of their horrible fate, with a calm fortitude, and pious resignation that are *sublime*; and which effaces from one's thought of them all *painful* sense of degrading sufferings . . . I feel proud of my sex – and of my countrywomen – for the first time in my life![15]

By the end of 1857, after much petitioning by individuals like Caroline Norton and Marian Evans's feminist friend Barbara Leigh Smith, the passing of the Matrimonial Causes Act, or Divorce Act, as it was usually known, took the dissolution of marriage out of the ecclesiastical court into a new secular court, and made divorce slightly easier (and simpler).[16] But since women were still disadvantaged by having no right over property or earnings acquired *before* the divorce, the economic problem for them remained acute. In addition, husbands might now sue for divorce on grounds of adultery alone, whereas a wife was required to prove not only adultery but also the 'additional aggravation' of desertion, cruelty, incest, rape, sodomy, or bestiality.[17] The Act was a small step towards a humane and equal law on marriage and property, but it made little or no difference to most marriages and most lives in the short term.

Jane returned home in September, a little better in health. Robert Tait was in the house every day during October and November, she told Mary Russell, working on his painting.[18] Tait's attention to detail knew no bounds. In January 1858 Carlyle reported to Jack that he was 'still painting away at that interminable "interior"; but happily he now does it at his own house; and gives no bother *here* for many weeks past. Only borrows my "dressing-gown"; sent yesterday for "the pair of shoes" I had on, more power to his elbow!'[19]

Jane committed a lively narrative to paper on 23 November, telling her Haddington friend Agnes Howden the story of the black beetle that got into her servant Ann's ear. Ann had rushed in 'with her head *tumbled off* (as at first it looked to me) and carrying it in her hands!!'

She was holding down her head as low as her waist, her cap off, her hair flying, and her hand pressed to her right ear. I sprang forward and pulled her fingers from her ear which was full of blood. 'What *animal?*' I gasped. 'Oh, I think it is a black-beetle!!' – And the screams went on, and she declared the beetle was 'running into her brain'. Her ignorance of anatomy was very unfortunate at the moment! I called up Mr Carlyle, for I had lost all presence of mind as well as herself. He took it coolly, as he takes most things. 'Syringe it' he said; 'syringing will bring out *any amount of black beetles.*'

Ann was dispatched to the apothecary at the bottom of the street, Jane following, where she found the girl covered in soap-suds and the beetle 'extracted piece meal (with a probe)'.[20]

In the same letter which contained in passing this tribute to Carlyle's sang-froid in an emergency, Jane bestowed a rare word of praise on another admirable aspect of his character – his utter lack of cupidity:

Mr C has or *had* some money in America. He *doesn't recollect how much*! and doesn't feel even a natural *curiosity* what is become of it!! – I have never heard a word out of his head about it except to say *once*, 'I suppose *my* money will have gone in the crash, and poor *Butler* (the gentleman who invested it for him) will be very sorry!' – Being a Philosopher's wife has some advantages![21]

Carlyle later noted that this winter of 1857–8 was 'none of the best' for Jane in terms of health, and that he was 'deep all the while in Frederick proofs'. In January 1858 he spent three days with Lord Ashburton at the Grange, where he felt the lack of Lady Ashburton on his first entrance into 'the empty drawing-room in silence of dusk'.[22]

He took a little more notice of Jane's complaints this winter, telling Jack on 22 January that she had 'a particular pain about a handbreadth below the heart – rather sore to the touch'.[23] And he pitied his 'poor little sick partner' when she and Ann, after five and a half years as mistress and servant, fell out seriously enough for notice to be given and accepted for the end of March.[24] Jane's good friend Ellen Twisleton was in Rome, and Geraldine, though still visiting often at Cheyne Row, had, in the sense of being a good companion, 'all but as good as gone out of my life!' as Mary Russell was told on 16 January. 'She has been making "a considerable of a fool" of herself, to speak plainly.' The cause was Geraldine's throwing herself at Walter Mantell, a scientist and explorer visiting England from New Zealand, where he was a government administrator. Jane saw with unsparing and unsympathetic eyes how unmarried men took fright at Geraldine's 'impulsive demonstrative ways'. Mantell, it was clear, had no intention of marrying Geraldine. 'It is making herself so small!' she exclaimed to Mary, 'openly making the craziest love to a man who having eight hundred a year may *marry* her at any moment'.[25]

Some consolation for her loss of female friendship came early in 1858, when the Edinburgh publisher John Blackwood sent Jane a copy of a new work, three stories entitled *Scenes of Clerical Life*, with the compliments of the author, 'George Eliot'. Marian Evans, who had not even revealed her identity to Blackwood yet – though he guessed – had specified Jane as the only female recipient of her first published work of fiction. Copies were also sent to Dickens, Thackeray, Tennyson, Ruskin, Froude, and Faraday.[26]

Dickens had replied warmly to his new unknown rival, saying he was 'strongly affected' by the stories and adding that, judging from certain 'womanly touches', he felt inclined to address the author as a woman. To Joseph Langford, the manager of Blackwood's London office, he was even more direct, declaring that if the writer was not a woman, 'I should begin to believe that I am a woman myself'.[27]

As for Jane, she was ecstatic, writing on 21 January to the mysterious author:

Dear Sir,
I have to thank you for a surprise, a pleasure, and a – *consolation*(!) all in one Book! and I *do* thank you most sincerely. I cannot divine what inspired the good thought to send *me* your Book; since (if the name on the Title Page be your real name) it could not have been personal regard; there has never been a *George Eliot* among my friends or acquaintance. But neither I am sure could you divine the

circumstances under which I should read the Book, and the particular benefit it should confer on me! I read it – at least the first volume – during one of the most (physically) wretched nights of my life; sitting up in bed, unable to get a wink of sleep for fever and sore throat; and it helped me through that dreary night, as well – better than the most sympathetic helpful friend watching at my bedside could have done!

It was, she continued,

a *human* book – written out of the heart of a live man, not merely out of the brain of an author – full of tenderness and pathos without a scrap of sentimentality, of sense without dogmatism, of earnestness without twaddle – a book that makes one *feel friends*, at once and for always, with the man or woman who wrote it!

On the question of gender, Jane hedged her bets, deciding that the author was most probably 'a man of middle age, with a wife from whom he has got those beautiful *feminine* touches in his book'.[28] Her praise, bestowed unawares on the strong-minded woman of the *Westminster Review* who had set up home with Lewes, was delightful to the sensitive author, who had chosen to write under a pseudonym largely because of society's disapproval of Marian Evans.[29]

*

In February Jane reported to Mrs Russell that there were two artists in the house. Not only was Tait still finishing off his *Interior,* destined for the Royal Academy Exhibition, but another artist, 'a certain charming Mrs Hawkes', was determined to do a portrait of Jane, also intended for the Exhibition.[30] Emilie Hawkes, born Ashurst, had been Mazzini's closest woman friend for several years past. It was she who gave Mazzini the 'little interior' of the Carlyles in January 1861 – either a photograph or a copy of Tait's painting. Though Emilie's portrait of Jane appears not to have been completed, she visited often to work at it, and she and Jane became friendly over the next few years. Mazzini, it seems, no longer wrote to Jane when he was away, but he always asked after her in his letters to Emilie.[31]

A Chelsea Interior was shown in the summer. Jane's new servant, sixteen-year-old Charlotte Southam, later remembered being taken to the Exhibition by Jane, who told her to walk round and look at the pictures for herself. Charlotte came running back, exclaiming, 'Oh mum, Mr Carlyle and you and Nero are all in the other room. Come and see them.' Jane noticed that Charlotte was so excited that her eyes were as big as saucers, and Carlyle, when told of the afternoon's jaunt, was tickled by Charlotte's saying to Jane, 'Come and see *them.*'[32]

By one of those ironies of life Jane and Carlyle were thus exhibited to the public, together in their own famous, if modest, house, at a moment when they were at their most fragile as a couple. When Carlyle, having finished reading the proofs of volumes one and two of *Frederick*, escaped to his sister Mary's at the Gill towards the end of June 1858, he left Jane more morbid and hysterical than ever. Though she no longer had to suffer the constant irritation of seeing him go off to Bath House or the Grange to be with the woman of his rather childish dreams, she still felt neglected, and was in a state of real anxiety about her health. Her ill health, if still not properly diagnosed, was plain for all to see. The photographs of her show it, and her contemporaries noticed it too. Thomas Woolner, for example, told Emily Tennyson on 7 June that Carlyle was blind to his wife's weak state, though it was staring him in the face.[33]

Jane herself made the point through a dramatic story spun out of a surprise visit by her earliest friend Eliza Stodart, now Mrs Aitken, soon after Carlyle had gone to Scotland. There is something both pathetic and perverse about the energy Jane could put into a description of her own weakness in order to impress a husband whose chief failing was inability to be moved by such a spectacle. Jane had found Eliza about to knock at the door:

'Is this Mrs Carlyle's?' she asked of *myself* while I was gazing dumfoundered! 'My goodness!' cried I – at the sound of my voice she knew me – just think! *not* till then! tho at my own door! and certainly the recognition was the furthest from complimentary I ever *met* – She absolutely staggered – screaming out '*God* preserve me! – Jane! – *That* you!' – Pleasant![34]

Shortly before leaving London, Carlyle had mentioned in a letter to Emerson the gossip about Dickens's marriage:

If you read the Newspapers, they will babble to you about Dickens's 'Separation from Wife' &c &c: fact of Separatn (Lawyer's *Deed* &c) I believe is true; but all the rest is mere lies and nonsense. No crime or misdemeanour specificable on either side: *unhappy* together, these good many years past, and they at length end it.[35]

It was true that the marriage was unhappy, though the dissatisfaction was all on one side – Dickens's – and he did have a relationship, with the young actress Ellen Ternan, which he went to great lengths to conceal. Nevertheless, many knew or suspected the secret, and the Garrick Club was full of rumours, with Thackeray at the heart of the gossiping. On 12 June Dickens made a disingenuous and ill-advised public statement in his newspaper, *Household Words*, announcing the separation and denying the 'most monstrous, and most cruel' reports circulating about him.[36] Jane and Carlyle knew about the rumours, and Jane at least may have believed them, for she jotted down a riddle in a notebook, probably at this time, which read: 'When does a man really ill-use his wife? Ans. – When he plays the Dickens with her.'[37]

Or, she might have said, though at the expense of her neat piece of wordplay, when he plays the Bulwer-Lytton with her. Bulwer-Lytton had been separated from Rosina since 1836; he had custody of their two children, whom he neglected, and he kept Rosina short of money. She pursued him for years with letters and petitions, wrote novels with undisguised Bulwerish hero-villains, and in 1851 had threatened to disrupt performances of *Not So Bad As We Seem*.[38] If Rosina was a nuisance, her husband was a monster, though Dickens and Forster unaccountably remained his staunch friends and supporters. (Dickens even named a son after him in 1852.) Forster, now Secretary of the Lunacy Commission looking into asylums and committals, gave Bulwer-Lytton procedural advice this June 1858, when, infuriated by Rosina's dramatic appearance on the hustings at Hertford to denounce him as he stood for re-election to Parliament, he had her committed to a lunatic asylum. The deed was done on 22 June; under pressure to submit to a public inquiry into his actions, he was forced to have her released again on 17 July.[39]

The Carlyles, like everyone else, discussed the scandal, Jane asking Carlyle on 9 July if he had heard about Bulwer-Lytton 'putting his wife into confinement', to which Carlyle replied from the Gill two days later:

What is all that of Bulwer & Wife in *confinement*? Jean, when I questioned her, had heard from the Newspapers, of the furious Lady's spring up upon the Public Stage, and clutching her Phantom Husband in sight of the world, at some sublime acme of his Harangue. But nothing more is yet known here.[40]

Jane passed on what she knew from Forster. Bulwer-Lytton, on discovering Rosina's presence at the hustings, rushed down from the platform, jumped into his carriage, 'almost fainting', and 'was gallopped back to Knebworth – leaving his friends to speak for him!' 'Don't you think the Lady had the best of the day here?' Jane asked, before telling of Rosina's being 'handed over to a *mad doctor*'.[41]

In his reply Carlyle gave his opinion that Rosina was 'no more *mad* than I am, tho' unwise, ill-guided to a high degree, and plunging wildly under the heavy burden laid on her'. As for her husband:

No man of real humanity, I think, in any case would or could have kept the once Partner of his life, if he could have possibly helped it, in a state of *poverty*, for one thing . . . why does he not, like Herodotus's man, in a like or not nearly so bad case, 'go to his father's grave', and there honestly 'fall upon his sword' (theatrical rapier, Kean or Mathews wd lend him one), and *finish* in the Devil's name![42]

Though Carlyle and Jane were entirely in agreement that Rosina was the wronged partner, this Bulwer-Lytton business was to be resonant for

Jane. Towards the end of 1863, when she was so ill and desperate that even Carlyle was alarmed, she begged him, 'on two occasions, with such a look and tone as I shall never forget', as he recalled, ' *"promise* me that you will not put me into a mad-house, however this go. Do you *promise* me, now?" I solemnly did.'[43] Even now, in the summer of 1858, the Dickens and Bulwer-Lytton discords arose during a particularly unharmonious period for the Carlyles, though as before they corresponded themselves and one another into warmer feelings and better relations by the end of it.

Carlyle had opened the summer's correspondence with a friendly letter on 24 June to say he had arrived safely at the Gill. He appealed to Jane, in a tone more pathetic than tactful, as 'my dear one friendkin (what other have I left really?)' – she would surely read a reference to the loss of Lady Ashburton in that – and assured her that a very short letter from her would be welcome, 'if it only tell me you begin to profit by being left alone'.[44] Jane replied immediately, in one of those letters without endearments; she pounced on Carlyle's phrase about being left alone and threw it back at him:

'*Let alone*'; with a sort of vengeance! Exhausted human nature could not desire more perfect letting alone! . . . to see *you* constantly discontented and as much so with *me* apparently, as with all other *things*, when I have neither the strength and spirits to bear up against your discontent, nor the obtuseness to be indifferent to it, *that* has done me more harm than you have the least notion of. You have not the least notion what a killing thought it is, to have put into one's heart, gnawing there day and night, that one *ought* to be *dead*, since one *can* no longer make the same exertions as formerly! – that one was taken only 'for better' – not by any means 'for worse'! and in fact, that the only feasible and dignified thing that remains for one to do is to just *die*, and be done with it!

'Alas! alas! sinner that I am', wrote Carlyle in the margin here as he read her letters after her death.[45]

On 27 June Jane wrote again, still without any 'my dears' or 'affectionately yours', but thawing sufficiently to tell Carlyle with relish the story of Lord Ashburton's giving the 'fancy' sum of £500 for *A Chelsea Interior*.[46] Meanwhile Carlyle was responding to her outburst about his being discontented with her. 'Depend upon it', he wrote, 'that is a *mistake* once for all'. He had been discontented with himself, with 'hot fetid London', with 'all persons and things (and my stomach had struck work withal), but not discontented with poor *you* ever at all'.[47]

Hot and fetid London certainly was, so much so that this became known as the summer of 'the Great Stink'. For years the rapid growth of London's population (doubling in the first forty years of the century) had put a strain on its primitive sanitation arrangements. Chadwick had done his best to improve things, with his 1842 *Report* on sanitary conditions and his agitation to have house drains and cesspools connected to sewers. But he was hampered by a combination of factors ranged against him – the vested interests of paving boards, vestries, private water companies – and by the prevalent but mistaken belief, which he shared, that diseases such as cholera were airborne rather than water-borne. His efforts at laying new sewers in 1853–4, therefore, on which Carlyle had commented admiringly when one was being laid in Cheyne Row, were well intentioned but mistaken, since the sewers discharged their filth straight into the Thames, which was also the source of London's drinking water. His actions contributed to pollution and to the spread of cholera during its periodic outbreaks.[48]

In June 1858 the Thames stank so dreadfully right under the noses of MPs at Westminster that, according to *The Times* on 18 June, members were 'driven to retreat, each man with a handkerchief to his nose'. Desperate measures were at last called for; warring factions were obliged to co-operate; and the result was the great project to introduce leak-proof sewers to run alongside the Thames and discharge their contents into specially constructed outfalls to the east of London. Joseph Bazalgette, the chief engineeer, enclosed these sewers in a series of embankments during the 1860s and 1870s – the Albert, Victoria, and finally (in 1874) the Chelsea Embankment.[49]

One body which was trying to improve matters, the Public Health Section of the Social Science Association, had recently invited Carlyle to become a member of its board. Arthur Helps wrote in December 1857 saying the committee would consist of 'very eminent men in many ways' – surgeons, physicians, engineers, politicians such as Lord Stanley, men of science like Michael Faraday, and 'resolute sanitarians such as Chadwick'. Anticipating correctly that Carlyle would refuse, as he now refused all such requests for the sake of getting *Frederick* done, Helps concluded flatteringly, 'Whether you accept this invitation or not, I think you would have been pleased to see the way in which your name was received – as that of a man who had already done good services.'[50]

Carlyle escaped the worst of the stink by being in Scotland, but not before he had smelt the smell and connected it metaphorically with the condition of England. He wrote to Forster on 17 June: 'Temperature 82 in the shade; Thames River with a stink worse than Acheron; a gilt Old-Clothes-man [Disraeli] ruling the Empire of Britain.' A week later he reported to the same correspondent that he was off to Scotland, glad to get out of '*this* thrice-infernal element' with its 'Italian Organ-boys, tepid dirtyish water, stinking river, stinking Parlt', and other unspecified horrors.[51]

From Scotland Carlyle continued writing steadily to the alienated Jane, apologising for upsetting her and gradually moving away from sensitive subjects. Jane was prepared to follow suit. She told him about Tait and the extravagant Lord Ashburton on 1 July, urging him to stop worrying:

I cant understand your fretting about the sale and wishing to stop it any more. Neither you nor I are responsible for Lord Ashburton's imbecility . . . Let someone else tell him that Posterity will look with more interest at this Picture than any other in his possession (and I, for one, think so) and his impressionable Lordship would be enchanted with his purchase! Unless you had a hand in the original making of *Lord A* I can't see that you need vex yourself about this five hundred pounds, which he has not spent to please you but himself.[52]

Carlyle replied with a description of his difficulties with the Dumfries-shire tailors from whom he always ordered his clothes (not trusting London clothiers for anything).[53] Then Jane wrote of curling up to read some 'delightful volumes of Tourgueneff's' while Emilie Hawkes came (to paint her, presumably). On 11 July she struck boldly into a set piece, headed 'Notes of a Sitter-still':

Botkin (what a name!) your Russian translator, has called. Luckily Charlotte had been forewarned to admit him if he came again . . . He burst into the room with wild expressions of his 'admiration for Mr Carlyle' – I begged him to be seated, and he declared 'Mr Carlyle was the man for Russia'[.] I tried again and again to 'enchain' a rational conversation but nothing could I get out of him but rhapsodies about *you* in the frightfulest English that I ever heard out of a human head! It is to be hoped that (as he told me) he *reads* English much better than he *speaks* it – else he must have produced an inconceivable translation of *Hero Worship*. Such as it is, anyhow, 'a large deputation of the Students of St Petersburg' waited on him (Botkin), to *thank* him in the strongest terms for having translated for them Hero Worship, and made known to them Carlyle – *and* even the young Russian Ladies now read *Hero Worship*, and 'unnerstants – it – thor-lie' – He was all in a perspiration when he went away – and so was I![54]

Soon Jane was calling Carlyle 'dear' again. A few days later she sent on another proof of his international celebrity in the form of the map of the new Carlyle Township in Australia which Duffy had posted.[55]

★

Carlyle had long ago realised that he needed to visit Germany again. He could not get enough books, though he despised all those he did read, especially the Dryasdust German histories, 'hideous imbroglios without vestige of Index', as he wrote in exasperation in the margin of one of them.[56] He also knew he ought to visit more battlefields. As he confessed to Varnhagen von Ense in October 1857, 'The truth is, I should have *come to Berlin* to write this book.'[57] He wondered if Lord Ashburton knew of anyone with a yacht who might take him to the Baltic coast.[58] Jane reported back on 27 July that a member of the Ashburton circle, Lord Dufferin, was sailing to the Mediterranean, and could land Carlyle at Trieste.[59]

After the usual dithering, Carlyle decided to go from Scotland, sailing to Hamburg with a Welsh acquaintance, Frederick Foxton, who 'offers himself as escort', as Carlyle told Neuberg on 22 July.[60] Carlyle set off on 21 August to spend a month in Germany, first as a guest of the Baron von Usedom on the Baltic island of Rügen, then in Berlin, where the loyal Neuberg met him and smoothed his path in the tiresome matters of accommodation and transport. Varnhagen and others helped to find military men who would accompany Carlyle to the twelve battlefields he wished to visit. In letters to Jane, and in a memoir of his journey written soon after his return in October, he described the usual trials with beds and food, but indicated that he had done well on his research visits to Breslau, Prague, and Dresden.[61] He was less grateful to his volunteer companions than he ought to have been, complaining to Jane from Prague on 14 September:

Poor Neuberg has fairly broken down by excess of yesterday's labour, and various misery: he gave up the Hradschin ('Rad*sheen*', they pronounce it [the castle at Prague]) to Foxton and me . . . He is the mainspring of every enterprise: I cd not *do* it with[ou]t him; – and Foxton is good for absolutely nothing except to neutralize him, whh he pretty much does.[62]

The ungrateful traveller came back to Chelsea on 22 September to be greeted by Nero, but not Jane, who had gone on her own travels in the meantime, first spending most of August with Lord Ashburton's sisters, the Misses Baring, at Bay House, then venturing north once more to visit a second cousin, Mrs Pringle, in Dumfriesshire, the Russells at Thornhill, James and Isabella Carlyle at Scotsbrig, and Mary Austin at the Gill. She had even gone to Craigenputtoch for a day's outing with Mrs Pringle, letting Carlyle know on 10 September that she experienced 'the most ghastly sensations' while there.[63]

Jane did not disclose her motive in revisiting the place of her nightmares, but it surely had something to do with the fact that Carlyle himself had gone to Craigenputtoch on business on 5 August, writing to Jane that the house was 'now quite buried in woods', that 'our old dining-room is now the state apart[men]t', but '*your* old paper is on the other two rooms, dim like the fading memories'. He had added in his fatal way, 'I looked with emotion upon my old *Library closet*, and wished I cd get thither again to finish my *Friedh* under fair chances!'[64] This revelation 'made me feel *choked*', Jane replied.[65] She may have been piqued by curiosity, as well as combativeness, into going to see the old place for herself.

She arrived back in Chelsea at the end of September, laden with eggs and other delicacies pressed on her by Mary Austin, as well as 'an enormous bundle of new clothes' Carlyle had left for her to take with her, 'the produce of the indefatigable exertions of *three tailors*, whom he had kept sewing for him at the Gill for *four weeks!*' as Mary Russell was told on 1 October. Thanks to young Charlotte Southam's efforts, Jane had arrived home to a well-ordered household:

A perfectly-cleaned house and a little maid radiant with 'virtue its own reward'. And oh unexpected joy! a jet-black kitten added to the household . . . Charlotte said yesterday, 'I think Scotland must be such a fresh, airy place! I should like to go there! You did *smell so beautiful* when you came in at the door last night'!! She is quite a jewel of a Servant. Far more like an adopted Child than a London maid-of-all-work.[66]

Jane had written to Charlotte from Mrs Russell's house on 16 September, giving her the minutest instructions about how to prepare the house for the return from Germany of its exacting master, and how to manage with him for a week or so until Jane herself got back. We learn from this letter that Carlyle cast a critical eye over all housekeeping matters:

You know his ways and what he needs pretty well by this time. Trouble him with as few questions as possible. You can ask him whether he will take tea or coffee to breakfast? – and whether he would like broth, or a pudding to dinner? you must always give him one or other with his meat and either an egg to breakfast or a slice of bacon. I think you can now cook most of the things he takes oftenest boiled fowl, mutton broth, chops and bread and ground rice puddings – If you take pains to please him I have no doubt you will. And if he look fussed and *cross*, never mind, so long as you are doing your best; travelling always puts him in a fever, and nobody can look and speak *amiably* with sick nerves . . .

Heaven help you and him well through it! Take care your kitchen be in order – When he goes to light his pipe, – he will see.[67]

Jane's delight with Charlotte lasted for another two years only; she was dismissed in August 1860, being in need, Jane thought, of 'some *stricter* superintendence than mine'.[68] Jane's tendency to quarrel with her servants, but also to quasi-mother and spoil them until they presumed too much on her good nature, resulted in the hiring and firing of more than thirty servants in as many years.[69]

Carlyle's German trip was neatly distilled by Jane in a letter to Lady Stanley at the end of October. He had not lingered more than three weeks

in a country destitute of '*Christian* Beds' and anything in the shape of '*human* food'! Ten days of the three weeks he passed in a Calypso Island (of Rügen), where Madame von Usedom spirited him away in a carriage and four, and where, (the Calypso being *scotch*), a certain approximation to Christianity in the Beds and humanity in the food appears to have been attainable. The other eleven days he was rushing from Battlefield to Battlefield, like a man chased by Devils! And arrived here in a condition that reminded one of *Cruiser* after his fight with Harry!

Jane apparently alludes here to a book advertised at this time with the provocative title *How I Tamed Mrs Cruiser by Benedict Cruiser MM (married man) now HH (happy husband).*[70]

The first two volumes of *Frederick* were published in late September. They sold well, earning Carlyle £2,800 by the end of the year. He had reason to be grateful to John Forster, who had accepted the job of negotiating the final financial settlement with Chapman and Hall. Carlyle had put the matter into his capable hands before going to Scotland in June, writing 'amid the agonies of packing' on the day he left, 23 June, to thank his friend for taking on the whole 'arithmetical-commercial' side of things.[71] Carlyle was fortunate in his assistants. Forster was an experienced negotiator. Neuberg not only escorted Carlyle round Germany for a second time and did research for him in libraries in London, but also translated *Frederick* into German, the first volume appearing in Berlin before the end of 1858, followed by the second in 1859.[72] And Larkin painstakingly compiled a running index and prepared the numerous maps and battle plans which adorned the book.

Though Carlyle made no acknowledgement to his assistants in *Frederick* itself, he did give Larkin a cheque for £100 when presenting him with a copy of volumes one and two on 30 September, and shortly afterwards sent him a life subscription to the London Library, saying, 'If I had been King Friedrich, I would have given you a pretty little Mansion and grounds, for your merits to me'; 'that not being so, I have on cheap terms procured you a small *spiritual freehold*'.[73]

Thanks to Larkin's exertions, Carlyle's *Frederick* came forth richly equipped with the kind of apparatus so lacking in the books he had used in his research. He had told Varnhagen in June 1852 that he was in desperate need of a topographical dictionary of Prussia to locate the hundreds of place names associated with Frederick's career, 'character of place, sequence of time, Topography and Chronology' being, as he said, 'the warp and woof of all historical intelligibility to me'. A biographical dictionary or 'old "Peerage Book" such as we have in England' would have been a help, too, in finding his way among 'these crowds of empty names'. 'There are such multitudes of different Schwerins', 'so many Brandenburg-Schwedl-Brunswick-Bewerns, half-dozens of Dukes of Würtemberg, &c &c – it becomes like a Walpurgis-Nacht'.[74] (Larkin's index to *Frederick* lists over twenty different Friedrichs – kings, dukes, princes, and margraves.) In a letter to Ruskin in May 1855 Carlyle, with despairing wit, had likened his 'Prussian affairs' to the fiasco of Balaklava, the more so as

I had no business at all to concern myself in such an adventure with such associates; and that a *good* result to it does not seem (for most part) so much as possible! 'the longer you look at it', as Sir John Burgoyne [second-in-command to Lord Raglan in the Crimea] says, 'the less you see your way through it.'[75]

If this was how he had felt after three years of working on Frederick, the appearance of the first two volumes after a further three and a half years of toil represented both success and failure. Success, because he had subdued the mountainous material sufficiently to write the first part of his huge narrative – the first half, as he fondly imagined, sending out the two volumes with a hopeful title-page reading: '*History of Friedrich II of Prussia, called Frederick the Great*, by Thomas Carlyle, in four volumes'. (In the end, six volumes were required.) Failure, because, after more than six years' labour, he had produced a narrative which brought Frederick only as far as the death of his father – a rough old tyrant whom Carlyle confessed he loved and admired – and his own accession to the throne in 1740. Failure, too, because he had published the first part of a six-volume work which was vast, unmanageable, detailed to a fault. *Frederick* was a caricature, or '*reductio ad absurdum*' of Carlylism, in William Allingham's words, though Allingham swiftly added that it contained 'a world of wit, humour, picture, narrative, character, history, thought, wisdom, shrewdness, learning, insight'.[76] And so it does for the reader with plenty of time and infinite patience.

Volume one opens in lively enough fashion. Carlyle asks us to view the palace of Sanssouci 'about fourscore years ago', where 'a highly interesting lean little old man, of alert though slightly stooping figure', saunters on the terrace. This old man, simply dressed, of no 'godlike physiognomy', is the king known as Frederick the Great, now approaching death in 1786. The French Revolution would follow soon, and Frederick be forgotten. But, Carlyle says, he is one of the most important phenomena of his century, which Carlyle personalises, as he had done in *The French Revolution* (a book which he assumes the reader knows):

To me the Eighteenth Century has nothing grand in it, except that grand universal Suicide, named French Revolution, by which it terminated its otherwise most worthless existence with at least one worthy act; – setting fire to its old home and self, and going up in flames and volcanic explosions, in a truly memorable and important manner.[77]

This hated century produced a number of lies, including 'poor'

Voltaire's work on Frederick's private life, a 'scandalous libel' written in a mad frenzy and not intended for publication. It is Carlyle's self-appointed task to make the period yield up some truths, a task which is hindered not only by worthless French and English books which misrepresent Frederick and all his doings, but equally by well-intentioned German histories by a species of 'Prussian Dryasdust' who 'writes big Books wanting in almost every quality; and does not even give an *Index* to them'. 'And so', Carlyle concludes this idiosyncratic opening chapter, 'we will end these pre-ludings, and proceed upon our Problem, courteous reader.'[78]

For the rest of the book – all six volumes – Carlyle adopts the unusual and fatally lengthening practice of including, as part of his text, remarks of scorn, scepticism, and disgust at the dishonesty or unscholarliness of his sources, rather than leaving these in his study in the form of private notes in the margins of his books, notes such as the following written on an anonymous English publication of 1758 on the life of Frederick the Great's grandfather, Frederick I of Prussia:

There is *nothing* absolutely in this Book but blundering stupidities and mis-informations; except what is copied (stolen) from poor Dilworth, I can recollect nothing deserving another character . . . Baddish print (from a good Picture); bad poor Map . . . Adieu, thou *other* stupid farrago! (29 Novr 1855; 11½ p.m.).[79]

Haranguing and arguing with such sources, as well as quoting liberally from them and letting them argue amongst themselves in his own pages, was surely a mistake. As Althaus wrote in his 1866 memoir of Carlyle, the work (the German translation of which Althaus completed in 1869, when Neuberg died shortly before finishing the final volume) shows the scaffolding as well as the edifice.[80] One example from many comes in Book VIII, chapter 5, in which Carlyle quotes from the published letters of Lieutenant-General Schulenburg, prefacing his quotation with the irritated remark, 'Schulenburg continues; not even taking a new para-graph, which indeed he never does.' A few pages later, having extracted what he needs, Carlyle bids farewell to Schulenburg – 'let the Lieutenant-General withdraw now into silence' – contemptuously (and somewhat self-defeatingly) adding that 'these glimpses' of Frederick as Crown Prince 'are not very luculent to the reader, – light being indifferent, and mirror none of the best'.[81] Though Carlyle can often be comic in his contempt, it is a questionable proceeding to put the reader vicariously through the torment, the mud-wrestlings, as he would say, which he himself had transacted for years in his rooftop study.

Worse than this, however, is Carlyle's plunging for half a volume into the dustiest depths of Frederick's ancestry among the dukes and princes of Brandenburg and Hohenzollern, at times going back as far as the eleventh century in an attempt to bring light out of darkness, order out of chaos. As Frederic Harrison later wittily remarked of the whole work:

As to *Frederick*, it is not a book at all, but an encyclopædia of German biographies in the latter half of the eighteenth century . . . Who cares to know how big was the belly of some court chamberlain, or who were the lovers of some unendurable Frau? What a welter of dull garbage! In what dust-heaps dost thou not smother us, Teufelsdröckh! O, Thomas, Thomas, what Titania has bewitched thee with the head of Dryasdust on thy noble shoulders?[82]

Carlyle himself was not particularly interested in the trivia of 'court gossip and *Potsdamiana*', in Harrison's phrase. But his sources were. He therefore devised a method of relaying such minutiae in a comically weary tone of irony, not very different from the tone he and Jane had long ago adopted in their letters to one another, in which they reduced their acquaintances to a set of repeated coterie quotations – Jeffrey 'the little dear', Lewes 'the Ape', Mazzini the speaker of comically foreign English. Frederick's arranged marriage to a woman he scarcely knew and cared nothing about is treated in this way. The Princess Elizabeth of Brunswick is described as an 'insipid Brunswick specimen'; thereafter her every appearance is accompanied by a variation on this label – 'your Insipidity of Brunswick', 'insipid *Corpus delicti* herself', 'Insipidity's private feelings are not known to us'.[83]

Frederick's relations with his father, Friedrich Wilhelm, form for Carlyle – and for the reader – much the most interesting part of these first two volumes, which end with the death of the old king. The relationship is presented throughout as similar to that of Shakespeare's Henry IV and Prince Hal: a tragicomic tale of mutual misunderstandings, filial rebellion, and fatherly displeasure and disappointment. Carlyle resorts to comic chapter titles of a Fieldingesque sort – 'Crown-Prince Falls into Disfavour with Papa' – and refers directly to *Tom Jones* when asking us to imagine Frederick's father:

Conceive a rugged thick-sided Squire Western, of supreme degree, – for this Squire Western is a hot Hohenzollern, and wears a crown royal; – conceive such a burly *ne-plus-ultra* of a Squire, with his broad-based rectitudes and surly irrefragabilities; the honest German instincts of the man, convictions certain as the Fates, but capable of no utterance, or next to none, in words; and that he produces a Son who takes into Voltairism, piping, fiddling and belles-lettres, with apparently a total contempt for Grumkow and the giant-regiment! Sulphurous rage, in gusts or in lasting tempests, rising from a fund of just implacability, is inevitable.[84]

Frederick not only sold surprisingly well, but was also widely reviewed. Most reviewers were respectful about this first publication of Carlyle's since the *Life of Sterling* in 1851, but many thought the subject unworthy of Carlyle's enormous labour (as he did himself, at bottom).[85] George Gilfillan, a Scottish clergyman, calculated in the *Scottish Review* that the 'two enormous volumes' might have been reduced by more than half 'on the easy plan of excluding all the oaths, one half of the exclamations, a third of the repetitions, and a fourth of the needless minutiae'.[86]

Among Carlyle's friends the verdict was mixed. Clough told Charles Eliot Norton on 7 October that he had just begun 'Carlyle's big book, of which hitherto the report is good'.[87] Two weeks later he was part way through reading the second volume, and wrote to the same correspondent: 'There can be no doubt of the research & diligence – whatever else may be said.'[88] By 29 October Clough had finished the book. 'I cannot say that as yet I have much liking for the hero, though indeed the hero may be said to be the hero's father – old Friedrich Wilhelm; – whom certainly one comes to like.'[89] In Mazzini's opinion, the book was '*feudalism*; worships [*sic*] of force, intellectual or brutal'.[90]

Others who were less than enthusiastic were FitzGerald and Browning. The former wrote to a friend in January 1859 that he did not 'care much about it', but that it was successful enough to have 'got to a second Edition rapidly, of which Mudie [of the circulating library] took a thousand Copies'. To Carlyle himself he wrote in his friendly but offhand and rather pithy way in June 1859, craftily eliding book and protagonist: 'You don't care what one thinks of your Books: you know I love so many: I don't care so much for Frederick so far as he's gone: I suppose you don't neither.'[91] Browning's comment, relayed by his wife, who reported from Rome in February that he was cursing and swearing over *Frederick*, was 'Never was there a more immoral book in the brutal sense.'[92]

There were warmer responses. Emily Tennyson recorded in her journal on 7 December 1858 that Alfred had begun reading *Frederick* aloud to her.[93] And Herzen sent a copy of his edition, in French, of Catherine the Great's *Memoirs* (1859), with the following inscription on the title-page: 'A Monsieur Thomas Carlyle témoignage d'estime et de respect', signed A. Herzen and dated 30 November 1858.[94] Carlyle read and annotated Herzen's book; he was also to bestow some rare praise on it in volume six of *Frederick*, where he called it 'a credible and highly remarkable little Piece: worth all the others, if it is knowledge of Catharine you are seeking'.[95] Emerson responded graciously, if belatedly, in May 1859, to Carlyle's gift of the two volumes, with its dedication 'To R. Waldo Emerson Esq (Concord, Massachusetts), From an old Friend, Chelsea, 6 December 1858'. 'We think you the true inventer of the stereoscope, as having exhibited that art in style, long before we had yet heard of it in drawing.'[96]

★

On 28 December 1858 Carlyle had noted in his journal that sales of *Frederick* were already over 4,000. 'I am fairly richer at this time than I ever was, in the money sense.' He felt rich enough to arrange for Jane to go out twice a week in a hired carriage, 'an expensive luxury', she told Mary Russell, but one Carlyle thought she had a right to enjoy.[97] In the same journal entry Carlyle observed that Lord Ashburton had married again and gone off to Egypt on his honeymoon. Carlyle was probably shocked that Lord Ashburton had found another wife so soon after Lady Harriet's death; in his journal he merely quotes Burns – 'The changes of this age, which fleeting Time procureth!' adding, 'Ah me ! ah me!'[98]

It was only a few months since Carlyle had written to Lord Ashburton from the Gill, diffidently reminding him of a bequest Lady Ashburton had made to him – £1,000 and a commission to distribute £50 each year to 'distressed literary Persons':

About the 10th of May gone a year, – the first time I drove with you to Addiscombe after an Event which can never be forgotten, – you took from your pocket a little Paper, drawn up as you said in far other days; in which was some bequest to me, among others.

Carlyle had felt unable to discuss it then, and now supposed that Lord Ashburton had mistaken his silence for refusal. It had been on his mind since, and he brought the subject up now, since 'no wish or command of *hers* but must be sacred to whoever was the object of it'. Lord Ashburton had replied the same day, and the bequest was honoured.[99] Now, a few months later, Lord Ashburton had taken a new wife, Louisa Stewart Mackenzie, to whom both Carlyle and Jane became attached in due course, though Carlyle had written innocently to Lord Ashburton a year earlier, describing Miss Mackenzie as a flirt, 'a bright vivacious damsel' who was 'fond of doing a stroke of "artful dodging"'.[100]

Jane's first reaction to the news of Lord Ashburton's impending second marriage was also sceptical. 'Oh dear', she wrote to Lady Stanley, 'the most brilliant of women are missed no longer than the most insignificant!' Old Lady Sandwich, she added admiringly, 'takes it beautifully', being prepared to accept any daughter-in-law who would make 'dear Ashburton' happy.[101] To Mary Russell she was even more disapproving. Louisa Mackenzie had been setting her cap at Lord Ashburton within six weeks of his wife's death. '*He* is very *trusting*, and has been very lonely – like a child that had lost its mother in a wood!' 'I shall never like the new Lady Ashburton – that I am sure of!'[102]

In spite of the relative decline in Carlyle's reputation during the 1850s, and his increasing reclusiveness, he was still one of the most respected men of his day. Old friends and admirers remained loyal, and new generations of young people read his works and joined the ranks of his admirers. This was particularly the case at Oxford and Cambridge. Macaulay, who could not stand Carlyle or his writings, resenting, as Carlyle also did, the fact that reviewers regularly compared and contrasted the historical methods and styles of the two men, wrote with satisfaction in April 1859 that his nephew, George Otto Trevelyan (who was also to become a celebrated historian), was doing well as a Cambridge undergraduate. In particular, Macaulay says, 'it is owing to me' that Trevelyan 'lives in the very midst of an atmosphere reeking with Carlylism, Ruskinism, Browningism, and other equally noxious isms, without the slightest taint of the morbific virus'.[103]

The painter Ford Madox Brown renewed a request for Carlyle to sit for a photograph to be used in his monumental painting entitled *Work*. Carlyle tried to wriggle out of it. 'I think it a pity you had not put (or should not still put) some other man than me into your great Picture', he wrote in spring 1859. But he remembered having promised 'to sit for some photographs', and so agreed to give up one hour of his time, either at Cheyne Row or at Brown's Chelsea studio.[104] The picture, completed in 1863, depicts in realistic style, yet with allegorical significance, a scene in Heath Street, Hampstead. At the centre is a group of brawny, handsome labourers digging a water main; they are surrounded by representatives of other groups and classes, from ragged children to fashionable ladies and a gentleman on horseback. In a prominent position on the right of the picture stand two gentlemen, watching the labourers approvingly; they are F. D. Maurice, who had become founder and principal of the Working Men's College in 1854, and Carlyle, the apostle of work, who is shown grinning rather demonically.[105]

Jane was singled out to receive a copy of George Eliot's next work, her first full-length novel, the enormously successful *Adam Bede*, which was published on 1 February 1859. Once again Jane fired off an enthusiastic letter, treating the unknown author to a blow-by-blow account of the novel's arrival and reception at Cheyne Row:

I must again offer you my heartfelt thanks. Since I received your *Scenes of Clerical Life* nothing has fallen from the skies to me so welcome as *Adam Bede, all to myself*, 'from the author'.

My Husband had just read an advertisement of it aloud to me, adding: '*Scenes of Clerical Life? That* was *your* Book wasn't it?' (The '*your*' being in the sense not of possession but of predilection) 'Yes', I had said, 'and I am so glad that he has written another! *Will* he send me this one, I wonder?' – thereby bringing on myself an utterly disregarded admonition about 'the tendency of the Female Mind to run into unreasonable expectations'; when up rattled the Parcel Delivery cart, and, a startling double-rap having transacted itself, a Book-parcel was brought me. 'There it is!' I said, with a little air of injured innocence triumphant! – 'There

is *what*, my Dear?' – 'Why, *Adam Bede* to be sure!' . . . The Book was actually
Adam Bede, and *Adam Bede* 'justified my enthusiasm'; to say the least!

Oh yes! It was as good as *going into the country for one's health*, the reading of that
Book was! – Like a visit to Scotland *minus* the fatigues of the long journey, and
the grief of seeing friends grown old, and Places that knew me knowing me no
more! . . .

In truth, it is a beautiful most *human* Book! Every *Dog* in it, not to say every
man woman and child in it, is brought home to one's 'business and bosom', an
individual fellow-creature! I found myself in charity with the whole human race
when I laid it down – the *canine* race I had *always* appreciated.[106]

Jane and Carlyle may have had a shrewd suspicion that George Eliot
was a woman, a fact which did not become generally known until June,
when Marian Evans reluctantly bowed to Garrick Club gossip and
persistent rumours in her native Warwickshire, and divulged her author-
ship.[107] Jane, writing to her Edinburgh friend Major David Davidson on
14 February about the fashion among 'young ladies of the present day' for
writing books, adds that *Adam Bede* has been sent by 'an Unknown Entity,
who is pleased to pass by the name of *George Elliot*' [*sic*].[108] William
Allingham later observed that the only time Carlyle mentioned George
Eliot's fiction to him was when he claimed to have 'found out in the first
two pages that it was a woman's writing – she supposed that in making a
door you last of all put in the *panels*!'[109]

This is a reference to the activity of Adam and Seth Bede and their
fellow carpenters in the opening chapter, entitled 'The Workshop'. If
Carlyle had been less prejudiced against novels in general, indeed if he had
read this novel through, he might have noticed that *Adam Bede*, unusually,
contains many scenes of people at work, carrying on their daily lives in an
unremarkable manner. As the advocate of honest toil, he might have
appreciated George Eliot's innovation. But there is no evidence that he
read any of her novels. By October 1859 the Carlyles knew what everyone
else did, namely that Marian Evans was the author; it appears that they
never visited her, despite their continuing friendship with Lewes, though,
according to Alexander Gilchrist, Carlyle was heard to say to Jane about
this time, 'Well, I don't know why you shouldn't call on Miss Evans.'[110]

Gilchrist recorded at the same time a conversation about Mill, whose
book *On Liberty* had been published earlier in 1859. Carlyle's response to
this influential work was succinct. He told Jack in May that he had never
in his life read 'a serious, ingenious, clear, logical Essay with more perfect
and profound dissent from the basis it rests upon, and most of the
conclusions it arrives at'. His answer to Mill's famous argument that each
individual's liberty should be limited only by the need for tolerance and
forbearance towards the opinions and actions of other individuals having

equal freedom, was to say incredulously, 'As if it were a sin to control, or coerce into better methods, human swine in any way.'[111] Intemperate though Carlyle's view was, he did make a shrewd point, in a note written in October 1865, about Mill's relative silence on the positive, rather than negative, duties of human beings towards one another: 'Seldom read a book by a serious sincere man, which surprised me more. It appears then that the *summum bonum* of a man is to be well let alone by other men.'[112]

The talk with Gilchrist in October 1859 turned to Mill and his wife, the erstwhile Harriet Taylor, who had died towards the end of 1858. The story of the burning of *The French Revolution* manuscript came up, and Jane told Gilchrist that the name of the perpetrator had been kept secret for a long while, 'but ultimately the Mills themselves let it out. Very uncomfortable affair for Mill before the name was known.' Sarah Austin had 'said in his presence, there seemed to her only one plan open to the man – to have gone home and shot himself',[113] which is much what Mill had felt like doing at the time.

Relations between the Mills and the Carlyles had been virtually non-existent for many years, though Carlyle had written from the Gill in June 1858, passing on an inquiry about an Indian appointment from an 'ingenuous-looking young man' who had asked Carlyle for advice. He appealed to Mill for old times' sake:

As it lies partly in your old department, and your old Humanity is still memorable to me, I consider it possible you might consent to invest half an hour (not more) of your time . . . in this speculation of a young inquiring spirit and his bit of 'progress in life', all-important to himself at least! . . .

I often think, if you were in the next cottage, half a mile off, what discoursing we should still have, in front of the ancient Selgovian Sea [the Solway Firth], and the Cumberland Mountains rising dumb and grand to rear of it . . . I send many unchangeable regards to Mrs Mill.[114]

The reply was polite, but cool. Mill had seen the young man, a Mr Russell, and given him some advice; but his response to Carlyle's appeal to his comradeship was not encouraging:

You are well out of dusty London at this season; though we by no means find it necessary to go so far as Annan for the calm and silence you speak of. We have a quiet corner down here [in Blackheath, south-east of London], where we shall be at any time happy to see you.[115]

In May 1859 both Carlyles were unwell. Jane told Mary Russell that she had called in a new doctor, 'the *nearest* General Practitioner', a Dr Barnes, who had a '*human practical* look'. He pleased Jane because he took her seriously, spending 'half an hour instead of the official three minutes' when visiting her; he flattered her by approving of her self-dosing, though he also warned against its 'audacity'. He also opened Carlyle's eyes to the real weakness of her condition, though he does not seem to have given a name to it, any more than her other doctors had done.[116] The result was the removal of the whole household from Cheyne Row to Fife, with Carlyle, Charlotte the maid, Nero the dog, and Fritz the horse leaving on 22 June by steamer, and Jane setting out alone by overnight train.[117]

They all came together for the first six weeks in a house near the coast at Aberdour and then in Auchtertool House, a large mansion not far from Walter Welsh's Kirkcaldy manse. Jane reported to George Cooke, William Allingham's friend, to whom she now wrote frequently. Charlotte was 'the happiest of girls', delighted at being called 'Bonnie wee lassie' by young men passing her on the road. As for the rest of the party:

The horse also liked 'the change'. Mr C says 'he is a much improved horse; is in perfect raptures over his soft food (grass and new hay) but incapable of recovering from his astonishment at the badness of the Fife roads!' Nero bathes with his master from a sense of duty; and is gradually shaking off the selfish torpor that had seized upon him in London: he snores less, thinks of other things besides his food; and shows some of his old fondness for me.

Though she herself had 'derived the least benefit hitherto', she hoped to do better now that she had hired a donkey to ride on, after Carlyle had tried her twice, with mixed success, on 'the enraptured and astonished' Fritz.[118]

Dr Barnes's daughter had written to tell Jane that she was engaged to be married. Like so many other young women, she had chosen Jane as her chief confidante, a role about which Jane had mixed feelings. She relished the tribute, but could scarcely bring herself to congratulate the girl in an uncomplicated way, the more so as she remembered only too well the youth of another doctor's daughter. She could only be gloomy about 'the Triumphal-Procession air which, in our Manners and Customs, is given to Marriage at the outset – that singing of *Te Deum* before the battle has *begun*'. And she confessed that Miss Barnes 'reminded me so vividly of my own youth, when I, also an only daughter – an only child – had a Father as fond of me, as proud of me' as Dr Barnes was of his daughter.[119]

Jane was home before the end of September, while Carlyle went to Scotsbrig to see his family and to console James, whose wife Isabella had died in June.[120] Back in Cheyne Row in October, he wrote to Forster lamenting the recent death of his old friend and neighbour, Leigh Hunt. He also asked Forster to tell Dickens that his latest novel, *A Tale of Two Cities*, was 'wonderful',[121] the very epithet Dickens had used in his Preface to describe Carlyle's *French Revolution*, with which the novel has a rhetorical affinity. Thackeray, too, was in touch this autumn, begging on 16 October in his capacity as editor of the new *Cornhill Magazine*: 'Is there any hope? Can you help an old friend? Have you never a chapterkin, or a subject on wh. you wish to speak to the public?'[122] To which Carlyle replied that he would gladly help if he could, but was so 'crushed to death amid Prussian rubbish' that he had 'nearly lost the power of thinking'.[123]

Other honours came Carlyle's way. In November Karl Alexander, Grand Duke of Saxe-Weimar-Eisenach, who had visited Cheyne Row in June 1847, wrote saying he had long admired Carlyle's genius and his writings, especially as they 'reflect the intellectual life of Germany to the minds of your countrymen'. He was reminded by the current celebrations in Germany of the centenary of Schiller's birth that Carlyle had been 'one of the earliest of Schiller's biographers', and now wished Carlyle to accept 'the accompanying token' of his admiration. With the letter came a note from the Duke's British secretary, Carlyle's acquaintance James Marshall, announcing that Carlyle was 'now (in spite of your teeth, as it were) a Knight-Commander of the Order of the White Falcon, otherwise called "the Order of Vigilance" – a mere toy in itself, if you will, – but, as the symbol of the recognition of your work in Germany, I trust it will give you some satisfaction.'[124]

It certainly gave Jane satisfaction, since she could report on it comically to Mary Russell:

Did you see in your newspaper that Mr Carlyle was made a 'Knight of the White Falcon'? Consequently I am a Lady of the White Falcon! Charlotte told our charwoman, with great glee, that the Master might call himself 'Sir Thomas, if he liked'. 'My!' said the charwoman, 'then the Mistress is Lady, now!' 'Yes', said Charlotte, 'but she says she won't go in for it! Such a shame!' – The *Order*, however, which Mr C immediately made over to *me*, is beautiful! A solid enamelled White Falcon, on a green star, attached to a broad red ribbon.[125]

★

In October 1859 Nero was run over by a butcher's cart while out with Charlotte. He never fully recovered, and Dr Barnes put him down on 31 January 1860. Jane thanked the doctor the next day, begging him not to think her grief absurd. 'Nobody but myself can have any idea what that little creature has been in my life.' He had been her 'inseparable companion during eleven years, ever doing his little best to keep me from feeling sad and lonely'.[126] Nero was buried in the garden, and even Carlyle was moved at the loss of his old companion on his nightly walks.[127]

Jane's loneliness was noticed by Carlyle's helper Vernon Lushington, who described a conversation with her in a letter to friends on 4 March:

She gave me an account of her daily life, which struck me as very sad – so lonely it seemed to be – breakfast in silence, dinner separate, & *he* absorbed in his work;

out of reach of fireside talk. This between ourselves. Must it ever be that those who give most to the world are themselves strangers to household joys? . . . in our time Dickens is another instance; he & Mrs D must have led a sad life of it, yet scarcely any writer writes so much of family happiness.[128]

Carlyle was grimmer than ever as he toiled on with *Frederick*. He managed a little wit when turning down an invitation from Thackeray in May 1860: 'Alas, dear Thackeray, I durst as soon undertake to dance a hornpipe on the top of Bond Steeple, as to eat a white-bait dinner in my present low and lost state!'[129] He was 'visited by sleeplessness' and a 'dark, cold, vague, yet authentic-looking feeling of terror' that he would 'never get my sad book on Friedrich finished, that it would finish me instead'.[130] Jane, with Neuberg's help, got him to Brighton for a week in July, first going there herself to try out some lodgings, testing the food, the beds, the cleanliness, and the dangers of noise.[131] Then in August he went to the far north of Scotland to stay at Thurso Castle with Sir George Sinclair.

Jane meanwhile was, most unusually, in raptures over the birth at the end of June of a daughter to the Ashburtons. She had met the new Lady Ashburton during a week spent at the Grange in January, when, having 'set my mind against liking her, [I] could not resist the pains she took to make me'. Neither could she resist telling Mary Russell that Lord Ashburton's 'devotion to the new Lady is perfect. And really he never was so "made of" before! – I can't wonder that he likes it!'[132] She assured Lady Ashburton in July that the baby, Mary, was 'the first human child' to have 'awakened what is called *the maternal instinct* in me – me whose lines have always been cast in Babyless Places!'[133]

Having decided to go to Scotland herself, Jane set off in August to stay with the Russells and the Austins, stopping on the way to visit her friends the Stanleys of Alderley in Cheshire. Here, in a misunderstanding due to the crossing of letters between her and Carlyle in Thurso, she got hold of the idea that he was intending to come home suddenly at the end of the month. He had written that he was about to 'sail South' from Thurso. He meant as far as Scotsbrig and the Gill, but Jane rushed back to Chelsea to prepare the house instead of carrying on towards Scotland. Lady Stanley wrote to her husband on 26 August: 'Poor Mrs Carlyle, who was going to Scotland Tuesday has heard from the Philosopher that he returns to Chelsea like a cannon ball and so she goes to meet him. She is very amusing and tells no end of stories.'[134]

Though she wrote humorously to friends like Lady Ashburton – 'my mischances of late have been so outrageous, that I think of working them up into a Farce, to be called *the Unlucky Woman*'[135] – she punished Carlyle with furious letters accusing him of failing to make his intentions clear. He made things worse by addressing her as 'my unfortunate, dear, infatuated

Goody!' and telling her she had made a mistake.[136] Jane's temper was not improved by having Charlotte Southam, whom she had dismissed, 'hanging on' at her mother's nearby, hoping to be reinstated, while Jane tried to cope with two new servants, a cook and a housemaid. On 19 October she told Mary Austin that she did not feel she would ever get used to the 'improvement' of having two servants instead of one. 'It is just as if one had taken lodgers into one's lower story.'[137]

Carlyle was back in Chelsea by this time, writing encouragingly to Ruskin, who was publishing 'Unto This Last' in the *Cornhill Magazine*. The work, a fierce attack on Mill, Ricardo, and political economy in general, was inspired by Carlyle's own writings, as Ruskin acknowledged to a friend in November – 'Carlyle having led the way, as he does in all noble insight in this generation'.[138] Naturally Carlyle responded positively (though so few other readers did that the *Cornhill* ceased to publish the papers in November), using his favourite purgative metaphor to signify his praise: 'You go down thro' those unfortunate Dismal-Science people, like a Treble-x of Senna, Glauber and Aloes [three contemporary laxatives]; like a fit of British Cholera, – threatening to be fatal!' Recognising that such writing, so like his own, was not likely to find widespread agreement, he welcomed Ruskin to 'a minority of *two*'.[139]

It was a phrase he had shared with Jane years ago, when he had been struggling to get his work published and to make a name for himself when she was almost his only champion. Things were different now. They lived together, but each was increasingly alone. Silent breakfasts, separate dinners, a shortfall of sympathy for each other's mental torment, both strangers to household joys – that was the story which lay behind the couple captured by the meticulous Tait in his *Chelsea Interior*.

CHAPTER 17

In Sickness and in Health 1861–1866

Thanking Emilie Hawkes, now Venturi, in January 1861 for the 'little interior' she had sent him, Mazzini reflected that he had now been 'too long away from Carlyle for me to begin anew':

Our paths are too widely apart, and the attempt would prove a fruitless one. But I too feel the same esteem and affection for Mrs C and any little thing I might do for her or to please her would be a pleasure to me.[1]

It was exactly twenty years since Mazzini had first-footed the Carlyles on New Year's Day 1841.

This New Year they spent a few days at the Grange, now no longer the scene of incessant 'making wits' or of Jane's jealous torment. Carlyle noted that the party was 'small and insignificant; nobody but ourselves and Venables, an honest old dish, and Kingsley, a new, of higher pretensions, but inferior flavour'.[2] Kingsley's father had been the Carlyles' parish clergyman; a new man, the Reverend Gerald Blunt, was appointed Rector in 1860. He and his wife called on Jane one afternoon in April 1861, to find her resplendent in a black velvet dress, with pearl necklace and bracelets. She wrote comically to Dr Barnes's daughter, whom she called 'Carina', about the strange impression she must have made, all because she had been shopping in Regent Street in the rain, had got wet through, and had to change her clothes on her return. 'It being within a couple of hours of the time when I was engaged to dine at Forster's, with Dickens and Wilkie Collins', she explained, 'I thought I had best make one dressing do for all'; and so she was sitting on her sofa at half-past four looking 'stunning' in black velvet when the Blunts came to call.[3]

Jane was much taken back to her youth at this time, not just by 'Carina's' engagement, but also by a new relationship with Margaret Oliphant, a thirty-one-year-old widow with three young children who had undertaken to write a *Life* of Edward Irving. Naturally she approached the Carlyles for help. Jane was willing, though anxious not to have too many confidential details revealed. She was also concerned, touchingly, for Irving's reputation. She therefore offered, in April 1861, '*one* letter that may be printed. It is an extremely characteristic letter, and contains nothing fatal.' She promised to show Mrs Oliphant the one other letter of

Irving's which had been 'spared unburnt' and the romantic sonnet he had addressed to her. She had consulted Carlyle about the letter she was enclosing, in which Irving had called her 'lovely'. Carlyle thought the word should not be omitted, *'for the letter would'nt [sic] be the least like a letter of Irvings without it'*. But both she and he were of the opinion that Mrs Oliphant should not quote

the two lines about the 'antique cast' of his head – which those who didn't know him might find ridiculous & vain. He *was* vain – there is no denying it! – but it was a vanity proceeding out of what was best and most loveable in him, his childlike simplicity and desire to be *loved* – even to the 'cast of his head' – his *crystal transparency* of character, letting every little weakness show thro' it as grandly as his noblest qualities.[4]

Where Irving had been the first eccentric genius in the Carlyles' lives, Ruskin was the latest one. Carlyle's feelings towards him were warm, and he often rode over to Denmark Hill, where Ruskin was living with his parents once more. John Ruskin senior was astonished and delighted by both Carlyle and Fritz, as he told a friend on 28 January 1861:

Thomas Carlyle rode over yesterday for a call but remained till after seven talking as only he can talk in a most marvelous manner. When a boy of 15 I drank tea with his namesake Dr Carlyle called by Walter Scott Jupiter Carlyle whose autobiography is now going through the reviews. A man also never to be forgotten but the Chelsea one is the Jupiter – he has a Horse allowing for the difference betwixt Man & Beast, as extraordinary as himself – I was pleased to hear it knows this House and when at the Top of Tulse Hill it pricked up its ear, set off at a rapid pace & stopped at the gate.

The original 'Jupiter Carlyle' was the eighteenth-century Scottish divine, playwright, and pamphleteer, Dr Alexander Carlyle.[5] One sees why Mr Ruskin applied the name to Carlyle from an extremely handsome photograph of him on Fritz, taken on 2 August 1861 in Hyde Park. Both horse and rider have a strong, lean, upright bearing, all the more remarkable in Carlyle, who was now sixty-five.[6]

The elder Ruskin sent Carlyle gifts of cognac and cigars, while the younger relied on his older friend for support. Carlyle took the trouble to attend a lecture Ruskin delivered on 19 April at the Royal Institution on Albemarle Street, reporting to Jack on this strange event:

Lecture on Tree Leaves as physiological, pictorial, moral, symbolical objects. A crammed house, but tolerable to me even in the gallery. The lecture was thought to 'break down', and indeed it quite did *'as a lecture'*; but only did from *embarras des richesses* – a rare case.[7]

On 4 July G. H. Lewes noted in his journal that Anthony Trollope had come to dinner, 'bringing the sad news of Mrs Browning's death' a few days earlier at Florence. After dinner, Lewes took Trollope to introduce him to the Carlyles. 'Woolner, the sculptor, there. Capital talk.'[8] Carlyle and Trollope got on well, agreeing that West Indian blacks were vain and lazy, an opinion Trollope had expressed in his recent book, *The West Indies and the Spanish Main* (1859).[9] It is not clear from Lewes's description of the evening whether George Eliot accompanied them to Cheyne Row. She, for her part, noted in a brief journal entry for 26 July that she 'sat next to Mrs Carlyle' that evening at a performance of *Hamlet* at the Princess's Theatre.[10] Jane's view of her, based on a reading of the novels perhaps more than on personal contact, was reported by Margaret Oliphant in November. She apparently said that 'Mrs Lewes', as Marian Evans liked to be known, 'has mistaken her rôle – that nature intended her to be the properest of women, and that her present equivocal position is the most extraordinary blunder and contradiction possible'.[11]

While Carlyle worked on, Jane escaped to Ramsgate in August, accompanied by Geraldine, towards whom she had thawed since Walter Mantell's return to New Zealand in October 1859.[12] She regaled Carlyle with the horrors of Ramsgate: nasty smells consisting of 'spoiled shrimps complicated with cesspool!', nasty people, noises from morning till night, 'cries of prawns, shrimps, lollipops – things one never wanted, and will never want', as well as brass bands, female fiddlers, barrel organs, and French horns. These daytime noises were replaced at night by 'hundreds of cocks', 'three steeple clocks', slamming gates, wailing cats, and barking dogs. With all this, she told him triumphantly, she was actually able to sleep: 'I think "roar away", "bark away", "slam away"; you can't disturb Mr C at Cheyne Row, that can't you! and the thought is so soothing, I go off asleep.'[13]

To Blanche Airlie she was frank on her return about the disadvantages of going to a seaside resort where the masses also went and where the men sat 'in their shirt sleeves, at open windows, eating shrimps! The women mostly in the family-way! It was *"truly* disgusting" (as Countess Pepoli says).'[14] She and Geraldine stayed only a week, partly because of her fellow holidaymakers, partly because, as she told Mary Russell on 30 August, 'the letter that came from [Carlyle] every morning was like the letter of a Babe in the Wood, who would be found buried with dead leaves by the robins if I didn't look to it'.[15]

In September they both tried a spell in Windsor Forest as guests of Lady Sandwich in 'a pretty lodge she had hired', as Carlyle remembered. But though 'Windsor Forest sounded something Arcadian when I started', he came to realise that it should now be called 'Windsor Cockneydom unchained'.[16] More mass tourism, it seems. Jane blamed the failure of this trip rather on Carlyle's foolishness in sitting on wet grass with only a pocket handkerchief for protection, which resulted in lumbago, bad temper, and a precipitate return home, as Miss Barnes was told, with the added meaningful remark that Carlyle required 'perfect liberty' to be disagreeable: 'And that consolation – that happiness, that liberty reserves itself for the domestic hearth! As you will find well when you are married, I daresay.'[17]

The wedding of this much warned young lady finally took place in February 1862. Carlyle begged Jane to ensure that he did not receive an invitation, 'for it would be a real vexation to me to refuse that bonnie wee lassie', but if he went 'it would be the ruin of me for three weeks!' Jane managed the affair by simply telling Carina all this on 24 January.[18] She herself attended. On being asked afterwards 'to acknowledge how superior the English way of marrying was to the Scotch', she, who had been married with hardly half a dozen people in attendance, replied that her feelings were mixed. She relayed the conversation with Mr Blunt to Mary Russell:

'Mixed?' the rector asked, 'mixed of what?' 'Well', I said, 'it looked to me something betwixt a religious ceremony and a – pantomime!' So it is. There were forty-four people at the breakfast![19]

At the Grange in January 1862 rather more guests gathered than the previous year. Old regulars like Venables, Milnes, and the Bishop of Oxford were there; among the newer visitors were the Kingsleys and the Duke and Duchess of Argyll. As Jane was unwell, only Carlyle went, reporting that 'the most agreeable man among us is the Duke; really a good, solid, Scotch product'. Carlyle was wary of the Duchess, finding 'the Nigger question much a topic with her, and by no means a safe one'.[20] By which he meant that she (and her husband, who was a prominent Liberal politician) took the side of the Northern States in the American Civil War, which had begun in April 1861 after the abolitionist Abraham Lincoln had been elected President, leading to the secession of the Southern States and the declaration of war. Opinion was divided in Britain, with Carlyle siding with the slave-owning South.

So preoccupied was Carlyle with his work that he seemed scarcely to take notice of such large events as the War or, indeed, the publication in November 1859 of the culminating work on evolution, Darwin's *Origin of Species*. Jane had written scornfully in January 1860 that, regardless of the 'ecstasy' of 'all the scientific world', she did not feel that 'the slightest light would be thrown on my practical life for me, by having it ever so logically made out that my first ancestor, millions of millions of ages back', had been an oyster. Sounding very like Carlyle, and also like Carlyle's amiable Grange opponent, 'soapy' Sam Wilberforce, she reduced the issue of evolution to its simplest terms in order to gain a victory over it:

It remained a plain fact that I was no oyster, nor had any grandfather an oyster within my knowledge; and for the rest, there was nothing to be gained, for this world, or the next, by going into the oyster-question, till all more pressing questions were exhausted![21]

This response was not very different from the Bishop of Oxford's in his famous exchange with Darwin's champion T. H. Huxley at the Oxford meeting of the British Association for the Advancement of Science in the autumn of 1860. Wilberforce asked Huxley whether it was on his grandfather's or his grandmother's side that he claimed descent from an ape, to which Huxley replied that he saw no reason to be ashamed of having an ape for an ancestor. On the contrary:

If there were an ancestor whom I should feel shame in recalling, it would be a *man*, a man of restless and versatile intellect, who, not content with an equivocal success in his own sphere of activity, plunges into scientific questions with which he has no real acquaintance, only to obscure them by an aimless rhetoric, and distract the attention of his hearers from the real point at issue by eloquent digressions, and skilled appeals to religious prejudice.[22]

The opponents of Darwinism, in the popular and religious press in particular, made play of the idea of the descent of man from apes, or fish, or birds, often with illustrations to match. *Punch* carried several caricatures of the scientists themselves as animals, as well as lampoons such as the one published on 18 May 1861 entitled 'Monkeyana', a poem written by 'Gorilla' of 'Zoological Gardens', who appeared in caricature with a placard reading 'Am I a Man and a Brother?'[23] According to Froude, Carlyle dreaded that Darwin's theory of the adaptation of species might turn out to be right, though he rejected it as unproved, and disliked the idea that man was no more than a developed animal and 'God and religion no more than inferences'.[24]

★

Volume three of *Frederick* was published at the end of April 1862. Once more Carlyle shows himself everywhere. Describing the early days of Frederick's reign, he takes us on an excursion with the new king. An account 'out of Voltaire's and other people's waste-baskets . . . fished-up, patch by patch, and pasted together by victorious modern Editors', is passed on by a scornful Carlyle.[25] Even his adroit present-tense presentation of the Battle of Mollwitz, in which he accompanies the troops in imagination much as he had accompanied the actors in the drama of the French Revolution, is vitiated by despairing interpolations about blockheads and their 'chaotic pamphlets'.[26]

The more he attempted to conquer his material, the less successful he seemed to be. As for the human cost at home, his rueful remarks in his reminiscence of Jane demonstrate the horrible irony of his and her situation as he persisted with his mad task. He recalls that he worked almost all the time, only venturing from his study to ride on Fritz in the evening, then spending a mere half-hour in the drawing room with Jane. She would lie on the sofa while he told her of his day's work:

After tugging and wriggling through what inextricable labyrinth and sloughs-of-despond, I still well remember, it appears I had at last *conquered* Mollwitz, saw it all clear ahead and round me, and took to telling her about it, in my poor bit of joy, night after night. I recollect she answered little, though kindly always. Privately, she at that time felt *convinced she was dying*: – dark winter, and such the weight of misery, and utter decay of strength; – and, night after night, my theme to her, *Mollwitz!*[27]

Jane did not read this volume, or the next three. Emerson did, and wrote half admiringly, half disapprovingly, in December, thanking Carlyle for his copy. He could not really approve of the author 'sitting as Demiurgus, trotting out his mannikins, coaxing and bantering them', nor of Carlyle's wilful shutting of his eyes to anything he did not wish to see. Emerson also made it clear that he hated slavery and supported the North in the War, on which Carlyle commented when sending the letter on to Jack, 'Emerson's Letter will rather disappoint you; nothing in it abt the Practical State of America, that is not more or less chimerical, – conquering the South, and becoming celestial by emancipating Niggers, and so forth'.[28]

In May 1862 Jane's charming young friend Ellen Twisleton, 'so young, and beautiful, and clever, so admired in society and adored at home', died, aged thirty-four, after a 'long terrible illness'.[29] Several of the Carlyles' friends had died in recent years, many of them at a young age. There was Clough, who died in Florence in November 1861, aged forty-two; their neighbour Alexander Gilchrist succumbed to scarlet fever in the same month, aged thirty-three. Jane had lost her beloved Kate Sterling, Mrs Ross, in December 1860 – she was only twenty-six. Older friends had also gone recently – Elizabeth Pepoli and Lady Sandwich in April 1862. And now Ellen. Carlyle rode with Browning, back in England since the death of his own wife, to Broughton Castle in Oxfordshire on 24 May to attend the funeral.[30]

After a brief stay in July 1862 in Folkestone, where she joined the Ashburtons and a new acquaintance, Caroline Davenport Bromley, 'who is amiable and an acquisition',[31] Jane set off to see the Russells in their new house, Holm Hill, still in Thornhill, but a little nearer to her old home at Templand. She was met on the way at Dumfries by Jean Aitken, who 'had actually brought a little jar of "warm tea" ' and some biscuits – 'the most practically kind thing I ever saw Jean do', she told Carlyle with her usual sharpness where Jean was concerned. Mary Austin, the most congenial of his sisters, had rushed out to meet Jane's train when it stopped briefly at Ruthwell, near the Gill.[32]

While at Holm Hill, Jane met 'Arthur Burnet, the Sheriff of Lanarkshire, whom you may remember', she wrote on 15 August. She had some gossip to pass on to Carlyle:

Now he has got transformed into the most ridiculous, yet touching likeness of Jeffrey! The little shock grey head, and round brow, the arching of his eyebrows, the settling of his chin in his neckcloth, the jerking movements, the neither Scotch nor English speech bring Jeffrey before one as if he were alive again! I have been instituting searching inquiries as to the *character* of *Mrs* Burnet of Monboddo; for I have not the slightest doubt in my own mind that Arthur Burnet is Jeffrey's son (unofficially). I find that this Mrs Burnet was the *Daughter* of Monboddo, and contracted a *secret marriage*, with her Father's Secretary, one *Williamson*, who had 'eventually' to take *her* family name. A woman who commenced with an irregular marriage, you see! quite easy to arrive later at an irregular Baby![33]

Her interest in Mazzini had been aroused again by a letter he wrote on 22 August telling her of his plans to go to Italy to help Garibaldi try to take Rome once more. 'I go sadly', he confided; 'I do not feel fit for any task; neither morally nor physically. But I think I *must* try'. He was sorry not to have been able to shake Carlyle's hand before going, but he had been 'overwhelmed with work'. He would send Jane news from time to time: 'I know that, spite of my sins towards you, you will welcome them.'[34] The news on 2 September was that Garibaldi had been 'wounded and captured already', as Jane told Carlyle from Edinburgh, where she was now staying with her aunts. 'Mazzini will be thankful he must have reached Garibaldi; it is to be hoped he is not taken also, but he went with his eyes perfectly open to the madness.'[35]

During her stay in Edinburgh Jane discovered in a stationer's shop a horrible photograph of Carlyle for sale. The stationer had told her it 'came from Dumfries, Mem; we thought it had been like!' When she got back to London in the middle of September, she insisted on having a new commercial photograph taken. Carlyle told Jack that 'under guidance of Woolner, and a selected chief Artist here, there is now coming out a genuine article, which will cut up the Dumfries traitor'.[36] Jane sent the new photograph to Mary Russell, along with two of herself, also done by the 'chief Artist', Mr Jeffray of Oxford Street, 'who had been for years soliciting [Carlyle] to come and be *done*, – for nothing!' She also sent one of Tennyson and one of Mazzini. Mr Jeffray, she added, 'will make a *good thing* of supplying the shops with Mr C's'.[37]

An old friend of the Carlyles, their first London servant Bessy Barnett, had turned up at Cheyne Row while Jane was in Scotland. Carlyle, who had remained fond of Bessy, after defending her against Mrs Montagu's gossip nearly thirty years before, told Jane about the visit on 21 August. The maid had announced 'a Lady who says you will know her by the name of *Bessy*!' 'Not a bit of it!' said Carlyle, till he thought of her, and said if she was 'Bessy *Barnet*; yes, for a few moments!' And in she sailed, looking 'highly respectable' and giving a succinct narrative of her life since her return to Birmingham and Dr Badams. She had met another doctor, called Blakiston, now widowed, whom she was about to marry. With a request to be allowed to visit Jane when she was married, Bessy went, leaving Carlyle feeling, as he said, 'quite gratified by the adventure'.[38] Carlyle's kindness is demonstrated by a letter he wrote on the same day to Dr Blakiston, saying he was delighted to have seen Miss Barnett and to hear that she had made such good friends and was about to marry. 'May your marriage be happy, dear Sir and Madam'; 'it will give us much pleasure to see you and her'.[39]

More photography was transacted in October, when the Carlyles spent some time at the Grange. Jane was amused by the photographer, Vernon Heath, who was there 'taking "Views" and "Interiors" at the easy rate of five guineas a day and as much french cookery and champagne as he could stow into him'. Then

Lady A made him take Lord A and Mr C sitting on one bench; which was intended to come out a touching illustration of modern friendship, but – she tells me – it has come out a picture of two criminals in one dock; the one (Lord A) having *received* his sentence of death, and sinking away into insensibility; the other (Mr C) in the act of receiving his, and glaring back uneasy defiance![40]

This was written to Eliza Forster, the wealthy widow of the publisher Henry Colburn who had married John Forster in September 1856, to the astonishment of Forster's friends. (Dickens reacted to this 'prodigious, overwhelming, crushing, astounding, blinding, deafening, pulverizing, scarifying' news by lying down flat, 'as if an Engine and Tender had fallen upon me'.)[41] Jane at first thought Eliza too talkative – 'she gabbles like a mill-clapper', she wrote in July 1858[42] – but soon became as confidential with the wife as she had always been with the husband. Now in this lively letter recounting the photographic exploits at the Grange, she wrote encouragingly to Mrs Forster, who had left London in search of health:

The wisest Dr I know (a Scotch one of course) told me when I was in Nithsdale the other day, 'whenever you feel to be getting weak and low – nervous, sleepless – all that sort of thing; don't sit still, listening to your sensations – don't send for a Doctor, and take 'mixtures', but pack your carpet-bag and put yourself on a railway – *to anywhere!*' . . . Hang it! Why might not we go sometimes, with a mutual carpet-bag, and spend a day and night at some way-side Inn, when we feel to need 'a change' from our own comfortable homes, and men-of-genius Husbands.[43]

By the end of October 1862 Lord Ashburton was seriously ill. For the next two months, at the Grange and then in Paris, he hung between life and death, ill with an inflammation of the lungs. Carlyle was despondent, declaring he was about to lose 'the kindest, gentlest, friendliest man in my life', until better news came from Paris towards the end of November.[44] Jane had thought she might have to conquer her fear of seasickness and go to Paris to help Lady Ashburton nurse him. 'It was', she told Mary Austin on 23 October, 'a serious undertaking for me, at this season, who had never crossed the Channel, and suffering so from sailing'. She had offered to go and had been relieved at Lady Ashburton's declining.[45]

Mazzini was back in London in October after the failure of Garibaldi's expedition against Rome. Browning heard about him from Jane, who told him 'Joseph' was here under an assumed name. Sharing Carlyle's distaste for the cloak-and-dagger aspect of Mazzini's doings, Browning had expressed his lack of sympathy, whereupon Jane defended Mazzini. Browning told the story to Isabella Blagden on 19 November, enjoying the fact that he had seen through Mazzini's disguise:

'J' told her long ago he had done all he could to *protest* the expedition, wrung his hands over G[aribaldi]'s folly &c &c whereto I replied, of course, that 'J' was the little boy who had stuck a pin into a horse to get him to move on gently – & now was amazed at his . . . doing no end of damage. Well, last Monday, being at Chelsea to see Rossetti, who has taken a huge old house there which he is mediaevalising, I called at Carlyle's – when, lo, there was 'J' tête-à-tête with Mrs C: I spoke to him in Italian at once, naming him – his hesitation & replies in English were funny – he had forgotten me & no wonder. I said, 'I should know you anywhere!'[46]

★

A new danger at home was capturing newspaper headlines. It had become fashionable for thieves to 'garrotte' their victims, to approach from behind and half strangle them while robbing them. An MP suffered such an attack one evening between Parliament and his club, causing John Carlyle to warn his brother about his solitary late-night walks. 'The garrotting is more a terror and a rumour than anything very practical', Carlyle assured him in December 1862. 'But I do generally leave my watch; carry a thick stick, and keep a sharp eye in these night walks.'[47]

Carlyle's walks were soon replacing his evening rides on Fritz, as he told Jack on 13 February. His 'excellent old horse' had had an accident the previous week,

came smash down, lying flat on the ground for one quarter of an instant, had done me no mischief at all, sprang up and trotted half a mile (greatly ashamed of himself, I suppose); when looking over his shoulder I saw the blood streaming over his hoof, drew bridle, dismounted, found the knees quite smashed, and except slowly home have ridden no more since. Jane will not hear of my ever riding him again, nor in real truth is it proper. *Finis* therefore in that department. I have been extremely sorry for my poor old fourfooted friend. *Ganz treu* [absolutely loyal] he constantly and wonderfully was; and now, what to do with myself! or how to dispose of poor Fritz. Of course I can sell him; have him knocked down at Tattersall's for a 10*l* or an old song; and then (as he goes delirious under violent usage and is frightened for running swift in harness) get the poor creature scourged to death in a horrible way, after all the 20,000 faithful miles he has carried me, and the wild puddles and lonely dark times we have had together. I cannot bear to think of that.[48]

Fritz was sold for £9, Carlyle carefully choosing his new owner, as Jane explained to Lady Ashburton on 1 May:

He didn't sell poor Fritz for *the money*! the money was but *nine pounds*!! But he thought him too young for being invalided at grass – said to turn him out for the rest of his life would be 'like turning an old servant *into the Workhouse*'. So he sold him for anything he liked to offer to a respectable man in the next street who meant to *ride* him, not punish him into *drawing*. The poor brute looks so well in his new service, was brought to our door this morning to report himself.[49]

Before parting with Fritz Carlyle had ridden him one last time, 'just *to soothe the poor quadruped's feelings*, by showing him he was forgiven', as Jane told Lady Ashburton, adding, 'I wonder what *Biped* he would have done as much for?'[50] Lady Ashburton had offered to replace Fritz, and on 17 May Carlyle wrote to thank her for the arrival of 'a beautiful bay-chestnut horse' whom he called Noggs.[51]

Jane told Mary Austin in February 1863 that though as a rule she never went out 'after sunset, at this season', she had gone to Ealing, 'some seven miles out of London', the day before to visit Margaret Oliphant, and had stayed the night there. 'She is a dear little homely woman, who speaks the broadest East Lothian Scotch, though she has lived in England since she was ten years old!'[52] Mrs Oliphant's biography of Irving had been published the previous spring, when Jane wrote warmly to her with Carlyle's opinion of the book:

Darling woman, I never heard him praise a *woman's* book, hardly any man's, as cordially as he praises this of yours! You are 'worth cartloads of Mulocks [Dinah

Mulock, Mrs Craik, author of *John Halifax, Gentleman*, 1856], and Brontes, and *things* of that sort'. 'You are full of geniality and genius even'!

Honesty compelled her to include one characteristic criticism from Carlyle, namely, '*a certain dimness about dates and arrangements of Time!*'[53]

There was disdain in Cheyne Row for the 'noise about that Royal marriage' in March between Victoria's son Albert Edward (later King Edward VII) and Princess Alexandra of Denmark.[54] Jane thanked Lady Ashburton for sending tickets to watch the procession from a scaffold erected outside Bath House, but she could not face going, she said, with the Ashburtons themselves still in Paris. In any case, she had 'a good deal of the *Great Original Oyster*' in her and could 'not get up a sentiment' about the procession.[55]

A topic which kept all London chattering was the visit in March of John Colenso, Bishop of Natal, whose first volume of critical commentary on the Pentateuch had appeared at the end of 1862 to a chorus of disapproval. In translating and explaining the Bible to the Zulu people, he had begun to doubt the literal truth of the Old Testament, and had now published his doubts. Naturally he came to visit the Carlyles, with Froude as his chaperon. Jane was unimpressed; in her view he was not 'worth talking about for five minutes, except for the absurdity of a man making arithmetical onslaughts on the Pentateuch, with a bishop's little black silk apron on!'[56] Froude must have remonstrated with her after the visit, for she defended herself in a letter, reminding him of her supposed descent from a daughter of John Knox:

Oh! my dear Mr Froude! I surely couldn't have looked so bored as that. I couldn't because I wasn't. I own to feeling rather antipathetic to the anomalous bishop. A man arrived at the years of discretion wearing an absurd little black silk apron, disturbs my artistic feelings to begin with. Then consider whom I am descended from, the woman who when King James offered to make her husband a bishop if she would persuade him to return to his country and be a peaceable subject, held up her apron and answered '*I would rather kepp his head in there!*'[57]

Carlyle was wrestling his fourth volume to completion in the isolation of his study. He gave a brief example of that energy of metaphorical detail which so characterises his writing in a letter to Alexander Ireland, editor of the *Manchester Examiner*, on 18 March. Someone had forwarded a clipping from a newspaper – Ireland's, he thought – about

a wonderful self-condemnatory manuscript by Frederick the Great, gathered at Berlin by some Duc de Rovigo, for the endless gratitude of the curious. I had not heard of the monstrous platitude at all till then, but guessed then what it would be, – an *old* acquaintance of mine, truly a thrice-brutal stupidity, which has had red-hot pokers indignantly run through it about ten times, but always revives and steps forth afresh, with new tap of the parish-drum.[58]

Though mainly staying at home and refusing invitations, Carlyle ventured out in April to hear Dickens do a public reading of the trial scene in *Pickwick Papers*. When inviting him, Dickens had said he hoped 'you would find a healthy suggestion of an abuse or two, that sets people thinking in the right direction'.[59] The reading was of chapter 34, in which simple Mr Pickwick is wrongly convicted in a breach of promise case brought by the conniving Mrs Bardell, aided by a set of corrupt lawyers and a stupid judge. Jane was too unwell to accompany Carlyle, so he took Woolner instead, and rather enjoyed the outing, as he reported the following day to his sister in Canada, Jenny Hanning:

I had to go yesterday to Dickens's Reading, 8 p.m., Hanover Rooms, to the complete upsetting of my evening habitudes and spiritual composure. Dickens does do it capitally, such as *it* is; acts better than any Macready in the world; a whole tragic, comic, heroic *theatre* visible, performing under one *hat*, and keeping us laughing – in a sorry way, some of us thought – the whole night.[60]

Bessy Barnett, now Blakiston, called on Jane in May, delighted to see her, but horrified at how ill she looked. Jane was warmly invited to visit the Blakistons at St Leonard's on the Sussex coast, where Dr Blakiston had his practice. She gladly 'fled from Chelsea' for a few days, describing to Blanche Airlie how Dr Blakiston applied his 'miraculous medicine' and Bessy, 'the Heroine of the very most interesting Romance I ever came across', nursed her, fed her with jellies, and generally 'made much' of her. 'My only regret is, that I must go home on Saturday and take up with the opposite of all that!'[61]

Carlyle was full of travel plans which came to nothing, his fellow planner being Jack, who was visiting London. Jane wrote laughingly to Lady Ashburton on 13 August:

You have seen children building card-houses as eagerly as if it were houses to live in? and you have seen, at some push against the table, the *Houses* become a shower of cards? With just such an absurd suddenness and completeness did your letter yesterday morning sweep down the schemes of travel, which Mr C and his Doctor-Brother had been building up, and hithering and thithering amongst for the two preceding days . . . We were sitting at breakfast, which, to judge from the look of the table, consisted mainly of pocket maps and Bradshaws, with a supply of which my Brother-in-law *always* surrounds himself; and for the twentieth time Dr C had just urged on Mr C that, 'say what he liked, to sail to *Jersey* would be the most feasible thing, *or* to – *Denmark*!' and Mr C had just detailed the superior advantages of 'taking a look at Orkney and Shetland' – or 'perhaps better, after all, sail to Plymouth, and go by land to Froude's; tho' it *would* be a nicer thing a cruise round – the Western Isles'!!! the only point of agreement between them being that they should start for *somewhere* tomorrow; – when your letter was brought in, which, when I had read it in silence, I handed to Mr C, who, having read the first page, said quite simply, 'Oh! that is all right! we are going to The Grange Sir'. 'And you won't *sail* anywhere?' 'Certainly not! I tell you we are going to The Grange'! I could hardly help laughing, as the Dr swept together, in an indignant manner, his aids to locomotion![62]

Lord Ashburton was still unwell, and Dr Richard Quain was in attendance at the Grange. Jane was impressed by him, telling Lady Ashburton on 13 September, after her return home, that her friend Lady William Russell talked of him as the 'most rising' medical man in London. She was always hearing of cases 'where he had at once hit the nail on the head when other Drs were puzzling to find it'. Jane went on cheerfully:

It always does one good to visit Lady William! she has such an unsurpassable gift of flattery! However *Cindarella*ish may be my opinion of myself in entering her room, I always come away thinking myself 'one and somewhat'! Yesterday, for example, I found a Colonel Percy with her whom she 'begged to introduce to Mrs Carlyle – the wife of Mr Carlyle the *distinguished Philosopher* and herself a very distinguished woman *altho' she was not aware of it*'! What more delicate compliment could be devised? the '*altho' she was not aware of it*' at once investing me with an *admirable modesty* to my own eyes! and anticipating any doubts I might feel as to the fact! She must have made a first-rate Ambassadress in her time![63]

Carlyle had published a brief piece in the August number of *Macmillan's Magazine*, edited by his admirer David Masson. Entitled 'Ilias (Americana) in Nuce' (American Iliad in a Nutshell), this parable on the American Civil War reads in its entirety:

Peter of the North (to Paul of the South). – 'Paul, you unaccountable scoundrel, I find you hire your servants for life, not by the month or year as I do! You are going straight to Hell, you——!'
Paul. – 'Good words, Peter! The risk is my own; I am willing to take the risk. Hire you your servants by the month or the day, and get straight to Heaven; leave me to my own method.'
Peter. – 'No, I won't. I will beat your brains out first!' (*And is trying dreadfully ever since, but cannot yet manage it.*)
T. C.
May 1863.[64]

Several newspapers reprinted this, since it chimed in with reports of hardship at home; the death in June of a young milliner 'from simple overwork' raised a storm about 'our white slaves' who are 'toiled into the grave'. A leader in *The Times* on 2 July declared that 'while we work our own young women to death, using the scourge of starvation, instead of the crack of the whip, as the instrument of compulsion, we have scarcely a right' to complain of American slave-owners, who at least feed their slaves. Marx was working on *Das Kapital* at this time, and quoted several of these newspaper remarks in the first volume (published in Germany in 1867), culminating with Carlyle's piece. 'Finally', he wrote, 'spake the oracle, Thomas Carlyle'. 'In a short parable, he reduced the one great event of contemporary history, the American Civil War, to this level.'[65]

Marx was not alone in disliking Carlyle's short article. Horace Howard Furness, abolitionist and son of the Reverend W. H. Furness, a Unitarian minister and friend of Emerson who had helped get Carlyle's early works published in America,[66] wrote to a friend on 31 August that nearly all the British newspapers had 'joined in the howl against us, urged on by such men as Thackeray and Carlyle!' In November he told the same friend that he had sent Carlyle a photo of the 'Scourged Back'. 'Wonder what he thought when he saw it.'[67] The photograph, which Carlyle seems to have passed on to the Ashburtons, shows a black slave with his naked back to the camera, covered in a criss-cross of weals. Furness's letter reads:

Philadelphia Aug 29

Mr Carlyle
London
Sir,
   Pray observe an instance of '*hiring* for life'.
      God forgive you for your cruel jest, and blindness!
         Horace Howard Furness.[68]

As Furness indicates, and Marx too, Carlyle's comparing of the two kinds of 'slave labour', black and white, was not unusual, though his rhetoric was particularly vehement. An abolitionist who was visiting England in 1863, Moncure Conway, argued with him about slavery. Conway disliked Carlyle's views, but liked the man, and even half defended him. 'Abhorring the condition of the mass of labourers around him, Carlyle idealised the condition of the negroes in the Southern States; that was all.'[69]

Palmerston's Government adopted an official position of neutrality towards the Civil War, though many in the Cabinet favoured the South, and there was concern about the Lancashire cotton mills, which depended on cheap cotton from the slave states. Conway noticed that the War was the occasion for much ignorance and prejudice in Britain; it was also a source of entertainment. At Christmas 1863 Astley's Theatre put on a show in which the two American Presidents, Lincoln for the North and Davis for the South, were represented as a pair of prize fighters.[70]

★

Towards the end of September 1863 Jane had an accident in the street. She 'was plashed down on the pavement of St Martin-le-Grand (five miles from home)' while trying to board an omnibus.[71] Falling on her already 'neuralgic' right arm, she had to be picked up, in great pain, 'by *two Roughs* and a Policeman',[72] and put into a cab. When she got home, she asked her maid to call her neighbour Henry Larkin – not Carlyle – to help her upstairs.[73] She did not wish to disturb her husband's work. Perhaps a little vengefulness was mingled with her consideration; he had excluded himself from her for so long, and now she excluded him, showing him that she had no faith in his care for her welfare.

Dr Barnes was called in and assured her that no bones were broken. There followed weeks of extreme pain and sleeplessness. Jane was convinced she was dying, and Carlyle feared so too.[74] Though he was shocked into trying to help, Jane refused to see much of him. 'She speaks little to me', he wrote sadly to Jack, 'and does not accept me as a sick nurse, which, truly, I had never any talent to be.'[75] Dr Quain was called in. Like Dr Barnes he was unable to discover the cause of Jane's torment; he merely prescribed quinine for her neuralgia.[76]

Something of the old Jane sparked out in a letter to Mary Russell of 26 October, written laboriously in pencil. She reported that the pain in her leg was lessening, but her arm was still agonisingly sore:

Mr Barnes can throw no light on that for me, or suggest any remedy: at least he doesn't. It seems to me he regards my leg as his patient, and my arm as Dr Quain's patient, which he has nothing to do with; and he is rather glad to be irresponsible for it, seeing nothing to be done![77]

On 1 November Dr Barnes's daughter, now Mrs Simmonds, gave birth to a girl. Jane wrote her congratulations, but refused the honour of being a godmother. 'I don't belong to the English Church, and the Scotch Church, which I do belong to, recognises no Godfathers and Godmothers. The father takes all the obligations on himself (serves him right!).' Besides, 'how could I dream of binding myself to look after the spiritual welfare of any earthly baby? I, who have no confidence in my own spiritual welfare!'[78] She did allow Carina to name the baby after her; Ethel Jane Carlyle Simmonds was christened with a present of a brooch from Jane.[79]

In a letter telling the story of her accident to Blanche Airlie on 2 November, Jane launches with gusto into a current scandal involving the sexual exploits of the seventy-nine-year-old Prime Minister. A divorce suit by one Timothy O'Kane, naming Palmerston as his wife's partner in 'criminal conversation', was brought, to the amusement of Palmerston himself.[80] Jane commented:

What on earth is the meaning of this absurd scandal about Lord Palmerston? Surely it must be either a political conspiracy or an attempt to extort money! I have heard nothing like it, since the old Lord Buchan insisted on appearing before the Kirksession and being '*rebuked*' for a child that some young woman had laid to him![81]

Despite such moments of epistolary fun, the pain continued throughout the winter. Jane was confined to her room, which she came to hate, and saw no one. It was at this time that she feared insanity and made Carlyle promise never to put her in an asylum, as he recalled with a shudder in his reminiscence of her. In December Carlyle asked her cousin Maggie Welsh to come and nurse her. He reported to Jack that Dr Blakiston had visited and 'confirmed Barnes in every particular: – indeed the case seems medically plain, – nothing wrong internally, but the irritation, restlessness, pain and nervous weakness very great'.[82] Geraldine came often, writing to Mantell in February 1864 that Jane was '*very* ill and nobody knows what is the matter with her'. In March she reported that Jane was a little better physically, but still could not sleep, 'and she cannot be roused to interest or pleasure in anything'. As for Carlyle, he was 'killing himself over *Frederick*. He has aged very much since his wife's illness.'[83]

Volume four of *Frederick* was published in February 1864, Neuberg having prepared it for the printer. Carlyle has to deal here with the 'scandalous rumours' about Frederick's homosexuality, which he does by labelling a contemporary observer 'the Demon Newswriter', whom he quotes with running disparagement before setting out to say 'what little I have to say' on this 'most melancholy portion of my raw-material'. Accepting Frederick's lack of interest in his wife from the beginning, he says of the homosexuality claim that 'proof of the *negative*, in this or in any such case, is by the nature of it impossible'. As for 'proof in the affirmative', it has, as far as Carlyle knows, 'not anywhere turned-up'. That being the case, 'the present Editor does not, for his own share, value the rumour at a pin's fee'. And if the public is disappointed, hoping for 'obscene details', then the public is depraved. 'Thus, too, you will observe of dogs: two dogs, at meeting, run first to the shameful parts of the constitution; institute a strict examination, more or less satisfactory, in that department', then separate.[84] While this volume was being seen through the press by Neuberg during the winter of 1863-4, and Carlyle was writing volume five, the 'horrible' truth dawned on him that there would have to be a sixth volume.[85]

Publication day passed almost unnoticed in the Carlyle household, where Jane was in despair and the doctors powerless. Early in March she was persuaded to move to St Leonard's to the care of the Blakistons. A special 'invalid carriage' was hired, 'hideous to look upon', as Carlyle wrote in his reminiscence of Jane, 'black, low, base-looking – and you entered it by a window', as if it were a hearse.[86] Maggie Welsh stayed with Jane; Carlyle wrote daily and visited every few days. Her state was so bad that at first Maggie did not tell her of Lord Ashburton's death on 23 March. When she learned in early April she wrote to comfort Lady

Ashburton on the loss of such a kind man, and could not resist saying she thought her own condition fatal.[87]

To Carlyle she wrote on 8 April, addressing him for once as 'my own darling', and saying she was wretched. 'So, God help me, for on earth is no help!' She had heard from Lady Ashburton that Lord Ashburton had left Carlyle £2,000. 'Money', she added, 'can do nothing for us now', before signing herself 'Your loving and sore suffering Jane W. Carlyle'.[88] Carlyle told Lady Ashburton that Lord Ashburton's bequest was 'so *like* the Doer of it: – the last finish to 20 years of friendly acts and offices on his part, – all done in the same gentle, quiet and fine way'.[89] In his own quiet way, Carlyle over the years gave away the money in small amounts to people he saw in need.[90]

Desperate notes came from Jane, such as the one on 25 April when she wrote, 'Oh, my husband! I am suffering torments! each day I suffer more horribly. Oh, I would like you beside me! I am terribly alone.'[91] A few days later Carlyle hired lodgings in St Leonard's and moved there, taking his books with him and leaving his good neighbour Larkin in charge of the house in Cheyne Row. John Carlyle went too, and various concerned visitors turned up – the Forsters, Edward Twisleton, Woolner, Miss Davenport Bromley – but Jane could not see any of them.[92]

Finally, in July, she decided on one last effort; she wanted to go to Scotland, where she would be in her homeland and where the Russells, the husband her favourite doctor and the wife her best friend, might help her through her torture. The journey was daunting, but she set off by train under the less than ideal escort of John Carlyle – 'we quarrelled incessantly', she told Carlyle on her safe arrival at the Gill, where Mary Austin was her usual kind self.[93] John, who rubbed her up the wrong way at the best of times, was hardly the right company for her now. She never forgave him for saying, as she reported to Carlyle from the haven of the Russells' house on 23 July, that 'if I had ever done anything in my life this would not have been; that no poor woman with work to mind had ever such an ailment as this of mine since the world began!'[94] There may have been some truth in this, though it was certainly cruel of John to make the remark just at this moment; it also did not come very appropriately from a man as idle and aimless as Carlyle's sanguine and irritating brother.

More despairing notes, written shakily with her left hand, came to Carlyle during July and August. He replied lovingly, agreeing with her that John had been callous, and that his 'sympathy is dull and coarse, – and he has great vanity'.[95] Carlyle was receiving daily letters from Jane detailing her lack of hope, and almost daily notes from John saying she looked better, had slept well, and so on. John had discussed the case with

Dr Russell and they agreed that she should not be given opium.[96] She herself told Eliza Forster on 25 August that she was sleeping better, and dreaming normally, 'for I do not count my horrible opium visions as *dreams!*'[97] She also complained to Mrs Forster about John's circulating a 'flourishing account' of her immediately after her arrival in Scotland. 'It did not need an MD to ones name to have perceived in that extraordinary *Wellness*, after such fatigues and agitations, neither more nor less than a terrible *flare up* of bilious excitement.'[98]

Mary Austin, who, as Jack observed after Jane's death, was the only one of Carlyle's siblings who got on well with her sister-in-law,[99] was worried by Jane's religious scepticism and despair. She gently urged Jane to 'call on God's help':

He is able to support and has never said to any seek ye my face in vain try to cast your cares on him he will never leave you nor forsake you. My dear forgive me if I have said anything offensive to you . . . your ever loving Mary.[100]

Carlyle was also anxious about Jane's lack of faith, endorsing Mary's remarks and begging Jane to believe in God. 'In your good moments, you too strive that way, don't you? We shd both of us, you *and* I, to whom it is the easier of the two. God help us, Darling!'[101]

With gentle nursing and country food, Jane did improve, even putting on some weight, but her spirits remained low, and by the end of September, when she was due to return to Chelsea, once more with John for escort – Carlyle having carefully ascertained that she would accept his offer[102] – she was naturally afraid of the journey. Though Carlyle was at last being as solicitous as she had always longed for him to be, she dreaded home life with him once more, though now because she would be a 'burden' on his spirits rather than the other way round. Her inability to gain comfort from any religious faith seemed to her like bitter poetic justice: 'Nobody can help me! Only God – and can I wonder if God take no heed of me when I have all my life taken so little heed of Him?'[103]

*

Eliza Forster had undertaken to oversee painters and decorators to cheer up Jane's bedroom – her prison for six months the previous winter – and the drawing room. Carlyle kept her informed of progress during September, and also of the energetic preparations of the maids to get the house fit for Jane's return. 'The girls are raging and scrubbing', he told her on 25 August. The front windows were clean, and the curtains 'all on a rope in the Garden; – Cat, with miniature black Likeness of herself contemplatively wandering among the skirts of them'. Other news he passed on concerned Forster's work as a Lunacy Commissioner: 'Fuz I am told is doing the Colney Hatch Asylum, near 2,000 *mads* in it.' On coming home from his ride the previous evening he had found Mr Morison, '*Son* of the Morrison's Pills, I believe', waiting for him, 'an innocent, polite, intelligent kind of man; – who kept me talking till 11 o'clock (sorrow on him) instead of *reading* for my task of today!'[104]

He also had comic news about barrel organs, one of the many sources of noise nuisance to him over the years. Michael Bass, MP for Derby, had introduced a Bill for the Suppression of Street Music earlier in the year, supported by a letter in May from Dickens and twenty-seven other signatories, including Carlyle.[105] The Bill was passed in July. Now, in late August, Carlyle reported that the 'yellow demons' – organ-grinders, mainly Italian – seemed to be 'rifer than ever, after Bass's triumphant Act of Parliament'. 'Think of Parliament's sitting debating', he wrote with refreshing amusement, 'passing Act after Act; about the beautiful melody I now hear saluting me not far off!'[106]

Jane's arrival at Cheyne Row on 1 October was greeted with joy and kisses from Carlyle and the maids, and with champagne sent by Lady Ashburton.[107] A few days later she told Mary Austin how astonished and pleased her friends were to see her looking so much better, especially 'the men'. 'They take me in their arms, most I have seen, and kiss me, and – burst into tears!! or are struck speechless.' George Cooke, Richard Monckton Milnes (now Lord Houghton), Woolner, and the expressive Forster all went through this gratifying procedure on seeing her.[108] Carlyle, too, pleased her. Jane told his sister Mary on 18 October that he was 'gentle and good'. 'He is as busy as ever, but he studies my comfort and peace as he never did before.' She also mentioned recent changes to the domestic staff. 'I have engaged a new housemaid, and given warning to the big beautiful blockhead who has filled that function here for the last nine months; this has been a worry too.'[109]

The 'blockhead' was the servant Mary, about whom Jane had just been told a most astonishing story, which she passed on to Mary Russell on 12 November. Of the two maids, Mary and Helen, Jane had supposed the latter to be guilty of stealing various items of food, napkins, and crockery which had been disappearing from the house, and so gave her notice. It transpired, however, that Mary was the thief. Not only that but, on 29 July, during Jane's absence in Scotland, she had given birth to an illegitimate child in the house. 'Now, my Dear', wrote Jane to her friend, 'if you had seen the creature Mary you would just as soon have suspected the Virgin Mary of such things!'

While she was in labour in the small room at the end of the dining room, Mr Carlyle was taking tea in the dining room with Miss Jewsbury talking to him!!!

Just a thin small door between them! The child was not born till two in the morning when Mr C was still reading in the Drawingroom.[110]

Jane told Kate Stanley the story, expressing her shock but also her amusement at the thought of Carlyle sitting innocently at tea 'while his Cook and Housekeeper was taking the liberty' of producing a baby in the adjoining room.[111] She now engaged a sensible older woman, Mrs Warren, as her cook and housekeeper. Telling Mrs Russell this in November, she also mentioned that she had avoided 'reporting herself' to Dr Quain:

He was very kind and attentive to me last Winter, and couldn't be persuaded ever to take a fee! But now that the torment, which burnt up all delicacy in me, is abated, I 'think shame' to see him, after all the dreadful questions and answers that passed between us![112]

In February 1865 Jane again told Mary Russell how embarrassed she was with Dr Quain, remembering 'how wildly I used to talk to him, imploring him to give me poison, etc., etc., and all the horrid questions he had to ask!'[113]

From these two confessions one thing is clear, and another may be – and has been – conjectured. Jane, in her maddening pain during the winter of 1863–4, had asked Quain to help her to die. As to the 'horrid questions', since one medical theory was that she had a disease of the womb, as she had told her aunts in April 1864,[114] Quain may have asked her about her menstrual history and possibly also about her sexual history. Quain's name was used by the scandal-monger Frank Harris in connection with his own unlikely story of Carlyle's having told him in the last year of his life that he was impotent. Harris said that he had it from Quain's own lips that Mrs Carlyle had died a virgin.[115] It is possible that Quain examined Jane in 1864, and again on her death, but we cannot be sure what he found, nor whether he told anyone.

That Jane's illness had taken its emotional toll on Carlyle is illustrated by an account given by Annie Thackeray in October 1864. Her beloved father had died suddenly, aged fifty-two, on Christmas Eve 1863. She and her sister Minny – who liked visiting Jane because she gave them hot chocolate and told them never to marry a dyspeptic man of genius[116] – had met Carlyle 'the other day on his horse & he suddenly began to cry. I shall always love him in future, for I used to fancy he did not care about Papa.'[117] Carlyle had attended Thackeray's funeral. On 29 December 1863 he wrote to Milnes that their friend had 'many fine qualities, no guile or malice against any mortal: a big mass of a soul, but not strong in proportion'.[118] Carlyle's weeping on meeting the Thackeray girls in October 1864 was partly for Thackeray, partly for his orphaned daughters, and partly, we may suppose, for himself and Jane.

Yet Jane appeared to have made a remarkable recovery, as Edward Twisleton noticed in December 1864. 'I see her very often', he told Ellen's sister Mary, observing also that 'the great peril from which she has escaped has infused the most touching tenderness into Carlyle's relations with her'.[119] Because of this new attention from him, augmented by visits and gifts from numerous friends, Jane's life this winter was a very different one from the previous tortured one. As she wrote happily to Mary Russell on 20 October, 'It is a wonder I have not been knocked up by the heaps of people who come and make such rejoicing over me, as if I were a Queen bee!'[120]

Lady Ashburton was treated to the story of the sudden arrival on 17 October of the artist George Frederic Watts and the photographer Julia Margaret Cameron, both of whom were later to do portraits of Carlyle, Watts a loathed 'Blotch-Portrait' in 1868–9, and Mrs Cameron her famous photographic studies of him in 1867.[121] These two made 'an *inburst*' into the house, and Mrs Cameron was 'hardly to be restrained from forcing her way into Mr C's bedroom while he was changing his trousers!!'[122]

Not only was Jane cosseted at home, but she now went out and about. Mary Russell heard on 10 October of her visit to her dressmaker, Madame Elise, to 'get a velvet bonnet she made me last year, stripped of its finery. White lace and red roses don't become a woman who has been looking both death and insanity in the face for a year.'[123] A few weeks later she visited Elise once more to have a fitting for a new dress, refusing the fashionable crinoline, but being fussed over by the dressmaker in a satisfactory manner.[124]

Carlyle was intent on adding some luxury and comfort to her life, hiring a brougham for her with a feeling of guilt – if he had taken the trouble a year earlier, she would not have had the street accident which seemed to have brought on her dreadful illness. He had begrudged taking time off from *Frederick* to make the arrangements, but now he went ahead, though characteristically he asked Neuberg to do the work of finding a suitable brougham and horse.[125] Jane, too, joined in the search, going to 'half-a-dozen coachmakers' yards seeking that carriage', and finally getting 'a nice little Brougham', 'all to myself, with a smart grey horse and an elderly driver (in Mr C's old brown surtout)!'[126] They named the little mare Bellona. Jane told Mary Russell with glee in the 'gloomy month of November' that she was driving out every day. Having the brougham 'enables me to do my shopping (at the carriage window) and to make visits (on the new principle of calling out the person visited to sit in the carriage with me!)'[127]

One person she visited in this way was Mazzini, who described such an occasion in March 1865:

Mrs Carlyle – who comes in a coach, stops invariably at some distance in the road and compels me to go to her and exhibit myself to a very inquisitive neighbourhood in slippers and hat – came two days ago with the modest request of twelve autographs of mine for a Bazar, consisting of quotations, etc. The first I wrote was: England, with all thy faults I love thee still.[128]

Jane still loved Mazzini too, and she loved his crazy English, sending on to Carlyle in July 1865 a report of Mazzini's description of a dinner he had eaten – 'A crushed Fish; some conspicuous Bird – Goose – what shall I say? A viscous fabric, and a Pie whatever!'[129]

An important moment arrived for both Carlyles in January 1865. Carlyle finished *Frederick*, with a feeling of thankfulness and exhaustion after thirteen years of internal struggle and discord which had contributed mightily to the domestic disharmony at Cheyne Row.[130] Volumes five and six were published in March, 3,000 copies of each being printed. Carlyle earned £1,675 from these two volumes; in April he told Jack that he had £2,000 to invest, which John Chorley advised putting into 'the *Indian Guaranteed* (something)' – what did Jack think?[131] He had seen his work through to the end, but had written not only himself and his wife, but also his subject, into the ground. The final volume concerns itself rather half-heartedly with the last fourteen years of Frederick's life, after the end of the Seven Years War in 1763. With this last Herculean task, he wrote, Frederick's contribution to 'World-History' comes to an end, and the rest is mere Prussian history.[132]

As a hostile but respectful review by Herman Merivale in the *Quarterly Review* pointed out, Carlyle 'has become in the sixth volume thoroughly tired of his work'. He has given fine accounts of Frederick's big battles, but seems to think 'that every forgotten skirmish in the Bohemian mountains requires to be embalmed in long pages, while the various stages of social progress and civil administration are below the notice of the historian of a hero'. Nevertheless, writes Merivale fairly, one must respect 'the extraordinary power which he has lavished on what seems to us so intractable a subject':

Enough to say, that, after forming the literary taste of England and America to an extent which no contemporary (unless, possibly, one of a very different class, Macaulay) has approached, he has become, while yet alive and at work among us, something of a classic.[133]

Frederick the Great became a classic in Germany too. Neuberg's translation, completed in 1869 by Althaus, was greeted enthusiastically in Bismarck's Prussia. The book, supplemented by extracts in German newspapers of Carlyle's pro-German comments during the Franco-Prussian War of 1870–1,[134] led to Carlyle's 'sublime elevation to the Prussian Order of Merit' in February 1874. He had no desire for such honours, and put the decoration away after graciously accepting it; later in the same year he was to decline Disraeli's offer of a Grand Cross of the Bath.[135]

In 1916, during the First World War, the Neuberg translation was reissued to an eager German public. Thomas Mann wrote a review of 'Carlyle's *Friedrich*' in the same year, expressing his amazement at the thoroughness of the research and his approval of Carlyle's novelistic techniques, the 'heroic humour' towards the material he had worked on so laboriously, and his unique readability. Mann's own short study, *Frederick and the Great Coalition* (*Friedrich und die grosse Koalition*), had been published in 1915, its cumulative, detailed, breathless, dramatic, and ironic narrative bearing strong similarities to Carlyle's method.[136]

Most famously, or infamously, Goebbels read aloud a passage from volume six to a despairing Hitler in his Berlin bunker in April 1945. Towards the end of the Seven Years War, Frederick is in deep gloom, when news comes from Russia of the death of the Czarina Elizabeth, his implacable enemy, and the succession of the friendly Peter III. Carlyle, who has been consoling Frederick in his dismay, declares this 'a wonderful star-of-day' for the King. Hitler, hearing of the death of Franklin D. Roosevelt, briefly believed a similar miracle was about to happen to him. In his case history did not repeat itself, and he committed suicide before the month was out.[137]

★

Geraldine Jewsbury wrote to Walter Mantell in March 1865 that Carlyle had finished *Frederick*. 'And his wife, who ought to know, declares "that he has been kicking up his heels in a wonderful way ever since!" '[138] In April Carlyle agreed to go to Woolner's studio to sit for a bust which Lady Ashburton had commissioned, 'a botheration' and not likely to be any good, he told Jack.[139] Jane was also sceptical:

It seems he 'is as difficult to catch a likeness of as a flash of lightning' is; so that it is a trying business for both sitter and sculptor and I am afraid the Bust will never be worth the hundred guineas Lady A will pay for it.[140]

Exhausted by *Frederick*, Carlyle made for Scotsbrig. As he told Emerson, he had not been in his old home region since 1860. 'My work was getting desperate at that time; and I silently said to myself, "We won't return till *it* is done, or *you* are done, my man!" '[141] While he was away, Jane took the opportunity once more of rearranging the house. The sound-proofed study was to be abandoned now *Frederick* was done; Carlyle was to use the dining room as his study from now on. She was still cheerful, but her right hand was useless. She felt strong enough, however, to set off in June for the Russells at Holm Hill, where Carlyle visited her. They treated one another gently this year, as if they had both learned something from the terrible summer of 1864.

Carlyle wrote rather sadly to Jane, suggesting changed relations – probably because of her – with John and Jean, who came over together on a brief visit from Dumfries, just as he was setting out for his daily ride on the sands on Noggs:

Poor souls, they were very kind and gentle to me, – all the more as they had hardly two hours and a half to stay; perhaps the best length of visit, as times now go! I strolled with them thro' the woods to near Cummertrees, saw, as I strode back, a white handkerchief flying from the window of the next up train (Dr John's); to which I waved my hat in reply, – and there was finis on those poor terms.[142]

Alick had sent a photograph of himself, which set Carlyle musing on his brother's 'tenderness, the old vein of melancholy, of pathos with affectionate sorrow', as well as the 'fiery indignations and manifold sarcastic ruggednesses' of character.[143] He had sent Alick a photo in return. It 'represents me pretty truly, well on in my 70th year', he wrote on 6 August. He had gone to Craigenputtoch with Jamie, he said, where he found 'your old Cattle-House, still *standing* by the woodside in the hollow, walls still standing, roof long since gone'.[144]

Released from Prussian history, Carlyle was reading Charles Lyell's *Elements of Geology* (1865), which Ruskin had sent him. Ruskin had become interested in geology and had a 'superb mineralogical collection' at Denmark Hill, which Carlyle went to see.[145] Carlyle could not be persuaded by Lyell's gradualist theory of the evolution of the earth's crust. He wrote scornfully to Jane on 9 June that it was 'the dullest thick book, long-winded, though intelligent', the tendency of which was more or less 'to prove that we are much the same as the apes; that Adam was probably no other than a fortunate ourang-outang who succeeded in rising in the world'.[146]

Ruskin continued to court Carlyle assiduously, and he knew how to please Jane too, sending her a copy of his new book, *Sesame and Lilies*, for her sixty-fourth birthday on 14 July. She was delighted, remembering that he had once given her strawberries and cream on her birthday, and enthusing about his 'talent for *naming*', as evidenced in *Sesame and Lilies* by its two parts, 'Of King's Treasuries' (about the importance of good books) and 'Of Queen's Gardens' (on the influence of good women). 'The names', she wrote on 15 July, 'lift me already into the sphere of Arabian Nights!'[147] Carlyle saw a review by Trollope in the *Fortnightly Review* which displeased him, as it declared that Ruskin had become 'essentially

Carlylesque', but that only Carlyle could get away with the literature of denunciation. Ruskin should stop preaching sermons and go back to giving us 'wonderful words on Art'. Carlyle considered this insolent and stupid.[148]

While he stayed on in Scotland till the end of August, Jane was back in London by the end of July. There she saw what she took to be a great sign of his celebrity, namely her own photograph stuck up in a shop window where the women on show were mostly authoresses, murderesses, actresses, or courtesans.[149] It seems that Miss Davenport Bromley, with whom Jane spent some time in Folkestone in August, persuaded her to accept a little dog, a pug named Tiny.[150] Though not the heroic character that Nero had been, he was soon to play a dramatic part in the Carlyles' lives.

Because Carlyle no longer sequestered himself in his study every day and every evening, they had frequent visitors during the winter of 1865–6. Despite Jane's difficult arm, they went out too, dining with the Froudes, the Forsters, and Lady William Russell, and seeing Woolner, Ruskin, Tennyson, Geraldine, and Margaret Oliphant, among other friends. Forster insisted on giving a party for Carlyle's seventieth birthday on 4 December. 'We had to go', Carlyle told Jack simply the following day: Forster, though ill with gout, 'would take no denial'.[151]

Edinburgh and its university, which had been so inhospitable to Carlyle in his youth, now honoured him by electing him Rector, with 657 votes to his rival Disraeli's 310.[152] Carlyle's composure was not 'overset by joy' when he heard the news, as he told Jack, but he accepted the honour and agreed to go to Edinburgh the following March to be invested.[153] Jane was pleased for him; she told her mother's old servant Betty Braid that 'if the weather happened to be remarkably mild, and if I happened to be remarkably well, I should like to go with him'.[154]

Her story-telling talent was as sharp as ever, as Mary Russell found when she received a well-spun tale in a Christmas letter. Carlyle was as usual the villain of the piece, but the tone was both comic and indulgent. Neighbour noise from number 6 was the subject. There had been a sudden

importation of nine hens, and a magnificent cock, into the adjoining garden! For years back there has reigned over all these gardens a heavenly quiet – thanks to my heroic efforts in exterminating nuisances of every description. But I no longer felt the hope or the energy in me requisite for such achievements. Figure then my horror, my despair, on being waked one dark morning with the crowing of a cock, that seemed to issue from under my bed! I leapt up, and rushed up to my dressing-room window, but it was still all darkness. I lay with my heart in my mouth, listening to the cock crowing hoarsely from time to time, and listening for Mr C's foot stamping frantically, as of old, on the floor above. But, strangely enough, he gave no sign of having heard his enemy, his whole attentions having been, since his visit to Mrs Aitken [at Dumfries], morbidly devoted to – railway whistles. So soon as it was daylight I looked out again, and there was a sight to see – a ragged, Irish-looking hen-house, run up over night, and sauntering to and fro nine goodly hens, and a stunning cock! I didn't know whether Mr C remained really deaf as well as blind to these new neighbours, or whether he was only magnanimously resolved to observe silence about them; but it is a fact, that for a whole week he said no word to enlighten me, while I expected and expected the crisis which would surely come, and shuddered at every cock-crow, and counted the number of times he crowed in a night – at two! at three! at four! at five! at six! at seven! Oh, terribly at seven!

For a whole week I bore my hideous secret in my breast, and slept 'none to speak of'. At the week's end I fell into one of my old sick headaches. I used always to find a sick headache had a fine effect in clearing the wits. So, even this time, I rose from a day's agony with a scheme of operation in my head, and a sense of ability to 'carry it out'. It would be too long to go into details – enough to say my negotiations with 'next door' ended in an agreement that the cock should be shut up in a cellar, inside the owner's own house, from three in the afternoon till ten in the morning; and, in return, I give the small boy of the house a lesson every morning in his 'Reading made Easy', the small boy being 'too excitable' for being sent to school! It is a house full of mysteries – No 6! I have thoughts of writing a novel about it.[155]

Jane was amused in a shuddering sort of way by the Edinburgh rumour that because Carlyle had been made Rector, he and Jane would 'tear ourselves up by the roots, and transplant ourselves *there*!' She told one of her Edinburgh aunts on 23 January 1866 that she had been remarkably well all winter, and had taken her daily three-hour drive in the brougham most days.[156] But as the time for Carlyle's going to Edinburgh approached, she began to dread both the journey and the speech at the end of it. Thanking Henry Inglis for his invitation to stay with him, she declared that she was

now, what is pleasantly called 'a *Living Miracle*!' – That is a woman who ought in the course of Nature to have been dead and buried, but has come alive again; for *some* purpose; – *what*? one does not see! – But surely it could not have been for the *purpose* of killing myself after all, by outrageous fatigues and agitations, wilfully encountered – to hear my own Husband *speak*!![157]

As the day of the inauguration, 2 April, drew near, Carlyle became more and more apprehensive about his speech, remembering how nervous he had been when giving lectures nearly thirty years before. Anticipation was high. The Royal Scottish Academy showed Tait's *Chelsea Interior*, graciously lent by Lady Ashburton to coincide with his visit.[158] Mary Dods, wife of Jane's old Haddington schoolfellow William

Dods, sent a newspaper cutting reproducing the painting with a commentary. In her reply on 12 March, Jane accused the critic of

an almost unpardonable omission, in failing to point out *the Dog* – '*thinking*'! – thinking, to most purpose of the three, it strikes me! Could anybody look in that dear little quadruped's face; without seeing that *he* was '*thinking*' all this nonsense of keeping him motionless on a sofa-cushion, to be painted, a great bore! and I'll be hanged if either Mr C or I were *thinking* anything more profound!

'Mr C', she added, with reference to the number of dinner parties she had been attending recently, 'said this morning "really my Dear I think it is time you drew bridle in the Career of Dissipation you have entered on!" But it helps me to – *sleep!*'[159]

As the two scientists, Huxley and Carlyle's ardent admirer John Tyndall, were also going to Edinburgh to receive honorary degrees, they agreed to travel together. Tyndall called for Carlyle on 29 March and they set off for Yorkshire, where they stopped over at Fryston as guests of Lord Houghton. Carlyle spent a sleepless night there – due to railway whistles – then a few days later, having been joined by Huxley, they continued to Edinburgh. There they were greeted by Sir David Brewster, who as Principal of the University was to preside over the installation of the man to whom he had given his first paid work when he employed Carlyle on the *Edinburgh Encyclopædia* in 1820.[160]

When the great day came Jane wrote to say she was suffering vicariously, imagining Carlyle 'getting up to speak to an awful crowd of people' and 'dropping down dead'.[161] In fact he gave an extempore speech to a rapt audience of students, professors, and invited ladies. Having processed into the hall with Brewster, dressed in gold-laced ceremonial robes, he 'threw off his robe, like an ancient David declining the unproved armour of Saul', in Tyndall's romantic words. He spoke largely to the students in the audience, encouraging them to keep their youthful enthusiasm, but also to cultivate diligence, frugality, and patience. He talked of his love of history and of its importance. There were characteristic moments, as when he scorned 'clap-trap books' which affected 'the minds of foolish persons', or gave his opinion that 'there is a nobler ambition than the gaining of all California, or the getting of all the suffrages that are on the planet just now!'[162]

Carlyle ended with a quotation from the writer from whom he had learned first and most – not one of his university teachers, but Goethe. Quoting from the old favourite 'Symbolum' in his own translation, he called it 'a modern psalm', 'a kind of marching music of mankind'. The last two verses rang out:

> But heard are the voices,
> Heard are the Sages,
> The worlds and the Ages:
> 'Choose well, your choice is
> Brief, and yet endless.
>
> Here eyes do regard you
> In Eternity's stillness:
> Here is all fullness,
> Ye brave, to reward you!
> Work, and despair not.'[163]

The Address was published in *The Times*, and as a shilling pamphlet in Edinburgh; a more elaborate version, called *On the Choice of Books*, was printed in London, 'with additional articles, a memoir of the author, and two portraits', by the bookseller John Camden Hotten of Piccadilly.[164] After delivering the speech, Carlyle was followed through the Edinburgh streets by students uttering 'vivats and vociferations'. His brothers John and James were there, and Carlyle had to do much more socialising than he liked. 'I am like a man killed with kindness', he told Jane on 4 April; 'ah me, all the world coming tumbling on. "Do me this, see me that; above all, dine, dine!"'[165]

Tyndall had sent a telegram to Jane as soon as the ceremony was over, stating merely, 'a perfect Triumph'. 'He is a Jewel, that man', she wrote delightedly of Tyndall when telling Lady Ashburton the good news.[166] The maids and her cousin Maggie danced and clapped when they heard. Jane had gone to dinner at Forster's house, where Dickens and Wilkie Collins were also invited, all of them happy to drink Carlyle's health with 'hearty good-will'. Forster even sent a glass of brandy out to the coachman, Sylvester.[167]

Jane's joy at Carlyle's success shines out from her letters for the next two weeks. He did not come straight home, but went to Scotsbrig to recuperate from all the wining and dining. She sent him news of the congratulations that were pouring in. On 12 April she told him she had sent the previous day a 'charming' *Punch*, but was not sure whether he would have received it, for 'Geraldine undertook the posting of it, and as Ann said of her long ago, "*Miss* can write Books but I'm sure it's the only thing she's fit for"'. 'There you are', she wrote, 'in the chief place' in *Punch*, 'cape & wideawake, making a really creditable appearance'.[168] Carlyle is presented as 'Wisdom', set against 'Wind-Bag', the radical Birmingham MP John Bright. *Punch* first calls him, with only a touch of sarcasm, 'Chancellor Silvertongue', then apostrophises the seventy-year-old sage, more seriously, as 'brave old man, wise old man'.[169]

Meanwhile, Carlyle was writing to her from Scotsbrig: 'I have

" 'appened a misfortune" (to keep me in the level of common humanity, and take any undue conceit out of me)'; he had sprained his ankle.[170] This delayed his departure for home, which he eventually fixed for 23 April, going first to stay with Jean in Dumfries. Jane was planning to give a tea party on Saturday, 21 April. The Froudes were to be there, and also Geraldine Jewsbury and Margaret Oliphant; Jane was to lunch with the Forsters on the same day.[171] She had given a successful tea party a couple of days before, consisting of one of her Italian protégés, Mazzini's fellow patriot Aurelio Saffi, his wife, Miss Bromley, Geraldine, Edward Twisleton, and George Cooke. Her matchmaking instinct had been aroused, but was disappointed: 'Mr Twisleton "was meant" to *take to* Miss Bromley, but, instead, he took – very decidedly too – to the bright little Patriot's Wife!'[172]

On the morning of 21 April Jane wrote again, wondering how she was to make ten matching cups do for eleven guests. She reported that Frederick Chapman, of Carlyle's publishers Chapman and Hall, who were co-publishing the inaugural speech with an Edinburgh firm, was furious that his rival Hotten of Piccadilly had 'got the start of him' with the booksellers. 'Smith and Elder had bought five hundred copies from Hotten! And poor Frederick did not receive his copies from Edinburgh till he had "telegraphed", six-and-thirty hours after I had received mine!'[173]

This letter reached Carlyle on the afternoon of Sunday, 22 April; it had been preceded on the Saturday evening by two telegrams which came while he 'was sitting in Sister Jean's at Dumfries; thinking of my Railway to Chelsea on Monday'.[174] Jane had left Forster's house at about three o'clock on the Saturday afternoon with her dog Tiny. Sylvester had driven her through Hyde Park, where she let Tiny out for a run. The dog was knocked over by another brougham, and Jane had lifted him up and taken him into the carriage. The brougham went on, and when Sylvester heard no instructions about leaving the Park, he looked back over the blinds, where he could see Jane's hands. A few yards further on he looked again, and noticed that the hands had not moved. He asked a lady to look into the carriage; she summoned a man to confirm her suspicions, and Sylvester was advised to drive to the nearby St George's Hospital. Jane was dead.

Froude and Geraldine, preparing for the evening tea party, were called to the hospital. Froude then went to Cheyne Row, where he found Forster. Resourceful as usual, though distraught, Forster used his position as Lunacy Commissioner to prevent the inquest which would have been normal in such cases.[175] Dr Quain provided a certificate of the probable cause of death, which was thought to be a 'spinal disease'.[176]

Her last letter, which Carlyle read after receiving the news of her death, was cheerful, even warm. Her sharpness, for so long aimed directly at him, especially during the long years of Ashburton and *Frederick* misery, was now pointed elsewhere. Her last words to the other partner of this difficult marriage were generous ones, though not without that spice of wit which so characterised her, early and late:

I saw in an old furniture-shop window at Richmond a copy of the Frederick picture that was lent you – not bad; coarsely painted, but the likeness well preserved. Would you like to have it? I will, if so, make you a present of it, being to be had 'very equal'. I 'descended from the carriage', and asked, 'What was that?' (meaning what price was it). The broker told me impressively, 'That, ma-am, is Peter the Great.' 'Indeed! and what is the price?' 'Seven-and-sixpence.' I offered five shillings on the spot, but he would only come down to six shillings. I will go back for it if you like, and can find a place for it on my wall.[177]

And so ended the life and writings of Jane Welsh Carlyle. Carlyle, though struck as if by lightning, found some comfort in knowing that she had taken pleasure in his success, that she had been lunching 'with the Forsters (old friends), was never seen more brilliantly cheerful, *well* beyond wont, and seemed to *eat* better than usual'; that she had, in short, died happy and – in the word the Carlyles valued perhaps too highly in life – 'victorious'.[178]

Dickens, whom Jane had been delighting with the beginning of a verbal 'half romantic' novel about a neighbouring house (undoubtedly number 6) when they had drunk Carlyle's health together on the day of his speech, wrote to Forster when he heard of her death: 'How often I have thought of the unfinished novel. No one now to finish it. None of the writing women come near her at all.'[179] Carlyle thought so too, as he went through as many of her letters as he could collect in the lonely months after her death. 'Not all the *Sands* and *Eliots* and babbling *cohue* [band] of "celebrated scribbling Women" that have strutted over the world' could equal the genius of Jane's letters, he believed.[180]

Well, in Jane's case her letters *are* her novels. She never wrote a novel; some combination of character and circumstances prevented her from achieving the fame of a George Sand or a George Eliot in that genre. As a letter writer, however, she was – Carlyle was right – unsurpassed. It is one of the many ironies of their in some ways rather terrible relationship that Jane's epistolary talent was fed, fostered, and also in the end preserved, by the one great fact in her life, namely that she was, for better or worse, for richer or poorer, in sickness and in health, the wife of no other man than the impossible, meticulous, magnetic genius, Thomas Carlyle.

Epilogue

John Carlyle accompanied his brother home from Dumfries on Monday, 23 April. He and Forster made the funeral arrangements. Jane had asked to be buried with her father in the nave of the old Abbey Kirk at Haddington. They took her body by train on the Wednesday; Edward Twisleton travelled by the same train, which was stopped by special arrangement at Longridding, where William Dods met it with the hearse.[1] The funeral, a quiet one in accordance with Carlyle's wishes, took place on Thursday, 26 April. The night before he 'went out to walk in the moonlit silent streets of Haddington', and looked up at the windows of the room where he had first seen Jane in 1821, 'on a summer evening after sunset', when Edward Irving and he had walked to Haddington together.[2]

On his return home, he found letters of condolence 'from the Queen downwards'.[3] One of their earliest London friends, Erasmus Darwin, wrote that he was unable to come and see Carlyle, but wanted to say that his acquaintance with Jane had been 'one of the great pleasures of my life & I shall never cease thinking of her with gratitude & affection'.[4] Dickens wrote simply that he loved and honoured Carlyle: 'To your great heart and mind, little can come out of mine but sympathy. – That has been with you from the first, and ever will be while I live.'[5]

In order to give himself something to do, and to honour Jane's memory, Carlyle set about writing his reminiscence of her, which he finished at the end of July 1866. That led naturally to the long reminiscence of Irving, his friend and rival so long ago, to which he added the shorter, sharper, less emotional sketches of Jeffrey, Southey and Wordsworth, 'Christopher North' (John Wilson), and Sir William Hamilton, finishing these loosely connected memoirs in February 1868. By this time he had decided to make a selection of Jane's letters, partly to keep busy, and partly because he thought them 'among the cleverest ever written'.[6] He therefore became Jane's historian and editor, collecting, sorting, dating, and annotating as many of her letters as he could find, including the many hundreds written to himself.

It was his last work, though he could not bring himself to publish either the letters or his reminiscences, leaving both, and his own journals, to Froude, with equivocal half-instructions about publication. His editorial work is like all his other writings – meticulous, detailed, idiosyncratic, done straight from the heart. He felt remorse when he read Jane's complaints about him, especially in her miserable journals of 1855–6, and to his credit he preserved the documents which he was surely tempted to destroy, such a black picture did they paint of him. He stopped short, however, of writing a full confession, leaving Jane's desperate remarks about his relations with 'Bath House' unannotated.

Carlyle survived Jane by nearly fifteen years. He died on 4 February 1881, aged eighty-five. Westminster Abbey was suggested as a suitable resting place for such an influential figure, but his will requested that he should be buried beside his parents in the churchyard in Ecclefechan. Both he and Jane therefore returned to their roots. The couple who had been so famous as one entity, 'Mr and Mrs Carlyle', and so associated with Chelsea, were separated once more, though both were laid to rest in their native Scotland. With the publication by Froude of *Reminiscences* (1881), the four volumes of Carlyle's *Life* (1882–4), and the three volumes of Jane's *Letters and Memorials*, annotated by Carlyle (1883), the world soon knew of the neuroses and dissatisfactions inside number 5, Cheyne Row. The world then commented freely on the Carlyles' larger-than-life personalities and impossibly sensitive reactions – like two Othellos bellowing about life and death over the dropping of a handkerchief – their hypochondria and selfishness, his cruel neglect and her treacherous complaints, the possibility that their marriage had remained unconsummated. It also recognised their kindness and fun, the genius of both, the wit, the way with words with which husband and wife were abundantly gifted.

The sheer quantity of their writing, quite apart from its sparkling quality, impresses and informs later generations who are interested in the Victorian period. We cannot but be struck by the number and variety of those contemporaries, British and foreign, in the literary, political, and domestic spheres, who were attracted to the two magnets residing in Cheyne Row. Everyone knew them, or wanted to know them. Unlike Dickens, Carlyle made no bonfire of letters to keep them from the eyes of curious posterity; unlike George Eliot, he did not take the letters of his life's partner to the grave with him. We can read more letters of Carlyle and Jane, and above all more letters between Carlyle and Jane, than perhaps of any other couple in history.

And yet, as is their right, they retain their joint and individual mystery. What were their feelings for one another? Did they have a sexual relationship? Was Carlyle ever physically violent? How far did his domestic tyranny go – was it worse than that of other husbands of genius, such as Dickens or Marx, or that of the grim fathers of the Brontës and Elizabeth Barrett? How addicted was Jane to morphine, opium, and other medicines, and how distorted were her perceptions as a consequence? Did she seriously contemplate leaving Carlyle? Was she ever really in love with any man, be it Irving or Carlyle or Mazzini? What was the true nature of Carlyle's feelings for Lady Ashburton – those of a sexually frustrated husband or of an emotionally immature romantic?

That he was a tortured genius is clear. It is equally clear that, like most of his contemporaries, he considered women as the inferior sex, whose place was to serve the men to whom they belonged. He was no John Stuart Mill, no progressive advocate of sexual equality. Nor, really, was Jane, though she resented her subjection. She made no valiant effort at independence, though she knew (and half envied, half despised) women who did – Geraldine Jewsbury, for example, and George Eliot. She chose to marry Carlyle, believing, when few others cared to, that his genius would eventually be recognised, and she shared the lean times in Edinburgh and Craigenputtoch, while he struggled, slowly and sometimes perversely, to make a living and a name.

Jane's reward was to share the years of success – phenomenal success – when all the world, British, American, European, made for their shabby-genteel corner of Chelsea. She got her chance to sparkle and shine before literary lions and political leaders; most were fascinated by her wit, though some feared or disliked it. These celebrities provided the raw material, along with a succession of servants, neighbours, shopkeepers, beggars, 'mads', and social flotsam and jetsam, for her fluent letters, of which one might say, as Walter Bagehot said of Dickens's fiction, that they were written as if by a special correspondent for posterity.

When we add her letters to Carlyle's, and to his published writings, from the early essays, through *Sartor Resartus*, *The French Revolution*, and *Past and Present* to the great white elephant *Frederick the Great*, we have the most striking body of non-fictional prose of the nineteenth century. It can be said without exaggeration that together the Carlyles present a uniquely detailed picture, a Vandyke portrait in words to match Tait's visual one, of the age in which they lived, and of their always interesting individual selves.

Notes

Abbreviations

The following frequently cited works are given in abbreviated form in the Notes:

CL	*The Collected Letters of Thomas and Jane Welsh Carlyle*, 28 vols so far (1970—)
Froude, I, II	James Anthony Froude, *Thomas Carlyle: A History of the First Forty Years of his Life 1795–1835*, 2 vols (1882)
Froude, III, IV	James Anthony Froude, *Thomas Carlyle: A History of his Life in London*, 2 vols (1884)
Houghton	Houghton Library, Harvard University
Letters and Memorials	*Letters and Memorials of Jane Welsh Carlyle*, ed. J.A. Froude, 3 vols (1883)
NLS	National Library of Scotland
New Letters and Memorials	*New Letters and Memorials of Jane Welsh Carlyle*, ed. Alexander Carlyle, 2 vols (1903)
New Letters	*New Letters of Thomas Carlyle*, ed. Alexander Carlyle, 2 vols (1904)
Two Note Books	*Two Note Books of Thomas Carlyle*, ed. Charles Eliot Norton (1898)
Wilson, I	David Alec Wilson, *Carlyle till Marriage (1795–1826)* (1923)
Wilson, II	David Alec Wilson, *Carlyle to 'The French Revolution' (1826–37)* (1924)
Wilson, III	David Alec Wilson, *Carlyle on Cromwell and Others (1837–48)* (1925)
Wilson, IV	David Alec Wilson, *Carlyle at his Zenith (1848–53)* (1927)
Wilson, V	David Alec Wilson, *Carlyle to Threescore-and-Ten (1853–65)* (1931)
Wilson, VI	David Alec Wilson and David Wilson MacArthur, *Carlyle in Old Age (1865–81)* (1934)

Introduction

1 See, for example, W. M. Thackeray to Edward FitzGerald, [?February] 1846, *The Letters and Private Papers of William Makepeace Thackeray*, ed. Gordon N. Ray, 4 vols (Cambridge, Mass., 1945–6), II, 227.

2 JC to Mary Russell, 20 November 1857, *I Too Am Here: Selections from the Letters of Jane Welsh Carlyle*, ed. Alan and Mary McQueen Simpson (Cambridge, 1977), pp. 125–6. Corrected from MS 606, National Library of Scotland (henceforth referred to as NLS).

3 JC to Thomas Woolner, [June 1858], Amy Woolner, *Thomas Woolner, RA, Sculptor and Poet: His Life in Letters* (London, 1917), p. 150.

4 John Ruskin to JC, c. November 1857, *The Correspondence of Thomas Carlyle and John Ruskin*, ed. George Allan Cate (Stanford, California, 1982), pp. 78–9.

5 JC to Mary Russell, 29 March 1858, *I Too Am Here*, p. 145.

6 Robert Tait, quoted by Alastair Laing of the National Trust in his application on behalf of the Trust for a National Art Collections Fund grant to help buy *A Chelsea Interior* for Carlyle's House, 1999 (quoted here by kind permission of Alastair Laing and the National Trust).

7 See Sidney C. Hutchison, *The History of the Royal Academy 1768–1986* (London, 1986), p. 100.

8 *Art-Journal*, IV n.s. (1 June 1858), 161, 171. See also *The Times*, 1 May 1858, for a comparison of Frith's painting with Hogarth's works; *Athenaeum*, 1 May 1858, on Frith's 'dazzling picture'; *Illustrated London News*, 8 May 1858, for a long appreciation of Frith's work.

9 K. J. Fielding, 'Robert Scott Tait: His Portraits and Photographs of the Carlyles in their "A Chelsea Interior"', *Review of Scottish Culture*, XIII (2000), 112–16.

10 Giuseppe Mazzini to Emilie Venturi, January 1861, *Scritti editi ed inediti*, Edizione Nazionale, 106 vols (Imola, 1906–90), LXX, 264.

11 Francis Espinasse, *Literary Recollections and Sketches* (London, 1893), p. 102. Millais sold his *Lorenzo and Isabella*, exhibited at the Royal Academy in 1849, for £150, and William Holman Hunt sold *Rienzi* for £100, see Hutchison, *History of the Royal Academy*, p. 94.

12 JC to TC, 27 June 1858, MS 606 (NLS).

13 See Ian Campbell, 'Carlyle House', *Carlyle Annual*, XII (1991), 65–90. The house has been owned since 1936 by the National Trust, which purchased Tait's picture with the aid of a grant from the National Art Collections Fund (information from Alastair Laing of the National Trust).

14 Papers of the Carlyle's House Purchase Fund Committee, in the collection of Carlyleana (Carl 244.2) in the Houghton Library, Harvard University (henceforth referred to as Houghton).

15 John Nichol, *Thomas Carlyle* (London, 1892), p. 63.

16 See Mark Stocker, 'Joseph Edgar Boehm and Thomas Carlyle',

Carlyle Newsletter, VI (Spring 1985), 11–22.

17 See Reginald Blunt, *By Chelsea Reach: Some Riverside Records* (London, 1921), pp. 265–6.

18 David Masson, *Memories of London in the 'Forties* (London, 1908), pp. 47–8.

19 Frederic Harrison to John Morley, 11 January 1872, F. W. Hirst, *Early Life and Letters of John Morley*, 2 vols (London, 1927), I, 209–10.

20 TC to JC, 17 May 1834, *The Collected Letters of Thomas and Jane Welsh Carlyle*, Duke–Edinburgh Edition, ed. C. R. Sanders, K. J. Fielding, Clyde de L. Ryals, Ian Campbell, Aileen Christianson, et al., 28 vols so far (Durham, North Carolina, 1970–), VII, 152–3 (henceforth referred to in the notes as *CL*).

21 TC to JC, 21 May 1834, ibid., VII, 170–3. For the history of Cheyne Row see *The Homes and Haunts of Thomas Carlyle* (London, 1895), p. 118ff; Thea Holme, *The Carlyles at Home* (London, 1965), p. 2ff; and Reginald Blunt, *The Carlyles' Chelsea Home* (London, 1895), p. 1.

22 TC to his mother, Margaret Carlyle, 12 June 1834, and to John Carlyle, 17 June 1834, *CL*, VII, 206, 212.

23 See Algernon Graves, *The Royal Academy of Arts: A Complete Dictionary of Contributors and their Work from its Foundation in 1769 to 1904*, 4 vols (London, 1905), IV, 317; JC to John Sterling, 11 July 1838, *CL*, X, 117–18 and note.

24 See TC to his sister Jean Aitken, 2 March 1851, *CL*, XXVI, 39;

Woolner, *Life in Letters*, p. 65.

25 See JC to TC, 18 and 22 July 1858, *Jane Welsh Carlyle: A New Selection of her Letters*, ed. Trudy Bliss (London, 1950), pp. 276–7; Sir Charles Gavan Duffy, *Conversations with Carlyle* (London, 1892), p. 202.

26 Daniel Maclise exhibited one portrait of Catherine Dickens in 1848 as a pendant to one of Dickens, see Richard Ormond, *Early Victorian Portraits*, 2 vols (London, 1973), I, 140.

27 JC to TC, 30 July 1865, *I Too Am Here*, pp. 65–6.

28 W. M. Thackeray to his mother, 4 August 1848, *Letters and Private Papers*, II, 418.

29 TC, 'National Education' (February 1835), *CL*, VIII, 29–31.

30 TC Journal, March 1835, and TC to John Carlyle, 23 March 1835, ibid., VIII, 80n, 81.

31 JC to Jeannie Welsh, 28 December 1843, ibid., XVII, 220–1.

32 TC to his brother James Carlyle, 21 February 1844, ibid., XVII, 280–1.

33 JC to Jeannie Welsh, 26 February 1844, ibid., XVII, 282.

34 Statistics about marital status were included for the first time in 1851; see Michael Mason, *The Making of Victorian Sexuality* (Oxford, 1994), pp. 237–9.

35 Samuel Butler to Miss Savage, 21 November 1884, *Letters between Samuel Butler and Miss E. M. A. Savage 1871–1885*, ed. Geoffrey Keynes and Brian Hill (London, 1935), pp. 349–50.

36 See David Alec Wilson, *Carlyle to Threescore-and-Ten (1853–65)*, vol. V of Wilson's six-volume

biography of Carlyle (London, 1931), pp. 117–18, 269.

37 Frank Harris, 'Talks with Carlyle', *English Review*, VII (February 1911), 432; see also Philippa Pullar, *Frank Harris* (London, 1975), p. 54. For an overview of the whole controversy see Trev Broughton, 'Froude: The "Painful Appendix" ', *Carlyle Studies Annual*, special issue, XV (1995), 65–79.

CHAPTER I

Strange Meeting 1821

1 See *CL*, III, 420n, where it is explained that Jane Welsh's father was descended not from the John Welsh who married Knox's daughter, but from his brother David.

2 See TC, *Reminiscences*, ed. K. J. Fielding and Ian Campbell (Oxford, 1997), pp. 118, 74; Virginia Surtees, *Jane Welsh Carlyle* (Salisbury, 1986), p. 7.

3 JC, *'The simple Story of my own first Love'*, ed. K. J. Fielding and Ian Campbell with Aileen Christianson (Edinburgh, 2001). The story was first published, with editorial changes and omissions, in *New Letters and Memorials of Jane Welsh Carlyle*, ed. Alexander Carlyle, 2 vols (London, 1903), II, 48ff.

4 Thomas Erskine to JC, 23 July 1855, MS 1774 (NLS).

5 See Mrs Alexander Ireland, *Life of Jane Welsh Carlyle* (London, 1891), pp. 10–11; JC to Helen Welsh, 6 December 1850, *CL*, XXV, 303; Geraldine Jewsbury, memoir of JC, 20 May 1866, printed in *Reminiscences*, p. 42.

6 See Margaret Oliphant, *The Life of Edward Irving*, 2 vols (London, 1862), I, 37–8.

7 Geraldine Jewsbury's memoir of JC in *Reminiscences*, p. 44.

8 JC's footnote to her *'simple Story'*, ed. Fielding et al., pp. 23–4. The note was printed, with changes and omissions, in James Anthony Froude, *Thomas Carlyle: A History of the First Forty Years of his Life 1795–1835*, 2 vols (London, 1882), I, 121–2.

9 See *CL*, I, 3n, 92n.

10 *New Letters and Memorials*, II, 207. Dr Welsh's account book is in the Haddington house, since 1984 a museum dedicated to JC.

11 See *CL*, I, 357n. J. M. Sloan, *The Carlyle Country* (London, 1904), p. 35ff, gives an account of the complications of the secession movement.

12 *Reminiscences*, p. 213.

13 JC to TC, 24 July 1825, *CL*, III, 357.

14 Edward Irving to JC, 6 March 1822, Lawrence and Elisabeth Hanson, *Necessary Evil: The Life of Jane Welsh Carlyle* (London, 1950), p. 47.

15 *Reminiscences*, p. 259.

16 Quoted by David Alec Wilson, *Carlyle till Marriage (1795–1826)*, vol. I of his six-volume biography (London, 1923), p. 171.

17 JC to TC, 21 July 1823, *CL*, II, 403, 404.

18 JC to Helen Welsh, 6 December 1850, ibid., XXV, 303–4.

19 For examples of Irving's flattery of Mrs Welsh, see Froude, I, 161.

20 *Reminiscences*, p. 70.

21 TC to William Graham, 12 June 1821, *CL*, I, 305. For TC's own account of William Graham, see *Reminiscences*, pp. 252–8.

22 TC to Alick Carlyle, 6 June 1821, *CL*, I, 363.

23 See TC's reminiscence of James Carlyle (1832), *Reminiscences*, p. 17ff.

24 Richard Herne Shepherd (ed.), *Memoirs of the Life and Writings of Thomas Carlyle*, 2 vols (London, 1881), I, 7; Moncure Daniel Conway, *Autobiography, Memories, and Experiences*, 2 vols (London, 1904), II, 153.

25 *Reminiscences*, pp. 6, 9, 14, 10–11.

26 *Two Reminiscences of Thomas Carlyle*, ed. John Clubbe (Durham, North Carolina, 1974), p. 27. Althaus's article, 'Thomas Carlyle: Eine biographisch-literarische Characteristik', was published in *Unsere Zeit* in July 1866.

27 See *CL*, I, 139n.

28 Ibid. See also Sloan, *Carlyle Country*, pp. 31–2.

29 Froude, I, 232, 285.

30 Sigmund Freud, *The Interpretation of Dreams* (1900), The Pelican Freud Library, vol. IV (Harmondsworth, 1980), pp. 362–8.

31 For a succinct account of the many biographical works on TC with particular reference to their relation to Froude's biography, see Carlisle Moore's essay on TC in *The English Romantic Poets and Essayists: A Review of Research and Criticism*, ed. C. W. Houtchens and L. H. Houtchens (London, 1966), p. 344ff.

32 *Two Reminiscences*, p. 27.

33 TC to his mother, 4 December 1853, MS 521 (NLS).

34 See *Reminiscences*, p. 13; TC to his mother, 27 July 1836, *CL*, IX, 23 and n.

35 See TC to John Carlyle, 18 May 1834, and to his mother, 30 May 1834, *CL*, VII, 163, 198.

36 Margaret Carlyle to TC, n.d., MS 1763 (NLS).

37 *Two Reminiscences*, p. 30.

38 *Reminiscences*, p. 34.

39 *Two Reminiscences*, p. 28.

40 *Reminiscences*, p. 34.

41 *Sartor Resartus*, Book II, chapter 3 ('Pedagogy').

42 *Two Reminiscences*, p. 32.

43 *Sartor Resartus*, Book II, chapter 3 ('Pedagogy').

44 Coleridge to Robert Southey, 13 September 1803, *The Collected Letters of Samuel Taylor Coleridge*, ed. Earl Leslie Griggs, 6 vols (Oxford, 1956–71), II, 988.

45 TC's reminiscence of Francis Jeffrey (1867), *Reminiscences*, p. 350.

46 TC to John Carlyle, 10 February and 9 March 1821, *CL*, I, 325, 339.

47 See Sloan, *Carlyle Country*, p. 89.

48 TC to JC, 19 May 1824, *CL*, III, 66.

49 See Janet Browne, *Charles Darwin: Voyaging*, vol. I of a projected 2-volume biography (London, 1995), pp. 44–50. For a history of Edinburgh University, see *Four Centuries of Edinburgh University Life 1583–1983*, ed. Gordon Donaldson (Edinburgh, 1983).

50 TC to Thomas Murray, 22 August 1815, and to Robert Mitchell, 11 December 1815, *CL*, I, 60, 65.

51 TC's note on Althaus, *Two Reminiscences*, p. 35.

52 TC's reminiscence of Irving (1866), *Reminiscences*, p. 226. See also TC to Robert Mitchell, 31 March 1817, *CL*, I, 97–8.

53 TC's note on Althaus, *Two Reminiscences*, p. 35.

54 TC's reminiscence of James Carlyle, *Reminiscences*, p. 14.

55 Teufelsdröckh attends a 'Rational University', where religious scepticism is taught, *Sartor Resartus*, Book II, chapter 3 ('Pedagogy').

56 TC to Robert Mitchell, 5 July 1817, *CL*, I, 103, 104.

57 TC to Robert Mitchell, 16 February 1818, ibid., I, 119.

58 TC to Robert Mitchell, 5 July 1817, ibid., I, 103.

59 *Reminiscences*, pp. 212–13.

60 Ibid., pp. 220, 348.

61 Ibid., p. 239.

62 Ibid., p. 240.

63 Margaret Gordon to TC, 4 and 28 June 1820, R. C. Archibald, *Carlyle's First Love: Margaret Gordon Lady Bannerman* (London, 1910), pp. 73, 76; part quoted in Froude, I, 32–3.

64 See TC to Robert Mitchell, 6 November 1818, *CL*, I, 144.

65 TC to Thomas Murray, 19 February 1819, ibid., I, 163. For TC's frequent change of lodgings, see ibid., I, 399n.

66 *Reminiscences*, p. 262.

67 See TC to Robert Mitchell, 27 November 1818, *CL*, I, 148.

68 TC, 'Wotton Reinfred', published in *Last Words of Thomas Carlyle* (London, 1892), p. 31. See also TC's note on Althaus, *Two Reminiscences*, p. 41.

69 See *CL*, I, 229n.

70 TC to Alick Carlyle, 29 March 1819, to Robert Mitchell, 14 July 1819, and to John Fergusson, 25 August and 25 September 1819, ibid., I, 172–3, 190, 193, 196.

71 Ibid., I, 197.

72 TC to John Carlyle, 11

November 1819, ibid., I, 206. For Irving's sympathy with the Glasgow weavers see TC's account in *Reminiscences*, pp. 246-8.

73 TC to Robert Mitchell, 30 December 1819, *CL*, I, 218.

74 TC to Alick Carlyle, 26 January 1820, ibid., I, 222.

75 JC to Eliza Stodart, [early 1820], ibid., I, 219, 220.

76 See ibid., I, 269n.

77 TC's reminiscence of Jeffrey, *Reminiscences*, p. 358. For details of the work TC is reviewing, see Ian Campbell, 'Carlyle, Pictet and Jeffrey Again', *The Bibliotheck*, VII (1974), 1–15.

78 See *CL*, I, 289n; TC to Alick Carlyle, 2 January 1821, ibid., I, 301.

79 TC to Alick Carlyle, 23 December 1820, and to John Carlyle, 25 January 1821, ibid., I, 299, 314.

80 TC to John Fergusson, 22 October 1820, ibid., I, 285.

81 TC to John Carlyle, 9 January 1821, ibid., I, 303.

82 TC to Edward Irving, 3 June 1820, ibid., I, 255.

83 TC to Thomas Murray, 4 August 1820, ibid., I, 268.

CHAPTER 2

Negotiating Romance 1821–1824

1 TC to JC, 4 June 1821, *CL*, I, 359, 360, 361.

2 JC to TC, late June 1821, ibid., I, 366.

3 The editors of *CL* estimate the number of surviving letters TC wrote to JC at nearly a thousand; hers to him were fewer, but number several hundred, see *CL*, I, xxv.

4   TC, 'Wotton Reinfred', *Last Words*, pp. 32–3.

5   TC to JC, 28 June 1821, *CL*, I, 367.

6   JC to TC, 6 July 1821, ibid., I, 368.

7   TC to JC, 16 July 1821, ibid., I, 368, 369.

8   JC to TC, 18 July 1821, ibid., I, 370.

9   JC to Jeannie Welsh, 8 January 1843, ibid., XVI, 12.

10 TC, Journal, 21 September 1825, ibid., III, 382n.

11 TC to Alick Carlyle, 5 December 1820, ibid., I, 290–1.

12 TC to John Carlyle, 19 July 1821, ibid., I, 371.

13 TC to Edward Irving, 14 August 1821, ibid., I, 379, 378.

14 Coleridge to Henry Crabb Robinson, 18 November 1811, *Collected Letters*, III, 347.

15 Coleridge's use of the word comes in a MS of about 1812, published in *Inquiring Spirit: A New Presentation of Coleridge from his Published and Unpublished Prose Writings*, ed. Kathleen Coburn (London, 1951). For Darwin's ill health see Browne, *Charles Darwin*, p. 372ff.

16 TC MS fragment (n.d.), MS 3823 (NLS).

17 TC, Journal, 21 September 1825 and 3 December 1826, *Two Note Books of Thomas Carlyle*, ed. Charles Eliot Norton (New York, 1898), pp. 66, 67.

18 *Sartor Resartus*, Book II, chapter 7 ('The Everlasting No').

19 TC's note to Althaus, *Two Reminiscences*, p. 49.

20 There has been some argument about whether TC's experience occurred in the summer of 1821 or that of 1822. Froude suggested June 1821, a date which TC's nephew Alexander Carlyle disputed. John Clubbe, in a footnote to the Althaus memoir, discusses the probabilities and opts for 1822, wrongly, I think (*Two Reminiscences*, p. 49n). Simon Heffer, in his recent biography, *Moral Desperado: A Life of Thomas Carlyle* (London, 1995), argues for 1821 (p. 57). See also *Thomas and Jane: Selected Letters from the Edinburgh University Collection*, ed. Ian Campbell (Edinburgh, 1980), p. 14.

21 See John Tyndall, 'Personal Recollections of Thomas Carlyle' (1890), in *New Fragments* (New York, 1892), p. 356. Goethe is called 'the Wisest of our time' in *Sartor*, Book II, chapter 9 ('The Everlasting Yea'). For a discussion of TC's relationship with Goethe, see Rosemary Ashton, *The German Idea: Four English Writers and the Reception of German Thought 1800–1860* (Cambridge, 1980, reprinted London, 1994).

22 TC to Goethe, 20 August 1827, *CL*, IV, 248.

23 Henry Crabb Robinson, Diary, 12 February 1832, *Diary, Reminiscences, and Correspondence*, ed. Thomas Sadler, 3 vols (London, 1869), III, 2.

24 TC to Thomas Spedding, 23 November 1851, *CL*, XXVI, 239.

25 TC, Journal, 31 December 1823, *Two Note Books*, pp. 56–7.

26 JC to Elizabeth Welsh, 5 October 1819, *CL*, I, 201.

27 TC's note, ibid., I, 202.

28 Charlotte Williams Wynn to William Brookfield, January

1856, Hansons, *Necessary Evil*, pp. 443–4.

29 Edward Irving to JC, 9 July 1821, and to TC, 24 July 1821, *CL*, I, 370n, 380n.

30 TC's reminiscence of Irving, *Reminiscences*, p. 347.

31 See JC to TC, 7 August 1821, and TC to JC, 27 May 1822, *CL*, I, 375, II, 121.

32 TC to JC, 1 September 1821, ibid., I, 383.

33 See JC to TC, 24 November and 29 December 1821, ibid., I, 400, 420.

34 Edward Irving to JC, 9 February 1822, Oliphant, *Life of Edward Irving*, I, 134, 135.

35 TC to John Fergusson, 11 February 1822, *CL*, II, 35.

36 *Reminiscences*, p. 269.

37 TC to his father, 12 January 1822, *CL*, II, 4.

38 *Reminiscences*, pp. 270, 272. See also TC to his father, 4 December 1822, *CL*, II, 217.

39 *Reminiscences*, pp. 269, 270, 271.

40 Ibid., p. 272.

41 JC to TC, *c.* 17 January 1822, and TC to JC, 30 January 1822, *CL*, II, 21, 20, 27.

42 JC to Eliza Stodart, *c.* 12 February 1822, ibid., II, 38.

43 TC to JC, 13 February 1822, ibid., II, 41.

44 JC to Eliza Stodart, January 1822, ibid., II, 17, 18.

45 JC to TC, 27 April 1822, ibid., II, 91.

46 See ibid., II, 285n.

47 JC to TC, 1 July 1822, ibid., II, 144.

48 TC to JC, 13 July 1822, ibid., II, 148.

49 *Reminiscences*, p. 272; TC to his mother, 23 September 1822, *CL*, II, 165.

50 TC to his mother [? December 1821], *CL*, I, 402.

51 TC to his mother, 4 December 1822, ibid., II, 219. The quotations are from Ezekiel, Jeremiah, and the Gospel of St John.

52 JC to TC, 11 November 1822, ibid., II, 196.

53 TC to JC, 28 July 1823, ibid., II, 409.

54 JC to TC, 23 January and 10 February 1823, ibid., II, 282, 285.

55 TC to JC, 18 February 1823, ibid., II, 289.

56 TC to JC, 31 August 1823, and JC to TC, 19 August 1823, ibid., II, 419, 416.

57 TC to JC, 31 August 1823, ibid., II, 420, 421.

58 JC to TC, 16 September 1823, ibid., II, 427.

59 TC to JC, 18 September 1823, ibid., II, 432, 433.

60 See TC to JC, 26 March 1823, ibid., II, 316.

61 See TC to his mother, 16 April 1823, ibid., II, 337.

62 *Reminiscences*, p. 277.

63 TC to John Carlyle, 17 September 1823, *CL*, II, 428.

64 TC to JC, 13 November 1823, ibid., II, 474.

65 JC to TC, 15 July and 19 August 1823, ibid., II, 397, 416, 417.

66 TC to JC, 10 August 1823, ibid., II, 413.

67 TC to John Carlyle, 2 September 1823, ibid., II, 425–6.

68 Oliphant, *Life of Edward Irving*, I, 158–9, 160.

69 Ibid., I, 169, 171–2, 173.

70 TC to his mother, 28 September 1823, *CL*, II, 441.

71 TC to JC, 6 April 1823, ibid., II, 326.

72 *Reminiscences*, p. 277.

73 TC, *Life of Friedrich Schiller*, ed. Jeffrey L. Sammons (Columbia, South Carolina, 1992), pp. vii–ix, 12. See also Ashton, *The German Idea*, pp. 91–4.

74 TC to John Carlyle, 20 October 1823, *CL*, II, 456.

75 Edward Irving to TC, 11 October 1823, ibid., IX, 385, 386.

76 TC to John Carlyle, 20 October 1823, ibid., II, 456.

77 JC to TC, 14 October 1823, ibid., II, 450.

78 TC to JC, 22 October 1823, ibid., II, 458.

79 Ibid., II, 459–60.

80 JC to TC, 14 October 1823, ibid., II, 450.

81 *Reminiscences*, p. 278.

82 TC, Journal, 14 and 31 December 1823, *Two Note Books*, pp. 54, 56.

83 See TC to JC, 22 December 1823, *CL*, II, 491.

84 See TC to Oliver and Boyd, 10 March 1824, and JC to TC, 29 February 1824, ibid., III, 45, 37.

85 JC to TC, 4 April 1824, ibid., III, 55.

86 TC, Preface to his translation of *Wilhelm Meister's Apprenticeship* (1824).

87 See George Eliot, 'The Morality of *Wilhelm Meister*' (1855) in George Eliot, *Selected Critical Writings*, ed. Rosemary Ashton (Oxford, 1992), pp. 129–32; Henry James, 'Carlyle's Translation of Goethe's *Wilhelm Meister*' (1865) in *Literary Reviews and Essays*, ed. Albert Mordell (New York, 1957), pp. 267–8. See also Ashton, *The German Idea*, pp. 76–91, 166–73.

88 *Reminiscences*, p. 278.

89 Edward Irving to JC, quoted in Froude, I, 190 (no date given, but probably May 1824, see *CL*, III, 69).

90 JC to TC, 20 and 25 May 1824, *CL*, III, 69, 70.

91 TC to his mother, 5 June 1824, ibid., III, 77.

92 JC to TC, 10 June 1824, ibid., III, 79.

CHAPTER 3

A Kind of Engagement 1824–1826

1 TC to his mother, 11 June 1824, *CL*, III, 80, 81.

2 TC to JC, 23 June, to John Carlyle, 24 June, and to Alick Carlyle, 25 June 1824, ibid., III, 84, 89, 93.

3 TC, *Reminiscences*, p. 295.

4 TC to his mother, 6 July 1824, *CL*, III, 104.

5 TC to his mother, 20 July 1824, ibid., III, 111.

6 TC to JC, 23 June 1824, ibid., III, 84.

7 *Reminiscences*, pp. 291–2.

8 TC to John Carlyle, 24 June 1824, *CL*, III, 90.

9 TC to JC, 23 June 1824, ibid., III, 84.

10 Froude, I, 218–19. Froude was widely criticised for publishing *Reminiscences*.

11 *Reminiscences*, pp. 286–7.

12 TC to JC, 23 June 1824, *CL*, III, 84.

13 *Reminiscences*, p. 282.

14 TC to JC, 23 June 1824, *CL*, III, 85.

15 TC to Thomas Murray, 24 August 1824, ibid., III, 139.

16 TC to John Carlyle, 27 September 1824, ibid., III, 161.

17 For Coleridge and German literature, see Ashton, *The German Idea*, pp. 27–66.

18 TC to John Carlyle, 24 June 1824, *CL*, III, 90–1.

19 For an account of Coleridge's career and how his contemporaries saw it, see Rosemary Ashton, *The Life of Samuel Taylor Coleridge: A Critical Biography* (Oxford, 1996).

20 TC to Thomas Murray, 24 August 1824, to John Carlyle, 22 January 1825, and to JC, 15 November 1824, *CL*, III, 139, 261, 199.

21 TC, undated MS fragment, MS 3823 (NLS).

22 See TC to George Boyd, 5 July, and to John Taylor, 29 July 1824, *CL*, III, 101–2, 117–18.

23 See ibid., III, 101n; TC to John Carlyle, 24 June 1824, ibid., III, 92.

24 TC to James Hessey, 6 August 1824, ibid., III, 119.

25 TC to JC, 22 July 1824, ibid., III, 113.

26 TC to his mother, 6 July 1824, ibid., III, 105–6.

27 TC to Alick Carlyle, 11 August 1824, ibid., III, 125.

28 Alick Carlyle to TC, 22 August 1824, ibid., III, 140n.

29 *Reminiscences*, p. 299.

30 TC to JC, 12 August 1824, *CL*, III, 135.

31 JC to TC, 11 August 1824, ibid., III, 128–9.

32 Ibid., III, 132.

33 TC to JC, 12 August 1824, ibid., III, 132, 134.

34 TC to JC, 2 September 1824, ibid., III, 145–6.

35 See TC, reminiscence of JC, *Reminiscences*, p. 161.

36 TC to his father, 4 October 1824, *CL*, III, 168–9.

37 Ibid., III, 166.

38 *Reminiscences*, pp. 284–5.

39 TC to JC, 5 October 1824, *CL*, III, 171.

40 JC to TC, 14 October 1824, ibid., III, 175.

41 Ibid., III, 176.

42 Ibid., III, 177.

43 TC to JC, 28 October 1824, ibid., III, 178–9.

44 Ibid., III, 180.

45 TC to John Carlyle, 7 November 1824, ibid., III, 187–8.

46 Ibid.

47 Ibid., III, 188.

48 TC, undated MS fragment, MS 3823 (NLS).

49 TC to John Carlyle, 7 November 1824, *CL*, III, 186.

50 TC to JC, 28 October 1824, ibid., III, 182–3.

51 JC to TC, 10 November 1824, ibid., III, 189, 191.

52 TC to George Boyd, 1 January 1825, and to Alick Carlyle, 8 January 1825, ibid., IV, 440, III, 242.

53 TC to JC, 9 January 1825, ibid., III, 244.

54 JC to TC, 19 December 1824, ibid., III, 231.

55 JC to TC, 13 January 1825, ibid., III, 249–50.

56 TC to JC, 20 January 1825, ibid., III, 255–7.

57 Ibid., III, 158–9.

58 JC to TC, 29 January 1825, ibid., III, 265–7.

59 Ibid., III, 291n.

60 Ibid., III, 197–8n.

61 Margaret Carlyle to TC, 18 December 1824, Froude, I, 267. Froude has regularised Mrs Carlyle's spelling.

62 TC to Alick Carlyle, 8 January 1825, *CL*, III, 243.

63 *Reminiscences*, p. 319.

64 TC to JC, 23 March 1825, *CL*, III, 308.

65 JC to TC, 3 April 1825, ibid., III, 311.

66 TC to JC, 6 May 1825, ibid., III, 322.

67 JC to TC, 8 May 1825, ibid., III, 322, 324.

68 *Reminiscences*, p. 320.

69 TC's note on Althaus, *Two Reminiscences*, p. 61.

70 TC to Henry Crabb Robinson, 29 April 1825, *CL*, III, 317–18.

71 TC to Goethe, 24 June 1824, ibid., III, 87.

72 TC to John Carlyle, 18 December, and to JC, 20 December 1824, ibid., III, 226, 235.

73 TC to his mother, 31 Janaury 1825, ibid., III, 273.

74 *Reminiscences*, p. 320.

75 Ibid., pp. 320–1.

76 See *CL*, III, 335n.

77 JC to TC, 19 July 1825, ibid., III, 355 and n.

78 JC to TC, 24 July, and TC to JC, 29 July 1825, ibid., III, 356–7, 361.

79 TC to JC, 24 June 1825, ibid., III, 339.

80 Ibid., III, 381n.

81 TC, note written in 1868, ibid., III, 378.

82 See TC, Journal, 21 September 1825, *Two Note Books*, pp. 65–6.

83 TC to his father, 4 October 1824, and to JC, 19 October 1825, *CL*, III, 167, 390.

84 TC to JC, 19 October 1825, ibid., III, 391.

85 See Negley Harte and John North, *The World of UCL 1828–1990* (London, 1991), pp. 9–10.

86 TC to JC, 19 October 1825, *CL*, III, 391.

87 JC to TC, 18 December 1825, ibid., III, 438.

88 JC to TC, 16 March, and TC to JC, 2 April 1826, ibid., IV, 60, 69–70.

89 See JC to TC, 10 April 1826, ibid., IV, 71.

90 Grace Welsh to TC, 10 April 1826, ibid., IV, 72–3.

91 JC to TC, 23 May 1826, ibid., IV, 97.

92 *Reminiscences*, p. 320.

93 See JC to TC, 31 August 1826, *CL*, IV, 128.

94 TC to JC, 19 September 1826, ibid., IV, 132.

95 JC to TC, 23 September 1826, ibid., IV, 135, 136.

96 TC's note, October 1866, ibid., IV, 143–4.

97 David Masson, article in *Macmillan's Magazine* (December 1881), quoted in Mrs Ireland, *Life of Jane Welsh Carlyle*, pp. 106–7.

98 JC to Mrs George Welsh, 1 October 1826, *CL*, IV, 140–1.

CHAPTER 4
Edinburgh 1826–1828

1 TC to his mother, 19 October 1826, *CL*, IV, 152–3.

2 TC to his mother, 16 November 1826, ibid., IV, 156–7.

3 Ibid., IV, 159.

4 John Carlyle to his mother, 9 December 1826, ibid., IV, 167.

5 JC to Jean Carlyle, 3 February 1827, ibid., IV, 186.

6 TC to his mother, 9 December 1826, ibid., IV, 165.

7 Anna Montagu to JC, 20 October and 8 December 1826, ibid., IV, 168n.

8 See TC to N. H. Julius, 4 December, to his mother, 9 December 1826, and to JC, 21 January 1826, ibid., IV, 161–2,

166, 23–4. For a detailed account of the crash, and Scott's part in it, see John Sutherland, *The Life of Walter Scott: A Critical Biography* (Oxford, 1995), pp. 284–98.

9   TC to Alick Carlyle, 3 February 1827, *CL*, IV, 184 and n. See also IV, 200.

10 See TC to Hunt and Clarke, 16 March, and to Alick Carlyle, 29 March 1827, ibid., IV, 193, 197–8.

11 TC to Alick Carlyle, 3 February 1827, ibid., IV, 185.

12 TC, *Reminiscences*, p. 353.

13 Ibid., p. 355.

14 Ibid., pp. 360, 362.

15 *Edinburgh Review* (August 1825).

16 TC to James Johnston, 26 October 1825, *CL*, III, 400.

17 TC's annotation on his copy of John Sterling, *Essays and Tales, Collected and Edited with a Memoir of his Life by J. C. Hare*, 2 vols (London, 1848), I, ix (Houghton Library Collection of TC's Books, Harvard University).

18 TC to his mother, 17 February 1827, *CL*, IV, 190.

19 TC to Anna Montagu, 7 May 1827, ibid., IV, 222.

20 See TC to Alick Carlyle, 3 June 1827, ibid., IV, 226.

21 TC to John Carlyle, 4 June 1827, ibid., IV, 228.

22 See TC's notes to Althaus, *Two Reminiscences*, p. 58.

23 TC, 'Jean Paul Friedrich Richter', *Edinburgh Review* (July 1827).

24 TC's notes to Althaus, *Two Reminiscences*, p. 59.

25 TC's reminiscence of Francis Jeffrey, *Reminiscences*, p. 360.

26 TC, 'Jean Paul Friedrich Richter'.

27 Francis Jeffrey to TC, undated but *c.* June–July 1827, David Alec Wilson, *Carlyle to 'The French Revolution' (1826–37)*, vol. II of his six-volume biography (London, 1924), p. 28.

28 See Carlyle's notebook for 1827, *Two Note Books* (London, 1924), pp. 103, 113; Ashton, *The German Idea*, pp. 91–9.

29 TC, 'The State of German Literature', *Edinburgh Review* (October 1827).

30 TC to his mother, 20 October 1827, *CL*, IV, 263.

31 TC's reminiscence of 'Christopher North' (1868), *Reminiscences*, pp. 414–15.

32 'Jane Welsh Carlyle' and 'Christopher North', ibid., pp. 73, 414.

33 The letters of TC and JC to Jeffrey have disappeared; his to them are in NLS (see *CL*, I, xxvi).

34 TC's reminiscence of Jeffrey, *Reminiscences*, pp. 360–1.

35 See TC to Alick Carlyle, 3 February 1827, *CL*, IV, 185; *Reminiscences*, pp. 73–4.

36 TC to Alick Carlyle, 29 March 1827, *CL*, IV, 198, 199, 200.

37 TC to JC, 14 April, and JC to TC, 16 April 1827, ibid., IV, 203–6, 213.

38 TC to Grace Welsh and JC, 19 April 1827, ibid., IV, 216–17, 218.

39 JC to Anna Montagu, 7 May 1827, ibid., IV, 220–1. The Carlyles spelt Craigenputtoch inconsistently, sometimes with a final 'h' and sometimes with a 'k'.

40 TC to Henry Crabb Robinson, 14 May 1827, ibid., IV, 225.

41 JC to Anna Montagu, 2

September 1827, ibid., IV,
250–1.

42 See TC to Alick Carlyle, 11
September 1827, ibid., IV, 256.

43 TC to John Carlyle, 5
September, and Edward Irving to
TC, 27 August 1827, ibid., IV,
253, 250n.

44 See JC to John Carlyle, 13
September 1827, ibid., IV, 259.

45 Francis Jeffrey to TC, 6
September 1827, Wilson, II,
30–1.

46 JC to John Carlyle, 13
September 1827, *CL*, IV, 259.
For Goethe's letter of 17 May
1827 see *Correspondence between
Goethe and Carlyle*, ed. Charles
Eliot Norton (London, 1887),
pp. 11–12, 13n.

47 JC to John Carlyle, 13
September 1827, *CL*, IV, 259.

48 TC to Alick Carlyle, 23 October
1827, ibid., IV, 265.

49 Ibid., IV, 266 and n; TC to John
Carlyle, 29 November 1827,
ibid., IV, 291–2.

50 TC to Anna Montagu, 20
November 1827, ibid., IV, 281.

51 See TC to John Carlyle, 5
September 1827, ibid., IV, 253
and n.

52 TC to John Carlyle, 25 October
1827, ibid., IV, 270, 272.

53 John Carlyle to TC, 3
November 1827, ibid., IV, 279n.

54 John Carlyle to TC, 6 February
1828, ibid., IV, 333–4n.

55 TC to John Carlyle, 7 March
1828, ibid., IV, 333–4.

56 *Two Note Books*, p. 102.

57 See Kant's Introduction to his
Critique of Pure Reason (*Kritik der
reinen Vernunft*), 2nd edition
(1787).

58 TC's reminiscence of Sir William
Hamilton (1868), *Reminiscences*,

p. 432.

59 TC to John Carlyle, 7 March
1828, *CL*, IV, 335–6.

60 TC to John Carlyle, 29
November 1827, ibid., IV, 290.

61 TC to Anna Montagu, 20
November 1827, ibid., IV, 283.

62 TC to John Carlyle, 29
November 1827, ibid., IV, 291.

63 TC to John Carlyle, 12 March
1828, ibid., IV, 342.

64 *Reminiscences*, p. 303.

65 Goethe to TC, 1 January 1828,
*Correspondence between Goethe and
Carlyle*, pp. 38, 43.

66 Goethe to TC, 20 July 1827,
ibid., pp. 17–18, 25–6. See also
CL, IV, 211n.

67 See *CL*, IV, 211–12n.

68 TC to Goethe, 20 August 1827,
ibid., IV, 247.

69 TC to Walter Scott, 13 April
1828, ibid., IV, 352–4.

70 TC to Walter Scott, 23 May
1828, ibid., IV, 375.

71 Ibid., IV, 375n.

72 TC to Goethe, 18 April 1828,
ibid., IV, 364.

73 TC to Goethe, 17 January 1828,
ibid., IV, 301.

74 Goethe's testimonial for TC, 14
March 1828, *Correspondence
between Goethe and Carlyle*, pp.
71–80.

75 See TC to Bryan W. Procter, 17
January 1828, *CL*, IV, 304.

76 TC to his mother, 26 January
1828, ibid., IV, 310.

77 See TC to Alick Carlyle, 29
January 1828, ibid., IV, 314.

78 Francis Jeffrey to TC, 24
December 1827, Wilson, II,
42.

79 TC to John Carlyle, 7 March
1828, *CL*, IV, 337.

80 TC to John Carlyle, 12 March
1828, ibid., IV, 340.

81 TC to John Carlyle, 16 April
    1828, ibid., IV, 359.
82 See TC to his mother, 20 April
    1828, ibid., IV, 369.
83 TC to John Carlyle, 4 June 1827,
    ibid., IV, 229.
84 Edward Irving to TC, 31 May
    1827, MS 3823 (NLS).
85 Francis Jeffrey to TC, 24
    December 1827, Wilson, II, 42.
86 TC's reminiscence of JC,
    Reminiscences, p. 77.

CHAPTER 5
Craigenputtoch 1828–1831

1   TC to John Carlyle, 25 August
    1828, *CL*, IV, 401.
2   TC to John Carlyle, 21 August
    1830, ibid., V, 144.
3   TC's notes on Althaus, *Two
    Reminiscences*, pp. 65–6.
4   Ibid., p. 66n.
5   TC to his mother, 11 September
    1828, *CL*, IV, 401, 402.
6   TC to John Carlyle, 5 March
    1829, ibid., V, 9, 10.
7   TC to his mother, 18 December
    1829, ibid., V, 42 and n.
8   John Carlyle to TC, 7 October
    1823, ibid., II, 453n.
9   TC to John Carlyle, 19 March
    1830, ibid., V, 79.
10 TC to John Carlyle, 6 August
    1830, ibid., V, 128–9.
11 JC to Eliza Stodart, 28 July 1828,
    ibid., IV, 385.
12 JC to TC, 19 August 1828, ibid.,
    IV, 393.
13 JC to Eliza Stodart, 21
    November 1828, ibid., IV, 418.
14 JC to Eliza Stodart, 22 December
    1828, ibid., IV, 435, 436.
15 JC to Eliza Stodart, 5 February
    1830, ibid., V, 70.
16 *The Autobiography of Mary Smith,
    Schoolmistress and Nonconformist. A*

*Fragment of a Life, with Letters from
Jane Welsh Carlyle and Thomas
Carlyle* (London, 1892), p. 307.
17 JC to Mary Smith, 11 January
    1857, ibid., pp. 309–11; reprinted
    in *Jane Welsh Carlyle: A New
    Selection of her Letters*, pp. 256–7.
18 Frederic Harrison, review of
    Froude's *Life of Carlyle*, reprinted
    in *The Choice of Books and Other
    Literary Pieces* (London, 1886),
    pp. 178–9.
19 Geraldine Jewsbury to J. A.
    Froude, 22 November 1876, MS
    copy (with ellipses) by Sara
    Norton, daughter of TC's
    American editor Charles Eliot
    Norton, bMS Am 1088, Norton
    Collection (Houghton).
20 Geraldine Jewsbury, 'In
    Memoriam J. W. C.' (20 May
    1866), TC, *Reminiscences*, pp.
    56–7.
21 TC, reminiscence of JC (1866),
    ibid., pp. 76, 77, 78.
22 Ellen Twisleton to Mary
    Parkman, 23 November 1855,
    Parkman Family Papers, MS
    *45M–98 (Houghton).
23 Ellen Twisleton, MS notebook
    [November 1855], bMS Am
    1408 (376) (Houghton);
    published by K. J. Fielding, 'The
    Cry from Craigenputtoch', *Times
    Literary Supplement* (13 August
    1999), p. 13.
24 Ibid., pp. 13–14.
25 Ibid., p. 14.
26 JC to Jean Carlyle, 11 September
    1827, *CL*, IV, 258.
27 Ellen Twisleton, MS notebook,
    p. 14.
28 See TC to John Carlyle, 1
    October 1833, *CL*, VII, 8.
29 TC's reminiscence of JC,
    Reminiscences, p. 76
30 TC to John Carlyle, 21 August

1830, *CL*, V, 141–2.

31 TC, Journal, early 1829, *Two Note Books*, pp. 138, 139–40.

32 Ibid., pp. 141, 154–5; TC to John Carlyle, 27 October 1829 and 10 April 1830, *CL*, V, 23 and n, 91.

33 TC to Goethe, 25 September 1828; TC to Goethe's secretary, Johann Peter Eckermann, 9 December 1828, *CL*, IV, 404, 407–8, 426–7.

34 TC to John Carlyle, 27 October 1829, ibid., V, 24.

35 JC to Margaret Carlyle, 15 December 1829, ibid., V, 39.

36 TC to Goethe, 3 November 1829, ibid., V, 29.

37 TC to Goethe, 31 August 1830, ibid., V, 152, 153 and n. See also TC to John Carlyle, 25 October 1827, ibid., IV, 271 and n.

38 TC to Goethe, 31 August 1830, ibid., V, 153–4.

39 Ibid., V, 44 and n; TC to David Aitken, 26 January 1830, to John Carlyle, 10 April 1830, and to William Tait, 24 July 1830, ibid., V, 59 and n, 92 and n, 125.

40 TC to William Tait, 23 August 1830, ibid., V, 147. See *Carlyle's Unfinished History of German Literature*, ed. Hill Shine (Lexington, Kentucky, 1951), for the portion TC completed.

41 TC, Journal, February 1831, *Two Note Books*, p. 183.

42 Francis Jeffrey to TC, 9 March 1830, Wilson, II, 138–9.

43 TC to John Carlyle, 19 March 1830, *CL*, V, 81.

44 TC, Journal, April 1830, *Two Note Books*, pp. 155–6.

45 Jeffrey to TC, 22 May 1830, Wilson, II, 153; TC to John Carlyle, 17 October 1832, *CL*, VI, 246.

46 TC's reminiscence of Jeffrey, *Reminiscences*, p. 371.

47 See John Carlyle to TC, 9 September 1830, *CL*, V, 163n.

48 TC, reminiscence of Jeffrey, *Reminiscences*, p. 369.

49 Jeffrey to TC, 16 September and 3 October 1828, Wilson, II, 65, 66.

50 Jeffrey to TC, 22 October 1828, ibid., II, 73.

51 TC to John Carlyle, 13 January 1829, *CL*, V, 6.

52 TC to John Carlyle, 7 July 1831, to John Stuart Mill, 12 January 1833, to his mother, 27 January 1833, and to JC, 21 May 1834, ibid., V, 297, VI, 301, 311, VII, 177.

53 See *CL*, V, 203n.

54 Macvey Napier to TC, 18 June 1832, MS in Charles Sumner Collection of Autographs, fMS Am 1301.2 (Houghton).

55 TC, 'Voltaire', *Foreign Review* (April 1829).

56 TC, 'Signs of the Times', *Edinburgh Review* (June 1829).

57 TC to Henry Inglis, 31 March 1829, *CL*, V, 15.

58 TC to Gustave d'Eichthal, 9 August 1830, ibid., V, 134–6.

59 TC to John Carlyle, 19 March 1830, ibid., V, 81.

60 Thomas Chalmers to his wife, 7 May 1827, Oliphant, *Life of Edward Irving*, I, 403.

61 Ibid., II, 5ff.

62 TC to John Carlyle, 25 August 1828, *CL*, IV, 400 and n.

63 TC to Anna Montagu, 13 November 1829, ibid., V, 34.

64 Oliphant, *Life of Edward Irving*, II, 88.

65 Edward Irving, dedication to *Daniel's Vision of the Four Beasts and of the Son of Man opened, and*

applied to our Present Crisis in Church and State (1829), quoted in Oliphant, *Life of Edward Irving*, II, 90. For Irving's dedications to Montagu and Coleridge, see ibid., I, 186, 204.

66 William Hazlitt, 'Rev. Mr Irving', *The Spirit of the Age* (1825).

67 Froude, I, 162.

68 TC, Journal, 30 June 1830, *Two Note Books*, p. 157.

69 TC to John Carlyle, 18 September 1830, to his mother, 10 October 1830, to John Carlyle, 19 December 1830 and 4 March 1831, *CL*, V, 165, 170, 199, 242. For Mary's 'stupid' husband, see *Reminiscences*, p. 263.

70 TC, reminiscence of JC, *Reminiscences*, p. 86.

71 JC to Eliza Stodart, late December 1830, *CL*, V, 207.

72 Geraldine Jewsbury, memoir of JC, *Reminiscences*, p. 56.

73 JC to Eliza Stodart, 16 January 1831, *CL*, V, 209.

74 TC to John Carlyle, 6 June 1831, ibid., V, 283.

75 TC, Journal, October 1830, *Two Note Books*, pp. 176, 177.

76 See Wilson, II, 183.

77 TC to John Carlyle, 21 January 1831, *CL*, V, 215.

78 John Carlyle to TC, 12 February 1831, ibid., V, 233n.

79 TC to John Carlyle, 4 March 1831, ibid., V, 243.

80 Ibid., V, 243–4.

81 Ibid., V, 244.

82 TC to John Carlyle, 17 July 1831, ibid., V, 305.

83 Jeffrey to TC, early August 1830, Hansons, *Necessary Evil*, p. 140. Wilson quotes the letter, omitting 'Blasted', II, 161.

84 Jeffrey to TC, 18 December 1830, Wilson, II, 188.

85 TC to John Carlyle, 21 January 1831, *CL*, V, 216 and n.

86 Ibid., V, 212–13.

87 Jeffrey to TC, July 1831, Wilson, II, 212.

CHAPTER 6

Closing the First Act 1831–1834

1 See TC to John Carlyle, 12 July 1831, *CL*, V, 303.

2 TC, 'Jean Paul Frederick Richter', *Foreign Review* (January 1830); *CL*, III, 16n. See also *OED*.

3 *Sartor Resartus*, Book I, chapter 9 ('Adamitism'); TC, Journal, August 1830, *Two Note Books*, p. 163.

4 TC to JC, 11 August 1831, *CL*, V, 318; TC, Journal, 11 August 1831, *Two Note Books*, p. 194.

5 TC to JC, 17 August 1831, *CL*, V, 341.

6 TC to JC, 22 August 1831, ibid., V, 353.

7 Ibid.

8 TC to JC, 24 August 1831, ibid., V, 362; see also TC to JC, 22 August 1831, ibid., V, 355.

9 TC to JC, 31 August and 4 September 1831, ibid., V, 381, 399.

10 Ibid., V, 399.

11 TC to JC, 8 September 1831; John Murray to TC, 17 September 1831, ibid., V, 404, 441n.

12 TC to JC, 19 September 1831, ibid., V, 440.

13 TC to JC, 23 September 1831, ibid., V, 444.

14. See John Carlyle to TC, 7 July, TC to Alick Carlyle, 18 August, and TC to JC, 24 August 1831,

ibid., V, 302n, 343, 364.

15 JC to TC, 18 August 1831, ibid., V, 345-6.

16 JC to TC, 1 September 1831, ibid., V, 392–3.

17 JC to TC, 6–9 August and 11–14 August 1831, ibid., V, 313, 320.

18 JC to TC, 6-9 August 1831, ibid., V, 313.

19 TC to Alick Carlyle, 15 October 1831, ibid., VI, 18.

20 JC to TC, 11-14 August 1831, ibid., V, 324-5.

21 JC to TC, 24 August 1831, ibid., V, 360.

22 JC to TC, 18 August 1831, ibid., V, 344, 345.

23 TC to JC, 31 August 1831, ibid., V, 382.

24 JC to TC, 1 September 1831, ibid., V, 393.

25 TC to JC, 14 September 1831, ibid., V, 433.

26 For the details of the family tradition about baby clothes, and its part in the controversy, see ibid., V, 433n.

27. JC to TC, 11–14 August 1831, ibid., V, 324.

28 Ibid., V, 123n.

29 TC to JC, 22 August 1831, ibid., V, 357.

30 JC to TC, 11 September 1831, ibid., V, 423.

31 JC to TC, 27 September 1831, ibid., V, 447.

32 TC, *Reminiscences*, p. 83.

33 Anna Montagu to JC, 30 September 1831, *CL*, VI, 8n.

34 TC to JC, 11 and 29 August 1831, ibid., V, 319, 377.

35 JC to Jean Carlyle, 23? January 1832, ibid., VI, 100.

36 Francis Jeffrey to JC, 17 and 21 November 1831, Wilson, II, 257, 258.

37 TC to JC, 22 August 1831, *CL*,

V, 351.

38 TC to his mother, 20 October 1831, ibid., VI, 24–5 and n.

39 TC to John Carlyle, 13 November 1831, ibid., VI, 51.

40 TC to JC, 22 August 1831, ibid., V, 350.

41 TC to John Carlyle, 13–14 November 1831, ibid., VI, 50–1.

42 *Reminiscences*, pp. 84–5.

43 TC to JC, 17 August 1831, *CL*, V, 337–8.

44 Ibid., V, 338.

45 TC to JC, 4 September 1831, ibid., V, 396–7.

46 TC, reminiscence of Jeffrey (1867), *Reminiscences*, pp. 375–6.

47 TC to JC, 4 September 1831, *CL*, V, 397–8.

48 John Stuart Mill, *Autobiography* (1873), ed. John M. Robson (Harmondsworth, 1989), pp. 27–36, 112 (chapters 1, 'Childhood, and Early Education', and 5, 'A Crisis in My Mental History').

49 Ibid., p. 130.

50 TC to JC, 4 September 1831, *CL*, V, 398.

51 TC to John Stuart Mill, 5 October 1831; JC to Helen Welsh, 26 October 1831, ibid., VI, 5, 36.

52 Mill to John Sterling, 20-22 October 1831, *The Earlier Letters of John Stuart Mill, Collected Works of John Stuart Mill*, ed. Francis E. Mineka et al., 33 vols (London, 1963–91), XII, 85.

53 TC to his mother, 10 November, and to John Carlyle, 13–14 November 1831, *CL*, VI, 37, 52.

54 TC to Alick Carlyle, 4 December 1831, ibid., VI, 61.

55 TC, 'Characteristics', *Edinburgh Review* (December 1831).

56 Robert Louis Stevenson to Alexander Ireland, 25 February 1882, *The Letters of Robert Louis Stevenson*, ed. Bradford A. Booth and Ernest Mehew, 8 vols (New Haven, Conn., 1994–5), III, 288–9.

57 TC, Journal, October 1831, *Two Note Books*, p. 213.

58 TC, Journal, 13 January 1832, ibid., p. 231.

59 Thomas Babington Macaulay to Macvey Napier, 1 February 1832, *The Letters of Thomas Babington Macaulay*, ed. Thomas Pinney, 6 vols (Cambridge, 1974–81), II, 113.

60 Francis Jeffrey to Macvey Napier, 7 February 1832, Wilson, II, 264–5.

61 TC to Leigh Hunt, 8 and 20 February 1832, *CL*, VI, 117–18 and n, 135–6; TC, Journal, *c.* 17 March 1832, *Two Note Books*, p. 257.

62 Henry Hart Milman to John Murray, 4 October 1831, see Thomas C. Richardson, 'John Murray's Reader and the Rejection of *Sartor Resartus*', *Carlyle Newsletter*, VI (Spring 1985), 39. For Murray's refusal to TC, see *CL*, VI, 6n.

63 TC to John Carlyle, 20 December 1831 and 10 January 1832, *CL*, VI, 70, 87.

64 TC to John Carlyle, 16 February 1832, ibid., VI, 125.

65 TC, Journal, 13 January 1832, *Two Note Books*, pp. 231, 232, 233.

66 Ibid., pp. 231–2.

67 TC to John Carlyle, 10 January 1832, *CL*, VI, 89.

68 TC, Journal, 21 January 1832, *Two Note Books*, pp. 250, 251.

69 TC, Journal, 13 January 1832,

ibid., p. 232.

70 TC to John Carlyle, 16 February 1832, *CL*, VI, 125.

71 JC to Mary Welsh, 27 December 1831, ibid., VI, 81.

72 JC to Jean Carlyle, 23? January 1832, ibid., VI, 100.

73 TC to his mother, 10 November 1831, ibid., VI, 40.

74 JC to Margaret Carlyle, November 1831, ibid., VI, 44.

75 James Carlyle to TC, 21 September 1831, ibid., VI, 11n.

76 TC to his mother, 24 January 1832, ibid., VI, 105.

77 TC, reminiscence of JC, *Reminiscences*, p. 84.

78 TC, reminiscence of James Carlyle, ibid., p. 7.

79 Ibid., p. 37.

80 TC, Journal, 13 January 1832, *Two Note Books*, p. 230.

81 TC, 'Biography', *Fraser's Magazine* (April 1832); for 'environment', see *OED*.

82 TC, 'Boswell's Life of Johnson', *Fraser's Magazine* (May 1832).

83 TC's note on Althaus, *Two Reminiscences*, p. 74; TC, Journal, March 1832, *Two Note Books*, p. 255.

84 TC to Alick Carlyle, 7 April 1832, *CL*, VI, 143.

85 Abraham Hayward to TC, 6 April 1832, Wilson, II, 284; for Hayward's translation of *Faust*, published in 1833, see *CL*, VI, 378n.

86 TC to John Carlyle, 31 July 1832, *CL*, VI, 193.

87 TC, 'Death of Goethe', *New Monthly Magazine* (June 1832).

88 TC, Journal, May 1832, *Two Note Books*, pp. 268–9.

89 TC to John Stuart Mill, 18 May 1832, *CL*, VI, 154.

90 TC, Journal, 16 May 1832, *Two Note Books*, pp. 274–5.
91 TC to John Carlyle, 31 July 1832, *CL*, VI, 196.
92 Mill to TC, 17 July 1832, *Earlier Letters, Collected Works*, XII, 113.
93 Mill, *Autobiography*, p. 139 (chapter 5, 'A Crisis in My Mental History').
94 JC to Eliza Miles, 16 June 1832, *CL*, VI, 172.
95 TC to John Carlyle, 2 July 1832, ibid., VI, 182–3.
96 See Froude, II, 291–2, where the poem is attributed to Jane. Alexander Carlyle, *The Love Letters of Thomas Carlyle and Jane Welsh*, 2 vols (London, 1909), II, 359–60n, attributes it to TC. The poem is reproduced, with editorial commentary, in *The Collected Poems of Thomas and Jane Welsh Carlyle*, ed. Rodger L. Tarr and Fleming McClelland (Greenwood, Florida, 1986), pp. 56–7.
97 TC to his mother, 3 December 1833; JC to John Carlyle, 25 February 1834, *CL*, VII, 49, 109.
98 TC, 'Goethe's Works', *Foreign Quarterly Review* (August 1832).
99 TC to John Carlyle, 31 August 1832, *CL*, VI, 216 and n.
100 JC to Margaret Carlyle, 18? September 1832, ibid., VI, 230.
101 JC to Eliza Stodart, 10 October 1832, ibid., VI, 235.
102 JC to Eliza Stodart, 4 December 1832, ibid., VI, 279.
103 TC to John Carlyle, 8–9 January 1833, ibid., VI, 291, 292.
104 TC to Mill, 12 January 1833, ibid., VI, 300, 301.
105 TC, Journal, 1 February 1833, ibid., VI, 327n; TC to John Carlyle, 10 February 1833, ibid., VI, 322.
106 TC to John Carlyle, 17 May 1833, ibid., VI, 387.
107 Ibid., VI, 388.
108 TC to John Carlyle, 2 December 1832, and John Carlyle to TC, 31 August 1832, ibid., VI, 268 and n.
109 TC to John Carlyle, 17 May 1833, ibid., VI, 388.
110 TC to Mill, 18 July 1833, ibid., VI, 414.
111 TC, Journal, 13 February 1833, ibid., VI, 327n.
112 JC to Eliza Miles, 15 July 1833, ibid., VI, 410, 411.
113 JC to Eliza Stodart, 28 July 1833, ibid., VI, 421.
114 Ralph Waldo Emerson, *English Traits* (1856, reprinted London, 1889), pp. 1–2 (chapter 1, 'First Visit to England').
115 Emerson, Journal, 11 and 13 May, 14 July, 14 September, 1, 27, and 28 October 1832, *The Journals and Miscellaneous Notebooks of Ralph Waldo Emerson*, ed. William H. Gilman et al., 16 vols (Cambridge, Mass., 1960–82), IV, 15, 18, 28, 40, 45, 52, 54–5.
116 Mrs Ireland, *Life of Jane Welsh Carlyle*, pp. 137–8.
117 TC to John Carlyle, 27 August, to his mother, 27 August, and to Mill, 10 September 1833, *CL*, VI, 425, 430, 438.
118 JC to Henry Inglis, 23 November 1833, ibid., VII, 44.
119 Emerson to Alexander Ireland, 30 August 1833, ibid., VII, 262–3n.
120 Emerson, Journal, 26 August 1833, *Journals and Miscellaneous Notebooks*, IV, 219–20.
121 Emerson, *English Traits*, pp. 11, 12.
122 Ibid., p. 13; see also Emerson,

Journal, 26 August 1833, *Journals and Miscellaneous Notebooks*, IV, 221.

123 Emerson, Journal, 28 August 1833, *Journals and Miscellaneous Notebooks*, IV, 223.

124 Francis Jeffrey to TC, 14 January 1834, MS 787 (NLS); part-published in Wilson, II, 353, and *CL*, VII, 84n.

125 TC to John Carlyle, 21 January 1834, *CL*, VII, 79.

126 'Thomas Carlyle', *Fraser's Magazine* (June 1833).

127 *Sartor Resartus*, Book I, chapter 10 ('Pure Reason').

128 Ibid., Book II, chapters 9 ('The Everlasting Yea') and 7 ('The Everlasting No'); Book III, chapter 8 ('Natural Supernaturalism').

129 Ibid., Book III, chapter 1 ('Incident in Modern History').

130 [Edward Lytton Bulwer], *Pelham; or, the Adventures of a Gentleman*, 2nd edition, 3 vols (1828), I, 69.

131 *Sartor Resartus*, Book III, chapter 10 ('The Dandiacal Body').

132 TC to James Fraser, 27 May 1833, *CL*, VI, 396.

133 TC to Macvey Napier, 20 January 1831, ibid., V, 211 and n.

134 Tennyson to Richard Monckton Milnes, 8 or 9 January 1837, *The Letters of Alfred Lord Tennyson*, ed. Cecil Y. Lang and Edgar F. Shannon, Jr., 3 vols (Oxford, 1982–90), I, 147–8.

135 Espinasse, *Literary Recollections and Sketches*, p. 57; Oscar Wilde to the Home Secretary, 2 July 1896, *The Complete Letters of Oscar Wilde*, ed. Merlin Holland and Rupert Hart-Davis (London, 2000), p. 660. For a comprehensive account of the composition, publication, and influence of *Sartor Resartus*, see Rodger L. Tarr and Mark Engel (eds), *Sartor Resartus* (Berkeley, California, 2000), in the ongoing Norman and Charlotte Strouse Edition of Carlyle's Works.

136 TC to John Carlyle, 18 November, and Jean Carlyle to TC, 22 October 1833, *CL*, VII, 38, 37n.

137 John Carlyle to Margaret Carlyle, 13 February 1834, ibid., VII, 100n.

138 TC and JC to John Carlyle, 25 February 1834, ibid., VII, 103, 108.

139 Ibid., VII, 104.

140 TC to Leigh Hunt, 1 May 1834, ibid., VII, 140.

141 TC, Journal, [14] May 1834, Froude, II, 425. (Froude misdates the entry.)

CHAPTER 7
Preparing to Astonish the World 1834–1835

1 TC to JC, 17 May 1834, *CL*, VII, 149, 150–1.

2 Ibid., VII, 153 and n.

3 TC, Journal, 14 May 1834, Froude, II, 426.

4 TC to Jean Aitken, 6 July 1834, *CL*, VII, 231.

5 TC to JC, 21 May 1834, ibid., VII, 176–7.

6 TC, Journal, 26 July 1834, Froude, II, 444.

7 TC to JC, 21 May 1834, *CL*, VII, 174.

8 TC, conversation with C. E. Norton in 1873, *Letters of Charles Eliot Norton*, ed. Sara Norton and M. A. De Wolfe Howe, 2 vols (London, 1913), I, 497.

9 See Michael St John Packe, *The*

Life of John Stuart Mill (London, 1954), p. 110ff.

10 Ibid., p. 153.

11 TC, conversation with C. E. Norton, 9 May 1873, *Letters of Charles Eliot Norton*, I, 499–500. Buller's name is left blank in the published version, but appears in the manuscript of this conversation, bMS Am 1088.5 (Houghton).

12 TC to John Carlyle, 22 July 1834, *CL*, VII, 245–6.

13 John Welsh to Grace Welsh, quoted in JC to TC, 22 May 1834, ibid., VII, 188.

14 JC to TC, 22 May 1834, ibid., VII, 186.

15 JC to TC, 26 May 1834, ibid., VII, 193.

16 TC's later note on a letter from Grace Welsh to Margaret Carlyle, 3 November 1834, ibid., VII, 332.

17 JC to Eliza Stodart, c. August 1834, ibid., VII, 250–1.

18 Ibid., VII, 251–2, 252–3.

19 TC to his mother, 12 June 1834, ibid., VII, 209.

20 TC to John Carlyle, 17 June 1834, ibid., VII, 216–17.

21 TC to his mother, 21 August 1832, and Journal, 21 August 1832, ibid., VI, 205, 206n.

22 Mill to W. J. Fox, 14 July 1834, *Earlier Letters, Collected Works*, XII, 228–9 and n.

23 TC to John Carlyle, 15 August 1834, *CL*, VII, 269–70.

24 Ibid., VII, 270.

25 TC to John Carlyle, 28 October 1834, ibid., VII, 327.

26 Lotte and Joseph Hamburger, *Contemplating Adultery: The Secret Life of a Victorian Woman* (New York, 1991), pp. 189, 214, 252.

27 Sarah Austin to Anna Jameson, 26–28 September 1835, Lotte and Joseph Hamburger, *Troubled Lives: John and Sarah Austin* (London, 1985), p. 129.

28 Leigh Hunt to TC, 28 May 1833, Charles Richard Sanders, *Carlyle's Friendships and Other Studies* (Durham, North Carolina, 1977), p. 112.

29 TC to John Carlyle, 28 October 1834, *CL*, VII, 327.

30 JC to Margaret Carlyle, 1 September 1834, ibid., VII, 287–8.

31 JC to Margaret Carlyle, 21 November 1834, ibid., VII, 338.

32 Ibid., VII, 337.

33 TC to Alick Carlyle, 27 June 1834, ibid., VII, 223, 225.

34 Ibid., VII, 223; TC to his mother, 6 July 1834, and JC to Margaret Carlyle, 20 November 1834, ibid., VII, 235–6, 338.

35 TC to John Bradfute, 29 July 1834, ibid., VII, 249.

36 See Ashton, *The Life of Samuel Taylor Coleridge*, pp. 248–9, 316–17, 360–1.

37 TC, Journal, 26 July 1834, Froude, II, 443–4.

38 TC to Alick Carlyle, 27 June 1834, *CL*, VII, 223 and n.

39 TC to his mother, 5 August 1834, ibid., VII, 261.

40 TC, reminiscence of Irving, *Reminiscences*, pp. 289, 333.

41 TC to John Carlyle, 15 August 1834, *CL*, VII, 272–3.

42 William Graham to TC, 22 August 1834, ibid., VII, 297n.

43 TC, 1866 note on letter of JC to Margaret Carlyle, ibid., VII, 340–1.

44 TC to David Hope, 19 December 1834, ibid., VII, 344.

45 TC, 'Death of Edward Irving', *Fraser's Magazine* (January 1835).

46 TC, reminiscence of Irving, *Reminiscences*, p. 347.

47 Oliphant, *Life of Edward Irving*, II, 434.

48 Jane Simpson to Edward Irving, 31 May 1832, Gordon Strachan, 'Carlyle, Irving, and the "Hysterical Women"', *Carlyle Annual*, XII (1991), 22.

49 Henry Crabb Robinson, Diary, 5 May 1825, MS Dr Williams's Library, London.

50 TC, note to Althaus (1866), *Two Reminiscences*, p. 38.

51 TC, reminiscence of Irving, *Reminiscences*, p. 346.

52 TC to John Carlyle, 1 October 1833, and to his mother, 6 July 1834, *CL*, VII, 6, 236. See also ibid., VI, 442n.

53 TC to John Carlyle, 17 June 1834, ibid., VII, 317.

54 TC, Journal, 26 July 1834, Froude, II, 445.

55 C. E. Norton, MS note of TC's conversation, 21 March 1873, bMS Am 1088.5 (Houghton).

56 TC to JC, 21 May 1834, *CL*, VII, 175.

57 Emerson to TC, 14 May 1834, *The Correspondence of Emerson and Carlyle*, ed. Joseph Slater (London, 1964), p. 98.

58 TC to Emerson, 12 August 1834, *CL*, VII, 264.

59 TC, reminiscence of Southey and Wordsworth (1867), *Reminiscences*, p. 395.

60 William Graham to TC, 17 December 1834, *CL*, VII, 348–9n.

61 TC to William Graham, 24 December 1834, ibid., VII, 350.

62 TC to John Carlyle, 22 July 1834, ibid., VII, 244, 245.

63 TC to William Graham, 14 September 1834, ibid., VII, 300.

64 TC to John Carlyle, 28 October 1834, ibid., VII, 325.

65 TC to his mother, 23 October 1834, and JC to Margaret Carlyle, 21 November 1834, ibid., VII, 314–15, 337.

66 JC to John Carlyle, 12 January 1835, ibid., VIII, 15.

67 TC to William Graham, 10 January 1835, ibid., VIII, 6.

68 TC to his mother, 20 November 1834, ibid., VII, 334.

69 TC to Jean Aitken, 28 January, to his mother, 29 January, and to John Carlyle, 30 April 1835, ibid., VIII, 23, 26, 106.

70 TC to Alick Carlyle, 27 February 1835, ibid., VIII, 59 and n.

71 TC to his mother, 30 May 1834, ibid., VII, 197 and n.

72 TC to Jean Aitken, 24 October 1834, ibid., VII, 317–18.

73 See Richard D. Altick, *The Presence of the Present: Topics of the Day in the Victorian Novel* (Columbus, Ohio, 1990), pp. 85, 88, 802.

74 TC, Journal, October 1834, Froude, II, 458.

75 TC, 'National Education', *c.* 3 February 1835, *CL*, VIII, 29–30, 31 and n.

76 TC to Mill, 1 June 1835, ibid., VIII, 125–6 and n.

77 Emerson to TC, 20 November 1834, 12 March and 30 April 1835, *Correspondence of Emerson and Carlyle*, pp. 110, 120, 122–5.

78 TC, Journal, 7 February 1835, James Anthony Froude, *Thomas Carlyle: A History of his Life in London*, 2 vols (London, 1884), I, 19; TC to John Carlyle, 12 January 1835, *CL*, VIII, 12, 9.

79 TC to John Carlyle, 27 November 1835, *CL*, VIII, 263.

80 Ibid., VIII, 139n.

81 Ibid., VIII, 144n; TC to his mother, 4 June 1835, ibid., VIII, 130.
82 TC to John Sterling, 4 June 1835, ibid., VIII, 136, 137 and n.
83 TC, Journal, *c.* June 1835, Froude, III, 42.
84 TC, Journal, 26 May 1835, ibid., III, 45–6; *CL*, VIII, 139n.
85 JC to John Sterling, 4 June 1835, *CL*, VIII, 138.
86 Ibid., VIII, 139.
87 JC to Jean Aitken, mid–August 1835, ibid., VIII, 193.
88 TC, Journal, 7 March 1835, ibid., VIII, 67n.
89 TC to John Carlyle, 23 March 1835, ibid., VIII, 75–6.
90 TC, Journal, 7 March 1835, ibid., VIII, 67n. A fragment of the burnt MS is in Carlyle's House.
91 TC to James Fraser, 7 March 1835, ibid., VIII, 69 and n.
92 TC to his mother, 25 March 1835, ibid., VIII, 83.
93 TC to James Fraser, 7 March, to John Carlyle, 23 March, to his mother, 25 March 1835, and to Emerson, 13 May 1835, ibid., VIII, 67, 76, 83, 121. See also TC's later note, ibid., VIII, 113.
94 TC to Mill's sister Harriet, May 1873, ibid., VIII, 68n. The editors of *CL* give a full account of the accident, ibid., VIII, 67-8n.
95 Charles Eliot Norton, 'Notes of Carlyle's Talk', bMS 1088.5 (Houghton).
96 W. H. Chesson, account of a conversation with Oscar Wilde, July 1898, *More Letters of Oscar Wilde,* ed. Rupert Hart-Davis (London, 1985), p. 202. For Oscar Wilde quoting from *The French Revolution,* see Richard

Ellmann, *Oscar Wilde* (London, 1987, reprinted 1988), p. 207.
97 TC, reminiscence of JC, *Reminiscences*, p. 92.
98 TC to Mill, 7 March 1835, *CL*, VIII, 70.
99 TC to Mill, 17 March, and to John Carlyle, 23 March 1835, ibid., VIII, 74, 76; TC, Journal, 17 March 1835, ibid., VIII, 74n.
100 TC to John Carlyle, 10 August 1835; JC to Jean Aitken, mid-August 1835, ibid., VIII, 188, 194–5.
101 TC to Mill, 10 September 1835, ibid., VIII, 204.
102 TC to William Graham, 25 September 1835, ibid., VIII, 215.
103 TC to JC, 6 October 1835, ibid., VIII, 219, 220.
104 JC to TC, 12 October 1835, ibid., VIII, 222, 224–5.
105 Leigh Hunt, 'Jenny kissed me', David Alec Wilson, *Carlyle on Cromwell and Others (1837–48),* vol. III of his six-volume biography (London, 1925), p. 30.
106 JC to TC, 12 October 1835, *CL*, VIII, 224.
107 TC to JC, 19 October 1835, ibid., VIII, 227, 231.
108 JC to TC, 26 October 1835, ibid., VIII, 242–3, 246.
109 TC to JC, 2 November 1835, ibid., VIII, 253.
110 TC to Jean Aitken, 4 December 1835, ibid., VIII, 265–6.
111 JC to Margaret Carlyle, 23 December 1835, ibid., VIII, 273–4.

CHAPTER 8
Changed Times 1836–1838

1 TC to John Carlyle, 26 January 1836, *CL*, VIII, 287, 288.
2 JC to John Carlyle, 26 January

1836, ibid., VIII, 292.

3   TC to his mother, 18 January
1836, ibid., VIII, 283.

4   JC to John Carlyle, 23 February
1836, ibid., VIII, 308.

5   See TC, *The French Revolution*
(1837), Part I, Book I, chapter 8.

6   TC to John Carlyle, 20 October
1836, *CL*, IX, 76.

7   JC to Eliza Stodart, *c.*29 February
1836, ibid., VIII, 313.

8   TC, Journal, 22 March 1836,
Froude, III, 69–70.

9   See TC to JC, 2 July 1837, *CL*,
IX, 235, 238.

10 TC to John Carlyle, 29 June
1836, ibid., VIII, 363.

11 TC to his mother, 22 March,
and to John Carlyle, 31 March
1836, ibid., VIII, 322, 328.

12 JC to Helen Welsh, 1 April 1836,
ibid., VIII, 330, 331.

13 TC to his mother, 5 May 1836,
ibid., VIII, 341, 342.

14 TC to JC, 24 August 1836, ibid.,
IX, 44.

15 See TC to JC, 24 July 1836,
ibid., IX, 23.

16 TC, later note on JC to TC, 16
July 1836, ibid., IX, 13.

17 JC to TC, 16 July 1836, ibid.,
IX, 10.

18 JC to TC, 30 July 1836, ibid.,
IX, 28, 29.

19 TC to JC, 6 August 1836, ibid.,
IX, 33.

20 Ibid., IX, 39.

21 TC to John Carlyle, 14 July
1836, ibid., IX, 9.

22 TC to JC, 24 July 1836, ibid.,
IX, 17–18.

23 JC to Mary Welsh, 4 September
1836, ibid., IX, 48.

24 TC to John Carlyle, 12
September 1836, ibid., IX, 60.
See also Packe, *Life of John Stuart
Mill*, pp. 206–8.

25 TC to John Sterling, 3 October
1836, *CL*, IX, 67.

26 Emerson to TC, 8 April 1836,
*Correspondence of Emerson and
Carlyle*, p. 142.

27 Ibid., pp. 17–18.

28 The copies of *Sartor* owned by
Longfellow, Holmes, and Lowell
are in the Houghton Library. So
also is that of another associate of
Emerson's, Elijah P. Clark of the
New England Bank, who was to
act as Carlyle's American
representative when his works
were being reprinted in America
in 1846. He owned a copy of the
1836 Boston edition, and
collected over 1,000 plates and
portraits to illustrate it, filling
eight large scrapbooks with
photographs, newspaper cuttings,
and engravings relating to *Sartor*
and its myriad allusions.

29 TC to Mill, late May 1836, *CL*,
VIII, 350 and n.

30 Emerson to TC, 17 September
1836, *Correspondence of Emerson
and Carlyle*, p. 149.

31 See TC to Jean Aitken, 29
December 1836, *CL*, IX, 109.

32 JC to TC, 17 July 1837, ibid.,
IX, 247.

33 TC to John Carlyle, 2 December
1836, ibid., IX, 102.

34 TC, reminiscence of JC,
Reminiscences, p. 141.

35 See JC to Eliza Stodart, 9 March
1833, *CL*, VI, 342.

36 Harriet Martineau, *Autobiography*,
2 vols (London, 1877, reprinted
1983), I, 350–1, 352.

37 Ibid., I, 377, 378.

38 Ibid., I, 381–2.

39 JC to John Sterling, 1 February
1837, *CL*, IX, 134.

40 Martineau, *Autobiography*, I,
382–3.

41 TC to Jane Wilson, 24 February 1837, *CL*, IX, 157.

42 TC, later note to JC, John Welsh, 4 March 1837, ibid., IX, 162.

43 T. Wemyss Reid, *Life, Letters, and Friendships of Richard Monckton Milnes, First Lord Houghton*, 2 vols (London, 1890), I, 192.

44 TC to Alick Carlyle, 23 April 1837, *CL*, IX, 196.

45 Ibid., IX, 194; Alick Carlyle to TC, 12 April 1837, ibid., IX, 194n.

46 TC to Jean Aitken, 2 April 1837, ibid., IX, 180.

47 TC to John Carlyle, 23 April 1837, ibid., IX, 190–1.

48 TC, Journal, 15 November 1837, Froude, III, 119–20.

49 *Reminiscences*, p. 145.

50 Martineau, *Autobiography*, I, 383.

51 Henry Taylor to Isabella Fenwick, 6 May 1837, *Correspondence of Henry Taylor*, ed. Edward Dowden (London, 1888), p. 81.

52 Fanny Wedgwood to Sarah Wedgwood, 3 May 1837, *CL*, IX, 202n.

53 TC to John Carlyle, 17 February 1837, ibid., IX, 148.

54 TC to his mother, 23 December 1837, ibid., IX, 375.

55 *The French Revolution*, Vol. I, Part I, Book I, chapter 2 ('Realized Ideals').

56 Ibid.

57 Walter Scott, *Waverley; or, 'tis Sixty Years Since* (1814), chapter 46.

58 *The French Revolution*, Vol. I, Part I, Book IV, chapter 4 ('The Procession').

59 Ibid.

60 Charles Dickens to John Forster, summer 1851, *The Letters of Charles Dickens*, ed. Madeleine House, Graham Storey, Kathleen Tillotson, et al., 12 vols (Oxford, 1965–2002), VI, 452.

61 Dickens, Preface to *A Tale of Two Cities* (1859).

62 TC to John Carlyle, 21 September 1834, *CL*, VII, 306.

63 *The French Revolution*, Vol. I, Part I, Book V, chapter 6 ('Storm and Victory').

64 Mill, review of *The French Revolution*, *London and Westminster Review* (July 1837), reprinted in *Thomas Carlyle: The Critical Heritage*, ed. Jules Paul Seigel (London, 1971), pp. 64, 65.

65 Frederic Harrison, *Autobiographic Memoirs*, 2 vols (London, 1911), I, 114–15; and 'Histories of the French Revolution', *North American Review* (October 1883), reprinted in *The Choice of Books*, p. 412.

66 Lady Sydney Morgan's review of *The French Revolution*, *Athenaeum* (20 May 1837), Seigel (ed.), *Critical Heritage*, pp. 46, 47, 49.

67 TC to John Carlyle, 30 May 1837, *CL*, IX, 213–14.

68 See TC to John Carlyle, 17 February 1837, ibid., IX, 145.

69 Mill to Robert Barclay Fox, 16 April 1840, *Earlier Letters*, *Collected Works*, XIII, 427.

70 Mill's review of *The French Revolution*, *London and Westminster Review* (July 1837), Seigel (ed.), *Critical Heritage*, p. 52.

71 Ibid., pp. 53, 54, 57, 58, 61.

72 Ibid., p. 68.

73 Thackeray's review of *The French Revolution*, *The Times* (3 August 1837), ibid., pp. 69, 71, 72, 73.

74 JC to TC, 3 August 1837, *CL*, IX, 271.

75 TC to John Carlyle, 12 August 1837, ibid., IX, 288.

76 W. M. Thackeray, Diary, 30 April, 21 June, and 1 July 1832, *Letters and Private Papers*, I, 196, 213, 214.

77 TC to John Carlyle, 30 May 1837, *CL*, IX, 215.

78 JC to TC, 3 August 1837, ibid., IX, 274.

79 See TC to John Carlyle, 7 July 1837, ibid., IX, 241.

80 TC, reminiscence of Southey and Wordsworth, *Reminiscences*, pp. 393–4.

81 JC to TC, 3 August 1837, *CL*, IX, 272.

82 JC to TC, 11 August 1837, ibid., IX, 281–2.

83 JC to TC, 29 August 1837, ibid., IX, 300.

84 Ibid., IX, 299.

85 TC to John Carlyle, 21 September 1837, ibid., IX, 311.

86 TC, 'Sir Walter Scott', *London and Westminster Review* (January 1838).

87 TC to John Carlyle, 21 September 1837, *CL*, IX, 312.

88 TC to John Carlyle, 12 August 1837, ibid., IX, 284.

89 TC to his mother, 22 September 1837, ibid., IX, 316.

90 TC to William Charles Macready, 17 October 1837, ibid., IX, 332–3 and in *Macready's Reminiscences, and Selections from his Diaries and Letters*, ed. Sir Frederick Pollock, 2 vols (London, 1875), II, 91n.

91 TC to John Carlyle, 7 November 1837, *CL*, IX, 343.

92 TC to John Carlyle, 23 March 1835, ibid., VIII, 81.

93 *Reminiscences*, pp. 391–2.

94 Ibid., p. 394.

95 Emerson to TC, 13 September 1837, *Correspondence of Emerson and Carlyle*, pp. 167, 168; Emerson, Journal, August 1837, *Journals and Miscellaneous Notebooks*, V, 358.

96 Emerson to TC, 2 November 1837, 9 February and 10 May 1838, *Correspondence of Emerson and Carlyle*, pp. 170, 177, 183–4. For a succinct account of the complicated arrangements for TC's American publications, see Slater's introduction, ibid., pp. 16–29.

97 Emerson to TC, 30 July 1838, ibid., p. 189.

98 TC to his mother, 7 December 1837, and Journal, 7 December 1837, *CL*, IX, 357–8, 358n.

99 See Rodger L. Tarr, *Thomas Carlyle: A Descriptive Bibliography* (Oxford, 1989), pp. 42–3, 73–4.

100 Martineau, *Autobiography*, I, 385–6.

101 Harriet Martineau to Fanny Wedgwood, 20 February 1838, *Harriet Martineau's Letters to Fanny Wedgwood*, ed. E. S. Arbuckle (Stanford, California, 1983), p. 11.

102 Martineau, *Autobiography*, I, 383–4; TC, Journal, 17 February 1838, *CL*, X, 30n.

103 TC to Mill [January–March 1838], and to John Carlyle, 1 February 1838, *CL*, X, 14 and n, 17.

104 Ibid., X, 18.

105 TC, Journal, 31 May 1838, ibid., X, 107n; TC to John Carlyle, 1 February 1838, ibid., X, 17.

106 Ian Campbell, 'Conversations with Carlyle: The Monckton Milnes Diaries', *Prose Studies*, VIII (May 1985), 48.

107 See James Pope-Hennessy, *Monckton Milnes: The Flight of Youth 1851–1885*, vol. II of a two-volume biography (London, 1951), p. 113ff.

108 Augustus J. C. Hare, *The Story of My Life*, 6 vols (London, 1896–1900), IV, 383.

109 TC to his mother, 15 February 1838, *CL*, X, 28–9.

110 TC to his mother, 12 April 1838, ibid., X, 68, 69.

111 JC to Fanny Wedgwood, 7 March 1838, ibid., X, 35.

112 See ibid., X, 48n.

113 TC to John Carlyle, 28 October 1834, ibid., VII, 327; TC to his mother, 29 January 1835, ibid., VIII, 26.

114 TC, Journal, 18 May 1838, ibid., X, 84n. For Leigh Hunt's reports of the lectures in the *Examiner*, see Shepherd, *Memoirs of Thomas Carlyle*, I, 176–96.

115 See TC and JC to Jean Aitken, 1 May 1838, *CL*, X, 70, 72–3.

116 Emma Wedgwood to Madame Sismondi, 21 July 1838, and Charles Darwin to Emma Wedgwood, 20 November 1838, *Emma Darwin: A Century of Family Letters 1792–1896*, ed. Henrietta Litchfield, 2 vols (London, 1915), I, 287, II, 13.

117 Barbara and Hensleigh Wedgwood, *The Wedgwood Circle 1730–1897* (London, 1980), p. 232.

118 JC to Jean Aitken, 6 July, and to TC, 18 September 1838, *CL*, X, 115, 181.

119 TC, 'Poor Thomas Cairel', *Collected Poems*, p. 61.

120 TC, Journal, 3 December 1838, *CL*, X, 230n.

CHAPTER 9
Rising into Fame 1839–1840

1 See TC to F. D. Maurice, 24 December 1838, *CL*, X, 245–6.

2 TC to John Forster, 17 January 1839, ibid., XI, 6–7.

3 *Examiner*, 27 January 1839, ibid., XI, 11n; TC to John Carlyle, 4 February 1839, ibid., XI, 19 and n.

4 TC to Henry Cole, [11 May 1838?], *CL*, X, 79–80 and n; see Aileen Christianson, 'Carlyle and Universal Penny Postage', *Carlyle Newsletter*, IV (Spring 1983), 16–19.

5 TC to Jean Aitken, 1 January 1840, and to John Carlyle, 15 February 1840, *CL*, XII, 3, 47.

6 TC to John Forster, 27 February 1839, ibid., XI, 34.

7 TC to the House of Commons, 7 April 1839, ibid., XI, 66–7, 67–8.

8 Wordsworth to Thomas Noon Talfourd, 8 April 1839, *The Letters of William and Dorothy Wordsworth*, second edition, ed. Chester L. Shaver, Mary Moorman, and Alan G. Hill, 7 vols (Oxford, 1967–88), VI, 678.

9 See Emerson to TC, 6 August 1838 and 13 January 1839, *Correspondence of Emerson and Carlyle*, pp. 190, 210.

10 TC to John Carlyle, 4 February 1839, *CL*, XI, 16.

11 TC to Jean Aitken, 13 February 1839, ibid., XI, 28.

12 TC to John Carlyle, 11 March 1839, and to his mother, 13 April 1839, ibid., XI, 46, 75.

13 See TC to John Sterling, 31 October 1841, ibid., XIII, 291 and n.

14 Dickens, *Our Mutual Friend* (1864–5), Book I, chapter 2

('The Man from Somewhere').

15 TC to John Carlyle, 11 March 1839, *CL*, XI, 48–9.

16 TC to his mother, 8 March 1839, ibid., XI, 39.

17 James Pope-Hennessy, *Monckton Milnes: The Years of Promise 1809–1851*, vol. I of his two-volume biography (London, 1949), pp. 40, 90. Pope-Hennessy describes the friendship between Milnes and Rio as 'passionate'.

18 JC to Grace Welsh, 7 April 1839, *CL*, XI, 69–70.

19 A. F. Rio, *Épilogue à l'Art Chrétien*, 2 vols (Fribourg-en-Brisgau, 1870), II, 336.

20 Ibid., II, 335.

21 Ibid., II, 334–5.

22 JC to Grace Welsh, 7 April 1839, *CL*, XI, 70–1.

23 TC to John Carlyle, 15 April 1839, ibid., XI, 85–6.

24 TC to John Carlyle, 26 May 1839, ibid., XI, 113.

25 See JC to Jane Wilson, 2 August 1839, ibid., XI, 162 and n.

26 John Hunter, Diary, 4 March 1839, part published in Walter C. Smith, 'Reminiscences of Carlyle and Leigh Hunt', *Good Words*, XXIII (1882), 99, 100. See also *CL*, XI, 51n.

27 *Catalogue of Important Autograph Letters, Historical Documents and Commemorative Medals*, Bloomsbury Book Auctions (November 1999), pp. 71–2.

28 Ibid., p. 72.

29 TC to his mother, 8 March 1839, *CL*, XI, 40.

30 TC to John Carlyle, 11 March 1839, ibid., XI, 46–7.

31 Charles Darwin, 'Autobiography' (1876), Francis Darwin, *The Life and Letters of Charles Darwin*, 3

vols (London, 1887), I, 77.

32 TC to John Carlyle, 4 February 1839, *CL*, XI, 19.

33 See Benjamin Woolley, *Bride of Science: Romance, Reason, and Byron's Daughter* (London, 1999), pp. 147–8, 153–5.

34 TC to Jean Aitken, 27 March, and to Emerson, 13 April 1839, *CL*, XI, 64, 81.

35 TC to Jean Aitken, 27 March 1839, ibid., XI, 64.

36 JC to Margaret Carlyle, 5 May 1839, ibid., XI, 93.

37 Leigh Hunt, *Examiner* (12 May 1839), in Shepherd, *Memoirs of Thomas Carlyle*, I, 202, 203.

38 Ibid., I, 204.

39 TC to Emerson, 29 May 1839, *CL*, XI, 120.

40 JC to Margaret Carlyle, 20 May 1839, ibid., XI, 102–3.

41 JC to Margaret Carlyle, 5 May 1839, ibid., XI, 94–5.

42 TC to his mother, 19 and 26 June 1839, ibid., XI, 129, 145.

43 TC to Emerson, 4 September 1839, ibid., XI, 180.

44 TC to John Carlyle, 13 September 1839, ibid., XI, 182.

45 See TC to John Carlyle, 20 June 1839, ibid., XI, 135.

46 JC to Helen Welsh, 22 September 1839, ibid., XI, 189.

47 John Sterling to R. C. Trench [1839], Anne Kimball Tuell, *John Sterling: A Representative Victorian* (New York, 1941), pp. 295–6.

48 TC to Sterling, 28 September 1839, *CL*, XI, 192.

49 TC, Journal, 23 October 1839, Froude, III, 171.

50 TC to Alick Carlyle, 2 February 1839, *CL*, XI, 12.

51 TC to John Carlyle, 11 March, and to Alick Carlyle, 13 March 1839, ibid., XI, 43, 52 and n.

52   TC to Lockhart, 20 May 1839, ibid., XI, 103–4.

53   TC to Henry Cole, 15? October 1839, ibid., XI, 203–4 and n.

54   TC, *Chartism* (1839), chapter 5 ('Rights and Mights').

55   Ibid., chapter 1 ('Condition-of-England Question'), and chapter 6 ('Laissez-Faire').

56   Ibid., chapter 9 ('Parliamentary Radicalism').

57   Mill to TC, early December 1839, *Earlier Letters, Collected Works*, XIII, 414.

58   TC to Jane Wilson, early December 1839, *CL*, XI, 220; Tarr, *Descriptive Bibliography*, pp. 80–1.

59   TC to Jean Aitken, 1 January, and to Sterling, 6 January 1840, *CL*, XII, 3–4, 7.

60   Harriet Martineau to Fanny Wedgwood, 17 January 1840, *Harriet Martineau's Letters*, p. 26.

61   TC to his mother, 17 January 1840, *CL*, XII, 18.

62   See Thomas Erskine to TC, 10 February 1840, ibid., XII, 21–2n.

63   Thomas Erskine to JC, 16 April 1838, fMS Am 1301 (Houghton). For Erskine as religious teacher, see Henry F. Henderson, *Erskine of Linlathen: Selections and Biography* (Edinburgh, 1899).

64   TC to Thomas Ballantyne, 24 January 1840, *CL*, XII, 22–5.

65   TC to Thomas Arnold, 9 January 1840, ibid., XII, 11-12 and n.

66   Giuseppe Mazzini to his mother, 11 November 1837, *Scritti*, XIV, 144.

67   For Mazzini's career, see Denis Mack Smith, *Mazzini* (London, 1994).

68   Mazzini to his mother, 4 and 11 December 1839, *Scritti*, III, 291, 297–8.

69   Mazzini to Eleanora Ruffini, 22 March 1840, ibid., XIX, 40–1. See also *CL*, XII, 82n.

70   Mazzini to his mother, 22 April, and to Eliza Fletcher, April 1840, *Scritti*, XIX, 76, 97–8.

71   Mazzini to his mother, 20 May, 18 June, and 15 July 1840, ibid., XIX, 131, 161, 188. See also Mack Smith, *Mazzini*, p. 29.

72   See TC to Sir William Hamilton, 16 March 1840, *CL*, XII, 74 and n.

73   Mazzini to his mother, 8 September and 8 October 1840, *Scritti*, XIX, 262, 304–5.

74   Giovanni Ruffini to his mother, 20 November 1840, *Giuseppe Mazzini e i Fratelli Ruffini*, ed. Carlo Cagnacci (Porto Maurizio, 1893), pp. 254–5 and n. See also Roland Sarti, *Mazzini: A Life for the Religion of Politics* (London, 1997), pp. 102–3.

75   TC to Henry Cole, 25 April 1840, *CL*, XII, 117–18.

76   TC to John Carlyle, 19 March 1840, ibid., XII, 82.

77   TC, *Reminiscences*, pp. 94–5.

78   Ibid., p. 95.

79   TC to John Carlyle, 12 October 1840, *CL*, XII, 285.

80   Thackeray to his mother, 18 January 1840, *Letters and Private Papers*, I, 413.

81   TC to his mother, 24 February 1840, *CL*, XII, 53.

82   TC to his mother, 17 March 1840, ibid., XII, 97.

83   TC to John Carlyle, 17 March 1840, ibid., XII, 80–1.

84   Harriet Martineau to Fanny Wedgwood, 8 March 1840, *Harriet Martineau's Letters*, pp. 31–2.

85   JC to Margaret Carlyle, 15 April 1840; TC to John Carlyle, 18

April, and to Thomas Aird, 1
May 1840, *CL*, XII, 113, 114,
129.

86 JC to Margaret Carlyle, 5 May
1840, ibid., XII, 133.

87 *Globe*, 9 May 1840, ibid., XII,
157n.

88 Robert Browning to Euphrasia
Fanny Haworth, May 1840, *The
Brownings' Correspondence*, ed.
Philip Kelley, Ronald Hudson,
and Scott Lewis, 14 vols so far
(Winfield, Kansas, 1984–), IV,
270.

89 Macready, Diary, 8 May 1840,
Macready's Reminiscences, II, 160;
12 May 1840, *The Diaries of
William Charles Macready
1833–1851*, ed. William Toynbee,
2 vols (London, 1912), II, 60.

90 Caroline Fox, Journal, 1 and 27
March 1840, *The Journals of
Caroline Fox 1835–1871*, selected
and ed. Wendy Monk (London,
1972), pp. 72, 78.

91 Caroline Fox, Journal, 19 May
1840, ibid., pp. 90–2.

92 Caroline Fox, Journal, 8 June
and 18 August 1840, ibid., pp.
96, 97, 101.

93 See Tarr, *Descriptive Bibliography*,
pp. 89–90.

94 TC to J. C. Hare, 1 August
1840, *CL*, XII, 208–9.

95 TC to Jean Aitken, 25 August
1840, ibid., XII, 233, 234.

96 TC to *The Times*, 27 June 1840,
ibid., XII, 178. For an account of
the meeting see ibid., XII,
173–5n.

97 TC and W. D. Christie to
Members of the London Library,
14 December 1840, ibid., XII,
362–3.

98 Geraldine Jewsbury to TC, 6
April 1840, ibid., XII, 103–4n.

99 TC to Geraldine Jewsbury, 12

April 1840, ibid., XII, 105.

100 TC to John Carlyle, 5 September
1840, ibid., XII, 239.

101 See *Letters of Tennyson*, I, xx,
xxxvi.

102 Milnes's Commonplace Book,
Pope-Hennessy, *The Flight of
Youth*, p. 59.

103 John Hunter, 1882 reminiscence,
quoted in *CL*, XII, 99–100n.

104 Longfellow's autographed copy
of *Sartor Resartus*, dated 1835, is
in the Houghton Library.

105 TC to H. W. Longfellow, late
December 1840, *CL*, XII, 379.

106 TC, Journal, 26 December 1840,
Froude, III, 200–1.

107 Sterling to Mill, 9 December
1840, Tuell, *John Sterling*, p. 306.

108 JC to Margaret Carlyle, 27
October 1840, *CL*, XII, 303.

109 Ibid., XII, 301–2. For the
Carlyles' servants, see Holme,
The Carlyles at Home, p. 185ff.

110 JC to Margaret Carlyle, 27
October 1840, *CL*, XII, 301.

CHAPTER 10

Lion and Lion's Wife 1841–1843

1 Mazzini to his mother, 6 January
1841, *Scritti*, XX, 4.

2 TC to James Carlyle, 24 March
1841, *CL*, XIII, 65.

3 TC to his mother, 2 January and
6 February 1841, ibid., XIII, 4–5,
31–2.

4 TC to John Carlyle, 5 February
1841, ibid., XIII, 30.

5 TC to Macready, 24 December
1841, ibid., XIII, 327.

6 Richard Monckton Milnes to
TC, n.d. (but probably 7 or 8
March 1841), MS 666 (NLS).
The MS has had the wrong date
– 9 July 1851 – added in pencil,
and is quoted under that date in

CL, XXVI, 105n. It clearly belongs to March 1841.

7 TC to Milnes, 9 March 1841, *CL*, XIII, 53.

8 TC to John Carlyle, 5 February 1841, ibid., XIII, 29.

9 TC to Thomas Murray, 2 April 1841, ibid., XIII, 72.

10 TC to his mother, 18 February 1841, ibid., XIII, 39.

11 Ibid., XIII, 56n.

12 JC to John Sterling, *c.* 9 March 1841, ibid., XIII, 56.

13 David Masson, *Carlyle Personally and in his Writings: Two Edinburgh Lectures* (London, 1885), p. 21.

14 JC to Susan Stirling, 8 January 1841, *CL*, XIII, 10.

15 JC to Mary Scot, late March 1841, ibid., XIII, 68.

16 See TC to Alick Carlyle, 21 March 1841, ibid., XIII, 60–1.

17 TC to Sterling, 4 August 1841, ibid., XIII, 208.

18 Emerson to TC, 14 October 1841, *Correspondence of Emerson and Carlyle*, p. 307; TC to Emerson, 19 November 1841, *CL*, XIII, 300.

19 W. H. Brookfield to Jane Elton, 2 April 1841, Charles and Frances Brookfield, *Mrs Brookfield and her Circle*, 2 vols (London, 1906), I, 88.

20 TC to JC, 5 and 7 April 1841, *CL*, XIII, 78, 79, 82.

21 JC to TC, 7 April 1841, ibid., XIII, 82, 85.

22 TC to JC, 9 April 1841, ibid., XIII, 88, 90.

23 TC to his mother, 11 April, and to JC, 12 April 1841; and Journal, 4 June 1841, ibid., XIII, 92, 97, 96n.

24 JC to TC, 22 April 1841, ibid., XIII, 109.

25 JC to TC, 15 and 22 April 1841,

ibid., XIII, 100, 110.

26 JC to TC, 15 April 1841, ibid., XIII, 101.

27 TC to John Carlyle, 3 March 1841, ibid., XIII, 50.

28 Geraldine Jewsbury to JC, 10 April 1841, *Selections from the Letters of Miss Jewsbury to Jane Welsh Carlyle*, ed. Mrs Alexander Ireland (London, 1892), p. 1. Mrs Ireland misdates the letter, and her collection is marred by errors and frequent editorial blanks for proper names. The original manuscripts of Geraldine's letters to JC have disappeared since Mrs Ireland used them, and Geraldine apparently destroyed most of JC's to her before she died, though the surviving ones are in the NLS. For an interesting, if not always accurate, account of Geraldine's life and loves, see Susanne Howe, *Geraldine Jewsbury: Her Life and Errors* (London, 1935).

29 Geraldine Jewsbury to JC, [July] 1841, and 6 July 1841, *Selections from Letters*, pp. 22, 24, 25.

30 TC to JC, 29 April 1841, *CL*, XIII, 119.

31 TC to Sterling, 13 May 1841, ibid., XIII, 131.

32 TC, notes on Cromwell, ibid., XIII, 266n.

33 Thackeray to JC, 25 February 1841, *The Letters and Private Papers of William Makepeace Thackeray*, Supplement to Gordon Ray's 4-volume edition, ed. Edgar F. Harden, 2 vols (New York, 1994), I, 94, 95.

34 Thackeray to JC, 20 March 1841, ibid., I, 101.

35 TC to JC, 9 April 1841, *CL*, XIII, 91.

36 TC to his mother, 16 June 1841, ibid., XIII, 150.
37 TC to John Sterling, 12 January 1841, ibid., XIII, 15.
38 TC to Robert Browning, 21 June 1841, ibid., XIII, 155.
39 Ibid., XIII, 156n.
40 Elizabeth Barrett to Mary Russell Mitford, 27 and 28 March 1842, and to George Moulton-Barrett, 30 March 1842, *The Brownings' Correspondence*, V, 281, 290.
41 TC to Henrietta Stanley, 6 July 1841, *CL*, XIII, 167.
42 TC to John Carlyle, 8 July 1841, ibid., XIII, 175.
43 JC to John Forster, 10 July 1841, ibid., XIII, 177.
44 JC to Fanny Wedgwood, 27 August 1841, ibid., XIII, 224–5.
45 TC to Milnes, 19 July, to John Carlyle, 28 July, and to Emerson, 18 August 1841, ibid., XIII, 193, 201, 218.
46 TC to Macvey Napier, 21 June 1841, ibid., XIII, 154.
47 JC to Fanny Wedgwood, 27 August 1841, ibid., XIII, 225.
48 JC to John Forster, 28 August, and TC to John Carlyle, 26 August 1841, ibid., XIII, 232, 222.
49 TC to Jean Aitken, *c.* 19 September 1841, ibid., XIII, 256.
50 TC to JC, 2 September 1841, ibid., XIII, 240.
51 TC to John Carlyle, 7 September 1841, ibid., XIII, 249.
52 See William Whewell to his sister, 8 April 1840, Mrs Stair Douglas, *The Life and Selections from the Correspondence of William Whewell DD* (London, 1881), pp. 196–7.
53 TC to Alick Carlyle, 8 April 1840, *CL*, XII, 99.
54 TC, *Reminiscences*, p. 144.
55 See *CL*, XIII, 259n.
56 TC to Jean Aitken, 5 October 1841, ibid., XIII, 270.
57 JC to Thomas Chalmers, [22 October?] 1841, ibid., XIII, 285.
58 TC to Henry Dunipace, 17 December 1841, ibid., XIII, 319.
59 TC to his mother, 17 December, and JC to her mother, 19 December 1841, ibid., XIII, 320, 324.
60 Ibid., XIV, 27–31 and n.
61 TC to JC, 27 March 1842, ibid., XIV, 97–8.
62 TC to JC, 3 and 7 April 1842, ibid., XIV, 113, 127–8.
63 TC to JC, 16 and 18 April 1842, ibid., XIV, 148, 152.
64 JC to John Welsh, 8 April 1842, ibid., XIV, 130.
65 Mazzini to his mother, 28 March 1842, *Scritti*, XXIII, 79–80.
66 TC to JC, 9 April 1842, *CL*, XIV, 134–5.
67 TC to JC, 23 April 1842, ibid., XIV, 161.
68 TC to Thomas Spedding, 10 May 1842, ibid., XIV, 183.
69 TC to Thomas Chalmers, 11 October 1841, ibid., XIII, 275.
70 TC to Jean Aitken, 10 May 1842, ibid., XIV, 185.
71 TC to Henrietta Stanley, 13 May 1842, ibid., XIV, 188.
72 TC to his mother, 4 June and 4 July 1842, ibid., XIV, 198, 215.
73 Caroline Fox, Journal, 6 June 1842, *Journals*, p. 130.
74 Ibid., p. 132.
75 JC to Maggie Welsh, 15 July 1842, *CL*, XIV, 226.
76 JC to John Sterling, 29 April 1841, ibid., XIII, 121–2.
77 Emerson to TC, 30 October 1842, *Correspondence of Emerson and Carlyle*, p. 308 and n.
78 Bronson Alcott, Journal, 21

August 1881, *The Journals of Bronson Alcott*, selected and ed. Odell Shepard (Boston, Mass., 1938), pp. 526–7.

79 Alcott, Journal, 25 June 1842, ibid., pp. 161, 162.

80 TC to John Sterling, 23 July 1842, *CL*, XIV, 235.

81 TC to John Sterling, 28 July 1842, ibid., XIV, 241.

82 Browning to Alfred Domett, 30 September 1842, *The Brownings' Correspondence*, VI, 89.

83 Mazzini to his mother, 15 July 1842, *Scritti*, XXIII, 220.

84 TC to Emerson, 29 August 1842, *CL*, XV, 58; Emerson to TC, 15 October 1842, *Correspondence of Emerson and Carlyle*, p. 331.

85 TC's note (*c.* 1866), *CL*, XV, 11n.

86 See TC to his mother, 24 February 1840, ibid., XII, 54 and n.

87 JC to TC, 12 August 1842, ibid., XV, 9.

88 JC to TC, 15 August 1842, ibid., XV, 20.

89 TC to JC, 26 August 1842, ibid., XV, 51–2.

90 See Nicolaas A. Rupke, *Richard Owen: Victorian Naturalist* (London, 1994), pp. 13, 40–1, 131–2.

91 T. H. Huxley to John Tyndall, 13 May 1887, Leonard Huxley, *Life and Letters of Thomas Henry Huxley*, 2 vols (London, 1900), II, 167; Charles Darwin to J. D. Hooker, 8 September 1868, *More Letters of Charles Darwin: A Record of his Work in a Series of Hitherto Unpublished Letters*, ed. Francis Darwin and A. C. Seward, 2 vols (London, 1903), I, 309.

92 See JC to Jeannie Welsh, 4 and 6 September 1842, *CL*, XV, 66, 71.

93 TC to his mother, 7 September 1842, ibid., XV, 74.

94 JC to Jeannie Welsh, 8 and 9 September 1842, ibid., XV, 77, 79, 80.

95 Edward FitzGerald to Bernard Barton, 16 and 22 September 1842, *The Letters of Edward FitzGerald*, ed. Alfred McKinley Terhune and Annabelle Burdick Terhune, 2 vols (Princeton, New Jersey, 1980), I, 340, 352; TC to FitzGerald, 18 and 24 September 1842, *CL*, XV, 89, 101–2.

96 TC, note, 5 October, and Journal, 25 October 1842, *CL*, XV, 118n, 139n.

97 JC to Jeannie Welsh, 19 October 1842, ibid., XV, 134.

98 JC to Jeannie Welsh, 29 October 1842, ibid., XV, 152, 153.

99 See JC to Jeannie Welsh, 8 and 12 December 1842, ibid., XV, 219, 226.

100 JC to Jeannie Welsh, 25 December 1842, and 18 (or 19) January 1843, ibid., XV, 250, XVI, 21.

101 JC to Jeannie Welsh, 24 February and 2 March 1843, ibid., XVI, 59, 60, 69.

102 JC to Jeannie Welsh, 12 March 1843, ibid., XVI, 79.

103 JC to Jeannie Welsh, 18 (or 19) January 1843, ibid., XVI, 22–3.

104 Ibid., XVI, 21.

105 MS letters of Buller, Milnes, Thackeray, Mill, and others are in the Ashburton Papers, Acc. 11388 (NLS).

106 Mill to Lady Harriet Baring, n.d. (but probably 1843), ibid.

107 TC to his mother, 6 January 1843, *CL*, XVI, 6.

108 See Ibid., XV, 129n.

109 TC to James Marshall, 1 February 1843, ibid., XVI, 40.

110 TC to Lady Harriet Baring, [18?]
     February 1843, ibid., XVI, 52.
111 TC to Lady Harriet Baring, 21
     April 1843, ibid., XVI, 134.

CHAPTER 11

Fascinations and Flirtations
1843–1845

1   TC, *Past and Present* (1843),
    Book I, chapter 1 ('Midas').
2   'Occasional Discourse on the
    Nigger Question', *Fraser's
    Magazine* (December 1849); see
    OED.
3   *Past and Present*, Book I, chapter
    1; see also TC to Thomas
    Chalmers, 11 October 1841, *CL*,
    XIII, 275.
4   *Past and Present*, Book I, chapter
    5 ('Aristocracy of Talent'), Book
    III, chapter 2 ('Gospel of
    Mammonism'), and chapter 3
    ('Gospel of Dilettantism').
5   Ibid., Book III, chapter 14 ('Sir
    Jabesh Windbag').
6   Ibid., Book II, chapter 7 ('The
    Canvassing').
7   William Henry Smith, review of
    Past and Present in *Blackwood's
    Magazine* (July 1843), Seigel
    (ed.), *Critical Heritage*, p. 215.
8   *Past and Present*, Book I, chapter
    3 ('Manchester Insurrection').
9   Ibid., Book III, chapter 7
    ('Over-Production').
10 Ibid., Book I, chapter 4
    ('Morrison's Pill'). For Morison's
    Pills see Altick, *The Presence of the
    Present*, pp. 550–1.
11 F. D. Maurice, letter to *Christian
    Remembrancer* (October 1843),
    Seigel (ed.), *Critical Heritage*, pp.
    193, 197.
12 Friedrich Engels, review of *Past
    and Present*, *Deutsch-Französische
    Jahrbücher* (1844), in *Marx-Engels*

    Collected Works, 50 vols so far
    (London, 1975–), III, 444–68.
13 *Past and Present*, Book IV,
    chapter 4 ('Captains of Industry')
    and chapter 5 ('Permanence').
14 Marx and Engels, *The Communist
    Manifesto* (1848), ed. A. J. P.
    Taylor (Harmondsworth, 1986).
    For an account of the life of
    German exiles in England,
    including Marx and Engels, see
    Rosemary Ashton, *Little
    Germany: Exile and Asylum in
    Victorian England* (Oxford, 1986).
15 Caroline Fox, Journal, 5 August
    1843, *Journals*, p. 145.
16 Elizabeth Barrett to Richard
    Hengist Horne, 1 May 1843, *The
    Brownings' Correspondence*, VII,
    100.
17 TC to James Marshall, 1
    February 1843, *CL*, XVI, 40.
18 J. A. Froude, 'The Oxford
    Counter-Reformation' (1882),
    Short Studies on Great Subjects, 4
    vols (London, 1892), IV, 339–40.
19 Froude, III, 290–1, 292.
20 Froude, autobiographical
    fragment, Waldo Hilary Dunn,
    *James Anthony Froude: A
    Biography*, 2 vols (Oxford, 1961,
    1963), I, 95.
21 T. H. Huxley to W. Platt Ball,
    27 October 1870, *Life and Letters
    of Thomas Henry Huxley*, II, 268.
22 Huxley, autobiographical
    fragment, ibid., I, 15.
23 George Eliot to Mary Sibree, 12
    March 1846, *The George Eliot
    Letters*, ed. Gordon S. Haight,
    9 vols (New Haven, Conn.,
    1954–5, 1978), VIII, 11.
24 George Eliot, 'Thomas Carlyle',
    Leader (27 October 1855), *Essays
    of George Eliot*, ed. Thomas
    Pinney (London, 1963), pp.
    213–14. See also Rosemary

Ashton, *George Eliot: A Life* (London, 1996), p. 35ff.

25 TC to James Carlyle, 28 April 1843, *CL*, XVI, 140.

26 JC to Jeannie Welsh, 18 April, 3 May, and 12 November 1843, ibid., XVI, 129, 151, XVII, 174.

27 John Carlyle to TC, 4 August 1845, ibid., XIX, 125n.

28 TC to Alick Carlyle, 23 June 1843, and JC to Jeannie Welsh, 30 June 1843, ibid., XVI, 213, 222.

29 TC to JC, 9 July 1843, ibid., XVI, 254; see also XVI, 281n.

30 Mazzini to his mother, 29 July 1843, *Scritti*, XXIV, 204.

31 JC to TC, 31 July 1843, *CL*, XVI, 329.

32 JC to TC, 18 and 27 August 1843, ibid., XVII, 62–3, 93.

33 Mazzini to George Sand, 20 September 1844, *Scritti*, XXVII, 26.

34 JC to TC, 23 August 1843, *CL*, XVII, 82.

35 JC to TC, 21 August 1843, ibid., XVII, 72–3; TC's note, ibid., XVII, 73n.

36 JC to Jeannie Welsh, *c.* 29 August 1844, and TC to John Carlyle, 20 September 1844, ibid., XVIII, 195, 214.

37 TC's note, ibid., XVII, 73–4n.

38 See TC to JC, 23 and 28 August and 7 September 1843, ibid., XVII, 79, 80, 100, 121.

39 JC to Jeannie Welsh, 25 October 1843, ibid., XVII, 159.

40 Geraldine Jewsbury to JC, 17 October 1843, *Selections from Letters*, p. 75.

41 TC, Journal, 10 October 1843, *CL*, XVII, 153n.

42 TC to Henry Cole, 25 October 1843, ibid., XVII, 156.

43 JC to Susan Stirling, 14

44 JC to Amely Bölte, 23 December 1843, ibid., XVII, 209–10.

45 JC to Jeannie Welsh, 28 December 1843, ibid., XVII, 219–20, 221.

46 JC to Jeannie Welsh, *c.* 9 January 1844, ibid., XVII, 238.

47 Dickens to JC, 27 January 1844, *Letters of Charles Dickens*, IV, 33.

48 Dickens to the editors of four American newspapers, 27 April 1842, ibid., III, 213.

49 TC to Dickens, 26 March 1842, *CL*, XIV, 93.

50 JC to Jeannie Welsh, 26 February 1844, ibid., XVII, 283.

51 JC to Jeannie Welsh, *c.* 9 January 1844, ibid., XVII, 238–9.

52 JC to Jeannie Welsh, 26 February 1844, ibid., XVII, 282–3.

53 JC to Jeannie Welsh, *c.* 5 March 1844, ibid., XVII, 298.

54 JC to John Forster, 17 April 1845, ibid., XIX, 55.

55 JC to Jeannie Welsh, 23 April 1844, ibid., XVIII, 22.

56 JC to Jeannie Welsh, 6 May 1844, ibid., XVIII, 37, 38.

57 Geraldine Jewsbury to JC, 21 June and 17 September 1844, *Selections from Letters*, pp. 133, 144.

58 JC to Jeannie Welsh, 19 June 1844, *CL*, XVIII, 77.

59 TC to the editor of *The Times*, 18 June 1844, ibid., XVIII, 73–4.

60 Mazzini to his mother, 21 June 1844, *Scritti*, XXVI, 213–14.

61 See *Letters of Charles Dickens*, IV, 151 and n.

62 JC to Jeannie Welsh, 31 May 1844, and TC to JC, 26 June 1844, *CL*, XVIII, 56, 86.

63 Mazzini to his mother, 21

September 1844, *Scritti*, XXVII, 30.

64 JC to Jeannie Welsh, 26 July 1844, *CL*, XVIII, 156; Mazzini to his mother, 26 July 1844, *Scritti*, XXVI, 256.

65 JC to Jeannie Welsh, 1 August 1844, *CL*, XVIII, 163–4.

66 JC to Jeannie Welsh, *c.* 12 June 1844, ibid., XVIII, 63–4.

67 JC to TC, 2 July 1844, ibid., XVIII, 99.

68 JC to TC, 26 June and 1 July 1844, ibid., XVIII, 87–8, 96.

69 JC to Jeannie Welsh, 26 July 1844, ibid., XVIII, 155.

70 See ibid., XVI, 137n.

71 TC to his mother, 14 August 1844, ibid., XVIII, 179.

72 Sterling to TC, 10 August 1844, ibid., XVIII, 179n.

73 TC to Sterling, 27 August 1844, ibid., XVIII, 193.

74 Anthony Sterling to TC, 30 August 1844, ibid., XVIII, 193n.

75 See ibid., XVIII, 192n, 214n, 215n.

76 See JC to Jeannie Welsh, 12 August 1844, ibid., XVIII, 176.

77 TC to JC, 14 September 1844, ibid., XVIII, 207.

78 Ibid., XVIII, 134n.

79 See JC to TC, 11 September 1844, ibid., XVIII, 199 and n.

80 TC to JC, 14 September 1844, ibid., XVIII, 207.

81 See ibid., XVIII, 208 and n.

82 JC to Jeannie Welsh, *c.* 12 September 1844, ibid., XVIII, 202.

83 JC to Helen Welsh, 25 September 1844, ibid., XVIII, 221.

84 Letters from Charles Buller to Bingham Baring, Lady Harriet Baring, and Mrs Buller, 1843–4, MSs Acc. 11388, Ashburton Collection (NLS).

85 JC to Helen Welsh, 16 October 1844, *CL*, XVIII, 244.

86 JC to Jeannie Welsh, 18 December 1844, ibid., XVIII, 289.

87 TC to Lady Harriet Baring, 22 December 1844, ibid., XVIII, 292–3.

88 Amely Bölte to Varnhagen von Ense, 27 February 1848, *Amely Böltes Briefe aus England an Varnhagen von Ense (1844-1858)*, ed. Walther Fischer and Antje Behrens (Düsseldorf, 1955), p. 57.

89 TC to Lady Harriet Baring, 22 December 1844, *CL*, XVIII, 293; Charlotte Williams Wynn to Ludmilla Assing, 23 June 1860, Walther Fischer, 'Thomas und Jane Carlyle im Spiegel der Briefe Amely Böltes an Varnhagen von Ense (1844–1853)', *Englische Studien*, LXIV (1929), 424–5. For an account of Amely Bölte's career in England, see Ashton, *Little Germany*, pp. 212–18.

90 See Alison Winter, *Mesmerized: Powers of Mind in Victorian Britain* (London, 1998), 221–5.

91 JC to John Welsh, 13 December 1844, *CL*, XVIII, 283–4.

92 JC to Jeannie Welsh, 14 May 1844, ibid., XVIII, 46–7.

93 JC to Helen Welsh, 12 November 1844, ibid., XVIII, 268.

94 JC to Jeannie Welsh, 23 December 1848, ibid., XXIII, 185. For JC's relationship with Anthony Sterling see K. J. Fielding, 'Captain Anthony Sterling's Photograph Album and his Relations with Jane Carlyle', *Carlyle Newsletter*, VI (Spring

1985), 42–50.

95 JC to Helen Welsh, 31 January 1845, *CL*, XIX, 15–16.

96 *A New Spirit of the Age* (1844), in *The Brownings' Correspondence*, VIII, 354, 355.

97 Elizabeth Barrett to TC, 14 August and late August 1844, and to Mary Russell Mitford, 1 September 1844, *The Brownings' Correspondence*, IX, 99, 115, 122.

98 Elizabeth Barrett to Robert Browning, 17 February 1845, ibid., X, 81.

99 See TC to Henry Field, 13 May 1844, and to Browning, 21 May 1844 and 13 February 1845, *CL*, XVIII, 40, 48, XIX, 30.

100 See Tarr, *Descriptive Bibliography*, pp. 108–10.

101 See James A. Davies, *John Forster: A Literary Life* (Leicester, 1982), pp. 105, 118–19, 200ff. See also Wilson, III, 292–9.

102 See Milnes to Varnhagen von Ense, 29 June 1845, *Die Briefe Richard Monckton Milnes' an Varnhagen von Ense (1844–1854)*, ed. Walther Fischer (Heidelberg, 1922), p. 108; Lewes to Varnhagen, 10 January 1846, *The Letters of George Henry Lewes*, ed. William Baker, 2 vols (Victoria, British Columbia, 1995), I, 120.

103 JC, notebook, 27 April 1845, *CL*, XIX, 64–5n.

104 JC to Jeannie Welsh, 15 June 1845, ibid., XIX, 79, 80.

105 JC to John Welsh, 28 June 1845, ibid., XIX, 88.

106 JC to Jeannie Welsh, 9 July 1845, ibid., XIX, 92, 93; see also XIX, 58.

107 JC to TC, 30 July and 3 August 1845, ibid., XIX, 119, 126.

108 JC to TC, 10 August 1845, ibid., XIX, 137–8.

109 JC to TC, 23 September 1845, ibid., XIX, 209.

110 JC to TC, 28 September 1845, ibid., XIX, 221, 222.

111 JC to Jeannie Welsh, 29 September 1845, ibid., XIX, 228.

112 TC to JC, 1 October 1845, ibid., XX, 4.

113 JC to Jeannie Welsh, 28 December 1845, and TC to Charles Redwood, 29 December 1845, ibid., XX, 82, 83.

114 JC to Mary Russell, 30 December 1845, ibid., XX, 85.

CHAPTER 12

Revolutions Domestic and Foreign 1846–1849

1 TC to Alick Carlyle, 2 January 1846, *CL*, XX, 91.

2 John Mitchel, review of *Cromwell*, *The Nation*, 6 January 1846, ibid., XX, 104–5n.

3 TC to Lady Harriet Baring, 24 March 1846, ibid., XXI, 188.

4 TC to Lady Harriet Baring, 20 February 1846, ibid., XX, 125.

5 See TC to John Carlyle, 3 March 1846; JC to Jeannie Welsh, 10 March 1846, ibid., XX, 134, 139.

6 JC to Helen Welsh, 24 April 1846, ibid., XX, 179.

7 JC to Jeannie Welsh, 19 May 1846, ibid., XX, 194.

8 JC to TC, 6 July 1846, ibid., XX, 222.

9 TC to JC, 13 July 1846, ibid., XX, 229.

10 Geraldine Jewsbury to Amely Bölte, [July] 1846, MS Jagiellonian Library, Cracow; JC to Amely Bölte, 14 July 1846, *CL*, XX, 235.

11 Mazzini to JC, 10 July 1846, *Scritti*, XXX, 70–1, 72–3.

12 Mazzini to JC, 15 July 1846,

ibid., XXX, 373, 375.

13 JC to TC, 15 July 1846, *CL*, XX, 240.

14 TC to JC, 16 July 1846, ibid., XX, 241.

15 TC to Lady Harriet Baring, 28 July 1846, ibid., XX, 261, 262,

16 TC to JC, 20 August 1846, ibid., XXI, 20.

17 Lady Harriet Baring to JC, 18 August 1846, ibid., XXI, 20–1n.

18 JC to John Stodart, 30 September 1849, ibid., XXIV, 258.

19 Lady Harriet Montagu to William Bingham Baring [1822] and [1844 or 1845], Ashburton Collection, MS Acc. 11388 (NLS).

20 TC, note to letters of September 1846, *CL*, XXI, 24, 25, 26.

21 JC to Helen Welsh, 29 September 1846, ibid., XXI, 62.

22 JC to Mary Russell, 29 December 1846, ibid., XXI, 126.

23 JC to Jeannie Welsh, 30 October 1846, ibid., XXI, 83–4.

24 TC to John Carlyle, 8 November 1846, ibid., XXI, 88.

25 JC to Jean Aitken, [2 February? 1847], ibid., XXI, 151.

26 JC to Helen Welsh, 17 February 1847, ibid., XXI, 161.

27 TC to Edward FitzGerald, 6 February 1847, ibid., XXI, 156, 157.

28 See ibid., XXII, 203n. For an account of the Squire Papers affair, see Clyde de L. Ryals, 'Thomas Carlyle and the Squire Forgeries', *Victorian Studies*, XXX (1987), 495–518.

29 TC, note at the end of vol. II of the third edition of *Cromwell*, 4 vols (1850).

30 TC to his mother, 14 April 1849, *CL*, XXIV, 22.

31 TC to Lady Harriet Baring, 25 December 1847, and 6 November 1847, ibid., XXII, 183, 152.

32 JC to Helen Welsh, 15 June 1847, ibid., XXI, 232.

33 Caroline Fox, Journal, 20 May 1847, *Journals*, pp. 171, 172.

34 Browning to TC, 14 May 1847, *The Brownings' Correspondence*, XIV, 200.

35 Elizabeth Barrett Browning to Henrietta Moulton-Barrett, 9 July 1847, ibid., XIV, 242; TC to Browning, 23 June 1847, *CL*, XXI, 239.

36 TC to Jean Aitken, 30 June 1847, *CL*, XXI, 246.

37 JC to Helen Welsh, 5 July 1847, ibid., XXII, 9.

38 TC to John Carlyle, 8 August 1847, ibid., XXII, 30.

39 W. E. Forster to Sarah Fox, 17 August 1847, T. Wemyss Reid, *Life of the Right Honourable William Edward Forster*, 2 vols (London, 1888), I, 208–9.

40 W. E. Forster to Sarah Fox, 16 August 1847, ibid., I, 207; JC to TC, 5 October 1847, *CL*, XXII, 116.

41 JC to W. E. Forster, 28 October 1847, *CL*, XXII, 142.

42 Emerson to his wife, 27 October 1847, *The Letters of Ralph Waldo Emerson*, ed. Ralph L. Rusk and Eleanor M. Tilton, 10 vols (New York, 1939–95), III, 423.

43 TC to Jean Aitken, 26 October 1847, *CL*, XXII, 138.

44 JC to Lady Harriet Baring, 28 October 1847, ibid., XXII, 139–40.

45 Emerson to his wife, 27 October 1847, *Letters of Emerson*, III, 424.

46 A. H. Clough to Tom Arnold, 31 January 1848, *The*

Correspondence of Arthur Hugh Clough, ed. Frederick L. Mulhauser, 2 vols (Oxford, 1957), I, 198.

47 JC to John Forster, 20 November 1847, *CL*, XXII, 165.

48 JC to Helen Welsh, 19 November 1847, ibid., XXII, 163.

49 JC to John Forster, [26?] February 1848, ibid., XXII, 255.

50 See JC to John Forster, 26 November 1847, ibid., XXII, 169.

51 JC to TC, 14 January 1848, ibid., XXII, 208.

52 TC to Browning, 23 June 1847, ibid., XXI, 241.

53 Thackeray to TC and JC [1851?], *Letters and Private Papers*, II, 775.

54 Thackeray, *Vanity Fair* (1847–8); wrapper to one of the original monthly numbers (1847), and chapter 8 ('Private and Confidential'), reproduced in World's Classics edition of the novel, ed. John Sutherland (Oxford, 1983), pp. li, 95, 881–2.

55 TC to Elizabeth Gaskell, 8 November 1848, *CL*, XXIII, 154.

56 See Fred Kaplan, 'Carlyle's Marginalia and George Henry Lewes's Fiction', *Carlyle Newsletter*, V (1984), 21.

57 JC to Jeannie Welsh, 18 or 19 January 1843, *CL*, XVI, 20.

58 JC to TC, 13 April 1848, ibid., XXIII, 18.

59 Kaplan, 'Carlyle's Marginalia', 23, 24, 25.

60 TC, Journal, 9 February 1848, Froude, III, 420, 421.

61 Ibid., III, 422.

62 Ibid., III, 423. See also TC to William Bingham Baring, 8 February 1848, *CL*, XXII, 242

63 and n.

64 Fred Kaplan, ' "Phallus-Worship" (1848): Unpublished Manuscripts III – A Response to the Revolution of 1848', *Carlyle Newsletter*, II (1980), 22.

64 TC, *Latter-Day Pamphlets* (1850), number II ('Model Prisons').

65 Lord John Russell to Queen Victoria, 29 February 1848, *The Letters of Queen Victoria*, ed. A. C. Benson and Viscount Esher, 3 vols (London, 1907), II, 182–3.

66 Dickens to Emile de la Rue, 29 February 1848, *Letters of Charles Dickens*, V, 254.

67 *The Times*, 25 February and 1 March 1848; Emerson gives an account of the extra copies printed on 1 March in *English Traits*, p. 214 (chapter 15, 'The "Times" ').

68 Thomas Frost, *Forty Years' Recollections: Literary and Political* (London, 1881), p. 129.

69 TC to Emerson, 28 February 1848, *CL*, XXII, 257.

70 See TC to John Forster, 5 March 1848, and to JC, 5 April 1848, ibid., XXII, 260–1, XXIII, 6.

71 TC to Jean Aitken, 6 March 1848, ibid., XXII, 262.

72 TC, 'Louis-Philippe', *The Times*, 4 March 1848, reprinted in Shepherd, *Memoirs of Thomas Carlyle*, II, 365, 368.

73 George Eliot to John Sibree, 8 March 1848, *The George Eliot Letters*, I, 253–4, 255.

74 JC to Jeannie Welsh, 20 March 1848, *CL*, XXII, 272.

75 TC to his mother, 19 May 1848, ibid., XXIII, 34 and n.

76 Dickens to Sir Edward Bulwer-Lytton, 10 April 1848, *Letters of Charles Dickens*, V, 274. For an account of the day see Henry

Weisser, *April 10: Challenge and Response in England in 1848* (London, 1983).

77 TC to JC, 10 April 1848, *CL*, XXIII, 10–11.

78 See Dickens to Emerson, April 1848, *Letters of Charles Dickens*, V, 275 and n.

79 Emerson to his wife, 4 May 1848, *Letters of Emerson*, IV, 66.

80 Emerson, Notebook, *Journals and Miscellaneous Notebooks*, X, 550.

81 George Eliot to Sara Hennell, 2 November 1851, *The George Eliot Letters*, I, 372.

82 Emerson, Notebook, *Journals and Miscellaneous Notebooks*, X, 552, 553.

83 JC to Lady Harriet Ashburton, 11 June 1848, *CL*, XXIII, 44.

84 TC to his mother, 6 July 1848, ibid., XXIII, 61.

85 TC, 'Repeal of the Union', *Examiner*, 29 April 1848, reprinted in Shepherd, *Memoirs of Thomas Carlyle*, II, 377, 373.

86 Ibid., II, 372, 373.

87 J. S. Mill, 'England and Ireland', *Examiner*, 13 May 1848, reprinted in Seigel (ed.), *Critical Heritage*, pp. 304–9; see Phyllis Harnick, 'Point and Counterpoint: Carlyle and Mill on Ireland in 1848', *Carlyle Newsletter*, VII (Spring 1986), 26–33.

88 W. M. Thackeray to Edward FitzGerald, *c.* 29 April 1848, *Letters and Private Papers*, II, 366.

89 Amely Bölte to Varnhagen von Ense, 7 May 1848, *Briefe*, p. 61.

90 TC to Lord Clarendon, 26 May 1848, *CL*, XXIII, 35–6 and n.

91 C. G. Duffy to TC, 13 October 1848, ibid., XXIII, 139n.

92 TC to John Forster, 6 July 1848, ibid., XXIII, 64.

93 JC to Helen Welsh, *c.* 16 July 1848, ibid., XXIII, 72, 71.

94 TC to John Forster, 22 August, and to John Carlyle, 26 August 1848, ibid., XXIII, 97, 98–9.

95 Amely Bölte to Varnhagen von Ense, 24 July 1848, *Briefe*, pp. 64–5.

96 TC to his mother, 19 May 1848, *CL*, XXIII, 33.

97 TC to his mother, 3 September 1848; JC to Jeannie Welsh, 28 September 1848, ibid., XXIII, 103, 125.

98 TC to John Carlyle, 11 September, and to his mother, 15 September 1848, ibid., XXIII, 107, 108, 111.

99 TC to John Carlyle, 19 September 1848, ibid., XXIII, 115.

100 JC to Jeannie Welsh, 28 September 1848, ibid., XXIII, 125–6.

101 Aubrey de Vere to JC, 30 September 1848, ibid., XXIII, 126n.

102 Froude, III, 449.

103 TC to Lady Ashburton, 29 November 1848, *CL*, XXIII, 164, 165.

104 TC, obituary of Charles Buller, *Examiner*, 2 December 1848, reprinted in Shepherd, *Memoirs of Thomas Carlyle*, II, 36, 37, 38.

105 TC, Journal, 4 December 1848, *CL*, XXIII, 164n.

106 TC, Journal, 29 December 1848, ibid., XXIII, 187n.

107 See TC to Lady Ashburton, 29 January 1849, ibid., XXIII, 208 and n.

108 JC to Jeannie Welsh, 17 May 1849, ibid., XXIV, 51, 52n; see also 78n.

109 TC to JC, 3 April 1849, ibid., XXIV, 6–7.

110 Froude to Clough, 28 February 1849, *Correspondence of Arthur Hugh Clough*, I, 246-7.

111 See Rosemary Ashton, introduction to J. A. Froude, *The Nemesis of Faith* (1849, London, 1988), pp. 7-8, 29-30.

112 Charles Kingsley to Friedrich Max Müller, 10 May 1852, MS Eng. c.2806/1 (Bodleian).

113 TC to John Forster, 4 April 1849, *CL*, XXIV, 13.

114 Froude, III, 458.

115 Ibid., III, 459.

116 TC to Emerson, 19 April 1849, *CL*, XXIV, 30.

117 J. S. Mill to Harriet Taylor, *c.* 31 March 1849, *The Later Letters of John Stuart Mill, Collected Works*, XIV, 23.

118 JC to Jeannie Welsh, 29 January 1849, *CL*, XXIII, 211.

119 JC to Jeannie Welsh, 5? February 1849, ibid., XXIII, 223, 224.

120 JC to Jeannie Welsh, 17 May 1849, ibid., XXIV, 50.

121 JC to Mary Russell, 22 February 1849, ibid., XXIII, 239-40.

122 Elizabeth Gaskell to Anne Green, 13 May 1849, *The Letters of Mrs Gaskell*, ed. J. A. W. Chapple and Arthur Pollard (Manchester, 1966), p. 828.

123 JC to Jeannie Welsh, 17 May 1849, *CL*, XXIV, 51.

124 JC to Jeannie Welsh, 15 June 1849, ibid., XXIV, 67-8.

125 See Sir James Crichton-Browne, introduction to Alexander Carlyle's edition of *New Letters and Memorials*, p. lvii; Leonard Huxley, introduction to *Jane Welsh Carlyle: Letters to her Family 1839-1863* (London, 1924), p. xii; Thea Holme, *The Carlyles at Home*, p. 52.

126 Caroline Fox, Journal, 13 June

1849, *Journals*, p. 191.

127 JC to Jeannie Welsh, 23 June 1849, *CL*, XXIV, 79.

128 JC to Jeannie Welsh, 17 May 1849, ibid., XXIV, 52.

129 JC to TC, 5 July 1849, ibid., XXIV, 100.

130 JC to John Carlyle, 11 and 23 July 1849, ibid., XXIV, 115, 143-4.

131 JC to TC, 16 July 1849, ibid., XXIV, 124.

132 JC to TC, 20 July 1849, ibid., XXIV, 137-8.

133 JC to John Carlyle, 28 July 1849, ibid., XXIV, 152-3.

134 JC, 'Much ado about Nothing', 2 August 1849, ibid., XXIV, 163, 164, 165.

135 Ibid., XXIV, 169.

136 Lord Clarendon to Lord John Russell, 31 July 1849, ibid., XXIV, 101n.

137 TC to JC, 6 July 1849, ibid., XXIV, 102.

138 TC to Lord Clarendon, 6 July 1849, ibid., XXIV, 104.

139 TC to Aubrey de Vere, 13 July 1849, ibid., XXIV, 118.

140 TC to JC, 17 July 1849, ibid., XXIV, 127-8.

141 TC to Lord Clarendon, 5 August 1849, ibid., XXIV, 173, 174 and n.

142 TC to JC, 5 August 1849, ibid., XXIV, 176.

143 TC to JC, 2 September 1849, ibid., XXIV, 210, 212, 213.

144 JC to TC, 5 September 1849, ibid., XXIV, 221.

145 TC to John Carlyle, 28 September and 1 October 1849, ibid., XXIV, 251, 260.

146 John Forster, *The Life of Charles Dickens*, 3 vols (1872-4), ed. and annotated in one vol. by J. W. T. Ley (London, 1928), p. 528.

147 TC to John Carlyle, 6 October 1849, *CL*, XXIV, 265–6.

148 JC to Jeannie Welsh, 6 November 1849, ibid., XXIV, 278.

149 JC to John Forster, 6 November 1849, ibid., XXIV, 280.

150 Dickens, letter to *The Times*, 14 November 1849; see *CL*, XXIV, 217–18n, 293n.

151 JC to Jeannie Welsh, 2 December 1849, *CL*, XXIV, 305.

152 TC to John Forster, 28 November 1849, ibid., XXIV, 298–9.

153 JC to John Carlyle, 10 December, and to John Forster, 11 December 1849, ibid., XXIV, 309, 310.

CHAPTER 13
Courting Controversy 1850–1852

1 See TC to J. W. Parker, 14 November 1849, *CL*, XXIV, 290.

2 TC to James Carlyle, 20 January 1850, ibid., XXV, 6.

3 See Tarr, *Descriptive Bibliography*, pp. 129–30.

4 TC, 'Occasional Discourse on the Negro Question', *Fraser's Magazine* (December 1849), reprinted in *Carlyle's Latter-Day Pamphlets*, ed. M. K. Goldberg and J. P. Seigel (Ontario, 1983), pp. 424, 425–6.

5 Dickens, *Bleak House* (1852–3), chapter 4 ('Telescopic Philanthropy').

6 TC, 'Occasional Discourse', *Latter-Day Pamphlets*, pp. 426, 427, 428.

7 Ibid., pp. 433, 460, 464.

8 See H. L. Malchow, *Gothic Images of Race in Nineteenth-Century Britain* (Stanford, California, 1996), p. 110.

9 See *OED*.

10 See Malchow, *Gothic Images*; also Christopher Herbert, *Culture and Anomie: Ethnographic Imagination in the Nineteenth Century* (Chicago, Illinois, 1991).

11 The descriptions are from Phyllis Rose, *Parallel Lives: Five Victorian Marriages* (London, 1984), p. 264. See also Patrick Jackson, *Education Act Forster: A Political Biography of W. E. Forster 1818–1886* (London, 1997), pp. 100–1.

12 TC to Jean Aitken, 26 January 1850, *CL*, XXV, 11.

13 Froude, IV, 25.

14 Thackeray to James Spedding, 5 January 1850, *Letters and Private Papers*, II, 628–9.

15 Thackeray to Lady Ashburton, 29 December [1849], MS Acc. 11388, Ashburton Collection (NLS).

16 TC, Journal, 7 February 1850, Froude, IV, 28; *CL*, XXV, 2n.

17 TC, *Latter-Day Pamphlets*, pp. 16, 23, 27, 28 (No. 1, 'The Present Time').

18 For example, Elizur Wright, *Perforations in the 'Latter-Day Pamphlets' by one of the Eighteen Million of Bores* (1850); see K. J. Fielding, 'Carlyle and the Americans: "Eighteen Million Bores"', *Carlyle Studies Annual*, XV (1995), 55–63.

19 TC, *Latter-Day Pamphlets*, p. 395 (No. 8, 'Jesuitism').

20. Ibid., pp. 113, 126, 128 (No. 3, 'Downing Street').

21 Emerson, notes on TC, *Journals and Miscellaneous Notebooks*, X, 553.

22 Edward FitzGerald to Frederick

Tennyson, 17 April 1850, *Letters of Edward FitzGerald*, I, 668.

23 Thomas Spedding to TC, 22 May, and TC to Spedding, 31 May 1850, *CL*, XXV, 87n, 87–8.

24 *Hansard's Parliamentary Debates*, third series, CX (8 April–13 May 1850), 225.

25 TC, *Latter-Day Pamphlets*, p. 211.

26 TC, Journal, 27 May 1850, *CL*, XXV, 81n.

27 TC, Journal, 3 July 1850, Froude, IV, 48.

28 *Punch*, XVIII (16 March and 6 April 1850), 107, 140.

29 See JC to Jeannie Welsh, 25 February 1849, *CL*, XXIII, 224.

30 TC, *Latter-Day Pamphlets*, pp. 69, 73, 72 (No. 2, 'Model Prisons').

31 Dickens, *David Copperfield* (1849–50), chapter 61 ('I am shown Two Interesting Penitents').

32 *Household Words*, I (27 April 1850), 97.

33 *Leader*, I (30 March 1850), 13, 14.

34 TC to John Forster, 17 February 1850, *CL*, XXV, 26.

35 TC to Jean Aitken, 26 April 1850, ibid., XXV, 72–3.

36 See TC to Edwin Chadwick, 3 April 1850, ibid., XXV, 59; Dickens to Henry Austin, 27 February, and to W. H. Wills, 12 March 1850, *Letters of Charles Dickens*, VI, 47 and n, 62 and n. See also *The Speeches of Charles Dickens*, ed. K. J. Fielding (Oxford, 1960).

37 See Mason, *The Making of Victorian Sexuality*, pp. 239–40.

38 Amely Bölte to Varnhagen von Ense, 7 April 1850, *Briefe*, p. 79.

39 JC to TC, 29 January 1850, *CL*, XXV, 15.

40 JC to Nero, 20 March 1850, ibid., XXV, 52, 53.

41 TC to JC, 15 September 1849, ibid., XXIV, 232; TC to JC, 30 March 1846, ibid., XX, 155.

42 JC to Helen Welsh, 2 June 1850, ibid., XXV, 93.

43 Moritz Hartmann, 'Mazzini' (1868), *Gesammelte Werke*, ed. Ludwig Bamberger and Wilhelm Vollmer, 10 vols (Stuttgart, 1873–4), X, 169.

44 TC to Leigh Hunt, 17 June, and to John Carlyle, 26 June 1850, *CL*, XXV, 97–8 and n, 102–3.

45 See TC to John Carlyle, 23 November 1850, ibid., XXV, 293 and n.

46 Leigh Hunt to TC, 30 June 1851, ibid., XXV, 293n.

47 JC to Helen Welsh, 4 July 1850, ibid., XXV, 95 and n, 113.

48 Anne Thackeray Ritchie, *Chapters from Some Memoirs* (London, 1894), pp. 60–3.

49 TC, Journal, 25 June 1850, *CL*, XXV, 112n.

50 JC to Helen Welsh, 4 July 1850, ibid., XXV, 111–12.

51 JC to TC, 4 August 1850, ibid., XXV, 135–6. For Lewes's domestic arrangements, see Rosemary Ashton, *G. H. Lewes: A Life* (Oxford, 1991, reprinted London, 2000).

52 JC to TC, 22–3 August 1850, *CL*, XXV, 168.

53 TC to JC, 13 September 1850, ibid., XXV, 211; TC to John Carlyle, 28 April, and to Jean Aitken, 29 April 1851; JC to Janet Hanning, 29 April 1851, ibid., XXVI, 73–4, 76, 77.

54 David Alec Wilson, *Carlyle at his Zenith (1848–53)*, vol. IV of his six-volume biography (London, 1927), pp. 313, 315.

55 JC to TC, 27 September and 8 October 1850, *CL*, XXV, 233–4,

257; see also Thackeray to Henry Taylor, 3 October 1850, *Letters and Private Papers*, II, 694–6 and n.

56 Thackeray to Jane Brookfield, 8 October 1850, *Letters and Private Papers*, II, 698.

57 Thackeray to Lady Ashburton, n.d. (but October or November 1849), MS Ashburton Collection, Acc. 11388 (NLS). The letter can be dated from Thackeray's references to his age, his illness, and, later in the letter, the trial of the Mannings.

58 JC to Helen and Jeannie Welsh, 3 November 1850, *CL*, XXV, 271.

59 Harriet Martineau to Fanny Wedgwood, [?November] 1850, *Harriet Martineau's Letters*, pp. 111–12, 116–17.

60 JC to Mary Russell, 25 November 1850; TC to John Carlyle, 30 November 1850, *CL*, XXV, 294, 297.

61 JC to Helen Welsh, 6 December 1850, ibid., XXV, 303.

62 TC to his mother, 14 December 1850, ibid., XXV, 307.

63 TC to John Carlyle, 23 November 1850, ibid., XXV, 293.

64 TC, Journal, 20 January 1851, Froude, IV, 67.

65 TC to JC, 28 September, and to John Carlyle, 18 December 1850, *CL*, XXV, 237, 312.

66 TC, Journal, 30 December 1850; TC to Lady Bulwer-Lytton, 31 December 1850, ibid., XXV, 324–5 and n.

67 Thackeray to JC, 9 July 1851, *Letters and Private Papers*, Supplement, ed. Harden, I, 422; Dickens to Sir Edward Bulwer-Lytton, 9 May 1851, *Letters of*

Charles Dickens, VI, 379–80 and n.

68 JC to Lady Bulwer-Lytton, early January 1851, *CL*, XXVI, 5.

69 Geraldine Jewsbury to JC, 7 February 1851, *Selections from Letters*, p. 390.

70 JC to John Welsh, 2 and 7 January 1851, *CL*, XXVI, 4, 5, 6–7 and n.

71 See Packe, *Life of John Stuart Mill*, pp. 348–51; *CL*, XXVI, 70n.

72 JC to Jeannie Welsh, 11 May 1851, *CL*, XXVI, 81–2.

73 TC to John Carlyle, 12 January 1851, ibid., XXVI, 13–14.

74 TC to John Carlyle, 29 March, and to Jean Aitken, 3 April 1851, ibid., XXVI, 53, 54.

75 Dickens and W. H. Wills, 'The Metropolitan Protectives', *Household Words*, 26 April 1851, reprinted in Dickens, *Uncollected Writings: Household Words 1850–9*, ed. Harry Stone, 2 vols (London, 1969), I, 255.

76 TC to his mother, 11 June 1851, *CL*, XXVI, 87.

77 JC to Helen Welsh, 5 June 1851, ibid., XXVI, 83–4.

78 Amely Bölte to Varnhagen von Ense, 11 June 1851, *Briefe*, p. 90; Caroline Fox, Journal, 12 June 1851, *Journals*, p. 201.

79 JC to Helen Welsh, 4 July 1851, *CL*, XXVI, 99.

80 Thackeray to JC, 9 July 1851, *Letters and Private Papers*, Supplement, ed. Harden, I, 421, 422.

81 TC to John Carlyle, 24 July 1851; James Gully to TC, 27 July 1851, *CL*, XXVI, 109 and n, 113–14n.

82 TC to John Carlyle, 5 August, and to his mother, 8 August 1851, ibid., XXVI, 120, 124.

83 Macaulay to Thomas Ellis, 24 August 1851, *Letters*, V, 182; TC to Emerson, 25 August 1851, *CL*, XXVI, 141; for Carlyle's later note about Malvern, see ibid., XXVI, 154n.

84 TC to Lady Ashburton, 13 September 1851, *CL*, XXVI, 173.

85 JC to Helen Welsh, 27 August 1851, ibid., XXVI, 143–4.

86 TC to John Carlyle, 24 September, and to JC, 28 September 1851, ibid., XXVI, 182, 185–6.

87 Elizabeth Barrett Browning to Mrs Martin, early August, and to Miss Mitford, 22 October 1851, *The Letters of Elizabeth Barrett Browning*, ed. Frederick G. Kenyon, 2 vols (London, 1897), II, 16, 27.

88 TC, 'Excursion to Paris', *Last Words of Thomas Carlyle*, pp. 156, 158, 159, 161.

89 Ibid., pp. 162, 163–4.

90 TC to JC, 28 September 1851, *CL*, XXVI, 187–8.

91 *Last Words of Thomas Carlyle*, p. 187.

92 Ibid., pp. 178, 179, 180.

93 Ibid., pp. 184, 191.

94 TC to Alick Carlyle, 10 October 1851, *CL*, XXVI, 199.

95 TC, *The Life of John Sterling* (1851), Part III, chapter 7 ('Conclusion').

96 Ibid., Part I, chapter 5 ('A Profession'); Part III, chapter 6 ('Ventnor: Death').

97 Ibid., Part I, chapter 8 ('Coleridge').

98 George Eliot, '*The Life of Sterling*', *Westminster Review* (January 1852), in *Essays of George Eliot*, pp. 47–51.

99 Geraldine Jewsbury to JC, 4 November 1851, *Selections from Letters*, p. 428; Emerson to Emily Drury, 19 November 1851, *Letters of Emerson*, IV, 265; Thackeray to Lady Stanley, 28? October 1851, *Letters and Private Papers*, II, 808.

100 Thackeray to Lady Ashburton, Wednesday [probably 22 October 1851], MS Acc. 11388 (NLS).

101 Thackeray, 'Carlyle's *Life of Sterling*', *Leader*, II (25 October 1851), 1021.

102 JC to Jeannie Welsh, 15 October 1851, *CL*, XXVI, 206.

103 TC to Lady Ashburton, 27 October 1851, ibid., XXVI, 217, 218.

104 JC to Julia Sterling, 18 December 1851, ibid., XXVI, 271.

105 Ibid., XXVI, 272.

106 TC to John Carlyle, 29 December 1851, ibid., XXVI, 286 and n.

107 TC to Lady Ashburton, 10 and 16 February 1852, ibid., XXVII, 39, 45–6.

108 TC to Jean Aitken, 11 October 1851, ibid., XXVI, 203.

109 See Ashton, *Little Germany*, p. 150ff.

110 Alexander Herzen, *My Past and Thoughts*, trans. Constance Garnett, 4 vols (London, 1968), III, 1058–9.

111 TC to John Carlyle, 23 February, and to Lady Ashburton, 28 February 1852, *CL*, XXVII, 52, 54.

112 TC to Arthur Helps, 12 May, and to John Carlyle, 14 June 1852, ibid., XXVII, 113–14, 144.

113 TC to Lady Ashburton, 16 February 1852, ibid., XXVII, 46.

114 TC, Journal, October 1852,

Froude, IV, 120.

115 TC to his mother, 19 September 1852, *CL*, XXVII, 293.

116 TC to JC, 20 and 25 September 1852, ibid., XXVII, 299, 302.

117 TC to John Carlyle, 3 October 1852, ibid., XXVII, 317, 319.

118 Amely Bölte to Varnhagen von Ense, 5 November 1852, *Briefe*, pp. 92–3; Varnhagen von Ense, Diary, 1 October 1852, *Aus dem Nachlass Varnhagen's von Ense, Tagebücher*, ed. Ludmilla Assing, 15 vols (Leipzig, 1861–70, Berlin, 1905), IX, 374.

119 JC to John Carlyle, 30 August 1852, and TC to Joseph Neuberg, 5 November 1852, *CL*, XXVII, 260, 349.

120 TC to his mother, 8 November 1852, ibid., XXVII, 352.

121 See K. J. Fielding, introduction to JC, 'The simple Story of my own first Love', pp. 3–5.

122 'The simple Story', p. 14.

123 Ibid., p. 20. Alexander Carlyle, in *New Letters and Memorials*, II, 47–57, omits the references to the Duchess of Devonshire and the pamphlet on the marriage question, and prints a slightly altered version of the rest.

124 JC to Helen Welsh, 14 November 1852, *CL*, XXVII, 359–60.

125 TC to Henry Hart Milman, 16 November 1852, ibid., XXVII, 362.

126 TC to John Carlyle, 17 December, and to his mother, 19 December 1852, ibid., XXVII, 367 and n, 368 and n.

127 TC, Journal, 9 November 1852, ibid., XXVII, 354n.

128 TC to Lady Ashburton, 10 November 1852, ibid., XXVII, 354–5.

129 JC to Helen Welsh, 14 November 1852, ibid., XXVII, 358.

130 JC to Kate Sterling, 23 October 1852, ibid., XXVII, 342.

CHAPTER 14

In the Valley of the Shadow of Marriage 1853–1854

1 TC to Alick Carlyle, 6 January 1853, *CL*, XXVIII, 6.

2 See TC to A. H. Clough, 25 February, and to his mother, 5 February 1853, ibid., XXVIII, 54, 32.

3 TC to Alick Carlyle, 8 April 1853, ibid., XXVIII, 100, 99.

4 JC to Kate Sterling, 28 January 1853, ibid., XXVIII, 22. See K. J. Fielding, 'Captain Anthony Sterling's Photograph Album', 42–50.

5 TC to John Carlyle, 9 April 1853, *CL*, XXVIII, 102.

6 TC to his mother, 6 May 1853, ibid., XXVIII, 129.

7 For information on the Carlyles' sanitary arrangements I am indebted to Uta Thompson, curator of Carlyle's House. See also Lawrence Wright, *Clean and Decent: The Fascinating History of the Bathroom and the Water Closet* (London, 1960); Daniel Pool, *What Jane Austen Ate and Charles Dickens Knew: From Fox Hunting to Whist – the Facts of Daily Life in Nineteenth-Century England* (New York, 1993), pp. 202–3; Stephen Halliday, *The Great Stink of London: Sir Joseph Bazalgette and the Cleansing of the Victorian Capital* (Stroud, 1999), p. 35ff.

8 See Thea Holme, *The Carlyles at Home*, p. 78.

9 TC to Joseph Neuberg, 28 July

1853, *CL*, XXVIII, 227.

10 See TC to Neuberg, 6 February, and to John Forster, 11 April 1853, ibid., XXVIII, 36, 104.

11 TC, *Reminiscences*, p. 153.

12 TC to Anthony Panizzi, 11 April 1853, *CL*, XXVIII, 105–6 and n.

13 TC, Journal, 13 April 1853, Froude, IV, 129.

14 *Reminiscences*, p. 149.

15 See Tarr, *Descriptive Bibliography*, pp. 129–30.

16 See TC to Edward Chapman, 18 May 1853, *CL*, XXVIII, 144.

17 TC to Clough, 29 December 1852, ibid., XXVII, 382.

18 TC to Clough, 12 May 1853, ibid., XXVIII, 134.

19 TC to Edward Chapman, 13 May 1853, ibid., XXVIII, 139; see Tarr, *Descriptive Bibliography*, pp. 159–65.

20 Lady Ashburton to Jane Brookfield, 1 January 1853; William Brookfield, Diary, 16 April 1853, *Mrs Brookfield and her Circle*, pp. 381, 391.

21 TC to Lord Ashburton, 3 March, and to John Carlyle, 10 March 1853, *CL*, XXVIII, 60, 69.

22 TC to Octavian Blewitt, 6 March 1853, ibid., XXVIII, 65.

23 TC to his mother, 27 May 1853, ibid., XXVIII, 155.

24 Blanche Smith to A. H. Clough, 13 March, and Clough to Blanche Smith, 2 April 1853, *Correspondence of Arthur Hugh Clough*, II, 408–9 and n.

25 Froude to Amely Bölte, 27 May [1882?], Manfred Eimer, 'Briefe an Amely Bölte aus Carlyles Freundeskreis', *Englische Studien*, XLIX (Leipzig, 1915–16), 271.

26 Ellen Twisleton to her sisters, 30 June 1852, *Letters of the Hon. Ellen Twisleton Written to her Family 1852–1862*, ed. Ellen Twisleton Vaughan (London, 1928), pp. 13, 14.

27 TC to Joseph Neuberg, 15 September 1853, *CL*, XXVIII, 272 and n.

28 Ellen Twisleton to her sisters, 1 July 1853, *Letters*, pp. 113–14.

29 TC to John Carlyle, 13 June 1853, *CL*, XXVIII, 171.

30 Mazzini to JC, 1 January 1853, *Scritti*, XLVIII, 111.

31 Mazzini to Aurelio Saffi, 28 March and (?) April 1853, ibid., XLIX, 4, 136–7.

32 TC to John Carlyle, 1 July 1853, *CL*, XXVIII, 181.

33 TC to JC, 8 July 1853, ibid., XXVIII, 186.

34 TC to JC, 9 July 1853, ibid., XXVIII, 193.

35 JC to TC, 8 and 15 July 1853, ibid., XXVIII, 189, 206.

36 TC, note to JC's letters, ibid., XXVIII, 210n.

37 TC to JC, 12 July, and to Isabella Carlyle, 12 July 1853, ibid., XXVIII, 198, 199.

38 JC to TC, 21 July 1853, ibid., XXVIII, 214.

39 See TC to JC, 18 July 1853, ibid., XXVIII, 209.

40 JC to Kate Sterling, 13? August 1853, ibid., XXVIII, 248.

41 JC to Kate Sterling , 26? August 1853, ibid., XXVIII, 253–4.

42 TC to Jean Aitken, 28 August 1853, ibid., XXVIII, 255.

43 See JC to [Cubitt's builder], 23? September 1853, ibid., XXVIII, 276.

44 TC, note on JC's letters, ibid., XXVIII, 214n.

45 See TC to John Carlyle, 14 September 1853, ibid., XXVIII, 268.

46 TC to Lord Ashburton, 8

September 1853, Wilson, V, 40, 41, 42, 43; published in part in *CL*, XXVIII, 264n.

47   See *Hansard's Parliamentary Debates*, 3rd series, CXL, 1772 (31 January to 11 March 1856).

48   TC to Jean Aitken, 18 November 1853, *CL*, XXVIII, 314.

49   TC to Lady Ashburton, 19 November 1853, ibid., XXVIII, 316.

50   TC to John Carlyle, 28 November 1853, ibid., XXVIII, 326.

51   TC to John Carlyle, 28 November, and to Lady Ashburton, 3 November 1853, ibid., XVIII, 327, 305 and n.

52   TC to Lady Ashburton, 28 November 1853, ibid., XXVIII, 327.

53   Froude, *Nemesis of Faith*, p. 130.

54   Emerson to TC, 10 August 1853, *Correspondence of Emerson and Carlyle*, p. 492.

55   See TC to J. W. Parker, 21 November, and to Lady Ashburton, 3 November 1853, *CL*, XXVIII, 320 and n, 305–6.

56   TC to his mother, 4 December 1853, ibid., XXVIII, 333, 334.

57   TC to Jean Aitken, 7 December 1853, ibid., XXVIII, 335.

58   W. H. Brookfield, Diary, 6, 8, and 10 December 1853, *Mrs Brookfield and her Circle*, pp. 395–6, 397–8.

59   Samuel Wilberforce, Journal, 10 December 1853, Wilson, V, 67.

60   Brookfield, Diary, 6 December 1853, *Mrs Brookfield and her Circle*, p. 394.

61   JC to Charles Redwood, 25 December 1853, and TC's note to JC's letters, *CL*, XXVIII, 350–1, 342n.

62   JC to Charles Redwood, 25 December 1853, ibid., XXVIII, 351.

63   TC, note on JC's letters, ibid., XXVIII, 358n.

64   TC to JC, 25 December 1853, ibid., XXVIII, 349.

65   TC to JC, 27 December 1853, ibid., XXVIII, 356.

66   JC to TC, 27 December 1853, ibid., XXVIII, 359.

67   See *Reminiscences*, pp. 196–7.

68   TC to John Carlyle, 31 December 1853, *CL*, XXVIII, 371.

69   JC to Mary Russell, 30 December 1853, ibid., XXVIII, 368.

70   TC to JC, 27 December 1853, ibid., XXVIII, 357.

71   TC, Journal, 28 February 1854, Froude, IV, 148.

72   TC to Jean Aitken, 14 February 1854, *New Letters of Thomas Carlyle*, ed. Alexander Carlyle, 2 vols (London, 1904), II, 163.

73   TC, Journal, April 1854, Froude, IV, 154.

74   TC to Lady Ashburton, 11 January 1854, MS Acc. 11388 (NLS).

75   TC to John Carlyle, 10 February 1854, MS 524 (NLS); published with omissions by Froude, IV, 147.

76   See *DNB*.

77   See K. J. Fielding, 'New Notes for *The Letters*: I. Carlyle's Sketch of Joseph Neuberg. II. "Leave it Alone; Time Will Mend It" ', *Carlyle Annual*, XIII (1992–3), 5.

78   George Eliot to Harriet Beecher Stowe, 29 October, and to John Blackwood, 3 November 1876, *The George Eliot Letters*, VI, 302, 304.

79   See Wilson, V, 86n.

80 TC to Lord Ashburton, 13 March 1854, ibid., V, 87.

81 Emerson to TC, 11 March 1854, *Correspondence of Emerson and Carlyle*, pp. 497–8.

82 Thackeray to Lady Ashburton, 8 March 1854, MS Acc. 11388 (NLS).

83 TC to Emerson, 9 September 1853, *CL*, XXVIII, 266.

84 See D. J. Trela, 'Carlyle, the Just War and the Crimean War', *Carlyle Newsletter*, IX (Spring 1988), 2–11.

85 TC, Journal, Spring 1854, Froude, IV, 151.

86 *The Times*, 23 December 1854; see Trela, 'Carlyle', 6.

87 TC, letter in *The Times*, 28 November 1876, reprinted in Shepherd, *Memoirs of Thomas Carlyle*, II, 308, 310.

88 TC to John Carlyle, 28 April 1854, MS 524 (NLS); published with omissions by Froude, IV, 152–3.

89 See Rupke, *Richard Owen*, pp. 132–3.

90 JC to Mary Smith, 16 January 1854, *Autobiography of Mary Smith*, p. 308.

91 JC to John Carlyle, 18 April 1854, Eric W. Nye, 'An Edition of John Sterling Uncovers New Carlyle Letters', *Carlyle Newsletter*, IX (Spring 1988), 46, 47.

92 JC to Mary Russell, 13 July 1854, *Letters and Memorials of Jane Welsh Carlyle*, ed. J. A. Froude, 3 vols (London, 1883), II, 247.

93 JC to Joseph Neuberg, 14 June 1854, *Letters of Jane Welsh Carlyle to Joseph Neuberg 1848–1862*, ed. Townsend Scudder (London, 1931), p. 22.

94 See *CL*, VII, 337.

95 JC to John Carlyle, 9 May 1854, *New Letters and Memorials*, II, 75, 76–7; corrected from the MS as transcribed by editors in preparation for publication of future volumes of *CL* (see Preface). Henceforth referred to as *CL* file.

96 Clough to C. E. Norton, *Correspondence of Arthur Hugh Clough*, II, 481.

97 Effie Ruskin to her father, 7 March 1854, Tim Hilton, *John Ruskin: The Early Years* (London, 1985), p. 197.

98 JC to William Allingham, 24 February 1856, MS 3823 (NLS).

99 TC to John Carlyle, 27 November 1855, *Correspondence of Carlyle and Ruskin*, p. 15.

100 See Ellen Twisleton to her sisters, 24 June 1853, *Letters*, pp. 97–9.

101 Ellen Twisleton to her sisters, 21 July 1852, ibid., pp. 34–6.

102 Ellen Twisleton to her sisters, 19 September 1852, ibid., p. 52.

103 Ellen Twisleton to her sisters, 7 July 1853, ibid., pp. 115, 116.

104 Ibid., p. 117.

105 Ibid., p. 118.

106 Ibid., p. 119.

107 Ellen Twisleton to her sisters, 22 June 1854, ibid., p. 203.

108 See Froude, IV, 160n.

109 Annie Thackeray, Journal, 22 March 1859, *Letters of Anne Thackeray Ritchie*, ed. Hester Ritchie (London, 1924), p. 110.

110 JC to Mary Russell, 13 July 1854, *Letters and Memorials*, II, 246.

111 See Susanne Howe, *Geraldine Jewsbury*, p. 136.

112 JC to Lady Airlie, 27 December 1851, *CL*, XXVI, 282.

113 JC to Joseph Neuberg, 22

December 1854, *Letters to Neuberg*, p. 24.

114 Ellen Twisleton to her sisters, 31 May 1855, *Letters*, p. 278.

115 Dickens to TC, 13 July 1854, *Letters of Charles Dickens*, VII, 367.

116 Dickens to Forster, 15 May 1854, ibid., VII, 332.

117 Columbia University Library has an album mainly of Tait's photographs of the Carlyles and their circle, apparently collected for JC by Geraldine Jewsbury; copies are in Edinburgh University Library and the National Portrait Gallery.

118 Browning, conversation recorded by Daniel Sargent Curtis, 6 October 1883, printed as Appendix C of *More Than Friends: The Letters of Robert Browning to Katharine de Kay Bronson*, ed. Michael Meredith (Waco, Texas, 1985), p. 168.

119 Robert Tait, typed extract from undated reminiscence of his 1854 visit to Weimar, Acc. 10915 (NLS); TC to Tait, 15 January 1855, MS Edinburgh University Library.

120 For accounts of the early relationship of Lewes and George Eliot, see Ashton, *G. H. Lewes*, p. 148ff, and *George Eliot*, p. 111ff.

121 TC to James Marshall, 14 July 1854, MS *CL* file.

122 G. H. Lewes to TC, 19 October 1854, *The George Eliot Letters*, II, 176.

123 TC to Edward FitzGerald, 19 October 1854, Ashton, *George Eliot*, pp. 118–19.

124 *The George Eliot Letters*, II, 177n.

125 Duffy, *Conversations with Carlyle*, p. 222.

126 George Eliot to Charles Bray, 12 November 1854, *The George Eliot Letters*, II, 185.

127 TC, fragment of 4 August 1854, MS 1798 (NLS).

128 See John Sutherland, *Victorian Fiction: Writers, Publishers, Readers* (London, 1995), p. 69.

129 See Tarr, *Descriptive Bibliography*, p. 163.

130 TC to Alick Carlyle, 6 September 1854, *The Letters of Thomas Carlyle to his Brother Alexander, with Related Family Letters*, ed. Edwin J. Marrs, Jr. (Cambridge, Mass., 1968), pp. 711, 712.

131 JC to Isabella Carlyle [n.d. but 28 August 1854], MS Acc. 7988 (NLS).

132 TC to Lord Ashburton, 30 September 1854, MS Acc. 11388 (NLS); part published in Sanders, *Carlyle's Friendships*, pp. 183–4.

133 TC to John Carlyle, 13 October 1854, *New Letters*, II, 166–7.

134 Thackeray to Lady Stanley, 4 December 1854, *Letters and Private Papers*, III, 404; Ellen Twisleton to her sisters, 6 April 1855, *Letters*, p. 266.

135 JC to Mary Russell, 7 November 1854, *Letters and Memorials*, II, 248; corrected from *CL* file.

136 Dickens to Macready, 1 November 1854, *Letters of Charles Dickens*, VII, 452.

137 TC to Lady Ashburton, 9 November 1854, MS Acc. 11388 (NLS), quoted by C. R. Sanders, 'Carlyle's Pen Portraits of Queen Victoria and Prince Albert', in *Carlyle Past and Present*, ed. K. J. Fielding and Rodger L. Tarr (London, 1976), p. 227.

138 TC to Lady Ashburton, 4 November 1854, MS Acc. 11388 (NLS).

139 TC to Emerson, *Correspondence of Emerson and Carlyle*, p. 505.
140 JC to Mary Russell, 30 December 1854, *Letters and Memorials*, II, 248.
141 TC, undated note, Wilson, V, 125.

CHAPTER 15
Breakdown 1855–1857

1 John Nichol, *Thomas Carlyle*, pp. 123–5.
2 Ruskin to TC, 23 January 1855, *Correspondence of Carlyle and Ruskin*, pp. 62, 63.
3 TC to Ruskin, 23 January 1855, ibid., p. 65.
4 See ibid., pp. 32, 35, 39, 177.
5 Ruskin to Charles Eliot Norton, *The Correspondence of John Ruskin and Charles Eliot Norton*, ed. John Lewis Bradley and Ian Ousby (Cambridge, 1987), p. 488.
6 JC, 'Budget of a Femme Incomprise', [12] February 1855, Froude, IV, 162–3, 163–4; corrected from *CL* file.
7 Ibid., IV, 164–5.
8 Ibid., IV, 165–7.
9 Ibid., IV, 168.
10 Ibid., IV, 169.
11 Ibid., IV, 170.
12 Ibid., IV, 170, 162.
13 Ellen Twisleton to her sisters, 30 April 1855, *Letters*, pp. 271–2.
14 TC to John Carlyle, 20 April 1855, Froude, IV, 174–5.
15 J. Studholme Brownrigg to TC, 30 April 1855, MS 1763 (NLS).
16 TC to Lady Ashburton, 15 December 1855, Wilson, V, 196.
17 Alexander Herzen to Aurelio Saffi, 14 April 1855, *Sobraniye Sochineniy [Complete Works]*, 30 vols (Moscow, 1954–65), XXV, 254.

18 TC to Alexander Herzen, 13 April 1855, published by Herzen in *My Past and Thoughts*, IV, 1797.
19 Herzen to TC, 14 April 1855, ibid., IV, 1797–8n ; *Sobraniye Sochineniy*, XXV, 256.
20 Thomas Erskine to JC, 23 July 1855, MS 1774 (NLS).
21 JC to William Allingham, 24 February 1856, MS 3823 (NLS); see also TC to Ruskin, 29 June 1855, *Correspondence of Carlyle and Ruskin*, p. 67.
22 JC to Ruskin, [6 or 13 July 1855], *Correspondence of Carlyle and Ruskin*, p. 69. Dates from *CL* file.
23 Elizabeth Barrett Browning to Anna Jameson, July–August 1855, *Letters of Elizabeth Barrett Browning*, II, 210.
24 JC to John Carlyle, 27 July 1852, *CL*, XXVII, 190.
25 JC, Journal, 4 July 1856, *New Letters and Memorials*, II, 108–9.
26 See *New Letters of Robert Browning*, ed. W. C. De Vane and K. L. Knickerbocker (London, 1951), p. 262n; Browning, conversation of 6 October 1883 with Daniel Sargent Curtis, *More Than Friends*, p. 168.
27 TC to John Carlyle, 25 September 1855, MS 525 (NLS), part published in Sanders, *Carlyle's Friendships*, p. 162.
28 TC to Browning, 4 December 1855, *Letters of Thomas Carlyle to John Stuart Mill, John Sterling, and Robert Browning*, ed. Alexander Carlyle (London, 1923), pp. 294–5; TC to Harriet Grote, 8 February 1855, MS 23167 (NLS).
29 TC to G. H. Lewes, 7 August

1855, *The George Eliot Letters*, VIII, 141; Ashton, *G. H. Lewes*, p. 162.

30 FitzGerald to TC, 1 August 1855, *Letters of Edward FitzGerald*, II, 171.

31 TC to FitzGerald, 7 August 1855, ibid., II, 173.

32 JC to TC, 11 August 1855, *New Letters and Memorials*, II, 80.

33 See TC to Robert Tait, 21 March 1855, MS Edinburgh University Library; TC to Joseph Neuberg, 22 January 1855, MS 551 (NLS).

34 JC to TC, 14 August 1855, *Letters and Memorials*, II, 250–1; corrected from *CL* file.

35 Ibid., II, 251–2.

36 Mrs Brookfield to Mr Brookfield, 18 August 1855, *Mrs Brookfield and her Circle*, p. 417; TC to JC, 17 August 1855, Froude, IV, 177.

37 TC to John Carlyle, 28 August 1855, MS 525 (NLS).

38 TC to Alick Carlyle, 29 August 1855, *Letters to Alexander*, pp. 717, 719.

39 TC to JC, 2 September 1855, Froude, IV, 178; corrected from *CL* file.

40 TC to FitzGerald, 15 September 1855, *Letters of Edward FitzGerald*, II, 182.

41 JC to TC, 12 September 1855, *New Letters and Memorials*, II, 82–3.

42 See Blunt, *By Chelsea Reach*, pp. 173–84.

43 JC to TC, 14 August 1855, *Letters and Memorials*, II, 253–4; corrected from *CL* file.

44 TC to Lady Ashburton, 23 September 1855, Wilson, V, 176.

45 JC, Journal, 21 and 22 October 1855, *Letters and Memorials*, II,

257, 258.

46 JC, Journal, 23, 31 October, 1 November 1855, ibid., II, 258, 260.

47 JC, Journal, 5, 6, and 7 November 1855, ibid., II, 261.

48 Elizabeth Dwight to Mary Parkman, 8 November 1855, Parkman Family Papers, MS *45M–98 (Houghton).

49 Elizabeth Dwight to Mary Parkman, 16 November 1855, ibid.

50 TC to Lady Ashburton, 13 November 1855, MS Acc. 11388 (NLS); published with omissions by Wilson, V, 188–9.

51 JC to Lady Ashburton, 14 November 1855, MS Acc. 11388 (NLS).

52 JC, Journal, 20 November 1855, *Letters and Memorials*, II, 263.

53 JC, Journal, 21 November 1855, ibid., II, 263–8.

54 Nero to Ellen Twisleton, 30 November 1855, bMS Am 1408 (Houghton).

55 JC, Journal, 11 December 1855, *Letters and Memorials*, II, 268; TC to Lady Ashburton, 15 December 1855, MS Acc. 11388 (NLS).

56 Elizabeth Dwight to Mary Parkman, December 1855, MS *45M–98 (Houghton).

57 Jane Brookfield, quoted in *Mrs Brookfield and her Circle*, p. 426.

58 Ibid., pp. 425–6.

59 W. H. Brookfield to Lord Lyttelton, 5 January 1856, ibid., pp. 431–2.

60 Ibid., p. 428.

61 JC to William Allingham, 24 February 1856, MS 3823 (NLS).

62 TC to Robert Browning, 27 January 1856, MS Huntington Library.

63 W. H. Brookfield, Diary, 6 January 1856, *Mrs Brookfield and her Circle*, p. 433.

64 John Tyndall to Thomas Archer Hirst, 12 January–7 February 1856, typescript copy in Tyndall Papers, Royal Institution of Great Britain. I am grateful to Professor K. J. Fielding for drawing my attention to this account of Tyndall's visit to the Grange.

65 TC to Lord Ashburton, 18 January 1856, Wilson, V, 209.

66 TC to Lady Ashburton, 19 January and 13 February 1856, MS Acc. 11388 (NLS).

67 JC to David Davidson, 2 February 1856, David Davidson, *Memories of a Long Life* (Edinburgh, 1890), p. 302.

68 JC to Mary Russell, 8 February 1856, *New Letters and Memorials*, II, 85.

69 TC to Lady Ashburton, 3 April 1856, Wilson, V, 223.

70 JC, Journal, 26 March and 11 April 1856, *Letters and Memorials*, II, 270, 271.

71 JC, Journal, 15 April 1856, *New Letters and Memorials*, II, 88.

72 JC, Journal, 14 April 1856, ibid., II, 91n.

73 JC, Journal, 25 and 28 April, 1 May 1856, ibid., II, 94, 95, 96.

74 TC to Ruskin, 2 May 1856, *Correspondence of Carlyle and Ruskin*, p. 76.

75 JC to Kate Sterling, 14 May 1856, MS Acc. 9086 (NLS; collection deposited by the National Trust).

76 JC, Journal, 15 and 17 May 1856, *New Letters and Memorials*, II, 98, 100.

77 JC to Kate Sterling, 14 May 1856, MS Acc. 9086 (NLS).

78 JC, Journal, 29 May 1856, *New Letters and Memorials*, II, 101.

79 JC, Journal, 15 and 18 May 1856, ibid., II, 97, 100; TC to Lady Ashburton, 20 May 1856, Hansons, *Necessary Evil*, pp. 445–6.

80 JC, Journal, 19 June 1856, *New Letters and Memorials*, II, 104.

81 Waldo Hilary Dunn, *Froude and Carlyle: A Study of the Froude–Carlyle Controversy* (London, 1930), pp. 93, 194–9, reproduces the entry for 26 June 1856 from a copy which remained in the possession of Froude's family. It is likely that Carlyle's nephew and niece, Alexander and Mary Carlyle, removed the passage from the notebook, which is now in the NLS (MS 533). Alexander Carlyle omitted the passage in *New Letters and Memorials*.

82 JC, Journal, 27 June 1856, *New Letters and Memorials*, II, 107.

83 See J. A. Froude, *My Relations with Carlyle* (London, 1903), p. 22.

84 TC, *Reminiscences*, pp. 157–8. On p. 446 the editors summarise the complicated history of Jane's journals, which were written in two notebooks. The first (from 21 October 1855 to 14 April 1856), published in part by Froude in *Letters and Memorials*, has not survived; the second (from 15 April to 5 July 1856), published in part by Alexander Carlyle in *New Letters and Memorials*, is the one Carlyle bound into his own notebook, and is MS 533 (NLS).

85 See Wilson, V, 269.

86 See Tarr, *Descriptive Bibliography*, pp. 447–8.

87 See *Anne Gilchrist: Her Life and Writings*, ed. H. H. Gilchrist (London, 1887), pp. 41–3.

88 Anne Gilchrist's memoir of her husband in Alexander Gilchrist, *The Life of William Blake*, 2nd edition, 2 vols (London, 1880), II, 373.

89 Vernon Lushington on TC, *Oxford and Cambridge Magazine* (January–December 1856); for TC's letters to Lushington see K. J. Fielding, 'Vernon Lushington: Carlyle's Friend and Editor', *Carlyle Newsletter*, VIII (Spring 1987), 8ff.

90 *Reminiscences*, p. 166.

91 Dickens to TC, 20 July 1856, *Letters of Charles Dickens*, VIII, 166.

92 Dickens to Washington Irving, 5 July 1856, ibid., VIII, 151.

93 JC to Mary Russell, 30 July 1856, *New Letters and Memorials*, II, 115; corrected from MS 605 (NLS).

94 TC to John Carlyle, 30 July 1856, MS 525 (NLS); *Reminiscences*, p. 158.

95 JC to TC, 29 July, 9 and 19 August 1856, *Letters and Memorials*, II, 280, 285, 287.

96 TC to Lady Ashburton, 7 August 1856, MS Acc. 11388 (NLS).

97 JC to TC, 30 August 1856, MS 605 (NLS); part published in *New Letters and Memorials*, II, 118 and n.

98 JC to TC, 18 September 1856, *Letters and Memorials*, II, 299; corrected from *CL* file.

99 Ibid., II, 300–1.

100 TC to JC, 23 September 1856, MS 614 (NLS); part published in Froude, IV, 186.

101 TC to Alick Carlyle, 3 October 1856, *Letters to Alexander*, p. 720.

102 JC to Mary Russell, [6 October 1856], MS 605 (NLS).

103 JC to Mary Russell, 10 October 1856, *Letters and Memorials*, II, 304, 305; corrected from *CL* file.

104 JC to Mary Russell, [24 October 1856], *New Letters and Memorials*, II, 124. Dated from *CL* file.

105 JC to Mary Russell, 28 November 1856, ibid., II, 126.

106 Ellen Twisleton to Elizabeth Dwight, n.d. [probably 24 and 31 October 1856], MS *45M–98 (Houghton).

107 Ellen Twisleton to Elizabeth Dwight, 3 December 1856, ibid.

108 JC to Elizabeth Dwight, 19 December 1856, MS *52M–179 (Houghton).

109 TC, 1866 note on Althaus's memoir, *Two Reminiscences*, p. 113.

110 JC to Emily Tennyson, 21 January 1857, Hansons, *Necessary Evil*, p. 456.

111 TC to Lord Ashburton, 20 December 1856, MS Acc. 11833 (NLS).

112 TC to John Carlyle, 21 March 1857, MS 525 (NLS).

113 TC to [Thomas Watts?], 8 April 1857, MS Acc. 6833 (NLS); TC to Frederick Martin, 7 June 1857, MS CM/C31b (New College, Edinburgh). Watts worked at the British Museum; the editors of *CL* suggest him as the recipient of TC's letter of 8 April.

114 See *CL*, IV, 184n; Wilson, V, 249–51; Fielding, 'Vernon Lushington', 14, 15; Slater, introduction to *Correspondence of Emerson and Carlyle*, p. 65ff.

115 Ellen Twisleton to Elizabeth Dwight, 11 and 12 December 1856, MS *45M–98 (Houghton).

116 TC to Lady Ashburton, 14 January 1857, MS Acc. 11388 (NLS).

117 TC to Lady Ashburton, 23 February 1857, ibid.

118 TC, Journal, 29 March 1857, *CL* file.

119 JC to Mary Russell, 20 April 1857, MS 606 (NLS).

120 Ellen Twisleton to Elizabeth Dwight, 5 February 1857, MS *45M–98 (Houghton).

121 JC to Mary Russell, March 1857, *I Too Am Here*, p. 240.

122 TC to John Carlyle, 22 May 1857, MS 525 (NLS).

123 JC to Mary Russell, *c.* 18 May 1857, *I Too Am Here*, pp. 241–2.

124 W. H. Brookfield, Diary, 12 May 1857, *Mrs Brookfield and her Circle*, p. 456.

125 Ellen Twisleton to Elizabeth Dwight, 14 May 1857, MS *45M–98 (Houghton).

126 Obituary of Lady Ashburton, *The Times*, 7 May 1857, p. 8.

127 *Reminiscences*, p. 105.

CHAPTER 16
A Chelsea Interior 1857–1860

1 JC to TC, 8 July 1857, *Letters and Memorials*, II, 314; corrected from *CL* file.

2 JC to Lady Airlie, 31 July [1857], MS 20767 (NLS).

3 TC to JC, 16 and 26 July 1857, *Thomas Carlyle: Letters to his Wife*, ed. Trudy Bliss (London, 1953), pp. 323, 324, 325.

4 JC to TC, 30 July 1857, Hansons, *Necessary Evil*, p. 463.

5 JC to TC, 3 August 1857, *Letters and Memorials*, II, 322–3.

6 JC to TC, 13 and 15 August 1857, ibid., II, 329.

7 JC to Mary Russell, *c.* 1 October

1857, *Jane Welsh Carlyle: A New Selection of her Letters*, p. 269; corrected from *CL* file.

8 JC to Lady Airlie [11 September 1857], MS Acc. 2427 (NLS).

9 JC to TC, 24 August 1857, *Letters and Memorials*, II, 332–3; corrected from *CL* file.

10 TC to JC, 25 August 1857, *Letters to his Wife*, p. 327.

11 See Henry Blyth, *Madeleine Smith* (London, 1975), pp. 183–5.

12 JC to TC, 26 July 1857, *Letters and Memorials*, II, 319, 320; corrected from *CL* file.

13 Froude, IV, 194.

14 TC to Varnhagen von Ense, 7 October 1857, *Last Words of Thomas Carlyle*, p. 282.

15 JC to Mary Russell [8? October 1857], MS Autograph file (Houghton).

16 See Lee Holcombe, 'Victorian Wives and Property: Reform of the Married Women's Property Laws, 1857–1882', in *A Widening Sphere: Changing Roles of Victorian Women*, ed. Martha Vicinus (London, 1977), pp. 11–12.

17 See Geoffrey Best, *Mid-Victorian Britain 1851–75* (London, 1971, reprinted 1989), p. 303.

18 JC to Mary Russell, 20 November 1857, *I Too Am Here*, p. 126.

19 TC to John Carlyle, 28 January 1858, MS 516 (NLS).

20 JC to Agnes Howden, 23 November 1857, *New Letters and Memorials*, II, 169–70; corrected from *CL* file.

21 Ibid., II, 171.

22 TC's note on JC's letters, *Letters and Memorials*, II, 344.

23 TC to John Carlyle, 22 January 1858, Froude, IV, 197.

24 TC to John Carlyle, 15 April

1858, ibid., II, 199; JC to Mary Russell, February 1858, *New Letters and Memorials*, II, 176–7.

25 JC to Mary Russell, 16 January 1858, *New Letters and Memorials*, II, 172, 173–4; Howe, *Geraldine Jewsbury*, p. 147ff.

26 See George Eliot, Journal, 8 January 1858, *The George Eliot Letters*, II, 418; Ashton, *George Eliot*, p. 172ff.

27 Dickens to George Eliot, 18 January, and to Joseph Langford, 18 January 1858, *Letters of Charles Dickens*, VIII, 506, 507.

28 JC to George Eliot, 21 January 1858, *The George Eliot Letters*, II, 425–6.

29 See Ashton, *George Eliot*, pp. 164ff, 189.

30 JC to Mary Russell, February 1858, *New Letters and Memorials*, II, 175.

31 Mazzini to Emilie Hawkes, August and 14 October 1856, *Scritti*, LVII, 13, 160.

32 Wilson, V, 331. For Charlotte Southam see Holme, *The Carlyles at Home*, p. 190.

33 Thomas Woolner to Emily Tennyson, 7 June 1858, *Life in Letters*, p. 149.

34 JC to TC, 11 July 1858, *Letters and Memorials*, II, 357; corrected from *CL* file.

35 TC to Emerson, 2 June 1858, *Correspondence of Emerson and Carlyle*, p. 523.

36 See Edgar Johnson, *Charles Dickens: His Tragedy and Triumph*, 2 vols (London, 1953), II, 920ff.

37 JC, miscellaneous notebook, *New Letters and Memorials*, II, 115.

38 See Michael Sadleir, *Bulwer: A Panorama; Edward Bulwer and Rosina 1803–1836* (London, 1931), p. 407ff.

39 See Davies, *John Forster*, p. 41.

40 JC to TC, 9 July 1858, *New Letters and Memorials*, II, 184; TC to JC, 11 July 1858, MS 615 (NLS).

41 JC to TC, 12 July 1858, MS 606 (NLS).

42 TC to JC, 14 July 1858, MS 615 (NLS).

43 TC, *Reminiscences*, p. 169.

44 TC to JC, 24 June 1858, Froude, IV, 207.

45 JC to TC, 25 June 1858, *Letters and Memorials*, II, 348 and n.

46 JC to TC, 27 June 1858, MS 606 (NLS).

47 TC to JC, 28 June 1858, MS 615 (NLS); quoted in part in Froude, IV, 208.

48 See Halliday, *The Great Stink of London*, pp. xii, 61.

49 Ibid., pp. 71, 77ff.

50 Arthur Helps to TC, 22 December 1857, John R. DeBruyn, 'Thomas Carlyle and Sir Arthur Helps', *Bulletin of the John Rylands University Library of Manchester*, LXIV (Autumn 1981, Spring 1982), 35–6.

51 TC to John Forster, 17 and 23 June 1858, MS Forster Collection (Victoria and Albert Museum).

52 JC to TC, 1 July 1858, MS 606 (NLS).

53 TC to JC, 2 July 1858, MS 615 (NLS).

54 JC to TC, 4 and 11 July 1858, *Letters and Memorials*, II, 354, 355–6.

55 JC to TC, 19 and 22 July 1858, *Jane Welsh Carlyle: A New Selection of her Letters*, pp. 276, 277.

56 TC, annotation in his copy of *Helden-, Staats-, und Lebensgeschichte des allerdurchlauchtigsten*

*und grosmachtigsten Fürsten und
Herrns, Friedrichs des Andern*
(Frankfurt, 1758–64), II, 117, in
the collection of TC's books in
Houghton Library.

57 TC to Varnhagen von Ense, 7
October 1857, *Last Words of
Thomas Carlyle*, p. 281.

58 See Wilson, V, 317.

59 JC to TC, 27 July 1858, *New
Letters and Memorials*, II, 187.

60 TC to Joseph Neuberg, 22 July
1858, MS 552 (NLS).

61 Froude, IV, 217; TC, *Journey to
Germany, Autumn 1858*, ed. R. A.
E. Brooks (New Haven, Conn.,
1940), 1, 9ff. For Foxton, see
Wilson, V, 247.

62 TC to JC, 14 September 1858,
Froude, IV, 224; corrected from
CL file.

63 JC to TC, 10 September 1858,
Letters and Memorials, II, 381.

64 TC to JC, 6 August 1858,
Froude, IV, 215; corrected from
CL file.

65 JC to TC, 9 August 1858, *Letters
and Memorials*, II, 377.

66 JC to Mary Russell, 1 October
1858, ibid., II, 385–6, 387.

67 JC to Charlotte Southam, [16
September 1858], *Thomas and
Jane: Selected Letters*, pp. 82–3.

68 JC to Mary Russell, 22 October
1860, *New Letters and Memorials*,
II, 236.

69 See Holme, *The Carlyles at Home*,
p. 185ff, for a list of the servants
at Cheyne Row.

70 JC to Lady Stanley [end October
1858], MS Duke University
Library; *CL* file, to which I am
indebted for the identification of
Cruiser.

71 TC to Forster, 23 June 1858,
Wilson, V, 316; Davies, *John
Forster*, p. 193.

72 See Tarr, *Descriptive Bibliography*,
pp. 181–2.

73 TC to Henry Larkin, 6 January
1859, MS Huntington Library;
part published in Henry Larkin,
'Carlyle and Mrs Carlyle', *British
Quarterly Review* (July 1881).

74 TC to Varnhagen von Ense, 6
June 1852, *Last Words of Thomas
Carlyle*, p. 268.

75 TC to Ruskin, 23 May 1855,
*Correspondence of Carlyle and
Ruskin*, p. 66.

76 William Allingham, Diary, 2
December 1873, *William
Allingham's Diary*, ed. H.
Allingham and D. Radford
(London, 1907, reprinted 1967),
pp. 229–30.

77 TC, *Frederick the Great*, Book I,
chapter 1 ('Proem: Friedrich's
History from the Distance We
Are At').

78 Ibid.

79 TC, marginal note on *The Life
and Actions of Frederic, the
Victorious King of Prussia, Elector of
Brandenburg, &c. Compiled from
Original Memoirs and Documents*
(London, 1758), in Houghton
Library.

80 Althaus memoir, *Two
Reminiscences*, p. 116.

81 *Frederick the Great*, Book VIII,
chapter 5 ('Interview of Majesty
and Crown-Prince at Custrin').

82 Frederic Harrison, 'Thomas
Carlyle', *Studies in Early Victorian
Literature* (London, 1895), p. 45.

83 *Frederick the Great*, Book IX,
chapter 1 ('Princess Elizabeth
Christina of Brunswick-Bevern').

84 Ibid., Book IV, chapter 12
('Crown-Prince Falls into
Disfavour with Papa').

85 See Arthur A. and Vonna H.
Adrian, 'Frederick the Great:

"That Unutterable Horror of a Prussian Book"', in *Carlyle Past and Present*, ed. Fielding and Tarr, pp. 188–9.

86 George Gilfillan, 'Frederick the Great', *Scottish Review* (January 1859), in Seigel (ed.), *Critical Heritage*, p. 438.

87 Clough to Charles Eliot Norton, 7 October 1858, *Correspondence of Arthur Hugh Clough*, II, 557.

88 Clough to Norton, 20 October [1858], bMS Am 1088 (Houghton).

89 Clough to Norton, 29 October 1858, *Correspondence of Arthur Hugh Clough*, II, 559.

90 Mazzini to Emilie Hawkes, 3 November 1858, *Scritti*, LXI, 332–3.

91 FitzGerald to E. B. Cowell, 13 January, and to TC, 20 June 1859, *Letters of Edward FitzGerald*, II, 324, 336.

92 Elizabeth Barrett Browning to Isabella Blagden, *Dearest Isa: Robert Browning's Letters to Isabella Blagden*, ed. Edward C. McAleer (Austin, Texas, 1951), p. 35.

93 Emily Tennyson, Journal, 7 December 1858, *Lady Tennyson's Journal*, ed. James O. Hoge (Charlottesville, Virginia, 1981), p. 128.

94 TC's copy of *Mémoires de L'Impératrice Catharine II, écrits par elle-même et précédés d'une préface par A. Herzen* (London, 1859), in Houghton Library.

95 *Frederick the Great*, Book XX, chapter 10 ('Friedrich in Breslau; has News from Petersburg').

96 Emerson to TC, 1 May 1859, *Correspondence of Emerson and Carlyle*, p. 527 and n.

97 JC to Mary Russell, 30 December 1858, *Letters and Memorials*, II, 393.

98 TC, Journal, 28 December 1858, Froude, IV, 229.

99 TC to Lord Ashburton, 28 and 29 July 1858, MS Acc. 11388 (NLS).

100 TC to Lord Ashburton, 15 September 1857, ibid.; quoted without date in Virginia Surtees, *The Ludovisi Goddess: The Life of Louisa, Lady Ashburton* (Salisbury, 1984), p. 57.

101 JC to Lady Stanley [end October 1858], MS Duke University Library.

102 JC to Mary Russell, 30 October 1858, MS 606 (NLS).

103 Macaulay to Thomas Flower Ellis, 1 April 1859, *Letters of Thomas Babington Macaulay*, VI, 206.

104 TC to Ford Madox Brown, [Spring 1859], Wilson, V, 339.

105 See *Art Treasures of England: The Regional Collections* (London, 1998), catalogue no. 130.

106 JC to George Eliot, 20 February 1859, *The George Eliot Letters*, III, 17–18.

107 See Ashton, *George Eliot*, p. 213ff.

108 JC to Major David Davidson, 14 February 1859, *New Letters and Memorials*, II, 205. (MS Mrs. Mary Davidson)

109 William Allingham, note on TC, MS 3823 (NLS).

110 *Anne Gilchrist: Her Life and Writings*, p. 73.

111 TC to John Carlyle, 4 May 1859, *New Letters*, II, 196.

112 TC, notes on *On Liberty*, 19 October 1865, D. J. Trela, 'A New (Old) Review of Mill's *Liberty*: A Note on Carlyle and Mill's Friendship', *Carlyle Newsletter*, VI (Spring 1985), 24.

113 *Anne Gilchrist: Her Life and Writings*, p. 71.

114 TC to Mill, 28 June 1858, *Letters to Mill, Sterling, and Browning*, pp. 184–5.

115 Mill to TC, 8 July 1858, *Later Letters, Collected Works*, XV, 556–7.

116 JC to Mary Russell, 12 May 1859, *New Letters and Memorials*, II, 212–13.

117 JC to Mary Russell, 27 June 1859, ibid., II, 214.

118 JC to George Cooke, [2 July 1859], *Letters and Memorials*, II, 397–8.

119 JC to Miss Barnes, 24 August 1859, ibid., III, 2,3; *I Too Am Here*, p. 80.

120 See TC to Alick Carlyle, 7 October 1859, *Letters to Alexander*, p. 733.

121 TC to John Forster, 26 October 1859, *New Letters*, II, 204, 205.

122 Thackeray to TC, 16 October 1859, *Letters and Private Papers*, Supplement, ed. Harden, II, 905.

123 TC to Thackeray, 20 October 1859, *Letters and Private Papers*, IV, 157-8.

124 Karl Alexander, Grand Duke of Saxe-Weimar-Eisenach, to TC, 9 November 1859, MS 1763 (NLS).

125 JC to Mary Russell, [November] 1859, *New Letters and Memorials*, II, 220.

126 JC to Dr Barnes, 1 February 1859, *Letters and Memorials*, III, 23.

127 See JC to Mary Russell, 24 February 1860, *New Letters and Memorials*, II, 224.

128 Vernon Lushington to Joanna and Helen Richardson, 4 March 1860, K. J. Fielding, 'Vernon Lushington', 17.

129 TC to Thackeray, 24 May 1860, *Letters and Private Papers*, IV, 187.

130 TC, note in *Letters and Memorials*, III, 25.

131 JC to Neuberg, 3 July 1860, *Letters to Neuberg*, p. 29.

132 JC to Mary Russell, 28 January 1860, Hansons, *Necessary Evil*, p. 483.

133 JC to Lady Ashburton, July 1860, ibid., p. 488.

134 Lady Stanley to Lord Stanley, 26 August 1860, ibid., p. 490.

135 JC to Lady Ashburton, early September 1860, ibid.

136 TC to JC, 28 August 1860, *Letters to his Wife*, pp. 352–3.

137 JC to Mary Austin, 19 October 1860, *Letters and Memorials*, III, 63.

138 Ruskin to John Brown, 11 November 1860, *Correspondence of Carlyle and Ruskin*, p. 89n.

139 TC to Ruskin, 29 October 1860, ibid., p. 89.

CHAPTER 17

In Sickness and in Health

1861–1866

1 Mazzini to Emilie Venturi, January 1861, *Scritti*, LXX, 264.

2 Froude, IV, 243.

3 JC to Miss Barnes, 3 April 1861, Blunt, *By Chelsea Reach*, pp. 186–7.

4 JC to Margaret Oliphant, [end of April 1861], D. J. Trela, 'Margaret Oliphant's "bravest words yet spoken" on Thomas and Jane Welsh Carlyle', *Carlyle Studies Annual*, XVIII (1998), 156–7.

5 John James Ruskin to W. H. Harrison, 28 January 1861, *Correspondence of Carlyle and Ruskin*, p. 20n. For Dr Alexander ('Jupiter') Carlyle, see *DNB*.

6 See Duffy, *Conversations with Carlyle*, p. 213. A copy of the photograph is at Carlyle's House.

7 TC to John Carlyle, 23 April 1861, Froude, IV, 245.

8 G. H. Lewes, Journal, 4 July 1861, *The George Eliot Letters*, III, 435.

9 See Lewes to Thomas Adolphus Trollope, 5 July 1861, ibid., VIII, 287.

10 George Eliot, Journal, 26 July 1861, *The Journals of George Eliot*, ed. Margaret Harris and Judith Johnston (Cambridge, 1998), p. 98.

11 Margaret Oliphant to John Blackwood, 4 November 1861, *Autobiography and Letters of Mrs Margaret Oliphant*, ed. Mrs Harry Coghill (London, 1899, reprinted Leicester, 1974), p. 180.

12 See Howe, *Geraldine Jewsbury*, p. 152.

13 JC to TC, 6 August 1861, *Letters and Memorials*, III, 81, 82.

14 JC to Lady Airlie, n.d. [1861], MS 20767 (NLS).

15 JC to Mary Russell, 30 August 1861, *Letters and Memorials*, III, 86.

16 TC, note on JC's letters, ibid., III, 88.

17 JC to Miss Barnes, 22 September 1861, ibid., III, 90.

18 JC to Miss Barnes, 24 January 1862, ibid., III, 94.

19 JC to Mary Russell, 23 February 1862, ibid., III, 97.

20 TC to JC, January 1862, Froude, IV, 248.

21 JC to Mary Russell, 28 January 1860, *Letters and Memorials*, III, 20–1.

22 Huxley's speech as reported by J. R. Green to Boyd Dawkins, see Francis Darwin, *The Life and Letters of Charles Darwin*, II, 322.

23 *Punch*, XL (18 May 1861), 206.

24 Froude, IV, 259.

25 *Frederick the Great*, Book XI, chapter 3 ('Friedrich Makes an Excursion, Not of Direct Sort, into the Cleve Countries').

26 Ibid., Book XII, chapter 10 ('Battle of Mollwitz').

27 TC, *Reminiscences*, p. 156.

28 Emerson to TC, 8 December 1862, *Correspondence of Emerson and Carlyle*, pp. 535, 536; TC to John Carlyle, 28 December 1862, ibid., p. 537n.

29 JC to Mary Russell, 5 June 1862, *Letters and Memorials*, III, 99.

30 See Browning to Richard Monckton Milnes, 23 May 1862, *New Letters of Robert Browning*, p. 145.

31 JC to TC, 29 June 1862, *New Letters and Memorials*, II, 247.

32 JC to TC, 12 August 1862, ibid., II, 250.

33 JC to TC, 15 August 1862, MS 607 (NLS).

34 Mazzini to JC, 22 August 1862, *Scritti*, LXXIII, 73, 74.

35 JC to TC, 2 September 1862, *Letters and Memorials*, III, 114.

36 TC to John Carlyle, 19 September 1862, *New Letters*, II, 212.

37 JC to Mary Russell, September 1862, *New Letters and Memorials*, II, 268–9.

38 TC to JC, 21 August 1862, *Letters to his Wife*, pp. 355–6.

39 TC to Dr Peyton Blakiston, 21 August 1862, K. J. Fielding and Peter Jackson, 'Carlyle's Reminiscences: Dr Peyton Blakiston and Bessy Barnet', *Carlyle Newsletter*, IX (Spring 1988), 54.

40 JC to Eliza Forster, 30 October

1862, MS 1797 (NLS).

41 Dickens to Georgina Hogarth, 11 March 1856, *Letters of Charles Dickens*, VIII, 70.

42 JC to TC, 9 July 1858, Hansons, *Necessary Evil*, p. 472.

43 JC to Eliza Forster, 30 October 1862, MS 1797 (NLS); part published in Davies, *John Forster*, p. 110.

44 See JC to Betty Braid, 25 December 1862, and to Mary Russell, 21 November 1862, *Letters and Memorials*, III, 144, 136–7.

45 JC to Mary Austin, 23 October 1862, ibid., III, 134.

46 Browning to Isabella Blagden, 19 November 1862, *Dearest Isa*, p. 136.

47 TC to John Carlyle, 4 December 1862, Wilson, V, 487.

48 TC to John Carlyle, 13 February 1863, Froude, IV, 269–70.

49 JC to Lady Ashburton, 1 May 1863, Hansons, *Necessary Evil*, p. 507.

50 JC to Lady Ashburton, 23 March 1863, ibid., p. 506.

51 TC to Lady Ashburton, 17 May 1863, ibid., p. 507.

52 JC to Mary Austin, 26 February 1863, *Letters and Memorials*, III, 154–5.

53 JC to Margaret Oliphant, Spring 1862, Trela, 'Margaret Oliphant's "bravest words yet spoken"', 159.

54 JC to Grace Welsh, 2 March 1863, *Letters and Memorials*, III, 157.

55 JC to Lady Ashburton, 7 March 1863, Hansons, *Necessary Evil*, p. 504.

56 JC to Grace Welsh, 2 March 1863, *Letters and Memorials*, III, 157.

57 JC to J. A. Froude, [March 1863], Hansons, *Necessary Evil*, pp. 504–5.

58 TC to Alexander Ireland, 18 March 1863, Shepherd, *Memoirs of Thomas Carlyle*, II, 187.

59 Dickens to TC, 13 April 1863, *Letters of Charles Dickens*, X, 233.

60 TC to Janet Hanning, 29 April 1863, *Letters of Thomas Carlyle to his Youngest Sister*, ed. Charles Townsend Copeland (London, 1899), pp. 228–9. See also Wilson, V, 504–5.

61 JC to Lady Airlie, 11 June [1863], MS 20767 (NLS).

62 JC to Lady Ashburton, 13 August 1863, Hansons, *Necessary Evil*, pp. 509–10.

63 JC to Lady Ashburton, 13 September 1863, ibid., p. 511.

64 TC, 'Ilias (Americana) in Nuce', *Macmillan's Magazine*, VIII (August 1863), 301.

65 Karl Marx, *Capital*, I, Part III, 'The Production of Absolute Surplus-Value', chapter 10 ('The Working Day'), published in German (Hamburg, 1867) and in English, edited by Friedrich Engels (London, 1887).

66 See Fielding, 'Carlyle and the Americans', 61.

67 Horace Howard Furness to Edmund K. Muspratt, 31 August and 24 November 1863, *Letters of Horace Howard Furness*, ed. H. H. F. Jayne, 2 vols (Boston, Mass., 1922), I, 145, 156.

68 Horace Howard Furness to TC, 29 August [1863], with photograph, MS Acc. 11388 (NLS).

69 Conway, *Autobiography*, I, 357, 365.

70 Ibid., I, 394.

71 JC to Grace Welsh, 20 October

1863, *Letters and Memorials*, III, 182.

72 JC to Lady Airlie, 2 November [1863], MS 20767 (NLS).

73 Larkin, 'Carlyle and Mrs Carlyle', 76–7.

74 See TC's reminiscence of Jane, *Reminiscences*, p. 169.

75 TC to John Carlyle, October 1863, Hansons, *Necessary Evil*, p. 514.

76 JC to Lord Ashburton, late October 1863, ibid., p. 513.

77 JC to Mary Russell, 26 October 1863, *Letters and Memorials*, III, 185.

78 JC to Mrs Simmonds, 3 November 1863, ibid., III, 190.

79 JC to Mrs Simmonds, 27 November 1863, *Jane Welsh Carlyle: A New Selection of her Letters*, p. 310; see also Blunt, *By Chelsea Reach*, p. 166.

80 See J. T. Delane to G. W. Dasent, 4 November 1863, Arthur Irwin Dasent, *John Thadeus Delane, Editor of 'The Times': His Life and Correspondence*, 2 vols (London, 1908), II, 73.

81 JC to Lady Airlie, 2 November [1863], MS 20767 (NLS).

82 TC to John Carlyle, 11 December 1863, *New Letters*, II, 217–18.

83 Howe, *Geraldine Jewsbury*, p. 171.

84 *Frederick the Great*, Book XVI, chapter 10 ('Demon Newswriter, of 1752').

85 TC to Neuberg, 12 November 1863, Wilson, V, 531.

86 *Reminiscences*, p. 173.

87 JC to Lady Ashburton, early April 1864, Hansons, *Necessary Evil*, pp. 517–18.

88 JC to TC, 8 April 1864, *Letters and Memorials*, III, 195–6.

89 TC to Lady Ashburton, 10 April 1864, MS Acc. 11388 (NLS).

90 See Wilson, V, 541.

91 JC to TC, 25 April 1864, *Letters and Memorials*, III, 196–7.

92 TC's notes, ibid., III, 195, 200.

93 JC to TC, 15 July 1864, ibid., III, 202.

94 JC to TC, 23 July 1864, ibid., III, 204.

95 TC to JC, 25 July 1864, MS 633 (NLS).

96 John Carlyle to TC, 28 July 1864, MS 1775B (NLS).

97 JC to Eliza Forster, [25 August 1864], MS 1797 (NLS).

98 JC to Eliza Forster, [17 August 1864], ibid.

99 John Carlyle to Alick Carlyle, 4 July 1866, *Letters to Alexander*, p. 754.

100 Mary Austin to JC, [26 July 1864], MS 608 (NLS).

101 TC to JC, 29 July 1864, MS 616 (NLS).

102 TC to John Carlyle, 24 September 1864, *New Letters*, II, 223.

103 JC to TC, 26 September 1864, Hansons, *Necessary Evil*, p. 523.

104 TC to JC, 25 August 1864, *Letters to his Wife*, p. 372.

105 Dickens et al. to Michael Bass, [?early May 1864], *Letters of Charles Dickens*, X, 388.

106 TC to JC, 25 August 1864, *Letters to his Wife*, p. 372.

107 JC to Mary Russell, 3 October 1864, *Letters and Memorials*, III, 216–17.

108 JC to Mary Austin, 9 October, and to Mary Russell, 24 October 1864, *New Letters and Memorials*, II, 303, 307.

109 JC to Mary Austin, 18 October 1864, *Letters and Memorials*, III, 228.

110 JC to Mary Russell, 12 November 1864, *I Too Am Here*, pp. 155, 156.

111 JC to Kate Stanley, 24 November [1864], *The Amberley Papers: The Letters and Diaries of Lord and Lady Amberley*, ed. Bertrand and Patricia Russell, 2 vols (London, 1937), I, 430.

112 JC to Mary Russell, November 1864, MS 609 (NLS); part published in *New Letters and Memorials*, II, 308–9.

113 JC to Mary Russell, 28 February 1865, *New Letters and Memorials*, II, 319.

114 JC to the Misses Welsh, late April 1864, *Letters and Memorials*, III, 197.

115 See Pullar, *Frank Harris*, p. 56.

116 Anne Thackeray Ritchie, *Chapters from Some Memoirs*, p. 136.

117 Annie Thackeray to Mrs Baxter, 24 October 1864, *Letters and Private Papers*, IV, 304.

118 TC to Milnes, 29 December 1863, Reid, *Life of Richard Monckton Milnes*, II, 113.

119 Edward Twisleton to Mary Parkman, 16 December 1864, MS *45M–98 (Houghton).

120 JC to Mary Russell, 20 October 1864, *New Letters and Memorials*, II, 305.

121 For TC's view of Watts's portrait, see Jude V. Nixon, ' "Return Alphias": The Forster/Carlyle Unpublished Letters and Re-tailoring the Sage', *Carlyle Studies Annual*, XVIII (1998), 93. Watts's painting and Mrs Cameron's photographs are in the National Portrait Gallery.

122 JC to Lady Ashburton, [18 October 1864], Hansons,

123 *Necessary Evil*, p. 525.

123 JC to Mary Russell, 10 October 1864, *Letters and Memorials*, III, 224.

124 JC to Mary Russell, November 1864, *New Letters and Memorials*, II, 312.

125 TC to Neuberg, 13 October 1864, Wilson, V, 559. See also TC's note, *Letters and Memorials*, III, 229–30.

126 JC to Mary Russell, 31 October 1864, *Letters and Memorials*, III, 230.

127 JC to Mary Russell, November 1864, *New Letters and Memorials*, II, 308.

128 Mazzini to Matilda Biggs, 4 March 1865, *Scritti*, LXXX, 124.

129 JC to TC, 12 July 1865, *Jane Welsh Carlyle: A New Selection of her Letters*, p. 323.

130 See TC's note, *Letters and Memorials*, III, 242–3.

131 See Davies, *John Forster*, p. 195; TC to John Carlyle, 26 April 1865, *New Letters*, II, 227.

132 *Frederick the Great*, Book XXI, chapter 1 ('Prefatory').

133 Herman Merivale, review of *Frederick the Great, Quarterly Review* (July 1865), Seigel (ed.) *Critical Heritage*, pp. 452, 454.

134 See Shepherd, *Memoirs of Thomas Carlyle*, II, 293ff.

135 See David Alec Wilson and David Wilson MacArthur, *Carlyle in Old Age (1865–81)*, volume VI of Wilson's six-volume biography, completed by his nephew after his death (London, 1934), pp. 321, 344–5.

136 Thomas Mann, *Friedrich und die grosse Koalition* (1915) and 'Carlyle's *Friedrich*' (1916), in Thomas Mann, *Gesammelte Werke*, 13 vols, 2nd edition

(Frankfurt, 1974), X, 76ff, 568–9, 570.

137 See Introduction to *Frederick the Great*, selected and edited by John Clive (Chicago, Illinois, 1969), p. xiii.

138 Geraldine Jewsbury to Walter Mantell, March 1865, Howe, *Geraldine Jewsbury*, p. 172.

139 TC to John Carlyle, 26 April 1865, *New Letters*, II, 227–8 and n.

140 JC to Mary Russell, 4 May 1865, *Jane Welsh Carlyle: A New Selection of her Letters*, p. 322.

141 TC to Emerson, 14 June 1865, *Correspondence of Emerson and Carlyle*, pp. 543–4.

142 TC to JC, 11 June 1865, *Letters to his Wife*, pp. 378–9.

143 TC to John Carlyle, 14 September 1865, *New Letters*, II, 231.

144 TC to Alick Carlyle, 6 August 1865, *Letters to Alexander*, pp. 742, 743.

145 Ruskin to TC, 23 or 24 February 1865, *Correspondence of Carlyle and Ruskin*, pp. 108–9; TC to John Carlyle, 1 March 1865, *New Letters*, II, 225.

146 TC to JC, 9 June 1865, *Letters to his Wife*, p. 378.

147 JC to Ruskin, 15 July 1865, *Correspondence of Carlyle and Ruskin*, p. 111.

148 TC to JC, 27 July 1865, *Letters to his Wife*, pp. 381, 404–5.

149 JC to TC, 30 July 1865, *Letters and Memorials*, III, 278.

150 Wilson, VI, 23. A different account of Tiny's arrival is given by John Carlyle in a letter to Alick of 3 May 1866, in which he says the dog was bequeathed to Jane in March 1866 by a friend, Mrs Chapman; see *Letters*

to *Alexander*, p. 751.

151 TC to John Carlyle, 5 December 1865, *New Letters*, II, 232.

152 Wilson, VI, 30.

153 TC to John Carlyle, 7 November 1865, Froude, IV, 296.

154 JC to Betty Braid, 28 December 1865, *New Letters and Memorials*, II, 343.

155 JC to Mary Russell, 25 December 1865, *Letters and Memorials*, III, 301–3.

156 JC to Grace Welsh, 23 January 1866, *I Too Am Here*, pp. 280, 279.

157 JC to Henry Inglis, March 1866, ibid., p. 281.

158 See *The Royal Scottish Academy Exhibitors 1826–1990*, ed. Charles de Laperriere, 4 vols (Calne, 1991), IV, 296.

159 JC to Mary Dods, 12 March [1866], MS 1797 (NLS).

160 See John Tyndall, *New Fragments*, pp. 358–9, 362.

161 JC to TC, 2 April 1866, *Letters and Memorials*, III, 317.

162 See Shepherd, *Memoirs of Thomas Carlyle*, II, 216.

163 See *Letters to his Wife*, p. 385.

164 See Tarr, *Descriptive Bibliography*, pp. 196–202.

165 TC to JC, 3 and 4 April 1866, *Letters to his Wife*, pp. 386, 387.

166 JC to Lady Ashburton, 2 April 1866, Hansons, *Necessary Evil*, p. 542.

167 JC to TC, 3 April 1866, *Letters and Memorials*, III, 318.

168 JC to TC, 12 April 1866, ibid., III, 328–9; corrected from MS 609 (NLS).

169 'Lord Rector', *Punch*, L (14 April 1866), 154; see Janice Carlisle, 'Shooting Niagara? Carlyle and *Punch* in the Late 1860s', *Carlyle*

Studies Annual, XVIII (1998), 21–3.

170 TC to JC, 11 April 1866, *Letters to his Wife*, p. 389.

171 JC to TC, 19 April 1866, *Letters and Memorials*, III, 334–5.

172 JC to TC, 17 April 1866, Hansons, *Necessary Evil*, p. 544.

173 JC to TC, 21 April 1866, *Letters and Memorials*, III, 336, 337.

174 TC, reminiscence of JC, *Reminiscences*, pp. 192–3.

175 Ibid., pp. 191–2; Geraldine Jewsbury to TC, 26 May 1866, *Letters and Memorials*, III, 338–40; Froude, IV, 313–14.

176 See John Carlyle to Alick Carlyle, 3 May 1866, *Letters to Alexander*, p. 752.

177 JC to TC, 21 April 1866, *Letters and Memorials*, III, 337–8.

178 TC to Jean Aitken, 28 April 1866, *New Letters*, II, 235–6.

179 Dickens to Forster, [?25 April 1866], *Letters of Charles Dickens*, XI, 192 and n.

180 *Reminiscences*, p. 161.

Epilogue

1 John Carlyle to William Dods, 24 April 1866, MS 1797 (NLS).

2 TC, *Reminiscences*, p. 193.

3 John Carlyle to Alick Carlyle, 3 May 1866, *Letters to Alexander*, p. 752.

4 Erasmus Darwin to TC, 2 May [1866], 'New Carlyle Letters', *Carlyle Newsletter*, VIII (Spring 1987).

5 Dickens to TC, 30 May 1866, *Letters of Charles Dickens*, XI, 207.

6 Carlyle, Journal, 30 November 1867, Froude, IV, 359–60.

Bibliography

1. MANUSCRIPT SOURCES

I have consulted the large collection of manuscript letters by, between, to, and about the Carlyles in the National Library of Scotland (NLS), including the recently acquired Ashburton Collection which contains letters by Lord and Lady Ashburton, as well as letters to them from the Carlyles, Mill, Thackeray, and other acquaintances.

The Houghton Library of Harvard University (Houghton) contains letters and journals relating to the Carlyles, as well as holding TC's annotated library of books used in his research for *Frederick the Great*. The Charles Eliot Norton Collection has letters and Norton's journals of conversations with TC; the Twisleton and Parkman Family Papers contain letters from Ellen Twisleton and her sister Elizabeth Dwight, with much interesting material on the Carlyles, as well as letters from JC. The Charles Sumner Collection of Autographs also has some Carlyle-related material.

Other libraries with unpublished material which I have consulted are:

Bodleian Library, Oxford (Kingsley letters).
Duke University Library, Durham, North Carolina (JC to Lady Stanley).
Edinburgh University Library (TC to Robert Tait).
Henry E. Huntington Library, San Marino, California (TC to Robert Browning and to Henry Larkin).
Jagiellonian University Library, Cracow (Geraldine Jewsbury to Amely Bölte).
National Art Library, Victoria and Albert Museum, London (Forster Collection).
New College Library, Edinburgh (TC to Frederick Martin).
Royal Institution of Great Britain, London (John Tyndall Papers).
Dr Williams's Library, London (Henry Crabb Robinson diary).

2. BOOKS AND ARTICLES

Adrian, Arthur A. and Vonna H., 'Frederick the Great: "That Unutterable Horror of a Prussian Book"', in *Carlyle Past and Present*, ed. K. J. Fielding and Rodger L. Tarr (London, 1976).

Alcott, Bronson, *The Journals of Bronson Alcott*, selected and ed. Odell Shepard (Boston, Mass., 1938).

Allingham, H. and Radford, D. (eds), *William Allingham's Diary* (London, 1907, reprinted 1967).

Althaus, Friedrich, 'Thomas Carlyle: Eine biographisch-literarische Characteristick', *Unsere Zeit* (July 1866).

Altick, Richard D., *The Presence of the Present: Topics of the Day in the Victorian Novel* (Columbus, Ohio, 1990).

The Amberley Papers: The Letters and Diaries of Lord and Lady Amberley, ed. Bertrand and Patricia Russell, 2 vols (London, 1937).

Archibald, R. C., *Carlyle's First Love: Margaret Gordon, Lady Bannerman* (London, 1910).

Art Treasures of England: The Regional Collections (London, 1998).

Ashton, Rosemary, *George Eliot: A Life* (London, 1996).

—— *The German Idea: Four English Writers and the Reception of German Thought 1800–1860* (Cambridge, 1980, reprinted London, 1994).

—— *G. H. Lewes: A Life* (Oxford, 1991, reprinted London, 2000).

—— *The Life of Samuel Taylor Coleridge: A Critical Biography* (Oxford, 1996).

—— *Little Germany: Exile and Asylum in Victorian England* (Oxford, 1986).

Best, Geoffrey, *Mid-Victorian Britain 1851–75* (London, 1971, reprinted 1989).

Blunt, Reginald, *The Carlyles' Chelsea Home* (London, 1895).

—— *By Chelsea Reach: Some Riverside Records* (London, 1921).

Blyth, Henry, *Madeleine Smith* (London, 1975).

Bölte, Amely, *Amely Böltes Briefe aus England an Varnhagen von Ense (1844–1858)*, ed. Walther Fischer and Antje Behrens (Düsseldorf, 1955).

Brookfield, Charles and Frances, *Mrs Brookfield and her Circle*, 2 vols (London, 1906).

Broughton, Trev, 'Froude: The "Painful Appendix"', *Carlyle Studies Annual*, special issue, XV (1995).

Browne, Janet, *Charles Darwin: Voyaging* (London, 1995).

The Brownings' Correspondence, ed. Philip Kelley, Ronald Hudson, and Scott Lewis, 14 vols so far (Winfield, Kansas, 1984–).

Browning, Elizabeth Barrett, *The Letters of Elizabeth Barrett Browning*, ed. Frederick G. Kenyon, 2 vols (London, 1897).

Browning, Robert, *Dearest Isa: Robert Browning's Letters to Isabella Blagden*, ed. Edward C. McAleer (Austin, Texas, 1951).

—— *More Than Friends: The Letters of Robert Browning to Katharine de Kay Bronson*, ed. Michael Meredith (Waco, Texas, 1985).

—— *New Letters of Robert Browning*, ed. W. C. De Vane and K. L. Knickerbocker (London, 1951).

Burdett, Osbert, *The Two Carlyles* (London, 1930).

Butler, Samuel, *Letters between Samuel Butler and Miss E. M. A. Savage 1871–1885*, ed. Geoffrey Keynes and Brian Hill (London, 1935).

Campbell, Ian, 'Carlyle House', *Carlyle Annual*, XII (1991).

—— 'Carlyle, Pictet and Jeffrey Again', *The Bibliotheck*, VII (1974).

—— 'Conversations with Carlyle: The Monckton Milnes Diaries', *Prose Studies*, VIII (May 1985).

Carlisle, Janice, 'Shooting Niagara? Carlyle and *Punch* in the Late 1860s', *Carlyle Studies Annual*, XVIII (1998).

The Collected Letters of Thomas and Jane Welsh Carlyle, Duke–Edinburgh Edition, ed. C. R. Sanders, K. J. Fielding, Clyde de L. Ryals, Ian Campbell, Aileen Christianson, et al., 28 vols so far (Durham, North Carolina, 1970—).

The Collected Poems of Thomas and Jane Welsh Carlyle, ed. Rodger L. Tarr and Fleming McClelland (Greenwood, Florida, 1986).

The Love Letters of Thomas Carlyle and Jane Welsh, ed. Alexander Carlyle, 2 vols (London, 1909).

Thomas and Jane: Selected Letters from the Edinburgh University Collection, ed. Ian Campbell (Edinburgh, 1980).

Carlyle, Jane Welsh, *I Too Am Here: Selections from the Letters of Jane Welsh Carlyle*, ed. Alan and Mary McQueen Simpson (Cambridge, 1977).

—— *Jane Welsh Carlyle: Letters to her Family 1839–1863*, ed. Leonard Huxley (London, 1924).

—— *Jane Welsh Carlyle: A New Selection of her Letters*, ed. Trudy Bliss (London, 1949).

—— *Letters and Memorials of Jane Welsh Carlyle*, ed. J. A. Froude, 3 vols (London, 1883).

—— *Letters of Jane Welsh Carlyle to Joseph Neuberg 1848–1862*, ed. Townsend Scudder (London, 1931).

—— *New Letters and Memorials of Jane Welsh Carlyle*, ed. Alexander Carlyle, 2 vols (London, 1903).

—— 'The simple Story of my own first Love', ed. K. J. Fielding and Ian Campbell with Aileen Christianson (Edinburgh, 2001).

Carlyle, Thomas, *Carlyle's Latter-Day Pamphlets*, ed. M. K. Goldberg and J. P. Seigel (Ontario, 1983).

—— *Carlyle's Unfinished History of German Literature*, ed. Hill Shine (Lexington, Kentucky, 1951).

—— *Correspondence between Goethe and Carlyle*, ed. Charles Eliot Norton (London, 1887).

—— *The Correspondence of Emerson and Carlyle*, ed. Joseph Slater (London, 1964).

—— *The Correspondence of Thomas Carlyle and John Ruskin*, ed. George Allan Cate (Stanford, California, 1982).

—— *Frederick the Great*, selected and ed. John Clive (Chicago, Illinois, 1969).

—— *Journey to Germany, Autumn 1858*, ed. R. A. E. Brooks (New Haven, Conn., 1940).

—— *Last Words of Thomas Carlyle* (London, 1892).

—— *The Letters of Thomas Carlyle to his Brother Alexander, with Related Family Letters*, ed. Edwin J. Marrs, Jr. (Cambridge, Mass., 1968).

—— *Letters addressed to Mrs Basil Montagu and B. W. Procter by Mr Thomas Carlyle*, ed. Anne Benson Procter (printed for private circulation, London, 1881).

—— *Letters of Thomas Carlyle to his Youngest Sister*, ed. Charles Townsend Copeland (London, 1899).

—— *Letters of Thomas Carlyle to John Stuart Mill, John Sterling, and Robert Browning*, ed. Alexander Carlyle (London, 1923).

—— *Life of Friedrich Schiller*, ed. Jeffrey L. Sammons (Columbia, South Carolina, 1992).

—— 'New Carlyle Letters', *Carlyle Newsletter*, VIII (Spring 1987).

—— *New Letters of Thomas Carlyle*, ed. Alexander Carlyle, 2 vols (London, 1904).

—— *Reminiscences*, ed. K. J. Fielding and Ian Campbell (Oxford, 1997).

—— *Sartor Resartus*, ed. Rodger L. Tarr and Mark Engel (Berkeley, California, 2000).

—— *Thomas Carlyle: Letters to his Wife*, ed. Trudy Bliss (London, 1953).

—— *Two Note Books of Thomas Carlyle*, ed. Charles Eliot Norton (New York, 1898).

—— *Two Reminiscences of Thomas Carlyle*, ed. John Clubbe (Durham, North Carolina, 1974).

Catalogue of Important Autograph Letters, Historical Documents and Commemorative Medals, Bloomsbury Book Auctions (November 1999).

Christianson, Aileen, 'Carlyle and Universal Penny Postage', *Carlyle Newsletter*, IV (Spring 1983).

Clarke, Norma, *Ambitious Heights: Writing, Friendship, Love – The Jewsbury Sisters, Felicia Hemans, and Jane Welsh Carlyle* (London, 1990).

Clough, Arthur Hugh, *The Correspondence of Arthur Hugh Clough*, ed. Frederick L. Mulhauser, 2 vols (Oxford, 1957).

Clubbe, John (ed.), *Carlyle and his Contemporaries: Essays in Honor of*

Charles Richard Sanders (Durham, North Carolina, 1976).

Coleridge, Samuel Taylor, *The Collected Letters of Samuel Taylor Coleridge*, ed. Earl Leslie Griggs, 6 vols (Oxford, 1956–71).

Collis, John Stewart, *The Carlyles: A Biography of Thomas and Jane Carlyle* (London, 1971).

Conway, Moncure Daniel, *Autobiography, Memories, and Experiences*, 2 vols (London, 1904).

Crichton-Browne, Sir James and Carlyle, Alexander, *The Nemesis of Froude: A Rejoinder to J. A. Froude's 'My Relations with Carlyle'* (London, 1903).

Darwin, Charles, *More Letters of Charles Darwin: A Record of his Work in a Series of Hitherto Unpublished Letters*, ed. Francis Darwin and A. C. Seward, 2 vols (London, 1903).

Darwin, Emma, *Emma Darwin: A Century of Family Letters 1792–1896*, ed. Henrietta Litchfield, 2 vols (London, 1915).

Darwin, Francis, *The Life and Letters of Charles Darwin*, 3 vols (London, 1887).

Dasent, Arthur Irwin, *John Thadeus Delane, Editor of 'The Times': His Life and Correspondence*, 2 vols (London, 1908).

Davidson, David, *Memories of a Long Life* (Edinburgh, 1890).

Davies, James A., *John Forster: A Literary Life* (Leicester, 1982).

DeBruyn, John R., 'Thomas Carlyle and Sir Arthur Helps', *Bulletin of the John Rylands University Library of Manchester*, LXIV (Autumn 1981, Spring 1982).

Dickens, Charles, *The Letters of Charles Dickens*, ed Madeleine House, Graham Storey, Kathleen Tillotson, et al., 12 vols (Oxford, 1965–2002).

—— *The Speeches of Charles Dickens*, ed. K. J. Fielding (Oxford, 1960).

—— *Uncollected Writings: Household Words 1850–9*, ed. Harry Stone, 2 vols (London, 1969).

Donaldson, Gordon (ed.), *Four Centuries of Edinburgh University Life 1583–1983* (Edinburgh, 1983).

Drew, Elizabeth, *Jane Welsh and Jane Carlyle* (London, 1928).

Duffy, Sir Charles Gavan, *Conversations with Carlyle* (London, 1892).

Dunn, Waldo Hilary, *Froude and Carlyle: A Study of the Froude–Carlyle Controversy* (London, 1930).

—— *James Anthony Froude: A Biography*, 2 vols (Oxford, 1961, 1963).

Eimer, Manfred, 'Briefe an Amely Bölte aus Carlyles Freundeskreis', *Englische Studien*, XLIX (Leipzig, 1915–16).

Eliot, George, *Essays of George Eliot*, ed. Thomas Pinney (London, 1963).

—— *The George Eliot Letters*, ed. Gordon S. Haight, 9 vols (New Haven, Conn., 1954–5, 1978).

—— *The Journals of George Eliot*, ed. Margaret Harris and Judith Johnston (Cambridge, 1998).

—— *Selected Critical Writings*, ed. Rosemary Ashton (Oxford, 1992).

Ellmann, Richard, *Oscar Wilde* (London, 1987, reprinted 1988).

Emerson, Ralph Waldo, *English Traits* (1856, reprinted London, 1889).

—— *The Journals and Miscellaneous Notebooks of Ralph Waldo Emerson*, ed. William H. Gilman et al., 16 vols (Cambridge, Mass., 1960–82).

—— *The Letters of Ralph Waldo Emerson*, ed. Ralph L. Rusk and Eleanor M. Tilton, 10 vols (New York, 1939–95).

Espinasse, Francis, *Literary Recollections and Sketches* (London, 1893).

Faderman, Lillian, *Surpassing the Love of Men* (New York, 1981).

Fielding, K. J., 'Captain Anthony Sterling's Photograph Album and his Relations with Jane Carlyle', *Carlyle Newsletter*, VI (Spring 1985).

—— 'Carlyle and the Americans: "Eighteen Million Bores"', *Carlyle Studies Annual*, XV (1995).

—— 'The Cry from Craigenputtoch', *Times Literary Supplement* (13 August 1999).

—— 'Froude and Carlyle: Some New Considerations', in *Carlyle Past and Present*, ed. K. J. Fielding and Rodger L. Tarr (London, 1976).

—— 'New Notes for *The Letters*: I. Carlyle's Sketch of Joseph Neuberg. II. "Leave it Alone; Time Will Mend It"', *Carlyle Annual*, XIII (1992–3).

—— 'Robert Scott Tait: His Portraits and Photographs of the Carlyles in their "A Chelsea Interior"', *Review of Scottish Culture*, XIII (2000).

—— 'Vernon Lushington: Carlyle's Friend and Editor', *Carlyle Newsletter*, VIII (Spring 1987).

—— and Jackson, Peter, 'Carlyle's Reminiscences: Dr Peyton Blakiston and Bessy Barnet', *Carlyle Newsletter*, IX (Spring 1988).

Fischer, Walther, 'Thomas und Jane Carlyle im Spiegel der Briefe Amely Böltes an Varnhagen von Ense (1844–1853)', *Englische Studien*, LXIV (1929).

FitzGerald, Edward, *The Letters of Edward FitzGerald*, ed. Alfred McKinley Terhune and Annabelle Burdick Terhune, 2 vols (Princeton, New Jersey, 1980).

Forster, John, *The Life of Charles Dickens*, 3 vols (1872–4), ed. and annotated by J. W. T. Ley (London, 1928).

Fox, Caroline, *The Journals of Caroline Fox 1835–1871*, selected and ed. Wendy Monk (London, 1972).

Freud, Sigmund, *The Interpretation of Dreams* (1900), The Pelican Freud Library, vol. IV (Harmondsworth, 1980).

Frost, Thomas, *Forty Years' Recollections: Literary and Political* (London, 1881).

Froude, James Anthony, *My Relations with Carlyle* (London, 1903).

—— *The Nemesis of Faith* (1849), ed. Rosemary Ashton (London, 1988).

—— *Short Studies on Great Subjects*, 4 vols (London, 1892).

—— *Thomas Carlyle: A History of the First Forty Years of his Life 1795–1835*, 2 vols (London, 1882).

—— *Thomas Carlyle: A History of his Life in London*, 2 vols (London, 1884).

Furness, Horace Howard, *Letters of Horace Howard Furness*, ed. H. H. F. Jayne, 2 vols (Boston, Mass., 1922).

Gaskell, Elizabeth, *The Letters of Mrs Gaskell*, ed. J. A. W. Chapple and Arthur Pollard (Manchester, 1966).

Gilchrist, Alexander, *Life of William Blake, with Additional Letters and a Memoir of the Author*, 2 vols (London, 1880).

Gilchrist, H. H. (ed.), *Anne Gilchrist: Her Life and Writings* (London, 1887).

Graves, Algernon, *The Royal Academy of Arts: A Complete Dictionary of Contributors and their Work from its Foundation in 1769 to 1904*, 4 vols (London, 1905).

Halliday, James L., *Mr Carlyle My Patient: A Psychosomatic Biography* (London, 1949).

Halliday, Stephen, *The Great Stink of London: Sir Joseph Bazalgette and the Cleansing of the Victorian Capital* (Stroud, 1999).

Hamburger, Lotte and Joseph, *Contemplating Adultery: The Secret Life of a Victorian Woman* (New York, 1991).

—— *Troubled Lives: John and Sarah Austin* (London, 1985).

Hansard's Parliamentary Debates, third series, CX (1850), CXL (1856).

Hanson, Lawrence and Elisabeth, *Necessary Evil: The Life of Jane Welsh Carlyle* (London, 1950).

Hare, Augustus J. C., *The Story of My Life*, 6 vols (London, 1896–1900).

Harnick, Phyllis, 'Point and Counterpoint: Carlyle and Mill on Ireland in 1848', *Carlyle Newsletter*, VII (Spring 1986).

Harris, Frank, 'Talks with Carlyle', *English Review*, VII (February 1911).

Harrison, Frederic, *Autobiographic Memoirs*, 2 vols (London, 1911).

—— 'The Carlyle House' (1895), in *Memories and Thoughts* (London, 1906).

—— *The Choice of Books and Other Literary Pieces* (London, 1886).

—— 'Thomas Carlyle', *Studies in Early Victorian Literature* (London, 1895).

Harte, Negley and North, John, *The World of UCL 1828–1990* (London, 1991).

Hartmann, Moritz, *Gesammelte Werke*, ed. Ludwig Bamberger and Wilhelm Vollmer, 10 vols (Stuttgart, 1873–4).

Hazlitt, William, *The Spirit of the Age* (London, 1825).

Heffer, Simon, *Moral Desperado: A Life of Thomas Carlyle* (London, 1995).

Henderson, Henry F., *Erskine of Linlathen: Selections and Biography* (Edinburgh, 1899).

Herbert, Christopher, *Culture and Anomie: Ethnographic Imagination in the Nineteenth Century* (Chicago, Illinois, 1991).

Herzen, Alexander, *My Past and Thoughts*, trans. Constance Garnett, 4 vols (London, 1968).

—— *Sobraniye Sochineniy [Complete Works]*, 30 vols (Moscow, 1954–65).

Hilton, Tim, *John Ruskin: The Early Years* (London, 1985).

Hirst, F. W., *Early Life and Letters of John Morley*, 2 vols (London, 1927).

Holcombe, Lee, 'Victorian Wives and Property: Reform of the Married Women's Property Laws, 1857–1882', in *A Widening Sphere: Changing Roles of Victorian Women*, ed. Martha Vicinus (London, 1977).

Holme, Thea, *The Carlyles at Home* (London, 1965).

The Homes and Haunts of Thomas Carlyle (reprinted from the *Westminster Gazette*, London, 1895).

Howe, Susanne, *Geraldine Jewsbury: Her Life and Errors* (London, 1935).

Hutchison, Sidney C., *The History of the Royal Academy 1768–1986* (London, 1986).

Huxley, Leonard, *Life and Letters of Thomas Henry Huxley*, 2 vols (London, 1900).

Ireland, Mrs Alexander, *Life of Jane Welsh Carlyle* (London, 1891).

Jackson, Patrick, *Education Act Forster: A Political Biography of W. E. Forster 1818–1886* (London, 1997).

James, Henry, *Literary Reviews and Essays*, ed. Albert Mordell (New York, 1957).

Jewsbury, Geraldine, *Selections from the Letters of Miss Jewsbury to Jane Welsh Carlyle*, ed. Mrs Alexander Ireland (London, 1892).

Johnson, Edgar, *Charles Dickens: His Tragedy and Triumph*, 2 vols (London, 1953).

Kaplan, Fred, 'Carlyle's Marginalia and George Henry Lewes's Fiction', *Carlyle Newsletter*, V (1984).

—— ' "Phallus-Worship" (1848): Unpublished Manuscripts III – A Response to the Revolution of 1848', *Carlyle Newsletter*, II (1980).

—— *Thomas Carlyle: A Biography* (Cambridge, 1983).

Larkin, Henry, 'Carlyle and Mrs Carlyle', *British Quarterly Review* (July 1881).

—— *Carlyle and the Open Secret of his Life* (London, 1886).

Lewes, George Henry, *The Letters of George Henry Lewes*, ed. William Baker, 3 vols (Victoria, British Columbia, 1995, 1999).

Macaulay, Thomas Babington, *The Letters of Thomas Babington Macaulay*, ed. Thomas Pinney, 6 vols (Cambridge, 1974–81, 1999).

Mack Smith, Denis, *Mazzini* (London, 1994).

Macready, William Charles, *The Diaries of William Charles Macready 1833–1851*, ed. William Toynbee, 2 vols (London, 1912).

—— *Macready's Reminiscences, and Selections from his Diaries and Letters*, ed. Sir Frederick Pollock, 2 vols (London, 1875).

Malchow, H. L., *Gothic Images of Race in Nineteenth-Century Britain* (Stanford, California, 1996).

Mann, Thomas, *Gesammelte Werke*, 13 vols (Frankfurt, 1974).

Martineau, Harriet, *Autobiography*, 2 vols (London, 1877, reprinted 1983).

—— *Harriet Martineau's Letters to Fanny Wedgwood*, ed. E. S. Arbuckle (Stanford, California, 1983).

Marx–Engels Collected Works, 50 vols so far (London, 1975—).

Marx, Karl and Engels, Friedrich, *The Communist Manifesto*, ed. A. J. P. Taylor (Harmondsworth, 1986).

Mason, Michael, *The Making of Victorian Sexuality* (Oxford, 1994).

Masson, David, *Carlyle Personally and in his Writings: Two Edinburgh Lectures* (London, 1885).

—— *Memories of London in the 'Forties* (London, 1908).

Mazzini, Giuseppe, *Giuseppe Mazzini e i Fratelli Ruffini*, ed. Carlo Cagnacci (Porto Maurizio, 1893).

—— *Scritti editi ed inediti*, Edizione Nationale, 106 vols (Imola, 1906–90).

Mill, John Stuart, *Autobiography* (1873), ed. John M. Robson (Harmondsworth, 1989).

—— *The Earlier Letters of John Stuart Mill*, vols XII and XIII of *Collected Works of John Stuart Mill*, ed. Francis E. Mineka et al., 33 vols (London, 1963–91).

—— *The Later Letters of John Stuart Mill*, vols XIV–XVII of *Collected Works*.

Milnes, Richard Monckton, *Die Briefe Richard Monckton Milnes' an Varnhagen von Ense (1844–1854)*, ed. Walther Fischer (Heidelberg, 1922).

Moore, Carlisle, 'Thomas Carlyle', in *The English Romantic Poets and Essayists: A Review of Research and Criticism*, ed. C. W. Houtchens and L. H. Houtchens (London, 1966).

Morrison, N. Brysson, *True Minds: The Marriage of Thomas and Jane Carlyle* (London, 1974).

Nichol, John, *Thomas Carlyle* (London, 1892).

Nixon, Jude V., ' "Return Alphias": The Forster/Carlyle Unpublished Letters and Re-tailoring the Sage', *Carlyle Studies Annual*, XVIII (1998).

Norton, Charles Eliot, *Letters of Charles Eliot Norton*, ed. Sara Norton and M. A. De Wolfe Howe, 2 vols (London, 1913).

Nye, Eric W., 'An Edition of John Sterling Uncovers New Carlyle Letters', *Carlyle Newsletter*, IX (Spring 1988).

Oliphant, Margaret, *Autobiography and Letters of Mrs Margaret Oliphant*, ed. Mrs Harry Coghill (London, 1899, reprinted Leicester, 1974).

—— *The Life of Edward Irving*, 2 vols (London, 1862).

Ormond, Richard, *Early Victorian Portraits*, 2 vols (London, 1973).

Packe, Michael St John, *The Life of John Stuart Mill* (London, 1954).

Park, Peter T., 'Thomas Carlyle and the Jews', *Journal of European Studies*, XX (1990).

Pool, Daniel, *What Jane Austen Ate and Charles Dickens Knew: From Fox Hunting to Whist – the Facts of Daily Life in Nineteenth-Century England* (New York, 1993).

Pope-Hennessy, James, *Monckton Milnes: The Flight of Youth 1851–1885* (London, 1951).

—— *Monckton Milnes: The Years of Promise 1809–1851* (London, 1949).

Pullar, Philippa, *Frank Harris* (London, 1975).

Reid, T. Wemyss, *Life, Letters, and Friendships of Richard Monckton Milnes, First Lord Houghton*, 2 vols (London, 1890).

—— *Life of the Right Honourable William Edward Forster*, 2 vols (London, 1888).

Richardson, Thomas C., 'John Murray's Reader and the Rejection of *Sartor Resartus*', *Carlyle Newsletter*, VI (Spring 1985).

Ricks, Christopher, 'Froude's Carlyle', *Essays in Appreciation* (Oxford, 1996).

Rio, A. F., *Épilogue à l'Art Chrétien*, 2 vols (Fribourg-en-Brisgau, 1870).

Ritchie, Anne Thackeray, *Chapters from Some Memoirs* (London, 1894).

—— *Letters of Anne Thackeray Ritchie*, ed. Hester Ritchie (London, 1924).

Robinson, Henry Crabb, *Diary, Reminiscences, and Correspondence*, ed. Thomas Sadler, 3 vols (London, 1869).

Rose, Phyllis, *Parallel Lives: Five Victorian Marriages* (London, 1984).

The Royal Scottish Academy Exhibitors 1826–1990, ed. Charles de Laperriere, 4 vols (Calne, 1991).

Rupke, Nicolaas A., *Richard Owen: Victorian Naturalist* (London, 1994).

Ruskin, John, *The Correspondence of John Ruskin and Charles Eliot Norton*, ed. John Lewis Bradley and Ian Ousby (Cambridge, 1987).

Ryals, Clyde de L., 'Thomas Carlyle and the Squire Forgeries', *Victorian Studies*, XXX (1987).

Sadleir, Michael, *Bulwer: A Panorama; Edward Bulwer and Rosina 1803–1836* (London, 1931).

Sanders, Charles Richard, *Carlyle's Friendships and Other Studies* (Durham, North Carolina, 1977).

—— 'Carlyle's Pen Portraits of Queen Victoria and Prince Albert', in *Carlyle Past and Present*, ed. K. J. Fielding and Rodger L. Tarr (London, 1976).

Sarti, Roland, *Mazzini: A Life for the Religion of Politics* (London, 1997).

Seigel, Jules Paul (ed.), *Thomas Carlyle: The Critical Heritage* (London, 1971).

Shepherd, Richard Herne (ed.), *Memoirs of the Life and Writings of Thomas Carlyle*, 2 vols (London, 1881).

Sloan, J. M., *The Carlyle Country, with a Study of Carlyle's Life* (London, 1904).

Smith, Mary, *The Autobiography of Mary Smith, Schoolmistress and Nonconformist. A Fragment of a Life, with Letters from Jane Welsh Carlyle and Thomas Carlyle* (London, 1892).

Smith, Walter C., 'Reminiscences of Carlyle and Leigh Hunt', *Good Words*, XXIII (1882).

Stair Douglas, Mrs, *The Life and Selections from the Correspondence of William Whewell DD* (London, 1881).

Sterling, John, *Essays and Tales, Collected and Edited with a Memoir of his Life by J. C. Hare*, 2 vols (London, 1848).

Stevenson, Robert Louis, *The Letters of Robert Louis Stevenson*, ed. Bradford A. Booth and Ernest Mehew, 8 vols (New Haven, Conn., 1994–5).

Stocker, Mark, 'Joseph Edgar Boehm and Thomas Carlyle', *Carlyle Newsletter*, VI (Spring 1985).

Strachan, Gordon, 'Carlyle, Irving, and the "Hysterical Women"', *Carlyle Annual*, XII (1991).

Surtees, Virginia, *Jane Welsh Carlyle* (Salisbury, 1986).

—— *The Ludovisi Goddess: The Life of Louisa, Lady Ashburton* (Salisbury, 1984).

Sutherland, John, *The Life of Walter Scott: A Critical Biography* (Oxford, 1995).

—— *Victorian Fiction: Writers, Publishers, Readers* (London, 1995).

Tarr, Rodger L., *Thomas Carlyle: A Descriptive Bibliography* (Oxford, 1989).

Taylor, Henry, *Autobiography of Henry Taylor 1800–1875*, 2 vols (London, 1885).

—— *Correspondence of Henry Taylor*, ed. Edward Dowden (London, 1888).

Tennyson, Alfred Lord, *The Letters of Alfred Lord Tennyson*, ed. Cecil Y. Lang and Edgar F. Shannon, Jr., 3 vols (Oxford, 1982–90).

Tennyson, Emily, *Lady Tennyson's Journal*, ed. James O. Hoge (Charlottesville, Virginia, 1981).

Thackeray, William Makepeace, *The Letters and Private Papers of William Makepeace Thackeray*, ed. Gordon N. Ray, 4 vols (Cambridge, Mass., 1945–6); Supplement, ed. Edgar F. Harden, 2 vols (New York, 1994).

Trela, D. J., 'Carlyle, the Just War and the Crimean War', *Carlyle Newsletter*, IX (Spring 1988).

—— 'Margaret Oliphant's "bravest words yet spoken" on Thomas and Jane Welsh Carlyle', *Carlyle Studies Annual*, XVIII (1998).

—— 'A New (Old) Review of Mill's *Liberty*: A Note on Carlyle and

Mill's Friendship', *Carlyle Newsletter*, VI (Spring 1985).

Tuell, Anne Kimball, *John Sterling: A Representative Victorian* (New York, 1941).

Twisleton, Ellen, *Letters of the Hon. Ellen Twisleton Written to her Family 1852–1862*, ed. Ellen Twisleton Vaughan (London, 1928).

Tyndall, John, 'Personal Recollections of Thomas Carlyle' (1890), in *New Fragments* (New York, 1892).

Varnhagen von Ense, Karl August, *Aus dem Nachlass Varnhagen's von Ense, Tagebücher*, ed. Ludmilla Assing, 15 vols (Leipzig, 1861–70, Berlin, 1905).

Victoria, *The Letters of Queen Victoria*, ed. A. C. Benson and Viscount Esher, 3 vols. (London, 1907).

Wedgwood, Barbara and Hensleigh, *The Wedgwood Circle 1730–1897* (London, 1980).

Weisser, Henry, *April 10: Challenge and Response in England in 1848* (London, 1983).

Wilde, Oscar, *The Complete Letters of Oscar Wilde*, ed. Merlin Holland and Rupert Hart-Davis (London, 2000).

—— *More Letters of Oscar Wilde*, ed. Rupert Hart-Davis (London, 1985).

Wilson, David Alec, *Carlyle till Marriage (1795–1826)*, vol. I of his six-volume biography of Carlyle (London, 1923).

—— *Carlyle to 'The French Revolution' (1826–37)*, vol. II (London, 1924).

—— *Carlyle on Cromwell and Others (1837–48)*, vol. III (London, 1925).

—— *Carlyle at his Zenith (1848–53)*, vol. IV (London, 1927).

—— *Carlyle to Threescore-and-Ten (1853–65)*, vol. V (London, 1931).

—— and MacArthur, David Wilson, *Carlyle in Old Age (1865–81)*, vol. VI (London, 1934).

Winter, Alison, *Mesmerized: Powers of Mind in Victorian Britain* (London, 1998).

Woolley, Benjamin, *Bride of Science: Romance, Reason, and Byron's Daughter* (London, 1999).

Woolner, Amy, *Thomas Woolner, RA, Sculptor and Poet: His Life in Letters* (London, 1917).

Wordsworth, William, *The Letters of William and Dorothy Wordsworth*, second edition, ed. Chester L. Shaver, Mary Moorman, and Alan G. Hill, 7 vols (Oxford, 1967–88).

Wright, Lawrence, *Clean and Decent: The Fascinating History of the Bathroom and the Water Closet* (London, 1960).

Wylie, William Howie, *Thomas Carlyle: The Man and his Books* (London, 1881).

Index